The Cave
and the Mountain

A Study of E. M. Forster

The Cave
and the Mountain

A Study of E. M. Forster

Wilfred Stone

Stanford University Press, Stanford, California   1966
London: Oxford University Press

148146

PR
6011
.O58
Z845
1966

To Cary, Greg, and Mimi

Preface

This book has been on the fire for almost eight years, and in that time I have been helped by more people than I can properly honor or ever repay. My first debt is to E. M. Forster, who during 1957–58 and again in 1965 shared with me conversation, books, mementos, pictures, clippings, and glasses of wine. Both my wife and I remember his genial kindness with pleasure and gratitude. Though he has not read or directly influenced this book, it has inevitably been colored by my memory of his voice and manner—and by the way I learned to listen for the backwash of his remarks, those pale casts of afterthought into which were often slipped his most memorable comments. To have known Forster personally is to feel his distinction, his toughness as well as his warmth, and to learn why his friends honor him not just as a writer, but as an influence.

Next I give thanks to those, on both sides of the Atlantic, who read and criticized the manuscript: to Noel Annan (now Lord Annan), who twice read the book and generously let me profit from his knowledge of Bloomsbury and his literary tact—as well as opening to me the resources of the King's College Library; to J. G. Bell, for his generous (and merciless) editorial scrutiny of versions early and late; to Robert Holloway, the editor who saw the book through the press and made it better as it went; to Sally Boyd, who took over where he left off; to Arthur Sale, for his wit, marginalia, and friendship—which sustained me and this enterprise in unrepayable ways; to Patrick Wilkinson, Kingsman and friend of Forster, whose sympathetic reading saved me from many an error of fact and taste; and to all those others who read this manuscript (in whole or part), or helped with ideas or information or encouragement, notably Charles Allen, Irving Howe, the late William Irvine, Thomas Moser, Lucio Ruotolo, and Ian Watt.

I am further grateful to all those kind and candid people who talked with me and answered my questions: to the late Clive Bell, Mr. and Mrs. David Garnett, F. L. Lucas, the late G. E. Moore and Mrs. Moore, and Leonard Woolf, all members of Bloomsbury; to Norman Routledge, Graham Hough, Mr. and Mrs. Arthur Tillotson, and Basil Willey; and to those kindly natives of Wiltshire, Noel and Dorothy Grudgings of Melksham, who showed me part of Forster's religion in their local countryside.

A special word of thanks goes to Oliver and Gunnvor Stallybrass: to Oliver (formerly of the London Library, now of Secker & Warburg) for sharing with me his excellent Forster bibliography (since completed by Miss B. J. Kirkpatrick), which saved me perhaps a year's work; and to Gunnvor, for taking us, bag, baby, and baggage, into her sunny home.

I thank the Guggenheim Foundation for the award that made possible the trip to England where this book was started; Stanford University for three grants-in-aid which paid for secretarial and research assistance (I remember with gratitude the work of Robert Eschbacher, Robert Hass, and Patricia McNees) and which partly supported my search for pictures. I wish also to thank the staffs of the King's and Trinity College Libraries at Cambridge, the Stanford Library, and the Hoover Institution for their many acts of kindness. Finally, I am grateful to Josephine Guttadauro, Mary Johnson, Caroline MacKinnon, Mary Nattkemper, Eleanor Higby, and Jeanne Kennedy for their able typing, proofreading, and indexing; and especially to Jack Werner Stauffacher for arranging the picture sections with such sympathy and taste.

My gratitude to those who have permitted me to use copyrighted material and have helped me in gathering illustrations is recorded under Acknowledgments and Credits, pp. 426–28.

Finally, I wish to thank my wife and two children, to whom this book is dedicated, for more gifts than I can mention.

W. S.

November 1965

Contents

PART I. THE INNER CIRCLE

1. Introduction: Poetry and Prose   3
2. Clapham: The Father's House   21
3. The Apostolic Ring   40
4. Goldsworthy Lowes Dickinson   72

PART II. THE EXPANDING RING

5. Forster's Esthetics: From Words to Music   101
6. The Stories: Fantasy   122
7. Where Angels Fear to Tread: The Fool as Prophet   162
8. The Longest Journey: The Slaughter of the Innocent   184
9. A Room with a View: Sex and Sensibility   216
10. Howards End: Red-bloods and Mollycoddles   235

PART III. THE GREAT ROUND

11. A Passage to Alexandria   279
12. A Passage to India: The Great Round   298
13. Criticism: The Near and the Far   347

Notes   391
Acknowledgments and Credits   426
Index   429

Photographs follow pages 52, 276, and 372.

Abbreviations

Abbreviation		First Published
WA	*Where Angels Fear to Tread*	1905
LJ	*The Longest Journey*	1907
RV	*A Room with a View*	1908
HE	*Howards End*	1910
GE	*The Government of Egypt*	1920
AHG	*Alexandria: A History and a Guide*	1922
PP	*Pharos and Pharillon*	1923
PI	*A Passage to India*	1924
AN	*Aspects of the Novel*	1927
GLD	*Goldsworthy Lowes Dickinson*	1934
AH	*Abinger Harvest*	1936
CS	*Collected Stories of E. M. Forster*	1948
TC	*Two Cheers for Democracy*	1951
HD	*The Hill of Devi*	1953
MT	*Marianne Thornton*	1956

The editions cited in this book are those published by Edward Arnold except AHG (Doubleday & Co.), PP (The Hogarth Press), and CS (Penguin Books).

Part I

The Inner Circle

Chapter one

Introduction: Poetry and Prose

There is a huge economic movement which has been taking the whole world, Great Britain included, from agriculture towards industrialism. . . . Personally I hate it.

— *E. M. Forster*

No great novelist can be a Benthamite. . . .

—*F. R. Leavis*

In 1840 John Stuart Mill declared that "Every Englishman of the present day is by implication either a Benthamite or a Coleridgean." It is a brilliant oversimplification, not only describing an age's self-division but also suggesting that division itself, self-alienation, is the essential character of that age. It is no new thing for a Westerner to view the human condition as divided, for dualism is an inseparable part of the Christian tradition. But the divisions that wracked Western society after the French Revolution were more than new arrangements of old antagonisms. They marked a society that was fundamentally split—a society out of touch with its ancient roots, speaking different moral languages, existing, as it were, on opposing sides of an abyss. "It may be," writes Alfred North Whitehead, "that civilisation will never recover from the bad climate which enveloped the introduction of machinery."[1] The worst thing about that climate was the breakdown in moral communication, the separation of men from their traditional roots and values.

The cleavage Mill saw helped make England "two nations," and forced some of its greatest artists into living double lives, torn between their public and private roles, uncertain of their true vocation or identity. Mill's is a specialized phrasing of what the early Marx called "the alienated consciousness"—that tendency to see man only as an economic creature, dominated by the drives of aggression and

possessiveness.[2] Mill also anticipates what Jung calls the "split consciousness" of modern man, that sense of unrelatedness resulting
from the rupture between faith and knowledge, between religious
or poetic truth and scientific or rational truth.[3] And the words
bring to mind T. S. Eliot's "dissociation of sensibility," that divorce
between thought and feeling which Eliot saw as one of our evil inheri-
tances from the Reformation.[4] Another way of seeing this split is Alfred North Whitehead's: he laments the attention the modern world
devotes "to *things,* as opposed to *values,*" attributing this distortion
of emphasis in large part to the materialistic basis of science. However it is seen, the split is fundamental; it is the essential meaning of
the word modern.

But to label the split with the names of Bentham and Coleridge is
to see it in a particularly useful and comprehensive way. These men
were, as Mill said, "the seminal minds," "the teachers of the teachers,"
and though their names were not always invoked in the great clashes
of the last century, their influence was present, for they had formu-
lated the two positions around which the age polarized its deepest
thought and feeling. Since 1840 those formulations have been
amended and altered, but they still mark the symbolic extremes of
the modern situation.

The contrast between the two is profound and complex, but essentially it is a contrast between a mechanical and an organic view of
life, between analysis and creative synthesis. Bentham, a son of the
Enlightenment, sought to discover social laws as immutable and
splendidly abstract as Newton's laws of physics. Coleridge, a romantic
idealist, sought to formulate a view of man and society compatible
with man's highest aspirations. It is the difference between ration-
alism and romanticism, Utilitarianism and anti-Utilitarianism, and
these are perhaps the best tags for the opposing sides. But the antagonism was less often labeled than felt and acted upon intuitively.
When little Sissy Jupe in *Hard Times* is asked for "the first law of
political economy," she naïvely recites the Golden Rule. The question is Benthamite, the answer Coleridgean. Neither party understands the other: they are isolates, morally incommunicado, and in
their confrontation we see the split personality of an age—a serious
and possibly tragic separation between the practical and the ideal.
Coleridge and other idealists wanted (more or less consciously) to

heal this schism by repudiating its causes—not through legislative reform or social action, but through ideas and art. In Mill's words:

The Germano-Coleridgean doctrine ... expresses the revolt of the human mind against the philosophy of the eighteenth century. It is ontological, because that was experimental; conservative, because that was innovative; religious, because so much of that was infidel; concrete and historical, because that was abstract and metaphysical; poetical, because that was matter-of-fact and prosaic.[5]

E. M. Forster is an implicit Coleridgean. Though neither a political conservative nor religious in a Christian sense, he shares essentially in all the values Mill lists, he is engaged in the same movement of thought and protest, and he is dedicated to the same search for ways (to take one instance) of joining poetry and matter-of-fact. In the long contention between Benthamite and Coleridgean, broadly and symbolically understood, he found the essential dialectic of his life and art. It is no exaggeration to say that nearly all the characters in Forster's novels are either Benthamites or Coleridgeans—opposing the mind to the heart, the letter to the spirit, efficiency to love. "Bentham's method," writes Mill, "may be shortly described as the method of detail; of treating wholes by separating them into their parts, abstractions by resolving them into the individuals of which they are made up; and breaking every question into pieces before attempting to solve it."[6] This is precisely the way of the male Wilcoxes in *Howards End*. Henry Wilcox "treated marriage like a funeral, item by item, never raising his eyes to the whole," and like his son, he used the methods of the committee room in dealing with emotion generally: "They did not make the mistake of handling human affairs in the bulk, but disposed of them item by item, sharply." (HE, 232, 103.)* In the questions Forster's characters ask themselves, in the attitudes they assume, we can see their author directing his attention to precisely the division that Mill named in 1840. And Forster the critic is as energetic an anti-Benthamite as Forster the artist.

2

A major literary aspect of that division is the antithesis between prose and poetry. A modern poet has defined poetry as "language married to music, reason embraced by imagination, intellect in the clasp of

* Works of E. M. Forster that are abbreviated in the text and Notes are listed on p. xi.

emotion, the outer world and the inner life united in metaphor."[7] The statement is Coleridgean. Coleridge was from childhood possessed, as Basil Willey says, with "a sense of the Whole as a living unity, a sense of God in all and all in God, a faith in a divine spiritual activity as the ground of all existence."[8] That wholeness was, for Coleridge, the essence of poetry, his great dread being that he might lose this vision and come to look upon the universe as a collection of parts, "an immense heap of *little* things."[9] His ideal poet is more than a maker of verses; he is a mediator between heaven and earth, the infinite and the particular, the unseen and the seen. His almost divine power is revealed "in the balance or reconcilement of opposite or discordant qualities: of sameness, with difference; of the general with the concrete; the idea with the image; the individual with the representative."[10]

Coleridge lived and wrote in an increasingly Benthamite society. "The nymphs are gone from the Regent's canal," lamented Hazlitt; the coal barges of industry had driven them out. Keats saw a "cold" scientific philosophy conquering "all mysteries by rule and line" and emptying "the haunted air."[11] Such writers feared man's severance from the springs of imagination, from the forces providing a culture with its myths and symbols, as a deplorable and fatal amputation. To the rationalists, material progress was unalloyed good. To the romantics "progress" brought with it a denial of something basic and eternal in human experience, a denial of what Carlyle, for one, called "unconsciousness": "Unconsciousness belongs to pure unmixed life; Consciousness to a diseased mixture and conflict of life and death: Unconsciousness is the sign of creation; Consciousness, at best, that of manufacture."[12] That denial continues. Jung's statement that "only an unparalleled impoverishment of symbolism could enable us to rediscover the gods as psychic factors . . . , as archetypes of the unconscious,"[13] is only another way of saying that the nymphs are still gone from the Regent's canal.

Forster's concern, like Coleridge's, is with restoring the nymphs, guarding them against further harm, and creating conditions in which they can flourish. To Forster, man's loss of respect for his own naïve experience, the withering of his capacity for wonder, the repression of feeling, and the denial of his myth-making powers are deadly serious matters. He has no plan of action (beyond the wish fulfillments of art) for bringing the nymphs back or for removing the barges, but he is convinced that somehow poetry must be joined to prose or we shall all shrivel up and die. "Only connect the prose and the passion and both will be exalted, and human love will be seen at its height. Live in fragments no longer." (HE, 197.)

Poetry to Forster, as to most romantics, is not only a literary form but a way of responding passionately to experience, a response to be found, as Hazlitt says, "wherever there is a sense of beauty, or power, or harmony."[14] In *Aspects of the Novel,* after discussing the relatively technical and mundane matters of story, people, and plot, Forster comes to what really interests him, "that vague and vast residue into which the subconscious enters," which he labels "poetry, religion, passion" (p. 98). The three words are not quite synonymous, but they are inseparable—the holy trinity of a romantic humanist. Forster talks of "poetry" in an evangelical, not a critical, sense; it is what makes "literature" out of "information," what transfigures matter-of-fact into beauty, what links the relative and the absolute. Poetry is a humanist's term for what is holy in a secular world. It is that which makes whole and sees whole: far from being just a literary exercise, it has to do with the entire ethical and spiritual life of man. The "Devil," as Forster defines him, is a Benthamite creature "blinded by arithmetic, deaf to the warnings of poetry, [who] assumes that a man is only the sum of his qualities." (GLD, 241.) To rout this doctrine is Forster's mission.

Forster's term for his own doctrine is Art with a capital A. Art is not simply a created work in painting, music, or literature; nor is it a term for all the arts thought of collectively. Art is an *idea* of wholeness, a wholeness that is greater and other than the sum of its parts. A work of art, writes Forster, "is a self-contained entity, with a life of its own. . . . It has internal order. It may have external form. That is how we recognise it."[15] Note: it *may* have external form. Art, with Forster, is a humanistic surrogate for God or the Divine Idea.

Unfortunately, however, there is no guarantee that this Idea will prevail in the social or the political realm. Art is valuable because it "creates little worlds of its own . . . in the bosom of this disordered planet,"[16] but those little worlds have no necessary impact on the great world; they may exist only as sanctuaries of private consolation. Consequently Forster reminds himself, as Tennyson was reminded by a friend, that one "cannot live in art." "Society," he writes, "can only represent a fragment of the human spirit, and . . . another fragment can only get expressed through art."[17]

Forster has heavy commitments in both directions: he is both artist and moralist, poet and prose writer, novelist and social critic. To recognize this tension in him is the first step in understanding his achievement. He is on the one hand a private sensibility, a unique individual talent, with esthetic allegiances outside of history and society—even in repudiation of them. Art, to him, means otherworldliness. On the other hand, he is a public and representative man, the product of a tradition, the self-conscious heir of a commercial and intellectual aristocracy stemming from the late eighteenth century. Both strains are strong: the private and the public, the unworldly and the worldly. In short, his life is divided even as the society of his time is divided.

This division has shown itself in a dramatic way: Forster published no fiction after 1924, when *A Passage to India* appeared. When he was forty-five the "poetry" virtually ceased and gave way to prose; the artist turned critic. "I somehow dried up after the *Passage*," he wrote. "I wanted to write but did not want to write novels."[18] If that kind of statement were peculiar to Forster, it would be nothing more than a confession of a personal failure. But it is not peculiar to him; it echoes a dozen similar confessions from the last century and this.

Coleridge, as Forster notes, "wrote all his best poetry when he was a young man of twenty-five, in a single year,"[19] after which a slow paralysis of his creativity set in. The poet gave way to the critic, the creator to the theorizer. Burdened though Coleridge was by the effort of seeking and hanging on to a religion, he managed, as Carlyle said, to save his "spiritual manhood," but this deliverance came at the cost of his art. No longer given his themes and values as part of a cultural inheritance, the poet had to discover them himself, a task often beyond his powers. The story of Coleridge's narcotic addictions and his clogged energies has become almost symbolic of an age's malaise—a fragmentation of purpose reflecting a cultural as well as a personal neurosis. A Benthamite world, equating poetry and pushpin, was spiritually starving its poets, and when it did not drive the artist from society into Bohemia, it forced him into apologizing for his vocation.

Crises more or less similar to Coleridge's afflicted Wordsworth, Carlyle, Browning, Tennyson, Ruskin, Arnold, Rossetti, Morris, Hopkins, Hardy, and T. S. Eliot—to name but a few. They all led divided lives.

If the role of the artist in the nineteenth century was a hard one, it was partly because the creative consciousness was sapped by the social conscience, by nagging demands on the artist's sense of responsibility. The need for education, poor relief, and humane working conditions made even temporary residence in the Ivory Tower seem self-indulgent; and Tennyson was typical in periodically abandoning his true poetic voice in order to heap versified abuse on poor laws, commercial greed, and the adulteration of bread. If Victorian writers agreed upon one thing, it was that their age was ugly. But the ugliness had political, social, and economic roots; it could not be corrected by pretty pictures or by books with happy endings, and it could not be decorated out of existence. Some artists were drawn to socialism; some translated their esthetic objectives into commercial and popular terms; most became part-time economists, political theorists, social critics. But nearly all of them suffered as artists.

Matthew Arnold is perhaps the most striking case. While still a young man, Arnold virtually abandoned poetry for literary, social, and religious criticism. Verses continued to come from his pen, but they were with rare exceptions the heavy-handed and heavy-hearted productions of an expired impulse, a talent made leaden with intellectual and moral freight. As early as 1853 he confessed to his friend Clough, "I am past thirty, and three parts iced over."[20] No writer of the century more successfully convinces his readers that he suffers from a drought of the age and not merely a personal drying-up. The Zeitgeist must be right if the artist is to be right, and this time was, for the poet, all wrong. In friends like Clough he saw the "strange disease of modern life"—the ratiocination, the morbid seriousness, the intense and unremitting self-analysis that was paralyzing his own poetic nerve. He tried to keep his distance, but he had caught the infection. The writing of poetry, Arnold wrote, "demands not merely an effort and a labour, but an actual tearing of oneself to pieces, which one does not readily consent to . . . unless one can devote one's whole life to poetry."[21] Such devotion, for Arnold, was impossible—partly because he had to earn a living as a school inspector, but more because, in one of his sharpest critical sentences, "The dialogue of the mind with itself has begun." This turning upon the self, the vicious circularity of the search for one's center of identity, bred a melancholy and ennui that Arnold never successfully combated. He once discarded one of his own poems because it presented a situation in which "there is everything to be endured, nothing to be done"; and he rightly saw that if art were to achieve "joy"—the aim that, following Schiller, he cherished for it—the conditions for that achievement must prevail in the world.* He strove, therefore, to create them, to make the world safe for art; and as the warmth departed from his poetry he tried to put it into his prose. His critical campaign was a great one, and no one has more brilliantly defined the essential terms of the Benthamite–Coleridgean contention as a cultural struggle. "Machinery" was not just something found in factories, but something in the souls of men and in their personal relations. Freedom, population, coal, wealth, religious organization—what are these, worshiped by the average Englishman as precious ends in themselves, but machinery, means toward ends?[22] To counter their force he proposed something that could be embraced as an end in itself, which he called *culture*. Culture is Arnold's final and all-embracing absolute, as Art is Forster's. Culture is man's perfection and the study of perfection; it is a condition achievable in society as a state of affairs, within the individual as a state of grace; it is both a being and a becoming, an ontological *Ding an sich* and a teleological expansion toward the perfect state:

Culture, then, is a study of perfection, and of harmonious perfection, general perfection, and perfection which consists in becoming something rather than in having something, in an inward condition of the mind and spirit, not in an outward set of circumstances.... The idea of perfection as an *inward* condition of the mind and spirit is at variance with the mechanical and material civilization in esteem with us, and nowhere, as I have said, so much in esteem as with us. The idea of perfection as a *general* expansion of the human family is at variance with our strong individualism, our hatred of all limits to the unrestrained swing of the individual's personality, our maxim of "every man for himself." Above all, the idea of perfection as a *harmonious* expansion of human nature is at variance with our want of

* In *A Room with a View*, Forster refers to "The sadness of the incomplete—the sadness that is often Life, but should never be Art" (p. 27).

flexibility, with our inaptitude for seeing more than one side of a thing, with our intense energetic absorption in the particular pursuit we happen to be following.[23]

Culture, in short, is Arnold's word for the ultimate Coleridgean synthesis, the Whole embracing all other wholes and rising above them. It is a term as full of contradictions and impossibilities as the Christian Trinity, but this is its mystery and value, for it is doing humanistic service in lieu of Christianity. Arnold could neither achieve this state of grace in his own poetry nor prevent the forces of prose from invading and dividing his life, but he gave the modern world an instructive look at what it means to be so deprived. Forster is deeply in Arnold's debt. Arnold's words again and again become Forster's, and the notion of a general and harmonious expansion is the very heart of Forster's esthetic ideal. Both are humanists, both are self-divided; Arnold more than any other Victorian helps us grasp Forster's dialectic of experience. "Matthew Arnold is of all the Victorians most to my taste: a great poet, a civilised citizen, and a prophet who has managed to project himself into our present troubles [1944], so that when we read him now he seems to be in the room."[24]

Nothing, however, unites them more than their early retirement as artists. Forster's only continuously productive period as an artist was the decade between 1902 and 1912, when all of his published fiction except *A Passage to India* was written. *Passage* (1924) was a kind of sport, the Indian summer of a talent that had shown marked faintness and weariness even before World War I. That novel was a superb flowering, but it was an end, not a beginning. With it the poetry stopped—though not absolutely—and the literary and social criticism began. There were, to be sure, other writings: histories, biographies, pageants, reviews, librettos, radio talks, letters. But they were not, in any serious sense, art.

3

Why did the springs dry up? When Forster asks himself this question, he nearly always strikes one note in his answers: events have moved too fast for him, he cannot handle artistically the kind of world that succeeded the one he grew up in: "As for the ends of *The Longest Journey* and *Howards End* they are certainly unsatisfactory, but perhaps were less so at the time. Then the English countryside, its reality, and creative retreat into it, were more plausible than they are today. Events have damaged my stock-in-trade as a novelist in this direction as they have in another: the existence, in an established home, of the family."[25]

Those two great historical changes—the passing of the countryside and the passing of the Victorian family—were main forces drawing Forster from fiction to exposition, from poetry to prose. "I don't fret over the changes in the world I grew up in. But I can't handle them," he wrote.[26] Near the conclusion of *Howards End* the "red rust," the smog of London, is seen on the horizon, a not-too-distant threat (in space or time) to the still unravaged countryside. The ugly cancer of suburban housing developments and industrial filth is moving in. Howards End is a house in Hertfordshire in which he lived as a boy (MT, 269), and a picture of it hangs in his rooms at King's College, Cambridge. (See Plate 25.) But by the end of the Second World War the house and much of the village it stood near were marked for destruction. The novel's prophecy had been fulfilled:

I was brought up as a boy in one of the home counties, in a district which I still think the loveliest in England. There is nothing special about it—it is agricultural land, and could not be described in terms of beauty spots. It must always have looked much the same. I have kept in touch with it, going back to it as to an abiding city and still visiting the house which was once my home, for it is occupied by friends. A farm is through the hedge, and when the farmer there was eight years old and I was nine, we used to jump up and down on his grandfather's straw ricks and spoil them. To-day he is a grandfather himself, so that I have the sense of five generations continuing in one place. [See MT, 274.] Life went on there as usual until this spring. Then someone who was applying for a permit to lay a water pipe was casually informed that it would not be granted since the whole area had been commandeered. Commandeered for what? Had not the war ended? Appropriate officials of the Ministry of Town and Country Planning now arrived from London and announced that a satellite town for 60,000 people is to be built. The people now living and working there are doomed; it is death in life for them and they move in a nightmare. The best agricultural land has been taken, they assert; the poor land down by the railway has been left; compensation is inadequate. Anyhow, the satellite town has finished them off as completely as it will obliterate the ancient and delicate scenery. Meteorite town would be a better name. It has fallen out of a blue sky.

"Well," says the voice of planning and progress, "why this sentimentality?

People must have houses." They must, and I think of working-class friends in north London who have to bring up four children in two rooms, and many are even worse off than that. But I cannot equate the problem. It is a collision of loyalties. I cannot free myself from the conviction that something irreplaceable has been destroyed and that a little piece of England has died as surely as if a bomb had hit it. I wonder what compensation there is in the world of the spirit, for the destruction of the life here, the life of tradition.[27]

That passage is a piece of the essential Forster—not only in what it says of his love of the country and the traditional, but in the "collision of loyalties" between those loves and his social conscience. He is too honest and serious to be concerned only with his own vested interest in a corner of England's loveliness, but the idea of a compromise between Hertfordshire and north London simply breaks his heart. He does not know the secret of making poetry from such a union any more than he knew how, in one of his novels, to bring the poor and the rich together. He does not avert his gaze from north London, he does not forget to include it in his picture of human reality, but at heart he wants to wipe it from the face of the earth and grow a Hertfordshire in its place.

The issue has no easy solution. The esthetic problem will not square with the problem of social justice, and the gap between the ideal and the social reality has grown too wide for art—at least Forster's art—to bridge. This sense of alienation from his world and subject, this "dissociation of sensibility," not only helped turn Forster the artist into a critic, but caused him to put his faith in individual rather than social salvation. "I wonder what compensation there is in the world of the spirit, for the destruction of the life here, the life of tradition." That is his essential question.

The basic problem is one of quality—how to maintain beauty, space, and human dignity in a leveling world, how to preserve the treasures of the privileged without sinking them in the anonymity of the insatiable mass. If selling all that one has and giving it to the poor would solve anything, Forster would doubtless do it, for he has a Protestant conscience and cares immensely about fair play. But it is not as simple as that. Forster cannot find solutions in political or economic terms because politics and economics do not deal in spiritual compensation, and the "red rust" is smothering not only Hertfordshire but the very soul of England. When he found the problem intractable, he stopped writing novels (at least novels with English settings) rather than falsify or sentimentalize it. The energy once directed into "poetry" was drawn off into polemics: "I am glad to have known our countryside before its roads were too dangerous to walk on and its rivers too dirty to bathe in, before its butterflies and wild flowers were decimated by arsenical spray, before Shakespeare's Avon frothed with detergents and the fish floated belly-up in the Cam."[28]

Such violations have, Forster claims, made him lose that "reverential" view of nature he felt so strongly in his early years,[29] and indeed most of his late writing on the subject has an elegiac tone. Nevertheless, nature, even nature remembered, can symbolize what is permanent, whole, and beautiful; and Forster's lament over its passing goes to the heart of his values. Destroy the old association between the land and the men who love her and you break a vital link with the instinctual life, with that sense of an ancient and unbroken heritage from the past which creates and enriches our cultural symbols. Forster values the English countryside (where it survives) because it has been handled gently, cherished over the mellowing centuries, whereas modern "progress" has been a rape. Abinger Hammer, the Surrey village where Forster once lived, can still evoke for him a time when men and nature knew a common rhythm, when the village and its fields were related as in a marriage, and a still earlier time when there were only unmolested trees: "Thousands of years before the Britons came, the ash grew at High Ashes and the holly at Holmwood and the oak at Blindoak Gate; there were yew and juniper and box on the downs before ever the Pilgrims came along the Pilgrims' Way."[30]

This "connection with the land"[31] is with Forster one of the primary meeting places of responsibility and faith. Unfortunately, the Benthamite commercial-mechanical juggernaut can bulldoze the connection out of existence in a day. But "preserving" the land in the form of public parks and greenbelts is, to Forster, not much better; it only puts the gods in a zoo. "The moment nature is 'reserved' her spirit has departed for me, she is an open-air annex of the school, and only the semi-educated will be deceived by her. The sort of poetry *I* seek resides in objects Man *can't* touch—like England's grass network of lanes a hundred years ago."[32] Like Arnold, he finds consolation in nature's "unmating things": "We want something honorable with which we are not naturally in contact, such as the rocks and the sea."[33] Destroy all visible evidences of a nature man cannot touch, and you destroy that sense of the vast which is an assurance that something is sacred, a promise from the physical world that a spiritual exists. The population explosion terrifies Forster not because it raises problems of housing or food supply, but because it threatens spiritual suffocation. "For some of us who are non-Christian," Forster writes, "there still remains the comfort of the non-human, the relief, when we look up at the stars, of realizing that they are uninhabitable."[34]

These may seem surprising words from a humanist, but the more we read Forster the more we become aware of what appears to be a negative, even nihilistic, side. Like D. H. Lawrence, he prizes that *otherness* to be found in nature and in the depths of the human psyche; and he values it not alone for its non-human peace, but even for "a sense of something vaguely sinister, which would do harm if it could . . . of something muffled up and recalcitrant; of something which rises upon its elbow when no one is present and looks down the converging paths."[35] Wordsworth knew those feelings too, and Forster is in some ways his heir. But such feelings come at a high ethical cost in the modern world. Few nature-lovers continuously face the antisocial implications of their love: in the crowded modern world, just to love space is to wish people elsewhere. And if there is nowhere else to go? As Forster said, he cannot equate the problem.

The second change that hurt Forster's artistic powers was the passing of the family. When Forster speaks of the family in an established home, he is speaking of two things: of his own particular family history, the faces and notations in the family album, and of the family as a value, as a symbol of a certain kind of integrity. We shall touch on that family history in the next chapter, but we should note here that his father's relatives were wealthy and eminent; and that at their center was Battersea Rise, the great house with its thirty-four bedrooms and spacious library (Plate 2). In his great-grandfather's house were many mansions, and Forster, though he never lived there, remembered it almost as a sanctuary, the temple of a lost wholeness, of a good life beyond reach. Forster's father died in 1880, when Forster was a baby, and the boy grew up as a tenant rather than a proprietor of the houses he lived in and loved. A sense of homelessness pervades his writing.* In *The Longest Journey* both Rickie and Agnes "needed a home to confront the menacing tumultuous world" (p. 159), and Rickie (one of Forster's avatars) "was extremely sensitive to the inside of a house, holding it an organism that expressed the thoughts, conscious and subconscious, of its inmates" (p. 176).

Houses, for Forster, were living symbols of an emotional and spirtual security that he had only tasted in his half-orphaned experience. The Hertfordshire house he loved as a child he left at the age of fourteen:

I took it to my heart and hoped, as Marianne had of Battersea Rise, that I should live and die there. We were out of it in ten years. The impressions received there remained and still glow—not always distinguishably, always inextinguishably—and have given me a slant upon society and history. It is a middle-class slant, atavistic, derived from the Thorntons, and it has been corrected by contact with friends who have never had a home in the Thornton sense, and do not want one. (MT, 269–70.)

This sense of loss, of partial disinheritance, is fundamental in understanding Forster. He longs for membership in some small community of faith as viable as the family was "when the Victorian fabric was still intact, and drawing-rooms seemed drawing-rooms and housemaids housemaids for ever."[36] The spiritual reality is not separable from the material. Forster is no sentimentalist about the family; he never pretends it is a frictionless bower of bliss, and often seems bored by the subject of marriage. But it provides a form, a setting, within which the individual can both be himself and be related, be free and yet belong. Life at Battersea Rise was to him a moving demonstration of how, in the right circumstances, "private decencies can be transmitted to public affairs."[37]

Another part of what Forster means by the passing of the family is the passing of manners, of the conventions. He reflects lovingly, for example, on how the Victorian upper-middle classes "adored death beds" (MT, 68). To Forster these were not routines but rituals, the

* Forster has lived in the following places (dates are approximate): Hertfordshire, 1883–93; Tonbridge and Tunbridge Wells, 1893–1901; Italy, 1901–2; Abinger Hammer, Surrey, 1902–45 (except for two visits to India, 1912–13 and 1921); King's College, Cambridge, 1945 to the present.

joining of private pieties to public gestures in a way the modern world
knows little about:

The bereaved and their comforters all write enormous letters, symptoms are
dwelt on, dying speeches and death-moments repeated and extended, the
Will of God is bowed to again and again, sorrow is so persistently exhibited
as joy that both become meaningless. The twentieth-century observer has to
remind himself that inside all this cocoonery of words there was love, there
was pain. It was the technique of the age and of a section of the middle
class; it lasted, as far as my own family were concerned, into the 1850's.
After that the technique of mourning shortens, it is now very brief and some
sensible people cut out mourning altogether. With it they cut down pain,
which has practical advantages, and with pain they cut down love. People
today love each other from moment to moment as much as ever their ancestors did, but loyalty of soul, such as the elder Thorntons possessed, is on the
decrease. (MT, 71.)

That loyalty of soul, exempt from the caprices of the passing moment,
is part of what Forster means by tradition—and it can exist only if
there are conventions and houses to hold it.

4

Forster's nostalgia for the old order is, of course, intimately tied up
with special privilege and class snobbery, and many people who have
known depressions and wars as their inheritance have great difficulty in sympathizing with Forster's sense of loss. Forster is the first
to acknowledge that Battersea Rise was a citadel of privilege maintained by a corps of underprivileged servants. The system was unfair,
even brutal, and had to go. But he cannot forget the values accruing
from the system—the beauty and space, the sense of order and continuance, the respect for the past*—and he wishes there were some way of
making those values consistent with social justice. Again, Forster cannot equate the problem. Fair play is important, but so is excellence;
the aristocracy of class, for all its faults, implies an aristocracy of spirit,
which we must not level out of existence. That is why he gives only
two cheers for democracy. The fragmentation of the modern world

* In 1934 Forster writes: "How much did the war destroy? It destroyed 'good
society.'... Will writers ever recover that peculiar blend of security and alertness
which characterises Mrs. Wharton and her tradition, and which has served her art
so well?" "Good Society," *The New Statesman and Nation*, VII (1934), 950.

has provided both form and subject for modern literature, but that is not the kind of literature Forster can write. Art, for him, is the creation of wholes, the harmonizing of contrarieties, not the celebration of lonely and unmended division.

It is significant that after *Howards End* (1910), the novel in which Forster most rigorously confronted the old with the new, he took up his next fictional residence in India, where life moved in more traditional rhythms and the past impinged on the present with less violence. After India the fiction ended (except for one unpublished novel); the search for poetry could no longer be sustained.

We must face the unpleasant truths that normal life to-day is a life in factories and offices, that even war has evolved from an adventure into a business, that even farming has become scientific, that insurance has taken the place of charity, that status has given way to contract. You will see how disquieting all this is to writers, who love, and ought to love, beauty and charm and the passage of the seasons, and generous impulses, and the tradition of their craft. And you will appreciate how lost some of them have been feeling during the last quarter of a century.[38]

Yet Forster has not given up. The modern world has forced him out of business as an artist, but not as a spokesman for Art. He does not raise his voice and his stance is unprophetic—that of one who looks away as he speaks, who "makes a perpetual slight displacement of the expected emphasis,"[39] who calls himself "old-fashioned." But, for all his gentleness, he is a tough-minded partisan who knows his own mind and puts his convictions on the line with energy and dedication. He was formed in a pre-1914 world and has scrapped few of the values derived from that sunny age, but he is no fossil. No antiquarian interest can account for his appeal to later generations, particularly the one of the Second World War. Though he has had no experience of trenches, breadlines, or concentration camps, he has not ignored this suffering; and his old-fashioned sensibility has seemed to many an astonishingly apt instrument for probing our present discontents.

Forster, in his own way, is an evangelist. His art, and his belief in art, are his religion, and he has simply gone on preaching what he could no longer practice. Besides art there is, of course, the social gospel, the joining of the body spiritual and the body politic. But ideally there is no conflict: the religion *is* a coming together, of the seen and the unseen, public affairs and private decencies. Another name for this religion is humanism. Christianity, writes Forster, "was a spiritual force once, but the indwelling spirit will have to be restated if it is to calm the waters again, and probably restated in a non-Christian form."[40] To make that restatement has been his life's work, in fiction and out of it. Like Roger Fry's, his art is one of "transformations"—an attempt to shape the crude clay of actuality into something divine, to transfigure the world of appearance into "value."

The crisis for Forster is whether this religion is translatable into any viable program of action. Can it exist except in idea—or outside an ivory tower? These are critical questions because of Forster's own deep aversion to the worldly and practical. "The more highly public life is organised the lower does its morality sink" he writes in 1939,[41] and his humanism is constantly threatened by his own fastidiousness, by a reluctance to come near the defiling pitch of the political or economic world. Still, Forster fights these tendencies, and his novels are not only chapters in a new gospel, they are dramatic installments in the story of his own struggle for selfhood—and for a myth to support it. They tell of a man coming out in the world, painfully emerging from an encysted state of loneliness, fear, and insecurity. Forster's evangelism springs as much from self-defense as from self-confidence, as much from weakness as from strength; but the style of his sermon always reflects those qualities about which there can for him be no compromise: tolerance and balance, sensitivity and common sense, and a loathing for everything dogmatic. In his own mild Arnoldian way, Forster is deeply committed, yet in the following passage we can see ennui fighting with engagement, decadence with puritan zeal. It is his own true style—a late version of the dialogue of the mind with itself. Why preach culture to the Philistines?

It is tempting to do nothing. Don't recommend culture. Assume that the future will have none, or will work out some form of it which we cannot expect to understand. Auntie had better keep her parcels for herself, in fact, and stop fidgeting. This attitude is dignified, and it further commends itself to me because I can reconcile it with respect for the people arguing upstairs. Who am I that I should worry them? Out of date myself, I like out of date things, and am willing to pass out of focus in that company, inheritor of a mode of life which is wanted no more. Do you agree? Without bitterness, let us sit upon the ground and tell sad stories of the death of kings, ourselves the last of their hangers-on. Drink the wine—no one wants it, though it came from the vineyards of Greece, the gardens of Persia. Break the glass —no one admires it, no one cares any more about quality or form. Without bitterness and without conceit take your leave. Time happens to have tripped you up, and this is a matter neither for shame nor for pride.

The difficulty here is that higher pleasures are not really wines or glasses at all. They rather resemble religion, and it is impossible to enjoy them without trying to hand them on. The appreciator of an aesthetic achievement becomes in his minor way an artist; he cannot rest without communicating what has been communicated to him. This "passing on" impulse takes various forms, some of them merely educational, others merely critical; but it is essentially a glow derived from the central fire, and to forbid it is to forbid the spread of the Gospel.[42]

The higher pleasures are not like wines or glasses, but like religion. So Mill told Bentham that pushpin is *not* as good as poetry, that there are degrees of pleasure, altruistic pleasure being among the highest. And so Coleridge preached the holiness of art. The Benthamite-Coleridgean war rages still, and the Benthamites are still ahead. Forster is not sure that art will have the victory over crude power very soon, but he is sure (if our world continues) that art will win in the long run. And his reason is the same as Arnold's—humanistic culture (including art) will survive because of a sense for "self-preservation" in the race: "I do not believe that this art business can be swept aside. No violence can destroy it, no sneering can belittle it. Based on an integrity in man's nature which lies deeper than moral integrity, it rises to heights of triumph which give us cause to hope."[43]

No violence? No sneering? Surely this argument, in the age of Hiroshima and Buchenwald, is mistaken. Yet the very extravagance of Forster's faith is what makes his achievement so interesting and important. No other modern English writer so bravely offers himself as a test of the proposition that art, created or appreciated, can be a surrogate for Christianity.

We must begin with Forster's roots, for the dialectic of his art began in the conflicts of his inheritance.

Chapter two

Clapham: The Father's House

Hate worldliness but love the world.

—E. M. Forster

People are trapped in history and history is trapped in them.

—James Baldwin

Forster is an ancestor-worshiper. This is not to say he loves his ancestors, but rather that he longs for their presence and feels their influence as something alive, something needed in his own character. The ancestor who is the archetype in this role and dominates the paternal line is Henry Thornton, Forster's great-grandfather and a leading figure in that "industry in doing good,"[1] the Clapham Sect. It is this strong man who is in Forster's mind as he writes "Recollectionism," the article in which he most clearly confesses his ancestor-worshiping. "In mythology, as in experience," he writes, "only a low barrier separates the present from all pasts." And then:

I can't myself manage chronology. The River of Time must be left to historians and Matthew Arnold. Most of us see the past as a swamp. Events do not flow past us; they neither go down into the mighty ocean nor are they lost in the sand; no . . . the moment they are out of our physical reach they begin to sway and interlock, and they remain quite near. It is no wonder that amateurs all through the ages have indulged in incantations, and hunted for the Word, the Gesture, the Sensation which should evoke their unburied dead. . . . The taste of a cake, the unevenness of a tile, were sufficient to regain all childhood, all Venice, for Proust. . . .

Events seem to die two deaths. The first occurs when they pass from us physically, the second when we remember them and so destroy their nature. And that is why . . . dreams, in spite of their silliness and horror, sometimes preserve an emotional truth which no waking moment can command. Dreams remember the essential past, however wildly they distort its forms. . . .

Still, there are solid reasons for remembering. . . . Memory gives mental

balance. That's partly why I practise it. The present is so heavy and so crude
and so vulgar that something has to be thrown into the opposite scale....
This is not a private fancy of mine: all races who have practised ancestor-
worship know about it.[2]

Henry Thornton, a "recollectionist" himself, would have had little
comprehension of "our quick jazzy minds, our trickiness with time,"
for he was at peace with time, as assured of an important place in the
hereafter as in the here—and his great-grandson clearly envies him.
Still, Henry Thornton and his circle would seem, on the surface, to
give Forster little to like: they were materialistic, pious, clannish, censorious, public-minded, antagonistic to art. But like or not like is
beside the point: they were strong, they had weight. "The world was
not so humorous then," writes Forster in *The Longest Journey* (pp.
106–7), "but it had been more important." And a sense of importance
is just what Forster lacked. Henry Thornton the individual can be
gently ridiculed, but Henry Thornton the institution, the ancestor, is
another matter. He is a form out of that "essential past," remembered
as well as dreamed, which can sustain the wanderer in the modern
wasteland. That Forster should see himself as that wanderer seems
strange, but the record, in fiction and out, reveals a man badly crippled by a lack of self-esteem, a man who felt himself to be weak, ugly,
and lost. To such a person the memory of that potent ancestor could
seem like the rising of another self.

But along with this paternal and masculine "past" was a maternal
and feminine one—and the two were powerfully, even destructively,
antithetical. Nor is the antithesis softened when we know that the
paternal line entered Forster's experience in the form of a woman, his
great-aunt, Marianne Thornton. His father was dead, and his mother
was, as we shall see, an almost defenseless pensioner on the good will
and generosity of the Thorntons, particularly of Marianne. The great-
aunt was a difficult and authoritative woman. Her attempt to usurp
the mother's role over the "Important One," Forster's ironic childhood title, seems to have accustomed Forster from his earliest days to
feeling like a victim, or at least like a fought-over prize.* "I had not

---

* Forster declared that his hated childhood curls were not cut off until the "old
lady" died (1887), at which time Forster was almost nine years of age. (Conversation with Forster, March 12, 1965.) "I... must have been almost the last of the
moppets thus to be tormented." MT, 267. See Plate 4.

really loved Aunt Monie—she was too old, and the masses of presents she had given me had not found their way to my tiny heart." (MT, 287.) It is an important sentence. Aunt Monie—Aunt Money: he took the presents but returned no love, and the guilt thus stirred was still being exorcised thirty years later. Stephen Wonham, one of Forster's fictional dream-selves, after running away from a female guardian (Rickie's aunt) as forbidding as Marianne, declares that he "would sooner die than take money from people he did not love" (LJ, 254). The fine simplicity of Stephen's gesture was not possible for Forster. For one thing, there is the second reason he gives in "Recollections" for remembering: there's money in it. "This is an age of autobiographies and recollections," he writes, and "there may be material and money in the past for a book or even two books."[3] The book that Forster made from the family records is, of course, *Marianne Thornton* (1956), a memorial to the benefactress whose bequest made Forster's writing career possible. There is a nice irony in the fact that Forster, by writing this book, is extracting one more gift from Marianne, a little more guilty tribute. There is even more irony in that Forster dedicates the book to his mother, that other woman in his life, Marianne's rival.

These tensions are all part of Forster's recollectionism. He delves into the past not only to seek "mental balance" but to settle old scores, and his fiction, obsessed as it is with the problem of continuance, is in large part one long negotiation with his inheritance. As we cross the four generations between worldly (but religious) Clapham and unworldly (but irreligious) Bloomsbury, we trace a span of history that, in Forster, is still being enacted as part of his inner drama. These are the poles of a psychological as well as a historical experience—the extremes of a mind's dialogue with itself—which constitute perhaps the fundamental dialectic of Forster's life and art. Forster was a "fringe" member of the Bloomsbury Group, in but not of it; likewise, in his sympathies, he was in but not of Clapham. This position of outsider is characteristic: to remain unaffiliated, to be furtive in one's comings and goings, is a way of staying free. Forster clung to such habits as he clung to an ideal amateurism, for to become specialized or committed is to reduce the sum of life's possibilities; it is to make choices, to abandon the dialogue for action—to grow up. Forster was not opposed to action, but for much of his life he was simply stymied, caught between alternatives too painful to be resolved—between money and honor, aunt and mother—and he tried to have it both ways. His fictions are the *exempla* of this dialectic, the dialogue turned to art, and they record the author's slow struggle for an identity and for a myth. We start with Clapham, for that "past," though not directly represented in his novels, is a presence in all of them, especially in their negotiations between God and Mammon, poetry and prose. Clapham gave Forster something to react against and an inheritance to justify; the distance he traveled from Clapham defined to a large extent who and what he became.

2

The Clapham Sect was a group of highly practical, intelligent, and wealthy Evangelical reformers who flourished between roughly 1790 and 1835. The account of their labors is staggering. Eminent in Parliament, the Church, the City, the universities, and the civil and military services,[4] this "brotherhood of Christian politicians"[5] was responsible for the abolition of the slave trade (1807); the emancipation of the slaves in the colonies (1833); the founding of the Missionary Society to sponsor Christian teaching in Australia, Africa, and the East (1799); the writing and distributing of edifying tracts for the lower classes; the establishment of *The Christian Observer* (1802), which became a journal of enormous influence; the founding of the British and Foreign Bible Society (1804), the Sunday School Society (1785), the Society for Giving Effect to His Majesty's Proclamation against Vice and Immorality (1799);* and the support of other good works dealing with prisoners, the blind, war widows, foreigners in distress, dueling, brutal sports, Sabbath observance, drunkenness, sedition, and blasphemy. On the night that Parliament passed the abolition bill—after years of agitation—William Wilberforce turned to Henry Thornton and asked, "Well, Henry, what shall we abolish next?" Thornton replied gravely, "The Lottery, I think."[6]

The men on this indefatigable committee worked through all the years of the French Revolution, the Napoleonic Wars, and the bad

---

* Sydney Smith, who did not like the Claphamites, called this "a Society for suppressing the vices of persons whose income does not exceed £500 *per annum*." Quoted by Howse, p. 120, from *The Edinburgh Review*, XIII (1809), 342.

times following, and within their number were some of the greatest
figures in England's intellectual aristocracy—centering in the four
families of Trevelyan, Macaulay, Huxley, and Arnold, a tradition
brilliantly studied by Noel Annan.[7] Nearly all of these families have
blood ties with Bloomsbury. But "the Agamemnon of the host, . . . the
very sun of the Claphamic system,"[8] was William Wilberforce, Henry
Thornton's cousin, who at twenty-six was converted and found his
life's work: "God Almighty has set before me two great objects, the
suppression of the slave trade and the reformation of manners."[9]
A personal friend of Pitt, and a magnificent speaker, he carried an immense moral authority in Parliament, even among his enemies. Unlike the provincial and obscurantist Wesleyans of the 1730's and
1740's, Wilberforce and his followers were men of the world, aristocratic, rich, well-bred; and though their latitudinarianism was anything but limitless, they did their best "to love the Quaker, to be kind
to the Presbyterian, to pity the Atheist, and to endure even the Roman
Catholic."[10]

Henry Thornton was Wilberforce's indispensable first lieutenant
and chief financier. "Before marriage," we learn from E. M. Howse,
"Henry Thornton gave away six-sevenths of what he earned; after
marriage two-thirds. In one year of distress he gave away £9,000."[11]
In the course of his life his gifts came to more than £150,000. The only
thing more wonderful than this giving is that there was this much
coming in. A banker and an astute man of business, he was also the
author of two books proclaiming his equal concern with treasure in
heaven and treasure upon earth: *Family Prayers* (published posthumously) and *An Enquiry into the Nature and Effects of the Paper
Credit of Great Britain*—the latter a work that went through thirty-
one editions between 1834 and 1854 and was so well done that Bentham gave up investigating the subject.

In a statement beginning with words from Thornton's friend and
executor, Sir Robert Inglis, Forster sums up the man:

"His piety was fervent, and yet sober; his liberality was magnificent and yet
discriminating; his charity was large and yet not latitudinarian; his self-
denial was rigorous yet unobtrusive." This is a very fair estimate. Like the
man himself, it does not go too far. There is also extant a charming portrait
of him by Hoppner, but this does not go too far either; calmness, modera-

tion and restraint dominate in its well-ordered scheme. Mr. Thornton's chin is firm without ferocity, his mouth ascetic without fanaticism, his forehead intelligent without fire, in his right hand is a parliamentary bill. The restless modern mind, skimming over all these solidities, finds nothing to laugh at, nothing to condemn, and nothing to die for, and becomes unsympathetic, partly through envy. Here is neither a sinner, a mystic, nor an artist—types which the modern mind can comprehend, and in whose presence it does not feel rebuked. Here is only a successful banker, an extensive philanthropist, a devout Christian, an affectionate husband and a judicious father, a loyal friend, an upright citizen, an incorruptible M.P.:

> No place or pension e'er got he
> For self or for connection;
> We shall not tax the Treasury
> By Thornton's re-election.[12]

Thornton gave not only his money and energy to the movement, but his house as well. Battersea Rise was the headquarters of the Sect,[13] and there for three decades the Saints, as they came to be called, gathered for their "Cabinet Councils" in the great oval library designed by Pitt. Thornton died in 1815, the group dwindled after the death of Wilberforce in 1833, and the great house passed out of existence in 1907. But these forces had injected something into the life of Victorian England—and into Forster's life—that continued to work. They taught their society something of the enormous power of a committee, how a small cell of dedicated and tireless believers could be a moral yeast, what Arnold called a "saving remnant." In their triumph over slavery, declared G. M. Trevelyan, lay the very origins of Victorian optimism, for "Mankind had been successfully lifted on to a higher plane by the energy of good men, and the world breathed a more kindly air."[14]

How much of this heritage does Forster accept? It is a complicated question, but clearly he was ambivalent: part he revered, and part he could not swallow. *Marianne Thornton* is a domestic, not a public, biography; and Forster chooses to make the subject of his book the unknown woman, Henry's daughter, rather than the great man himself. This is Forster's way of reading history. He seeks, with Proust, "the Word, the Gesture, the Sensation" that will evoke the past, and he wants it to come through as an "aroma" rather than as an accumulation of old fact. The following passage on Henry Thornton is typically full of those domestic details Forster chooses to remember. He has just quoted a prayer from Thornton's devotional volume offering thanks for the Almighty's "manifold and great mercies."

"Manifold and great mercies," indeed! What can the words have conveyed to the reader or to the family and the servants who listened to them from opposite ends of the great library at Battersea Rise? To us they mean nothing at all. We get something quite different out of them: no meaning, but an aroma, the aroma of a vanished society, the sense of well-to-do people on their knees, the solid chairs into which the elbows dig, the antimacassared backs against which the foreheads rest, the voice of the master of the house, confronting his Maker in a monotone, and, if the hour be morning, the great virgin breakfast table, clothed all in white like a bride.[15]

This is an attempt to make the past "live," as Proust did, in terms of small rather than great events. Forster does not focus on the public activities of Clapham, but on the family life; the rooms of Battersea Rise that interest him most are those dominated by the women and children.

The institution of Family Life, as Forster exalts it, is to him a value almost as absolute as Truth or Beauty, one of the eternal forms. Though the institution is now dead, along with the belief in immortality which propped it, Forster remembers and misses them both:

It is this belief [in personal immortality] that makes the "Clapham Sect" seem remote today, even to Christians. Personal immortality today may not be denied by orthodoxy, but it is played down, it is felt to be self-centered and anti-social, it is seldom conceived as a changeless background for family life as it was at Battersea Rise. Our hopes of continuance, when we entertain them, are arguably more spiritual. Then, they were a solid possession, to be maintained by prayers, self-questionings, and good deeds, and to be confirmed finally through the mercy of God. (MT, 29.)

Forster possesses, in the words of F. R. Leavis, "a kind of elemental hunger for continuance,"[16] but it is a hunger translated into humanistic terms, for most of the institutions that once fed it have crumbled.

Clapham was not only weighty, it was whole. It knew no self-alienating conflicts between private and public, meditation and action, money and spirit, the little society and the great world. To Forster Clapham represented an age when, in his words, "to get rich and to be good were harmonious."[17] Modern man has no such opportunity: "Utter, O someone, the word that shall reconcile outer and inner! In the realm of public battle a man is bound to lose his balance; in the private life he may keep it, but at the cost of becoming isolated."[18] And again, in 1939: "We are troubled to-day, each of us, because we can lead neither the private nor the public life with any decency. I cannot shut myself up in a Palace of Art or a Philosophic Tower and ignore the masses and the misery of the world. Yet I cannot throw myself into movements just because they are uncompromising, or merge myself in my own class, my own country, or anyone else's class or country, as if that were the unique good."[19] Forster is a relativist longing for absolutes, the absolutes that Clapham had never questioned. "Action is the life of virtue," wrote Hannah More, Clapham's most eminent bluestocking, "and the world is the theatre of action."* The men of Clapham acted without hesitation, for they moved as God's agents. Wilberforce declared in 1786 that "my shame is not occasioned by my thinking that I am too studiously diligent in the business of life; on the contrary, I then feel that I am serving God best when from proper motives I am most actively engaged in it."[20] By 1850 any connection between moneymaking and virtue had begun to seem a little quaint, by 1900 it seemed hypocritical, and by 1939 it could be regarded as an archaic delusion. "I must mix myself with action/Lest I wither by despair" cries one of Tennyson's heroes—the motive for acting being therapeutic rather than idealistic. Clapham would not have understood the meaning of action on such nervous grounds. Clapham did not feel this dichotomy; its tight little coterie was in active communication with the world of politics, business, and finance. But a century later the tight little coteries of Cambridge and Bloomsbury were far gone in seeking salvation by withdrawal, quarantining themselves spiritually from the contaminating world. Forster was affected by this tendency, but he recognized its dangers: "The sense of purity is a puzzling, and at times a fearful thing. It seems so noble, and it starts at one with morality. But it is a dangerous guide, and can lead us away not only from what is gracious, but also from what is good." (LJ,

* Hannah More's remarks preceding this statement are also instructive: "Let me not be suspected of intending to insinuate that religion encourages men to fly from society, and hide themselves in solitudes: to renounce the generous and important duties of active life, for the visionary, cold, and fruitless virtues of an Hermitage, or a Cloyster. No: the mischief arises not from our living in the world but from the world living in us; occupying our hearts, and monopolizing our affections." *The Works of Hannah More* (London, 1801), VI, 67.

159.) Asking, after Plato and Berkeley, "What is real?" Stewart Ansell of *The Longest Journey* grants the "great world" no true existence at all; and Forster, writing in 1960,[21] still endorsed Ansell's denunciation: "There is no great world at all, only a little earth, for ever isolated from the rest of the little solar system. The little earth is full of tiny societies, and Cambridge is one of them. All the societies are narrow, but some are good and some are bad—just as one house is beautiful inside and another ugly. . . . Fools . . . confuse 'great,' which has no meaning whatever, with 'good,' which means salvation." (LJ, 74.)

The sensitive individual, however, is not to be criticized for preferring a coterie. "The clique," writes Forster, "is a valuable social device, which only a fanatic would condemn."[22] But in our time cliques can be *good* only if they are *little*. Clapham's opportunity to be both good and great, to exist as a body of elect souls and at the same time operate in the dirty world, is now a lost chance. "For the world has not progressed as Henry Thornton hoped. The evils in human nature, which he realised, and the evils in commercialism, which he could not realise, have combined to pull it down, and the religious remedies he proposed seem to-day formal and trifling."[23]

3

But there is another, more personal, reason why the "little society" appeals to Forster: it is a remedy for homelessness. Rickie Elliot, about to leave Cambridge for the great world, laments: "I never shall come indoors again." (LJ, 75.) His is a fear of moving beyond a cordon sanitaire into corruption, but it is also a fear of exposure, of nakedness, of entering a hostile world with no arms of defense. Rickie tells Ansell: "You've got a house—not a metaphorical one, but a house with father and sisters. I haven't, and never shall have. There'll never again be a home for me like Cambridge. I shall only look at the outsides of homes." (LJ, 75.) Rickie is as close to an ego-character as Forster ever created, and this desire for a real house—not a metaphorical house but a real establishment like Battersea Rise—is the longing of one who felt not only spiritually orphaned, but orphaned in a personal family sense. There is real despair in the following confession:

The boy grew up in great loneliness. He worshipped his mother, and she was fond of him. But she was dignified and reticent, and pathos, like tattle, was disgusting to her. She was afraid of intimacy, in case it led to confidences and

tears, and so all her life she held her son at a little distance. Her kindness
and unselfishness knew no limits, but if he tried to be dramatic and thank
her, she told him not to be a little goose. And so the only person he came to
know at all was himself. He would play Halma against himself. He would
conduct solitary conversations, in which one part of him asked and another
part answered. It was an exciting game, and concluded with the formula:
"Good-bye. Thank you. I am glad to have met you. I hope before long we
shall enjoy another chat." And then perhaps he would sob for loneliness,
for he would see real people—real brothers, real friends—doing in warm life
the things he had pretended. (LJ, 32.)

"The only person he came to know at all was himself"! As his fiction
shows, even this knowledge was agonizingly partial.

Once again we are reminded that Forster inherited from a maternal
as well as a paternal line. He "worshipped" his mother, but the unconscious cruelty evident in the above passage suggests that "worshipped"
—with its hint of distance—may have been advisedly chosen in place
of "loved." There is an interesting episode in *The Longest Journey*
where Rickie is asked by his Cambridge friends if he hates his father.
He is silent, though we know the answer is yes. When they ask if he
hates his mother, he "turns crimson" (p. 28). We cannot tell whether
that flush is one of anger or one of shame (and, of course, the fiction
cannot be read as literal autobiography), but there are plenty of tales
from Forster's real life, some of them more painful than amusing, that
suggest how he was smothered under his mother's attentions.* Even

* In one of his early books William Plomer had described Forster thus: "In appearance he was the reverse of a dandy. Incurious fellow passengers on a train,
seeing him in a cheap cloth cap and a scruffy waterproof, and carrying the sort of
little bag that might have been carried in 1890 by the man who came to wind the
clocks, might have thought him a dim provincial of settled habits and taken no
more notice of him." When Forster's mother read these words she remarked,
"There! You see what Mr. Plomer says. How often have I told you, Morgan dear,
that you really ought to brush your coat?" *At Home* (London, 1958), pp. 107–8.

Forster's dislike of a father whom he never knew is a mystery for Forster's biographer to solve, but that it was in large part instilled by the mother seems beyond
question. The attack on the father in *The Longest Journey* is based partly on the
father's lack of taste. This same point is made in *Marianne Thornton*. Eddie Forster had studied under Arthur Blomfield, the same architect who taught Thomas
Hardy. Forster writes: "It is one of life's little ironies that I should have got to
know Mr. Hardy and stayed with him at Max Gate, and should have never known
my father, seven years his junior. My father . . . went abroad, and my treasured
relics of him are the architectural sketches he made of churches in France and

in his advanced years his mother would muffle him in scarves and coats, and there can be little doubt that the following conversation is, in essentials, remembered from life:

> "Put on your greatcoat, dearest," she said to him.
> "I don't think I want it," answered Rickie, remembering that he was now fifteen.
> "The wind is bitter. You ought to put it on."
> "But it's so heavy."
> "Do put it on dear."
> He was not very often irritable or rude, but he answered, "Oh I shan't catch cold. I do wish you wouldn't keep on bothering." (LJ, 35–36.)

Immediately after this in the novel, with no preparation, the mother dies—and the undutiful son suffers remorse. (Rickie did not tell his friends about the greatcoat, "for he could not have spoken of it without tears.") In order to find any familial love, Forster has to skip a whole generation to his maternal grandmother. Maternal love, like the paternal strength, is something distant, to be found by moving toward the past—but here at least it is unqualified: "How I adored my grandmother!—we played for hours together. In later life I became highminded and critical, but we remained friends, and it is with her —with them—that my heart lies." (MT, 250.)

Forster's mother, a Whichelo, "did not belong to Thornton circles" (MT, 249), and was never allowed by Marianne to forget her lower social station. She moved to Hertfordshire immediately following her husband's death—and did her best to stay away from Clapham after this move. It was not "an easy family to marry into," and in his book Forster tells of one "poor little bride" (possibly his mother) who declared that "If there was a spot upon the glorious Sun himself, the Thorntons would notice it."[24] Clapham was of the great world, and Forster was proud of his connections. But if Clapham fed his pride,

---

Italy. He developed a charming niggling pencil; the further up a spire a detail is, the more clearly it shows. . . . Whatever the merit of the sketches, they certainly stimulate one to visit the church portrayed, and I have never paid such a visit without disappointment—the church has been neither as gigantic nor as delicate as I hoped." (MT, 212.)

Forster was happy to grant me permission to reproduce photographs of his mother, but not of his father.

anti-Clapham fed his affections, for the Whichelos—easygoing, unorganized, untidy—were everything the Thorntons were not: "They had no enthusiasm for work, they were devoid of public spirit, and they were averse to piety and quick to detect the falsity sometimes accompanying it." (MT, 250.) Forster, like Dickens, always associates such qualities with warmth and humanity.

Still, the Whichelos offered him little protection against a threatening world. They "muddled through," yet the word "muddle" occurs again and again in Forster's work as a fearful thing, and only rarely as something pleasant. He loves their casual irreverence, but that does not help much in the pinches. He is partisan to their poverty, yet the money he inherited from the Thornton fortune gave him the freedom he needed to become a writer.

The whole conflict is another phase of that fundamental problem: how can one lay up both treasure upon earth and treasure in heaven? How can one connect love and power, joy and order? The contention is symbolized by the two women, the great-aunt with the military voice and the kind, gentle, fearful, conforming mother. "I hope in the next world," declared Forster's mother, "there will be a compartment labelled 'Thornton' and that it won't be anywhere near me." (MT, 253.) Forster made the same separation in his values, if not in his allegiances; and the statement about money at the end of *Marianne Thornton* is the nub of a conflict that nagged him throughout his career.

This £8000 has been the financial salvation of my life. Thanks to it, I was able to go to Cambridge—impossible otherwise, for I failed to win scholarships. After Cambridge I was able to travel for a couple of years, and travelling inclined me to write. After my first visit to India [1912] and after the first world war the value of the £8000 began to diminish, and later on it practically vanished. But by then my writings had begun to sell, and I have been able to live on them instead. Whether—in so stormy an age as ours—this is a reputable sequence I do not know. Still less do I know how the sequence and all sequences will end, with the storms increasing. But I am thankful so far, and thankful to Marianne Thornton; for she and no one else made my career as a writer possible, and her love, in a most tangible sense, followed me beyond the grave. (MT, 289.)

Forster refuses to be decorous about money, for it financed his richest spiritual opportunities. He talks about it bluntly, naming sums, as if to show that he has nothing to hide. But it worries him.

One of his most subtle and serious questions is an inversion of the orthodox Christian ethic: "Will it really profit us so much if we save our souls and lose the whole world?" (LJ, 256.) The answer is No. Treasure upon earth and treasure in heaven are both needed and needed together. Forster is fascinated by the possibility that Caesar's coin might be transmuted into the spirit's wealth—an alchemy attempted in *Howards End*. But can one take such coin without being corrupted? Clapham itself did not escape the defiling pitch:

> Thanks to the economic conditions of the times, wealth rushed down these worthy people's throats from morn to eve, and not being psychologists they thought it would have no effect upon their souls if they purged themselves promptly. The devil is subtler than that. He, like Christ, understands the deceitfulness of riches: the deceitfulness which many a bitter example now brings to the light. Wealth always fattens the person who swallows it, no matter how promptly he purges.[25]

It is by no means an easy alchemy. Forster is certain that poverty of pocket is related to poverty of spirit, that salvation is inseparable from the health and leisure and dignity that money buys. He would be entirely with Becky Sharp when she said, "I think I could be a good woman if I had five thousand a year." Still he does not like either the makers or the making of money, and he is harder than anyone else on his own ancestors. Witness Rickie and Ansell in *The Longest Journey*, listening to Ansell's father's cash register:

> "Listen to your money!" said Rickie. "I wish I could hear mine. I wish my money was alive."
> "I don't understand."
> "Mine's dead money. It's come to me through about six dead people—silently."
> "Getting a little smaller and a little more respectable each time, on account of the death-duties."
> "It needed to get respectable."
> "Why? Did your people, too, once keep a shop?"
> "Oh, not as bad as that! They only swindled. About a hundred years ago an Elliot did something shady and founded the fortunes of our house."
> "I never knew any one so relentless to his ancestors. You make up for your soapiness towards the living." (LJ, 39.)

In a confusing but provocative short chapter of *The Longest Journey* Forster plays with a metaphor of two kinds of currency—the soul's and not the soul's. The first is "spiritual coinage," which we stamp "with the image of some beloved face" (in this case Rickie's mother), some human ancestor that time and weak memory have made divine. But the soul can have her "bankruptcies," and we "but shift responsibility by making a standard of the dead" (LJ, 255), for we may find that the dead are not divine or infallible after all. We can meet this emergency by replacing man's image by God's (so the metaphor runs) and therefore make the coinage utterly incorruptible and trustworthy. But if this will purchase the soul's needs, it will by no means purchase the body's. This coinage "cannot give us friends, or the embrace of a lover, or the touch of children, for with our fellow-mortals it has no concern. It cannot even give the joys we call trivial—fine weather, the pleasures of meat and drink, bathing and the hot sand afterwards, running, dreamless sleep. Have we learnt the true discipline of a bankruptcy if we turn to such coinage as this?" (LJ, 256.)

This is the humanist's refusal to turn to God just because people let him down, the refusal to sacrifice the human relative to the divine absolute. It is another way of asking the question: Should one gather treasure in heaven or treasure upon earth? For Forster that problem is inseparable from the problem of his own inheritance, for the anxiety to join the two kinds of treasure is fundamentally an anxiety about continuance. Neither the dead past nor the dead God can alone serve the bankrupt individual; he must mint his own living coinage if he is in turn to make his own bequests.

Forster again and again uses a commercial vocabulary in dealing with spiritual problems.* Clapham, too, borrowed its language of devotion from the marketplace: "to close the deal with God," "to close with the offer of God in Christ," and "to acquire a saving interest in the Blood of Jesus" are representative Clapham metaphors.[26] But to Clapham the language of business connoted something good, a moral and character-building enterprise, whereas to Forster "commercialism" is a curse-word. His use of such language, therefore, is touched with irony—or at least with a deliberate down-to-earthness that in itself marks the wide distance between himself and Clapham. Forster belongs to the same culture that advised the young Edith Wharton: "Never talk about money, and think about it as little as possible."[27]

* The father of the Schlegel sisters in HE, for example, speaks of paying "rent to the ideal, to his own faith in human nature" (p. 44).

"In came the nice fat dividends, up rose the lofty thoughts, and we did not realise that all the time we were exploiting the poor of our own country and the backward races abroad, and getting bigger profits from our investments than we should. We refused to face this unpalatable truth. I remember being told as a small boy, 'Dear, don't talk about money, it's ugly'—a good example, that, of Victorian defence mechanism." (TC, 120.) Forster broke with that canon of taste in the name of honesty. Clapham, however, knew no such squeamishness, sensed no irony between its wealth and the squalor of the working classes.

Indeed, that squalor—when they were aware of it—stirred thankfulness rather than guilt. These are the words of Henry Thornton to Charles Grant after visiting some factories:

We have ... gone together to see a variety of Manufactures and have been learning to feel for those who dig in Mines, who toil in Quarries, perspire in Salt works, wear out their Eyes in looking at Furnaces, or pass their morning noon and Even in the limited Employment of putting on the head of a Pin, or drawing over and over the same pattern on a piece of China. I fear that the less pleasant part of Education has been neglected. I trust however that seeing the world in this sense will prove very useful. It has also not a little entertained Mrs. T. & I trust that the View which we have taken of our fellow creatures has inspired some thankfulness for the temporal as well as spiritual Advantages of our condition. (MT, 53–54.)

The "final question" with Clapham "always passed from material considerations to spiritual,"[28] but the process often involved, as above, the evasion of embarrassing questions, the censoring of speculation that might lead to revolutionary conclusions. Negro slavery was an atrocity to be abolished, but factory slavery was a law of life, and it took a generation stirred by Dickens and the horror-stories of Parliamentary investigating committees before conservative Evangelicals turned seriously to the charities needed at home.*

"The very poor," writes Forster in *Howards End,* "are unthinkable,

* Ebenezer Elliott was one contemporary who noted these contradictions:
        Their lofty souls have telescopic eyes,
        Which see the smallest speck of distant pain,
        While, at their feet, a world of agonies,
        Unseen, unheard, unheeded, writhes in vain.
"The Ranter," *The Poetical Works of Ebenezer Elliott* (London, 1876), I, 369.

and only to be approached by the statistician or the poet." (HE, 47.)
The position is close to Clapham's. It does not mean that Forster
refuses to think about the poor, but only that he cannot accommodate them in his art. His art is concerned with the creation of a spiritual aristocracy, not a welfare state, and the "very poor" are beyond his imaginative reach. On the whole he has clung to his class
and his prerogatives, not so much from selfishness as from the conviction that only the well-off can attend to spiritual concerns, and that
it is better to have some so occupied than none at all. His view is not,
after all, so very different from Wilberforce's when he said: "I declare my greatest cause of difference with the democrats, is their laying, and causing people to lay, so great a stress on the concerns of this
world, as to occupy their whole minds and hearts, and to leave a few
scanty and lukewarm thoughts for the heavenly treasure."[29]

In the world of practical politics and economics, however, the differences between Clapham and Bloomsbury were immense. Clapham
was fundamentally Utilitarian; its leaders believed, with Adam Smith
and Ricardo and Malthus, that any interference with the free market
or the iron law of wages was bound to be pernicious.* Bloomsbury,
led mainly by John Maynard Keynes, was ardently anti-Utilitarian;
its goal was the planned society. Clapham had never doubted that the
poor you have always with you; Keynes was the architect of full employment. Clapham had engaged in private charity; Keynes made
charity a function of the state. Perhaps most revolutionary of all, the
Utilitarian ethic called for thrift; Keynes called for spending. Forster,
adapting his convictions to Keynes's, took a position that would have
horrified Henry Thornton:

> It is childish to save; thrift was only a virtue so long as it paid, which it has
> ceased to do. And it is fantastic to spend too much on charity; all the money
> in England could not stay the world's misery now, or even solve the refugee
> problem. Spending on art has this advantage, apart from the pleasure to be
> gained from it; it does maintain an artistic framework which may come in
> useful in the future; it is connected with a positive hope.[30]

---

* Although they were, of course, opposed to Utilitarian freethinking. Wilberforce
writes in 1830: "The Westminster Review, of which [James] Mill is a principal
support, is a very mischievous publication, and this Review will be a death-blow to
Mill as a reasoner." *Life of Wilberforce*, V, 315.

In the days just before the Second World War, spending became for Forster not only a moral expedient but a psychological need: "Sensitive people" who have money, he recommends, "should start spending it at once—spending quiets the nerves—and should spend it as if civilisation is permanent."[31] Money, for Forster, is never entirely unassociated with guilt, but for Clapham it was the mark of God's favor.

It may seem strange that Keynes, who helped create the welfare state, should be on the same side as a man who makes "personal relations" the center of his creed and despises the esthetic and spiritual results of leveling. In fact, however, personal relations are valuable to Forster partly because of the bankruptcy of individualism in the Utilitarian sense.* The individualism he prizes, as he indicates in "The Challenge of Our Time," is exclusively personal and spiritual:

> The doctrine of *laissez-faire* will not work in the material world. It has led to the black market and the capitalist jungle. We must have planning and ration books and controls, or millions of people will have nowhere to live and nothing to eat. On the other hand, the doctrine of *laissez-faire* is the only one that seems to work in the world of the spirit; if you plan and control men's minds you stunt them, you get the censorship, the secret police, the road to serfdom,† the community of slaves ... [We are told] that when all people are properly fed and housed, they will have an outlook which will be right, because they are the people. I cannot swallow that. I have no mystic faith in the people. I have in the individual. He seems to me a divine achievement and I mistrust any view which belittles him.[32]

Finally, both Clapham and Bloomsbury made a passage to India—but with what a difference! Clapham found Hindu society loathsome and unclean. Wilberforce described the Hindu Gods as "absolute

---

* Thus Meacham, in *Henry Thornton of Clapham* (p. 65): "Convinced that only private morality could bring public virtue, the Evangelicals saw it their duty to enter Parliament." Forster shared this conviction, but took an exactly opposite course.

† *The Road to Serfdom* is the title of a book (published in 1944) by Friedrich Hayek, who edited Thornton's book on *Paper Credit*. Hayek lived in London when "The Challenge of Our Time" appeared in 1946, and has taught at the London School of Economics since 1931. The book is a kind of anti-planning tract advocating free competition in a capitalist society. Forster is half on his side, but criticizes him for not emphasizing the "importance" of love in his book. "A Clash of Authority," *The Listener*, XXXI (1944), 686. (Review of Hayek and of Harold Laski, *Faith, Reason, and Civilisation*.)

monsters of lust, injustice, wickedness and cruelty," and India's religious system as "one grand abomination."[33] The Evangelical mission
was nothing less than a "direct assault" on the Hindu mind in order to
redeem it from outer darkness and, incidentally, add to British rev-
enue. The two missions are typically mixed in Charles Grant's earnest
summary of why God had smiled upon the expansion of the Empire:
"Is it not necessary to conclude that [new territories] were given to us,
not merely that we might draw an annual profit from them, but that
we might diffuse among their inhabitants, long sunk in darkness, vice,
and misery, the light and benign influence of the truth, the blessings
of well-regulated society, the improvements and comforts of active industry?"[34] English clergymen continued to be shocked by the immorality of Indian deities well into the twentieth century, as Forster
indicated in a review of *The Gods of India* by the Reverend E. O.
Martin: "Deity after diety is summoned before the tribunal of Wes-
leyanism, and dismissed with no uncertain voice. Krishna stole butter
as a baby, and worse later. Jagganath is a goggle-eyed log. Brahama
'has an unenviable moral record,' and his head was once cut off by
the thumbnail of Siva's left hand. 'What a scene is this for the wonder
of the world!' Mr. Martin cries."[35] Forster, by contrast, went to India
to be taught, not to teach; to appreciate, not to condemn. Moreover,
he went not as an Englishman or a ruler or a missionary, but as an individual without vested interests or preconceptions—an individual
quite willing to assume foreign costume if it proved more comfortable
or sensible or beautiful. He went not to bring light, but to see if the
darkness held secrets and mysteries worth knowing.

And this brings us to Forster's one unqualified criticism of his Clapham sires: they had no taste for mystery, for ambiguity, for poetry:

This indifference to the unseen seems to me the great defect in my great-
grandfather's set, and the reason why they have not made a bigger name in
history. It came out in everything—in the books they collected, in the letters
my great-aunts wrote to one another, and in the comments which they made
upon life, which are surprisingly dry for people so pious. Poetry, mystery,
passion, ecstasy, music, don't count.[36]

Those five things, for Forster, do count, and his difference with
Clapham on this score is final and beyond negotiation. Clapham never

felt the need of being lifted into "a region outside money." Forster—
and most of Bloomsbury—put this need above all others. Clapham,
when all is said and done, was unacceptable not because it was too
rich or too political or too authoritarian, but because it was not religious enough.

Chapter three

The Apostolic Ring

O spare Cambridge! Is not the city a little one? Is she not unparalleled?

The strong are so stupid.

—*E. M. Forster*

At a time when the Clapham Sect was close to the height of its strength and influence, another little English subculture, which represented an almost antithetical set of values, appeared. This was "the Apostles," a secret discussion society[1] organized around 1820 at St. John's College by George Tomlinson (later Bishop of Gibraltar)[2] and originally called the "Cambridge Conversazione Society"—or just "the Society." In 1824 the Society moved to Trinity, where most of its "best talents" dwelt, and it has remained there or at neighboring King's ever since,[3] numbering in its ranks some of the most distinguished British thinkers of the nineteenth and twentieth centuries. Three stages are evident in the Society's evolution: the original pre-Victorian gathering; a midcentury stage beginning at the time of Henry Sidgwick; and a third stage beginning around the turn of the century —just after Forster's Cambridge years (1897–1901). Frances Brookfield, writing in 1906, puts the heyday of the Society between 1820 and 1840, when it could boast such members as Alfred and Frederick Tennyson, Arthur Hallam, F. D. Maurice, Connop Thirlwall, Monckton Milnes, John Kemble, and William Whewell. But the names on the fin-de-siècle roster are even more impressive. Among the dons and fellows of that time were G. Lowes Dickinson, Roger Fry, J. M. E. McTaggart, G. E. Moore, Bertrand Russell, Nathaniel Wedd, and Alfred North Whitehead; among the undergraduates were Forster, John Maynard Keynes, Desmond MacCarthy, Thoby Stephen, Lytton Strachey, and Leonard Woolf.

The original Bloomsbury Group—with almost the sole exceptions of Clive Bell and its famous women, Virginia and Vanessa Stephen—belonged to this brotherhood, and even these ladies have been described as "Apostles to the fingertips."[4] But Forster, as we have noted, was something of a fringe Bloomsburian; he came up to King's in 1897, almost four years before those other young men, and Keynes, Woolf, and Strachey* all testify to the irregularity of his attendance at Bloomsbury gatherings after his graduation in 1901.[5]

Forster was only slightly touched by the influences that so overwhelmed the others. He cannot remember having read Moore's *Principia Ethica*, the appearance of which in 1903 caused Keynes to herald "the opening of a new heaven on a new earth" and Strachey to exclaim, "The age of reason has come!"[6] Instead of the *Principia* he had fed on Dickinson's *The Meaning of Good* (1901), a far more amateur work, which Moore's totally overshadowed.† If Forster knew any particular renaissance in 1903, it doubtless owed more to Samuel Butler's *The Way of All Flesh,* which appeared posthumously in that year, than to the standard Bloomsbury gospels. He partook of an altogether milder and more gentle intellectual climate.

To understand Forster we do not go primarily to Bloomsbury, or to the Moorean renaissance that helped cement the interests and friendships forming that coterie; we go—as Clive Bell has suggested—to the Apostles.[7] It was through this society of friends that Forster entered Bloomsbury, insofar as he did so, and it was largely his fortuitous acceptance by the Apostles that made his coming to Cambridge such an epiphany.‡ His biography of Dickinson is dedicated *Fratrum Societati,* and the joys Forster attributes to Dickinson upon arrival at Cambridge were his own as well:

As Cambridge filled up with friends it acquired a magic quality. Body and spirit, reason and emotion, work and play, architecture and scenery, laugh-

---

* Strachey was as eminent in Bloomsbury as Forster was retiring. Noel Annan writes, "It says an immense amount for the extraordinary power of Strachey's personality that, although he showed no signs of doing anything or publishing anything before *Eminent Victorians,* which fully displayed that power, Bloomsbury accepted him as an arbiter." Letter from Annan to the author, June 5, 1963.

† In GLD Forster erroneously fixed the publication date of *Principia Ethica* as 1901, when Dickinson's book was in proof.

‡ Forster thinks he joined the Apostles in 1897, the year he came up to Cambridge. Conversation with Forster, March 10, 1965.

ter and seriousness, life and art—these pairs which are elsewhere contrasted were there fused into one. People and books reinforced one another, intelligence joined hands with affection, speculation became a passion, and discussion was made profound by love. When Goldie [Dickinson] speaks of this magic fusion he illumines more careers than his own, and he seems not only to epitomise Cambridge but to amplify it, and to make it the heritage of many who will never go there in the flesh. (GLD, 35.)

When Forster writes lovingly of the intellectual life of the societies at Cambridge, the importance of the Apostles in distilling the essential Cambridge for himself and for Dickinson is plain:

The young men seek truth rather than victory, they are willing to abjure an opinion when it is proved untenable, they do not try to score off one another, they do not feel diffidence too high a price to pay for integrity.... Certainly these societies represent the very antithesis of the rotarian spirit. No one who has once felt their power will ever become a good mixer or a yes-man. Their influence, when it goes wrong, leads to self-consciousness and superciliousness; when it goes right, the mind is sharpened, the judgment is strengthened, and the heart becomes less selfish. There is nothing specially academic about them, they exist in other places where intelligent youths are allowed to gather together unregimented, but in Cambridge they seem to generate a peculiar clean white light of their own which can remain serviceable right on into middle age. (GLD, 66.)

Could it have really been *this* good? Certainly it seemed so to Forster, and there is little doubt that here he found his essential home. (We get no hint here of the stridency sometimes heard in Bloomsbury discussions—where candor could be cruel—and there is every reason to suppose that Bloomsbury-in-Cambridge, away from the great world and its women, was a warmer enclave than the London branch.) Here was the little society *within* the little society—the core of that holy entity called Cambridge. And here took place those lightly structured rituals by which the elect were renewed in spirit and came to think of themselves as one body—a "saving remnant," in Arnold's phrase—that was preparing in some ill-defined way to cast its clean white light into the dark world of the "Stumpfs."* As Rickie declares in *The Longest Journey,* " 'I'm certain one ought to be polite, even to people who aren't saved.' ('Not saved' was a phrase they applied just then to those whom they did not like or intimately

* An early apostolic term for philistines.

know.)" (p. 23.) One can think of more vigorous ways of casting one's light among men; but the problem for the Apostles, and more particularly for Forster, was how to enter the world without being contaminated by it. (Clapham's easy solution could no longer be entertained.) Rickie wanted to end "sets" in the College, and his companions scoffed; he wanted to "love everybody" and they thought him a fool. Yet he persisted in dreaming that the great world could model itself on the little world of the Apostles instead of being, as he had been told it was, a magnified version of the public school.

Forster's extravagant thankfulness at being received in this company owes not a little to his unhappiness at school. His testimony differs little from that of dozens of others, including Bertrand Russell and Leonard Woolf, who felt euphoric relief in escaping to Cambridge (or Oxford) from the stupefying boredom of late-Victorian households and public schools. Russell speaks of the unbearable loneliness of a childhood spent "in a morbid atmosphere where an unwholesome kind of morality was encouraged to such an extent as to paralyse intelligence."[8] Woolf calls the public school "the nursery of British philistinism," where "use of the mind, intellectual curiosity . . . were violently condemned and persecuted"—by masters as well as by boys.[9] Forster's school was Tonbridge, which appears as Sawston in *The Longest Journey,* and like most places with Forster, Sawston is a set of values as well as a place on a map.* The place is upper-middle-class suburbia, the stronghold of orthodoxy, convention, and chauvinism, and the school at its center told its inmates one great lie: that it was "the world in miniature" (LJ, 178).[10] Years later Forster gave a mock public school commencement address: "School was the unhappiest time of my life. . . . For it hindered me from discovering how lovely and delightful and kind the world can be, and how much of it is intelligible. From this platform of middle age, this throne of experience, this altar of wisdom, this scaffold of character, this beacon of hope, this threshold of decay, my last words to you are: 'There's a better time coming.' "[11]

The Cambridge-Sawston opposition is one of those symbiotic dual-

* Forster was at Tonbridge from 1893 to 1897 (ages 14-17). In retrospect, he remembers his time at school as unpleasant but not tragic (conversation with Forster, March 8, 1965); and actually the Headmaster of Tonbridge let Forster go bicycle riding instead of making him take part in the required games.

isms in Forster's work. What he loves is intimately tied to and defined by what he hates. One whole phase of his moral position is rooted in opposition, in the memory of private deprivations comparable to those Dickens suffered in the blacking warehouse, of a sense of loneliness and betrayal far more intense than the actual situation would seem to warrant. Although Forster can joke about Sawston-Tonbridge (or "Snobston" as he sometimes tags it), the joking is only controlled contempt. A boy in *The Longest Journey* would not learn the school anthem on the grounds that "it hurt his throat" (p. 190), and Forster, whether he was that boy or not, had no easier time trying to swallow the belligerent and muscular ideals the song recommended. In later years he parodied it thus:

> Choose we for life's battle, harp or sword or pen,
> Perish every laggard, let us all be men.
> So shall Snobston flourish, so shall England be
> Serving King and Country, ruling land and sea.[12]

In contrast, Cambridge seemed "too good to be real," and there Forster learned "that there is something more compelling in life than team-work and more vital than cricket, that firmness, self-complacency and fatuity do not between them compose the whole armour of man, that lessons may have to do with leisure and grammar with literature" (GLD, 26). Cambridge, as Frank Swinnerton writes, was "the most wonderful thing that ever happened" to Forster,[13] and he never got over it. It was the break, and after it Forster could never go home again, for this was home.

2

The Apostles displayed across the century an astonishing homogeneity of attitude and spirit. They were a single communion, and the forces binding them together were far stronger than any separating them. The reasons for this homogeneity are obvious. For one thing, Apostles were members for life and kept returning—the Society prided itself on bringing young and old together. For another, Apostles selected Apostles, perpetuating a membership similar in taste, class, intelligence, and breeding.

Even the apostolic ritual remained relatively unchanged throughout the years. The members would gather on Saturday evenings in the rooms of one who was to read a paper or to present some views, the doors would be closed against the outside world, some light re- freshments would be handed round (usually coffee and "whales," or anchovies on toast), and the host would hold forth. When he finished "the others replied, agreed, disproved, criticized, as conscience or as humour dictated."[14] In the earliest days, the gatherings were anything but solemn, as Dean Merivale, whose Apostleship coincided with Tennyson's, recalled:

It was with a vague idea that it should be our function to interpret the oracles of transcendental wisdom to the world of Philistines, or Stumpfs, as we designated them, and from time to time to call forth from this world the great souls who might be found capable of sympathizing with them, that we piqued ourselves on the name of the "Apostles"—a name given us, as we were sometimes told, by the envious and jeering vulgar, but to which we presumed that we had a legitimate claim, and gladly accepted it. We lived, as I said, in constant intercourse with one another... but every Saturday evening we held a more solemn sitting, when each member of the society, about twelve in number, delivered an essay on any subject, chosen by him- self, to be discussed and submitted to the vote of the whole number. Alas! alas! what reckless joyous evenings those were. What solemn things were said, pipe in hand; how much serious emotion was mingled with alternate bursts of laughter; how everyone hit his neighbour, intellectually, right and left, and was hit again, and no mark left on either side; how much sentiment was mingled with how much humour![15]

By midcentury the Society had acquired a somewhat more sober cast—with emphasis on "candor" and "sincerity"—though other qual- ities were unchanged. Henry Sidgwick, representing the serious Cam- bridge so much admired by F. R. Leavis (who thinks Bloomsbury brought the downfall of that Cambridge), has left an illuminating account of the Society in 1856–57.* Questions of religious doubt were in the air, and Sidgwick resigned his Fellowship at Trinity rather than give assent to a Thirty-Nine Articles that he could no longer accept in good conscience. He is a kind of touchstone for Bloomsbury,

* Sidgwick became a kind of test case for the Leavises in their assaults on Blooms- bury. His moral seriousness, and his willingness to stand up and suffer for his be- liefs, made him in their eyes a symbol of Cambridge at her best: "Cambridge was ...a place where it was possible to be a moral hero and find plenty of backers." Q. D. Leavis, "Henry Sidgwick's Cambridge," Scrutiny, XV (1947), 8. I am indebted in this review of the Apostles to Harrod, Keynes, pp. 69–75.

for while those later Apostles admired his moral goodness, his solemnity and racked conscience were—at least for Strachey and Keynes—
too reminiscent of a repudiated Victorianism to be palatable. "I have
never found so dull a book so absorbing,"[16] wrote Keynes of Sidgwick's *Memoir* in 1906.

> I wonder what he would have thought of us; and I wonder what we think
> of him. And then his conscience—incredible. There is no doubt about his
> moral goodness. And yet it is all so dreadfully depressing—no intimacy, no
> clear-cut crisp boldness. Oh, I suppose he was intimate but he didn't seem
> to have anything to be intimate about except his religious doubts. And he
> really ought to have got over that a little sooner; because he knew that the
> thing wasn't true perfectly well from the beginning.

But for all their misgivings about their mid-Victorian predecessors,
the fin-de-siècle Apostles, especially those who formed the core of
Bloomsbury, had a great deal in common with them*—and even with
Clapham. No one has understood these persisting kinships better than
Noel Annan:

> On the surface there seems to be little to connect Leslie Stephen's daugh-
> ters ... or Henry Thornton's great-grandson, E. M. Forster, with the Clap-
> ham Sect. On the surface only. Bloomsbury, like Clapham, was a coterie. It
> was exclusive and clannish. It regarded outsiders as unconverted and was
> contemptuous of good form opinions. Remarks which did not show that
> grace had descended upon their utterer were met with killing silence. Like
> the Claphamites they criticised each other unsparingly but with affection.
> Like Clapham, Bloomsbury had discovered a new creed: the same exhilara-
> tion filled the air, the same conviction that a new truth had been disclosed,
> a new Kingdom conquered. Bloomsbury assumed that worldly values were
> grotesquely stupid and wicked. Its members despised wealth, power, popu-
> larity and success and were sharp to notice whether someone was on the
> make. For this reason both Clapham and Bloomsbury infuriated polite soci-
> ety and drew upon themselves a good deal of envious spite. The two sets,
> of course, held very different views about laughter. The Claphamites were
> cheerful but only Wilberforce can be said to have known the meaning of

---

* Leonard Woolf is one who feels that there has been little change in the Apostles
since Sidgwick's day: "I am writing today [1960] just over a century after the year
in which Sidgwick was elected an Apostle, and looking back to the year 1903 I can
say that our beliefs, our discussions, our intellectual behavior in 1903 were in every
conceivable way exactly the same as those described by Sidgwick." *Sowing,* pp.
150–51.

the word humour. Bloomsbury's sense of humour was exceedingly highly developed. . . . But they combined extreme frivolity with extreme serious-ness. . . . Finally, both Clapham and Bloomsbury were circles which influ-enced the whole outlook of their generation. They were each in their time responsible for spreading the new ideas of "modern" morality.[17]

However, to notice these similarities is not to ignore the profound differences between Clapham on the one hand and Bloomsbury and the Apostles on the other. The tradition of the Apostles, from the earliest days, was such as to give Forster a footing independent of Clap-ham, upon which he could negotiate with those formidable ancestors. Indeed, the contrast between Clapham and the Apostles—dramatizing as it does that conflict between prose and poetry, Bentham and Cole-ridge, with which we began—is crucial to an understanding of For-ster's intellectual and artistic development.

3

In the first place, Clapham and the Apostles showed marked differ-ences in what might be called their spiritual taste, or religious tone. The motto of that Claphamite-in-Cambridge, Charles Simeon (a Fel-low of King's and an incumbent of Holy Trinity for fifty-three years—from 1783 until 1836), was "Be serious—be in earnest—don't trifle,"[18] and he stirred up among the "Sims" (as his followers were called) an Evangelical revival paralleling in intensity the one Newman aroused at Oxford. But the Apostles could not stand him or his mannerisms.* As Monckton Milnes describes his preaching we are reminded of Strachey on Dr. Arnold (in *Eminent Victorians*): "He brandishes his spectacles when he talks of the terrible, and smirks and smiles when he offers consolation."[19] Tennyson, the most famous Apostle of all,

* Sir James Stephen thus describes him in 1844: "To a casual acquaintance he must frequently have appeared like some truant from the green-room, studying in clerical costume for the part of Mercutio, and doing it scandalously ill. Such ad-venturous attitudes, such a ceaseless play of the facial muscles, so seeming a con-sciousness of the advantages of his figure, with so seemingly an unconsciousness of the disadvantages of his carriage—a seat in the saddle so triumphant, badinage so ponderous, stories so exquisitely unbefitting him about the pedigree of his horses or the vintages of his cellar—the caricaturists must have been faithless to their call-ing, and the under-graduates false to their nature, if pencil, pen, and tongue had not made him their prey." "The Clapham Sect," *The Edinburgh Review*, LXXX (1844), 297–98.

doubtless had Simeon in mind as he caricatured that earlier saint, "St. Simeon Stylites":

> Altho' I be the basest of mankind
> From scalp to sole one slough and crust of sin,
> Unfit for earth, unfit for heaven, scarce meet
> For troops of devils, mad with blasphemy,
> I will not cease to grasp the hope I hold
> Of Saintdom, and to clamour, mourn, and sob,
> Battering the gates of heaven with storms of prayer,
> Have mercy, Lord, and take away my sin!

On his deathbed Simeon grandiloquently called himself "the chief of sinners and the greatest monument of God's mercy,"[20] and some of this self-confidence apparently washed off on his disciples. Samuel Butler (one of Forster's favorites) has fun with the Sims in *The Way of All Flesh* when Ernest Pontifex parodies a Simeonite tract by taking "Personal Cleanliness" as his theme and exhorting the Sims to "a freer use of the tub."[21]

Yet the early Apostles, although they mocked clergymen, respected what they felt to be true religion—and their successors retained this respect. John Sterling, that eminent apostate whose *Life* was written by Carlyle, writes to a fellow-Apostle asking to be commended to the brethren, "who, I trust, are waxing daily in religion and radicalism."[22] The two words belong together, but the Apostles' religious radicalism bore no similarity to the atheism or anticlericalism of the Benthamites (to whom religion was an opiate), or to such organized secularism of the later century as that of Bradlaugh. They were, instead, in the tradition of philosophic idealism, schooled in Goethe, Kant, and (later) Hegel, and deeply read in the English Romantics, who sought divinity in nature and man, apart from revelation. They were discovering, as T. H. Huxley did after them, how "a deep sense of religion was compatible with the entire absence of theology."[23] And they led an English generation that was beginning to see the Truth as "no longer absolute, . . . static, revealed once and for all, but as relative, genetic, and evolutionary. The birth of Christ became not *the* event in history, but *an* event on a globe in which Man was a transitory being."[24] The Word of God for the Apostles was writ as large in the literature of human history, and in the private soul, as in the Bible—a far cry from the Bible Christianity of the Clapham Sect, which, for all its spiritual individualism, would have been shocked at such apostolic exploration in the world of experience. It took the Apostle Tennyson to say, "There lives more faith in honest doubt/Believe me, than in half the creeds."

Furthermore, the Apostles differed from Clapham in being anti-Utilitarian, opposing not just Benthamism but Paleyism. Richard Trench, an early Apostle who had "never quite liked" the Society, referred derisively to "the whole band of Platonico-Wordsworthian-Coleridgean-anti-Utilitarians"[25] who opposed not only Benthamite social and economic theories but also Archbishop Paley, the orthodox "moralist of utility." That this opposition was fundamental is evident from Keynes's assertion a century later that he regards "the Benthamite tradition . . . as the worm which has been gnawing at the insides of modern civilisation and is responsible for its present moral decay."[26] In *Evidences of Christianity* (1794)—a book still set as an examination subject for admission to Cambridge as late as 1921[27]—Paley maintains that "the truths of religion are akin to scientific truths and defensible by the same methods," arguing for the dogmas of the Church "with the quiet efficiency of a mathematical demonstration."[28] Such cool complacency toward religion was, of course, as antipathetic to the Claphamites as to the Apostles, for the Evangelical could not dissociate religion from what fired it, "that caloric—the vital heat of the soul itself."[29] But Paley's argument from design, particularly as it touched on the social order, was Clapham's very own:*
"If these rules [of property] sometimes throw an excessive or disproportionate share to one man's lot, who can help it? It is much better that it should be so, than that the rules themselves be broken up."[30] The Apostles were by no means political radicals, but they rejected Paley for the same reason they rejected Bentham: they could not swallow an ethic of expediency and self-interest, they could not dissociate

---

* Standish Meacham tells how Henry Thornton drew the lesson "How beautiful is the order of society" from the Fifth Commandment: ". . . when every person adorns the station in which GOD has placed him; when the inferior pays willing honour to the superior; and when the superior is diligently occupied in the duties of his trust . . . when minister and people, when young and old, high and low, rich and poor, instead of each intruding into the place of others, sit down, each satisfied with his own condition." *Henry Thornton*, p. 141.

religion from poetry, they could not reduce evil to a matter of "false moral arithmetic."[31] William Whewell, a midcentury Apostle and clergyman-scientist who tried to mend the split between science and religion, compared Paley with that very different defender of the faith, Bishop Butler:* "Paley makes virtue depend upon the consequences of our actions; Butler makes it depend upon the due operation of our moral constitution. Paley is the moralist of utility; Butler of conscience."[32] Coleridge, as anti-Paley as he is anti-Bentham, voices a disgust that the Apostles fully shared: "Evidences of Christianity! I am weary of the word. Make a man feel the want of it, rouse him, if you can, to the self-knowledge, of his need of it; and you may safely trust it to its own evidence."[33] And Utilitarians like Malthus roused him to furious denunciation:

Is it not lamentable—is it not even marvellous—that the monstrous practical sophism of Malthus should now have gotten complete possession of the leading men of the kingdom! Such an essential lie in morals—such a practical lie in fact. . . . I solemnly declare that I do not believe that all the heresies, and sects, and factions which the ignorance, and the weakness, and the wickedness of man have ever given birth to, were altogether so disgraceful, to man as a Christian, a philosopher, a statesman, or citizen, as this abominable tenet.[34]

The latter-day apostolic commitment to individualism and personal relations rendered the Apostles all but impervious to the appeal of "economic bogus-faiths" peddled as substitutes for Christianity—especially, as Keynes said, to "the final *reductio ad absurdum* of Benthamism known as Marxism."[35] Clapham had been Utilitarian in a practical rather than in a doctrinaire sense, waxing prosperous in a free market which seemed scarcely distinguishable from the hand of God;[36] but Bloomsbury, at the other end of the century, though still living on some of the profits, had lost all faith in the market's divine sanctions.

4

Clapham and the Apostles also differ in their attitudes toward action. Although many Apostles became eminent in church, state, and

---

* From whom Moore borrowed the epigraph for *Principia Ethica*, "Everything is what it is, and not another thing."

academy, they tended to be men of ideas rather than social and political activists. When Sterling, Hallam, and Tennyson engaged in a Spanish revolutionary enterprise, it was behavior as distinctly unapostolic as Julian Bell's participation in the Spanish Civil War more than a century later.* The Apostles' emphasis was on the inner condition of the individual—on the dictates of conscience and right reason over convention or law—and Keynes's statement (though it slightly misrepresents Moore) that "nothing mattered except states of mind . . . [that] were not associated with action or achievement or with consequences" indicates the persistence of that emphasis.[37] It was Coleridge who, following Kant, led in dramatizing for his generation the operation of the "Conscience, or Moral Constitution"—that right reason which differentiates man from the brutes and idiots and issues its moral imperatives irrespective of considerations of utility. Utterly different in kind from sense impressions, which are "morally passive," this higher reason, when properly cultivated, commands man to the "love of the good for the good's sake, and the love of the truth for the truth's sake."[38] Man can become deaf and blind to these ends in themselves by allowing the "appetites, passions, and imaginations" to usurp reason's domination over the will, but the man who can be called a man fosters the highest development of reason and conscience in himself. This is the *act* of faith:

It appears, then, that even the very first step, that the initiation of the process, the becoming conscious of a conscience, partakes of the nature of an act. It is an act, in and by which we take upon ourselves an allegiance, and consequently the obligation of fealty; and this fealty or fidelity implying the power of being unfaithful, it is the first and fundamental sense of faith.[39]

This is an idea of enormous consequence. To regard a state of mind as an *act* is to internalize morality, putting being good over doing good, and reducing the whole notion of moral responsibility to a matter of sensibility. Yet on this idea, or emphasis, rests Bloomsbury's entire ethic and esthetic—and its belief in the value of things that are ends in themselves. But within this idea also lurks the chief danger in that ethic—its tendency toward solipsism.

* Although Apostles in the 'thirties tended toward Marxism and engagement, they were never revolutionists in any serious sense of the word.

The idea is clearly evident in Bloomsbury's peculiar liberalism, its penchant for apolitical politics. Frederick Crews has ably traced the political roots of this liberalism,[40] but it can also be explained in terms of a philosophic and religious bias. Annan has called Bloomsbury a "revolution," but in what sense can an internalized morality be considered an instrument of change? Forster cheerfully admits that Cambridge has played a comparatively small part in the "control of world affairs" (GLD, 66), and Arnold before him, in commenting on the members of this new class of intellectual aristocrats (which the Apostles perfectly represent), had said that they were "not much of a civilising force" and were "somehow bounded and ineffective."[41] Their liberalism is revolutionary only if we accept some such notion of revolution as that advanced by Lord Acton—who was Regius Professor of Modern History at Cambridge between 1895 and 1902, and was admired by Forster.* Liberalism, in Acton's view, is the reign of ideas, "the advent of general ideas which we call the Revolution."[42] "Facts must yield to ideas."[43] The notion that "history was, in its most significant sense, the history of ideas—rather than of institutions, events, or persons," writes Gertrude Himmelfarb, "was itself an affirmation of revolution, for ideas are, at least potentially, subversive of institutions and critical of events and persons."[44] But the nub of the question comes right here: just how is the historian (or the history-maker) to get from "the impersonal forces, the abstract ideas, that govern men"[45] to the backstairs realities of crude power? Acton does not answer, nor is it much help to hear, in his famous phrases, that "power tends to corrupt and absolute power corrupts absolutely" or that history is the "disclosure of guilt and shame" or that "great men are almost always bad men."[46] Forster would agree with all these sentiments, for his distrust of power and of great men— and of "history" in its institutional sense—is fundamental: "No, I distrust Great Men. They produce a desert of uniformity around them and often a pool of blood too." (TC, 82.) How, then, is righteousness to join with power?

---

* Forster attended two courses of lectures given by Acton, and always remembered one of his remarks: "Every villain is followed by a sophist with a sponge." Conversation with Forster, March 8, 1965.

1 Henry Thornton, M.P.,
Forster's great-grandfather.
Painting by John Hoppner, about 1814.

2 Battersea Rise from the garden, about 1907.

3 Marianne Thornton, Forster's great-aunt, the daughter of Henry **Thornton**.
  Painting by George Richmond, 1873.

4 Forster, aged about three years, with his mother.
September 1882.

5 The living room of West Hackhurst, Abinger Hammer, Surrey,
   the home of Forster and his mother from about 1903 until 1945.

6 Forster, aged twelve or thirteen, probably at Tonbridge.

7 Forster's "adored" grandmother, Louisa Graham Whichelo; the original of Mrs. Honeychurch in *A Room with a View*.

8 A crack at Bloomsbury: Caricature of Fry by Max Beerbohm.
   The caption reads: "We needs must love the highest when we see it."

9 Goldsworthy Lowes Dickinson,
about 1930.

10 Edward Carpenter,
about 1916.

Four Apostles *(top left to right)*:
J. M. E. McTaggart as a young don. Painting by Roger Fry.
G. E. Moore. Sketch by Percy Horton, 1947.
Nathaniel Wedd, about 1906.
Roger Fry, about 1930.   (Plates 11–14)

Ideas can be weapons. "In Acton's lifetime," writes E. H. Carr, "liberalism had not spent its force as a dynamic of social change,"[47] and Bloomsbury was a prime carrier of those "general ideas which we call the Revolution"—until, that is, the War killed the stable society that had nourished them. Every revolution needs its first principles, and Bloomsbury produced them in abundance: besides Moore's *Principia Ethica* (1903) there was Bertrand Russell's *Principles of Mathematics* (1903), Russell and Whitehead's *Principia Mathematica* (1910–13),* Leonard Woolf's *Principia Politica* (1953),† and John Maynard Keynes's *General Theory* (1936), not to mention Roger Fry's pioneering work in esthetics, notably *Transformations* (1926). Moreover, it has been argued that the ideas of the Apostles have had a profound effect on action in the sense that, seeping down through such organs as the *New Statesman,* the *Guardian,* and the *Observer,* they have created a climate in educated circles (Civil Service, etc.) that has made possible such things as the orderly transfer of control to colonial peoples.

Nevertheless Bloomsbury liberalism was emphatically a liberalism of ideas detached from political engagement. In 1903, Dickinson helped start a liberal journal, *The Independent Review,* "to combat the aggressive Imperialism and the Protection campaign of Joe Chamberlain; and to advocate sanity in foreign affairs and a constructive policy at home" (GLD, 115). But in Dickinson's own contributions, these political aims are scarcely touched on: he deals instead with religion and faith, materialism and morals. "It was not so much a Liberal review as an appeal to Liberalism from the Left to be its better self" (GLD, 115), and Forster, who published ten stories and articles in it between 1903 and 1906 (and one in 1908, when it had become *The Albany Review*), regarded it as an organ of political messianism and utopianism rather than as a call to political action. Although the journal "did not make much difference to the councils of the nation," Forster writes, those associated with the magazine

---

* Developed from Russell's *Principles* (1903).

† This is the third volume in a series, the first two of which were called *After the Deluge* (1931) and *Barbarians at the Gate* (1939). Keynes thought the whole series should bear the title of the third volume, and Woolf agrees. See *Principia Politica* (New York, 1953), p. vi.

saw avenues opening into literature, philosophy, human relationships, and
the road of the future passing through not insurmountable dangers to a
possible Utopia. Can you imagine decency touched with poetry? It was thus
that the "Independent" appeared to us—a light rather than a fire, but a light
that penetrated the emotions.... The first number lies on the table as I
write.... I bought it on a bookstall at St. Pancras thirty years back, and
thought the new age had begun. (GLD, 116.)

E. H. Carr calls the "exaltation of practical action over idealistic
theorizing" the very "hallmark of conservatism,"[48] and by this standard the Apostles have been radical indeed. Just as J. W. Blakesley
complained in 1830 that Hallam "was submitting himself to the influences of the outer world more than (I think) a man of his genius
ought to do,"[49] so the Bloomsbury coterie felt that Keynes mixed too
much with the "political and high official world." "Some of us,"
writes Clive Bell, "shook our heads ... over the new friendships.
Would they not encourage the growth of ... false values? Would he
not be attaching more importance to means (power, honours, conventions, money) than to ends—i.e., good states of mind (*vide Principia
Ethica passim*)?"[50] The inner light has usually looked dangerously
red to conservatives, and few conservatives are made comfortable by
remarks like Forster's in "What I Believe": "If I had to choose between betraying my country and betraying my friend, I hope I should
have the guts to betray my country." (TC, 78.) Yet the impulse behind
such "idealistic theorizing" is deeply conservative; it proceeds from
the notion that only by dramatically elevating the individual over
the state will the state be kept in its place—as the servant of the private man and not his master. What things are ends in themselves?
That is the persistent liberal question. The individual qualifies, but
the state—unless it is the ideal state of Plato or Arnold—does not.

Imbued with such attitudes, the fin-de-siècle Apostles cultivated a
pose of irreverence toward Queen and Country, war and imperialism, politics and patriotism (all the things that excited the patriots
who supported the Boer War).* In 1900 the following stanzas (and

* These attitudes were, however, far from being limited to avant-garde Cambridge undergraduates. Helen Merrell Lynd writes: "There was beginning to be
disaffection with politics and with political parties altogether, an attitude of cynicism about *political* action which was to reach more complete expression in Cham-

many more in the same vein) appeared in *Basileona*, an undergraduate magazine to which Forster often contributed. Though Forster
claimed not to have written them, they were included in his scrap-
book, and are easily within the scope of his poetic talents.[51]

> I fail to see the reason why
> Britannia should rule the waves,
> Nor can I safely prophesy
> That Britons never shall be slaves;
> It always gives me quite a pain
> Even to *think* about the main.
>
> Elusive prospects of renown
> Do not excite me in the least,
> A Lion fighting for a Crown
> Is hardly an attractive beast.
> If you are anxious to be shot
> For Queen and Country, I am not.
>
> I have no longing to be great;
> One island is enough for me,
> Conveniently situate
> Within the circum-ambient sea,
> Where I may—so to speak—recline
> At ease beneath my private vine.

This is the apostolic tone: the serious opinion delivered with comic
insouciance. But there is also foppery here—the aristocratic stance of a
ruling race grown too sensitive to rule, too highbrow to stoop to politics except as a diversion. Bloomsbury was saved from fatal smugness
by the lessons of two world wars; but liberalism is always threatened
by its own self-esteem, the factitious moral superiority that comes
from holding refined or noble ideas not tested in action. One of
Bloomsbury's younger members drove this point home.

Julian Bell, the son of Vanessa and Clive, recorded a serious disa-
greement with Bloomsbury values in his *Essays, Poems, and Letters*

---

berlain's 'Patriotism before politics' slogan of 1900. Awareness of social and economic problems was increasing and 'politics' had not solved them." Helen Merrell
Lynd, *England in the Eighteen Eighties* (London, 1945), p. 7.

However, Forster, like Dickinson, was for a brief time a supporter of the Boer
War. Conversation with Forster, King's College, November 6, 1957; see also GLD, 86.

(posthumously published in 1938). To turn one's back on a crumbling world, to take one's ease beneath a private vine in 1937 (if one was lucky enough to find one) was, he felt, no longer an honorable option. Charles Mauron, Bloomsbury's Gallic representative who wrote an appreciation for the volume, describes the seductive little world from which Bell felt he must escape:

> None of these . . . is a man of action, they are painters, writers, philosophers of liberal outlook. In their work and in their lives all have given the greatest importance to liberty of thought, expression and choice. They think, amuse themselves and suffer in the peaceful qualitative land of tastes and colours. This was Julian Bell's spiritual home. But as soon as the necessity to act and change the world arises, he knows that he must leave that happy valley.[52]

Bell did not utterly repudiate his apostolic inheritance, but he was convinced that the Bloomsbury ethos would gain social respect only "when its exponents were willing to defend it and, if necessary, die for it."[53] His death on the Spanish front in 1937 shocked Bloomsbury, but it did not convince them he was right.

Forster, in response to Bell's "Letter to E. M. Forster" in the volume, replies somewhat peevishly: "What did Julian intend me, personally, to do after reading this letter? Not to chuck gentleness, I think. He realised that the rebound from gentleness is into sadism and hysteria, not into strength, and that if one has been gentle, semi-idealistic and semi-cynical, kind, tolerant, demure and generally speaking a liberal for nearly sixty years, it is wiser to stick to one's outfit."[54] Bell's letter is confused, contradictory, and sometimes silly —as when he doubts that the "prolonged and violent activity" of a soldier "brutalizes quite as horribly as does idealism"[55]—but it raises questions that deserved a less defensive answer. Forster does not face the fact that the liberal outfit, and his own gentleness, exist partly because others have wielded bayonets; or that (in Kipling's words) one "making mock of uniforms that guard you while you sleep" has something to answer for. One cannot stick by one's outfit unless there is an outfit to stick by,* and Bell—less secure than Forster in his own good luck—strongly brought home this point:

---

* A friend close to Forster points out that Forster, like other English intellectuals, was on Goebbels's list of persons to be exterminated in the event that England was conquered. Thus Forster is particularly indebted to the "prolonged and violent activity" of the R.A.F.

The first weakness ... of liberal politics and the liberal view, above all recently, has been that they neglect these elements of force and power. The second is the disregard of real sources of power. Liberals think in terms of a stable world, limited opposition, limited reforms, and of reason, persuasion, agitation, intrigue and "public opinion" as methods of accomplishing their reforms.[56]

But Bell's return to the world did not entice his apostolic friends and relatives. With only minor concessions, they stuck to their liberalism, and that liberalism is still a force. It is so because the social outfit in which it was nurtured has by hook or by crook survived—maimed, bombed, and socialized, but still tolerant of its gadflies, still receptive to ideas, still sensitive to public opinion, still adroit enough to maneuver the vested interests into sporadic acts of decency. Forster has bet on this survival, and his mission has been to keep it civilized.

Forster's liberalism is beset by a contradiction pointed out by Trilling and others: as a liberal he sees life as a "progress"; as a humanist he conceives of it as "civilization."[57] The first involves a commitment to continuity, the second to justice; the first to the view that society is pragmatic and relative, the second to the view (or dream) that human organization can approach the condition of the City of God and know something like absolute justice. To get rid of all anomalies may result in tyranny, or in worse anomalies; to accept the ideal may involve a denial of the human. "Hence the humanistic belief, often delusive, that society can change itself gradually by taking thought and revising sensibility."[58] A passage from the story "The Point of It" brilliantly illustrates how Forster, by some stylistic sleight-of-hand, tries (and perhaps manages) to have it both ways. As a humanist he speaks of a love that is absolute, but as a liberal he puts off its full realization to a future time:

He cared for the universe, for the tiny tangle in it that we call civilization, for his fellow men who had made the tangle and who transcended it. Love, the love of humanity, warmed him; and even when he was thinking of other matters, was looking at Orion perhaps in the cold winter evenings, a pang of joy, too sweet for description, would thrill him, and he would feel sure that our highest impulses have some eternal value, and will be completed hereafter. (cs, 150.)

We have wandered far from any simple contrast between Clapham and Bloomsbury; but the question of the morality of action, of works

vs. grace, is so fundamental in the apostolic ethos and so deeply implicated in Forster's art that we need this reading in its history.

The apostolic religion, as it flourished around 1903, was a fantasy
of wishful thinking, a liberal meliorism compounded variously of
McTaggart, Dickinson, and Moore, and derived ultimately from such
romantic idealists as Plato, Jesus, Goethe, Kant, Hegel, and A. C.
Bradley. It was the dream of a coterie of lapsed Protestants (all the
Apostles of Forster's day came from Nonconformist families) who en-
visioned a guilt-free and virtually frictionless world. The faith, at
least in its conscious forms, was killed by the First World War, and
the wisest Apostles (Forster included) had doubted it before that.
Still, all of apostolic Bloomsbury had ridden for much the same fall,
and Keynes describes it uncommonly well. They had, he writes,
thrown Utilitarian hedonism out the window and with it any notion
of social action "as an end in itself." And they had thrown out "not
only social action, but the life of action generally, power, politics,
success, wealth, ambition with the economic motive and the economic
criterion less prominent in our philosophy than with St. Francis
of Assisi, who at least made collections for the birds."[59] He continues:

> We were among the last of the Utopians, or meliorists as they are sometimes
> called, who believe in a continuing moral progress by virtue of which the
> human race already consists of reliable, rational, decent people, influenced
> by truth and objective standards, who can be safely released from the out-
> ward restraints of convention and traditional standards and inflexible rules
> of conduct, and left, from now onwards, to their own sensible devices, pure
> motives and reliable intuitions of the good. . . .
>
> In short, we repudiated all versions of the doctrine of original sin, of there
> being insane and irrational springs of wickedness in most men. We were not
> aware that civilisation was a thin and precarious crust erected by the person-
> ality and the will of a very few, and only maintained by rules and conventions
> skilfully put across and guilefully preserved.[60]

It is Forster's distinction that he was never completely unaware of
that "thin and precarious crust." War shocked him as it did the others, but it did not entirely surprise him. Though he sees what he came
to call the "subconscious" partly as a benign force, a well of energies
feeding the artistic impulse and preventing mental sterility,[61] he
also knows its blind destructiveness. Intuition, he writes, "can make

dancing dervishes of us all, and . . . the man who believes a thing is true because he feels it in his bones, is not very far removed from the man who believes it on the authority of a policeman's truncheon" (AH, 52). Forster shared Bloomsbury's hopes, but not, in any naïve measure, its optimism; his novels show an increasing awareness of something dark and negative in man competing with his sweetness and light.

The crisis for Forster—as for liberal Bloomsbury generally—arises at that edge where society, the individual, and something perhaps describable as the holy spirit, meet. Forster has not always maneuvered those three terms satisfactorily, but he has always known them as a deep personal tension rather than a mere formal dialectic. That is why his work is exciting in a way that Dickinson's, for example, is not. It is a critique of his liberal inheritance, not a mere exposition of it.

In 1907 Forster read a paper to the Working Men's Council Literary Society (one of those Ruskinite efforts to bring culture to the lower classes) in which he set forth, with studied simplicity, the "three great questions that we can ask ourselves": (1) "How shall I behave to the people I know—to my relatives, friends, and acquaintances?" (2) "How shall I behave to the people whom I don't know, but who nevertheless exist and have claims on me—to the government, to society as a whole, to humanity as a whole?" (3) "How shall I behave to the Unknowable? What shall my attitude be towards God, or Fate, or whatever you like to call the invisible power that lies behind the world?"[62] Note the emphasis: How shall I *behave?* But the problem implied in the questions is whether the exercise of "conscience," as Coleridge conceived it, is an act. Forster is always the moralist, even when he is most the artist. And as Forster's private vineyard has become overrun and subdivided, he has gradually increased his tolerance for overt social and moral action. But he has never conceded that his duty to the "great world" should exceed his allegiance to the "little society"—or to the forces marshaled under the name of the "invisible power." This trinity is the basic structure of his thought and art: its elements must work together—and toward harmony. Whenever Forster gives us a novel divided into threes he is striving for that result.

Nikolai Berdyaev has phrased the liberal dilemma pointedly: "The fundamental contradiction in my thinking about social life is bound up with the juxtaposition in me of two elements—an aristocratic interpretation of personality, freedom, and creativeness, and a socialistic demand for the . . . dignity of every man, of even the most insignificant of men, and for a guarantee of his rights in life."[63] It is a contradiction for which there is no logical solution, only an existential one —namely, the acceptance of the contradiction itself as an ironic fact of life.

Bloomsbury, for the most part, met this problem by ignoring or by rationalizing it, but Forster has rejected such solutions. "We are here on earth," he writes, "not to save ourselves and not to save the community, but to try to save both." He has not been engaged enough to please a Julian Bell, but neither has he accepted domicile in the ivory tower. The situation permits neither commitment: "And we, in our trouble today, again look for a division which will render unto the community what is the community's, and to the self what is the self's. We have not found it, and the New Jerusalem cannot be built until we do."[64] The Biblical language is itself a reminder of the inheritance from Clapham that Forster can neither wholly accept nor wholly reject.

5

In Forster's biography of G. Lowes Dickinson, the names of four men stand out. They are J. M. E. McTaggart, G. E. Moore, Nathaniel Wedd, and Roger Fry, all Apostles and intimates of Dickinson, and all active in that pre-Bloomsbury world which Forster entered in 1897. Of the four, only Wedd had much direct influence on Forster as an undergraduate.* But together with Dickinson, they virtually *were* the culture that the young Forster lived and breathed, the most vital ingredients of that holy gestalt called Cambridge. We can only touch on them here, but they are essential background for the study of Forster's mind and thought.

If McTaggart was not the last, he was certainly one of the most

---

* Forster writes: "I knew Roger Fry well, but not till later years; McTaggart not at all; and I saw something of G. E. Moore, but at the end of his life. Wedd was the formative figure and I am . . . glad that this should be emphasised." Letter to the author, February 9, 1963.

extravagant, of the philosophic idealists; and he interests us here chiefly as the purveyor of certain idealist notions that, with much alteration, got embedded in the Bloomsbury ethos. Chief among them were, first, his notion of a millennial Absolute, a timeless harmony of (individualized) souls toward which the world of appearance—through one incarnation after another—is inevitably moving; and second, his related notions about love.[65] His Absolute, or ultimate Reality, was, in fact, nothing more than an idealized reflection of all that McTaggart desired (and felt he had found) on earth. His Heaven is "a timeless and endless state of love—love so direct, so intimate, and so powerful that even the deepest mystic rapture gives us but the slightest foretaste of its perfection. We know that we shall know nothing but our beloved, and those they love, and ourselves as loving them, and that only in this shall we seek and find satisfaction."[66] McTaggart has been called "the last of the great philosophers" to attempt "to comprehend the whole universe," but the attempt led him into what now seem preposterous excesses.[67]

McTaggart frequently had what he called a "Saul feeling," a kind of oceanic sense of being in love with the universe akin to that experienced by the young David in Browning's poem "Saul,"[68] and this feeling seems to have been a response (in part at least) to the homosexual implications of the Saul-David relationship. Though McTaggart married, he spent little time at home, and was as lukewarm on the subject of married life as he was hot on the subject of "friendship."* Love of friends, in fact, displaced love of God: "It can't be nice to believe in God," he conjectured. "It would be horrible to think that there was anyone who was closer to one than one's friends."[69]

Here, very likely, was one source of Bloomsbury's emphasis on "personal relations." The quiet dignity of Forster's style and the rapturous sentimentality (except for sober professional moments) of McTaggart's have almost nothing in common, but both men are extravagant individualists partaking of the same tradition. And on one point their tastes are firmly linked—they were both admirers of Swinburne's poem "Hertha." That poem contains a line, "Even love, the beloved

---

* Before marriage he made clear to his wife, writes Wedd, that their union was not to interfere with his "assiduous attendance" at Trinity. "He dined most nights at the College, did his work in his rooms there, and came home, as a rule, only for lunch and tea.... Not many wives would have tolerated it." *McTaggart*, pp. 47–48.

Republic, that feeds upon freedom and lives," which Forster repeats at least three times in his writings,* perhaps most conspicuously in *The Longest Journey*: "The Beloved Republic ... of which Swinburne speaks ... will not be brought about by love alone. It will approach with no flourish of trumpets, and have no declaration of independence. Self-sacrifice and—worse still—self-mutilation are the things that sometimes help it most." (LJ, 265.) The poem argues that, since man invented God, man has displaced God; but that man's soul is greater than man, and the name of that soul is freedom.[70] McTaggart seems to have found this useful in support of his belief in immortality without God. He wrote to a friend: "You are quite wrong about myself and G. A. [God Almighty], I mean most decidedly to outlive him. For my own part I propose to be immortal and if he is, I will believe in Herbert Spencer or in any other impossibility you like. Let me refer you to a poem by Mr. Algernon Charles Swinburne in *Songs Before Sunrise* entitled 'Hertha.' "[71]

Forster valued the Beloved Republic for some of the same reasons McTaggart did, but he was far more realistic about the trials of citizenship. "We can only love what we know personally," he writes in 1941. When people say that love is the "spiritual quality" needed to rebuild civilization, Forster "respectfully but firmly" disagrees: "Love is a great force in private life ... but love in public affairs does not work. ... The idea that nations should love one another, or that business concerns or marketing boards should love one another ... is absurd, unreal, dangerous. It leads us into perilous and vague sentimentalism." (TC, 56.) This not only repudiates McTaggart, but reminds us that Forster grew up in a way McTaggart never did.

McTaggart called himself a Hegelian, wrote three books on that philosopher[72] in addition to his own metaphysics, and for a time had as disciples both Moore and Russell.[73] But actually he used Hegel very much as Goethe used Spinoza—as an auxiliary to his own idealizing and poeticizing—and though McTaggart's personal forcefulness

* In "The Menace to Freedom" (1935) he writes: 'There is the Beloved Republic to dream about and to work for through our dreams; the better polity which once seemed to be approaching on greased wheels; the City of God." (TC, 23.) In "What I Believe" (1938) he writes: "So Two cheers for Democracy. ... Two cheers are quite enough: there is no occasion to give three. Only Love the Beloved Republic deserves that." (TC, 79.)

was considerable, it was not in the long run enough to sustain his reputation as a major philosopher. At this distance he seems a rather silly and even pathetic figure. He walked with a twist, it was said, because "he was always being kicked at school" (GLD, 72); yet, unlike his colleagues, he defended his public school (Clifton, the same as Fry's) and in late life became in most ways a solid reactionary—a Tory, a traditionalist, a lover of academic pomps and rituals, a patriotic drumbeater (he attacked Russell for his pacifism during the First World War). In his last years he was almost totally estranged from Dickinson, Fry, and Wedd.

Before Moore's rise, McTaggart and Dickinson were the darlings of the undergraduates. Moore's *Principia* not only dethroned those two,[74] but made the study of philosophy at Cambridge (and in the Western world) a far more serious and hardheaded matter. Moore began the trend toward linguistic analysis of the sort engaged in by Ludwig Wittgenstein and A. J. Ayer; and in some ways he eclipsed the tradition of nineteenth-century idealism.[75] Moore's philosophy has been often summarized,[76] and is not relevant here except as a point of reference. But in that respect it is indispensable.

The discussion about "reality" that begins *The Longest Journey* was, Forster admits, inspired by a "Moorean" philosophical discussion he had witnessed.[77] Though Forster was no student of Moore's philosophy, the Cambridge he knew and wrote about is inseparable from Moore, as a new Introduction to *Journey* attests: "Cambridge is the home of Rickie, the elder brother, the legitimate, his only true home: the Cambridge of G. E. Moore which I knew at the beginning of the century: the fearless uninfluential Cambridge that sought for reality and cared for truth."[78] Moreover, sly references to Moore's phrases appear as private jokes again and again in Forster's work. In the story "Other Kingdom," for example, there is a boy who dreams of going to another planet: "There are no footmen in this other earth, and the kettle-stands, I suppose, will not be made of silver, and I know that everything is to be itself, and not practically something else." (CS, 65.) As we know, the epigraph of the *Principia* reads: "Everything is what it is, and not another thing." Another phrase that was bandied about in Bloomsbury conversations was "on the whole"—

found in the context of that peculiar Moorean casuistry which tries
to discover, among many alternatives, what is good "on the whole."
This pops up as a pun in *Howards End* (p. 39). The word "good"
itself is another special term—not *the* good or goods, which involve
the arguer in a typical Benthamite error known as the Naturalistic
Fallacy, but good as a "simple, indefinable, unanalysable object of
thought" apprehended intuitively and directly, as one apprehends
the color yellow.[79] We are therefore not surprised to learn that "religion" to Rickie was "a service, a mystic communion with good; not
a means of getting what he wanted on the earth" (LJ, 217).

   But by far the most important thing to note is Moore's chapter on
"the Ideal," where he advances his intuitive assurance that "the pleasures of human intercourse and the enjoyment of beautiful objects"
are universally considered "the most valuable things which we can
know or can imagine."

No one, probably, who has asked himself the question, has ever doubted that
personal affection and the appreciation of what is beautiful in Art or Nature
are good in themselves; nor, if we consider strictly what things are worth
having *purely for their own sakes,* does it appear probable that anyone will
think that anything else has *nearly* so great a value as the things which are
included under these two heads. [Moore's italics.][80]

The implied incredulity that anyone could possibly disagree with
this is typical of the almost comic innocence of this spoiled and un-
disillusioned optimist. Bloomsbury read that text in different ways,
but it is the classic statement—and the chief warrant for the apostolic
faith in art and in personal relations.

   We should note two interesting derivatives of Moore's position.
The first is his distinction between judgment and taste, the second
his endorsement of what he calls the love of love. If the enjoyment
of a beautiful object is an "organic unity" made up of the *consciousness* of the object together with the emotion accompanying that consciousness, then what comment can we make about a person who
thought he saw beauty where it didn't exist? This deluded person
may be, according to Moore, (1) attributing to the object beautiful
qualities that it does not possess, or (2) feeling qualities that the object
does in fact possess but that are not beautiful. The first is a cognitive
error, an error in judgment; the second is an emotional error, an error

in taste. Which is worse? To Moore, the error in taste is far more serious, for it involves a false idea about value, whereas the error in judgment involves only a false idea about fact. This distinction appears
again and again, in many guises, in the literature of Bloomsbury.*
It is the same separation Dickinson allowed between religion (imagination) and truth (science), and it underlies Forster's distinctions between literature and information, imagination and fact, and the artist
and the critic.

In the course of discussing the "pleasures of human intercourse,"
Moore got boxed in by his conclusion that love, when reciprocal and
fully realized, is primarily the admiration each lover has for the "admirable mental qualities" of the other—in other words, the love of
love.[81] This is close to solipsism, a narcissistic circle, the ghostly embrace of self-images. In spite of Moore's insistence that such a love
includes an awareness of the body, he is really talking, much as Mc-
Taggart does, about the love of pure souls for each other. "The New
Testament is a handbook for politicians compared with the unworldliness of Moore's chapter on 'The Ideal,' "[82] writes Keynes, and others
have testified to the "inexperience, virginity, seriousness, intellectual
puritanism" of the undergraduate set of 1903, among whom Moore
found those early, enthusiastic converts.[83] By 1914 Bloomsbury
had lost a good deal of its Edwardian innocence, but evidence
abounds that the desire to understand love as some sort of timeless
ecstasy rather than as a human (and humanistic) investment of the
libido managed to survive even the Great War.[84] The love of love
may be no worse than a pleasantly tender—or comic—sensation; but
it may also be a neurotic dissociation from reality. It is clear from
his novels that Forster saw, even when he could not meet, this danger.

No one has ever called Forster a Moorist,† but at least one person
associated Forster with Moore. When Forster and some other Apostles

* Consider this comment by Virginia Woolf: "The critic, Roger Fry insists over
and over again, must trust his sensibility, not his learning." *Roger Fry, A Biogra-
phy* (London, 1940), p. 116.
† Leonard Woolf says the active Moorists were Strachey, Sydney-Turner, Thoby
Stephen, Keynes, and himself, with Clive Bell, J. T. Sheppard, R. G. Hawtrey, and
A. R. Ainsworth orbiting at some distance beyond. Forster and Desmond Mac-
Carthy, he writes, "moved erratically in and out of this solar system of intellectual
friendship, like comets." *Sowing*, p. 171.

visited Henry James in 1908, James laid his hand on the young man's shoulder and declared, "Your name's Moore." "I do not think," writes Forster, "I ever got disentangled from G. E. Moore in the Master's mind."[85]

Although Forster was surprised to learn of similarities between his own esthetic ideas and those Roger Fry advanced in *Vision and Design* (1920), *Transformations* (1926), and *Last Lectures* (posthumous, 1939),[86] the fact is that Fry's esthetic can almost be read as a gloss on Forster's *Aspects of the Novel*. It was Fry who (with Moore's philosophic support) gave art its place in the Bloomsbury ethos, and gave it its spiritual credentials. Before Fry came along, the Apostles and Cambridge generally had small tolerance for the arts of painting and drama, and not much more for music. "There is no evidence," writes Virginia Woolf,

that the young men who read so many books and discussed so many problems ever looked at pictures or debated the theory of aesthetics. Politics and philosophy were their chief interests. Art was for them the art of literature; and literature was half prophecy. Shelley and Walt Whitman were to be read for their message rather than for their music. Perhaps then, when Mr. [E. F.] Benson talks of the pallor of the Apostles, he hints at something eyeless, abstract, and austere in their doctrines.[87]

Fry's esthetics cannot be easily summarized, and we shall touch upon them later in the chapter on Forster's esthetics, but one point must be made in advance: the unworldliness of which Bloomsbury boasted was perhaps most clearly reflected in Fry. His continual emphasis was on what, in the work of art, was "self-contained, self-sufficing, and not to be valued by . . . references to what lies outside"[88]—what Moore would call "intrinsic qualities." This is exactly Forster's definition of art as well: "a self-contained entity, with a life of its own" (TC, 99). Representation may lure us into valuing a work "for an ulterior nonesthetic end,"[89] such as its moral message, its literary references, its psychological stimulation, its erotic stimulation (as in nudes), or its realism. These things are not evil, they are simply worldly, and art is their antithesis. Despite his originality as a critic, Fry had as much trouble as most of the other Apostles in adjusting his puritan inheritance to the new world of the visual arts. And when it came to Indian art, he could overcome his resistance to it no better than Clapham could. The flaccid curves, the sinuosity, of Indian sculpture seemed to him lacking in moral rigor, and he despised what he called the "pornography" and "gross sensuality" that appeared in temples dedicated "to the purest abstractions of divinity."[90] (See Plate 32.) It took Forster to make the "passage" to India.

Nathaniel Wedd, the least famous of the four, was the most immediate influence on Forster. Entirely a teacher, Wedd published nothing except an edition of Euripides' *Orestes*. He opposed the "researching don" and ardently backed the idea that King's should be an Athens and not an Alexandria. According to Dickinson, "He gave up all his time and energy to the undergraduates, was at home to them at all hours of the night, stimulated, comforted, amused, and generally maintained the best tradition at King's, that of friendship and intimacy between undergraduates and dons, but overworked and oversmoked himself so that in the end he fell seriously ill and many years of his life have been frustrated." (GLD, 74.) "When I was at King's," writes Forster, "Wedd taught me classics and it is to him rather than to Dickinson—indeed to him more than to anyone—that I owe such awakening as has befallen me." (GLD, 73.) It is a great distinction. The Cambridge that took up the young Rickie "and soothed him, and warmed him, and . . . laughed at him a little, saying that he must not be so tragic yet awhile" (LJ, 10), is a Cambridge that came to Forster largely as the gift of Wedd.

Wedd was certainly one of the liveliest of the Apostles. He was, as Forster describes him, "cynical, aggressive, Mephistophelian, wore a red tie, blasphemed, and taught Dickinson how to swear too—always a desirable accomplishment for a high-minded young don" (GLD, 73–74). He was in his early days an ardent Shavian,[91] he put Zola and George Moore on the King's Library shelves, and he was openly and scandalously anti-God. His unorthodoxy supplies some amusing bits of King's folklore. To complaints about his playing croquet on Sundays, he replied, "I deplore a faith so fragile that it can't survive the click of croquet balls heard on the way to Chapel."[92] Once when the meat in Hall was unusually tough, he reputedly said, "Why, this lamb is almost as hard to swallow as the Lamb of God!"

Allowed by his freethinking parents to select his own religion,

Wedd discovered as a child, after searching among Evangelicals, Congregationalists, Baptists, Methodists, Anglicans, and Catholics, a unique solution in the free thought of Moncure Daniel Conway, an American who held forth at the South Place Institute in Finsbury.[93] "There, the appeal was to reason solely, to reasonableness, to humanity. Instead of lessons from the Prayer-book or chapters from the Bible, he [Conway] read passages from Plato, from Positive Philosophy, from Buddhist writers, from Confucius and Zoroaster, from Hindu philosophers. The extracts were followed by good music."[94] "The effect of attending South Place Institute," writes Wedd,[95] "was that I became a strong partizan of the Cause of Freedom of Thought, and a correspondingly strong opponent of organized religion as an institution for limiting freedom."* These were Forster's lifelong views as well, and both men, as we might expect, were Shelley-worshipers in their younger years. "Shelley," writes Wedd, "is still to me the Poet of Poets . . . because to him poetry was not the final end, because he took his art as an amateur and a 'gentleman,' not as a professional, and was out to discover himself and reveal to others the secret of things. . . . For me the Choruses of the Prometheus were the highest expression of religion, and the Choruses in 'Hellas' almost reconciled me to Christianity."[96]

Although Wedd ended his life a Tory, it is hard to think of him as anything but a radical spirit. He was with Dickinson on the editorial council of *The Independent Review* and throughout his earlier career was passionately concerned with social justice and humanitarian causes. Ibsen's *Ghosts,* Edward Carpenter's *Towards Democracy,* Andrew Mearns's *The Bitter Cry of Outcast London* were a few of the books he read around 1881, and Toynbee Hall, the Primrose League, the Psychical Society, the Aesthetic Movement, and Randolph Churchill's Tory Democracy were a few of the causes that interested him.[97] He was also influential in bringing professional theater to Cambridge for the first time.[98]

---

* In "The Eternal Moment" (cs, 203) Forster describes an American holding forth on the need for "a new universal religion of the open air," and comments: "If the old religions had indeed become insufficient for humanity, it did not seem probable that an adequate substitute would be produced in America." Forster is most likely making the joke for Wedd's benefit. Such cracks at America were common in Forster's earlier writings.

In what ways did this man "awaken" Forster? First of all, he most certainly awakened Forster's interest in the classics and inspired him to edit Virgil's *Aeneid* (translated by E. Fairfax Taylor) in 1906—a work few remember that Forster did. Forster's introduction is an exercise in quiet irreverence and anti-pedantry, and it is not hard to read Wedd's influence in such lines as these: "When Rome came into contact with the Greek world, she became somewhat dissatisfied with her own mythology. Romulus and the she-wolf, pleasant as they were, seemed a little rustic, and had no connections with the stately and radiant heroes of Greece. Romulus, no doubt, had founded Rome. He was accepted and revered. But could nothing be done for his ancestors?"[99]

In the second place, Wedd was a good friend when Forster needed one. Three letters from Forster to Wedd reside in the King's College Library which, taken together, say a good deal about the trust and confidence between the two. Even in one of the earliest and most formal of these notes,[100] we can feel his relief at having someone to turn to besides Oscar Browning.*

---

* Oscar Browning was one of the most colorful and notorious of Cambridge teachers, a name-dropper and collector of royalty and something less than a dependable scholar. Dickinson described him as "Falstaffian, shameless, affectionate, egoistic, generous, snobbish, democratic, witty, lazy, dull, worldly, academic"—to which Forster adds "a bully and a liar." (GLD, 29.) He also possessed a "more or less pronounced homosexual bias" (Esmé Wingfield-Stratford, *Before the Lamps Went Out* [London, 1945], p. 157), for which he had been dismissed from Eton—together with a mountain of debts. When the *Saturday Review* exposed O.B. as a corrupter of youth comparable to Oscar Wilde, he was delighted; Wedd records that he said, "If you are built like me, you would rather be abused than ignored." ("King's in 1883," pp. 28–29.) Browning founded and ran the Day Training College for Teachers in Cambridge, along with a turkish bath in Cambridge and a chicken run in a corner of the Grantchester meadows—all devices to help pay off the enormous debts he had piled up at Eton. Once at a hotel he provoked Robert Browning into writing him the following letter (*ibid.*, pp. 29–30):
Sir:
    I do not understand how in any circumstances one gentleman can open a letter addressed to another, and it is still farther beyond my understanding how, having done so, he should communicate the contents of the letter to a third person.
                    Yours faithfully,
                    Robert Browning
O.B. would show this letter and refer to the poet as "not, I believe, a relation, but always a very dear friend."

In the third place, Wedd must certainly have stimulated Forster's sense of mockery and humor. In Dickinson Forster found an idol to worship, in Wedd a friend to like—and had the second not tempered the first Forster might have been a very different man and writer. When we hear one of Forster's characters say, "He seems to see good in every one. No one would take him for a clergyman" (RV, 17), we recognize one of the graces of Forster's wit. Wedd, that expert in irreverence, could have been Forster's teacher.

But unquestionably Wedd's greatest distinction lies in having encouraged Forster to write.* In a 1959 television interview Forster said:

> Oddly enough it was Cambridge that first set me off writing. And in this very room where I now am there was at one time my tutor, a man called Wedd, and it was he who suggested to me that I might write. He said it in a very informal way. He said in a sort of drawling voice, "I don't see why you should not write," and I being very diffident was delighted at this remark and thought, after all why shouldn't I write? And I did. It is really owing to Wedd and to that start at Cambridge that I have written. I might have started for some other reason.[101]

Dickinson, Fry, McTaggart, and Wedd, writes Forster, "were originally drawn together by their passion for philosophy, and they were fired by a belief . . . that philosophy explains the universe." (GLD, 66–67.) Forster does not say when Wedd abandoned that belief, but assuredly he did. All the evidence shows a man who delighted in the particular, the personal, the here-and-now. He seems to have been happily and normally married.† His religion was essentially down-to-earth. In his personal and academic life he was a befriender of the eccentric and the underdog—a "kindler of live sparks in many stubbles."[102] Forster was one of them: "He taught me," Forster says of Wedd, "most important in my case, that I knew more than I thought I did."[103] Among all the figures of affection brushed into the following passage, we can be certain that the "merry don" is Wedd himself:

---

* See the letter dated December 1, 1901, the second of the Forster-Wedd letters, in Note 100.

† Wedd married Rachel Evelyn White, the Classical lecturer at Newnham College, in 1906, when she was 39 and he 42.

In the morning he had read Theocritus, whom he believed to be the greatest of Greek poets; he had lunched with a merry don and had tasted Zwieback biscuits; then he had walked with people he liked, and had walked just long enough; and now his room was full of other people whom he liked, and when they left he would go and have supper with Ansell, whom he liked as well as any one. (LJ, 10.)

We must now turn to that fifth Apostle whose biography Forster wrote. G. Lowes Dickinson may not have been as merry a friend, but he probably seemed, at least to the young Forster, a more serious influence.

Chapter four

Goldsworthy Lowes Dickinson

> There was John Locke, the philosopher; there was Syd-
> ney Smith, the Liberal and liberalising divine; there
> was Lowes Dickinson, writer of *A Modern Symposium,*
> which might be called the Bible of Tolerance ...; there
> was Goethe.
>
> —*Two Cheers for Democracy*

Forster's biography of Dickinson is a labor of love more than of scholarship, the payment of a fraternal debt as *Marianne Thornton* was
of a filial one, and the author's partisanship shows on every page.
Dickinson is called "the best man that ever lived,"[1] is claimed to
have been "incapable of snubbing others" or of "resenting a snub"
(p. 154), and is unblushingly placed in the same company as Socrates,
Goethe, and even Jesus. Such extravagances may tell us more about
Forster's need for a father than about Dickinson (Forster certainly
made his subject at once too saintly and too gloomy), yet for certain
Cambridge undergraduates across several generations Dickinson was
a life-giver—a man possessing not only great personal charm, but a
unique Socratic integrity, which made him for them a kind of moral
touchstone.

One could, however, see another man, for the man was divided.
On the one hand was the idealist, the esthete, the homosexual—the
author of *The Magic Flute* (1920), who dreams of a spiritual completion to be attained without meeting worldly resistance. On the other
was the tough-minded moralist, the political realist and scholar who
—despite his loathing of the labors of documentation—wrote *The International Anarchy* (1926), a once-famous indictment of diplomatic
immorality. But if he was "Goldie" to some, he was "Dirty Dick" to
others;[2] and if some only remember his openness and integrity, others
remember a kind of decadence. Esmé Wingfield-Stratford, for one,

recalls the air of Grecian suggestiveness which he introduced into
apostolic gatherings, and his penchant for "the sort of half-feminine
innuendo that ended not in a guffaw, but a snigger."[3]

Forster remembered only the first man, yet his apologia, for all its
shortcomings, is essential reading for the student of his work. No
other piece so well conveys the tone of fin-de-siècle apostolic sensibilities and loyalties; and nothing that Forster has written is more
revealing of his own capacities for hero-worship. The mature Forster,
though he looks back nostalgically on Dickinson as on a discarded
self-image, is quite unlike the older man, excelling him in mind, talent, and taste (if not in the ability to face political realities). Yet
their kinship is deep, and Julian Bell's comment (to Forster) is just:
"It will seem no extravagant compliment, but common opinion, if
I praise in you certain qualities that were also Lowes Dickinson's:
tolerance, reasonableness, charity; a clear and deep conviction of the
value of certain states of mind; a readiness to listen to opponents and
a sympathy for the young."[4] The statement is judiciously selective of
those qualities Forster most admired in the man who influenced him
more deeply (and more ambiguously) than any of his other Cambridge
teachers.*

"The Beloved Disciple," as Esmé Wingfield-Stratford calls Forster,[5]
outgrew this master, but traces were left. A Dickinsonian aroma satu-
rates much of Forster's minor work, and some of the major. In a 1920
review, for example, we get an almost perfect (and doubtless unconscious) imitation of Dickinson's "poetic" style, that style which
prompted some critics to say that "his poetry is too philosophic and
his philosophy too poetical" (p. 82).

Loveliness and beauty are sisters, the two divine children that imagination
has created out of Fact. . . . Beauty is the elder of the pair and the less popular. Her head is in the sky, her feet in the mire. She comprises all existence,
even the remote and the loathsome, and all non-existence. . . .
But it is otherwise with Loveliness. . . . Though weaker than her sublime

---

* The issues of youth and age, softness and hardness, pliancy and rigidity, amateurism and specialization, are very evident whenever Forster discusses Dickinson.
See, in this connection, the interesting (and neglected) short story "The Point of
It," which may mark a point in Forster's life when he was pulling clear of Dickinson's influence. (See Chapter Six.)

sister, she haunts a few places that Beauty never visits—the fields of Fancy, for instance, and the springs of Pathos, and the playgrounds of Fun. She is popular in consequence, and Beauty does not envy her the popularity. For, despite all rumours to the contrary, there is complete harmony between the sisters. Indeed, they sometimes appear together, the elder bending over the younger's shoulder.[6]

Had Forster written only in this manner, he would scarcely be remembered today. Such cute mythologizing, reminiscent of the worst of Meredith and Swinburne—and bringing to mind the banal allegorical sculpture which adorned Victorian public buildings—is typical of that mandarin, soul-probing style which some members of an apostate (and pre-Freudian) Victorian generation resorted to instead of religion. Pater may have started it, but men like Ruskin, Rossetti, Yeats, McTaggart, and Logan Pearsall Smith encouraged it; its antithesis was the style of Mill and his tradition. Dickinson did not always write this way; but even when he is most lucid and least ornate, there is a quality to his writing that suggests a greater interest in artistic effect than in truth, a kind of straitened Cyrenaicism that attempts to make style carry the burdens of conscience. Dickinson perambulates easily between realism and fantasy, prose and "poetry," and it is not unusual for passages in his books to begin in logic and end in rhapsody. Nor does he apologize for these emotional leaps; he is essentially a "mystic" rather than a systematic thinker, and even history is for him essentially "poetry" (p. 88).*

Though a popular writer in his time, Dickinson is scarcely remembered today—the fate of so many polemicists whose eloquence exceeds their imagination and insight. In reading him one feels little intellectual advance, only the application to different contexts of a relatively unchanging moral sensibility and a fixed set of values. Read any ten of his 300-odd books and articles on religion, war, international politics, pacifism, civil liberties, or people: the subjects change but the writer does not.[7]

Dickinson's professional subject was politics, but his interests

---

* Both Forster and Dickinson use "mystic" and "mystical" in loose senses. A typical example is Dickinson in *The International Anarchy*: "The feeling in question may therefore be called mystical, if by that word we describe a position for which no reasoned defense can be made." (New York, 1926), p. 15.

ranged from ethics to mountaineering. He was an *amateur,* and an amateur on principle: "I believe," he wrote, "that there is a function for the amateur, and one that becomes more and not less important as specialisation increases."[8] And amateurism connects with "youth" as a value: "The personality is then freer, because it is inexperienced." (p. 60.) Like Wedd, he hated the "researching don."[9] Forster writes:

He mistrusted research . . . although it is in itself so admirable and so necessary, because research atrophies the mind and renders it incapable of human intercourse: "the spectacle of learning gets more depressing to me every year," he tells Mrs. Webb, "I care only for fruitful and vital handling of the eternal commonplaces or else for a new insight that will really help some one to internal freedom." If the schoolmaster teaches wrongly, the specialist cannot teach at all, and between the two of them what room is left for Socrates? (p. 104.)

This longing for "internal freedom" and "the eternal commonplaces" can be called, from one point of view, transcendental aspiration; from another it is escapism. Dickinson's idealistic upbringing joins with his peculiar temperament to produce a man strangely contorted between inwardness and outwardness—a man who finds it "necessary to cultivate a hard outside in order to keep alive my fire within" (p. 50). But his temptation was to shrink from life rather than engage with it. For all his liberal optimism he was a sad man, and a glimpse at his childhood helps to tell why.

Dickinson was born in London in 1862 of pious and moderately well-off parents, and brought up at Hanwell, a village near London. His father began as a lithographer and became a fashionable artist. He knew Ruskin (as a colleague at the Working Men's College) and was active in the Christian Socialist movement with Charles Kingsley and F. D. Maurice. Throughout his life he suffered spells of unaccountable gloom, as did his son after him (p. 3). Dickinson's mother, as Forster describes her, "was a woman of sweet but firm character, with strong opinions as to what is right and wrong, and with a narrow vein of piety running through the abundance of her natural goodness" (p. 4). She died when Dickinson was nineteen. Like Forster's own mother, she was affectionate toward her son, but not really close to him. It was a Victorian childhood like many another. Though

softened by art and music, travel and home theatricals, big houses
and a kindly nurse, Dickinson lived a lonely childhood with no
sense of intimacy with his parents. As a child he was educated almost
entirely by descendants of Coleridge: he attended a school—Beo-
monds, at Chertsey—run by Ernest and Christabel Coleridge (the poet's grandson and granddaughter); the rector at Hanwell was Derwent
Coleridge, a son of the poet; and the rector's niece, Edith, had taught
Greek to Dickinson's mother, who in turn taught it to her children.
But all of this Broad Church liberalism was no emancipation from
the repressions of a Victorian home.

There were bright intervals, but what stands out in Dickinson's
early years is his torment: guilt over minor misdemeanors, agonized
confessions and self-consciousness, fears and fascinations before "the
mystery of sex" (p. 16). Just before his confirmation, Dickinson went
through a period of particular anxiety and nervous confusion: "He
became more devout and attended Holy Communion with unreal but
conscientious religiosity, liking to feel good, and sometimes longing
to be bad. He was in a complete muddle, without any standards except what were imposed from outside and even his rebellions were
conventional. Left to himself he would have escaped into the lost
world of Ariel, where neither obedience nor disobedience existed,
and the only sacrament was beauty." (p. 21.)* Here is the standard
pre-Bloomsbury and Bloomsbury record: oppressions too subtle for
outright rebellion, yet a sense of overwhelming frustration; the iron
deep in one's soul, yet no one to see it or listen to one's lament. It
was a training in both love and hate, self-respect and self-loathing,
rebellion and submission. Ultimately Dickinson, like Ruskin, formed
a world view out of his wounded sensitivity, generating from bitterness and self-pity the conception of a frictionless world of beauty, a
conception that is, itself, almost a death wish. As Forster says, Dickinson as a boy "could not escape from the horrors of existence, and
. . . as a man he would not escape from them" (p. 22).

Like almost everyone else in his Cambridge circle, Dickinson had

---

* Forster's own stories record another young man's escapes from the trials of life
into a fantasy world "where neither obedience nor disobedience existed." Forster's
assumption that Dickinson "would have" done the same is some measure of his
identification with him.

a miserable time at his public school, Charterhouse. He felt "alien" among the other boys and said, late in his life: "I have never lost this feeling. Indeed in my old age I feel it as never before. Men become to me simply unintelligible." (p. 21.) The ideal of the sensitive man— "manly" in Plato's but not in Kipling's sense—found little currency in the school's official attitudes, and Dickinson's reaction to the athleticism, patriotism, and religiosity of the school is virtually the same as Forster's to Tonbridge:

I curse the time as I look back on it. It seems to me all evil and no good. Cut off from home life and they from me, without a root to hold that really sprang from myself, yet tormented by external ties of mere superstition, with none of those passionate friendships or loves which redeem school for many boys, despised, and as I think rightly, yet by people who themselves were despicable, with no intellectual interest and no moral conviction, alone as I have never been since, physically unfit, mentally undeveloped—was ever a sadder drearier more hopeless entry upon life? (p. 24.)

Cambridge, of course, changed all that. There, writes Forster, Dickinson moved "from the alien life to the real one." He made lifelong friends, particularly in Roger Fry and Ferdinand Schiller; he acquired new gods in Shelley, Plato, and Goethe; he was stirred to life (as Forster says, "awakened from nightmare," p. 32) by King's College's notorious Silenus, Oscar Browning; he rode a bicycle, dabbled in psychical research, and even tried his hand at various attempts to reform society—attempts deriving from the Christian Socialism of his childhood ("though Frederick Denison Maurice would disown him, and Charles Kingsley turn in the grave," p. 28).

At Cambridge, Dickinson was troubled at first by the well-meaning attentions of his older brother Arthur and his companions—who were "healthy, practical, and destined for worldly distinction." "I wasn't at home with that kind of man," wrote Dickinson, "and I hardly knew there were other kinds." "That kind of man" is surely represented in the comparison Dickinson made some years later between the Redbloods and the Mollycoddles or, as Forster reports it, "the smart and the smarting set" (p. 27).

In the universe and in society the Mollycoddle is "out of it" as inevitably as the Red-blood is "in it." At school, he is a "smug" or a "swat," while the Red-blood is captain of the Eleven. At college, he is an "intellectual," while the Red-blood is in the "best set." In the world he courts failure while the Red-blood achieves success. The Red-blood sees nothing; but the Molly-coddle sees through everything. The Red-blood joins societies; the Molly-coddle is a non-joiner. Individualist of individualists, he can only stand alone, while the Red-blood requires the support of a crowd. The Molly-coddle engenders ideas, and the Red-blood exploits them. . . . The whole structure of civilisation rests on foundations laid by Mollycoddles; but all the building is done by Red-bloods. The Red-blood despises the Molly-coddle; but, in the long run, he does what the Mollycoddle tells him.[10]

2

The division between the "sets" at Cambridge is a matter of some complexity. Nathaniel Wedd, for example, distinguishes between the "scallywags" and the "best set," two groups not easily aligned with Dickinson's broad-brush categories. The members of the best set were by no means philistine, anti-intellectual, or entirely given over to rowing; they were, as Wedd says, in some ways "even more highbrow" than the others.[11] Nevertheless, the best set on the whole stood for the traditional values: aristocratic pedigree, religious conformity, row-ing, football, public service, Etonian loyalties. Until about the 1860's King's consisted, in accordance with the Foundation Statutes, almost entirely of Etonians, and by the end of the century Etonians still dominated the best set. But there were beginning to be important dissenters. John Maynard Keynes, both a rower and a player of Eton's rugged "wall game," threw in his lot with the Mollycoddles.

These matters may appear trivial, but actually they are fundamen-tal: one cannot properly understand Dickinson, Forster, or Blooms-bury without taking them into account. Such a society as the Apostles was very largely a defensive alliance against those healthy, worldly conformists for whom the world had apparently been made. None of the best set were invited. Keynes, as we know, was deeply suspect; and Clive Bell, who came of a fox-hunting family, did not get in.[12] The Apostles were, of course, more than a huddle of envious intellectuals, but we do not know them if we fail to recognize their acute sense of social separateness and almost physical intimidation. They staked a good deal on the proposition that the meek shall inherit the earth, and Dickinson, going so far as to label the enemy Red-bloods, was perhaps the most threatened by their alien manliness.

When Forster came up to Cambridge in 1897, Dickinson had been a don for ten years and was still a young man of thirty-five. Forster saw little of him as an undergraduate, and close friendship probably did not develop until 1904, when Forster joined one of Dickinson's discussion societies.[13] But from their first meeting in 1898, Forster was taken by Dickinson's charm—which shone through the sadness and dowdiness and made him, at least to his worshipers, "indescribably beautiful":

The complexion was not good, the head bowed a little forward from the shoulders when he walked. . . . The hands were large. The clothes, except during the American visits, erred on the dowdy side—dark blue serges, shirts of indistinction, podgy ties. I dress like that myself, except for illogical flash-inesses, and once when I invited him to accompany me into one of these he replied that it is hopeless to dress well unless one's personal appearance cor-responds. This made me realise that he was at all events not contented with his own appearance. I did not understand why. There was a beauty about him which cannot be given that patronising label "spiritual," a beauty which, though it had nothing to do with handsomeness, did belong to the physical, so that his presence was appropriate amid gorgeous scenery or ex-quisite flowers. (p. 101.)

When we read Dickinson's works, it is difficult to understand his influence on minds that seem in retrospect to have been clearly supe-rior to his own. The main reasons were personal. For one thing, as Noel Annan suggests, his talk was probably more forceful than his writing.[14] For another, to young Victorians half-suffocated by public school pedantry, Dickinson came as a breath of fresh air. The classics were to him living literature, not dead languages: to him, as Forster records it, "Greek literature combined beauty and depth, wisdom and wit, gaiety and insight, speculation and ecstasy, carnality and spirit; it had variety; it had constructional power; it was the greatest literature the world had yet produced."[15] In *The Greek View of Life* (1896), his most popular and influential book, he records his convic-tion that "the Ancients are modern, and that Athens in particular had expressed our problems with a lucidity beyond our power" (p. 106). The book is neither history nor criticism but a new myth of the Golden Age. Dickinson belonged to that considerable band of Vic-torian Hellenists—sons of Jowett like Gilbert Murray and Gilbert

Norwood—who saw in Periclean Athens a happy balance of virtues (aristocracy and democracy, authoritarianism and freedom, heroism and sensitivity, moral strength and sexual latitude) corresponding to all their own liberal hopes for the human condition.

Dickinson's Athens offered not only a new gospel for "a scholarly caste betrayed by the Industrial Revolution,"[16] but a perfect creed for bored undergraduates trying to end their bondage to Mrs. Grundy. It allowed one to have one's cake and eat it—to be unorthodox and yet moral—for it was arguable that in pagan dress (or undress) the Christian ethic could be seen perfected, that the Greeks knew the music to go with the Word. "To be advanced Dickinsonially...," writes Wingfield-Stratford, "included a convention of cultivated irreverence, a habit of cocking refined snooks at the Persons of the Trinity." For rebels not prepared to run the risks of rebellion, it was an ideal belief. "We repudiated entirely," wrote Keynes, "customary morals, conventions and traditional wisdom. We were ... in the strict sense of the term, immoralists."[17] Actually they were passionate moralists, but their morality derived from a half-fanciful Greek ideal of virtue with which—since the Greeks had long since been admitted to British respectability—one could wage ironic war with parents and schoolmasters. Dickinson, for example, jettisoned the Christian call to "duty" and, appealing to the "characteristically Greek" ideas of Plato, replaced it with a call to "desire": "Duty emphasizes self-repression. Against the desires of man it sets a law of prohibition, a law which is not conceived as that of his own complete nature ... but rather as a rule imposed from without by a power distinct from himself, for the mortification, not the perfecting, of his natural impulses and aims. Duty emphasizes self-repression; the Greek view emphasized self-development."[18] Small wonder that he appealed to the young.

Learning, to Dickinson, is a passionate engagement between matter-of-fact and personal faith, and any attempt to view his work as a systematic body of thought is singularly unrewarding. But some of his ideas on religion, ethics, and politics deserve our attention.

3

From first to last Dickinson is a humanist, and it is with this ill-defined word that Forster locates his essential value: "He challenges the materialism of our age. He also challenges the religiosity, the revivalism, the insistence on sin that are so often offered as correctives to materialism. In place of those false goods and gods he offers the human spirit which tries to follow reason, knows that reason sometimes fails, yet when it does fail does not scuttle to take refuge in authority."[19] Although Dickinson is fundamentally unscientific, "science" and the "scientific method" are important words in his religious argument. They are what the humanist has in place of revelation and superstition—which Dickinson tirelessly denounces.[20] The Church "has invited men to lie, and punished them for adhering to the truth. . . . It has arrested, so far as it could, the nascent growth of science, and thwarted the only activity by which man may alleviate his material lot, and set himself free for the triumphs of the mind and the spirit."[21] The great defect of the prophets, for example, was that they "associated their moral teaching with theories about the world based upon no proper method of inquiry."[22]

But this is not to say that religion and science are one: "Truth is matter of science, religion of imagination and feeling."[23] There may be some adventitious connection between the two, but religion cannot teach what is *true*. Dickinson did not invent that distinction —it is part of the modern disjunction we noted earlier—but it is a distinction of great consequence. This loosening of the ties between religion and truth, this transformation of religion into esthetics and psychology (imagination and feeling), opens the way for a faith based on pure sensibility, a spiritual solipsism in which inner states are divorced from active life and wishes become the horses of belief. Such a faith is a form of solitude, a late version of that "inner isolation" which Max Weber saw as deriving from the religious individualism of Calvin,[24] and art is a way, if not out of it, at least of expressing it. Dickinson does not discuss the danger of this situation—indeed, except in his own melancholy, he seems unaware of it—but he is active in imagining ways that art can (and does) substitute for the old religious truth.

"Faith . . . is closer to music and poetry than to science," he writes, and—though unsure of his taste in the visual arts—Dickinson was convinced that music and literature were vehicles of the new gospel.[25] A new ritual was needed, a new myth. "Protestantism, in purifying its inner life," he declares, "has gone far towards destroying its outward form"; without that formal expression, without "the mediation of art," religion becomes "stagnant, sour, and corrupt."[26] Wagner is an example of the modern "development of art towards religion"[27] and the literary artists, though often skeptics, tend to be "more believing" the more they are in doubt. "George Meredith, for example, while rejecting God and Immortality, demands our worship for what he calls 'Earth.' Mr. Bernard Shaw, repudiating the whole of our morals and our science, announces a new religion of 'Life-Force.' Even Nietzsche, after denying all sense to the words 'good' and 'true,' propounds in the end a new ethics, and a new cosmology."[28] To these mythmakers Dickinson would add others like Goethe, Blake, Shelley, Browning, Arnold, and Whitman. They are all prophets of the new religion. And what is that religion? In one tortured and barely comprehensible sentence, Dickinson defines it as "a reaction of the highest imagination of the best men upon life and the world, so far as we know them by experience and science—a passionate apprehension, from the point of view of ideals, of the general situation in which we find ourselves."[29] The sentence proclaims an amateur's inheritance from the prophets of romantic idealism.

Dickinson's religion, like McTaggart's, is melioristic and optimistic. Heaven is translated into psychological and historical terms, into a state of mind and a future state of human society: it is "the ultimate term of a process in which we are engaged, of the end of which we can only say that it is Good."[30] Evil exists, it is not mere appearance as some meliorists claim, but Good, not Evil, is "increasing in the long run."[31] No evidence is introduced in support of these grand assertions. Dickinson's arguments are the wish fulfillments of an "intuitive optimism," a sense of something in himself "making for more life and better"; they are appeals from a deep-seated personal need for "some kind of friendly relation to the universe."[32] Thus he translates Christian cosmology and teleology into humanistic terms—with no small admixture of a specifically puritan egoism and sense of election. In place of the Last Judgment we have man perfecting himself; in place of Divine Grace we have human love; in place of Gospel we have the creative imagination:

As I read Man he is a creature not finished, even approximately; not definitely and once for all fitted out with what we call human nature.... He is a being in process of creating himself. What he is not is more important than what he is. . . . He has in him a principle of growth, what I will call Imagination. . . . And by this he stretches feelers into the Dark, laying hold there of stuff, and building mythologies and poems, the palaces of splendid hopes and desires.[33]

This Utopian vision has to be expressed in poetic terms because, by definition, it is unknowable: it is the Great Beyond. "Its proper language . . . is not assertion but suggestion, not logic but passion, not prose but poetry."[34]

Belief in an evolving perfection is what Dickinson means by "faith," and the particular way in which the evolution is visualized is what he means by "myth." Freethinking poets and artists, writes Dickinson, are now "constructing mythologies on a basis of faith."[35] It is an important intimation of the modern writer's function, and in his own limited way Dickinson tried to contribute to these mythologies.

One of his more frantic, and revealing, efforts is a piece called "Euthanasia," which appeared in *The Independent Review* in 1905. We are taken into the mind of an alpinist ascending from the valley of this world into the deathly thin upper air of spiritual completion. The allegory is a rhapsodic, almost orgiastic, experience of a death wish. At the halfway point, the climber begins to see all things as symbols: "The sounds and scents, the colours and forms, were not only lovely . . . they were significant of inward states. The bluebells hung their heads in adoration, the marguerites gazed upward rapt with joy."[36] The path to the ultimate was lined with pathetic fallacies. During his conquest of the peak (a symbolic wrestling with death) the climber experiences an assurance of immortality, a humanistic immortality which is, in some mysterious way, implied in the general melioristic completion.* Dickinson writes: "All things together, each in his kind, each in his rank, press upwards, moved by love, to a goal that is good. What that goal is, I do not too closely inquire; neither

---

* Compare Rickie's dream in LJ: "He had lost all sense of incident. In this great solitude—more solitary than any Alpine range—he and Agnes were floating alone and for ever, between the shapeless earth and the shapeless clouds. An immense silence seemed to move towards them. A lark stopped singing, and they were glad of it. They were approaching the Throne of God." (p. 128.)

do I ask after the origin or meaning of the Whole. I cling to the fact I know. . . . [Man] is discord straining to harmony, ignorance to knowledge, fear to courage, hate and indifference to love. He is a system out of equilibrium, and therefore moving towards it."[37] "All metaphysics," writes Paul Tillich, "reaches a point where its concepts are myths not only in fact but even in the sound of its words."[38] Dickinson's myths were in large part the hypnotic assurances of a man talking to himself.

Appropriately—and strangely—enough, one of Dickinson's passions was mountain-climbing. Like Leslie Stephen and Nathaniel Wedd, Dickinson belonged to the Alpine Club at Cambridge. "One does not think of him as an athlete," writes Forster, "but he had toughness and determination, and delighted in the life of the body provided it was unorganised; he could scramble, ride, boat, swim, and when he could combine any of these exercises with romance he was perfectly happy." (p. 76.) He loathed games involving competition with other men; but the act of climbing gave him, as it did other Victorian intellectuals, a release akin to love itself—and the opportunity to be an actor in his own myth.*

Dickinson's religion was essentially an attempt to join body and soul in idea, but to avoid anything but the most exquisite contact in reality. Mortification of the flesh was no part of his program, but mortification of Red-bloods was, and the following passage from Forster's biography hints at how Dickinson translated an old puritan restraint into his own kind of fastidiousness. Forster writes:

Silly and idle young men did not come his way, no more did hearties and toughs unless they had intellectual leanings. This was due partly to his own constitution and partly to that of King's, which only admits men who are reading for honours and does not duck an intellectual in the fountain oftener

---

* Noel Annan explains the phenomenon thus: "Like love, mountaineering makes it possible for the intellectual to experience things which would otherwise be impossible: danger, intense comradeship, manliness, physical pain in pursuit of a tangible objective, and the sensation of being at one with Nature. Psychologically the intellectual is always conscious of his isolation. . . . [But] plant him in the silence of the snows and his neuroses fall from his back like Christian's burden. . . . For the Victorians, mountaineering was one of the few ways in which pacifist liberals could experience emotions similar to those they envied in soldiers and mariners." (*Leslie Stephen*, pp. 82, 85.)

than once in twenty years, apologising elaborately to him afterwards. In its exquisite enclosure a false idea can be gained of enclosures outside though not of the infinite verities. Dickinson, pacing up and down with his arms behind him, kept in touch in his own fashion with the world, but he could never slap it on the back or stand it a drink. And he loathed its brutality and bullying—with them there could be no compromise; his objection to rowdiness was . . . its inability to flourish without a victim. (p. 104.)

The exquisite femininity of Mother Cambridge and the exquisite masculinity of the pure and windswept peaks both lead to true versions of the "infinite verities." These two symbols are implicit in all of Dickinson's myth-making, and in his idea of love. And that brings us to his ethics.

4

Dickinson was a homosexual and an outspoken apologist for homosexual love. "His opinions on sex ran contrary to Christian ethics," writes Forster (p. 117), and Dickinson's ethics must all be referred to that fact. Love was at their heart, and he believed—as Forster points out—not only in love in the abstract but in "love between two individuals."[39] "I think that all forms of love," writes Dickinson, "including the physical, point to something beyond." (pp. 218–19.) But the Good for him was not to be found "merely in union with one other person" (which might inhibit rather than expand the soul),* but in the capacity of such a relation to transcend itself and become a type of the final consummation, "a perfect union of all with all." With Dickinson, as later with Bloomsbury generally, marriage is one of the suspect conventions together with all that precedes and follows it—wooing, engagements, the rigamarole of the wedding, possessiveness, and family life.[40] Union with woman represents confinement, an acceptance of slavery, a withering of the soul; union with man, how-

---

* As we shall see, this is the idea behind the title of *The Longest Journey*, a title containing words borrowed from a poem of Shelley. René Wellek says, "Shelley would like us . . . to ignore or rather to transcend the boundaries of individuality between persons just as Indian philosophy or Schopenhauer wants us to overcome the curse and burden of the *principium individuationis*." ("Literary Criticism and Philosophy," in *The Importance of Scrutiny*, Eric Bentley, ed. [New York, 1948], p. 29.) This idea is continually put to use by Dickinson, and relates to his belief in amateurism and in youth.

ever, suggests all the expansive ideas of brotherhood—a sense of limitless love, a transcending of the barriers of time and place.

In one of his last books, *After Two Thousand Years* (1930), Dickinson presents a dialogue between Plato and a modern young man,
Philalethes. The discussion is concerned with the philosophic problem of separating "Means to Goods" from "Real Goods" (as distinguished from means). It is, of course, with those Goods which are ends
in themselves that Dickinson finds final value. In this preferred list,
homosexual love ranks with "Truth" and "Art," for homosexuality is, in Dickinson's ideal judgment, singularly free from worldly
motives. The dialogue is Platonically—and Dickinsonially—long-
winded.* He writes:

Philalethes: Well, to begin with, when you spoke of love, you were always
   thinking of the love of men for men, not of that between people of
   opposite sexes.
Plato: I do indeed remember that that was so in my youth.
Ph. Not only in your youth, I think; for up to middle life you seem still to
   have held the same view.
Pl. Indeed?
Ph. Yes, indeed! And that love you treated in a way which, if it has inspired
   some men, has horrified others. . . .
Pl. How was it that my doctrine produced these disturbing effects?
Ph. Well, to begin with, in many parts of the world, and especially in my
   own country, such love is regarded with reprobation and contempt.
Pl. Why so?
Ph. I must reply by another question. In your treatment of love did you not
   admit that the body has a part in it?
Pl. When souls are shut up in bodies do not the bodies, of necessity, take
   part in the affections of the soul?
Ph. I think they do. But most men among us think, or think they think,
   that men ought not to be attracted by the bodies of men, nor women
   by those of women.
Pl. Perhaps, in some sense, they ought not; but then they ought not to be
   men nor women. They ought to be, if they could, pure spirits. But we
   are speaking, I understand, of such love as men do in fact feel. Or are
   you now, on earth, so extreme in your idealism that you try to love
   without bodies?

---

* Forster feels it is significant that in Dickinson's dialogues "none of his dispu-
tants is a female, unless we may include the Queen of the Night [in *The Magic
Flute*], and she is the despair rather than the life of the argument" (p. 109).

Near the end, the dialogue takes a more personal turn:

Pl. Are you not, perhaps, one of those who, like me when on earth, are drawn in love to your own sex?
Ph. Yes.
Pl. You know then, as I did, the perils as well as the raptures.
Ph. I think so.
Pl. And you will escape, as I hope, in the end, to a world more real.
Ph. I do not know, dear master, that I want to. I want to love as you once did, and, if I dared, I would say that perhaps I do.[41]

The book is, wrote Forster, "one of his finest" and "is coloured by recent experience"—the "result of his friendship with the post-war generation." Dickinson himself called it his "testament" (p. 203).

"His nature was not only loving, but tenacious," writes Forster, and the friend who came to occupy "the supreme position in Dickinson's life" was Ferdinand Schiller, whom he had first met as an undergraduate and who figures as Philip Audubon in *A Modern Symposium* (1905). "Devoted to Schiller, but constantly parted from him," Dickinson suffered "from a sense of frustration which the sensitive will understand" (p. 76). "The sensitive" is a euphemism which, in reading the Bloomsbury record, we come to know more fully; it is certainly echoed in Forster's aristocracy of "the sensitive, the considerate and the plucky."[42] Later in the Dickinson biography Forster remarks, "He had for many years been offering affection where it was not needed, and the knowledge that he had made a mistake and was in a sense blameworthy sank into him and saddened him." (p. 182.) Clearly there is an unhappy story here.

Another of Dickinson's lifelong friends was the socialist Edward Carpenter, who, in books like *Homogenic Love and Its Place in a Free Society* (1894), *Love's Coming of Age* (1896), *The Intermediate Sex* (1908), and *Intermediate Types Among Primitive Folk* (1914), made a direct or implied association—in the manner of Walt Whitman—between masculine love and his democratic ideals. Carpenter's social dream was one of lowering class barriers, of bringing freedom and equality to all men and women so that they might participate fully in the creative forces of evolution.[43] Like Dickinson and Forster (Forster more than Dickinson), he wanted "to break down the barrier of class and get into close touch with working people."[44]

He was far from being a cold social theorist: "The key to Carpenter's Socialism," writes Dickinson, "is to be found in his personal affections. He wanted a society in which men and women could be lovers and friends, and he found our society badly organized for that purpose."[45] He felt the same urgency about the emancipation of "the intermediate sex" as he did about the emancipation of women; or perhaps more urgency, since he sees the "Uranian man" as the man of the future. The Uranian man will be "by no means effeminate," but "more sensitive . . . and artistic . . . than the original John Bull." In him will join "such a union or balance of the feminine and masculine qualities" that he will become the interpreter of men and women to each other, the mediator between "two poles of *one* group —which is the human race."[46] This "new man," this androgynous mediator, is deeply implied in the work of Dickinson and Forster (especially before 1914) and is involved in nearly everything they say about the act of mediation called Art. The artist is the sensitive man, and the sensitive man is the very type of the superman, the new Tiresias, in the process of creation.

With Dickinson, as with Carpenter, the ideal of masculine love is inseparable from political and social values. The Greek ideal, as Dickinson interpreted it, was anything but an invitation to effeminacy or license. Among the ancients, he believed, the homosexual experience had not only been the shaping force of heroes, it had also distinguished the aristocratic freeman from the barbarian slave. (Dickinson's personal claim to aristocracy and freedom was based on the same premise.) Forster, in his Preface to the 1957 edition of *The Greek View of Life,* drew special attention to the passage where Dickinson made this point:[47]

So much indeed were the Greeks impressed with the manliness of this passion, with its power to prompt to high thought and heroic action, that some of the best of them set the love of man for man far above that of man for woman. The one, they maintained, was primarily of the spirit, the other primarily of the flesh. . . .

It is in the works of Plato that this view is most completely and exquisitely set forth. To him, love is the beginning of all wisdom; and among all the forms of love, that one in chief, which is conceived by one man for another, of which the main operation and end is in the spirit, and which leads on and out from the passion for a particular body and soul to an enthusiasm for that highest beauty, wisdom, and excellence, of which the most perfect mortal forms are but a faint and inadequate reflection. Such a love is the initiation into the higher life, the spring at once of virtue, of philosophy, and of religion.[48]

To endorse the Greek view of women would have been, of course, somewhat more embarrassing, and Dickinson stuck by his liberal guns: "If women wanted a degree or a vote or anything else which men monopolised, it was his duty to help them to get it, even if they overwhelmed him afterwards." But in spite of this "suicidal sense of fairness," Dickinson was not, Forster admits, a "creditable feminist" (pp. 105–6).

5

Dickinson's views on love and art are inseparable from what we might call his "pacifist" politics, which were rooted in a temperamental aversion to competition and violence of all kinds, and not simply in a doctrinaire opposition to war (he was actually a believer in collective security). Dickinson's practical politics were not very practical. "What do we really want?" he asks in one of his articles. The answer is "liberty"—not personal or political liberty in the classical sense, but "the effective power to be developing self; to feel, to act, to know, to worship, to love; to grow by each exertion of power, to come into touch with new ranges of experience; to sail farther and farther upon the great ocean of life, and see always farther reaches beyond."*[49] This kind of "liberty," being achievable by no imaginable reform or revolution, has nothing to do with practical politics at all, but stands in defiance of them.

In reflecting on his book *A Modern Symposium* (1905), Dickinson wrote:

Still it does not solve the problem, which is perhaps insoluble, of making the bridge between speculation and art and that side of life, and what is called practical politics. For practical politics involves fighting, and the object of such a book as mine, as it was Plato's object long ago, is to raise the mind above the fighting attitude. There lies here obscurely the great problem of the relation of ideals to passion and interests which I do not seem able clearly to formulate. It seems impossible to go into active life of any kind without being ready to kill to lie or to cheat. (p. 112.)

---

* This cliché seems to be a remote echo of Tennyson's "Ulysses." It is an image Forster uses frequently, and frequently with reference to that poem.

When killing, lying, and cheating are seen to be the conditions of "active life of any kind," we are in the presence of a spiritual fastidiousness of no mean order.*

Dickinson hated anarchy in the social world,[50] but cherished it intensely in his private world—where it could be understood as the right to act and think autonomously. And this is what, really, his whole politics comes down to—a subjective individualism in which the sensitive individual is a law unto himself. Dickinson was a democrat, but "he wanted a democracy where everyone will be an aristocrat."[51] He was less than enthusiastic about the emancipation of the laboring classes (though he had friends among them): "He feared that there would be a levelling down, instead of a levering up, and that the Many, in the process of making themselves comfortable, would throw away the pearl of great price which has been handed down to them by the Few." (pp. 87–88.) This sentiment would of course win no support among the Many; Dickinson, with Bloomsbury generally, had no great talent for making the "not saved" feel wanted. He could handle outsiders as abstractions—he "loved humanity" and wanted to "help the human race" (with "truth" derived from Cambridge)—but he had trouble in liking "ordinary people," and did not want to become like them (p. 49).

Dickinson crossed racial and national boundaries no more easily than he crossed class boundaries. When he liked a country, it was because he met people in it like himself, sharing the values of the universal spiritual aristocracy. When he disliked a country, as he did the United States, it was because it was full of Red-bloods and Red-bloods' values. Dickinson's travels, like Forster's, are symbolic tests of his ideals. In 1912 he went around the world on an Albert Kahn

---

* There is a scene in *The Magic Flute* strongly reminiscent of the Grand Inquisitor episode in Dostoevsky's *The Brothers Karamazov*, in which Satan, speaking to Voltaire, almost reiterates the words of the Inquisitor as he describes the temptations in the wilderness. "Freedom," with both authors, is the word describing Jesus's gift to mankind—which Church and State have conspired to subvert. Jesus, writes Dickinson, "was a democrat, I might say an anarchist. He believed in freedom." *The Magic Flute* (London, 1920), p. 78. Philip Rahv's comment on the theme of the Grand Inquisitor fits Dickinson's ideas perfectly: "What it comes to in the end is a total rejection of power in all its forms, in its actuality as in its rationalizations." "The Grand Inquisitor," *The Partisan Review*, XXI (1954), 264.

Travelling Fellowship, and spent considerable time in India, China, and the United States. He loved China because of what he called its humanism, its capacity to remain in touch with the simple realities of material and human life, and to find its values there. He disliked India, strangely enough, because of its denial of the temporal world. One might have thought that Dickinson's religion—in which individuals tend to get thought of as dehumanized "souls"—is not so far from some aspects of Hinduism, but he did not see it so. Here he speaks as a homosexual, protesting a little shrilly against all the puritanism of his bringing-up, that the flesh, if not the world, really matters. Still, it is a mixed protest, since puritan egotism, with the high value it places on individual salvation and the private conscience, is still strongly in evidence; and the Hindu desire to escape from the wheel of life seemed dangerously incompatible with his own optimism. In *Appearances* (1914), his book of travel impressions, he recounts an argument he had with an Indian:

I protested that I loved individual souls, and did not want them absorbed in Parabrahma. He laughed ... but it was clear that he held me to be a child, imprisoned in the Ego. I felt like that, and I hugged my Ego. ... But it was the religion of the East, not of the West. It refused all significance to the temporal world; it took no account of society and its needs; it sought to destroy, not to develop, the sense and the power of Individuality. It did not say, but it implied, that creation was a mistake; and if it did not profess pessimism, pessimism was its logical outcome.[52]

Forster was to differ fundamentally here, to see a truth on the other side, beyond Dickinson's objections. Yet though they disagreed about India, they were at one on the subject of Anglo-Indians, those public school Red-bloods sent out by England to rule her unconquerable subcontinent. From Cairo to Bombay, Dickinson, Forster, R. C. Trevelyan, and G. H. Luce traveled together; and immediately the Anglo-Indians on the boat dubbed the foursome "The Professors" or "The Salon." "They recognised that we were gentlemen, sahibs even, yet there was a barrier." (p. 136.) Part of the barrier was created by their apostolic willingness to "talk to Indians," which these civil servants of the "best set" would never do. In this kind of confrontation, Bloomsbury—or pre-Bloomsbury in this case—looks good, though it is worth noting that neither Dickinson nor Forster ever

associated with any but wealthy, educated, or aristocratic Indians.
In recalling the sea voyage, Dickinson remembers how he tried to
explain the finer points of the English caste system to an Indian on
shipboard. He singles out as an example one of his companions,
probably Forster himself:

"Ah, but he, like myself, is a pariah. Have you not observed? They are quite
polite. They have even a kind of respect—such as our public school boys
have—for anyone who is queer, if only he is queer enough. But we don't
'belong' and they know it. We are outside the system. At bottom we are
dangerous, like foreigners. And they don't quite approve of our being let
loose in India." "Besides, you talk to the Indians." "Yes, we talk to the
Indians." "And that is contrary to the system?" "Yes, on board the boat;
it's all very well while you're still in England."[53]

The essentials of this experience are dubbed into *A Passage to India*,
where we observe that the old battle between the "sets" is still being
waged.

   Letters from John Chinaman (1901) is not, as we might suppose, a
product of Dickinson's round-the-world trip, but a purely imaginative satire written years before. It is an example of a common literary
genre, the idealization of a foreign country for heuristic purposes.
A Chinese traveler, after visiting Europe and England, denounces the
West and exalts the East in a series of letters—now Swiftian in their
invective, now redolent of almond blooms—in which we are invited
to discover not decadent over-ripeness but spiritual health. The traveler's invitation is couched in Dickinsonian raptures:

To feel, and in order to feel to express, or at least to understand the expression of all that is lovely in Nature, of all that is poignant and sensitive in
man, is to us in itself a sufficient end. A rose in a moonlit garden, the shadow of trees on the turf, almond bloom, scent of pine, the wine-cup and the
guitar; these and the pathos of life and death, the long embrace, the hand
stretched out in vain, the moment that glides for ever away, with its freight
of music and light, into the shadow and hush of the haunted past, all that
we have, all that eludes us, a bird on the wing, a perfume escaped on the
gale—to all these things we are trained to respond, and the response is what
we call literature.[54]

That such sentimentality was ever taken seriously seems incredible,
yet *John Chinaman* numbered among its admirers George Meredith,

George Trevelyan, and Logan Pearsall Smith. (William Jennings
Bryan, thinking the book to be by a native Chinese, wrote a reply
"in which he observed, among other things, that clearly the writer
had never seen the inside of a Christian home," p. 143.) The book is
pure Dickinson—the abstractions and the non-dramatic "fiction" are
stylistic confessions of his difficulty in coping with real facts about
real people in this real world. Did Dickinson really think that such
orchidaceous emotionalism could be an effective counterforce to materialism, philistinism, and mechanization? Whatever he thought, his
love for such expressions of sensibility held him like a narcotic addic-
tion.

Dickinson's views on war showed something of the same disparity
between wish and fact. He did not oppose bloodshed on religious
grounds, did not think it always immoral to kill (p. 157), and once
during his tour of India was so taken with the Royal West Kents
that, writes Forster, "militarism became permissible" (p. 138). But
the First World War shocked him, and his whole war effort was an
attempt to win support for the League of Nations.* He was distressed
—though not surprised—by the ease with which the churches sided
with the Red-bloods; but the betrayal of Cambridge cut even deeper:

Like the rest, moved by passion, by fear, by the need to be in the swim,
those who should have been the leaders followed the crowd down a steep
place. In a moment, as it were, I found myself isolated among my own
people. When I say isolated, I do not mean in any sense persecuted. . . . But
I learned once for all that students, those whose business it would seem to
be to keep the light of truth burning in a storm, are like other men, blindly
patriotic, savagely vigilant, cowardly or false when public opinion once begins to run strong. The younger dons and even the older ones disappeared
into war work. All discussion, all pursuit of truth ceased as in a moment.
To win the war or to hide safely among the winners became the only preoccupation. (p. 162.)

---

* Writes Forster: "It is possible that Dickinson invented the phrase 'League of
Nations'; it is certain that he was the first person in this country to formulate the
idea." (p. 163.) In November 1914 Dickinson stayed with a friend in Hereford and,
to beguile his misery, sketched out a draft of a League. This was most probably
the basis of the plan adopted by Lord Bryce and his group, who took it to President Wilson. Though "only one of the tiny streams which finally fell into the Lake
of Geneva" (p. 164), it was one of the most important.

Did he really believe Cambridge students could be so exempt from the normal human condition? Or was he just piqued at being abandoned? What, exactly, were the young men of Cambridge to do? Dickinson had no answer except "Follow truth." But to follow truth one needs a course of action, such as pacifism, treason, desertion, exile, or noncombatant duty. This, however, is just the kind of practical recommendation Dickinson could not, or would not, make. The pursuit of truth and the world of action have, for him, almost no connection; to bring ideals into league with machinery is to corrupt the ideals. The following comment in *War: Its Nature, Cause, and Cure* (1923) is characteristic: "The lie is organised and the truth is not. And to expect the truth to be organised is to expect too much. . . . Truth has only one power: it can kindle souls. But, after all, a soul is a greater force than a crowd. These words are written to you, the individual reader. If they strike a light in you, that light will shine, and shining, perhaps, may yet help to save mankind."[55] Again the generalizations, the obscurantism, the easy optimism. How can a soul be a force unless it joins with other souls, becomes organized? How can the reader help to save mankind unless he has influence and weight in human institutions? Dickinson never faces these questions. His is the liberal faith that a small group of elect intellectuals, propagandizing on behalf of certain civilized virtues, can change the world.[56] But, writes Roger Fry, "he had been far too optimistic and naïve in his conception of human nature before the war—he had no notion of how much a primitive and pre-logical mentality still survived in civilised man." (p. 163.) Forster thinks he had the notion "but refused to face its consequences" (p. 163). That kind of refusal was a rooted habit: he was an optimist to the end, in spite of all the evidence of man's depravity, because he never doubted that "the Real, to a progressive race, is not that which is or has been, but that which shall be. . . . As men become idealists, they will become practical."[57]

6

Two books written by Dickinson after the war—*The Magic Flute* (1920) and *The International Anarchy* (1926)—can be taken as the summation of his life and work. *The International Anarchy* (begun

in 1921) is a study of the pre-war diplomacy leading to the conflict—
a work of careful scholarship, remarkable, as Forster says, "for its
learning, logic and lucidity" (p. 193); it is unquestionably his strongest claim to objective scholarship. *The Magic Flute,* on the other
hand, is a work of fancy, an elaborate allegory that comes as close to
being a full-blown personal myth as Dickinson was ever to achieve.

Forster admired both books, but put the work of scholarship first.
The book is remarkable, he tells us, "because it contains no exhibition of emotion":

> The violent feelings which agitated the writer, the indignation and irrita-
> tion, the sorrow and despair, are suppressed, lest they endanger his appeal.
> He refuses to show his readers how much he suffers, in case they are diverted
> from the facts and discount the argument. And so, paradoxically enough,
> *The International Anarchy* ranks high as a work of art. It is supported by
> an intense emotion which is never allowed to ruffle the surface. It has the
> quality which, working through another temperament and in another medi-
> um, has produced Bach's fugues. (p. 193.)

By contrast, *The Magic Flute*—in spite of being "serious, profound,
inventive, fanciful, beautifully written"—has one defect: "as soon as
it describes war the writer's emotions get out of control, and we have
him lamenting or denouncing instead of creating" (p. 193). These
comments say much about what Forster strove for in his own style.

These two styles and these two approaches to reality mark the man,
but ultimately "poetry" dominates. What Dickinson needed and
wanted was a myth, a fiction that would externalize his drives and
aspirations. *The Magic Flute* does not manage to do so, but its shortcomings are deeply revealing. As might be expected of one who thinks
the truth is disorganized, Dickinson's view of life is disorderly and
confused—a gathering of prejudices and dreams rather than a systematic ethic or metaphysic. And since he rarely mustered either the
will or the talent to break free of subjectivism and confront crude
fact, his myth is a drama of evasive abstractions. In its failure to become an intelligible or convincing fiction, we have a case study in
neurotic humanism—one of many modern attempts to make the dialogue of the mind with itself yield artistic results.

The central issue of the allegory is the pursuit of Tamino ("Every
Youth") for Pamina ("The World's Desire"). She is the daughter of

Sarastro (who, Forster explains, "stands for reason—and for something else")[58] and "The Queen of Night" (who stands for instinct, guile, force, and possessiveness). Sarastro is separated from his Queen, and Pamina has escaped from her in order to live in her father's court. But Tamino, as his pursuit matures, discovers that he does not desire Pamina for himself, but *for the whole world*.[59] His ardor is now for no single woman but for the truth. (Pamina, as a docile personified abstraction, seems not to mind either his departure or her consignment to universal promiscuity.) In his search for truth he interviews Jesus, Candide, Satan, a Scottish Presbyterian, and others, and Jesus advises him to seek "Truth in Love."[60] Following this lead, he ends up—after many trials—in the Hall of Sarastro, where he is received by Aureole, "a young man of his own age," who greets him with a kiss. He is taken into the Order and then returns to the world, getting a glimpse of Pamina ("who smiled at him") as he departs. "And he passed out, and was lost in the bliss that lies beyond consciousness."[61]

Whatever else this allegory is, it is a rationalization for homosexual love. Males and females are without exception detoured around each other, and the only physical contact is the kiss of Aureole. Tamino as "Every Youth" represents what Dickinson describes in *The Greek View* as "an ideal expression . . . [of] what was stirring in the heart of every generous youth."[62] And Pamina as "the World's Desire" is tolerated only as a desexed spiritual absolute. Tamino, to be sure, returns to the world, but he almost literally "passes out" as he does so—suggesting something less than a robust ability to "connect" with the world of men.

It is hard to say exactly what the allegory means, but its homosexual theme certainly provides a reason for its evasiveness. By spiritualizing the passion, by exalting the experience to cosmic significance, one gets rid of the social guilt. But even so, it must remain a closet drama, the key to which rests with sympathetic readers and not with the public censor. Unquestionably Dickinson was burdened by the necessity of writing his myth in these terms, of making a secret of what must have been the most important thing in his life; it kept indoors a spirit that, in another culture, might have moved vigorously in the world of action. Forster, in discussing Dickinson's talents with the dialogue form, remarks that "the instincts and passions could be discussed . . . but they could not be illustrated" (p. 109).

So his life remained a contracted one—perhaps even a crippled one —and he had no means of expansion except via romantic idealism. He needed a *public* myth, but was constrained by public opinion to adopt a kind of double-talk—to refer to love as if it were the kind of love acceptable in a Victorian household, to mute his admiration for the Greeks so that it was fit for the ears of schoolchildren. It was a sad imprisonment, and Dickinson must be admired for such attempts at escape as he made. But his life is, finally, a little one, and a letter to a friend, reprinted in Forster's biography, describes its frustrations as well as its achievements in appropriate terms.

What you say about myth is very much what I also have felt. Many years ago I tried to say that, in a little book on religion. But the trouble about myths is, that they cannot now become generally credible. I believe men ought to find what they want in poetry and music. But then so many aren't sensitive to those things. My motion is, a little round of light illuminated by science, increasing, one hopes, in illumination and range; and outside, twilight and night, to be filled by art—I mean serious art. Perhaps I should say imagination. (pp. 221–22.)

However much Forster outgrew Dickinson, the older man introduces us to the younger. Forster, like Dickinson, tried to write his myth, and succeeded where Dickinson failed. But the way to that success was a tortuous one, and in such an early book as *The Longest Journey* we meet a hero suffering many of the inhibitions and frustrations that Dickinson suffered, a man thwarted and imprisoned in similar ways. That book is part novel, part autobiography, and part fantasy—mixed ingredients that advertise the author's moral and esthetic uncertainty. But with *A Passage to India* the myth was fully expressed, absorbing the values and anxieties that had previously resisted confinement in any one fable. That success meant, among other things, that Forster came to terms with what only embarrassed Dickinson, and that he found a symbolic rather than a merely euphemistic way of expressing it. "Love," "beauty," and "art" are with Forster far tougher words than they are with Dickinson, far more touched with the ambiguities of the human condition. This difference means not only that Forster lived after Dickinson into a tougher age, but also that Forster's is the greater talent and intelligence. And perhaps what measures that difference best is Forster's superior ability to laugh—to play the humorist as well as the prophet.

Although that measure is not definitive, it divides the sentimentalist from his opposite—and here is the difference we constantly feel between Dickinson's Cambridge generation and that led by Lytton Strachey. Forster is just as serious as Dickinson; he shares most of his ideas and ideals, but he brings to Dickinson's program a different style, one touched with gaiety, astringency, and irony. The style belongs to Bloomsbury, the ideas and ideals to pre-Bloomsbury, and Forster mediates between the two.

Part II

The Expanding Ring

Chapter five

Forster's Esthetics:
From Words to Music

"Our whole age is seeking to bring forth a sacred book."
                                                    —*Mallarmé*

Forster's ideas on art are in the nature of footnotes to the general esthetic notions advanced by Moore, Fry, and Dickinson. They do not amount to an "esthetic" but they are connected with one—and Forster's main contribution is to bring the novel within its range of consideration. Forster's book is an *Aspects* rather than a *Principia,* but in spite of its humble title it is an important reinforcement of Bloomsbury's body of first principles.

The notion that the novel could be an art form is relatively new in English criticism. A discussion on the subject was started in the 1880's by Walter Besant and continued by Henry James and Robert Louis Stevenson,[1] but the idea was not solidly established until the 1920's, when three notable books appeared: Percy Lubbock's *The Craft of Fiction* (1921),* Forster's *Aspects of the Novel* (1927), and Edwin Muir's *The Structure of the Novel* (1928). In France the Flaubertian notion that novels, like sonnets or sonatas, could possess artistic form had existed since the 1850's;[2] but English novelists—with the almost solitary exception of James—wrote their books with other things in mind. When Hardy had read J. W. Beach's *The Techniques of Thomas Hardy* (1922), he is said to have commented: "I found he had made no reference to my technique as a poet. There isn't any technique about prose, is there? It just comes along of itself."[3]

---

* Lubbock was a colleague of Forster's at King's, 1898–1901.

In spite of its popularity, and because of it, the novel had a reputation for keeping low company and late hours that not even Scott,
Dickens, and George Eliot had succeeded in removing. And when it
avoided such suspicions, it was often honored for extra-artistic reasons—as a vehicle for moral instruction, social protest, or the re-crea-
tion of history. But it was spiritually low-caste, and "wallowing in
the troughs of Zolaism" defined its possibilities for many puritans
besides Tennyson. Even Forster in 1926 was shocked by the "horror
and filth" of Joyce's *Ulysses* (though he tempered the judgment later),
and he did not wonder that poets "despise" the novel form (AN, 9).[4]

Forster's effort is to elevate the novel to the status of Art with a
capital A. But unlike those other critics of the twenties, he is less interested in the novel than in Art, less interested in the techniques of
fiction than in the ways fiction can transcend technique and become
something that might be considered an end in itself. When Forster
laments the difficulty of elevating "this low atavistic form"[5] to the
level of Art, the note of contempt can be taken quite seriously: he is
trying to raise up the diseased and the fallen. He is trying to do for
the novel what Fry tried to do for the plastic arts, and his esthetics are
largely a restatement of Fry's general principles. His esthetics begin,
one might say, at the point where Fry and Mauron link "plastic
values" with literature. To make one gospel of all the arts is a Bloomsbury ideal—and Forster is simply entering the novel in the game.

But his critical interest is, if anything, less secular than that of Fry
and Mauron—a fact that, incidentally, helps to explain his under-
valuation of James.[6] His criticism is a missionary enterprise: if the
novel can be made into Art, then perhaps life can too, for both begin
in the common clay. And unless this most popular form can be a value
in itself, as music, poetry, and painting are, then art and life can have
little connection. Forster, in fiction and in criticism, is coming to
terms with that crisis in apostasy described by Philip Rieff:

The cultured of this era strive to relate themselves to art as a way of recap-
turing the experience of the divine in which otherwise they no longer believe and in which they cannot feel themselves participants, even indirectly. Through the mediation of a writer, painter, composer, movie director, the work of art is experienced as a thing in itself, bracketed and raised

above the ordinary workaday world, yet related to that world as revelation is related to that which is revealed. . . . The work of art becomes that *wholly other,* present and yet inviolate, through which the cultivated may escape, for the time of the relation, their self-isolation. To some, the esthetic relation may become even more important than direct human contacts, because of the relative frequency with which passional communions occur in confronting the surrogates of life in art.[7]

"Imagination," writes Forster, "is as the immortal God which should assume flesh for the redemption of mortal passion."[8] The novel, in his esthetics, is this Incarnation; it exists to effect a transformation of the human into something like the divine.

2

Most of Forster's ideas on the arts are found in a few pieces: "Anonymity" (1925), *Aspects* (1927), "The Ivory Tower" (1938), "The Duty of Society to the Artist" (1942), "The Raison d'Etre of Criticism in the Arts" (1947), and "Art for Art's Sake" (1949). In all of these writings the subject is Art, the transcendent value that, like Moore's organic unity, is more than the sum of the values of its parts.

The transforming reagents in the artistic event are similar to those described by Fry. What Fry calls "the esthetic state of mind" (and Moore "admirable mental qualities") Forster calls (in one place) "the creative state of mind."[9] This state of mind comes into being when a viewer confronts what Fry would call "pure art," or when the artist is in the act of creating. With the impressionists, Forster and Fry both hold that no knowledge is independent of the knowing subject, but to this relativistic position they bring two hypothetical absolutes: the "pure" work of art, and the "perfect" spectator. "The work of art," Forster writes,[10] "assumes the existence of the perfect spectator, and is indifferent to the fact that no such person exists."* Between spectator and artist—with the work of art as meeting ground—occurs what Fry described as a liaison and Forster a miracle of transformation:

---

* Fry said: "It nowise invalidates this conception if such a thing as an absolutely pure work of art has never been created." "Some Questions in Esthetics," *Transformations,* p. 3.

A work of art [writes Forster] is a curious object. Isn't it infectious? Unlike machinery, hasn't it the power of transforming the person who encounters it towards the condition of the person who created it? (I use the clumsy phrase "towards the condition" on purpose.)* We—we the beholders or listeners or whatever we are—undergo a change analogous to creation. We are rapt into a region near to that where the artist worked, and like him when we return to earth we feel surprised. . . . Something has passed. I have been transformed towards his condition, he has called me out of myself, he has thrown me into a subsidiary dream.[11]

If the work of art is an objective "reality," then the creative state of mind is that same reality in its subjective or psychological form. And the binding force in this union is love. The three elements are a restatement, in non-Christian terms, of the Trinity. "I would not suggest," writes Forster, "that our comprehension of the fine arts is or should be of a nature of a mystic union. But, as in mysticism, we enter an unusual state, and we can only enter it through love. Putting it more prosaically, we cannot understand music unless we desire to hear it."[12] Love as the transforming agent in the esthetic (or spiritual) experience is proclaimed more loudly by Dickinson, McTaggart, and Moore than by Fry; but they all agree that Art is the subjectively based realization of human desire, an "I" far more than an "it"— which is another way of saying that God is cast in man's image.

Since nearly all of Forster's writings on art appeared after his last published novel, they are inevitably a comment (at least in part) on his own practice. Our main purpose here will be to understand his esthetic ideas, rather than to criticize them.

3

If we substitute the word "Art" for "Poetry" in the quotation from "Poetry for Poetry's Sake" by A. C. Bradley—perhaps the greatest English critic in the Coleridgean tradition†—we have all the main

* That "clumsy phrase" echoes a similarly clumsy phrase in Shelley's "A Defence of Poetry": "Sounds as well as thoughts have relation both between each other and *towards that* which they represent." (My italics.) Forster was unquestionably influenced by this essay.

† "What then does the formula 'Poetry for Poetry's sake' tell us about this experience? . . . First, this experience is an end in itself, is worth having on its own account, has an intrinsic value. Next, its poetic value is this intrinsic worth alone. Poetry may have also an ulterior value as a means to culture or religion; because

items of Forster's esthetics before us. First of all, the experience of
Art is "an end in itself, is worth having on its own account, has an
intrinsic value." Forster confirms his agreement with this basic premise again and again: "A work of art—whatever else it may be—is a
self-contained entity, with a life of its own imposed on it by its creator. It has internal order. It may have external form. That is how
we recognise it."[13] Second, "its poetic value is this intrinsic worth
alone." Fry called this intrinsic worth "plasticity"; Forster evokes
the same notion with such words as *form, order, harmony, variety,
rhythm*. For example, after agreeing with Shelley that poets are "the
unacknowledged legislators of the world," Forster writes: "He [the
artist] legislates through creating. And he creates through his sensitiveness and his power to impose form.... Form ... of some kind is
imperative. It is the surface crust of the internal harmony, it is the
outward evidence of order."[14] What is that internal order and harmony? Forster never analyzes the question, but answers in a metaphysical analogy.

No longer can we find a reassuring contrast to chaos in the night sky and
look up with George Meredith to the stars, the army of unalterable law, or
listen for the music of the spheres. Order is not there. In the entire universe
there seem to be only two possibilities for it. The first of them ... is the
divine order, the mystic harmony, which according to all religions is available for those who can contemplate it....

The second possibility for order lies in the aesthetic category.... [It is]
the order which an artist can create in his own work.... A work of art
... is a unique product.... It is unique not because it is clever or noble or
beautiful or enlightening or original or sincere or idealistic or useful or educational—it may embody any of those qualities—but because it is the only
material object in the universe which may possess internal harmony. All the
others have been pressed into shape from outside.[15]

Again, the internal order and harmony is a kind of rhythm that
"stitches" a work of art internally, shapes it from the inside out; and

---

it conveys instruction or softens the passions, or furthers a good cause; because it
brings the poet fame, or money, or a quiet conscience. So much the better: let it
be valued for these reasons too. But its ulterior worth neither is nor can directly
determine its poetic worth....For its nature is to be not a part, nor yet a copy,
of the real world (as we commonly understand that phrase), but to be a world by
itself, independent, complete, autonomous." *Oxford Lectures on Poetry* (London,
1950), p. 5. Quoted in "Some Questions in Esthetics," *Transformations*, p. 10.

part of what rhythm does in novels it also does in music: "There's an insistence in music—expressed largely through rhythm; there's a sense that it is trying to push across at us something which is neither an aesthetic pattern nor a sermon."[16]

Bradley's third point is that ulterior ends tend to lower poetic value. The nature of Poetry, writes Bradley,[17] "is to be not a part, nor yet a copy, of the real world . . . but to be a world by itself, independent, complete, autonomous; and to possess it fully you must enter that world, conform to its laws, and ignore for the time the beliefs, aims, and particular conditions which belong to you in the other world of reality."* The existence of those two worlds is a fundamental presupposition of Forster's art and criticism, and the dualism gets labeled in different ways. The dichotomy between the critical and the creative state of mind is one. The critical mind is in this world, conscious, cerebral, knowing; the creative mind moves out of this world to an autonomous realm, and takes direction from the unconscious as well as from the conscious. Criticism can prepare us to meet art and "educate us to keep our senses open," but "she has to withdraw when reality [Art] approaches."[18]

Another is the dichotomy between music "that reminds me of something" and "music itself."[19] In "Not Listening to Music," Forster confesses his tendency to wool-gather at concerts, blaming Wagner for getting him into the habit: "he never let the fancy roam; he ordained that one phrase should recall the ring, another the sword, another the blameless fool. . . . I accepted his leitmotiv system much too reverently† and forced it on to other composers whom it did not

---

* Compare Coleridge's "The willing suspension of disbelief that constitutes poetic faith." Consider also D. H. Lawrence's parody of this theory in *Women in Love*. Loerke speaks of his painting: "It has nothing to do with anything but itself, it has no relation with the everyday world of this and other, there is no connection between them, absolutely none, they are two different and distinct planes of existence, and to translate one into the other is worse than foolish, it is a darkening of all counsel, a making confusion everywhere. Do you see, you *must not* confuse the relative work of action, with the absolute world of art. That you *must not do*." (Lawrence's italics.) (New York, 1922), pp. 490–91.

† Forster writes, "Reverence is fatal to literature. My plea is for something more vital: imagination." "Anonymity," TC, 96–97. Cf. Fry: "Reverence is . . . as inimical to true esthetic experience as it is to the apprehension of truth." "Culture and Snobbism," *Transformations*, p. 79.

suit."[20] The mistake of looking for "meaning" in music is the same mistake as looking for "representation" in painting: "When music reminded me of something which was not music [writes Forster], I supposed it was getting me somewhere. 'How like Monet!' I thought when listening to Debussy, and 'how like Debussy!' when looking at Monet. I translated sounds into colours, saw the piccolo as apple-green, and the trumpets as scarlet. The arts were to be enriched by taking in one another's washing."[21] Such synesthetic cross-referencing is a Symbolist as well as a Bloomsbury habit,* but with Forster "music itself" is always the highest value. It is "more 'real' than anything," and the sort of music that is "untrammeled and untainted by reference is obviously the best sort of music to listen to."[22]

To be "untainted by reference" is the whole point, for as soon as the work of art begins to call attention to what exists outside its own independent, complete, autonomous reality, it is leading from the spiritual to the secular. Forster, however, is deeply concerned lest art, in the act of transcending the human and the actual, repudiate them; and he invokes music to demonstrate that art can at once belong to Caesar's realm and rise above it. "Music, more than the other arts," he writes, "postulates a double existence. It exists in time, and also exists outside time, instantaneously."[23] We must listen to it on these two levels—just as we should read books and look at pictures on these two levels. "We ought to perform a miracle the nature of which was hinted at by the Almighty when he said he was always glad to receive Mephistopheles in Heaven and hear him chat."[24] Forster never defines the upper level more clearly than that. "With no philosophic training," he writes, "I cannot put my belief clearly"—and the heart of the problem is "super-rational."[25] But one does not need much philosophic training to see, in this esthetic "double existence," an echo of the Kantian distinction between the reason and the under-

* Margaret Schlegel says, "Now, doesn't it seem absurd to you? What *is* the good of the Arts if they're interchangeable? What *is* the good of the ear if it tells you the same as the eye? Helen's one aim is to translate tunes into the language of painting, and pictures into the language of music.... If Monet's really Debussy, and Debussy's really Monet, neither gentleman is worth his salt—that's my opinion" (HE, 41). Following this statement Margaret adds: "But, of course, the real villain is Wagner. He has done more than any man in the nineteenth century towards the muddling of the arts."

standing, between noumena and phenomena—and of the Kantian
effort to connect them. To connect this "double existence" in his own
art is Forster's ideal.

These two realms are perhaps most dramatically dealt with in Forster's essay "Anonymity," where a distinction is drawn between "information" and "creation"—between words that point to something
else and words (in art) that point to nothing but themselves. "Information is relative. A poem is absolute." The statement, although it
is nonsense as criticism, makes sense as religion. But what is unique
here is the emphasis on the "subconscious," an emphasis that allows
Forster to change the metaphor from one of rising to value to one of
descending to it.

Just as words have two functions—information and creation—so each human
mind has two personalities, one on the surface, one deeper down. The upper
personality has a name. It is called S. T. Coleridge, or William Shakespeare,
or Mrs. Humphry Ward. It is conscious and alert, it does things like dining
out . . . and it differs vividly and amusingly from other personalities. The
lower personality is a very queer affair. In many ways it is a perfect fool,
but without it there is no literature, because unless a man dips a bucket
down into it occasionally he cannot produce first-class work. . . . Although
it is inside S. T. Coleridge, it cannot be labelled with his name. It has something in common with all other deeper personalities, and the mystic will
assert that the common quality is God, and that here, in the obscure recesses
of our being, we near the gates of the Divine.[26]

That is one of Forster's most important critical statements; the notions it utters underlie both his myth-making and his social criticism.
The force that comes from the lower depths "makes for anonymity"
and has something "general" about it; it is like what Jung calls the
collective unconscious, and it corrects the egoistic excesses of the
"upper personality." In any event, it is a reminder that Forster believes in something quite other than—even antagonistic to—individuality and personal relations. Greater than the poet is the beauty he
creates, greater than the words of the artist is the universal Word:
"Lost in the beauty where he was lost . . . we reach what seems to be
our spiritual home, and remember that it was not the speaker who
was in the beginning but the Word."[27] Call it God or the esthetic
emotion, it is the same psychological event.

It is in this essay that Forster most clearly passes from a consideration of Art in general to a study of literature in particular. The word "literature" is, with Forster, a value term; it is not simply what is written with words, it is an organization of words that conveys something beyond information. "What is this element in words that is not information?"[28] Forster calls it "atmosphere," then "style," then the "power that words have to raise our emotions or quicken our blood," but none of these is quite the answer: "It is also something else, and to define that other thing would be to explain the secret of the universe. This 'something else' in words is undefinable."[29] This is nothing other than Moore's undefinable, unanalyzable concept of "good." As music exists in time but carries us to the timeless, so literature "exists neither in space nor time though it has semblances of both."[30] With *literature itself,* the world of appearance fades to the unseen, the author (and the reader) to anonymity, the words to wordlessness. We encounter something universal and ineffable:

Before we begin to read the *Ancient Mariner* we know that the Polar Seas are not inhabited by spirits, and that if a man shoots an albatross he is not a criminal but a sportsman, and that if he stuffs the albatross afterwards he becomes a naturalist also. All this is common knowledge. But when we are reading the *Ancient Mariner,* or remembering it intensely, common knowledge disappears and uncommon knowledge takes its place. We have entered a universe that only answers to its own laws, supports itself, internally coheres. . . . We can best define it by negations. It is not this world, its laws are not the laws of science or logic, its conclusions not those of common sense. And it causes us to suspend our ordinary judgments.[31]

The negations of the above passage again raise the old questions: How far can one go in worshiping things not of this world, and yet remain a humanist and a novelist? The desire to lose oneself in Art may be a kind of death wish. To seek beauty in the autonomous realms of the general, or to know love as a transcendence of identity and personality, may be only a formula for *Liebestod.* Forster has often been criticized for the number of sudden deaths in *The Longest Journey*—which one critic estimated as "forty-four percent of the fictional population."[32] But though he tried to mend his ways in later books, those sudden deaths seemed right to him; they were part of his artistic vision. The characters must be able to come and go like phrases in a musical composition. How else, save as rhythmic functions, can people live in an abstracted world of Art, a world "that only answers to its own laws, supports itself, internally coheres"?

I was not inspired to put anything vital in the place of the sudden deaths. The only remedy for a defect is inspiration, the subconscious stuff that comes up in the bucket. A piece of contemporary music, to my ear, has a good many sudden deaths in it; the phrases expire as rapidly as the characters in my novel, the chords cut each other's throats, the arpeggio has a heart attack, the fugue gets into a nose-dive. But these defects—if defects they be—are vital to the general conception. They are not to be remedied by substituting sweetness.[33]

Not sweetness, perhaps, but what about sympathy and compassion? There may be some covert malice in using people like musical notes, just as there may be reason to wonder, when people love only the divine in each other, whether they are loving each other as human beings at all.

4

Aspects of the Novel, Forster's most ambitious esthetic statement, applies these general ideas to the novel. The Table of Contents is a hierarchy of value, a Jacob's ladder up the routes we have been tracing from a seen to an unseen world. We move from *story* through *people, plot, fantasy,* and *prophecy,* to *pattern* and *rhythm.* It is an irregular ascent from the actual to the abstract, from the human to the divine.

Forster begins by locating the novel as a "spongy tract" of land bounded by two chains of mountains, "the opposing ranges of Poetry and of History" (p. 10). Poetry is art in an extreme and pure form, but "the mixed art of fiction" is impure, largely because of the alluvial wastes descending upon it from the range called History. That range exists, its importance cannot be ignored, and occasionally we must make business trips in that direction, but it should not be confused with final "reality." To escape History and Time is the main urge of Forster's theory of art ("Time, all the way through, is to be our enemy," p. 12). Consequently, he does not discuss the novel as an event in literary history, a product of influences and schools; but he visualizes the novelists he discusses as seated in a circular room writing their novels simultaneously in a contemporaneous moment.

He wants to find the *novel itself* (if such an essence exists)—the novel freed as completely as possible from its temporal and historical allegiances.

Yet he admits that the novel cannot escape time. In real life timelessness can be found through dreams or love or lunacy, but in a novel "there is always a clock" (p. 31). That is to say, there is always the story, the lowest of the novel's aspects, which Forster defines as "a narrative of events arranged in time sequence" (p. 31). The story stirs our curiosity, makes us want to know what happens next—and no novel can be free of this base substructure. Wearily, Forster laments, "Yes—oh dear yes—the novel tells a story" (p. 27), and he heartily wishes it could escape this low estate and aspire to something higher and purer—to "melody" or "the perception of truth."* Our daily lives, writes Forster, reveal a double allegiance: to "the life in time and the life by values." We measure the life by values "not by minutes or hours, but by intensity" (p. 30). Cannot the novel be like that? "The life in time is so obviously base and inferior that the question naturally occurs: cannot the novelist abolish it from his work, even as the mystic asserts he has abolished it from his experience, and install its radiant alternative alone?" (p. 41.)

No, he concedes, the novel cannot be like that. Gertrude Stein made the absolute experiment—"going much further than Emily Brontë, Sterne or Proust" (p. 42)—and she failed. To abolish the "sequence in chronology" is to abolish the "sequence between the sentences," so that the novel setting out to express values alone becomes unintelligible. But this honest admission does not hide Forster's disappointment: his "heart goes out" to Gertrude Stein for having made the attempt. Forster's taste for Idealist absolutes can be as unabashed as McTaggart's.

In two chapters on "People," Forster plays variations on this theme. How does Homo Fictus differ from Homo Sapiens? He differs by being more "real." This paradoxical statement follows logically from

---

* In two deft sentences in *A Room with a View* most of these esthetic principles are invoked: "She was like a woman of Leonardo da Vinci's, whom we love not so much for herself as for the things that she will not tell us. The things are assuredly not of this life; no woman of Leonardo's could have anything so vulgar as a 'story.' " (p. 109.)

Forster's esthetic principles: he is more real because "a novel is a work of art, with its own laws ... and a character in a novel is real when it lives in accordance with such laws" (p. 61); and because a fictional character, unlike his true-life counterpart, can keep no secrets from the reader, stands fully revealed. The novelist knows everything about the characters he creates, though he may keep mum, and as a result of this omniscience we get "a reality of a kind we can never get in real life" (p. 61). In real life, intimacy is "makeshift" and perfect knowledge an "illusion"—we see as in a glass, darkly. But in the novel "we can know people perfectly"—we can see them face to face. "If God could tell the story of the Universe," writes Forster (p. 55), "the Universe would become fictitious."*

But the differences between Homo Fictus and Homo Sapiens are only half the problem. The other half consists of differences between characters within the novel itself, and here Forster draws his well-known and useful distinction between flat and round characters. Flat characters are types, two-dimensional, "little luminous discs of a pre-arranged size" (p. 66) that are incapable of development. Round characters are three-dimensional and "capable of surprising in a convincing way" (p. 75). Flat characters, those walking *idées fixes,* are usually the stuff of comedy; only round people "are fit to perform tragically for any length of time,"and only they "can move us to any feelings except humour and appropriateness" (p. 70). Though the distinction is not new, Forster employs it in perceptive ways. Lady Bertram of Jane Austen's *Persuasion,* for example,

... "did not think deeply." Exactly: as per formula. "But guided by Sir Thomas she thought justly on all important points." Sir Thomas' guidance, which is part of the formula, remains, but it pushes her ladyship towards an independent and undesired morality. "She saw therefore in all its enormity what had happened." This is the moral fortissimo—very strong but carefully introduced. And then follows a most artful decrescendo, by means of negatives. "She neither endeavoured herself, nor required Fanny to advise her, to think little of guilt or infamy." The formula is reappearing, because

---

as a rule she does try to minimize trouble, and does require Fanny to advise her how to do this; indeed Fanny has done nothing else for the last ten years. The words, though they are negatived, remind us of this, her normal state is again in view, and she has in a single sentence been inflated into a round character and collapsed back into a flat one. How Jane Austen can write! (p. 73.)

How E. M. Forster can write! The most interesting thing here is the way Forster describes Austen's passage in musical terms. In the rising and falling of Lady Bertram we have a character becoming—or being understood as—rhythm. The fortissimo and decrescendo are musical equivalents for the geometry of round and flat, and it is through these changing relationships that we approach the novel's "centre of reality."[34] We learn to know Lady Bertram as a moral gesture, a movement through what Mauron would call "psychological volumes."

The plot, which Forster discusses next, is the novel in its "logical, intellectual aspect." It is a story with causality added:

"The king died and then the queen died," is a story. "The king died, and then the queen died of grief" is a plot. The time-sequence is preserved, but the sense of causality overshadows it. Or again: "The queen died, no one knew why, until it was discovered that it was through grief at the death of the king." This is a plot with a mystery in it, a form capable of high development. (pp. 82–83.)

Mere curiosity can keep a story going, but "a plot demands intelligence and memory also" (p. 83). It demands that the reader remember what has been written, conjecture, make cross-references, try to solve the novel's mysteries and surprises. These mysteries and surprises involve "a suspension of the time-sequence"—and for that, of course, Forster likes them. Nevertheless, the reader seeks to solve the mysteries, to drag them back into the realm of time, space, and causality. But the ultimate effect ("if the plot has been a fine one") will not simply be satisfactory solutions to the mysteries, but "something aesthetically compact, something which might have been shown by the novelist straight away, only if he had shown it straight away it would never have become beautiful" (pp. 84–85). This "something aesthetically compact" is nothing other than an organic unity, a whole that cannot be known by its parts and must be grasped entire, simultaneously. And that something is as much in the mind of the reader as in the book he reads—a gestalt created by the reader's imagination, memory, and intelligence.

Forster opened his discussion of plot by denying the Aristotelian notion that character is revealed in action. Like D. H. Lawrence, he is primarily interested in the novel's capacity to explore "the *passional* secret places of life" (Lawrence's italics); plot interests him mainly as a foil to the forces of anti-plot. "We believe that happiness and misery exist in the secret life, which each of us leads privately and to which (in his characters) the novelist has access. And by the secret life we mean the life for which there is no external evidence, not, as is vulgarly supposed, that which is revealed by a chance word or a sigh." (p. 80.) To accept something without evidence is, as Forster reminds us, to accept it on faith, on "the evidence of things not seen."[35] Forster wants to tap this unseen evidence, and the novelist has special opportunities for doing so: "He can show the subconscious short-circuiting straight into action ... he can show it in its relation to soliloquy. He commands all the secret life." (p. 81.) But while Forster cherishes this privilege, he cares little about the techniques for entering this secret life. To get there is what counts. Questions of point of view, so important to Percy Lubbock, merely bore Forster—they have "too much the atmosphere of the law courts about them."[36] He cannot care less whether the author is outside or inside his characters, omniscient or limited. "All that matters ...," he insists, "is whether the shifting of attitude and the secret life are convincing." (p. 81.) All that matters, in short, is the realm of value, not how we reach it.

Between character and plot is a struggle for domination. Living things do not gracefully submit to the machinery of plot—to "the triple process of complication, crisis, and solution so persuasively expounded by Aristotle" (p. 82). The critical question is whether people can be stretched on that Procrustean bed and still live.* Sometimes the plot, in the "losing battle" it fights with the characters, "takes a

---

* "In most literary works," writes Forster, "there are two elements: human individuals ... and the element vaguely called art" (p. 81); the question of which comes first is, with Forster, fundamental. In *E. M. Forster: The Perils of Humanism* (Princeton, 1962), Frederick C. Crews criticizes H. J. Oliver for claiming that Forster so sacrifices his own characters. See p. 90.

cowardly revenge": it rounds things off, it winds them up. Need this happen? Forster wants the novel to be like a natural organism rather than like a machine, and protests the sacrifice of its vitality to the demands of its "logical, intellectual aspect." "After all, why has a novel to be planned? Cannot it grow? Why need it close, as a play closes? Cannot it open out? Instead of standing above his work and controlling it, cannot the novelist throw himself into it and be carried along to some goal that he does not foresee?" (p. 92). Once again the answer is no—or not quite. But these wistful questions remind us of the spiritual ambitions behind Forster's esthetics. He wants the work of art to show God's handiwork, not man's; and ultimately he wants it to escape even nature's laws for a "timeless, spaceless universe."[37]

With fantasy we take a first step into this other region, into a world that brings together "the kingdoms of magic and commonsense" (p. 109). "There is more in the novel," writes Forster, "than time or people or logic or any of their derivatives," and that something he labels fantasy and prophecy (p. 100). Fantasy is a middle kingdom (often ruled by the god "Muddle") manifested in books like *Tristram Shandy, Zuleika Dobson, Lady into Fox* (David Garnett), and *The Magic Flute*. Such miniature mythologies, mixtures of realism and make-believe, "imply" the supernatural but "need not express it" (p. 105). When the supernatural enters, it comes as "the introduction of a god, ghost, angel, monkey, monster, midget, witch into ordinary life; or the introduction of ordinary men into no man's land, the future, the past, the interior of the earth, the fourth dimension; or divings into and dividings of personality; or finally the device of parody or adaptation" (pp. 105–6). Fantasy is a low cousin to the mock-epic, as the mock-epic is to the epic, and both show stages of corruption in the relations between the human and the divine. Forster's stories will be our best illustration of fantasy's insecure spirituality.

Prophecy, however, takes us all the way into the noumenal world. Prophecy has nothing to do with foretelling the future.* It is, instead,

---

* See Shelley's *Defence of Poetry*: "Not that I assert poets to be prophets in the gross sense of the word, or that they can foretell the form as surely as they foreknow the spirit of events. . . . A poet participates in the eternal, the infinite, and the one; as far as relates to his conceptions, time and place and number are not."

"an accent in the novelist's voice, an accent for which the flutes and saxophones of fantasy may have prepared us" (p. 116). Indeed, foretelling is out of place because words are out of place; choiring angels have replaced human conversation. The "tone of voice" that is prophecy has nothing to do with any particular religious faith; its theme is "the universe, or something universal." But the prophetic author "is not necessarily going to 'say' anything about the universe; he proposes to sing, and the strangeness of song arising in the halls of fiction is bound to give us a shock." If, however, this "bardic influence" is to be effective, both the prophet and the prophet's audience must be in a particular frame of mind:

> The prophetic aspect demands two qualities: humility and the suspension of the sense of humour. . . . Without [humility] . . . we shall not hear the voice of the prophet, and our eyes will behold a figure of fun instead of his glory. And the sense of humour—that is out of place: that estimable adjunct of the educated man must be laid aside. Like the school-children in the Bible, one cannot help laughing at a prophet—his bald head is so absurd*—but one can discount the laughter and realize that it has no critical value and is merely food for bears. (p. 117.)

This is one of Forster's most important critical distinctions. Humor, which can live in no world but that of space, time, and causality, will obviously be a force dragging the spiritual back to earth— or preventing its rise. If the two are allowed into the same book, we shall witness some strange and interesting contradictions. When Forster admits that "one cannot help laughing at a prophet," we wonder whether, when he dons his own prophetic singing robes, he will be able to keep from laughing at himself. The bardic strain is strong in him, but so is the comic; he is devoted to Dostoevsky and D. H. Lawrence, but also to Jane Austen and Mrs. Gaskell. It is not easy to see how the battle of the teacups and the battle of the gods can take place in the same setting and be absorbed in the same moment of vision, and Forster himself has recognized that joining the worlds of prophecy and common sense can create a comic-opera effect: "The singer does not always have room for his gestures, the tables and chairs get broken, and the novel through which bardic influence

---

* Compare T. S. Eliot's "The Love Song of J. Alfred Prufrock": "Though I have seen my head (grown slightly bald) brought in upon a platter/I am no prophet— and here's no great matter."

has passed often has a wrecked air, like a drawing-room after an earthquake or a children's party." (p. 116.) The *sens commun*, the soul of comedy, is antithetical to the romantic *sens propre*, the soul of tragedy (and prophecy). Forster has strong commitments in both directions—to the public and to the private, to decorum and to disorder, to the conscious and to the subconscious. His divided loyalties here are only another version of that fundamental problem: can art and human beings cohabit and survive?

There is no doubt, however, that prophecy is for Forster the greatest achievement. It is the breakthrough, the seeing of the visible world as the living garment of God, the miracle of natural supernaturalism. Forster eschews such Carlylean language, but these terms are appropriate to his meaning. Prophecy does not repudiate the phenomenal world so much as realize the spirit embedded in it. Prophetic writers like Dostoevsky, Melville, Emily Brontë, or D. H. Lawrence are meticulous about the "little things in the foreground" while the "essential" thing, the "prophetic song," simultaneously "flows athwart the action and the surface morality like an undercurrent" (p. 128). That essential thing "lies outside words."

Is that just a metaphor or can that double life really coalesce in the novel to form an esthetic whole? Forster is convinced that it can. Characters do not cease being people when prophecy touches them: they simply expand, continuing the kind of spiritual growth demonstrated so stingily by Lady Bertram. In Dostoevsky, for example, "the characters and situations always stand for more than themselves; infinity attends them; though they remain individuals they expand to embrace it and summon it to embrace them; one can apply to them the saying of St. Catherine of Siena that God is in the soul and the soul is in God as the sea is in the fish and the fish is in the sea." (p. 123.) "Dostoevsky's characters," writes Forster, "ask us to share something deeper than their experiences," something beyond what the empiricist would recognize as knowledge. They take us "far back." "They convey to us a sensation that is partly physical—the sensation of sinking into a translucent globe and seeing our experience floating far above us on its surface, tiny, remote, yet ours. We have not ceased to be people, we have given nothing up, but 'the sea is in the fish and the fish is in the sea.' " (p. 124.)

Through such images Forster—like Coleridge—argues the compatibility of human with absolute values, and provides meeting-places for the dualisms of his esthetics and his art. "Any metaphor" silenced the young Rickie (LJ, 21), and his creator is prodigal with metaphors, which he uses as propositions in his argument.

Prophecy is unlike fantasy "because its face is towards unity, whereas fantasy glances about" (p. 126). And the prophetic vision is usually below or behind ordinary experience rather than above it.* But the final distinguishing mark of prophecy is that it always "gives us the sensation of a song or of sound." It is literature turned to music. Conrad is not prophetic, because the voice of Marlow "is too full of experiences to sing." Hardy, though "a philosopher and a great poet," is not prophetic because his novels "do not give out sounds." And in Joyce, says Forster, "it is talk, talk, never song." But D. H. Lawrence makes the grade, even though he is a preacher: "His greatness lies far, far back, and rests, not like Dostoevsky's upon Christianity, nor like Melville's upon a contest, but upon something aesthetic. The voice is Balder's voice, though the hands are the hands of Esau. The prophet is irradiating nature from within, so that every colour has a glow and every form a distinctness which could not otherwise be obtained." (p. 133.) That "something aesthetic" is close to what Fry called the plastic values. "What is valuable about him," says Forster of Lawrence, "cannot be put into words; it is colour, gesture and outline in people and things." (p. 133.) And the definition drifts off into the language of esthetic abstraction, where solidities fade into relations. The language borrows from painting as well as from music, but this is, as we know, Bloomsbury's kind of critical terminology.

"Pattern and Rhythm," the chapter that follows, descends to talk about these matters in terms of technique. It borrows a term first from painting and then from music. By pattern, Forster means the shape the plot takes, such as the "hourglass" shape of Anatole France's *Thaïs,* in which the two main characters "converge, cross and recede with mathematical precision" (p. 138). Other patterns (though they are not always describable in pictorial images) are "the grand chain or converging lines of the cathedral or diverging lines of the Cather-

* Melville, for example, "reaches straight back into the universal, to a blackness and sadness so transcending our own that they are undistinguishable from glory" (p. 132).

ine wheel, or bed of Procrustes—whatever image you like as long as it implies unity" (p. 149). Patterns, like plots, are sometimes beautiful, but often that beauty comes at enormous cost. Henry James, for example, sacrifices his characters to the pattern, limiting their number and limiting their attributes:

They are incapable of fun, of rapid motion, of carnality, and of nine-tenths of heroism. Their clothes will not take off, the diseases that ravage them are anonymous, like the sources of their income, their servants are noiseless or resemble themselves, no social explanation of the world we know is possible for them, for there are no stupid people in their world, no barriers of language, and no poor.... Maimed creatures can alone breathe in Henry James' pages—maimed yet specialized.[38]

It is an astonishing misjudgment, but the reasons for it are not hard to find—or guess. First, Forster considered James a hopeless snob, probably never forgetting that day in Rye when the Master mistook him for Moore and seemed a bit stuffy about the bad dress and grooming of his young Cambridge visitors.[39] Forster again and again makes wisecracks at James's expense,* and he parodies his manner in the early pages of *Aspects*: "Of course as I say this I hear Henry James beginning to express his regret—no, not his regret but his surprise—no, not even his surprise but his awareness that neighbourliness is being postulated of him, and postulated, must he add, in relation to a shopkeeper." (p. 18.) But James's fundamental offense is implied in the quotation above: he is too *secular*. Bad as it is to curtail the novel's life for the sake of pattern, it is positively evil when "this castrating is not in the interests of the Kingdom of Heaven"—and in James it is not: "There is no philosophy in the novels, no religion (except an occasional touch of superstition), no prophecy, no benefit for the superhuman at all." (p. 148.) In short, if one is going to sacrifice people, it must be to a god. This objection—surprising as it may at first seem—is the voice of the quintessential Forster.

"Rhythm" is Forster's chief word for describing the technical prob-

* For example, in *The Longest Journey*, Agnes says: "At our Dorcas we tried to read out a long affair by Henry James—Herbert saw it recommended in 'The Times.' There was no doubt it was very good, but one simply couldn't remember from one week to another what had happened." (p. 85.) Agnes is not a sympathetic character, but Forster never suggests that her memory is defective.

lem of expressing prophecy in the novel. The perfect example of rhythm is the appearance and reappearance of the "little phrase" of the Vinteuil sonata in Proust's *A la recherche du temps perdu.* The phrase "has a life of its own, unconnected with the lives of its auditors. . . . It is almost an actor, but not quite, and that 'not quite' means that its power has gone towards stitching Proust's book together from the inside." (p. 153.) Why the "not quite" should have that meaning is a mystery, but then a mystery is exactly what Forster is trying to put in words. A symphony has an obvious rhythm that we "can all hear and tap to," but Forster is interested in another rhythm, one "which some people can hear but no one can tap to." This other rhythm derives from "the relation between its movements" (p. 151). He wants a literary equivalent for this relationship, one that will allow the novel to depend less on external form.[40] "Is there any effect in novels," he asks, "comparable to the effect of the Fifth Symphony as a whole, where, when the orchestra stops, we hear something that has never actually been played?" (p. 154.) If we can answer yes, we have passed in fiction into the noumenal world—beyond time, space, words, sight, sound, causation. This is where Forster ideally wants to go—into a world very like that of Moore's and Dickinson's "good," McTaggart's "absolute," and Fry's "plastic relations." Only there is found the true reality and freedom:

Expansion. That is the idea the novelist must cling to. Not completion. Not rounding off but opening out. When the symphony is over we feel that the notes and tunes composing it have been liberated, they have found in the rhythm of the whole their individual freedom. Cannot the novel be like that?* (p. 155.)

In short, if we were to take Forster at his word, we would have to conclude that he does not like novels much. He wants to transcend them, to wash his hands of their earthly clay. More than any other art form, the novel is committed to this world—to human beings in human society. But Forster not only wants an alchemy that will trans-

---

* Compare Shelley on the miracle of expansion in poetry: "It is a strain which distends, and then bursts the circumference of the reader's mind, and pours itself forth together with it into the universal element with which it has perpetual sympathy." *A Defence of Poetry*, p. 307.

form those elements into something as unworldly as music,* he wants
that music to be *unheard*—what one hears (if one has Forster's ear)
after the orchestra stops playing. The esthetic unity he cherishes for
the novel has almost nothing to do with technical considerations; it
is a vision of ontological completion, which would require that the
novel be a kind of bodiless transparency, flying off like a butterfly
into divine realms. This is idealism indeed. And had Forster really
practiced what he preached, his books could not have existed except
in idea.

He is a novelist because he does not, or cannot, take his own idealism too seriously. His sense of humor continually pulls him by the
leg back to earth. But more than that, for all his talk about the unseen and the timeless, for all his evasiveness and fastidiousness about
experience (the "shy crablike sidewise movement"), Forster likes it
here. With the Christian who does not doubt that heaven is of first
importance but hates to die, Forster—in his art and in his esthetics—
lives a paradox. That paradox is what makes him interesting and
important, for it involves an earnest effort to realize the timeless and
the relative, the eternal and the human, as parts of an organic whole.
His whole conviction is that there is something larger and of greater
value than dualism, conflict, division—and that nations and individuals (as well as novels) might express it. But to come to that wholeness we must, as it were, be already immersed in it; we must perceive
the wholeness with one part of our mind, all the while observing the
tentative, human solutions of plots and stories with another part.
Art, in short, is the writing of a new gospel, and Forster's esthetics are
a kind of theology—an attempt to find the formula by which that sacred book might be written. In trying to live and write this gospel,
Forster has been engaged in one of the central efforts of art in our
time, the attempt to find esthetic equivalents for a moribund Christian tradition.

* Consider D. H. Lawrence's search for "the strange ... *invisible* beauty ... which
is undeniably there, but which seems to lurk just beyond the range of our white
vision." *Kangaroo* (Harmondsworth, 1950), p. 87.

Chapter six

The Stories: Fantasy

He was entrapped by the commonplaces of idealism, by
the strange notion that only the make-believe could lib-
erate the spirit from the bonds of actuality.

—Roger Fry

Even fantasy must subdue a real world.

—G. Armour Craig

Forster's fiction, from the stories to *Passage,* describes a transition
from the subjective to the objective. Although the stories, thirteen
in all, appeared throughout the greater part of his fiction-writing
career, from 1903 until 1920, they are nevertheless youthful productions and deal with problems of youth—problems of revolt and belief, of self-justification and self-discovery.* Any study of Forster's
fiction must begin with these tales, for here is the unformed author
seeking his identity, testing himself in fictional roles, probing for his
subject and style—and giving voice, under a dozen fictional disguises,
to an agonized self-confession. The stories attempt to objectify personal experience, but the objectification does not get very far. Awkward, self-conscious, and amateurish, these tales are no more distant
from the author than persona is from person in a home theatrical.
Their trials and errors are personal as well as fictional.

In an interview for *The Paris Review,* Forster said: "In no book
have I got down more than the people I like, the person who I think
I am, and the people who irritate me. This puts me among the large

* All the stories were written before 1914, the earliest being "The Story of a
Panic" in 1902, and Forster began to publish them in periodicals in 1903. All but
one of the stories were published between 1903 and 1912; "The Story of the Siren"
appeared in 1920. See inside cover of cs.

body of authors who are not really novelists, and have to get on as best they can with these three categories."[1] If that is true of the novels, it is doubly true of the stories, since none of the novels, except possibly *The Longest Journey*, comes so close to the bare nerve of personal experience as the stories do. The tales have three voices or inflections: warmth and affection for the saved, self-pity for the unloved victim, and scorn for the oppressors—this last being especially conspicuous. They exist, in large part, as vehicles of deliverance—to deliver their author, with the help of Pan or celestial omnibuses, to visions of Paradise, but especially to deliver a merciless comeuppance to his tormentors. They record the first stage of a rebellion against school, church, and the intolerable chaperonage of loving parents and guardians. The last novel completes that rebellion, but there the scene has become cosmic rather than suburban, and the pain and rage of a personal indictment have given way to the objectivity of a universal symbolism.

2

Forster calls his stories fantasies. "I like that idea of fantasy," he writes, "of muddling up the actual and the impossible until the reader isn't sure which is which."[2] Such muddling may be play, a game of blindman's buff, but it may also be the sleight of hand of a man with something to hide—or with something he cannot or dare not show directly. "The young writer usually begins with fantasy, doesn't he?" Forster has asked.[3] Doubtless because of his own early practice, he puts this as a rhetorical question. But it can also be heard as an appeal for approval. In acknowledging his debt to another fantasist, the author of *Erewhon*, Forster says that Butler's spirit saves him from "scandal": "we both tend to be non-intimate on the subjects of letters and life, and to saddle Seneca or Ibsen with anything which we do not quite want to say."[4] Seneca and Ibsen are hardly figures of fantasy, but fauns and dryads, more indigenous to the form, get saddled in the same way. But why "scandal"? What sort of shame does the spirit of fantasy save Forster from? The stories reveal one answer: it is the scandalous act of cutting the silver cord, of biting the feeding hand. Both Butler and Forster knew this shame well, and both used fantasy as an unction for disobedience. How does fantasy so serve? What is its nature?

Fantasy, as a psychological phenomenon, is a means of getting via dream, imagination, or wishful thinking what one cannot get in reality. As a literary phenomenon, it is the record of this achievement, somewhat tidied up for public appearance. Fantasy is a device whereby old and young alike (but particularly young) escape or make tolerable an environment they cannot cope with in a mature way. It always springs from frustration: "We may lay it down," writes Freud, "that a happy person never fantasies, only an unsatisfied one. The motive forces of fantasies are unsatisfied wishes, and every single fantasy is the fulfillment of a wish, a correction of unsatisfied reality."[5] When Rickie in *The Longest Journey* achieved happiness, the "ghosts" of his childhood were laid: "When real things are so wonderful, what is the point of pretending?" (p. 71.) One of the agonies of growing up has always been the child's desire to escape parental authority, to cast off the status of ward; and that desire inevitably breeds guilt and confusion. The child is ashamed of his secret disloyalties toward those on whom he still depends, yet his own self-respect—indeed his very identity—hangs on his having the courage to establish his independence. He is desperate at once for some means of atonement and for some means of escape.

Fantasy provides these means; it is a substitute for action, a way of facing imaginatively what one cannot face in reality. It provides cheap atonement for the sin in one's heart without exposure to the heavy penalties that actual revolt would involve. It is a way of gratifying one's desires, however illicit or taboo, in a private world from which all authority and rule-makers, save the fantasist himself, are excluded. "You know with what People we are obliged in the course of Childhood to associate, whose conduct forces us into duplicity and falsehood to them," wrote Keats to his sister Fanny, in a passage quoted sympathetically by Forster.[6] Fantasy is one of the forms such duplicity and falsehood can take, and a great many puritan parents who have seen fantasy simply as harmless "play" have been taken in.

If these generalizations hold for any age, they were especially valid for upper-middle-class Victorians. Never were children more cruelly suffocated by morality and overprivilege than the poor little rich children of Forster's class and generation. Leonard Woolf puts their case: "People of a younger generation who from birth have enjoyed the results of this struggle for social and intellectual emancipation cannot realize the stuffy intellectual and moral suffocation which a young man felt weighing down upon him in Church and State, in the 'rules and conventions' of the last days of Victorian civilization."[7] Neither Woolf nor Forster nor any other members of Bloomsbury actually left the Establishment. Irreverent rather than iconoclastic, malcontents rather than revolutionaries, none of them in the long run refused the stocks and bonds of their cultural indenture. Fantasy is well equipped to express this moral ambiguity, to dignify, by translating them into a kind of art, disloyalties that one is not ready to act out.

Forster worked hard to keep his fantasies unportentous and light on the wing, invoking on their behalf only the lesser gods and the more trivial presences of fancy—"all beings who inhabit the lower air, the shallow water, and the smaller hills, all Fauns and Dryads and slips of the memory, all verbal coincidences, Pans and puns, all that is mediaeval this side of the grave" (AN, 103). All the gods, in short, that are out of favor, that powerful people only laugh at, that are dismissed by old ladies as cute and by stuffy gentlemen as time-wasters and frauds. But those on the inside know these gods to be anything but sweet and innocent. They are mischievous, irresponsible, and polytheistic; they despise churches, drawing-rooms, and schools; they inspire untidiness, natural manners, even sexual honesty. What a treat for a Victorian child to have a set of gods like these! They are the born enemies of Mrs. Grundy and all her household deities; they stand for everything one is not supposed to believe in. Yet who will disturb their worshiper? What parent or teacher will deign to notice such a whimsical apostasy?

Nevertheless these gods of fantasy are real gods and play an important role in Forster's private drama of belief. Fantasy is not only make-believe, it is also make-*belief*. It is the creation of a myth—or the preliminary probings in that direction—and since it has to do with matters "this side of the grave," with what is mortal and sublunary, it tends to dramatize a humanist religion. In contrast is the religion of prophecy—and the distinction is important:

> When we come to prophecy we shall utter no invocation, but it will have been to whatever transcends our abilities, even when it is human passion that transcends them, to the deities of India, Greece, Scandinavia and Judaea, to all that is mediaeval beyond the grave and to Lucifer son of the morning. By their mythologies we shall distinguish . . . [them].
> The power of fantasy penetrates into every corner of the universe, but not into the forces that govern it—the stars that are the brain of heaven, the army of unalterable law, remain untouched. (AN, 103–4.)

Fantasy makes jokes, prophecy does not; fantasy is ironic, prophecy rises above contrast; fantasy is quasi-human and domestic, prophecy is universal. The religion of fantasy, then, is useful rather than sublime—good when one needs to settle old scores or to get some mild revenge on second-rate enemies. But it remains, nevertheless, a vehicle of belief.

Indeed, fantasy can be understood as the dying expression of an epic or tragic impulse, of those literary forms making grand assertions, justifying God's ways to man, or showing heroes contending with the forces of the universe. It may be, as Forster said of Lampedusa's *The Leopard*, "an epic of worry rather than of high tragedy,"[8] but in its diminished way fantasy, no less than real epic, traffics between the human and the divine, the natural and the supernatural—or, to use Forster's special terms, the actual and the impossible. Although the gods and heroes of fantasy may seem more like anti-gods and anti-heroes, they are not fake; their confrontations have symbolic significance; they exist as the agents of petty causes. Like the sylphs of *The Rape of the Lock*, or like Puck or Oberon—who are the great gods descended into folk nuisances or dairymaid's helps—they concern themselves with worry rather than with sin, with the frustrated rather than the fallen, and they minister to symptoms rather than to causes, hovering "an inch or two above the surface of things."[9] Nevertheless, justice is still their work, though it may only be the justifying of a boy's ways to parents or the avenging of nature scorned. Even the tone of fantasy (as Forster conceives it) rings with a surviving echo of heroic aspiration and resolve. Listen to

Rickie the artist* lamenting his unsuccessful stories: " 'I can't soar;
I can only indicate. That's where the musicians have the pull, for
music has wings, and when she says "Tristan" and he says "Isolde,"
you are on the heights at once.' " (LJ, 162.)

Whatever else that says, it declares that the author of these stories
aimed not just at an epic of worry but at something more elevated.
Fantasy, however, always confesses a degree of spiritual poverty; it is
religion in a clown's tattered pantaloons, and hence uniquely suited
to an age in which the forms and gestures of belief are still visible, but
archaic. Fantasy mimics those forms and gestures, parodying the old
motions of aspiration. Its words are a language of low rather than
high confidence.

The true myth-making impulse, says Forrest Reid, is free of any
"will to believe"—like the artless and unselfconscious folklore of
Western Ireland. But Forster's stories are heavy with that will. Even
when they do leave the ground and fly between earth and heaven,
their harbingers are gods or men or omnibuses out of the machine,
creaking and groaning with their loads of messages. The one thing
needful to the butterflies and beetles of fantasy, says Forster, is "the
absence of a soul." But that is just what his creatures always have
too much of. They have wrongs to right and scores to settle, and
though Forster also makes laughter an article of their faith, it seems
superimposed—almost like a disguise—on their serious purposes.

In "Mr. Andrews," for example, we are taken on an epic ride from
this world to the next, and the heaven we reach is that of the joke-
books or of Byron's "The Vision of Judgment." The late Mr. Andrews, "kind, upright, and religious," finds himself floating upward
in company with a Moslem, "so godless, so lawless, so cruel, so lustful," and is, of course, surprised to find that both souls may enter
heaven. Parts of the story are quite funny, as when Mr. Andrews announces that he is "broad church" and his author declares, "The

---

* One of Rickie's stories, called "The Bay of the Fifteen Islets," takes place off
the coast of Sicily and bears some similarity, thematic as well as geographic, to
"Albergo Empedocle," Forster's first published story. Another, untitled, clearly refers to "Other Kingdom." Rickie called his collection of (eight or nine) stories "Pan
Pipes," a title which brings strongly to mind "The Story of a Panic." See LJ, 71, 83–
84, 161.

word 'broad' quavered strangely among the interspaces." But the poetic justice is more than frivolous; the fantasy mixes serious criticism with its fun:

Mr. Andrews saw Buddha, and Vishnu, and Allah, and Jehovah, and the Elohim. He saw little ugly determined gods who were worshiped by a few savages in the same way. He saw the vast shadowy outlines of the neo-Pagan Zeus. There were cruel gods, and coarse gods, and tortured gods, and, worse still, there were gods who were peevish, or deceitful, or vulgar. No aspiration of humanity was unfulfilled. There was even an intermediate state for those who wished it, and for the Christian Scientists a place where they could demonstrate that they had not died. (cs, 169.)

All the gods of orthodoxy have become gods of fantasy, tossed indiscriminately into the same heaven. This is not to ridicule religion or the religious impulse, but to make a case for the religion of humanism. This pantheon, wisecracks included, is almost exactly the one Wedd encountered at South Place Institute, and we are far afield if we think Forster did not take it seriously. But the promiscuous universality that can equate Vishnu and Jehovah, Buddha and Zeus, is revolutionary, just the kind of spiritual permissiveness most disturbing to the parochial Christian mind. Thus fantasy becomes a weapon in a holy skirmish, if not a holy war, and Forster joins that category of fantasists who cannot be wholly frivolous, cannot "prostitute all their powers," but are always implying "I am capable of higher things."[10] In one of his essays, he admits the soul and the conscience to his "unserious treatment of the unusual" (fantasy), and this is the result:

With the soul we reach solid ground. As soon as it enters literature, whether in full radiance or behind a cloud, two great side-scenes accompany it, the mountains of Right and of Wrong, and we get a complete change of *décor*, adapted for writers who likewise treat the unusual, but who treat it mystically or humanistically. Butterflies and beetles may survive the soul's arrival, but they serve another purpose: they bear some relationship to Salvation.[11]

3

Forster has published two books of stories, *The Celestial Omnibus* (1911) and *The Eternal Moment* (1928), which were gathered into

The Collected Tales of E. M. Forster in 1947.* There are doubtless stories (besides "Albergo Empedocle," which Forster did not think "good enough" for reprinting)[12] unrepresented here; it seems likely that such unpublished juvenilia as "Ear-rings through the Keyhole" and "Scuffles in a Wardrobe" (written "between the ages of six and ten")[13] have their more mature counterparts. The eight stories published before 1910 (all but two of which are in *The Celestial Omnibus*) are by far the best,† and include two of the three stories that Forster says came to him in moments of inspiration. With "The Story of a Panic" and "The Road from Colonus" he had the experience of "sitting down on the theme as if it were an anthill,"[14] but with a third story, called "The Rock," his luck did not hold: "Not an editor would look at it. My inspiration had been genuine but worthless, like so much inspiration, and I have never sat down on a theme since."[15] The stories not inspired by the *genius loci* are especially freighted with the "will to believe" and wear an air of conscious contrivance; all the stories of the first collection except "The Curate's Friend," for example, include a physical transference from this world to another. The very word "other" appears in two titles—"The Other Side of the Hedge" and "Other Kingdom"—and the title story takes us on a bus ride from a small boy's suburban hell to his private heaven.

The title story of the second collection, "The Eternal Moment" (1905), was also nearly "sat down on": this, he writes, "though almost an honest-to-God yarn, is a meditation on Cortina d'Ampezzo."[16] It is the best of the lot. The next, in quality and time, is "The Machine Stops" (1909), which Forster calls "a reaction to one of the earlier heavens of H. G. Wells."[17] The others—"The Point of It" (1911), "Mr. Andrews" (1911), "Co-Ordination" (1912), and "The Story of the Siren" (1920)—are slight. All but the last are expressions of a talent

---

* Published in Britain as *Collected Short Stories* (1948).
† They are: "The Road from Colonus" (1904), "The Story of a Panic" (1904), "The Other Side of the Hedge" (1904), "The Eternal Moment" (1905), "The Curate's Friend" (1907), "The Celestial Omnibus" (1908), "Other Kingdom" (1909), and "The Machine Stops" (1909). The two appearing in *The Eternal Moment* are the title story and "The Machine Stops." The others in that volume are: "Mr. Andrews" (1911), "The Point of It" (1911), "Co-Ordination" (1912), and "The Story of the Siren" (1920).

that was stiffening and hardening. In them Forster tends to slip from
fantasy into fable, rendering fictional object-lessons with the moral
underlined.

If one takes up the stories in order of writing, three classifications
suggest themselves. The five stories between 1903 and 1905 can best
be characterized by the title "The Eternal Moment," for they all center in an epiphany, a moment of illumination—and incidentally all
but the first originally appeared in that journal of the liberal "best
self," *The Independent Review*. The four stories between 1907 and
1909 make a less personal and a more social comment: their heroes
are at odds with the status quo, and, as in "The Celestial Omnibus,"
more openly rebellious. The last group, the tales published between
1911 and 1920, are more philosophical and ratiocinative, qualities
perhaps best suggested by the title "The Point of It." Forster, in describing his story-writing habits, declared: "As a rule, I am set going
by my own arguments or memories, or by the motion of my pen."[18]
We might say of the stories in the first set that they were, in the main,
set going by his memories (containing as they do the three he "sat
down on"); those in the second by his arguments with family, class,
and church; and those in the third, it would seem, by the motion of
his pen, for they least seem to know where they are headed. As
Bloomsbury asked, "What *is* the point of it?"[19]

4

Collected Short Stories begins strongly with "The Story of a Panic"
(1904), which Forster says is the first story he ever wrote,[20] and ends
just as strongly with "The Eternal Moment" (1905). Not only are
these tales among the liveliest and longest of the collection (each has
three "chapters"), but they also stake out some boundaries of the
author's personal myth. Each presents a moment of spiritual illumination and transformation, but the differences between these moments are great. In the first, the epiphany comes with emotional violence, in the second with philosophic calm. The first describes a
naturalistic, even primitive, event; the second a sophisticated, urbane
one. The first is a story of youth, the second of maturity. But more
essentially, although both cross the line between the human and the

divine, the one shows the god entering the man and the other the man
(or the woman) rising to the god. (If these incarnations seem a little
sexually confused, it is because the author wears now a male mask
and now a female one.)

"The Story of a Panic" is one of the few that came to Forster in a
moment of inspiration. In May of 1902 he visited a certain valley—
the Vallone Fontana Caroso—above Ravello, and "the first chapter
of the story rushed into [his] mind as if it had waited for [him]
there." (CS, 5; see Plate 15.) That mountainous cul-de-sac is the story's
basic symbol:

> The valley ended in a vast hollow, shaped like a cup, into which radiated
> ravines from the precipitous hills around. Both the valley and the ravines
> and the ribs of hill that divided the ravines were covered with leafy chest-
> nut, so that the general appearance was that of a many-fingered green hand,
> palm upwards, which was clutching convulsively to keep us in its grasp. (pp.
> 10–11.)

This is like his Cambridge "dell" (of a later book but of an earlier
experience), a feminine enclosure of seductive beauty and safety—but
here more clearly seen in its threatening and clutching aspect. It is
a perfect symbol of feminine enslavement, and the story is about
a small boy's escape from this womb—the assertion, however ineffectual, of his manhood against this death-in-life.*

The main event of the story is the appearance of the Great God Pan
to Eustace, a fourteen-year-old English boy. The boy is imprisoned
in the circle of the "nice" people, mostly English, who surround him
in the "delightful" little hotel at Ravello. There are his aunts, the
two Miss Robinsons; Mr. Sandbach, the curate; Mr. Leyland, "a

---

* It is interesting to note that Forster makes a great deal of nature as landscape
and vegetation, but almost never describes animals. Freud includes flora but not
fauna in his list of female sexual symbols—landscapes (including hollows, pits,
dells, and caves) representing the topography of sexual organs, and woods and
thickets representing pubic hair. See Sigmund Freud, *A General Introduction to
Psychoanalysis* (New York, 1935), p. 139. This female symbolism dominates Forster's work.

The clutching hand is a favorite image with Forster. Compare the story
described in LJ: "Fingers burst up through the sand-black fingers of sea devils"
(p. 71). See also *Passage*: "Fists and fingers thrust above the advancing soil" (p. 131).

would-be artist"; "the nice landlady, Signora Scafetti, and the nice English-speaking waiter, Emmanuele"—who was, at the time of the story, replaced by Gennaro, who was not nice.* This circle is joined by the narrator of the tale, his wife, and his two daughters. We never meet the wife (she is only referred to as "my poor wife") but one of the daughters achieves some identity.

It is significant that the events described by the narrator are said to have occurred "eight years ago." The publication date of the story is 1904, but it was written, according to Forster himself, in 1902.[21] Eight years before that would have been 1894, when Forster was fifteen. Eustace, we remember, was "about fourteen," and near the end of the story Gennaro says he is fifteen. The nearness of those two ages suggests that Eustace may be identified as the boy Forster was eight years earlier—and the narrator as the young man he is at the time of writing. The narrator's comments then become part of an ironic dialogue between a present and an outgrown self, and give a sharper edge to passages like this one:

> I would not have minded so much if he had been a really studious boy, but he neither played hard nor worked hard. His favourite occupations were lounging on the terrace in an easy chair and loafing along the high road, with his feet shuffling up the dust and his shoulders stooping forward. Naturally enough, his features were pale, his chest contracted, and his muscles undeveloped. His aunts thought him delicate; what he really needed was discipline. (p. 10.)

The narrator, mixing pity and contempt, takes the lad in charge and tries to do something about his muscles and disposition. For Forster to cast himself in the role of disciplinarian and athletic coach is itself a good joke; and when, in observing Eustace's strange behavior after Pan's visit, the narrator says, "I began to see that the young gentleman wanted a sound thrashing," we smile at the possibility that this is the author ironically disapproving of his own childhood

---

* It is of interest that a John Brown Sandbach came up to King's in 1897, the same year as Forster. A brother, F. E. Sandbach, came up in 1899, and another, E. Sandbach, in 1900. It is of interest, too, that Gennaro (Januarius) is the name of a saint who once saved Naples at the cost of his life. His blood is extant and liquefies several times a year (but only when important people visit the church).

This cast of characters is obviously similar to that in *A Room with a View*, the first part of which Forster was working on about this time.

personality. But there may be other and deeper ironies. Though the narrator's voice of masculine authority seems assumed and unconvincing, might it not represent Forster's attempt to provide Eustace with the paternal protection he himself longed for as a counterforce to the dreadful aunts and guardians? Here Forster may be giving himself that father, a pathetically inadequate one, to be sure, and one who never does administer the "wanted" thrashing. But the narrator is able to sympathize with Eustace's strange awakening, and had he exerted himself, he might have saved Eustace from the necessity of such a violent experience of self-discovery.

The experience occurs during a picnic in the very palm of that clutching hand above Ravello. The cup of the valley lies ready for Pan's violation. The beauty of the scene impresses everyone except the artist Leyland, a hopeless snob, who thinks "it would make a very poor picture" (p. 11), and Eustace, who has been dragged along on the expedition and sulks at everything. In the course of conversation, Mr. Sandbach retells the Plutarchan tale of the death of Pan, and repeats, in chorus with Leyland, the famous lament heard by the mariners: "The Great God Pan is dead." At this instant a sense of foreboding sweeps through the party; a "cat's-paw of wind" turns "the light green to dark" as it travels down one of the ridges opposite, and a total silence settles on everything. The picnickers flee in panic: "It was not the spiritual fear that one has known at other times, but brutal, overmastering, physical fear, stopping up the ears, and dropping clouds before the eyes, and filling the mouth with foul tastes. And it was no ordinary humiliation that survived; for I had been afraid, not as a man, but as a beast." (p. 15.)

But Eustace does not panic, and the others find him stretched on the turf in a half-conscious state, as if stunned by an electric shock. When they touch him he opens his eyes and, instead of his usual "peevish, discontented frown," shows a disquieting Giaconda smile.* A goat's footmarks are found in the moist earth under the trees, and Eustace rolls over them, "as a dog rolls in dirt" (p. 18). These are the early signs of the god's possession. On the way back Eustace "stepped

---

* The narrator says, "I have often seen that peculiar smile since, both on the possessor's face and on the photographs of him that are beginning to get into the illustrated papers." (p. 17.)

out manfully, for the first time in his life, holding his head up and taking deep draughts of air into his chest" (p. 19). He races about "like a real boy," scurrying in front of the others "like a goat." More surprising, he kisses a peasant woman as they pass, for which she blesses him. Yet more strange is his behavior toward Gennaro, the poor fisherman turned waiter: "Eustace sprang to meet him, and leapt right up into his arms, and put his own arms around his neck." (pp. 21–22.) "Ho capito," the boy says, "I have understood," though Eustace has said nothing to him. Among those who know Pan, there is a mysterious affinity.

The narrator finds this "promiscuous intimacy" to be "perfectly intolerable," and the group as a whole, believing Pan to be dead, attribute Eustace's strange behavior to a visitation of the devil. They thank God for their own "merciful deliverance."

The irony is patent and the Pan myth is ideal for Forster's purposes. "The spirit of the living Pan," writes W. R. Irwin, "can ... be made a convenient reproach against the disorders of modern living —industrialization, urbanization, sheer money or prestige valuation, the neuroses of over-civilized sensibility—against anything, indeed, of which it can be said, 'This is bad because it is unnatural.' "[22] Not only is the Great God Pan not dead, he is actively threatening the pieties of these smug gentlefolk. In the literature of the subject,* Pan is often depicted as a kind of pagan Christ, the chief contender against the new god's power and the only deity of the ancient world surviving into the Christian era.[23] Sandbach acknowledged and cursed him, as a licensed Christian should; Leyland, the esthetic snob, modishly lamented his passing, but without passion or love: "We are all hopelessly steeped in vulgarity. . . . It is through us, and to our shame, that the Nereids have left the waters and the Oreads the mountains, that the woods no longer give shelter to Pan." (p. 13.) But the others could not even credit his existence. They, not Pan, are

---

* Turn-of-the-century literature is full of Pan, even boasting a periodical of that name. Late Victorian paganism usually saw him as horrific, the suppressed part of the mind breaking out in revenge. The literature includes Arthur Machen's *The Great God Pan* (1894), Francis Bourdillon's *A Lost God* (1891), T. Sturge Moore's *Pan's Prophecy* (1904), and Bliss Carman's *Pipes of Pan* (1906). "Of Pan and the elemental forces," writes Forster, "the public has heard a little too much—they seem Victorian." (HE, p. 114.)

dead. But Forster again and again invokes this goatish god; he is almost the perfect actor for the ceremonies of rebellion.

The character of Pan has changed through the centuries, but he has never lost his impulsive, lustful quality. Though gentleness and benevolence may be among his qualities, he is essentially undisciplined and brings no guarantees of justice, fair play, or freedom from dirt. But he does bring a primal energy that fearfully threatens those who try to keep such energies in chains. As a pagan Christ he is Christ the tiger rather than Christ the lamb, and he may equal those forces Freud called the id. Those who fearfully cover their nakedness are likely to feel his coming as a kind of rape; those who do not may know him as release and fulfillment. Though he comes without warning and without courtship, he usually violates only those who resist him; to those who invite him in he can be a healing power, provoking "the kindly disorder which is needed for the triumph of life."[24] But he is always a "power-figure":

The power is in himself and can be gained by men intelligent enough to ignore brain and to follow instead the promptings of blood, muscle, viscera, and glands. But, still fearsome, Pan can also be a punisher and a destroyer, an embodiment even of the diabolic. Many, however, see in him benevolence and protection, not only of flocks and the creatures of the forest but of sorrowing humanity as well.[25]

Above all else, he is essentially human, the embodiment of human impulses we repress at our peril.

Eustace knows Pan not as "panic," but as the liberator of his spirit from the prudery and caution and stuffy morality that are about all his class had left of a once-vital faith. After being possessed by the god, Eustace increasingly takes to the out-of-doors. He becomes a wild thing, and his "promiscuous intimacy" with Gennaro grows more open and shameless. One night after he is found running about the hotel gardens and swinging through the trees like some arboreal animal, he is literally captured by the forces of convention—Gennaro playing Judas in a parody of Gethsemane—and is dragged screaming to his room. "Not to my room," he pleads. "It is so small." (p. 30.) He has been born again, and to return to the womb (to a room without a view) is a horror. Claustrophobia besets him—a fear not only of small places but of the small people who live in them. Its antidote (since his civilization offers no satisfying compromises) is another and opposite absolute: infinity. The story ends with Eustace, shouting and laughing, running from his prison into the far distance of an endless landscape.

On one level Eustace's experience is an adolescent sexual awakening, and its homosexual bent is not surprising. Just as the violence of his Pan-inspired sexual release grew from rebellion against the aunts and guardians (and the conspicuously absent father), so the nature of the cathexis is antisocial as well. His love is male because his whole problem is a search for manhood. He takes this direct and literal route, perhaps, because the female proprieties with which he was surrounded blocked all other alternatives. It was, quite literally, the path of least resistance. But his nympholepsy is a spiritual as well as a physical event. Eustace found not just freedom from social restraints, but freedom to move toward a boundless and ineffable ideal. He is intoxicated with a desire for absolutes that, to normal conceiving, are not to be had except in fantasy or dreams. And his final endless flight into endless open spaces—from time to eternity, from place to infinity—typifies one of the ways Forster translates present oppressions into future delights. Eustace, with the help of this pagan Christ, is creating a private religion out of the archetypes but not the substance of old orthodoxy. The essence of this religion is limitlessness and expansion, the refusal to be hemmed in—ideals which are also those of Forster's art. They remind us of the irrational faith of Tennyson's Ulysses, a tired old man setting out again with no destination or purpose except "To sail beyond the sunset, and the baths / Of all the western stars, until I die." Such an ambition has nothing to do with getting anywhere; its objective is, as Lionel Trilling has pointed out, experience for experience's sake, "a passing through events for the sake of knowledge."[26] But Eustace's religion, like Ulysses's, is essentially a flight from reality rather than an encounter with it, and can be thought of as bringing "knowledge" only in the most idealistic sense. His rebellion is just and necessary, but his problem is untouched. For it is, after all, only a fantasy rebellion; it exists as feeling rather than action, and such rebellion is, finally, only a form of suffering. "The more perfection a thing possesses, the more it acts and the less it suffers," said Spinoza, but Eustace is possessed by rather than the possessor of a will. He confronts nothing and escapes from everything—from his guilty love, from the philistines, even from his human identity. To flee from the actual to the impossible is fantasy's way, but we do not end convinced that Eustace, even in a fiction, got what he wanted. He has avenged himself on his tormentors by, in a sense, dying on them, but he had to dehumanize himself to do it.

Gennaro is also something of a martyr. When his work as Eustace's savior is done, his author commits him to sudden death without hesitation or preparation. Why is *he* sacrificed rather than some of the English prigs and snobs? The answer would seem to be that the weak must die in order to win their arguments; the others must live in order to absorb their lessons.

Though Pan does not appear in "The Eternal Moment," his spirit is present; *Pan Pipes* (the title Rickie gave to a collection of "eight or nine" of his stories) could appropriately contain this one.

"The Eternal Moment" deals with the return after many years' absence of a Miss Raby, a successful novelist, to the little Italian town of Vorta (Cortina d'Ampezzo), which she had made famous by her books.* Twenty years before, Vorta had been quiet and unprogressive, with the Biscione its best and virtually its only hotel. But progress and the spirit of commerce have descended. Hotels now abound and the town is overrun with English tourists. The "mildly unconventional" Miss Raby arrives in the company of Colonel Leyland, to whom she is neither married nor engaged and who is, except for his military bearing, indistinguishable from Leyland the artist. "Their friends laughed; their acquaintances gossiped; their relatives were furious" at this breach of convention. But, like so many of Forster's rebels, they are nonconformists only on the surface. There is nothing "wrong."

How could he explain the peculiar charm of the relations between himself and Miss Raby? There had never been a word of marriage, and would probably never be a word of love. If, instead of seeing each other frequently, they should come to see each other always it would be as sage companions, familiar with life, not as egoistic lovers, craving for infinities of passion which they

---

* Her double appears as Miss Lavish in *A Room with a View*.

had no right to demand and no power to supply. Neither professed to be a
virgin soul, or to be ignorant of the other's limitations and inconsistencies.
... Colonel Leyland had courage of no mean order: he cared little for the
opinion of people whom he understood.... Miss Raby was an authoress, a
kind of Radical; he a soldier, a kind of aristocrat. But ... he was ceasing to
fight, she to write. They could pleasantly spend together their autumn. ...
   He was too delicate to admit, even to himself, the desirability of marrying
two thousand a year. (pp. 197–98.)

   This autumnal story is as preoccupied with problems of age as
"The Story of a Panic" is with problems of youth. But their resolutions are not fundamentally different. Miss Raby and Colonel Leyland escape—or exempt themselves—from the commitment to marriage or love very much as Eustace escapes the confines of a particular love into the love of all (Pan). Thus they keep, if not their virginal, at least their amateur status, and leave the doors of possibility
open. However much the flesh is honored in these stories when it
appears as athletic vigor or physical beauty, it is only an embarrassment when it appears in its sexual aspect. Yet it is far from true to
say that Miss Raby did not crave "infinities of passion." It is precisely an infinity of passion—a spiritualized and eternalized abstraction of love—that she does crave, and obtain. That is the point of the
story.
   Miss Raby discovers that the Grand Hôtel des Alpes, where they
register, is owned by the son of her old friend, the proprietress of the
Biscione, and that the son is trying to run his mother out of business.
More important, she discovers that the son's concierge is the same
man who, twenty years before, as a porter, had declared his love for
her and panicked her into flight.* Then she saw him as a godlike
primitive, strong, passionate, and beautiful. Now, modern and progressive, he seems to her a decadent, middle-class vulgarian, possessed
by the Great God Mammon rather than by the Great God Pan. Two
problems present themselves: the problem of class and the problem
of sex. By abandoning his natural aristocracy for rank in the bour-
geoisie, he has lost his simple beauty, and by rising from near-peasan-
try to the middle class he has ascended the social scale. His social rise

* Miss Raby's screaming retreat from this sexual encounter is very like Adela's
screaming retreat from the cave in *Passage*.

has measured a moral fall, for which Miss Raby blames herself and "the gentle classes." She determines to make amends by recalling him to what he once was—or at least to make him remember that day on the mountain twenty years before.

This is her penance, an act of noblesse oblige; but it is also an act of appalling spiritual presumption, a presumption that neither she nor her creator seems embarrassed about. No question is made of her right to make absolute moral judgments or to play the goddess. "A great tenderness overcame her—the sadness of an unskilful demiurge, who makes a world and beholds that it is bad. She desired to ask pardon of her creatures, even though they were too poorly formed to grant it." (p. 212.)

The Eternal Moment is the title of the novel that brought the money to the place, and Feo is a product of that money. "He had not made himself. It was even absurd to regret his transformation from an athlete: his greasy stoutness, his big black kiss-curl, his waxed moustache, his chin which was dividing and propagating itself like some primitive form of life." (p. 212.) In the face of these physical signs of his inner decay, Miss Raby feels a sexual revulsion; but the class barrier between them is—Miss Raby tells herself—more spiritual and moral than social. Her motive is to elevate him to such a condition of grace that he will be worthy of—well, of herself: "After much pain, respectability becomes ludicrous. And she had only to overcome the difficulty of Feo's being a man, not the difficulty of his being a concierge. She had never observed that spiritual reticence towards social inferiors which is usual at the present day." (p. 214.)

In attempting to overcome the difficulty, she bullies Feo into remembering his old indiscretion and presents him to Colonel Leyland as "the man who fell in love with me when I was young." Feo is flabbergasted, at first thinking she is trying to threaten or trap him and then that she is making a pass. Under this last misapprehension, he makes the mistake of winking—a vulgarity affecting her as "a ghastly sight, perhaps the most hopelessly depressing of all the things she had seen at Vorta" (p. 216).

The reader is never allowed to think well of Feo, but he has an even harder time (contrary to the author's intentions) thinking well of Miss Raby. Though occasionally ridiculous, she is Forster's spokes-

woman; and the reader is not encouraged to disapprove of her un-
scrupulousness. Her assumption of responsibility for Feo's moral condition, and for that of the town, is a specious moral gesture: she does
not ultimately accept responsibility for these conditions. Instead, she
just stirs things up, hurts a few people in order to busy an unem-
ployed conscience, and then escapes. Trying to revive Feo's "love" is
at best an act of self-deception, at worst an act of sadism, and probably a little of both. She would seem to be attacking men in general
rather than any state of moral corruption.

At any rate, after the wink she is relieved to realize she is no longer
under any obligation to pretend love for his person. In place of the
love of Feo she substitutes the love of love; in place of an object
toward which emotion is directed she substitutes the emotion as an
end in itself:

> For she realized that only now was she not in love with him: that the inci-
> dent upon the mountain had been one of the great moments of her life—
> perhaps the greatest, certainly the most enduring: that she had drawn un-
> acknowledged power and inspiration from it, just as trees draw vigour from
> a subterranean spring. Never again could she think of it as a half-humorous
> episode in her development. There was more reality in it than in all the
> years of success and varied achievement which had followed. For all her cor-
> rect behaviour and lady-like display, she had been in love with Feo, and she
> had never loved so greatly again. A presumptuous boy had taken her to the
> gates of heaven; and, though she would not enter with him, the eternal re-
> membrance of the vision had made life seem endurable and good. (pp. 216–
> 17.)

The lady is making a very little go very far. Clearly, life has not shown
her much about love, and if she had "never loved so greatly again,"
the reader must be excused for suspecting that she has never tried, or
wanted to try, very hard.

The key word here is "reality," and we can understand Miss Raby's
thoughts on love only in idealist terms. As we know, Forster is no
realist in fiction, but one who wishes to take his reader "through"
his material to a real world of value on the other side of it. The crucial question for Forster, as Virginia Woolf has seen, is whether he
can successfully relate the material world and the world of value,
whether he can manage "to connect the actual thing with the mean-

ing of the thing and to carry the reader's mind across the chasm which divides the two without spilling a single drop of its belief."[27] Her verdict is that usually he cannot, that the two worlds remain distinct and divorced: "He has given us an almost photographic picture on one side of the page; on the other he asks us to see the same view transformed and radiant with eternal fires."[28]

The problem is philosophical as well as technical. When Descartes, for example, made the pineal gland the nexus of body and soul—body refined from matter into "animal spirits" and thus translatable into idea or spirit—he failed to solve this same problem, since matter made infinitesimally small does not cease to be matter. Philosophers before and after him—until matter became equated with energy—had no better luck. But "the eternal moment" provides one way of imagining the connection between the actual here-and-now and the world of transcendent value. Plato, Wordsworth, Browning, Pater, Proust, and Virginia Woolf* come immediately to mind as among those making the eternal, or supreme, or remembered, or intensely realized "moment" of experience a means of passage from a material world of mutability and flux to a world of fixed and timeless value. This notion can only be brushed here, but it was deeply sunk in Forster's intellectual inheritance. As the promises of orthodoxy became less accessible to intelligent people, doctrines such as this became more attractive. Like Descartes's space-occupying animal spirits, moments of time could be conceived as being so small in dimension as to approach the timeless. Thus could permanence be achieved amid impermanence, and flux stabilized. Browning's poem "Cristina," for example, has the same theme as Miss Raby's confession above, and Pater's famous conclusion to *The Renaissance* is perhaps the classic defense of the intensely realized moment:

Every moment some form grows perfect in hand or face; some tone on the hills or the sea is choicer than the rest; some mood of passion or insight or

---

* The notion of the single moment was almost obsessive with Virginia Woolf. She wrote in 1928: "The idea has come to me that what I want now to do is to saturate every atom. I mean to eliminate all waste, deadness, superfluity: to give the moment whole; whatever it includes." *A Writer's Diary*, ed. Leonard Woolf (New York, 1954), p. 136.

intellectual excitement is irresistibly real and attractive to us,—for that moment only. Not the fruit of experience, but experience itself, is the end.
A counted number of pulses only is given to us of a variegated, dramatic
life. How may we see in them all that is to be seen in them by the finest
senses? How shall we pass most swiftly from point to point, and be present
always at the focus where the greatest number of vital forces unite in their
purest energy?

To burn always with this hard, gem-like flame, to maintain this ecstasy,
is success in life.

Even apostate puritans like William Hale White, in seeking compensation for a lost faith in immortality, stumbled upon the same doctrine: "As I got older I became aware of the folly of this perpetual
reaching after the future, and of drawing from tomorrow . . . a reason for the joyfulness of today. I learned . . . to live in each moment
as it passed over my head."[29]

Forster, as Virginia Woolf saw, vacillates between realism and im-
pressionism, between the world of Mr. Bennett and the world of Mrs.
Brown,* between the life in time and the life that exists as a moment
of pure meaning. It is such a moment that Miss Raby achieves—and
in so doing transports this story from the realm of fantasy to that of
prophecy. That moment of time—though Forster does not, in the
manner of Joyce and Proust, dramatize it in a discontinuous narrative—is the same as Bergsonian "real time," which, as Joseph Frank
says, "when intuited by the sensibility, places us in contact with ultimate reality."[30] Miss Raby's book is "written round the idea that man
does not live by time alone, and that an evening gone may become
like a thousand ages in the court of heaven—the idea that was afterwards expounded more philosophically by Maeterlinck" (p. 199). This
is the essence of her experience of "love": love eternalized, exempted
from the ravages of time, uninvolved in any human investment or
in the uncertainties of human history. Like such moments in the
poems of Browning, it is a success-in-failure: failure in the world's
eyes (no physical marriage), success in the narrator's (a soul-marriage).
In Leyland's opinion she has disgraced herself, but Leyland turns out
to be no better than Feo, so encased in conventions that his indi-

* The title of a famous essay by Virginia Woolf in which she contrasts her fictional methods with those of realists like Arnold Bennett.

viduality cannot get through. So at the end Miss Raby transfers her
affections from men to values beyond them. To the sound of Vorta's
new campanile (which is, for symbolic reasons, being destroyed in a
slow landslide), "she turned from the men towards it with a motion
of love" (p. 221). "There is no nationality in sound" (p. 193), she had
earlier observed, and here as elsewhere in Forster, music is the bridge
between the particular and the infinite, between body and soul: "In
that moment of final failure, there had been vouchsafed to her a vision of herself, and she saw that she had lived worthily. She was conscious of a triumph over experience and earthly facts, a triumph magnificent, cold, hardly human, whose existence no one but herself
would ever surmise." (p. 221.)

She achieves love without men and in defiance of sex. The solution
is a rather startling anticipation of the theme of *Howards End*. Miss
Raby asks Feo to give her one of his children*—just like that—because she needs a spiritual heir. Miss Raby does not get the boy, but
in *Howards End* the spiritual heir comes almost that gratuitously
(one of Forster's "sudden births"). In both instances the women are
very reluctant to bear a child themselves. Miss Raby seems to feel
that it is really up to the lower classes to do this kind of dirty work.
Hers is the job of education, not procreation, and had the heir been
given she would have trained him to teach the rich "not to be stupid
to the poor" (p. 219). This is evasive liberalism, but it reminds us how
seriously some of the Victorian "saving remnant" could take their
mission. "All poetry," wrote Browning to Ruskin, is the problem of
"putting the infinite within the finite."[31] With Miss Raby the emphasis was the other way—putting the finite into the infinite, a difficult
alchemy to achieve without scorning the dross you have transmuted.

A lady much like Miss Raby presents herself in an autobiographical book to which Forster wrote an indulgent foreword—*Flowers and
Elephants* (1927) by Constance Sitwell. She too made moments into
eternity: "I do want, while I travel, to write of the unforgettable little
spaces of time that come when imagination is merged into living in
a special way, and the thing seen becomes like a work of art, intense,

---

* See *Where Angels Fear to Tread*, in which another Englishwoman tries to buy
an Italian baby.

significant, separate. They come suddenly, these perfect moments of perfect life, and they remain with me forever."[32] As her sense of loveliness deepens, "all things become symbolic"[33]—even people. Though she has moments of loneliness, she maintains her apartness from the several men who love or desire her. She is as successful as Miss Raby in keeping her detachment inviolate. She remains to the end one to whom "experience" is the gathering of exquisite impressions, one who has an eye for landscapes and beautiful things but who never describes a human face. She dramatizes, even more vividly than Miss Raby, the close connections between estheticism and decadence. Her sensitivity seems bought with frigidity, and Miss Raby—though a much tougher specimen—suffers a similar curtailment.

The other stories of this early period must be treated briefly. "Albergo Empedocle," though amateurish, is a better tale than some that Forster felt were good enough to reprint. Its main characters, Harold and Mildred, are an engaged couple traveling in Sicily. They are surrounded by the usual group of boring relatives and chaperones. Harold, the innocent, knows nothing of Empedocles or the Pythagorean theory of transmigration of souls, but he knows what he likes—beauties in land, sea, and people. He is a natural; Pan and he would have hit it off very well. One afternoon, after napping on a hillside near Girgenti with Mildred near, he awakens to the knowledge that he has lived there before, in another life. Mildred, romantically excited by the idea, pretends that she too has lived there before. He calmly calls her bluff: "No, Mildred darling, you have not."[34] Offended, Mildred withdraws and sides with the others, who think him insane. At the end he slips back entirely into that "better" past, losing touch with his modern dress and language, and is ultimately lodged in an asylum. There he is visited—and loved—only by his friend Tommy. His creator passes judgment: "The greater has replaced the less, and he is living the life he knew to be greater than the life he lived with us."[35] But that "greater life" might have been available in the here-and-now, had he not been cast among prigs and fools. "That is why," writes the author, "I shall never forgive Mildred Peaslake as long as I live."[36]

Forster is always hard on women of the Mildred Peaslake–Agnes Pembroke variety. They are the sexually threatening managers, the

apprentice chaperones and guardians, from whom his fantasy is a strategy of escape. The stuffiness of the world they made is suggested in a
passage like the following:

> "It's a beautiful idea, isn't it, that the soul should have several lives."
> "But, Mildred darling," said the gentle voice of Lady Peaslake, "we know
> that it is not so."
> "Oh, I didn't mean that, mamma. I only said it was a beautiful idea."
> "But not a true one, darling."
> "No."
> Their voices had sunk into that respectful monotone which is always con-
> sidered suitable when the soul is under discussion. They all looked awkward
> and ill at ease. Sir Edwin played tunes on his waistcoat buttons, and Harold
> blew into the bowl of his pipe. Mildred, a little confused at her temerity,
> passed on to the terrible sack of Acragas by the Romans. Whereat their faces
> relaxed, and they regained their accustomed spirits.[37]

The story is not very good, but fragments like this one bear comparison even with Wilde's satire on the pharisaism of the late Victorian
haute monde.

"The Road from Colonus" (1904)—one of the stories Forster "sat
down on"—is about Mr. Lucas, a henpecked old man, "tired of attention and consideration," who is traveling in Greece with his unimaginative, conventional, schedule-loving family.* "Greece is the land for
young people . . . ," he says to himself, "but I will enter into it, I will
possess it."[38] He does so by entering the hollowed-out bole of a plane
tree (from whose roots a spring of water gushes) that the local people
have turned into a shrine. There he experiences an epiphany: "His
eyes closed, and he had the strange feeling of one who is moving, yet
at peace—the feeling of the swimmer, who, after long struggling with
chopping seas, finds that after all the tide will sweep him to his goal.
So he lay motionless, conscious only of the stream below his feet, and
that all things were a stream, in which he was moving." (p. 98.) This
is a return to the womb, the blissful abandonment of selfhood in the
oblivion of the perfect environment—and it is of interest that the old

---

* The fictional setting is given as Platiniste, in the Province of Messenia. Since
there is no town of that name in Messenia, and since that would be off the travelers' route, the literal setting is probably Platiana, in the Province of Ilia, which is
near Mt. Platonos and about fourteen miles from Olympia, the evening destination of the party.

man plays at being Oedipus and the (despised) daughter at being Clytemnestra. But in that chthonic place the old man, like Lazarus, encounters some unforgettable wisdom, and when he is born again to time, the most ordinary movements of the Greek peasants about him take on symbolic meanings. He has tapped the source of myth: "To Mr. Lucas, who, in a brief space of time, had discovered not only Greece, but England and all the world and life, there seemed nothing ludicrous in the desire to hang within the tree another votive offering—a little model of an entire man." (pp. 98–99.)

But his vision does not transform his English guardians, nor do they share it. He is carried off, a passive resister, from the place of his inner transformation; thenceforth he becomes a pouting and disobedient child who uses withdrawal as a weapon—in striking anticipation of the behavior of Mrs. Wilcox and Mrs. Moore. He is an anarchist, if we remember that anarchism may express its discontent not only through the destruction of society, root and branch, but also through withdrawal from it.[39] The moment he had seen "was so tremendous that he abandoned words and arguments as useless, and rested on the strength of his mighty unrevealed allies: silent men, murmuring water, and whispering trees" (p. 103). But his heroism (and we are clearly supposed to regard him as heroic) is unconvincing. It is the heroism of the child who meets resistance by hiding his head under the pillow—and dreaming puckish revenge. Mr. Lucas playing Oedipus is a charade of "tragedy"—and an example of Forster's lazy use of that word.* His return to the mother is no agonizing fate but a deliberate choice of second childhood as the easiest way out of his difficulties. Pitiful rather than tragic, he illustrates one of the things wrong with fantasy as a means of redemption: instead of resolving anything it gives itself a narcotic. He suffers rather than acts. Though he has seen a "supreme event" which would "transfigure the face of the world" (p. 103), he is a strangely enervated prophet to receive such overwhelming visions. It is worth remember-

---

* Quite erroneously, I believe, does Frederick P. W. McDowell claim that "Mr. Lucas just misses the tragic stature of a dying Oedipus through the officiousness of his daughter." "Forster's 'Natural Supernaturalism': The Tales," *Modern Fiction Studies*, VII (1961), 274. His suffering resembles that of Prufrock far more than that of Oedipus.

ing that Dante's symbol of death by suicide (*Inferno*, XIII) was a human soul imprisoned in a tree.

"The Other Side of the Hedge" (1904) presents what might be called Forster's fundamental metaphor of belief. The story is built around two concentric circles, an outside and an inside, the outside being the actual world where the race of life is run, and the inside a still, timeless center where one escapes from that race. The hero, feeble of body and wind (whose pedometer told him that he was "twenty-five"), sits down to rest by the side of the road—as "Miss Eliza Dimbleby, the great educationalist, swept past, exhorting [him] to persevere" (p. 34). Ashamed of giving up like his brother, who "had wasted his breath on singing and his strength on helping others" (p. 34), he nevertheless does give up, for the story is an argument against life as competition. He crawls through the hedge bounding the highway and enters a world not absolutely divorced from the actual, but comfortably far away. "Behind the hedge," wrote Virginia Woolf, "he always hears the motor horn and the shuffling feet of tired wayfarers."[40]

The other side of the hedge is a vast arena of freedom. When the boy asks his guide, "Where does this place lead to?" the guide answers: "Nowhere, thank the Lord!" (p. 35.) There is no progress, machines won't work, and advance is never thought of, but such pastoral simplicities as singing, talking, gardening, hay-making are all approved. The paradise reminds us a little of B. F. Skinner's utopia in *Walden II,* where people have all freedoms but one—the freedom to be unhappy. "What does it all mean?" asks the boy. "It means nothing but itself" is the Moorean reply.

It is, in short, an ontological whole, a fictional representation of a McTaggartian *Absolute* or a Moorean *Organic Unity.* It is the geographical counterpart of an eternal moment, and an attempt to visualize a lost wholeness. "It is through this gate that humanity went out countless ages ago, when it was first seized with the desire to walk." (p. 38.) The story ends with a prophecy that someday "humanity— all that is left of it—will come in to us." (p. 40.) Although the place was meant for "all mankind," not many opt to join the inner elite, but the regrets of the saved do not seem overwhelming. The hero, almost to the end, continues to play Gulliver in defending the world

outside ("Give me life, with its struggles and victories, with its failures and hatreds, with its deep moral meaning and its unknown
goal!" [p. 39]), but this is only the irony of a talking parrot. After
an unconvincing spasm of final struggle, the lad accepts this life-in-
death as his true and everlasting home, and the story ends with the
rediscovery of the lost brother and the drinking of a can of beer:
"Though my senses were sinking into oblivion, they seemed to expand ere they reached it. They perceived the magic song of nightin-
gales, and the odour of invisible hay, and stars piercing the fading sky.
The man whose beer I had stolen lowered me down gently to sleep
off its effects, and, as he did so, I saw that he was my brother." (p. 40.)

Fainting (Forster's early heroes usually faint in crises) plus expansion plus music is a fairly normal formula for salvation in Forster.
His early heroes tend to go limp in the face of opposition, seemingly
in the hope that the ravening wolf will take pity, smile, and walk
away. Since the wolves usually do exactly that, these stories are rightly
called fantasies. They are wish fulfillments, hiding any real opposition from sight as if it were something unclean, discounting courage
and even making a virtue of spinelessness. Inside the hedge, the will-
less inherit the earth.

5

The stories between 1907 and 1909 continue to take passage from
the actual to the ideal, but their social satire is sharper and their
heroes show somewhat less reluctance to take up arms against their
troubles.

"The Celestial Omnibus" is one of the best and most personal. Its
subject is the escape of a small boy from spiritual imprisonment in
his parents' home at Agathox Lodge, 28, Buckingham Park Road, Surbiton. Surbiton is suburbia and "Agathox" (a corruption of Greek
agathos, "good") is one of its suffocating cells. Near the house a sign-
post reading "To Heaven" points up an alley.[41] The boy's mother
explains that the sign is the bad joke of some naughty men, one of
whom "wrote verses and was expelled from the University and came
to grief in other ways." A family friend, Mr. Bons ("Snob"), is more
specific: it was "the joke of a person named Shelley."[42]

The story invokes a literary pantheon—Homer, Dante, Sir Thomas

Browne, Jane Austen, Keats, Achilles, the Duchess of Malfi, Tom Jones, Mrs. Gamp, and some of the creations of Tennyson and Wagner. Shelley and his spirit, however, are central. "But is there no Shelley in the house?" asks Mr. Bons, who is president of the Literary Society. Mr. Bons can boast "seven Shelleys" (to Agathox Lodge's two), and this quantifying betrays the degree to which both establishments possess poetry but are not possessed by it. The boy hangs his head as he confesses to Bons that he has never heard of Shelley. It is Harold again, who had never heard of Pythagoras. But of course the boy is the one who mounts on Shelley's wings.

Shelley, the effectual angel, the acknowledged legislator, is the one who masterminds the boy's rebellion and escape to freedom. The poet serves the boy exactly as he served G. Lowes Dickinson—and Forster:

What he wanted was a song which would transport him out of the world in the right direction, wings that would carry him out of the body into a region where good and evil are more clearly opposed than on earth, and where good triumphs everlastingly. Sincere, enthusiastic, and fired with the same social hopes, Shelley provided him with exactly the right pair of wings. It was possible, in that enchanting company, to shake off the flesh. It was possible to shake it off in the company of many other poets, but Shelley remained unique because, however high he soared, he never rejected humanity. (GLD, 37.)

The boy's Shelleyan flight (omnibus replacing skylark) is the main event of the story.

It is a flight into poetry and out of oppression, the oppression of parents, of respectability, of bourgeois order. The boy is being killed not with kindness but with the appearance of kindness. He is given everything he needs except what he needs most: the chance to be himself. "His father, though very kind, always laughed at him—shrieked with laughter whenever he or any other child asked a question or spoke."[43] The mother, by joining in, becomes his accomplice. If this is one of the stories set going by Forster's "memories," then those memories must have been bitter indeed. The parents in the story are cruelly paid off for failing to understand their child.

The boy's flight is (fantastically speaking) a literal one. The boy discovers a notice posted by the "Surbiton and Celestial Road Car Company" that an omnibus leaves daily at sunrise and sunset from the alley near his home. He is "determined to settle once for all which was real: the omnibus or the streets" (p. 44), and the Platonic reality wins out. The omnibus, driven by Sir Thomas Browne, takes him upward. Within two hours they encounter thunder and lightning, the sound and sight mingling to create a "rainbow bridge" leading into heaven. The synesthesia of the event ("that sounds like a rainbow") is no small part of its esthetic importance, for by such transformations prose becomes poetry, and slavery freedom: "The colour and the sound grew together. The rainbow spanned an enormous gulf. Clouds rushed under it and were pierced by it, and still it grew, reaching forward, conquering the darkness, until it had touched something that seemed more solid than a cloud." (p. 49.) As they pass over the gulf between the actual and the ideal, they hear Wagner's music and the singing of the Rhinemaidens.[44] The Wagnerian rainbow bridge appears again in *Howards End,* where it serves an identical purpose.

For running away and for lying about where he had been, the boy is caned and set to "learning poetry for a punishment." His father could "pardon anything but untruthfulness." To the rhythm of the switch, the father chants: "There is *no* omnibus, *no* driver, *no* bridge, *no* mountain; you are a *truant,* a *gutter-snipe,* a *liar.*" (p. 50.) It is a savage indictment, and the pressure of hate reminds us of Butler's *The Way of All Flesh.* The mother, standing by, begs the boy to say he is sorry, but he will not. Forster adds a fine touch of irony: "It was the greatest day of his life, in spite of the caning and the poetry at the end of it." (p. 50.) Mr. Bons, however, is puzzled by the amount of literary lore the boy has picked up and decides to check his story.

He too is given a ride in the omnibus—this time the driver is Dante and the words *Lasciate ogni baldanza voi che entrate* are over the door. Mr. Bons explains to the boy that *baldanza* is a mistake for *speranza,* not guessing that this is a journey toward the consequences of innocence, not toward the consequences of sin. Abandon all self-importance, ye who enter here, for only the simple in heart will see God. As they travel heavenward the boy recounts his earlier experiences, while Mr. Bons lectures him on his errors—his preferring Sir Thomas Browne to Dante, Mrs. Gamp to Homer, and Tom Jones to Shakespeare—and tells him how to behave toward the immortals:

The lad bit his lip. He made a hundred good resolutions. He would imitate Mr. Bons. . . . He would not laugh, or run, or sing, or do any of the vulgar things that must have disgusted his new friends last time. He would be very careful to pronounce their names properly, and to remember who knew whom. Achilles did not know Tom Jones—at least, so Mr. Bons said. The Duchess of Malfi was older than Mrs. Gamp—at least, so Mr. Bons said. He would be self-conscious, reticent, and prim. He would never say he liked anyone. (pp. 55–56.)

"Suffer little children, and forbid them not to come unto me, for of such is the kingdom of heaven." The story reinforces that invitation and argues for the divinity of all literature that is inspired, that attains to "poetry." Only those artists who are pure in heart, who erect no barriers against the imagination, can live in this place. Mr. Bons, of course, cannot face the reality of poetry; it is for him not a faith to hold but a phylactery to wear. He panics and begs to return, imploring Dante: "I have honoured you. I have quoted you. I have bound you in vellum. Take me back to my world." Dante replies: "I am the means and not the end. I am the food and not the life. Stand by yourself, as that boy has stood. I cannot save you. For poetry is a spirit; and they that would worship it must worship in spirit and in truth." (pp. 57–58.) Attempting to escape, Mr. Bons crawls out on a moonlit rock; and since he does not really believe in its existence, he falls through it. His fall is the result of his snobbery—the secular word for pride. His shockingly mutilated body is discovered near the Bermondsey gas works.

The poetic justice is absolute and savage. The boy remains, for Mr. Bons had the return tickets in his pocket and without them one cannot go back. But the boy has no regrets—the only reason he returned the first time was to fetch his parents (who, of course, refused to come). So, through fantasy, the tyrants are punished and the hero is transported (with very little effort of his own) to glory—to an apotheosis of self-justification. One need only believe to be saved.*

No story more explicitly illustrates the workings of fantasy, and none more vividly shows fantasy's feet of clay. In spite of Dante's sensible reminder ("I am the means, not the end. I am the food and not the life")—which echoes not only Jesus's words but Forster's belief that

* Just as love wins in *Prometheus Unbound* without meeting resistance. When Asia (love) visits Jupiter, he merely falls down without a struggle.

one cannot truly live in art[45]—the story makes a total separation between "society" and "art." When things get too bad, it seems to say, one can really live only in art. The idealist may believe, with Joyce, that "the soul, in one sense, is all there is,"[46] but the practical humanist must know that this way leads to isolation and solipsism.

But why is Mr. Bons killed off and not the parents? For one thing, death would, of course, have exempted them from the torment of remorse. But a second reason may be even more persuasive. Perhaps the author is simply reluctant to reward himself with too much poetic justice. After all, the real parent-guardians might read the story—a consideration which returns us to the quite unfantastic fact that, ticket or no ticket, the author of this tale did get back to earth. And as time went on, he increasingly liked it there.

"The Machine Stops" (1909), Forster's only attempt at science fiction, is a small masterpiece in the genre, though most critics do not like it. Unlike H. G. Wells's *The Time Machine* (1895), to which it is a "reaction," the story is anti-Utopian, and takes its place alongside *Brave New World* and *1984* as a moral allegory warning men not to become the tools of their tools. But its main interest is personal, not social; it is another tale of the psychic escape of a boy hero. This time, however, he really is something of a hero: he actually wills his escape and suffers for it.

We are introduced to a civilization that has moved underground. It lives in the "machine"—a vast complex of tunnels and rooms and strange devices in and by which all human wants are supplied. Most of the inhabitants never leave their cells:

Imagine, if you can, a small room, hexagonal in shape like the cell of a bee. It is lighted neither by window nor by lamp, yet it is filled with a soft radiance. There are no apertures for ventilation, yet the air is fresh. There are no musical instruments, and yet, at the moment that my meditation opens, this room is throbbing with melodious sounds. An arm-chair is in the centre, by its side a reading-desk—that is all the furniture. And in the arm-chair there sits a swaddled lump of flesh—a woman, about five feet high, with a face as white as a fungus. It is to her that the little room belongs. (p. 109.)

The main conflict is between this woman, Vashti, and her son, Kuno. The mother is a devotee of the establishment and lectures on it. *The Book of the Machine* is her Bible. She loathes wasting time, bodily contact, and all experiences which fail to give her "ideas" (i.e., all experiences not connected with the machine). She has a "horror of direct experience" of any kind. The son's escape from the machine is, therefore, a symbolic escape both from a suffocating society and from a woman who represents it. His claustrophobia ("I had got back the sense of space and a man can't rest then") is as much a fear of the one as of the other.

In the early days of the machine, people still spoke directly to each other, took physical exercise, raced airplanes on the surface. But over the years they became soft, desexed, and unathletic; the desire to touch, speak to, or look at another human being came to be regarded as vulgar—"not mechanical." And people had so long ceased going to the surface that finally egress through the vomitories had been forbidden on pain of "homelessness" (exile above). When the machine was established, religion had no part in its life; but now (like the machines of *Erewhon*) it compels its inhabitants to worship it.

Kuno is a heretic. Not only does he take exercise and have hair on his body ("On atavism the Machine can have no mercy"), not only does he entertain the idea that man is the measure of all things, but he finds a way up to the surface without an egression-permit. As Kuno later describes this treasonable escape to his shocked mother, it assumes the character of an actual birth. He had found an abandoned elevator shaft and got the idea that, by climbing out, he could climb back in time to a humanity that communicated via hearts and bodies, not via machines. As he dug at the rotting mortar, he felt that "a protest had been lodged against corruption":

I felt that humanity existed, and that it existed without clothes. . . . It was naked, humanity seemed naked, and all these tubes and buttons and machineries neither came into the world with us, nor will they follow us out, nor do they matter supremely while we are here. Had I been strong, I would have torn off every garment I had, and gone out into the outer air unswaddled. But this is not for me, nor perhaps for my generation. I climbed with my respirator and my hygienic clothes and my dietetic tabloids! Better thus than not at all. (p. 127.)

This process of birth—or rebirth—took him from a symbolic womb to the outer air of the world. And the mother, unconscious of this symbolism, nevertheless is outraged and disgusted—"ashamed at having borne such a son"—and seems to contract in pain as her son describes the travail of an experience she cannot honor. After climbing through the tubes of darkness and silence, he unscrewed, with heroic effort, "one of those pneumatic stoppers that defend us from the outer air" (p. 128). It is the birth itself: " 'I cannot describe it. I was lying with my face to the sunshine. Blood poured from my nose and ears and I heard a tremendous roaring. The stopper, with me clinging to it, had simply been blown out of the earth, and the air that we make down here was escaping through the vent into the air above.' " (p. 129.)

He found himself in a grassy dell in Wessex, not unlike the dell of *The Longest Journey,* and he remained that day and night "on the boundary between two atmospheres," trying to learn to breathe the sharp air of earth. Then the "Mending Apparatus" went to work:

"Out of the shaft—it is too horrible. A worm, a long white worm, had crawled out of the shaft and was gliding over the moonlit grass.

"I screamed. I did everything that I should not have done, I stamped upon the creature instead of flying from it, and it at once curled round my ankle. Then we fought. The worm let me run all over the dell, but edged up my leg as I ran. 'Help!' I cried. (That part is too awful. It belongs to the part that you will never know.) 'Help!' I cried." (p. 133.)

He has been castrated, and the mother will never know—though it was done through her will and her instruments. The mother is responsible as well for the death of the woman who might have been Kuno's mate—a figure who appeared in the twilight as Kuno called for help; one of the worms killed her by "piercing her throat." The mother hears Kuno's story to the end and predicts that the machine will punish him with "homelessness" for his apostasy.

But Kuno wins after all—or at least is proved right. The machine itself falls victim to its own decadence. Over the years part after part breaks down and cannot be mended, for no one understands its total workings: "Humanity, in its desire for comfort, had overreached itself." (p. 138.) During the last moments of its history, Kuno makes his way over dead bodies, finds his mother, and kisses her. They finally talk and touch each other directly, unencumbered by the third presence of convention, religion, or propriety. Her spirit has at last escaped its prison and she shares with Kuno, who is now ecstatically happy, his vision of a new humanity:

They wept for humanity, those two, not for themselves. They could not bear that this should be the end. Ere silence was completed their hearts were opened, and they knew what had been important on the earth. . . . The sin against the body—it was for that they wept in chief; the centuries of wrong against the muscles and the nerves, and those five portals by which we can alone apprehend—glozing it over with talk of evolution, until the body was white pap, the home of ideas as colourless, last sloshy stirrings of a spirit that had grasped the stars. (p. 145.)

"Out of the Flesh," writes D. H. Lawrence, "cometh the Word, and the Word is finite . . . and hath an end. But the Flesh is infinite and has no end."[47]

But although the author makes these claims for the body, this hero can only advocate, not demonstrate, them. Kuno is a maimed and impotent prophet who from his sufferings brings only the confidence (based on no evidence) that future generations will possess the Word in the Flesh as he himself is unable to do. "Oh, I have no remedy—or, at least, only one—to tell men again and again that I have seen the hills of Wessex as Aelfrid saw them when he overthrew the Danes." (p. 131.) This is to look unto the hills for more help than they are likely to provide, and we can only repeat after Virginia Woolf that, in Forster's fiction, "the disease, convention, and the remedy, nature, are provided if anything with too eager a simplicity, too simple an assurance."[48]

Kuno dreams rather than enacts his final successes; he is heroic by virtue of having the right attitudes rather than of doing the right things. To be sure, his spirit is uncorrupted: he did not acquiesce in his mother's denaturing pruderies, and she finally loves him on his own terms, not on hers. But her final kiss is in every sense the kiss of death: she bestows it on a son who, thanks to her, can love no other woman; and she admits she is wrong only when the whole social structure falls on her head to prove it. Here is *Liebestod*. However noble the sounds, this is no tragic victory, but defeat, for nothing comes after. The hero leaves no heirs and no instructions, and he is far too anxious to forgive the hateful parent. He even seems glad that things end this way. Maybe death is the only atonement for the guilt of having opposed the mother-defender of the establishment. Yet this hero did put up something like a fight—even though it was in the act of running away.

"The Curate's Friend" (1907) is about a faun which is discovered in Wiltshire. The creature is visible to Harry, the clergyman who narrates the story, but not to his more secular friends. Harry is one of Forster's honorary Greeks or Italians who can "see" because he is possessed of that "certain quality, for which truthfulness is too cold a name and animal spirits too coarse a one" (p. 86). This is the same charismatic power that Forster associated with "the developed heart,"[49] that sweetness and light, the "aerial ease, clearness, and radiancy" which Arnold found in Hellenism. The faun becomes "modern" just as the classics, when taught by Wedd or Dickinson, become modern—they are felt as present experience.

The faun appears at a picnic on the downs attended by Emily, her mother, a friend, and the curate. The curate is vaguely in love with Emily and so is the friend. "Emily was at that time full of vague aspirations, and, though I should have preferred them all to centre in me, yet it seemed unreasonable to deny her such other opportunities for self-culture as the neighbourhood provided." (p. 87.) The faun provides these opportunities. As Harry converses with the beast (which he alone can see), the others think he is indulging in his customary clowning. The creature tries to tempt him with "blackberries, or harebells, or wives," but the curate answers: " 'Get thee behind me!' He got behind me. 'Once for all,' I continued, 'let me tell you that it is vain to tempt one whose happiness consists in giving happiness to others.' " (p. 90.) The faun, unfamiliar with sin, wants to know "What is to tempt?" When he claims that he can make Emily happy, the curate assumes that he will bring Emily to him. Instead, the faun lays hands on Emily and the "friend," and they, "who had only intended a little cultured flirtation, resisted him as long as they could, but were gradually urged into each other's arms, and embraced with passion" (p. 91).

Harry's reaction is interesting. Furious at first, cursing the perfidy of the faun and the falseness of Emily, he gradually realizes that he is experiencing nothing but joyful relief at his escape from conventional behavior and from sex. He becomes one who swears when he is cross and laughs when he is happy, and this ability to behave in a natural way affiliates him irredeemably with the faun's world. But in spite of these pagan affiliations, he, like a latter-day Robert Herrick, does not leave his pulpit: his real and social selves remain distinct. In justifying the wearing of his public mask he drops an interesting reason for writing short stories:

Though I try to communicate that joy to others—as I try to communicate anything else that seems good—and though I sometimes succeed, yet I can tell no one exactly how it came to me. For if I breathed one word of that, my present life, so agreeable and profitable, would come to an end, my congregation would depart, and so should I, and instead of being an asset to my parish, I might find myself an expense to the nation. Therefore in the place of the lyrical and rhetorical treatment, so suitable to the subject, so congenial to my profession, I have been forced to use the unworthy medium of a narrative, and to delude you by declaring that this is a short story, suitable for reading in the train. (pp. 93–94.)

The story, then, is a covert love poem, and the spirit of that love is illicit. Fantasy saves the curate from scandal.

"Other Kingdom" (1909),* appearing one year before *Howards End,* anticipates some of that novel's issues—in particular whether a rich man can enter the Kingdom of Heaven. This is the first story in which a narrator describes not his own deliverance, but that of another, suggesting that its author may be freeing himself from the malaises that gave rise to his early fantasies.

The story is about an Irish girl, Miss Beaumont, who escapes her fiancé, Mr. Worters, by turning—like Daphne—into a tree. Worters, anticipating Mr. Wilcox of *Howards End,* is a stiff-necked materialist who wants to make of the girl a compliant and well-mannered piece of property. She resists: " 'Oh, fence me out, if you like! Fence me out as much as you like! But never in. Oh, Harcourt, never in. I must be on the outside . . . where anyone can reach me.' " (p. 74.) He cannot handle such spiritual promiscuity, let alone the climactic revelation she makes at the moment of metamorphosis—when she tells him that she has had an actual lover. Her return to the natural, to the tree, is a protest like that of Mr. Lucas or of Eustace; and her transformation is skillfully wrought, nature fading into myth as Io the woman fades into Io the dawn in Tennyson's *Tithonus:*

---

* F. R. Leavis confidently states that the "source" of "Other Kingdom" is Meredith's *The Egoist,* though he does not demonstrate the connection. *The Common Pursuit* (Harmondsworth, 1963), p. 263.

She danced away from our society and our life, back, back through the centuries till houses and fences fell and the earth lay wild to the sun. Her garment was as foliage upon her, the strength of her limbs as boughs, her throat the smooth upper branch that salutes the morning or glistens to the rain. Leaves move, leaves hide it as hers was hidden by the motion of her hair. . . . "Oh Harcourt! I never was so happy. I have all that there is in the world." (pp. 82–83.)

But except for such gracious bits, the story is self-conscious and academic, weighted by heavy-handed private jokes, like the pun on the epigraph of *Principia Ethica*,[50] and by rather bland "secrets" such as the naming of many characters after Jacobean dramatists.* The dreams are getting more robust, and so perhaps is the dreamer. As the poetic justice becomes, in story after story, more complete and satisfying, the frustrations giving rise to fantasy may be also coming to an end—and with them fantasy itself.

6

The remaining four stories, "Mr. Andrews" (1911), "The Point of It" (1911), "Co-Ordination" (1912), and "The Story of the Siren" (1920) need not detain us long. Except in the last, the narrative gift is slipping, the themes are getting too heavy for the light wings of fantasy, and the essayist is moving in on the story-writer. The years following *Howards End* (1910) were, until the writing of *Alexandria*, a time of failures and false starts.[51] In the spring of 1914, for example, Forster began a novel with the working title "Arctic Summer," which he discarded after a few chapters.[52] One of the reasons he gave for not finishing it suggests some of the troubles in these late stories: "I had got my antithesis all right, the antithesis between the civilized man . . . and the heroic man. . . . But I had not settled what is going to happen."[53] To know the antithesis, the thematic diagram, but not know how to dramatize it, is to confess a usurpation by intellect of the creative function. The themes of these stories tend to exist apart from the action—a disjunctivity that ultimately turned Forster from fiction to criticism.

"Co-Ordination" is perhaps the least interesting and most pointless

* Forster has denied that "Ford" is drawn after Ford Madox Ford, the editor of *The English Review*, in which the story appeared.

story Forster ever wrote. Its theme seems to be that the abstractions "melody" and "victory" are greater than the particulars creating them, but neither the theme nor the fable supporting it seems valid or interesting. "The Point of It" is only slightly clearer, though it has been rated very highly by some critics.* The point of it seems to be that one should stay young in spirit, whole, unfragmented by analysis or specialization. The story offers a clear contrast between the heroic man and the civilized man, between one who, though a cripple, experienced the ecstasy of an epiphany, and then died, and another who lived a long, pointless, Prufrockian death-in-life. We can see here a search for personal identity, because Forster is not only drawn to both roles, he is also committed to the diverse literary environments in which the heroic and the civilized operate—to tragedy as well as to comedy, to prophecy as well as to fantasy. Here is his judgment on the soft old man:

He traced his decomposition—his work had been soft, his books soft, he had softened his relations with other men. He had seen good in everything, and this is itself a sign of decay. Whatever occurred he had been appreciative, tolerant, pliant. Consequently he had been a success; Adam was right; it was the moment in civilization for his type. He had mistaken self-criticism for self-discipline, he had muffled in himself and others the keen, heroic edge. (pp. 161–62.)

If this is a partial self-portrait, it is nevertheless a self that Forster sometimes defends with uncompromising vigor: "The education I received in those far-off and fantastic days made me soft and I am very glad it did, for I have seen plenty of hardness since, and I know it does not even pay."[54] But he repeatedly defends another image as well—the healthy, natural man of strength, the naked athlete, even the bully: "I like people who are well-made and beautiful." (LJ, 82.) Perhaps one reason nothing could "happen" from this antithesis was that it represented a locked struggle within himself.

"The Story of the Siren," published in 1920, seems in many ways an attempt to prove the thesis of "The Point of It": that one can recapture the spirit of youth, which "all men" have had but which all

* For instance, Frederick P. W. McDowell, in "Forster's 'Natural Supernaturalism': The Tales," gives it very high marks. *Modern Fiction Studies*, VII (Autumn 1961), 271–83.

forget. Forster was especially touched by the people in T. S. Eliot's early poems, "who seemed genuine because they were unattractive or weak."[55] Those people are subsumed in Prufrock, and the narrator of this story is a Prufrock to the letter: he has heroic impulses but unheroic capacities. He is an English boy who, escaping the guardians, meets a beautiful Italian boy who has seen a siren. When the boy is asked if he has heard her sing, he replies, with charming simplicity, "How can she sing under the water? Who could? She sometimes tries, but nothing comes from her but great bubbles." (p. 181.)

It is the old theme. The spiritually dead, the middle-class enemies of poetry, youth, imagination, and beauty, rise up against those who see and believe in sirens. The hero believes but does not confess that he does. At the end he returns, so far as we know, to his aunts and chaperones, to his thesis on the "Deist Controversy," and to his life of appearances. Sawston will never know the extent of his enormous disloyalties. He has heard the mermaids singing, each to each, but he does not think that they will sing—again—to him.

"Here, then," writes Virginia Woolf, "is a difficult family of gifts to persuade to live in harmony together: satire and sympathy; fantasy and fact; poetry and a prim moral sense."[56] The stories show these conflicting elements, and more, for they are, like their leading characters, in disequilibrium, without a center of identity. They are anything but pure fantasies: for all their artistry of escape, their aim is to put away rather than take up childish things. And except for touches here and there, not one is really funny or lighthearted. Though they are full of little people facing domestic trials, they are not comic, for we sense throughout a discontent with littleness and a tug toward heroism and prophecy. And their implicit Arminianism (that faith, not works, will save us) seems born of desperation. In accordance with his own formula, the author dutifully toots on the flutes and saxophones of fantasy, but the sounds are full of the effort to be gay, rather than of gaiety, and they evoke the emptiness and panic below the civilized surface. They are all, in short, attempts to solve Prufrock's dilemma, which, if not the most representative problem of our time, lies too close to the common nerve for laughter. Kierkegaard has said, "Generally the fantastical is that which so carries a man out into the infinite that it merely carries him away from himself and therewith prevents him from returning to himself."[57] As an artist Forster strove both to make the escape and to make the return, but the vehicle for the return had to be the novel, not fantasy.

One last point: although fantasy happened to serve Forster's own purposes, it was also a widely popular form in the decades around the turn of the century, and many of the weaknesses in Forster's tales can be traced to weaknesses in this literature generally. Dickinson was a fantasist whose influence on the manner of Forster's stories is undoubtedly great, as we can see in "The Point of It," which is heavily brushed with the style of *Letters from John Chinaman* and *The Magic Flute*. By and large that influence was bad, encouraging the indulgence of the sententious and sentimental moralizing that went along with the genre generally—in such productions as George Macdonald's *Phantastes* or the fairy tales of Oscar Wilde. Forster had outgrown the puerility implicit in the form, and it was time for him to be moving on.

Chapter seven

Where Angels Fear to Tread:
The Fool as Prophet

No! I am not Prince Hamlet, nor was meant to be.
                                        —*T. S. Eliot*

Cambridge told the young Rickie Elliot that "he must not be so tragic yet awhile" (LJ, 10). If Forster is Rickie, then *Where Angels Fear to Tread* (1905), his first novel, shows how seriously he tried to follow the advice. It is a gay book, boldly and simply plotted, carrying its slight themes with an easy poise. Sententiousness and solemnity are allowed no head, and in almost no other novel of Forster do we enjoy as full a sense of the author's complete competence, his command of subject and intention. This is his own world, and he is at home in it. Although we are constantly aware that the book is being managed, it is managed like a good party, full of calculated social risks that our host brings off.

It is a comedy, no doubt about it. The plot is a contrived sequence of cause-and-effect relationships, based on an irregular marriage. The characters range from earthy Italians to English virgins twitching with morality—but all are alike in being flawed, incomplete, and unheroic. The tone is ironic, the appropriate voice for a book that sets out to separate sheep from goats and that lives indoors, in the bedrooms and drawing rooms and first-class carriages and *caffès* which are the spaces for domestic argument. As with Jane Austen, serious social and political issues enter only by implication, and though some of the characters are poor, squalor is kept out of sight. "Vulgarity," not right or wrong, is the prevailing term of judgment; even the death of a baby who is being kidnapped gets passed off as "an unlucky accident," criminal delinquency fading into social error. And comic irreverence informs the book throughout. Here is Santa Deodata, the presiding saint of Monteriano* (where most of the action takes place):

So holy was she that all her life she lay upon her back in the house of her mother, refusing to eat, refusing to play, refusing to work. The devil, envious of such sanctity, tempted her in various ways. He dangled grapes above her, he showed her fascinating toys, he pushed soft pillows beneath her aching head. When all proved vain he tripped up the mother and flung her downstairs before her very eyes. But so holy was the saint that she never picked her mother up, but lay upon her back through all, and thus assured her throne in Paradise. She was only fifteen when she died, which shows how much is within the reach of any schoolgirl. (p. 112.)

Nevertheless, what is most interesting about the book is the ambiguities in its comedy, the flaws in its pose of intellectual detachment. Real passions occasionally erupt, and alongside the fools and their antics are found "round" characters capable of development (though they sometimes choose not to develop), characters who undergo a real struggle for self-realization and who suffer a real, if quiet, kind of pain. Nor is this a secure social world. Through a hundred clues we are told that the society of *Where Angels Fear to Tread* has an uncertain lease and is so unsure of its values that it must substitute the rigidity of etiquette for the spontaneity of taste. Feeling dissolution in the air, we sense that we are having a kind of last fling, a last laugh. It is not so much a lost generation as one that cannot find its way home among familiar landmarks. Comedy exists, as Bergson tells us, where the social norms are intact, where *common* sense can be appealed to as a way of bringing the erring or the eccentric

---

* Monteriano is in reality San Gimignano near Florence, the town of many towers, and Santa Deodata is in reality Santa Fina (A.D. 1253), who is celebrated in two fine frescoes by Ridolfo Ghirlandaio (1483–1561), to be found (as Forster explicitly tells us in the book) in the fifth chapel on the right of the Collegiate Church (the Collegiata). Santa Fina's claim to sainthood rests, according to *Butler's Lives of the Saints* (New York, 1956), on "the perfect resignation with which she accepted bodily suffering." A lovely child, she was as an adolescent attacked by some horrible, disfiguring diseases, and—desiring to be like Jesus—she lay for six years on a plank in one position, never complaining. When, after her death, her body was removed from the rotting plank, white violets were said to have been found growing where she had lain, and to this day the peasants of San Gimignano call white violets "Santa Fina's flowers." (See Plate 16.)

back to the center of things. But when we begin to care more about individuals than about the values of the social establishment, then we are no longer in that conservative world where comedy is a possibility, but in a revolutionary, or at least a romantic, one. Revolutionary ages are seldom calm or confident enough to permit the self-criticism of laughter, and romantic ones almost never take a comic view of experience. Likewise, the artist who has not yet found his identity or theme, or who is sheltering in a clique, is not likely to be a comic artist; anxiety, for the anxious, is a serious—not a comic—business.

Forster, as his stories tell us, can be torn between the civilized and the heroic, can feel the tug of a comic as well as a romantic impulse. This book measures that tension. If it succeeds as comedy, it is because the author has turned his laughing side toward us, not because he has no other side. But occasionally the "flutes and saxophones" are muted and we begin to hear a more "universal" music; and whatever the gain in this exchange, one of the costs is some "suspension of the sense of humour."[1] To observe the crossings of this divide is to discover the drama and meaning of this book. We can observe them best in the career of Philip Herriton, one of Forster's "civilized" avatars, but first we must recall some main events.

2

Ten years before the story commences, Lilia Theobald had married Charles Herriton, which is to say, in Herriton terms, that vulgarity had married respectability.[2] A daughter, Irma, was born, Charles died, and both daughter-in-law and granddaughter fell into the power of Mrs. Herriton and her daughter Harriet. Mother and daughter resolved that Lilia was to be "pushed through life without bringing discredit on the family into which she had married" (p. 13). But Lilia was a poor learner.* She continued to be frivolous

---

* It is of interest that Forster's mother was also called "Lily" (MT, 249), for the relations between Lilia and Mrs. Herriton could well caricature the struggles between Forster's mother and his great-aunt. Mrs. Herriton's statement, "It is mortifying to think that a widow of thirty-three requires a girl ten years younger to look after her" (WA, 11) is exactly the sort of thing the sharp-tongued Marianne Thornton would say. Whether Forster's mother ever thought of remarrying, Forster does not tell us; but the widow (aged about 45) was in Italy at about the time this story takes place.

and flirtatious, notable mainly for her "blowsy good spirits" and "the knack of being absurd in public." When she showed signs of becoming engaged, the Herritons panicked and (on Philip's suggestion) sent her to Italy out of harm's way—harm being Mr. Kingcroft, a curate with damp hands. The frustrated merry widow, aged thirty-three, goes off to the libidinous South under the chaperonage of Caroline Abbott, a sensible girl ten years her junior.

The first chapter opens with the departure; it closes with the telegraphed news that Lilia is engaged to "Italian nobility" (only Lilia, thought Mrs. Herriton, would have the "fatuous vulgarity" to say "nobility" rather than "noble"), and Philip is dispatched to save both the family name and Lilia from a fate worse than death. Mrs. Herriton, the dreadful guardian, defines his mission with exquisite clarity: "The man may be a duke or he may be an organ-grinder. That is not the point. If Lilia marries him she insults the memory of Charles, she insults Irma, she insults us. Therefore, I forbid her, and if she disobeys, we have done with her forever." (p. 24.) That is the voice of Sawston, the suburb of all the deadly virtues; its authentic stridency resounds throughout the book. Harriet, even more rigid and overwrought than Mrs. Herriton, parrots her mother, often missing the tune but never the hateful words. Her education had been "almost too successful": "Though pious and patriotic, and a great moral asset for the house, she lacked that pliancy and tact which her mother so much valued, and had expected her to pick up for herself." (p. 18.)

Lilia is discovered married to the impecunious and handsome Gino. Far from being a scion of the nobility, he is the son of a dentist. His character mixes avarice, insolence, and vulgarity with an equal measure of gentleness and charm.* His existence is profoundly disturbing to Philip, who has fallen in love with a Baedeker Italy but fears the unmediated reality that Gino represents. "Philip had seen that face before in Italy a hundred times—seen it and loved it, for it was not merely beautiful, but had the charm which is the rightful heritage of all who are born on that soil." On the other hand, Philip did not want to see that face at dinner: "It was not the face

* Compare D. H. Lawrence's *The Lost Girl* (1920), in which a middle-class English girl is carried off by an Italian to a rigorous life in which she is, though "lost," vitally alive.

of a gentleman." (p. 37.) This ambivalence tears at him. He had ro-
manticized Italy, believing that it "really purifies and ennobles all
who visit her" (p. 12), and that was why he had urged Lilia to go
there. But to discover dentistry at Monteriano—"false teeth and
laughing gas and the tilting chair at a place which knew the Etruscan League, and the Pax Romana, and Alaric himself, and the Countess Matilda, and the Middle Ages"—threatened his illusions, and "he
feared that Romance might die" (p. 32). But Romance, the author
tells us, was just beginning; it is not something that lives behind fastidious defenses: "Romance only dies with life. No pair of pincers
will ever pull it out of us. But there is a spurious sentiment which
cannot resist the unexpected and the incongruous and the grotesque.
A touch will loosen it, and the sooner it goes from us the better. It
was going from Philip now." (pp. 32–33.) To love Italy truly is to be
false to Sawston. Both Philip and Caroline Abbott are touched by
this guilt, and even enjoy it, but for the moment they must leave
Monteriano and return home to face the wrath of Mrs. Herriton.

The next critical event is Lilia's unhappiness—and moral growth.
"Italy is . . . a delightful place to live in if you happen to be a man"
(p. 54), but Lilia is doubly unfortunate in being both a woman and
an Englishwoman. "I mean to wake you all up," she tells Gino, "just
as I woke up Sawston" (p. 52), but she only stirs some sleeping dogs.
After a little bemused tolerance of her foreign ways and privileges,
Gino becomes a normal Italian husband, abandoning her for his male
friends at the Caffè Garibaldi, refusing to bring people to the house,
and forbidding her to take solitary walks. Like other Italian women,
she has her house and the Church (which she soon joined), but she
is utterly shut out from that "true Socialism" which Italy reserves for
its men, a Socialism based "not on equality of income or character,
but on the equality of manners" (p. 55). Moreover, she is also abandoned by Sawston, which forbids the disgraced mother even to write
to her own daughter. Then she discovers two things: that Gino has
married her for money and that he is unfaithful. She is trapped and
broken:

She had given up everything for him—her daughter, her relatives, her
friends, all the little comforts and luxuries of a civilized life—and even if
she had the courage to break away, there was no one who would receive her
now. The Herritons had been almost malignant in their efforts against her,

and all her friends had one by one fallen off. So it was better to live on humbly, trying not to feel, endeavouring by a cheerful demeanour to put things right. "Perhaps," she thought, "if I have a child he will be different. I know he wants a son."

Lilia had achieved pathos despite herself, for there are some situations in which vulgarity counts no longer. Not Cordelia nor Imogen more deserve our tears. (pp. 69–70.)

Humility, we remember, is one of the requirements for entering the realm of prophecy. To achieve pathos is not to achieve tragedy, but it is to leave the world of comedy and humor behind. Lilia is never transformed into a heroic figure, but, as she furiously indicts the husband who has unthinkingly and without malice become her tormentor and jailer, she acquires almost another self: "She was beside herself with passion, and though she could hardly think or see, she suddenly attained to magnificence and pathos which a practised stylist might have envied." (p. 75.) In achieving this transcendence, Lilia fulfills her function in the book. She takes us to the limits of comic possibility and beyond. By providing opposition, she characterizes Gino and the Herritons, the antagonists that make the book go. Finally, she delivers to the plot the one property it could not do without—a baby boy—and dies in the effort.

3

With this, the second phase of the Italian campaign opens. "Here beginneth the New Life," Philip had remarked when Lilia first departed for Italy (p. 11). He says it again now, as Mrs. Herriton instructs him in the new tactics: he is "to tell no one about the baby, not even Miss Abbott" (p. 81). The mother, ignoring the defeat and ennui in her son's voice, lectures him: " 'Yes, dear; but now it is really a New Life, because we are all at accord. Then you were still infatuated with Italy. It may be full of beautiful pictures and churches, but we cannot judge a country by anything but its men.' " (p. 82.) The ironies in that are popping like firecrackers.

The New Life lasts seven months, ending when a postcard that Gino sends Irma from her "lital brother" is not intercepted in time. But before this new crisis there is an important development in the relations between Philip and Caroline; he discovers that she too hates Sawston—"the idleness, the stupidity, the respectability, the petty unselfishness" (p. 86)—and that this hate had made her love Italy. After

the imprisonment of Sawston, Italy's beauty and splendor had dizzied
her. Why had she backed Lilia in the marriage? "We were mad—
drunk with rebellion. We had no common sense." (p. 88.) It is the
usual confession of one who has encountered Pan, or one of his descendants, and with the abandonment of common sense we abandon
—momentarily, at any rate—comedy also. In Italy she had known an
epiphany, an orgiastic awakening, but one that she had to enjoy vicariously, through the love of Gino and Lilia rather than through
any love of her own. The voyeur is common in Forster's fiction—the
generous (or perhaps masochistic) neutral who makes no sexual
claims, and so loves the world that he virtually drives his beloved
into the arms of another.[3] The only way to dignify a love of this character is to idealize it and thus remove it from any possibility of earthly
fruition or collision. This both Caroline and Philip do. The sexual
lovers have had their fling; these asexual, spiritual lovers come together (at least for the moment) as fellow victims, drawn as much by
their common antipathies and losses as by any liking for each other.
They are rebels who do not rebel. Philip retreats into "splendour and
beauty," into a solipsism that betrays at once his sensitivity and his
despair. The following exchange between Caroline and Philip is extremely important:

"You see, Mr. Herriton, it makes me specially unhappy; it's the only time
I've ever gone into what my father calls 'real life'—and look what I've made
of it! All that winter I seemed to be waking up to beauty and splendour. . . .
I actually hated society for a day or two at Monteriano. I didn't see that all
these things are invincible, and that if we go against them they will break
us to pieces. Thank you for listening to so much nonsense."
    "Oh, I quite sympathize with what you say," said Philip encouragingly;
"it isn't nonsense, and a year or two ago I should have been saying it too.
But I feel differently now, and I hope that you also will change. Society *is*
invincible—to a certain degree. But your real life is your own, and nothing
can touch it. There is no power on earth that can prevent your criticizing
and despising mediocrity—nothing that can stop you retreating into splendour and beauty—into the thoughts and beliefs that make the real life—the
real you." (pp. 88–89.)

    In short, one need never lose the battle between the individual and
society if one never engages in it. If "reality" is defined as an idealized
state of mind divorced from any interaction with the social world,
then one can, of course (so long as one has the luck to be fed, housed,

and clothed), be exempt from any of the claims of that world. But such an exemption is not victory, it is escape; and Philip is too entangled in his rationalizations to know the difference. That is precisely his personal problem—and his creator's. Insofar as the plot is concerned, his attitude serves a useful purpose in pointing up the book's most crucial social antithesis: that between "civilization" as conventional England knows it (Sawston and the rules) and "heroism," the complex of attitudes and assumptions that can be subsumed under Italy, love, or "real life." Philip is the go-between serving the antithesis. Although he acts the meek executor of Mrs. Herriton's super-egotistic vanities, and although he abstracts Italy's pagan flesh to "splendour and beauty," he keeps us and his fellow-characters reminded that there are better—or at least other—things to do. His tragedy is that he does not seem to know how to do them. Will he dream his final victories, like Kuno, or will he actually engage in the battle? That question is by far the most interesting of the book.

But these serious issues do not bog down the comedy. Irma makes the most of having an Italian brother, and her persecution of the Herritons on this score has a satanic brilliance. "Oh, I do long to see him," she remarks to Harriet, "and be the first to teach him the Ten Commandments and the Catechism." (The remark "always made Harriet look grave.") Worse still, the little Irma (aged about nine) asks if she might include him among those she mentions in her prayers. Mrs. Herriton, punctilious as always, sticks to the law:

"Of course I allowed her," she replied coldly. "She has a right to mention any one she chooses. But I was annoyed with her this morning, and I fear that I showed it."
"And what happened this morning?" [asked Philip].
"She asked if she could pray for her 'new father'—for the Italian!"
"Did you let her?"
"I got up without saying anything."
"You must have felt just as you did when I wanted to pray for the devil."
"He is the devil," cried Harriet.
"No, Harriet; he is too vulgar" [said Philip].
"I will thank you not to scoff against religion!" was Harriet's retort. (p. 91.)

Caroline decides the child must be brought up in England, away from that Monteriano which she now thinks of as "a magic city of vice, be-

neath whose towers no person could grow up happy or pure" (p. 99).*
In a fine burst of impertinence, she confronts Mrs. Herriton and asks
her what she intends to do about the baby. Mrs. Herriton—since
"she could not bear to seem less charitable than others" (p. 99)—is
shamed into taking action. She writes Gino and offers him money if
he will give up the baby, and Gino refuses, at which point she would
have dropped the matter. But the superconscientious Caroline will
not settle for this, thus forcing Mrs. Herriton to pretend that she
really cares about the baby's welfare. Once again Philip is given his
marching orders for Italy (this time with Harriet as first lieutenant),
and together they are to bring the baby back.

Philip picks up his sister† in the Tirol, "in a dense cloud five thousand feet above the sea, chilled to the bone, overfed, bored, and not
at all unwilling to be fetched away" (p. 105). As they descend into
Italy, the old enchantment touches Philip again. The Sawston brain-
washing drains away, and once again he acquires the courage to love
what he wishes to love: "Italy was beastly, and Florence station is the
centre of beastly Italy. But he had a strange feeling that he was to
blame for it all; that a little influx into him of virtue would make
the whole land not beastly but amusing." (p. 108.) But Harriet's feeling about the thirteen-hour descent from the virginal mountains is
unambiguous: it is a descent into hell. "Foreigners are a filthy nation," she cries, almost insane with the heat and the sweat. They meet
a hot Italian lady who confesses that she has never before "sweated
so profusely" (p. 107). Harriet gets smuts in her eye, finds puppies
asleep on her hotel bed at Bologna, and is revolted by the blowing
of bladder whistles at a religious *festa*. Everything about the country
assaults the senses of this straight, brave, and peevish woman. Her
screaming revulsion is directly counter to Philip's growing love and
pleasure. She condemns "the whole lot"—Frenchmen as well as Italians—to which Philip replies, more to himself than to her, "Things
aren't so jolly easy." (p. 111.) For all his sensibility, he lacks and perhaps even envies the obtuse Harriet's sublime self-confidence.

---

* Monteriano (San Gimignano) indeed has a phallic aspect with its "seventeen
towers—all that was left of the fifty-two that had filled the city in her prime" (WA,
33–34). See Plate 18.

† A Miss Herriton also appears briefly in *The Longest Journey* as a possible mate
for Herbert Pembroke, also of Sawston. See LJ, 170.

The whole episode is a comic masterpiece, comic because for Harriet "things were easy, though not jolly" (p. 111). She is the oversimplifier, the woman of one idea, one set of prejudices; but Philip is once again threatening the comedy with his moral growth. For the moment, however, Harriet keeps him to his duty: to get the baby. They arrive at the hotel, Harriet bawling and screaming, to discover that, of all people, Caroline Abbott has got there before them.

Caroline had taken it into her head to come and fix things up. When Philip sees the two women face to face, he simply runs away, without even paying the cabman. "Tear each other's eyes out!" he cries (p. 116). Though he likes Miss Abbott, he is not happy to have her in Monteriano—her presence "spoilt the comedy: she would do nothing funny" (p. 116). Nevertheless, the chapter ends in a scene of pure comic opera. The three of them attend a performance of *Lucia di Lammermoor* (in which the "hot lady of the Apennines" sings the leading role).* The vulgarities of the performance are manifold and undisguised—in particular the bamboo clothes-horse stuck all over with bouquets, mostly of artificial flowers, which Lucia embraces with joy—but this audience suspends its disbelief in these feigned gestures of chivalry and generosity with hilarious ease. Philip slips out of his withdrawn Sawston character and joins the party, but Harriet stiffens. She is struck full in the chest by a bouquet hurled by the prima donna, out of which falls a billet-doux. " 'Call this classical?' " she shrieks, " 'it's not even respectable!' " (p. 135.) And she leaves the hall. Philip, seeking the inamorato for whom the note was intended, finds Gino and is pulled by the family enemy up into his box—and embraced like a brother.

In the course of these events, though Harriet has been the same as she was in England, Caroline has followed Philip in being touched by the old fearful enchantment, and the chapter ends as she and Philip once again come together in sympathy and mutual respect. Philip has earlier seen that "there were two Miss Abbotts—the Miss Abbott who could travel alone to Monteriano, and the Miss Abbott

* The whole scene was remembered, I am told by Ian Watt and Lucio Ruotolo, from an actual performance by Luisa Tetrazzini at San Gimignano around the turn of the century. It reminds one too of Forster's description of a Sunday concert at San Stephano during the War—a concert for the eye rather than the ear. See below, p. 283.

who could not enter Gino's house when she got there" (p. 122). But she has a wonderful evening:

Her head . . . was full of music, and that night when she opened the window her room was filled with warm sweet air. She was bathed in beauty within and without; she could not go to bed for happiness. Had she ever been so happy before? Yes, once before, and here, a night in March, the night Gino and Lilia had told her of their love—the night whose evil she had come now to undo.

She gave a sudden cry of shame. "This time—the same place—the same thing,"—and she began to beat down her happiness, knowing it to be sinful. She was here to fight against this place, to rescue a little soul who was innocent as yet. She was here to champion morality and purity, and the holy life of an English home. (pp. 138–39.)

This is no girl fighting what she knows to be sinful, but one who has lost the ability to distinguish good from evil. She represents a transitional generation trying to get shut of its inhibiting puritanism, and yet feeling lost and fearful in the open spaces of its new freedom. This is not the prude faced with temptation—that old farcical situation—but a live woman reduced to moral absurdity by cultural restraints that have lost their meaning. Thus she becomes anti-comic, not comic. She and Philip are not partial people in a healthy society; they are what remains of life in a society already touched with rigor mortis. Although they are no heroes, they participate deeply in that conflict between what Freud calls the reality principle and the pleasure principle, in terms of which the rebellion against Victorianism can perhaps best be understood.[4] Sawston against Italy is morality against sexuality, duty against joy, order against disorder, and even— in a comically diminished sense—the Apollonian against the Dionysian. It is a familiar duality. For the last century and a half, such northern Europeans as Goethe, Arnold, Butler, Lawrence, and Mann have in their writings made Italy a powerful symbol for release from repression, for all the sensuous and passionate side of life that Protestant restraints have made illicit. Italy is the unconscious avenging itself on the repressive conscious, and since Philip and Harriet have strong commitments in both directions, they suffer an uncommonly hard struggle between desire and duty. If the issue of "society" versus "real life" is to be decided in action, then Philip and Caroline must decide whether to escape into exile, to face things through rebellion, or to return in moral defeat to Sawston. Whatever they do, we know by this time that their author is an expert on their inhibitions.

The last three chapters of the book, which contain some of Forster's most effective dramatic writing, test these alternatives. When Caroline decides that only she can get the baby from Gino, she bravely crosses his threshold alone, and receives two shocks: first, she sees the baby and realizes it as a living creature and not just as a concept; second, she witnesses Gino's physical beauty and capacity for paternal love: "This cruel, vicious fellow knew of strange refinements. The horrible truth, that wicked people are capable of love, stood naked before her, and her moral being was abashed. It was her duty to rescue the baby, to save it from contagion, and she still meant to do her duty. But . . . she was in the presence of something greater than right or wrong." (p. 152.) Gino, while bathing the baby, becomes a transcendent, almost god-like figure in her eyes: "The man was majestic; he was a part of Nature; in no ordinary love scene could he ever be so great." (p. 155.)

By such glib translations Caroline misses her moment of truth. Why must an "ordinary love scene" be inferior to this? Because Caroline is still not emancipated enough to face the human reality; she must spiritualize it in order to make it palatable, to get it past her moral sentries. She must, in other words, turn life into art before she can accept it. And so must Philip. When he enters he finds Caroline kneeling before the naked baby alongside the adoring father: it was "to all intents and purposes, the Virgin and Child, with Donor" (p. 157).

The moment is intense, yet that "to all intents and purposes" strongly qualifies the scene's transcendence. The Virgin, after all, is Caroline Abbott and the Donor Gino. It is a half-comic tableau, a parody—one of the places where this book turns away, as if on impulse, from seriousness. But toward the end of the scene, it loses its church-pageant quality, and the tone again plunges into ambiguity. When Miss Abbott, shocked by Philip's entrance, arises speechless and raises her hands to her mouth, "like one who is in sudden agony" (p. 157), we recognize this as real pain. And Gino, whatever he is in himself, is allowed to participate in a transfiguration, a kind of love-

agony in which the streams of "physical and spiritual life" mingle.
Has the scene passed from comedy to prophecy? The answer depends
on how seriously we take Caroline's tears, and her experience generally. Philip, looking back on her failure to get the baby, refers to the
"gush of sentimentalism which had carried her away,"[5] and he may
be right; her "agony" may be only her excessive embarrassment before so much nakedness.

Another moment of high drama—or melodrama—occurs when Harriet kidnaps the baby. Infuriated at the weaknesses of her confeder-
ates (who have decided that Gino loves the baby and will not part
with it), Harriet secretly takes things into her own hands. Pretending
resignation over their failure, she orders the retreat from Monteriano—Miss Abbott to go ahead in the first carriage, Harriet to follow
with Philip. At the last minute Harriet cannot be found and Philip,
searching her room, discovers only her purple prayerbook open on
the bed—to Psalm 144: "Blessed be the Lord my God who teacheth
my hands to war and my fingers to fight." (p. 175.) (Clearly, Forster
knows his Bible.) As we watch Harriet doing her Christian "duty,"
the scene takes on qualities of nightmare. A grotesque mute delivers
a note from Harriet ordering Philip to pick her up at one of the city
gates. When he does so she is carrying a bundle—the baby, more dead
than alive. "I suppose he breathes, and all that sort of thing?" Philip
asks when she has got into the carriage. Before the question is well
answered, the carriage collides with Miss Abbott's in the rain and
overturns. The baby is killed and Philip's arm is broken.

The story is now heavy with presentiments of prophecy. As Harriet
explains how the baby ("crying and [yet making] no noise") came into
her hands, Philip is swept by a powerful if passing emotion: "She
crooned harshly as they descended, and now and then she wiped up
the tears, which welled inexhaustibly from the little eyes. Philip
looked away, winking at times himself. It was as if they were traveling with the whole world's sorrow, as if all the mystery, all the per-
sistency of woe were gathered to a single fount." (p. 180.) This
strongly recalls the scene from *The Brothers Karamazov* that Forster
quotes in *Aspects* as an illustration of prophecy. Mitya dreams of
driving in the steppes past a burned-out village where a row of starving peasant women stand along a road. One of them holds a baby

against her dried-up breasts, and "the child cried and cried, and held out its little bare arms, with its little fists blue from cold." Mitya's dream will not yield him answers. "Tell me, why is it those poor mothers stand there? Why are people poor? Why is the babe poor? Why is the steppe barren? Why don't they hug each other and kiss? Why don't they sing songs of joy? Why are they so dark from black misery? Why don't they feed the babe?" (AN, 121.) He feels an enormous passion of pity, and when he awakens he finds that some kind person has put a pillow under his head as he slept, and he says, "I've had a good dream, gentlemen." We have the feeling, writes Forster, "that the whole universe needs pity and love" (AN, 122)—exactly as Philip feels that "they were traveling with the whole world's sorrow."*

A final dramatic scene follows Gino's learning of the baby's death. Gino violently attacks Philip, who bears the news, cruelly twisting his broken arm and trying to choke him. Philip is saved from death by the intervention of Miss Abbott. There is no similar scene of violence and pain in all of Forster's work, and the author, in *propria persona,* breaks in with the comment: "Physical pain is almost too terrible to bear. We can just bear it when it comes by accident or for our good —as it generally does in modern life—except at school. But when it is caused by the malignity of a man, full grown, fashioned like ourselves, all our control disappears." (p. 189.) That unbenign aspect of the natural man is too much to take. If evil is mere appearance, as the idealist tends to claim, then pain can be an acute embarrassment to his faith, the provoker of inescapable doubts. Forster, optimistic and pacifistic, is invariably overwrought in the presence of pain, and is quick to avert his gaze from the sufferer. Nevertheless, there is a good deal of implied violence in his books, and a good deal of masochism. Those who suffer most—the Philips, Rickies, and Cecils—

---

* See LJ, 125: "He loved Agnes, not only for herself, but because she was lighting up the human world." In the discussion of "prophecy" in *Aspects,* Forster contrasts the Dostoevsky scene with that from George Eliot's *Adam Bede* where Dinah goes to Hetty's cell to get the condemned prisoner to confess. The difference is that the one seems to invoke love enough for the space of Hetty's cell and the other for the whole universe. This brings to mind the fact that in Forster's fictional mythology, the "enemy" is space as well as time. The achievement of prophecy (and the cessation of humor) tends to involve a transcendence of both.

those who are most walked on, misunderstood, or cast away as re-
dundant by a strong world, are those closest to their author in character and temperament. To the degree that they are pitiful, their
creator seems to be pitying himself, and registering the sensitive man's
protest against the hard world symbolized by "school." Caroline
speaks for all the favored characters when she cries, "I will have no
more intentional evil." (p. 191.)

In a technical sense, the story ends happily. The fools, Philip and
Caroline, are morally victorious over the knaves, Harriet and Mrs.
Herriton. But the crucial question of the book is, what is the nature
of their victory?

4

The book, as we know, hovers indecisively between comedy and
prophecy. The female Herritons never deviate from flatness; but the
rebels or would-be rebels continually threaten to achieve roundness,
and actually do achieve it at moments. Lilia, for example, begins flat
and inflates to roundness; when she finally turns on the Herritons
("For once in my life I'll thank you to leave me alone," p. 42), she
achieves, in Forster's term, "pathos." But by far the most important
transformations are those of Caroline and Philip, especially Philip.
When Forster was asked, "Do any of your characters represent yourself at all?" he replied, "Rickie more than any. Also Philip. And Cecil
(in *A Room with a View*) has got something of Philip in him."[6] Earlier in the same interview, Forster said, "Philip Herriton I modeled
on Professor [E. J.] Dent. He knew this, and took an interest in his
own progress."[7] How can we explain this apparent contradiction?
The answer is very likely to be found in Forster's formula for turning a real person into a fictional one:

A useful trick is to look back upon such a person with half-closed eyes, fully
describing certain characteristics. I am left with about two-thirds of a human being and can get to work. A likeness isn't aimed at and couldn't be
obtained, because a man's only himself amidst the particular circumstances
of his life and not amid other circumstances. So that to refer back to Dent
when Philip was in difficulties with Gino . . . would have ruined the atmosphere and the book.[8]

Such a procedure gives us all the more warrant to look upon Philip
as a kind of experimental self for Forster, a portrait of the artist as

a young man exploring his own possibilities for experience. One phase of that exploration involves a most explicit kind of self-scrutiny —the examination of his physical endowments to see if they will do. Forster almost never shows us close-ups of the faces of his characters, but Philip Herriton is an exception:

> His face was plain rather than not, and there was a curious mixture in it of good and bad. He had a fine forehead and a good large nose, and both observation and sympathy were in his eyes. But below the nose and eyes all was confusion, and those people who believe that destiny resides in the mouth and chin shook their heads when they looked at him.
>
> Philip himself, as a boy, had been keenly conscious of these defects. Sometimes when he had been bullied or hustled about at school he would retire to his cubicle and examine his features in a looking-glass, and he would sigh and say, "It is a weak face. I shall never carve a place for myself in the world." But as years went on he became either less self-conscious or more self-satisfied. The world, he found, made a niche for him as it did for every one. Decision of character might come later—or he might have it without knowing. At all events he had got a sense of beauty and a sense of humour, two most desirable gifts. (p. 78.)

This is, quite obviously, Forster's own looking glass.* As we watch Philip's progress we sense that a somewhat bemused Forster is taking, like Professor Dent, "an interest in his own progress." Philip is no hero, but from the beginning his author has asked us to take him seriously.

The last phase of Philip's progress is most revealing. When Philip returns from Italy the second time, he falls again under his mother's sway. "All his life he had been her puppet. She had let him worship Italy, and reform Sawston—just as she had let Harriet be Low Church.

---

* Consider Rickie's reflection (LJ, 78): "Love in return—that he could expect from no one, being too ugly and too unattractive." Between the ages of 25 and 30 (1904–1909) Forster was "violently" worried about growing old, and kept a diary recording his "despair." "After twenty-five decay starts, one is not what one was, hair thins or might thin, one is unattractive, is a bore, finds examination papers more difficult to finish, gets rattled by the lapse of time, etc. etc." "De Senectute," *The London Magazine*, IV (1957), 16. One of the more ironic "secrets" of Forster's work is the fact that Henry Wilcox of HE, an unsympathetic character, looks very much like Philip Herriton: "His face was not as square as his son's, and, indeed, the chin, though firm enough in outline, retreated a little, and the lips, ambiguous, were curtained by a moustache.... The forehead, too, was...high and straight." HE, 95. Finally, one might consider Forster's passing comment on one of two noble savages in "Happiness!": "But he was chinless, like all truly good men." AH, 47–48.

She had let him talk as much as he liked. But when she wanted a thing she always got it." (p. 98.) He is her prisoner, though not her fool. During her fight with Caroline about the baby, Philip's eyes were opened to his mother's real nature:

Though she was frightening him, she did not inspire him with reverence. Her life, he saw, was without meaning. To what purpose was her diplomacy, her insincerity, her continued repression of vigour? Did they make anyone better or happier? Did they even bring happiness to herself? Harriet with her gloomy peevish creed, Lilia with her clutches after pleasure, were after all more divine than this well-ordered, active, useless machine. (p. 98.)

Though this is close to utter damnation, it is followed by the despairing comment: "But he could not rebel. To the end of his days he would probably go on doing what she wanted." (p. 98.)* Is this, we wonder, his last word?

On his second trip to Italy—now taking orders from Harriet—he recognizes himself as "a puppet's puppet," but one who "knew exactly the disposition of the strings" (p. 106). This ought to be stock comedy: the male dominated by the weaker sex. But the weakness we see is more disconcerting than funny. This is no Walter Mitty taking umbrage in daydreams of cliché heroics, but a highly intelligent, sensitive, and self-conscious young man. This puppet knows how he got that way and is far from certain that he wants to change. If he is a flat character in any sense, it is because he wills his own flatness, not because he lacks the character to be otherwise. But the reader knows that his deliverance hangs on whether he can break the strings, whether he can act his rebellion as well as feel it. Caroline—infuriated with his willingness to fail as long as he fails "honorably"—puts the issue squarely:

Oh, what's the use of your fairmindedness if you never decide for yourself? Anyone gets hold of you and makes you do what they want. And you see through them and laugh at them—and do it. It's not enough to see clearly. ... Your brain and your insight are splendid. But when you see what's right you're too idle to do it. You told me once that we shall be judged by our intentions, not by our accomplishments. I thought it a grand remark. But we must intend to accomplish—not sit intending on a chair. (p. 167.)

---

* Santa Deodata, in her inaction and in her passive hostility toward her mother, can be seen as a kind of metaphor for Philip.

This reminds us of Keynes's remark that in the Bloomsbury credo there was not a very intimate connection between "being good" and "doing good," and Forster, in casting Caroline Abbott as devil's advocate, shows himself highly conscious of the consequences of that moral position and keenly aware of its personal cost. Philip knows his inertia is a state of disgrace, not grace; but though he is a conformist without faith, he is neither a hypocrite nor an opportunist. Neither deluding nor deluded, he has simply surrendered. "You appreciate us all—see good in all of us," Caroline bursts out. "And all the time you are dead—dead—dead." She concludes, significantly, "I can't bear—she has not been good to you—your mother." (p. 168.) She is fighting for his moral life—as, against Gino, she has fought for his physical life—and he needs such a defender, for he will not fight for himself.

"Miss Abbott, don't worry over me. Some people are born not to do things. I'm one of them; I never did anything. . . . I never expect anything to happen now, and so I am never disappointed. You would be surprised to know what my great events are. Going to the theatre yesterday, talking to you now —I don't suppose I shall ever meet anything greater. I seem fated to pass through the world without colliding with it or moving it. . . . I don't die— I don't fall in love. And if other people die or fall in love they always do it when I'm just not there. You are quite right; life to me is just a spectacle, which—thank God, and thank Italy, and thank you—is now more beautiful and heartening than it has ever been before. (p. 168.)*

This is accidie, the sin of despair. In fantasy, which by definition avoids reality, Forster at least gave his heroes some pleasant rewards. Here, where his hero is cast in a realistic world, he gives him nothing —no rewards and almost no character. Philip is about as close to being all sensibility, all spirit, as a character could be and still remain recognizably human on the pages of a novel. He does not, however, want to die. Accidie is not that kind of despair: it is rather an indifference comparable to that of stones or plants, and Caroline is right to call him "dead." He perfectly exemplifies what Ortega y Gasset

* Philip's state is very like that of John Marcher in James's "The Beast in the Jungle": "The fate he had been marked for he had met with a vengeance—he had emptied the cup to the lees; he had been the man of his time, *the* man, to whom nothing on earth was to have happened." Henry James, *Seven Stories and Studies*, ed. Edward Stone (New York, 1961), p. 240.

calls the sentimental modern morality by which "anything becomes preferable to the thought of dying," and by which life is "prolonged in proportion as it is not used," gaining "extension at the cost of vitality."[9] Philip in effect reduces life's meaning to an esthetic design, and encloses himself within a chrysalis of female domination. But his imprisonment is particularly frightful because he is in part his own jailer, victimized by the feminine in himself, and he can hardly recognize in Caroline a woman who is ready to assist his escape. He is an archetype of the unheroic hero in modern fiction, related to such morally crippled or half-emasculated males as Ralph Touchett, Jude Fawley, Clifford Chatterley, Prufrock, and "Sainty"—the anti-hero of Howard Sturgis's *Belchamber* (1904). (Forster is an admirer of *Belchamber,* in which Sainty "fails because he lives among people who can't understand what delicacy is; at the best they are dictators, like his mother, and miss it that way; at the worst they are bitches, like his wife.")[10]

But Philip knows how unheroic he is—there is no failure of intelligence here. Caroline tells him, "I wish something would happen to you, my dear friend; I wish something would happen to you" (p. 168); and before the novel is finished, her wish is in a sense fulfilled. Something happens when Philip sees Caroline embrace Gino, just after she has prevented Gino from committing a murder. This to Philip is a great moment, a moment of transfiguration, and Caroline undergoes apotheosis. Only thus, vicariously, can he experience love—by looking upon it as one might look upon a work of art. The embrace reminds him of things he had seen "in great pictures but never in a mortal":

Philip looked away, as he sometimes looked away from the great pictures where visible forms suddenly became inadequate for the things they have shown to us. He was happy; he was assured that there was greatness in the world. There came to him an earnest desire to be good through the example of this good woman. He would try henceforward to be worthy of the things she had revealed. Quietly, without hysterical prayers or banging of drums, he underwent conversion. He was saved. (p. 192.)

Saved, needless to say, by faith and not by works.

But something more than this happens when, in the last chapter, Philip not only observes others in love but falls in love himself. For a moment it appears that Forster will wind the book up as a romantic comedy, for the male and female protagonists approach each other almost as sexual beings. Philip seems about to overcome his solipsistic despair and, by a peculiar reversal of the Platonic route, to find his way at last from the beauties of Caroline's soul to those of her body. He seems to discover, with Wallace Stevens, that "Beauty is momentary in the mind. . . . But in the flesh it is immortal."[11] "By this time he loved her very much. . . . He had reached love by the spiritual path: her thoughts and her goodness and her nobility had moved him first, and now her whole body and all its gestures had become transfigured by them. The beauties that are called obvious—the beauties of her hair and her voice and her limbs—he had noticed these last." (p. 196.) The conversion comes in a railway carriage: "The train seemed to shake him towards her"[12]—as though he or his author were trying to blame the machine for the all-but-shameful act. Stirred, he turned to embrace her, even in this public place. "Their faces were crimson, as if the same thought was surging through them both." He begs her to "say the word plainly," and she does, uttering what ought to be the novel's crowning irony and most painful experience. She says that she is in love with Gino, crudely and carnally in love with him. She rubs the point in: "I love him, and I'm not ashamed of it. I love him, and I'm going to Sawston, and if I mayn't speak about him to you sometimes, I shall die." And later: "Get over supposing I'm refined. That's what puzzles you. Get over that." (pp. 202–4.)

Philip is not shocked, dismayed, or even disappointed. "He did not lament" and at the moment of her confession he too bursts out, almost joyously, "Rather! I love him too!" Thus he makes common cause with the woman, both the woman there on the seat beside him and the woman within himself. For one passing instant he knows something like jealousy, when the thought of Caroline and Gino together reminds him of Pasiphae, mated with a bull by the "cruel antique malice of the gods." But this turns out to be more a lament for the "centuries of aspiration and culture" that seem to him repudiated and mocked by the persistence of the sexual drive than a lament for the loss of Caroline's person. Caroline too, though her love is unrequited, speaks like a Beatrice or a Laura of being "saved" by Gino's regarding her as "a superior being—a goddess" (p. 204). They have both found the love of love, and G. E. Moore would have been proud of them. Philip's brief carnal blush fades to a saintly pallor. The undutiful son still manages to be the good boy.

The novel ends with the pair gazing intently toward the past. For Philip "all the wonderful things had happened." For Caroline, Philip "had made her life endurable" (p. 205). Endurance may be the more creditable solution, but actually both are barely enduring. In spite of editorial protestations about their quasi-mystical happiness, the novel fairly screams their panic and emptiness, especially Philip's. His father is nonexistent; his mother is a witch. He had identified with the mother and been her slave, but now that identification is finished. Instead, he identifies with the other woman, the *donna angelica,* a kindly goddess of love who will return him something for the loss of his manhood. He cannot be her mate because, between the two of them, these women have taken all his maleness, and rather than face this awful fact he puts them both out of reach—the one in Hell, the other in Heaven. But it is because he has so dispatched them that he is so little jealous of Gino. He loves Gino just as Caroline does, but he has (imaginatively) put his feminine rival out of the competition. Even in his weak and unfocused homosexuality, he needs his goddess to lead the way.

So the comedy of this book is mainly a study in the devices whereby the leading character can avoid facing the "tragedy" within himself. Philip has two resources, to find life "funny" and to find it "beautiful" (p. 201), and these are the resources we discover as comedy and prophecy. But comedy and prophecy do not go well together, and when both appear in the same book each undercuts the other. "It is a pity," writes Forster, "that Man cannot be at the same time impressive and truthful."[13] Philip, having no center, prevents our laughing at his prophetic stances by being so quick to laugh at himself; yet at the same time he lets us know that this laughter is his truth. He cannot be both impressive and truthful. His tone is exactly that of Prufrock: "I am no prophet—and here's no great matter." By this ambivalence he at last acquires something we can recognize as a character, a character that continually tears itself down as it builds itself up.

There is something horrible, as well as amusing, about this continual suicide and rebirth, this laughing at one's own spiritual funeral.

His plight is an existential absurdity, since his frustration is so fundamental: it is not that he cannot find the right woman or the right
man, it is that he cannot find himself. He wanders in his inner
labyrinth piecing together the clues that will interpret what he sees
in the mirror. We may say that the persona is comic while the person
is not, but in the long run we have trouble telling the masks from
the man. The quality of the book (Philip's quality) is exactly suggested by passages like the following, which again and again stain
the comic surface, only to disappear:

Philip gazed after her mournfully, and then he looked mournfully out of
the window at the decreasing streams. All the excitement was over—the in-
quest, Harriet's short illness, his own visit to the surgeon. He was convalescent, both in body and spirit, but convalescence brought no joy. In the look-
ing-glass at the end of the corridor he saw his face haggard, and his shoulders
pulled forward by the weight of the sling. Life was greater than he had supposed, but it was even less complete. He had seen the need for strenuous
work and for righteousness. And now he saw what a very little way those
things would go. (p. 197.)

In no other novel by Forster does a character so often look at himself in the mirror. Yet in the next book, Forster gives us a far more
intimate portrait of the artist, and shows a far more desperate search
for the self. If Philip Herriton is the observer of life, Rickie Elliot
tries to become a participant.

Chapter eight

The Longest Journey:
The Slaughter of the Innocent

The greatest poverty is not to live
In a physical world, to feel that one's desire
Is too difficult to tell from despair.
—Wallace Stevens

A self, every instant it exists, is in process of becoming,
for the self . . . does not actually exist, it is only that
which it is to become.
—Kierkegaard

For all their talk about Art and Poetry as absolutes, Bloomsbury produced no poets, no respectable critics of poetry, and very few practicing artists. In literature, only Forster and Virginia Woolf are eminent, and the works of both are sapped by a moral anxiety to sacrifice dramatic representation for some swifter, purer, more direct statement of truth. Forster resists this anxiety more successfully than Virginia Woolf (whom he characterizes as "a poet, who wants to write something as near to a novel as possible"),[1] but both have a strong tendency toward what we might call anti-art or at least anti-literature: a tendency to be so interested in life as a spiritual event that one feels a kind of contempt for the display of its body. It cannot be said of Forster, as it has been of Norman Mailer, that he "radically distrusts art,"[2] yet often in his work cross-purposes seem as active as purposes—and give the hint of impish censors at work.

If this seems a surprising statement, one should re-read *The Longest Journey*: it demonstrates more clearly than any other Forster novel the war between his moral and esthetic impulses. In this confused and fascinating book, art as a redemptive device clashes continually with art as a dramatization of experience. It is a flawed novel because the forces of anti-literature drain its strength, and those forces derive from the mixed motives behind it. Dangerous as it is to tax a novelist with doing in his own book what he did not fully understand he was doing, that is very nearly what we must say of this book.

The Longest Journey is a portrait of the artist, but it is also a portrait of the non-artist, a negation of art that foreshadows Forster's own retirement. It clearly serves Forster as a way of assuming surrogate roles, of trying on new experience, of working, mole-like, out of a deep and crushing psychological repression. These uses are not, of course, antithetical to art. But as the book does its author these services, it does him an equal and opposite disservice by so surrounding Rickie, the ego character, with an ironic chorus (in which Forster participates) that we end by seriously wondering whether Rickie is supposed to be all or nothing, somebody or nobody, and whether there is any way of reconciling in one fiction his author's confusing overplus of self-love and self-hate. Forster, in short, is a part of Rickie's confusion, and the book shows it.

2

Forster's own statement about the book is the best place to begin:

> *The Longest Journey* is the least popular of my five novels but the one I am most glad to have written. For in it I have managed to get nearer than elsewhere towards what was in my mind—or rather towards that junction of mind with heart where the creative impulse sparks. Thoughts and emotions collided if they did not always co-operate. I can remember writing it and how excited I was and how absorbed, and how sometimes I went wrong deliberately, as if the spirit of anti-literature had jogged my elbow.* For all its faults, it is the only one of my books that has come upon me without my knowledge. Elsewhere I have had to look into the lumber-room of my past, and have found in it things that were useful to be sure; still I found them, they didn't find me, and the magic sense of being visited and of even returning the visit was absent.[3]

This intriguing statement raises as many questions as it answers. What does he mean by saying that the book came upon him without his "knowledge"? Probably that it came in a flow of inspiration, without much conscious planning—that he "sat down" on it.† But if that

---

* Forster, when asked to explain what was meant by "the spirit of anti-literature," replied: "In those immature days I enjoyed the idea of doing flattering imitations of literature." Conversation, March 8, 1965.

† In a piece called "Inspiration" Forster writes: "Experiences vary, but most writers when they compose seem to go through some such process as follows. They start pretty calm. . . . They write a few sentences very slowly and feel constricted and

is so, what purpose could possibly be served by the perversity of going wrong "deliberately" (which seems to contradict the idea of inspiration)? Whatever the reason for such tricks, the first critics of the book found plenty here that seemed wrong. The sudden deaths, the laxity of the construction, the anemic quality of the hero, the "abnormality" of the author's invention, the "almost brutal cynicism" of some of his humor, the contrived crises (which needed but a "slight geniality" in the author in order to have been avoided), were some of the evidences of anti-literature the reviewers found.[4] Even granting that not all these blemishes were intentional, why the practice at all? Did he have something to hide, some "scandal" from which the reader's attention might be deflected by these irritating decoys? Or did he perhaps not want readers looking too closely at Rickie as an authorial self-portrait (or at other characters drawn closely from life), and hence entangled them in awkward, but unmistakably fictional, contrivances?

That there is some validity in the second supposition is evident. To the question, "Do any of your characters represent yourself at all?" Forster replied, "Rickie more than any."[5] And other characters, often in bits and pieces, have been modeled on members of his family or his friends. Mrs. Failing (Rickie's Aunt Emily), Forster tells us, was created from an actual Uncle Willie, but the name may have been borrowed from that real Aunt Emily in the Thornton history who eloped to Denmark, as Rickie's mother did to Stockholm.[6] Ansell was the name of a childhood friend, a young garden boy, who, writes Forster, "probably did more than any one towards armouring me against life" (MT, 275). The Elliots, Rickie's parents, bear the name (in altered spelling) of two eminent Clapham families; Wonham, Forster tells us, was a remembered country name;[7] and Mr. Jackson,

---

used up. Then a queer catastrophe happens inside them. The mind, as it were, turns turtle, sometimes with rapidity, and a hidden part of it comes to the top and controls the pen. Quicker and quicker the writer works, his head grows hot, he looks far from handsome, he spoils the lunch and he lets out the fire. He is not exactly 'rapt'; on the contrary he feels more himself than usual, and lives in a state which he is convinced should be his normal one, though it isn't. On returning to his normal state, he reads over what he has written. It surprises him. He couldn't do it again. He can't explain to the reader how it was done. He can't remember whether plot or character was considered first, whether the work was conceived as a whole or bit by bit. If he started with a plan it is all forgotten or faded. . . . It is a reality outside his ordinary self." "Inspiration," *The Author*, XXII (1912), 281.

the enthusiast for the classics who "makes the past live" and knows the difference between "the golden mean and the pinchbeck mean,"[8] undoubtedly owes some of his qualities to Nathaniel Wedd. Forster likes "secrets from the reader" and there are doubtless more than these. The Uncle Willie* mentioned above, "a meddlesome tease of a man," bought up some remaindered copies of the book "and sent them to those of my relations whom they were most likely to upset."[9] This would not be a likely procedure unless the book were in some sense a *roman à clef,* hiding identities that beg to be discovered by those in the know. "When the book of life is opening," muses the young Rickie, "our readings are secret, and we are unwilling to give chapter and verse." (p. 42.) Maybe so. But some secrets are prized to be lost; and this book of life is coy rather than truly private, making of reticence an appeal for attention and sympathy.†

In a sense, however, the book's malformations give form to its theme. Just as the book cannot decide whether to become (in Northrop Frye's terms) a confession, a romance, or a novel,[10] so Rickie is tormented about what kind of man to become—a monk, a hero, or a solid citizen. "To write one kind of book is always to some extent a repudiation of other kinds,"[11] writes Wayne Booth, and these generic indecisions may offer the most useful way to approach the book's peculiar travail. In its confessional phase the book reflects the tradition of the *Künstlerroman,* that modern literature of the mind in dialogue with itself represented by Rousseau's *Confessions,* Goethe's *Sorrows of Young Werther,* Mark Rutherford's *Autobiography,* Joyce's *Portrait,* Gide's *Counterfeiters,* and, to take a memorable recent instance, Doris Lessing's *The Golden Notebook.* These books are drops in a flood. The last century and a half could well be named the era of self-confession, for no major writer has failed to present, as a significant part of his work, his own examined life—in auto-

---

*Uncle Willie is directly mentioned at least once in the book when Agnes implores Rickie, "Couldn't you make your stories more obvious? I don't see any harm in that. Uncle Willie floundered hopelessly." (p. 162.)

† If the people are disguised, the places are not. The three geographical settings that name its three parts—Cambridge, Wiltshire, and that universal suburb Sawston (the name of a town near Cambridge)—are obviously drawn from memory. They too are "in" the plot, for, as Forster emphasizes, "places have a genius, though the less we talk about it the better." (p. 69.)

biographies and memoirs, or in the pseudonymous or anonymous shadows of novels or poems. "All serious work in literature is auto-biographical," writes Thomas Wolfe, and this literature (though it serves all kinds of private motives) dramatizes more than anything else the modern sense of alienation, the sense of separation from God, from tradition, from a community, from one's self. It is not safe to generalize about a literature so various, but it is incontestable that much of it is the appeal of lonely or isolated individuals to a reading public for sympathy, approval, and justification. It addresses itself to a human audience as, in an earlier day, men would have addressed themselves to God; it implicitly reminds us that we are all in the same boat. It has, of course, been remarked that these "personal" motives often are too great a freight for the novel or the poem to bear. "The more perfect the artist," writes T. S. Eliot, "the more completely sepa-rate in him will be the man who suffers and the mind which creates."[12] The confusions of *The Longest Journey* would seem to indicate that Forster, when he wrote this book, was barely able to make the separa-tion at all.

In the confession, the first-person speaker is more often than not a self-examining weakling and a failure—drawn, of course, from real life. But in romance the leading figure is usually heroic; he is intui-tive, impulsive, and even stupid, and he engages neither in self-analy-sis nor in confessing his mistakes.* He is a man of faith and action, a larger-than-life figure who confidently confronts the ghosts, giants, and dragons of experience with a courage that does not calculate the odds. "The romancer," writes Northrop Frye, "does not attempt to create 'real people' so much as stylized figures which expand into psy-chological archetypes. It is in the romance that we find Jung's libido, anima, and shadow reflected in the hero, heroine, and villain respec-tively."[13] The reader of *The Longest Journey* is soon aware that this is no ordinary novel striving for realism.[14] Rickie's father, for ex-ample, who remarks of his son, "He worries me. . . . He's a joke of

---

* The term romance is here used broadly, as Northrop Frye uses it, and includes such forms as allegory, fairy tale, prophecy, myth, romantic tragedy, gothic fiction, and epic. In it character and action tend to be symbolic rather than realistic, and its leading figures to be, if not heroic, at least representative of more than them-selves.

which I have got tired" (p. 33), is so fiercely drawn, so hateful in
every way, that we recognize him as a projection of the author's conscious or unconscious hatred, a figure out of fairy tale or allegory
rather than a "character" from realistic fiction. For all his conventional dress, he is a satanic monster, an oedipal grotesque;* and
Rickie himself, most of the time, reads his own experience not prag-
matically but symbolically: " 'It seems to me that here and there in
life we meet with a person or incident that is symbolical. It's nothing
in itself, yet for the moment it stands for some eternal principle. We
accept it, at whatever cost, and we have accepted life. But if we are
frightened and reject it, the moment, so to speak, passes; the symbol
is never offered again.' " (p. 157.) It is part of the hero's "test" to recognize such symbols and interpret them correctly as well as to act
upon that knowledge. It is also the hero's duty to stand fast against
those who would destroy his faith in his own insights and visions—
as Agnes Pembroke constantly tries to destroy Rickie's: " 'My own
boy won't be fantastic, will he?' Then she fought the fantasy on its
own ground. 'And, by the bye, what you call the "symbolic moment"
is over.' " (p. 158.)

Rickie is tested, and his test is traditional in having three phases,
here suggested by the three parts of the book: Cambridge, Sawston,
and Wiltshire. The triad itself should be noted. Such a division is
fairly common in Forster's work,† invariably serving to bring the
reader into touch with some large, ordering generalities; and it has
a cultural history that Forster may be unconsciously reflecting. Robert Lee Wolff has shown that the habit of thinking in triads was popu-
larized in the West by Joachim of Fiore (1145–1202), who advanced
the notion that "the third age of the universe, the age of the third
member of the Trinity, would find its revelation in a third Testament, as the first two ages had been respectively that of the Father and
the Old Testament, and that of the Son and the New."[15] Modern re-
appearances of the same habit of mind occur in Comte's notion of

---

* When Forster was asked why he made Rickie's father so hateful, he replied:
"He just suited the book." Conversation with Forster, March 8, 1965.

† In *Angels* we find "the Palazzo Pubblico, the Collegiate Church, and the Caffè
Garibaldi: the intellect, the soul, and the body" (see Plate 17). *Passage* is divided
into three main sections: Mosque, Caves, Temple.

the theological, metaphysical, and scientific phases of history; Hegel's idea of thesis, antithesis, and synthesis; the Marxian dialectic of primitive communism, class society, and the classless society; and even Hitler's notion of the Third Reich, a title adopted by the Nazis "because they sensed that it retained the age-old emotional impact of the third and final member of a triad."[16] Forster senses the emotive and mystical force of the triad, and this book and others are in a sense versions of the Third Testament that Joachim called for. In the symphonic interplay of the book's three movements (corresponding to Aristotle's triad of complication, crisis, and solution) we have the instrument, if not the matter, for a grand assertion.[17]

But is Rickie a hero, or is he only pathetic? The word "tragedy" is used generously throughout the book,* and tragedy, as Joseph Wood Krutch has pointed out, must have a hero "if it is not to be merely an accusation against, instead of a justification of, the world in which it occurs."[18] Does Rickie qualify? At first glance he appears to be almost as Prufrockian as Philip Herriton. Lonely, introverted, shy, despised by his father—who called him Rickie ("rickety") because he was lame—and loved by a gentle but ineffectual mother, he grows up with a profound sense that he is ugly and no good. Yet, unlike Philip, he is not simply a puppet or victim. He makes decisions and acts on them (with plenty of advice, pro and con, from the chorus of guardian friends), and these decisions are based on his own intuitions. Moreover, he ends by giving his life for a cause. His final act is, to be sure, so ambiguous that it could indicate accident-proneness as much as courage; nevertheless, it arises from an exercise of will.

But in one fundamental respect he is not tragic, and this qualification must affect our whole reading of the book. He lives and dies in no real hope of setting his present lands in order, but in the name of a future kingdom. He is, therefore, insofar as he is a hero at all, what we might call a prophetic hero. The literature of tragedy differs from that of prophecy in that the one makes a statement about things as they are and the other about things as they might be. Hamlet says of man, "how infinite in capacities, in understanding how like a god,"

---

* Agnes Pembroke, for example, "is not conscious of her tragedy, and therefore only the gods need weep at it." Rickie has a "tragic" marriage. Even the death of Gerald Dawes is called a "tragedy." (pp. 224, 302, 65.)

and the play proceeds to justify human existence by demonstrating that these encomiums are deserved. But the prophetic writer, like Nietzsche, is unhappy with man as he is and makes human perfection an extremely distant event, justifying human existence in terms of the Superman, a hypothetical projection of human possibilities, rather than in terms of its present condition.[19]

To distinguish between the prophetic and the tragic hero is vital, for the theme of this book is reality, and prophecy and tragedy look at reality in radically different ways. The one is, so to speak, Platonic and idealistic, the other Aristotelian and realistic. The tragic hero accepts the reality of the world of appearance and comes to terms with it. The prophetic hero, however, is essentially romantic: he wants to transcend the world of appearance and expects fulfillment not in his own epoch, but in a distant millennium. His reality is an idea—an idea not yet realized. One of Rickie's deepest problems, as he faces his ordeals, is to decide whether his reality is to be found in terms of a now or in terms of a not-yet; whether he will accept his own nature and its consequences, or be content with himself only as an idealized wish-fulfillment.

But before witnessing some of those ordeals, we must note the book's third phase—that of the realistic novel itself. Quite simply, the book assumes the qualities of a novel, as opposed to a romance, when Rickie is trying hardest to become a solid citizen, to live in Sawston and abide by its laws. "The novel," writes Northrop Frye, "tends to be extroverted and personal; its chief interest is in human character as it manifests itself in society," whereas the romance tends to be "introverted and personal," dealing with characters in a more subjective way.[20] Rickie crosses these lines many times; but he makes a serious effort to adjust to society, and when he is in those suburbs we are at our greatest distance from characters and actions viewed symbolically. Then, far from rising to tragic heights, he sinks to bourgeois depths; tragedy (even if Rickie were capable of it) becomes anomalous among the Biedermeier trivialities of that social environment.

But none of these phases—confession, romance, or novel—is distinct. The forms, and the impulses creating them, constantly fade one into another, and occasionally we are struck by a particularly bold transition. Here, for instance, is romance moving toward the novel: "And so Rickie deflected his enthusiasms. Hitherto they had played on gods and heroes, on the infinite and the impossible, on virtue and beauty and strength. Now, with a steadier radiance, they transfigured a man who was dead and a woman who was still alive." (p. 71.) Transfiguration is still involved, but it is occurring closer to human society.

In writing this book Forster was at once bedeviled by "the spirit of anti-literature" and blessed by "the magic sense of being visited." These contradictory experiences can be explained as clashes between the different kinds of fiction the book tries to accommodate. Forster himself attributed the clogged quality of the book to the plethora of "ideas" that accumulated around his basic notion of writing about "a man who discovers he has an illegitimate brother":

> There was the metaphysical idea of Reality ("the cow is there"); there was the ethical idea that reality must be faced (Rickie won't face Stephen); there was the idea, or ideal, of the British Public School; there was the title, exhorting us in the words of Shelley not to love one person only; there was Cambridge, there was Wiltshire. I did not list the above notions consciously, but they were whirling around me as I wrote.[21]

But the trouble arose not so much from the number and clutter of these ideas as from their nature: some invite comic and some prophetic treatment; some take us inside the mind and some outdoors; some are natural conductors to the novel, some to the confession, and some to the romance. How then shall we drag this rich, amorphous book into the center of our minds?[22] An arbitrary but useful way is to read the book as a romance, studying Rickie's three tests or ordeals, and then to note deviations from the norms of romance as they arise.

3

The problem before Rickie is the discovery of his true nature, his "reality." As James said of Browning, the "real is his quest, the very ideal of the real, the real most finely mixed with life, which *is* in the last analysis the ideal."[23] Although the search for this grail is the point of the book, Rickie is not without intimations of his true nature from the beginning—and Forster, joining the chorus of Rickie's friends (who replace the chaperones of earlier fiction), is an ardent partisan whispering in his ear. Rickie knows, for example, that he has a talent for writing and that "the important thing" is freedom to create. He knows too (with Dickinson) that he is strongly pulled toward "friendship" as opposed to marriage. This is one of the critical passages of the book:

Nature has no use for us; she has cut her stuff differently. Dutiful sons, loving husbands, responsible fathers—these are what she wants, and if we are friends it must be in our spare time. Abram and Sarai were sorrowful, yet their seed became as sand of the sea, and distracts the politics of Europe at this moment. But a few verses of poetry is all that survives of David and Jonathan.

"I wish we were labeled," said Rickie. He wished that all the confidence and mutual knowledge that is born in such a place as Cambridge could be organized.... He wished there was a society, a kind of friendship office, where the marriage of true minds could be registered. (LJ, 75–76.)

This latent homosexuality is one of the realities of his nature. He must either courageously face this knowledge and its consequences or else try to force his life into an alien, conventional mold. On one side the great "world" urges him to be a dutiful son, a loving husband, and a responsible father, and on the other the voices of his inner being counsel him not to risk the agony of these trials. Either way, he faces a test—the one of his courage to defy convention, the other of his courage to endure it. He chooses the second course.

The book opens with a debate. A group of Cambridge undergraduates, with Stewart Ansell as philosophic high priest, are considering the question of appearance and reality: Is the cow they are looking at really there? Forster claims to have had G. E. Moore in mind as he wrote this passage,[24] but he may have meant the Cambridge of G. E. Moore rather than the man or his philosophy. But what matters is the problem itself, which stems in its modern phases from Locke's distinction between the secondary qualities, begotten on the mind through the senses, and the primary qualities, like size and shape, which are really *in* the object. What is "out there" and what is "in here"? That, in greatly oversimplified terms, is the problem which fostered the *Künstlerroman* and the other varieties of the modern psychological novel, for it made current the notion that reality (or truth) might be found by examining personal experience—indeed, could be found in no other way—and that reality could be understood in terms of ideas. God is an idea, the moon is an idea, blue is an idea; and for Rickie, his fiancée and marriage and friendship were all ideas, which must be weighed and tested and judged. The innocent Rickie is a poor judge of ideas (he begins with the idea that he can "love everybody"), but his friends in the chorus, Ansell in particular, constantly warn and instruct him. The burden of such constant analysis of experience is enormous, and occasionally Forster intrudes like an affectionate elder brother to help Rickie along with his lessons:

Love, say orderly people, can be fallen into by two methods: (1) through the desires, (2) through the imagination. And if the orderly people are English, they add that (1) is the inferior method, and characteristic of the South. It is inferior. Yet those who pursue it at all events know what they want; they are not puzzling to themselves or ludicrous to others; they do not take the wings of the morning and fly into the uttermost parts of the sea before walking to the registry office; they cannot breed a tragedy quite like Rickie's.

He is, of course, absurdly young—not twenty-one—and he will be engaged to be married at twenty-three. He has no knowledge of the world; for example, he thinks that if you do not want money you can give it to friends who do. He believes in humanity because he knows a dozen decent people. He believes in women because he has loved his mother. And his friends are as young and as ignorant as himself. They are full of the wine of life. But they have not tasted the cup—let us call it the teacup—of experience. . . . Oh, that teacup! To be taken at prayers, at friendship, at love, till we are quite sane, quite efficient, quite experienced, and quite useless to God or man. We must drink it, or we shall die. But we need not drink it always. Here is our problem and our salvation. There comes a moment—God knows when—at which we can say, "I will experience no longer. I will create. I will be an experience." But to do this we must be both acute and heroic. For it is not easy, after accepting six cups of tea, to throw the seventh in the face of the hostess. And to Rickie this moment has not, as yet, been offered.[25]

But the moment comes, and the hostess in whose face he throws the tea is Cambridge herself. Against all her wisest admonitions and ad-monitors, he marries Agnes Pembroke—the woman who Ansell insists does not exist.[26] In doing so he betrays both alma mater and mater, as well as the friends who have helped him to learn what it means to be "both acute and heroic." This heresy is the first phase of his grow-ing-up, and we must try to understand his motives.

As we know, Cambridge has welcomed the friendless Rickie with open arms, giving him freedom, her essential "reality." But it is too much to receive all at once. The frightened boy thaws slowly. During the first term he loves his rooms "better than any person" and often runs to them as to a sanctuary—feeling "almost as safe as he felt once when his mother killed a ghost in the passage by carrying him through it in her arms" (pp. 69, 70). It is the very womb of alma mater. Gradually he gains the self-confidence to emerge from his cell and to make friends. But he is still cautious, guarding his retreat, and his first step is merely to substitute an outdoor sanctuary for an indoor one. "A little this side of Madingley, to the left of the road," Rickie finds a secluded dell*—a place that looks "as big as Switzerland or Norway" and that becomes for him "a kind of church—a church where indeed you could do anything you liked, but where anything you did would be transfigured" (p. 25). (See Plate 21.)

Where anything you did would be transfigured! This is to enjoy election indeed. Such freedom is everything Rickie's childhood was not, and there is rebellion in his love of it. But it is a romantic and childish notion of freedom, ultimately self-annihilating, and Rickie is only half-consciously aware that hiding in dells is a way of confining as well as freeing oneself, that such circles contract as well as expand.† The dell is a symbol of self-defense as well as self-confidence, and within it Rickie ambiguously feels both "extremely tiny" (like a baby) and "extremely important" (like a god). It is, so to speak, a geographical "eternal moment"—a corner of space that exists beyond time.

---

* The "dell" is located just north of the American Cemetery in Cambridge on the road to Madingley. It is a few acres of land overgrown with thickets, the reserve of the Botany Faculty. Though symbolically important, the dell plays only a small part in the action of the novel.

† Circles and rings play an important symbolic role in the book. An incident referred to more than once involves Ansell drawing squares within circles and circles within squares. Rickie asks if they are "real." Ansell replies: "The inside one is— the one in the middle of everything, that there's never room enough to draw." (p. 24.) This is comparable to finding the reality of music in something existing after the music stops playing. In medieval symbolism, to square the circle is to see how the flesh fits into divinity. Ansell's portentous explanation suggests that his doodling has some such mystical overtone.

But no sooner does Rickie find his dell than he is beset by guilt. Should he keep it a secret or share it? Who should be let in and who kept out? In this sanctuary he knows for the first time the joy of intimacy with his guardian-friends, and there is no question about their rights of entry. But he cannot stop there. He has come upon the dell "at a time when his life . . . was beginning to expand" and when he is trying "to love every one equally" (a notion the friends ridicule) (pp. 25, 27). But these ideals of confident, infinite expansion are fundamentally at odds with his almost obsessive need for a well-guarded closeness, the defensive security of a few elect friends, little rooms, little dells.* Rickie sees the problem as a conflict between vulgarity and coarseness ("coarseness revealing something; vulgarity concealing something"),† and he prefers coarseness: " '*Procul este profani!*' exclaimed a delighted aesthete on being introduced to it [the dell]. But this was never to be the attitude of Rickie. He did not love the vulgar herd, but he knew that his own vulgarity would be greater if he forbade it ingress, and that it was not by preciosity that he would attain to the intimate spirit of the dell." (p. 25.)‡ Rick-

---

* Compare *Passage*, p. 41: "We must exclude someone from our gathering, or we shall be left with nothing."

† The distinction is made by Mr. Failing, Rickie's deceased uncle, in one of his notebooks: "Vulgarity, to him, had been the primal curse, the shoddy reticence that prevents man opening his heart to man, the power that makes against equality. From it sprang all the things that he hated—class shibboleths, ladies, lidies, the game laws, the Conservative party—all the things that accent the divergencies rather than the similarities in human nature." (p. 234). (It is only in terms of this definition that we can understand Forster's surprising statement that "the Ninth Symphony . . . may be regarded as an essay in coarseness." "Word-making and Sound-taking," AH, 122.) The distinction has been made in similar terms by a number of other Victorians. Ruskin declared that the true idealist conveys "a *whole* truth, however commonplace. . . . Vulgarity is only in concealment of truth, or in affectation." (Italics in original.) *The Works of John Ruskin*, ed. E. T. Cook and Alexander Wedderburn, V (London, 1903–1912), pp. 112–115, 118. Shaw remarked that "universality of character is impossible without a share of vulgarity" —a statement carrying the same meaning but reversing the terms. Preface to "Man and Superman" in *Nine Plays* (New York, 1948), p. 488. Edward Carpenter writes, "You try to set yourself apart from the vulgar. It is in vain. In that instant vulgarity attaches itself to you." *Towards Democracy* (London, 1912), p. 41.

‡ "*Procul este profani*" stood over the door of a summerhouse on the estate of Countess von Arnim of Nassenheide, in Pomerania, where Forster was a tutor in 1904. See Leslie de Charms, *Elizabeth of the German Garden* (London, 1958), p. 103.

ie's ethical fastidiousness forces him to behave contrary to his taste and sensibility. He becomes the possessor of a Nietzschean "bad conscience," that generator of one of the greatest and most disastrous of modern maladies: man's "sickness of himself, brought on by the violent severance from his animal past . . . [and his] old instincts." "Bad conscience," writes Nietzsche, "the desire for self-mortification, is the wellspring of all altruistic values."[27] Rickie goes against his own grain and chooses the hard way: he invites in people he does not like. It is a perverse altruism, entirely consonant with his puritan heritage: the path of justification is still not the path of desire.

But it is not just a matter of conscience, or at least not of conscience as usually understood. It is a matter, almost, of psychological compulsion. Who should be let in? The implied answer is unequivocal: *everybody*—not just this and that individual, but everybody, however lowbrow or unwashed. Why such universality and absoluteness? The answer would seem to lie in what Jung describes as the incest-guilt— an explanation particularly interesting in that it allows one to see a strong connection between the other uses of this book and its use as a private myth, an instrument of redemption.

The desire to hide in dells is the desire to hide in the mother. Such a desire is a normal expression of infantile sexuality, but in the grown boy or man it is felt as shameful, for this fantasy-return symbolically violates the strictest of our taboos, that against incest. Though the return to the womb is *only* symbolic, the desire to return—however unconscious—carries some heavy penalties of guilt. In a chapter of *Psychology of the Unconscious* called "The Sacrifice," Jung perfectly describes the Rickie of the dell: "This hero, of many words, who performs few deeds and indulges in futile yearnings, is the libido which has not fulfilled its destiny, but which turns round and round in the kingdom of the mother, and, in spite of all its longing, accomplishes nothing."[28] Maturity is achieved only by breaking out of this magic circle and by investing the libido elsewhere; failure to do so breeds melancholy, guilt, a death-in-life. Jung continues:

It is the striving of the libido away *from the mother towards the mother.* This paradoxical sentence may be translated as follows: as long as the libido is satisfied merely with fantasies, it moves in itself, in its own depths, in the mother. When the longing . . . rises in order to escape the magic circle of the incestuous, and therefore pernicious, object, and it does not succeed in finding reality, then the object is and remains irrevocably the mother. Only the overcoming of the obstacles of reality brings the deliverance from the mother, who is the continuous and inexhaustible source of life for the creator, but death for the cowardly, timid and sluggish.[29]

Rickie wants to let everyone into his dell (though, presumably, not everyone wants to come) because once everyone is within that symbolic hollow his guilt will go away. If all mankind makes this return and shares this shame, then we shall have wiped out contrast, this and that, good and evil—we shall have gotten, with Ansell and Rickie, "behind right and wrong" (p. 278). The need for this universal companionship nags at Rickie, for it is either this everything or something close to nothing. If we are all gathered together in the Garden, then we shall antedate sin. He wants, in short, his own version of McTaggart's Absolute or Moore's Good. The passage from Shelley's *Epipsychidion* from which the book gets its title exhorts us "not to love one person only,"[30] for such spiritual monogamy inhibits the possibilities of universal brotherhood. Shelley would have us "transcend the boundaries of individuality between persons just as Indian philosophy or Schopenhauer wants us to overcome the curse and burden of the *principium individuationis*."[31] The poem's exhortation fits perfectly with Rickie's idealization of the dell—and with the filial hostilities behind it:

> I never was attached to that great sect
> Whose doctrine is that each one should select
> Out of the world a mistress or a friend,
> And all the rest, though fair and wise, commend
> To cold oblivion,—though it is the code
> Of modern morals, and the beaten road
> Which those poor slaves with weary footsteps tread
> Who travel to their home among the dead
> By the broad highway of the world,—and so
> With one sad friend, perhaps a jealous foe,
> The dreariest and the longest journey go.[32]

But Rickie is not so deluded as to think that life can be simplified to the confines of a dell; this fantasy only sets the stage for a test. He "believes in women because he has loved his mother,"[33] but can he love a woman? This must be the test not only of his virility, but also of his manhood in a greater sense—his power to resist the lotus-like charms of a perpetual return and to stand free as an independent human being. In trying to love Agnes, he defies the advice and invites the wrath of Ansell. Ansell sees her (when he admits that she is visible at all)[34] as Rickie's true enemy, the female predator who will use him, partly as a replacement for her earlier lover and partly "to make something" out of him. Then, says Ansell, she will tire of this and come to see only how thin and lame he is: "Having made him thoroughly miserable and degraded, she will bolt—if she can do it like a lady." (p. 94.) In Ansell's opinion, friendship is Rickie's "reality," not marriage, and following Rickie's engagement he declares "war"— motivated partly by sexual jealousy of Agnes and partly by a hatred of the female sex. His words stir the suspicion that he has recently been reading *Man and Superman*:[35]

"You are not a person who ought to marry at all. You are unfitted in body: that we once discussed. You are also unfitted in soul: you want and you need to like many people, and a man of that sort ought not to marry. 'You never were attached to that great sect' who can like one person only, and if you try to enter it you will find destruction.... Man wants to love mankind; woman wants to love one man. When she has him her work is over. She is the emissary of Nature, and Nature's bidding has been fulfilled. But man does not care a damn for Nature—or at least only a very little damn." (p. 95.)

Rickie shares this misogyny, but he is also fighting that other ghost, the fear of sexual inadequacy, which Ansell knows almost nothing about. Half-paralyzed by the very fear he is facing, Rickie can neither deny the woman nor acknowledge her. Agnes is the aggressor; and it is in his own dell that she snares him. At first he refuses to enter the sacred place with her, but when she calls to him, he follows as if bewitched. Their first words recall the story "Other Kingdom":

"Did you take me for the Dryad?" she asked. She was sitting down with his head on her lap. He had laid it there for a moment before he went out to die, and she had not let him take it away.
   "I prayed you might not be a woman,"* he whispered.
   "Darling, I am very much a woman. I do not vanish into groves and trees. I thought you would never come to me."[36]

---

* Compare Birkin in Lawrence's *Women in Love*: "I want a woman I don't see." (New York, 1922), p. 167.

"Before he went out to die"—it is a sexual death in the sense of the
old pun, but it is also for Rickie, the initiate into the "great sect,"
a spiritual dying. He acts like one in the grip of some painful moral
compulsion, doing what he knows he must do, though it nauseates
him. To admit this woman is to betray the mother, whose temple the
dell really is; but not to admit her would be to abandon his own
chances for manhood. However wrong she is for him, however false
he is to his own "reality" in taking her, it would be suicidal in Rickie
not to make the experiment.

Still, Rickie's misogyny is powerful, and one of the strangest scenes
in this strange book is the one in which Rickie accidentally witnesses
a passionate embrace between Agnes and Gerald Dawes, her first
fiancé. An athlete and a swaggerer, Gerald had bullied Rickie at
school, and a certain tension still exists between them: "The bully
and his victim never quite forget their first relations" (p. 47). Gerald
is so unregenerate in his boorishness and physicality that, like Rickie's
father, he becomes an archetypal figure, more a scapegoat for Rickie's
unconscious hatreds and fears than a person in his own right. But,
though he is repelled by Gerald, Rickie is attracted as well. He is
stirred by Gerald's physical beauty—"Just where he began to be beautiful the clothes started" (p. 43)—and is tempted to idealize him.
Rickie, says Forster, has "escaped the sin of despising the physically
strong—a sin against which the physically weak must guard" (p. 46).
But he has not escaped; he despises and envies at once, and the only
way he can acknowledge his attraction is to transfigure it, to translate
lust into transcendent love. The embrace of Gerald and Agnes is a
signal for the prose to burst into a riot of color and music, which
mounts to an orchestral triumph almost embarrassing in its excess.
Rickie is able to tolerate the shock only by receiving it as "poetry."
One glimpse of the carnal facts filled this Acteon with guilt rather
than with desire, and drove him, hysterically rhapsodizing, to the
safety of an over-ripe empyrean:

He thought, "Do such things actually happen?" and he seemed to be looking
down coloured valleys. Brighter they glowed, till gods of pure flame were
born in them, and then he was looking at pinnacles of virgin snow. . . . Music flowed past him like a river. He stood at the springs of creation and heard
the primeval monotony. Then an obscure instrument gave out a little

phrase. The river continued unheeding. The phrase was repeated, and a listener might know it was a fragment of the Tune of tunes. Nobler instruments accepted it, the clarionet protected, the brass encouraged, and it rose to the surface to the whisper of violins. In full unison was Love born, flame of the flame, flushing the dark river beneath him and the virgin snows above. . . . Creation, no longer monotonous, acclaimed him, in widening melody, in brighter radiances. Was Love a column of fire? Was he a torrent of song? Was he greater than either—the touch of a man on a woman?

It was the merest accident that Rickie had not been disgusted. But this he could not know. (p. 49.)

It is a fascinating passage and shows, among other things, the technique of "rhythm" in an early stage of development—that "little phrase" serving somewhat as the little phrase of the Vinteuil sonata does over a wider space in Proust's book. If, as Pater says, "All art constantly aspires towards the condition of music,"[37] then we have here a remarkable instance of such aspiration. But more interesting is the palinode of the last paragraph, the return from prophecy to realism, from the romance to the novel; it reminds us that Forster is not Rickie merely, but Rickie's brother, friend, and psychoanalyst. We are relieved to know that Rickie's creator recognizes this explosion of fair images to be the defensive show of one in panic fear about his own potency. But we are disturbed by the feeling that Forster believes in both the passage and its retraction, that the irony is no literary device for making a thematic point, but the inadvertence of an author who has simply not yet made up his mind whether he is or is not going to side with his fictional self. Some of these ambiguities are intensified in the action that follows the passage just quoted.

Soon after the great embrace, Gerald—his use as scapegoat exhausted—meets sudden death ("He was broken up in the football match"). Rickie seizes the opportunity and transfigures what he has seen of their love into an eternal moment.* "Mind it," he says of

---

* That their transfiguration provides Rickie with a rationalization for not facing his sexual trauma is clear in the following passage: "He thought of her awake. He entertained her willingly in dreams. He found her in poetry and music and in the sunset. She made him kind and strong. She made him clever. Through her he kept Cambridge in its proper place, and lived as a citizen of the great world. But one night he dreamt that she lay in his arms. This displeased him. He determined to think a little about Gerald instead. Then the fabric collapsed." The continuation of the passage is equally relevant: "It was hard on Rickie thus to meet the

Gerald's death to Agnes. "It's the worst thing that can ever happen to you in all your life, and you've got to mind it—you've got to mind it." (p. 63.) A cruel thing to say, yet only if someone minds it can the event, which a modern pain-killer would reduce to insignificance or absurdity, have tragic implications. And only by having Agnes "mind it" can Rickie be saved, for his deliverance hangs on the vicarious potency represented in that *minded* reality. The memory of that embrace is Rickie's life in the body (or most of it), the half of life he tolerates as beauty but detests as touch, and to make it real he is willing even to invite Gerald's ghost to share his marriage bed. "His love desired not ownership but confidence, and to a love so pure* it does not seem terrible to come second." (p. 190.) Long after Agnes becomes his wife and the fatal corruption of marriage has begun its work, that splendid moment is still desired: "Love had shown him its infinities already. Neither by marriage nor by any other device can men insure themselves a vision; and Rickie's had been granted him three years before, when he had seen his wife and a dead man clasped in each other's arms. She was never to be so real to him again." (p. 189.) Earlier Rickie had said, "Never forget that your greatest thing is over. . . . What he gave you then is greater than anything you will get from me." (p. 87.)† It is perfectly true. This is one of Forster's horribly unfair marriages, designed, so it would seem, primarily to make the partners suffer, to teach them both a lesson (though Forster does not pity each of the sufferers equally). When a

---

devil. He did not deserve it, for he was comparatively civilized, and knew that there was nothing shameful in love. But to love this woman! If only it had been any one else! Love in return—that he could expect from no one, being too ugly and too unattractive. But the love he offered would not then have been vile. The insult to Miss Pembroke, who was consecrated, and whom he had consecrated, who could still see Gerald, and always would see him, shining on his everlasting throne —this was the crime from the devil, the crime that no penance would ever purge. She knew nothing. She never would know. But the crime was registered in heaven." LJ, 77–78. A more vivid instance of self-loathing would be hard to find in modern literature.

  * It is one of the ambiguities of this book that we cannot be sure whether phrases like this one are meant ironically or not.

  † Such great moments are frequent in Forster's fiction. Consider Caroline to Philip in WA: "The wonderful things are over" (p. 199).

child is born, the event seems as improbable as one of the book's sudden deaths, for Rickie has cast himself as a voyeur at the foot of the bed rather than as a man in it.

4

The second part of the book concerns Rickie's encounter with Sawston and his slow destruction by marriage and middle-class conventions. Ansell has washed his hands of him. He is at the mercy of Agnes, her brother Herbert (Headmaster of Sawston School), and—less directly—a third "unreal" person, his aunt Emily, Mrs. Failing. Sawston, where the parents live, stands for all that would confine the soul, kill the imagination, and put respectability before honesty. Herbert, its chief male representative, "had but one test for things—success: success for the body in this life or for the soul in the life to come" (p. 188). Rickie, since he is expected to teach these values at Herbert's school,* tries to assume them, to surrender his freedom to the "beneficent machine." It is the downward path ("he lost his independence—almost without knowing it"), and Agnes becomes Herbert's accomplice in hastening Rickie's disintegration. Since his writing has not sold, Agnes—who has always "mistrusted the little stories"[38] even as she "pushed" them—is delighted that he must now climb a more ordinary ladder of success. "How could Rickie, or any one," she asks, "make a living by pretending that Greek gods were alive, or that young ladies could vanish into trees?" (p. 172.) Though the self-doubting Rickie half believes her, he feels joy flowing out of him and prays "to be delivered from the shadow of unreality that had begun to darken the world." In his weakness (and his extreme, if unconscious, hostility) he is both deceived and self-deceived: "It was as if some

---

* In a review of *The Old School* edited by Graham Greene and containing autobiographical reminiscences of public-school experiences by Sean O'Faolain, E. Arnot Robertson, Stephen Spender, and Graham Greene, Forster writes an imaginary dialogue between Herbert and Agnes. He closes with this important remark: "Mr. Herbert Pembroke and his sister fade away into ghosts. They have been evoked for a moment from a forgotten novel in which, nearly thirty years back, I tried to write about this same topic of one's old school. I did not like mine. I felt towards it what most of the contributors to this volume feel towards theirs, and the Pembrokes were what is now called a compensation-device. I invented them in order to get back a bit of my own." "The Old School," *The Spectator*, CLIII (1934), 136.

power had pronounced against him—as if, by some heedless action, he had offended an Olympian god." This deception, tragic in his author's eyes, leads Rickie from a preoccupation with reality (or good) as an end in itself to the unreality of "doing good." He thinks to appease the god by "hard uncongenial work": "To do good! For what other reason are we here? Let us give up our refined sensations, and our comforts, and our art, if thereby we can make other people happier and better. The woman he loved had urged him to do good! With a vehemence that surprised her, he exclaimed, 'I'll do it.' " (p. 173.) That resolution echoes (and travesties) a major Victorian resolve. Next to "God," conjectures Walter Houghton, the most popular word in the Victorian vocabulary must have been "work," and work, to an extraordinary extent, had an ideal of service attached to it.[39] Rickie's impulses toward moral action may seem puny and almost funny compared with those of the great Victorians, but they spring from a similar moral anxiety, and they divided him from his art.

With such allies as Herbert and Agnes, Rickie learns to lie, to be habitually false to what he slowly comes to know as his true self, to live without friends. The deterioration sets in during their engagement. Mrs. Failing, who had ignored Rickie, grows attentive now that he seems happier, and she invites him to Wiltshire. Agnes and he visit her at Cadover, "the perilous house" (see Plate 23), which is indeed Rickie's Chapel Perilous. Mrs. Failing is the sister of Rickie's dead and hated father, and one of Forster's most complicated portraits. Vindictive and generous, sympathetic and cruel, intelligent and cold, she elicits from her creator a deeply felt ambivalence.* Pretending to be advanced, she manifests in one mood "a facile vein of Ibsenism" and imagines herself to be "a cold-eyed Scandinavian heroine." Actually, writes Forster, she is "an English old lady, who did not mind giving other people a chill provided it was not infectious." (p. 143.) It seems likely that Marianne Thornton, the dominant busybody, the moneybags who could give and withdraw favors (to the

---

* This ambivalence registers itself in the description of her face: "Her age was between elderly and old, and her forehead was wrinkled with an expression of slight but perpetual pain. But the lines round her mouth indicated that she had laughed a great deal during her life, just as the clean tight skin round her eyes perhaps indicated that she had not often cried." (pp. 99–100.) See the portrait of Marianne Thornton (Plate 3).

mother as well as to the son), sat for at least part of this portrait, and it is a good guess that Mrs. Failing was one of the reasons why the book might have been upsetting to some of Forster's relatives. Mrs. Failing likes to play Lady Bountiful, and one of her human playthings is Stephen Wonham, who turns out to be Rickie's half-brother. Unlike his sophisticated guardian, he is an uncomplicated child of nature—rough, handsome, simple, impulsive, and savagely noble. She keeps him like a pet animal: "It amused her when her *protégé* left the pew, looking bored, athletic, and dishevelled, and groping most obviously for his pipe. She liked to keep a thoroughbred pagan to shock people. 'He's gone to worship Nature,' she whispered. Rickie did not look up." (p. 142.)

Aunt Emily represents all the lovelessness of the father's line, whose defects are symbolized by the lameness appearing in all its members.* Although there is no escaping this physical disability, Rickie has gradually begun, with the help of Cambridge, to escape from the spiritual curse that lies upon his father's house. But now, especially since Agnes has joined forces with Aunt Emily, he is once again being helplessly drawn back under its influence:

Weakly people, if they are not careful, hate one another, and when the weakness is hereditary the temptation increases. Elliots had never got on among themselves. They talked of "The Family," but they always turned outward to the health and beauty that lie so promiscuously about the world. Rickie's father had turned, for a time at all events, to his mother. Rickie himself was turning to Agnes. And Mrs. Failing now was irritable, and unfair to the nephew who was lame like her horrible brother and like herself. ... She longed to shatter him,† but knowing as she did that the human thunderbolt often rebounds and strikes the wielder, she held her hand. (p. 140.)

---

* Perhaps her most characterizing speeches are these: "I say once more, beware of the earth. We are conventional people, and conventions—if you will but see it—are majestic in their way, and will claim us in the end. We do not live for great passions or for great memories or for anything great.... My age is fifty-nine, and I tell you solemnly that the important things in life are little things, and that people are not important at all." (pp. 304–5.)

† In response to Angus Wilson's observation that passivity and gentleness can be "actively used as weapons of defence and be ... destructive to others," Forster declared: "Yes. Indeed they can. But that surely is part of my dislike for cruelty. Yes, Rickie—I could kick him for his lame leg, you know." Angus Wilson, "A Conversation with E. M. Forster," *Encounter*, IX (1957), 55.

Rickie slowly discovers that Agnes's "health and beauty" are only
baits to his destruction. As she makes up to Aunt Emily, she comes
to share in the corruption of the old lady, who so loves to mislead
others that "in the end her private view of false and true was ob-
scured, and she misled herself" (p. 307). Agnes ends by betraying
Rickie: she urges him to "make it up" with Aunt Emily and to "fall
in" with her just because she had given them hospitality. It turns out
that Agnes is only after Aunt Emily's money: "She was legacy-hunt-
ing." (p. 214.)

The crisis between Rickie and Agnes comes when Mrs. Failing
casually and maliciously drops the remark that Stephen is Rickie's
half-brother. Rickie has always longed for a brother. At the age of
twelve he said, " 'Shall I ever have a friend? I don't see how. They
walk too fast. And a brother I shall never have.' " (p. 32.) The news
that he has one causes Rickie to faint dead away. The setting for this
event is important, for his creator also experienced an epiphany on
the very spot where Rickie is struck down.

Aunt Emily reveals the secret during an outing to the "Cadbury
Rings." These are really the Figsbury Rings, prehistoric earthworks
about five miles northeast of Salisbury, which Forster visited on September 12, 1904, and many times thereafter. These Rings, and the
Wiltshire countryside generally, became symbolic for Forster, and his
personal myth is inseparable from them: they are dells with wider
vistas. The Rings are two great circular earthen mounds, an inner
and an outer, topping a sweeping rise overlooking Salisbury and the
Wiltshire downs; a single small tree grows in the center. (See Plate
22.) Like the Marabar Caves of *Passage,* no history connects with
them; their purpose is but dimly known; they seem a silent testimony
of an existence before time and space.* Those earthen circles stirred
Forster profoundly:

I caught fire up on the Rings. A similar experience had already befallen me
in Italy and had produced my first short story. This time it wasn't just looking at a view, it was breathing the air and smelling the fields, and there was

---

* According to Dr. J. K. S. St. Joseph, the earthwork is probably a fort of Iron
Age date. The double ring is unusual in such forts, the inner work doubtless being
the more ancient. James McConkey erroneously calls the Rings "graves of the
ancient dead." See *The Novels of E. M. Forster* (Ithaca, New York, 1957), p. 110.

human reinforcement from the shepherds who grazed up there. They and I talked about nothing—still one of my favourite subjects; I offered a tip of sixpence which was declined, I was offered a pull at a pipe and had to decline. The whole experience was trivial in itself but vital to the novel, for it fructified my meager conception of the half-brothers, and gave Stephen Wonham, the bastard, his home.[40]

As Rickie views the earthworks, he is reminded of that other circle, the dell, where Agnes had ensnared him. She is with him again in this place, among these Rings symbolizing both the possibility of infinities of expansion, and his marital imprisonment. They are a larger version of the ring on her hand, yet they also imply that ultimate, unseen circle of Ansell's diagram—the one there is never any room to draw.* Both horror and splendor reside in these enclosures, and Rickie's moral trial is in large part his unspoken need to understand this symbolism. When Mrs. Failing makes her terrible announcement, the horror becomes uppermost, taking in his mind the form of wheels spinning within wheels. The tree in the center revolves and disappears into a vision of the London room where, he imagines, his father's indiscretions had occurred; the double entrenchment of the Rings gapes wider and wider, "like an unhallowed grave," and "encircled him" (p. 150). The unheroic hero has returned to the mother.

When Mrs. Failing, who had merely wanted to shock Rickie, considers the consequences of her disclosure, she decides, with Agnes concurring, that all knowledge of the relationship should be kept from Stephen. He would simply tell everyone: "His paganism would be too assertive; it might even be in bad taste." (p. 154.) The ladies close ranks and Agnes goes "white with horror" when Rickie urges that Stephen be told. "Tell him now, when everything has been comfortably arranged?" Agnes asks (p. 157). Rickie has no rebuttal to this argument, only an appeal—that this is one of those "symbolical" moments which should not be denied. But when he asks Agnes, "Is this nonsense?" she agrees that it is.

He is again defeated. His lifelong prayer for a brother has been

---

* Compare Nietzsche: "Oh, how could I not be ardent for eternity, and for the nuptial ring of rings—the ring of the return! Never yet have I found the woman from whom I wish children, unless she would be this woman whom I love; for I love thee, O eternity." Quoted in Jung, *Psychology of the Unconscious*, p. 447.

answered, but this brother, the illegitimate spawn of a hated father, becomes part of a nightmare—the nightmare of his own vulgarity. Throughout the book Agnes is haunted by fear of the "abnormal,"[41] and she infects Rickie with the same insidious poison:

She could not feel that Stephen had full human rights. He was illicit, abnormal, worse than a man diseased. And Rickie, remembering whose son he was, gradually adopted her opinion. He, too, came to be glad that his brother had passed from him untried, that the symbolic moment had been rejected. Stephen was the fruit of sin; therefore he was sinful. He, too, became a sexual snob. (p. 160.)

After this, Rickie has a curious breakdown and spends much of the following year in bed. But the crisis of his agony comes months later when he discovers the venality that underlies Agnes's desire to maintain "the family connection." He begs her to stop acting the lie and, with him, to write to Stephen "and tell him he is my father's son," but she refuses. "It was the last time he attempted intimacy." (p. 216.)

Just before this he had entertained one last hope. A child was to be born to them, and though "the glamor of wedlock had faded . . . it dawned on him, as on Ansell, that personal love and marriage only cover one side of the shield, and that on the other is graven the epic of birth."[42] But this "supreme event" proves another horror. His daughter is born lame—her defect is worse than Rickie's—and she soon dies. Agnes "got over the tragedy," as she gets over everything, and Rickie undergoes his ordeal alone. In dreams he sees the threatening faces of his enemies, "his aunt's, his father's, and, worst of all, the triumphant face of his brother" (p. 218). Stephen, the father's bastard, would have children and contribute to the stream of generations, whereas he, the mother's son, would not. He has another dream in which he hears the mother crying, and he speaks to her: " 'Never mind, my darling, never mind,' and a voice echoed, 'Never mind—come away—let them die out—let them die out.' " What fight this hero had has gone out of him: "Henceforward he deteriorates. Let those who censure him suggest what he should do. He has lost the work that he loved, his friends, and his child. He remained conscientious and decent, but the spiritual part of him proceeded towards ruin." (p. 218.)

In preparation for the third section of the book, Stewart Ansell and

Stephen Wonham—like the intellectual and physical halves of Rickie's estranged soul, the Apollonian and the Dionysian*—converge on Sawston to succor their foundering friend and brother. Stewart comes because he senses that his old friend is in trouble. Stephen comes to share the "tremendous news" that he is Rickie's brother—and only incidentally because Mrs. Failing has kicked him out of Cadover for breaking windows and getting drunk. The two emissaries meet for the first time in the garden of Dunwood House and promptly have a fight—thus unconventionally achieving an intimacy that, we are asked to believe, is far more "real" than anything Sawston will ever know. Herbert and Agnes cannot understand or cope with these strange guests. They immediately make the vulgar assumption that Stephen has come to extort money in return for silence about his illegitimacy, and a blank check (already signed by the demoralized Rickie) is waiting for him. Stephen, appalled by such grossness, wanders off muttering "I've made a bad mistake." (p. 250.) When Ansell realizes they have driven Rickie's brother away, he rises like "a Hebrew prophet passionate for satire and the truth," and denounces the Pembrokes before the astonished and delighted boys of the school:

"You're a little afraid Stephen may come back. Don't be afraid. I bring good news. You'll never see him nor any one like him again. I must speak very plainly, for you are all three fools. I don't want you to say afterwards, 'Poor Mr. Ansell tried to be clever.' Generally I don't mind, but I should mind today. Please listen. Stephen is a bully; he drinks; he knocks one down; but he would sooner die than take money from people he did not love." (pp. 253–54.)

---

* It may be of some significance that Ansell is doing a paper on Schopenhauer, a fact mentioned twice in the book (on pp. 76 and 88); Nietzsche quotes Schopenhauer in *The Birth of Tragedy* by way of illustrating the Apollonian and the Dionysian principles. Though Forster denies having read Schopenhauer (conversation, May 14, 1958), there are many parallels in the shape of their thought. Schopenhauer's idea of the dualistic nature of man, divided between compulsive sexual force (akin to the Freudian id) and a yearning toward the transcendence of Idea, is one way of expressing the essential symbolic dichotomy in Forster's work: Pan vs. Sawston, Stephen vs. Rickie, etc. And Schopenhauer's notion, derived indirectly from Kant, that the esthetic state offers the one hope of unity between these contending forces, the one chance for the mind to escape the bondage of the will, seems very close to Forster's notions about the uses of art. Compare Forster's "T. S. Eliot," AH, 106: "Oh, the relief of a world which lived for its sensations and ignored the will." See also Crews, *E. M. Forster: The Perils of Humanism*, pp. 124–32.

It is a speech straight out of melodrama or fairytale, and the author may be not only vindictively paying off old scores, but also trying to atone vicariously for some sins of his own. Forster, we remember, accepted £8,000 from people he did not love, and that may be one reason Stephen, throughout the book, is always called a hero.*

The climax of Ansell's speech is the turning point of the book. He reveals that Stephen is not the son of Rickie's hated father after all, but the son of the beloved mother.† Rickie predictably faints. The rest of the book is an account (by means of a long flashback) of Stephen's birth and of Rickie's attempt to accommodate this unbearable new knowledge to his—now thoroughly corrupted—sense of reality. He had gone along with Agnes in damning Stephen for the sins of his father; now, unless he is to repudiate his love for his mother as well, he must reverse this judgment and the values supporting it. He tries to do so. His first act is to leave his wife and her brother and go off with Stephen and Stewart.

5

The final section of the book, "Wiltshire," is mainly given over to the efforts of Rickie and Stephen to come together. Forster acknowledged that he had trouble with their "junction," with how to make them "intimate"—though "it is all right once they are together."[43] The trouble, which is more psychological than technical, lies in the difficulty of making Rickie's inner experience convincing. Rickie experiences a kind of regeneration, but the Sawston rot has gone too deep to be arrested. He cannot "face" Stephen, just as he has never really faced himself; all his Victorian pruderies about class, sex, and drunkenness are drawn to the surface by this confrontation with a brother who refuses to be idealized. He wants to reform Stephen, to transform him into a "symbol of redemption" (as Caroline did Gino), but Ste-

---

* In early drafts of the book, "Stephen was at one time called Harold and at another Siegfried," suggesting that Byronic and Wagnerian heroes were in Forster's mind. See "Aspect of A Novel," p. 1229.

† There is a suggestive similarity between Mrs. Elliot's adultery—from which Stephen was born—and the marriage of Henry Thornton with Emily Dealtry, his deceased wife's sister, which, under the Marriage Act of 1835, was legally a crime. Henry and Emily eloped probably to Denmark; Mrs. Elliot and her Robert (a farmer) elope to Stockholm. See MT, 174-98.

phen refuses to be used. You can't "own people," he tells Rickie, and he will not let him escape into poetry: "Come with me as a man. . . . Not as a brother; who cares what people did years back? We're alive together and the rest is cant." (pp. 285–86.) Stephen boldly penetrates Rickie's defenses and unconscious hypocrisies: "You don't care about *me* drinking, or to shake *my* hand. It's someone else you want to cure —as it were, that old photograph [of Rickie's mother]. You talk to me, but all the time you look at the photograph." The astuteness of Stephen's insight is only too clear to Rickie:

Then Rickie was heroic no longer. . . . The man was right. He did not love him, even as he had never hated him. In either passion he had degraded him to be a symbol for the vanished past. . . . He longed to be back riding over those windy fields, to be back in those mystic circles, beneath pure sky. Then they could have watched and helped and taught each other, until the word was a reality, and the past not a torn photograph, but Demeter the goddess rejoicing in the spring. Ah, if he had seized those high opportunities! For they led to the highest of all, the symbolic moment, which, if a man accepts, he has accepted life. (pp. 283–84.)

But this is still double-talk. Demeter the goddess is as much a device for not facing Stephen as the torn photograph is, and Rickie goes on passionately fooling himself. He loves Stephen, but he can handle that love only in ideal terms, only by translating Stephen into a romantic hero. But this Rickie's brother will not permit: "Look me in the face. Don't hang on me clothes that don't belong—as you did on your wife, giving her saint's robes, whereas she was simply a woman of her own sort, who needed careful watching." (p. 296.)

Rickie, however, cannot let Stephen *not* be a hero, for Stephen is (as Gerald was in another way) his instrument of sexual deliverance. One of Rickie's anxieties is the question of continuance: Will the father's or the mother's line (and all that each symbolizes) succeed in inheriting the earth?* Rickie, emasculated by women, cannot be that fleshly continuator. He is mama's boy, but Stephen is the mother's son, and it is he who fathers the daughter whose existence guarantees that the maternal line will survive, although the paternal line

* Consider Nietzsche: " 'I want heirs'—thus speaks all that suffers; 'I want children, I do not want *myself*.' " "Thus Spoke Zarathustra," *The Portable Nietzsche*, Walter Kaufmann, ed. (New York, 1954), p. 434.

(which Rickie represents but Stephen does not) will "die out." This is why Stephen is a hero—he can act, he is potent—and this is why Rickie in his moral benightedness despairs over Stephen's drinking, for the hero's defilement is the defilement of the mother and her line. "To yield to temptation is not fatal for most of us. But it was the end of everything for a hero." (That is to say, the end of everything for the hero's ward.) His faith in Stephen slipping away, Rickie

> leant against the parapet and prayed passionately, for he knew that the conventions would claim him soon. God was beyond them, but ah, how far beyond, and to be reached after what degradation! At the end of this childish detour his wife awaited him, not less surely because she was only his wife in name. He was too weak. Books and friends were not enough. Little by little she would claim him and corrupt him and make him what he had been; and the woman he loved [his mother] would die out, in drunkenness, in debauchery, and her strength would be dissipated by a man, her beauty defiled in a man. She would not continue. (pp. 311–12.)

Yet thanks to Rickie, this fear is not fulfilled. In one of the last scenes of the book, Stephen and Rickie are sailing a burning paper boat down a stream at night. The flame makes the arch of a railroad bridge "a fairy tunnel, dropping diamonds," and the two brothers experience the closest intimacy they will ever know. That same night Rickie is killed saving the drunken Stephen from death at the railway crossing. Rickie acts no hero's part—"wearily he did a man's duty" (p. 312), that is all—but from that day onward, Stephen the hero apparently is never to backslide again.

What, if anything, does Rickie's death mean? Rickie is an almost perfect illustration of Jung's infantile hero, who, unable to withstand the retrogressive longing for the mother ("the incestuous libido"), is sacrificed by the author—the ritual sacrifice of a childish self that releases the libido for active life.[44] But how, if Rickie is dead, can he have an active life? He can have it through Stephen, the illegitimate brother, who is Rickie's libido, his sexual vicar, and who assumes for Rickie the entire burden of heroism. "Stephen was a hero. He was a law to himself, and rightly. He was great enough to despise our small moralities." (p. 309.) Rickie is none of these things, and on his deathbed he reaches his moral low in saying to Mrs. Failing, that meanspirited defender of small moralities, "You have been right." (p. 312.) Forster makes his moral collapse savagely complete. Rickie is nothing

—a husk. But it is appropriate that he be a husk, for it is his function to be thrown away, to be shed like an unwanted skin. In a sense, the worse he is, the better. He exists to be sacrificed; he is a totem for all those childish disabilities that his creator hates in himself—the weakness, self-contempt, and repressed hostility that must be got rid of if he is ever to achieve a man's estate. His death is sudden, in that it is gratuitous and unmotivated, but it is absolutely essential to the theme of the book. Had it been carefully motivated and prepared for, Rickie would not have played his ritual part in Forster's redemptive myth, for such symbolic roles do not sort well with psychological realism. Still, Rickie must remain credible as a character. Forster wants him to look like the man on the street even though he is a moral zombie, for novels must, after all, be readable on the train. Rickie is the author's ego-character as well as his anti-ego; it is out of such totally incompatible intentions that this book is made. The healthy, emerging ego is, of course, Stephen, who becomes Rickie's deputy in far more than just a sexual sense. Perhaps man hath no greater love than to lay down his life for his friend, but what Rickie really lays down his life for (or has it laid down for) is the possibility that in a later generation people made like him might love rather than loathe themselves. Rickie, who is nothing, becomes Stephen, who is everything, and if this seems an extravagant conclusion, we should ponder these humble Wonhamian thoughts on the last page of the book: "Though he could not phrase it, he believed that he guided the future of our race, and that, century after century, his thoughts and his passions would triumph in England." (p. 320.)

Perhaps all heroes, tragic or prophetic, exist to be sacrificed, but the tragic hero tends to meet his end at the height of his powers, whereas the prophetic hero (or his prophetic predecessor) tends to be washed up before his end, his death being hardly more than the disposal of some waste matter. But if during his active life the prophetic hero is physically weak and morally decayed, he is not so intellectually; his ideas are all right, even if they are moral ideas. The prophetic hero (or his annunciator) lives, we remember, for the not-yet rather than the now, exempting himself from the normal human condition as if he were a kind of aristocrat who is, in Nietzsche's terms, "beyond good and evil." Thus Rickie, shortly before his death, is vouchsafed a vision: he journeys (with Ansell's help) until he stands "behind right and wrong" (p. 278). From this unique vantage point he sees that the mother "whom he loved had risen from the dead, and might rise again," and this gives him a kind of warrant to be nothing: "Let me die out. She will continue." (p. 278.) Stephen gives the child the name of "their" mother—thus allowing the prophetic hero, in the name of a future possibility, his share of fulfillment, his success-in-failure.

For Stephen continuance is effected through the body, glands, and muscles; for Rickie it is agamic, denatured to a spirit, a word, a voice. When Stephen asks Rickie to leave his wife and follow him into the open world, Rickie follows the promise of the voice, not the words, for therein he hears the voice of the mother:*

The words were kind, yet it was not for their sake that Rickie plunged into the impalpable cloud.† In the voice he had found a surer guarantee. Habits and sex may change with the new generation, features may alter with the play of a private passion, but a voice is apart from these. It lies nearer to the racial essence and perhaps to the divine; it can, at all events, overleap one grave. (p. 286.)

Thus does the novel drift into prophecy, and literature into a music beyond words. Though the word "tragedy" is used throughout the book, Forster fails to give us tragedy for the same reason that, as Krutch has said, "all moderns must fail when they attempt . . . to embrace the tragic spirit as a religious faith."[45] The book is essentially apocalyptic rather than tragic, a book of revelation. And at the heart of that revelation is the vaguely adumbrated faith that the real hero is yet to come—a synthesis of Stephen's body, Ansell's mind, and Rickie's soul into a new being, and perhaps into a new sex.

Although it fails to rise to tragic heights, the book has its moments of brilliant satire. Agnes and Mrs. Failing are impaled like bugs, and Herbert in particular is stripped of the last shred of honor or respect. When Herbert is caught trying to cheat Stephen out of his share of the royalties on Rickie's stories, Stephen collars the dumfounded

---

* In an interview for *The Paris Review* Forster declared, "I find it difficult to recognize people when I meet them; though I remember about them. I remember their voices." "The Art of Fiction," p. 36.

† Compare Luke 9:35: "And there came a voice out of the cloud, saying, This is my beloved Son: Hear him."

schoolmaster and delivers a lecture on retributive justice. Here is
Forster getting back a bit of his own:

Then he went to harness the horse, while Mr. Pembroke, watching his
broad back, desired to bury a knife in it. The desire passed, partly because
it was unclerical, partly because he had no knife, and partly because he soon
blurred over what had happened. To him all criticism was "rudeness": he
never heeded it, for he never needed it: he was never wrong. (pp. 317–18.)

But on the whole the book does not succeed; it tries to do too many
things at once and struggles vainly, as Rickie does, to achieve an
identity. Though of surpassing interest as a private ritual of redemption, its prophetic aspects call for an excessively generous suspension
of disbelief; and, because the book is neither this nor that, we cannot
forgo entirely our judgment of it as a novel, that is to say as an account of experience in which the reader should be able to find some
vicarious satisfaction or meaning. The book is rich in incidental sat-
isfactions and meanings—among which are its stylistic graces—but in
asking us to feel sympathetic toward Rickie (as the author openly
does), the book asks too much. Not only does Forster's sympathetic
identification with Rickie seem a kind of private affair from which
the reader is excluded, but it is nearly impossible to have much fel-
low-feeling for a character who is almost totally obsessed with himself
and yet will take no responsibility for his own existence. Rickie's failure implicitly warns us of what Philip Rieff has called "the personal
position of advanced sensibility: feeling divorced from responsibility,"[46] but that is not a warning his author intended. Rickie moves in
ten days "from disgust to penitence, from penitence to longing, from
a life of horror to a new life, in which he still surprised himself by
unexpected words" (p. 276). But he surprised himself with words, not
acts, just as he had satisfied himself with the idea of love instead of
love, and with a vicarious heroism instead of the real thing. These
abandonments of responsibility suggest that, before we acknowledge
the rights of the meek to inherit the earth, we should check to see
whether their meekness is the expression of virtue or of exhaustion.

But whatever else this book is, it is the record of a rite of passage,
a coming-of-age ceremony; and the writer has clearly shown his witnesses that he has a man and an artist locked within him, struggling
to be let out.

Chapter nine

A Room with a View:
Sex and Sensibility

Who among you can at the same time laugh and be exalted?

—Nietzsche

Forster's fiction is essentially an experiment in self-confidence. One after another his main characters, like so many groundhogs, poke their heads out of their sanctuaries to see whether it is safe to emerge further. Rickie uncautiously goes too far, and dies before he can get back to safety; Philip plays it safe and hardly goes out at all, except in imagination; Kuno gets out momentarily but is hauled back, repentant, into his mother's hold. Of course, not all the books have a main character who so clearly undergoes this particular process of trial and error, but they are all to some degree concerned with the experiment of emergence into the world. And Forster is particularly interested in how those who are too timid or too hurt to emerge very far view the world outside. Hence rooms with views are important; and this book provides a metaphor that illumines a pervasive theme in Forster's fiction.

Forster calls it his "nicest"* book, and the term fits, though it was perhaps meant ambiguously. Forster's fiction is always in some way testing values and roles; here he tries on conventional happiness, the happiness of actual marriage and sexual joy. "Will all the poetry in the world satisfy the manhood of Forster, when Forster knows that his implicit manhood is to be satisfied by nothing but immediate

* "It is not my preferred novel—*The Longest Journey* is that—but it may fairly be called the nicest." "Anniversary Postscript, 'A View Without a Room,'" *The Observer,* July 27, 1958, p. 15.

physical action?"[1] asks D. H. Lawrence. That question haunts *The Longest Journey* like a ghost, but here it is faced—not, indeed by Cecil Vyse, the character with whom Forster acknowledges a distant kinship, but by two remoter avatars: Lucy Honeychurch and George Emerson.*

If it is a nice book, it is so partly because its experiment in self-discovery occurs as it were in the open. It is Forster's most *objective* work; it goes outdoors, is filled with sunshine and light and space, and although the room of *Journey* is still there, it is no longer preferred to people, and it has a view. Instead of trying, as Lawrence says, "to soothe with poetry a man raging with pain which can be cured,"[2] the book transmutes the pain, and relieves it through the presentation of "a hero and heroine who are supposed to be good, good-looking and in love—and who are promised happiness."[3] Although the two do not exactly live happily ever after—since, as Forster indicates in his "Anniversary Postscript," they survived into an age when even decent rooms were hard to come by—they broke out of their isolation and ended still "fond of each other and of their children and grandchildren."[4]

As a piece of writing, *A Room with a View* (1908) is less a new departure for Forster than a cleaning up of old business. The two parts of the book, the Italian and the English, were written years apart, and their contrast makes an interesting measure of Forster's development as an artist. The first half, "almost the first piece of fiction" Forster attempted,[5] recalls the manner of *Angels* with its bold confrontations of comedy and prophecy, pharisees and poets, Sawston and Italy. It tries hard to be romantic comedy and succeeds about as well as *Angels,* the gaiety being constantly threatened by prophetic earnestness.

But the second half, which returns us entirely to England and introduces Cecil Vyse, is *Angels* with the breath of *The Longest Journey* blowing through it. The characters of the first half reappear, but in a different light: now we are invited to see past their frivolities into their souls, to watch the play of motive, and to read their actions and

---

* Forster mentions two characters as drawn from life: "Miss Lavish was actually a Miss Spender. Mrs. Honeychurch was my grandmother." "The Art of Fiction," *The Paris Review,* I (1953), 37, 38.

characters symbolically. Part II explains Part I, and though the momentum of comedy drives deeply into the second half, the two parts dramatize rather sharply the author's ambivalent desire both to wear a comic mask and to let us see behind it. In Part I Lucy Honeychurch gets a kiss that she wants but cannot accept; she is playing the part of the stock Edwardian lady. But in Part II we learn so much of her powers of self-deception that the stock Edwardian becomes a round, living, and no longer comic individual. Again, in Part I we meet Mr. Emerson, a sententious egalitarian whom we accept as a rather funny bore (and author's pet), but in Part II, where he is featured as a serious philosopher and truth-sayer, he becomes an uncomic pain.

Finally, in Part I the room with a view is a hotel room overlooking the Arno, and the people are idle tourists. In Part II it is the drawing room of a villa in Summer Street, a fancy country suburb in Surrey, and the people are serious citizens trying to work out their destinies. The view has become a vista, and the setting has broadened to admit more complication and sophistication—on that home ground that is to be the whole setting of *Howards End*. Yet for all its increased and sometimes heavy earnestness, Part II contains writing that for sheer competence has not been equaled earlier. In the following passage, the symbolism may be a bit labored and the comedy may be sinking toward the "subconscious," but the conversation has a nervous vitality, some important developments in character are taking place, and comedy and seriousness achieve a successful, if precarious, intimacy. Lucy and her fiancé are taking a walk:

"I'd rather go through the wood," said Cecil, with that subdued irritation that she had noticed in him all the afternoon. "Why is it, Lucy, that you always say the road? Do you know that you have never once been with me in the fields or the wood since we were engaged?"

"Haven't I? The wood, then," said Lucy, startled at his queerness, but pretty sure that he would explain later; it was not his habit to leave her in doubt as to his meaning.

She led the way into the whispering pines, and sure enough he did explain before they had gone a dozen yards.

"I had got an idea—I dare say wrongly—that you feel more at home with me in a room."

"A room?" she echoed, hopelessly bewildered.

"Yes. Or, at the most, in a garden, or on a road. Never in the real country like this."

"Oh, Cecil, whatever do you mean? I have never felt anything of the sort. You talk as if I was a kind of poetess sort of person."

"I don't know that you aren't. I connect you with a view—a certain type of view. Why shouldn't you connect me with a room?"

She reflected a moment, and then said, laughing:

"Do you know that you're right? I do. I must be a poetess after all. When I think of you it's always as in a room. How funny!"

To her surprise, he seemed annoyed.

"A drawing-room, pray? With no view?"

"Yes, with no view, I fancy. Why not?"

"I'd rather," he said reproachfully, "that you connected me with the open air."

She said again, "Oh, Cecil, whatever do you mean?"

As no explanation was forthcoming, she shook off the subject as too difficult for a girl, and led him farther into the wood. (pp. 129–30.)

Cecil, who can love light and openness as ideals, cannot tolerate them as part of his physical life.

2

The book is about a girl who lies. Lucy Honeychurch lies to others and to herself. It is the second kind of lie, the one that separates the true self from the conscious, social self, that interests her creator most. Like that other quasi-puritan, André Gide, Forster is fascinated by the problem of honesty and the difficulties of being honest, and Lucy, who finds it "too dreadful not to know whether she was thinking right or wrong" (p. 60), badly needs guardians. She is provided with two: Miss Charlotte Bartlett, a middle-aged Sawstonian cousin and paid companion; and Mr. Emerson, with his echoing son George, a pair of freethinking humanists. The problem she faces, until she achieves an identity of her own, is to know which of these guardians to believe and follow.

That problem is met in the first chapter. No scene in Forster's fiction brings home more vividly the stuffiness of upper-middle-class Edwardian society than the encounter between Sawston and the Emersons in the Pension Bertolini. Lucy and her formidable chaperone arrive to discover that their promised rooms with views are not available. Mr. Emerson, hearing their laments and ignoring decorum—

which requires English tourists to observe two or three days of pro-
bationary silence before speaking to other English tourists—offers to
swap his and his son's rooms (with views) for the ladies'. George
gloomily goes along with the offer: "It's so obvious they should have
the rooms. . . . There's nothing else to say." (p. 11.) But Miss Bartlett
will not hear of such an exchange. Although her own unselfishness is
notorious (Lucy never speaks of it without exclamation marks), such
unpremeditated openness is a kind of assault, and she draws her skirts
about her. The offer reeks with a threatening masculinity, and Miss
Bartlett, "powerless in the presence of brutality," finds it impossible
"to snub anyone so gross" (p. 12). Lucy, however, reacts less simply.
Perplexed rather than shocked, she has an odd feeling that "whenever these ill-bred tourists spoke the contest widened and deepened
till it dealt, not with rooms and views, but with—well, with something
quite different, whose existence she had not realized before" (p. 11).

That, in brief, is the plot—Lucy's gradual escape from her Sawstonian confinement (the lie) into Emersonian freedom (the truth).
The defining of that "something quite different" is the chief interest
of the book, and that alternative has as much to do with the Emersons' maleness as with their openness. When at last they take the
rooms, Miss Bartlett, with a chaperone's mania for propriety, takes
the larger because " 'it belongs to the young man, and I was sure your
mother would not like it' " (p. 21). This comic glimpse into Edwardian sexual repression brings to mind the scene in *Silas Lapham* where
Silas, showing the hero around his half-finished new house, says,
"This is my girls' room," and causes one of the daughters to blush
deeply.[6] Miss Bartlett guards the gates with comparable delicacy—
and appalling singlemindedness. Always angling for flattery, with her
insincere laments that she is a bore and an encumbrance, this "pre-
maturely aged martyr" oppresses Lucy with her rain of reminders
that, after all, the wishes of a paid companion are not to be considered (p. 97). When her "long, narrow head drives backward and forward like a hammer, "as though demolishing some invisible ob-
stacle,"[7] she is—though frightful—an altogether comic character. Later
she emerges from her flat old-maidishness into roundness. But through
most of the book she is rigid, Sawston's superego in a state of near
hysteria, and not until her moral change does she relax. In the early

chapters, as Lucy opens out, Miss Bartlett becomes ever more des-
perately repressed. Lucy wonders whether the acceptance of the rooms
"might not have been less delicate and more beautiful,"* but Charlotte does not even see the distinction. As they part for the first night
we are symbolically shown the lie she is teaching Lucy to live:

> Miss Bartlett . . . enveloped her in a protecting embrace as she wished her
> good night. It gave Lucy the sensation of a fog, and when she reached her
> own room she opened the window and breathed the clean night air, think-
> ing of the kind old man who had enabled her to see the lights dancing in
> the Arno. . . .
> Miss Bartlett, in her room, fastened the window-shutters and locked the
> door, and then made a tour of the apartment to see where the cupboards
> led, and whether there were any oubliettes or secret entrances. (pp. 21–22.)

Their decision to take the room is influenced by Mr. Beebe, a clergyman who will take over the parish at Summer Street on his return
home. He has all his life "loved to study maiden ladies," but his interest is only academic: "Girls like Lucy were charming to look at,
but Mr. Beebe was, from rather profound reasons, somewhat chilly
in his attitude towards the other sex, and preferred to be interested
rather than enthralled." (p. 44.) His motto is, with Mr. Woodhouse
of Jane Austen's *Emma*, "They that marry do well, but they that refrain do better." (p. 229.) Unlike Miss Bartlett, he is detached rather
than defensive, and he is gifted with a sense of humor. To him, the
Emersons are more to be disagreed with than deplored, and it is this
mild advocacy that props Lucy's guilty affection for them. " 'It is so
difficult,' " he says, speaking of the Emersons, " 'at least I find it difficult—to understand people who speak the truth.' " (p. 16.)

That ingenuous slip goes to the heart of the book. Some people
have no tolerance whatever for "truth," whereas others, like Mr. Emerson (and his satellite, George), are apparently in permanent possession of it. They are the book's absolutes, the possessors of the true
"views." What is their truth? It is a humanistic religion, not unlike
that of Dickinson or Wedd, but apparently in this case derived from
Samuel Butler. These parallels have been carefully demonstrated by

---

* Reminding us of Forster's statement: "I am with the old Scotsman who wanted
less chastity and more delicacy." "What I Believe," TC, 83.

Lee Elbert Holt.[8] Holt notes that Butler was just the man to speak up if struck by a generous notion, such as offering his rooms to strangers, and that Butler and Mr. Emerson have in common a love of Italy and music, and a loathing of hypocrisy and cant. At least once Mr. Emerson preaches directly from Butler as a text:* " 'Life,' wrote a friend of mine, 'is a public performance on the violin, in which you must learn the instrument as you go along.' "[9] Godly people who have "a great knowledge of divinity, but no sense of the divine"[10] are among Butler's chief aversions, and are equally despised by Mr. Emerson, who is "profoundly religious, and differed from Mr. Beebe chiefly by his acknowledgment of passion."[11] This difference is what makes it hard for Mr. Beebe to understand people who speak the truth. He is a helpful guide, but Mr. Emerson is the true prophet.

Absolutes, however, are not easy to accommodate in a novel, and saints are out of place in a comedy of manners. Mr. Emerson is as rigid in his own way as Miss Bartlett is in hers, yet we are not allowed to laugh at him. At times his talk has the homespun charm of the cracker-barrel philosopher, but more often it is the dreary monotone of one who cannot shake loose from a kind of professional holiness. Here is a sample of his stupefying sententiousness: " 'There is a certain amount of kindness, just as there is a certain amount of light,' he continued in measured tones. 'We cast a shadow on something wherever we stand, and it is no good moving from place to place to save things; because the shadow always follows.' " (p. 186.) He is always threatening to turn the comedy into a morality play, and George, his melancholy parrot, is simply incredible as a romantic lead. He too speaks in gnomic adages—"Italy is only an euphuism [sic] for Fate" (p. 223)—and he spends the greater part of the book pouting in the wings. Nevertheless, the book, if it is to be comedy at all, needs some firm standards of value, and these pontificating sages provide them.

Lucy has to choose between Miss Bartlett, the woman of rooms, and Mr. Emerson, the man of views. And the choice is complicated by the presence of other guardians. On one side are ranked the Emersons and Mr. Beebe; on the other are Miss Bartlett, the two Miss

---

* It is interesting that Forster says, "I think I have a more poetical mind than Butler's." "The Art of Fiction," p. 35.

Alans, and Miss Lavish. These last three minor rigidities are among the best touches of the book. Miss Alan (there are two of them but only one talks) is a gossip who is always "being charitable against her better judgment" (p. 47). Miss Lavish is another Miss Raby, a novelist and fake Bohemian who collects views as if they were postcards and takes a sentimental delight in "dear, dirty" back streets, "sweetly squalid" places, and what she calls "adventures" (pp. 14, 27). Her liberalism is outrageous: "Take the word of an old woman, Miss Lucy: you will never repent of a little civility to your inferiors. *That* is the true democracy." (p. 26.) Miss Catherine Alan is the last to join this female entente, for Mr. Emerson has been kind to her and she is susceptible. But when the others learn that he has given her violets, this "early Victorian" is forced to protect her character: "No, I have quite changed. I do *not* like the Emersons. They are *not* nice." (p. 49.)

The Reverend Mr. Cuthbert Eager, who also sides with Miss Bartlett, is the most vicious of the lot. A permanent resident of Florence, he is contemptuous of the tourists and of almost everyone else.* Florence is to him a museum, not a place for life. What bothers him most about the murder that Lucy witnesses in the Piazza Signoria (see Plate 24) is not the murder itself, but the "portentous" desecration it offers to "the Florence of Dante and Savonarola" (p. 65). Esthete, pedant, and snob, he is James's Gilbert Osmond in a clerical collar. Later on, Lucy contrasts him with the other clergyman, Mr. Beebe: Mr. Beebe has no "fences," but Mr. Eager " 'does have fences, and the most dreadful ones' " (p. 121). Of the book's chaste males, he is the most "medieval" (the term is important later), the most ascetic and obsessed with sin. His Italy is not classical and pagan, but the Italy of the Church, of darkness rather than light. He loathes Mr. Emerson so much that he shuts his eyes when the old man speaks to him, and it is he who spreads the rumor that Mr. Emerson had murdered his wife—later adding the afterthought, "in the sight of God" (p. 70). What he means is that Mr. Emerson had not granted his wife's wish (which resulted from Mr. Eager's good offices) to have

---

* A pleasant private joke of Forster's is the information that one of the English residents—one Eager can tolerate—is working on Gemistus Pletho. In 1905 Forster wrote a long essay on Pletho that was published in *The Independent Review*. See AH, 205–18.

George baptized, and that consequently she died heavy with a sense of sin.

The central event of the first half (as in "The Story of a Panic" and *Passage*) is an expedition, which is to Forster's fiction what the picnic is to Jane Austen's. The expedition is proposed and led by Mr. Eager, who wants to show a select few the view of Florence from the high hills, one "far better than the hackneyed view from Fiesole" (p. 64). On three occasions before this critical event, Lucy has been thrown into close proximity with George Emerson; she has even found herself in his arms just after she witnessed the stabbing in front of the shadowy Loggia d'Anza. As a result of these encounters she avoids him, "not because she disliked him, but because she did not know what had happened" (p. 75). But the expedition throws them together again. From the beginning "the little god Pan" rules the proceedings. The party's carriage is driven by a beautiful Italian boy (whom Mr. Beebe recognizes as "Phaethon"), who picks up a girl he calls his sister (Mr. Beebe recognizes her as "Persephone"). The god drives with one arm around the goddess, but Mr. Beebe, whose back is to them, is not aware of the deception until later. "Victory at last!" shouts Mr. Eager when the lovers are parted. Mr. Emerson replies: "It is not victory.... It is defeat. You have parted two people who were happy." (p. 79.) In his defense he quotes Lorenzo de' Medici— "Don't go fighting against the Spring." He is corrected by Mr. Eager, who translates the quotation with more elegance and less passion: " 'Non fate guerra al Maggio' ... 'War not with the May' would render a correct meaning." (p. 80.)

In the course of some delightful confusions that occur when the party stops for a ramble halfway up to Fiesole, Lucy gets lost and, searching for Mr. Beebe, asks the driver in her tourist's Italian, " 'Dove buoni uomini?' " Italians being intuitive about such things, he takes her through the woods to the only good man he has seen, George Emerson, who is standing by himself on a violet-covered ledge. Lucy falls down to the ledge, the driver shouts "Courage and love," and George advances and kisses her.* At that moment her name is called. Miss Bartlett—"brown against the view"—has witnessed the unspeakable offense.

* The driver's shout recalls the cry "Freedom and truth" uttered by the Dryad in Rickie's short story. LJ, 84.

This is the first crisis of Lucy's opening out. Earlier, when Mr. Beebe heard Lucy play Beethoven on the piano, he said, " 'If Miss Honeychurch ever takes to live as she plays, it will be very exciting—both for us and for her.' "[12] But life and art are not yet to join. Miss Bartlett moves in and takes command: " 'I have been a failure . . . , failed to make you happy; failed in my duty to your mother. She has been so generous to me; I shall never face her again after this disaster.' " (p. 97.) Lucy cannot bear up before such moral superiority and promises "absolute secrecy" about the kiss. It is her most conscious act of deceit, and leads to lies more serious. "Lucy was suffering," writes Forster, "from the most grievous wrong which this world has yet discovered: diplomatic advantage had been taken of her sincerity, of her craving for sympathy and love." (pp. 98–99.) Nevertheless, music and Italy, working together, gradually lead her to suspect that her social world is a conspiracy. Mr. Beebe notes that she "never knew her desires so clearly as after music," and when she played she found a solid world where she was "no longer either deferential or patronizing; no longer either a rebel or a slave. . . . Like every true performer, she was intoxicated by the mere feel of the notes: they were fingers caressing her own; and by touch, not by sound alone, did she come to her desire." (pp. 40–41.)

Lucy is beginning to say, with Rickie: "I will experience no longer. I will create. I will be an experience." (LJ, 72.) A later chapter is called "Lucy as a Work of Art," and here is an intimation of how she will become what hitherto she has only played—the miracle of the performer transformed into a performance, like Milton's poet conceived as a "true poem." She will experience what Nietzsche calls the Dionysian afflatus, when "Man is no longer an artist and has become a work of art."[13] Lucy finds through the touch of George Emerson a way of making the word (or music) flesh.

Miss Bartlett, an artist of another sort, senses the contagion of George Emerson's touch, and packs their bags for a flight to Rome. Lucy goes along, muddled and cowed, but not brainwashed:

At the moment when she was about to judge him her cousin's voice had intervened, and, ever since, it was Miss Bartlett who had dominated; Miss Bartlett who, even now, could be heard sighing into a crack in the partition wall; Miss Bartlett, who had really been neither pliable nor humble nor inconsistent. She had worked like a great artist; for a time—indeed for years—

she had been meaningless, but at the end there was presented to the girl the complete picture of a cheerless, loveless world in which the young rush to destruction until they learn better—a shame-faced world of precautions and barriers which may avert evil, but which do not seem to bring good. (p. 98.)

3

The second half of the book takes place in England, with some important new characters added to the old cast: Cecil Vyse, Mrs. Honeychurch, and her son Freddy, a healthy and level-headed medical student. Above all, there is Cecil Vyse. Mrs. Honeychurch likes him because "he's good, he's clever, he's rich, he's well connected . . . and he has beautiful manners," a speech which causes Freddy to kick the piano (p. 104). Forster gives him a formal introduction:

Appearing thus late in the story, Cecil must be at once described. He was medieval. Like a Gothic statue. Tall and refined, with shoulders that seemed braced square by an effort of the will, and a head that was tilted a little higher than the usual level of vision, he resembled those fastidious saints who guard the portals of a French cathedral. Well educated, well endowed, and not deficient physically, he remained in the grip of a certain devil whom the modern world knows as self-consciousness, and whom the medieval, with dimmer vision, worshipped as asceticism. A Gothic statue implies celibacy, just as a Greek statue implies fruition, and perhaps this is what Mr. Beebe meant. (pp. 106–7.)*

Medieval versus classical, ascetic versus pagan, and Gothic versus Greek—these are some of the important sets of contrasts that create the "rhythm" of the novel. Along with truth versus lies, light versus darkness, and views versus rooms, these are the symbolic antitheses that make up the book's tapestry of interwoven themes. The Emersons, who despise the Church and prefer honesty to chivalry, are classical. Lucy, who wonders why most "big things" are unladylike (p. 52), is becoming so. But most of the others and all of the clergymen (even, at the end, Mr. Beebe) are medieval; Miss Bartlett is a caricature of the type. She hopes for a knight in shining armor who will avenge George's kisses (which occur with increasing frequency): " 'Oh, for a real man! We are only two women, you and I. Mr. Beebe is hopeless. There is Mr. Eager, but you do not trust him. Oh, for your brother! He is young, but I know that his sister's insult would

---

* Mr. Beebe had called him "an ideal bachelor" (p. 105).

rouse in him a very lion. Thank God, chivalry is not yet dead.'" (p. 95.)

Her prayers seem answered when Lucy becomes engaged to Cecil, who is so old-fashioned as to ask Freddy's permission for her hand. But the engagement is simply proof that she does not yet know her true nature, nor he his. Since she is not ready for George, the handsome, cultured, and anti-clerical Cecil seems far from impossible. "If they were hypocrites they did not know it," Forster writes; and their discovery of each other is one of Forster's minor triumphs of psychologizing. Like Lucy, Cecil is ready to rebel against the narrowness of Summer Street society, and tries "to substitute for it the society he called broad." But, Forster tells us, he does not realize that "if she was too great for this society, she was too great for all society, and had reached the stage where personal intercourse would alone satisfy her."[14]

Apparently Forster conceives of personal relations as antithetical to social relations, and does not recognize their close dependency on each other. (If the separation of the two seems, in this book, only comic exaggeration, some of Forster's later work shows that he takes it very seriously indeed.) But Cecil is not yet ready for Lucy's kind of freedom, and by degrees Lucy realizes that his love of books, music, and Italy is only the pedantry of a defensive and withered nature. Cecil, in other words, is a slightly more snobbish, slightly more romantic Philip Herriton, and from the beginning theirs is a nervous relationship. Whereas Lucy's Italy is a place where "the senses expanded," Cecil's Italy quickens him "not to tolerance, but to irritation." A sentence in *The Longest Journey* ("Their love ... was not dependent on detail: it grew not from the nerves* but from the soul") gives a clue to why they are not suited for each other.[15] Lucy craves such a love, a love as free of "detail" as panoramic views are, but when George Emerson moves into Summer Street, she attributes the restlessness caused by her suppressed desires to "nerves," and looks no further:

---

* Compare D. H. Lawrence: "Some inscrutable bond held them together. But it was a strange vibration of the nerves, rather than of the blood. A nervous attachment, rather than a sexual love. A curious tension of will, rather than a spontaneous passion.... This attachment of the will and the nerves was destructive." *St. Mawr* and *The Man Who Died* (New York, 1960), p. 6.

She never gazed inwards. If at times strange images rose from the depths, she put them down to nerves. When Cecil brought the Emersons to Summer Street, it had upset her nerves. Charlotte would burnish up past foolishness, and this might upset her nerves. She was nervous at night. When she talked to George . . . she wished to remain near him. How dreadful if she really wished to remain near him! Of course, the wish was due to nerves, which love to play such perverse tricks upon us. (p. 174.)

Those same nerves reappear in T. S. Eliot's *The Waste Land,* where they are the sign not only of sexual frustration but of a class that has lost its social relevance, and is left with no vocation except the keeping up of appearances. "Nervousness" is not unique to the twentieth century, but it is astute of Forster to see the association between nerves and the reduction of life to "detail."

As a practical joke, Cecil entices the Emersons to Summer Street. Lucy (to keep her mother from finding out that Mr. Emerson is the man who has murdered his wife "in the sight of God") tells another lie—that the name of the man in Italy was Harris. She feels stupidly compromised in doing so, for hitherto "truth had come to her naturally" (p. 141). The social lie, the nervous lie, is the result of the soul's falsehood, and she must continue her course of mendacity until she is ready to regard truth as a total commitment of her being, and not merely a matter of manipulated details. But she is not ready, and she permits Mr. Harris, "never a very robust criminal, to droop his head, to be forgotten, and to die" (p. 145).

George, since he is in the neighborhood, kisses Lucy again at the earliest opportunity, thus compounding the irony of Cecil's practical joke. Lucy's first response is to slam shut all the doors of her defenses, and Miss Bartlett, who is visiting, assists her. Lucy's contest, her author tells us, lies between "the real and the pretended," and her first aim is to defeat herself: "Tampering with the truth, she forgot that the truth had ever been. Remembering that she was engaged to Cecil, she compelled herself to confused remembrances of George. . . . The armour of falsehood is subtly wrought out of darkness, and hides a man not only from others, but from his own soul" (p. 198). The darkness (of the room) and the brightness (of the view) are counterpointing symbols that show Lucy's struggle between outer convention and inner truth. Hence she experiences the break with Cecil as a falling of scales from her eyes: she can now "see clearly." George's passionate kiss brings back the sunlight of Italy, whereas Cecil's one belated kiss (for which she calmly lifts her veil) is only a small glimmer in the suburban darkness.

Although she is through with Cecil, she is not yet ready for George —Cecil being for Forster a rejected self much as Rickie was, and George a clumsily contrived ideal self, halfway between Stephen Wonham and Fielding (of *Passage*). Therefore, "the night received her, as it had received Miss Bartlett thirty years before" (p. 214). Forster, who is here as much a preacher as a novelist, evaluates her action:

She gave up trying to understand herself, and joined the vast armies of the benighted, who follow neither the heart nor the brain, and march to their destiny by catch-words. The armies are full of pleasant and pious folk. But they have yielded to the only enemy that matters—the enemy within. They have sinned against passion and truth, and vain will be their strife after virtue. As the years pass, they are censured. Their pleasantry and their piety show cracks, their wit becomes cynicism, their unselfishness hypocrisy; they feel and produce discomfort wherever they go. They have sinned against Eros and against Pallas Athene,* and not by any heavenly intervention, but by the ordinary course of nature, those allied deities will be avenged. (p. 214.)

This author is clearly finding relief in the notion that, since nature will exact revenge, he does not have to. Forster wants defenders against those who have pushed him around; he wants decency without having to fight for it; he wants all the Christian virtues to prevail as if by magic. A passage like this one is the voice of these desires. It asks for a great deal, but we need to remember that Forster's generation was brought up by cultural guardians enacting a worn-out charade of Pauline virtue. Here Forster is reminding them, as well as Lucy, how wrong they were, and reminding them in something very much like their own Calvinistic tones of righteousness.

The rejected Cecil rises to the occasion: "Nothing in his love became him like the leaving of it." (p. 213.) In casting off this medieval knight, Lucy tells him some plain truths that he cannot deny:

* Holt quotes Butler as saying: "The poet is not known by knowledge alone—not by *Gnosis* only—but also, and in greater part, by the *Agape* [wonder] which makes him wish to steal men's hearts." "E. M. Forster and Samuel Butler," p. 812.

" 'Cecil, . . . you may understand beautiful things, but you don't know how to use them; and you wrap yourself up in art and books and music, and would try to wrap up me. I won't be stifled, not by the most glorious music, for people are more glorious, and you hide them from me.' " " 'It is true,' " he replies. " 'True on the whole,' " she corrects him, "full of some vague shame"—which perhaps has something to do with her misquoting G. E. Moore (p. 211). Still, her emancipation is incomplete because she must deny her love for George.

One of the book's dramatic surprises is Miss Bartlett's exposure, the confrontation of her own lie. Although she has enjoined Lucy not to tell anyone about the kiss among the violets, Miss Bartlett tells Miss Lavish. And Miss Lavish, as novelists will, puts the scene into a book. Thus Miss Bartlett has betrayed both herself and Lucy; she is thoroughly discredited, and "the days of her energy were over" (p. 200). Yet the prophecy of Mr. Beebe that "she might yet reveal depths of strangeness, if not of meaning" is fulfilled. Against all Summer Street she supports Lucy's plan to go to Greece, Greece being a psychological state as well as a country. " 'It is absolutely necessary. . . . I know—I *know*,' " Miss Bartlett tells Mr. Beebe. "The darkness was coming on, and he felt that this odd woman really did know." (p. 228.) But as she moves out of the darkness, Mr. Beebe edges into it:

He . . . felt that Miss Bartlett knew of some vague influence from which the girl desired to be delivered, and which might well be clothed in the fleshly form. Its very vagueness spurred him into knight-errantry. His belief in celibacy, so reticent, so carefully concealed beneath his tolerance and culture, now came to the surface and expanded like some delicate flower. "They that marry do well, but they that refrain do better." So ran his belief, and he never heard that an engagement was broken off but with a slight feeling of pleasure. (p. 229.)

Mr. Beebe's development is equally important. Early in Part II, he, George, and Freddy go swimming in a "salad"—a grassy pool that the Honeychurches call "The Sacred Lake" and that is very much like the pond described by Forster in "The Last of Abinger."[16] It is another dell, another sacred fount,* and when George enters the water

---

* Compare "The Road from Colonus."

we are told that "he followed Freddy into the divine" (p. 159). But Mr. Beebe hesitates on the brink of this nakedness; what would the world of motor-cars and parishioners think? When he finally does shed his clothes, it is entirely fitting that the boys run off with them, for he is a timid Greek indeed. Before the trio departed for the Sacred Lake, Mr. Emerson had given them this Butlerian advice: "The Garden of Eden, . . . which you place in the past, is really yet to come. We shall enter it when we no longer despise our bodies.* . . . In this— not in other things—we men are ahead. We despise the body less than women do. But not until we are comrades shall we enter the garden." (pp. 154–55.) How far Mr. Beebe is from approving of bodies male or female is evident at the end of the book. When Lucy admits that she loves George, Mr. Beebe, standing like "a long black column," expresses his incredulity and disgust to Mr. Emerson: " 'I am more grieved than I can possibly express. It is lamentable, lamentable— incredible.' 'What's wrong with the boy?' fired up the other again. 'Nothing, Mr. Emerson, except that he no longer interests me. Marry George, Miss Honeychurch. He will do admirably.' " (p. 249.) Jealousy or fastidiousness? Doubtless a little of both, and the tone is exactly that of Dickinson on the occasion of Fry's marriage. Mr. Beebe has gone over to the Middle Ages. His face is that of an ascetic saint, whereas Mr. Emerson's is "the face of a saint who understood," who has shown her "the holiness of direct desire."[17]

George and Lucy marry, and though the Honeychurches have not forgiven her, there is a strong probability that they will. Lucy is confident that "if we act the truth, the people who really love us are sure to come back to us in the long-run" (p. 253). As the book closes, the person on her mind and George's is Miss Bartlett, who by her very pruderies and inhibitions has, they fancy, been the instrument of their coming together. In a strange and sudden desire to think well of her, they resort to the unconvincing argument that evil is really good if we only understand God's providence. George's optimism has a note of grim determination in it: " 'She is not frozen,

* In a canceled "fantasy-chapter" of *The Longest Journey*, Stephen bathes in a river by a train-crossing and is abused "in the filthiest language for wearing no costume" by a passing engine driver. The same thing once happened to Dickinson in Hertfordshire, Forster adds. See "Aspect of a Novel," p. 1229.

Lucy, she is not withered up all through. She tore us apart twice, but in the Rectory that evening she was given one more chance to make us happy. We can never make friends with her or thank her. But I do believe that, far down in her heart, far below all speech and behaviour, she is glad.' " (p. 256.)

Forster, like George Eliot, believes that the vibrations of one life are received, though not as simple echoes, in others. "There's never any knowing," says Caroline Abbott in *Angels,* "which of our actions, which of our idlenesses won't have things hanging on it forever" (WA, p. 171). If Mr. Emerson represents the holiness of direct desire, Miss Bartlett represents the hell of repressed desire; and it is a puzzle why her spinsterhood should produce good fruit while Mr. Beebe's celibacy is death on the vine. But Forster's comic universe is a complex one—which is not to deny such simple considerations as that he likes maiden ladies better than parsons.

4

This is the only one of Forster's books in which the problem of continuance (which always appears) is met in a straightforward sexual way. Although there is a hint of prudery in George's later kisses,* no surrogate breeder is needed to provide the heir for this holy family. George as the virile male is incredible; his author never gets inside him or even close to him, just as in his next book he never genuinely realizes Leonard Bast. But these prudish distances only emphasize how urgently Forster's personal myth needed this experiment in direct desire. The Sacred Lake and the male swimming party could have been the book's symbol rather than the room with a view and the lovers in their chamber. But the Sacred Lake could not issue into the stream of the generations, and Forster quite obviously needs to talk about continuance in a social as well as mystical sense. We may lament, though, that George has to be such a rough diamond. Sex and sensibility might have made a more graceful pair.

It would be a shame, however, to let these serious themes obscure the book's fine comedy. The serious characters are those who change, but some of the most delightful are those who do not. Cecil, though

---

* " 'Kiss me here.' He indicated the spot where a kiss would be welcome." (p. 252.)

a humorist rather than a clown, stays in character.* But the greatest of these unchanging figures is Mrs. Honeychurch, who is drawn after Forster's maternal grandmother, Louisa Graham Whichelo (see Plate 7). "How I adored my grandmother!" he writes of her (MT, 250), and Mrs. Honeychurch reflects this affection. She is totally loyal to the values of her class, yet she stands for all that is good and free about "family." Her Windy Corner is a house with a *view*; and though she worries about detail, she knows how to forget about it as well. Pious and inconsistent, she rules her brood with charming eccentricity. Hoping "to cure her children of slang by taking it literally," she says to Freddy, who has declared he is "getting fairly sick" of the carryings-on of Lucy and Cecil: "For goodness' sake go out of my drawing-room, then!" (p. 101.) Her ear for blasphemy is even more delicate. To Cecil's tale about the man who had murdered his wife "in the sight of God," she replies with pious absent-mindedness: "Hush, dear!" (p. 121.) And her Sabbath is as tolerantly "amphibious" as her daughter's: "She kept it without hypocrisy in the morning, and broke it without reluctance in the afternoon."† (p. 191.)

She and her family are among the warmest and most pleasant people in Forster's fiction. They are relatively relaxed, and their virtues are a result of this rare quality. Lucy, of course, has her tensions

---

* Cecil's clowning continues after the book is over. In an "Anniversary Postscript" Forster imagines Cecil's later career, and in doing so tightens the comparison with his own. Cecil was sent to Alexandria in 1914 as Forster was in 1915, and the "mischief and culture" in Cecil's character are qualities Forster shares. "[Cecil Vyse] moved out of the Emersons' circle but not altogether out of mine. . . . and in 1914 he was seconded to Information or whatever the withholding of information was then entitled. I had an example of his propaganda, and a very welcome one, at Alexandria. A quiet little party was held on the outskirts of that city, and some one wanted a little Beethoven. The hostess demurred. Hun music might compromise us. But a young officer spoke up. 'No, it's all right,' he said. 'A chap who knows about those things from the inside told me Beethoven's definitely Belgian.'

"The chap in question must have been Cecil. That mixture of mischief and culture is unmistakable. Our hostess was reassured, the ban was lifted, and the Moonlight Sonata shimmered into the desert." "A View Without a Room," *The Observer*, July 27, 1958, p. 15.

† Those other famous old ladies of Forster's fiction, Mrs. Wilcox of *Howards End* and Mrs. Moore of *Passage,* are really developments of Mrs. Honeychurch—good old ladies who, as they approach advanced age, become querulous and queer and irresponsible.

and is somewhat estranged from her family, but we know that she will return to it. Again the issue is that of *The Longest Journey*, the triumph of the mother's line. But this time no father and no aunt, no unpleasant Thorntons, are within the circle. He has reached back to the grandmother, and one senses that with her Forster feels securely home. One scene in the book shows Lucy, in a moment's respite from nerves and worry, looking across the table and considering her inheritance in its ideal permanency. She is here undoubtedly Forster's spokesman: "To-day she felt she had received a guarantee. Her mother would always sit there, her brother here. The sun, though it had moved a little since the morning, would never be hidden behind the western hills." (p. 189.)

But there is another mood slanting away from this one: "It will not last, this cheerfulness." The view from Windy Corner over the Weald to the South Downs is like the view from Fiesole across the Tuscan Plain, but the sense is strong that although these views suggest eternity, they have no eternal lease. The suburban villas of Summer Street are gobbling up the country, cosmopolitanism is invading the precincts of simplicity and honesty. As cities grow, the divine becomes more distant. The happiness this book depicts is based on precarious memories, precarious incomes, and precarious space, and the question must soon come up whether love and art are by themselves enough to meet the encroachments of an alien world. In his Anniversary Postscript to this novel, Forster continues the career of Lucy and George. They survive, and credibly, but nothing is the same after the First World War, "the war that was to end war—and spoilt everything."[18]

Forster's next novel takes us nearer to the catastrophe. There the enemies moving in on Windy Corner are seen at closer quarters. And never again will the problems of continuance be presented in the form of a romantic comedy. Edwardian youth, as Canon C. E. Raven has said, had the best chance since civilization began of leading a decent life, and even as early as 1908 (the date of this book) Forster could hardly suppress a note of nostalgia. By the date of the next (1910), the note was more like desperation.

Chapter ten

Howards End:
Red-bloods and Mollycoddles

Life without Industry is sin, and Industry without Art,
brutality.
                                        —Ruskin

Culture without character is ... something frivolous,
vain, and weak; but character without culture is ...
something raw, blind, and dangerous.
                                        —Matthew Arnold

With *Howards End* Forster broadened his subject from a private to
a public world, confronting for the first time not just personal or
domestic antagonists, but representatives of England's social, political, and economic power. The motto of Margaret Schlegel, who can
be said to speak for Forster, is "Only connect," and the book is a
test of the ability of Bloomsbury liberalism to survive a marriage with
the great world. Can personal relations and public relations join in
creative harmony? This crucial problem has worried Forster from the
beginning. Unless liberalism can show a more edifying view of reality
than the Christian warfare between the flesh and the spirit, the world
and the soul, unless it can effect some healing of the ancient dualisms,
then it has small hope, or reason, for survival—nor should we lament
its passing. Margaret's plea is a distant echo of the "Only believe" of
St. Mark:[1]

Only connect! That was the whole of her sermon. Only connect the prose
and the passion, and both will be exalted, and human love will be seen at
its height. Live in fragments no longer. Only connect, and the beast and the
monk, robbed of the isolation that is life to either, will die. (p. 197.)

The sermon is not new; versions of it have been preached by romantics from Blake to D. H. Lawrence, and Arthur Koestler has more
recently seen the opposition of the yogi and the commissar as defining
the polarities of the modern predicament.[2] But as a dominant emphasis, connection is something new with Forster. His earlier work

dramatized salvation mainly in terms of separation and escape—separation of sheep from goats, escape from earthly cross-purposes into the womb-like Eden of some frictionless eternity. Salvation, more often than not, was found through a delicate exclusiveness, through fulfilled dreams of spiritual sanitation. Of course, the earlier work made some connections, but almost the only serious attempt to bring marked opposites together was Rickie's marriage, a union described as a mistake and dramatized as a failure.

But now the ideal of inclusiveness, of connection, is given a deliberate and extensive trial, and in doing so Forster is testing not just a moral thesis, but himself. Alfred North Whitehead, commenting on the modern alienation of material from esthetic values, states what may be taken as the essential theme of this novel: "Sensitiveness without impulse spells decadence, and impulse without sensitiveness spells brutality."[3] All of the book's experiments in connection—Margaret Schlegel's marriage with the boorish materialist Henry Wilcox; Helen Schlegel's idealistic reach down through her class to the poor clerk Leonard Bast; and Leonard's attempts to cross class lines via "culture"—are symbolic testings of that slippery walk between decadence and brutality, ivorytowerism and concentration camps, which has been the frightful, and paradoxical, road of modern history. The book is therefore a kind of morality play, though its people and situations never altogether degenerate into the flatness of allegory. And its marriages and liaisons are symbolic crossings of moral divides of enormous historical and philosophical importance.

But this great theme, this joining of power and sensibility, the heroic and the civilized,* male and female, springs directly from a personal worry; and whatever universality the theme has is due in part at least to the representative nature of Forster's personal experience. We evoke that problem immediately if we remember Dickinson's dichotomy between the Red-bloods and the Mollycoddles. The Red-bloods had their originals in the wellborn bullies and roughs of the "best set," those cricket-playing conformists of the public school (and university) who were destined to rule Britain and her Empire; the Mollycoddles were those, like Dickinson and Forster,

---

* This is the basic division in Forster's unfinished novel, *Arctic Summer*. See "A Novel that 'Went Wrong,' " *The Manchester Guardian*, June 13, 1951, p. 3.

almost as wellborn, who hated and envied the strong ones and con-
soled themselves with dreams that one day the meek and the sensitive
would inherit the earth. The issue of crude power pervades everything Forster writes: how can one handle the authorities, the bosses,
the parents? This book confronts that issue and broadens its scope.
But it is interesting to note that here for the first time Forster relin-
quishes the hero-role entirely to women. The two Schlegel sisters, and
especially Margaret, are his personal representatives, and they take
on the male adversaries, the Wilcox Red-bloods, with feminine weapons. The attempt to compete as a man, abandoned with *The Longest
Journey,* is not resumed; instead the author pours his contempt into
that lost identity, lets it live briefly as Henry Wilcox, and takes shelter
in female bodies that men do not normally strike.

So it might be said that Forster is hiding out in this book—in the
very book that seems in some ways to move most bravely into the
public arena. His doing so would be in keeping with his well-known
"shy crablike sideways movement" (AN, 158), that oblique and feminine way of meeting opposition, and would suggest that Forster may
be facing the great world more out of duty than inclination. Such
possibilities make one question whether Forster will be able to give
the problem of connection, especially connection between men and
women, a fair trial. Lionel Trilling calls *Howards End* Forster's masterpiece because it "develops to their full the themes and attitudes
of the early books and . . . justifies these attitudes by connecting them
with a more mature sense of responsibility."[4] But is the book more
responsible than the earlier ones? Does it represent a summit or a
crisis of achievement?[5] These are critical questions. Connection, not
division, is the theme, and Forster's fictional transvestism does not
increase our confidence that he will be an impartial mediator between Red-bloods and Mollycoddles, or indeed that he will even try
to be. But in spite of these misgivings—and because of them—this book
commands an unusual degree of interest and respect.

2

Houses have the symbolic role in this novel that rooms had in the
last. Howards End is modeled on the house in Hertfordshire where
Forster and his mother lived for ten years, but it is also, like Windy

Corner, a symbolic house, a house with a view.* Of the three principal houses in the book, this one is the most important: it is the country house, and represents all of England and her spiritual inheritance
that can be implied in the phrases "the English countryside" and "the
existence, in an established home, of the family." Wickham Place is
the city house, the urban home of the Schlegels, which along with its
traditions and family memories is leveled by the bulldozer of "progress" to make room for the flats required by the "civilization of luggage." A third house, Oniton—located near Clun Castle in Shrop-
shire[6] (see Plates 26, 27)—represents the kind of real estate that the
likes of Henry Wilcox buy and sell for weekend purposes, a priceless
commodity used like a prostitute, owned but never truly possessed.

Houses are feminine symbols. Will any "key" of Henry Wilcox open
Howards End, or any house?† Can Leonard be more than a nervous
intruder at Wickham Place? Will Oniton ever possess what Margaret
calls "the power of Home" (HE, 234), since Henry does not know how
to love it? The novel really leads to an overwhelming question: Do
any men, in fact, possess the credentials for inhabiting these houses?
The Schlegels, as the moral arbiters of the novel, are strongly given
to seeing sensitiveness as female and brutality as male. Not only does
Margaret hold a feminist idea of politics ("I am sure that if the mothers of various nations could meet, there would be no more wars," p.
94), but she sees the extremes of Whitehead's aphorism as dangers
that could be avoided by female domination: " 'So with our house—
it must be feminine, and all we can do is to see that it isn't effeminate.
Just as another house [the Wilcoxes'] that I can mention, but won't,
sounded irrevocably masculine, and all its inmates can do is to see
that it isn't brutal.' " (p. 46.)

* "The garden, the overhanging wych-elm, the sloping meadow, the great view
to the west, the cliff of fir trees to the north, the adjacent farm through the high
tangled hedge of wild roses were all utilised by me in *Howards End,* and the interior is in the novel too." (MT, 269.) (See Plate 25.)

† The key is, of course, an ancient symbol representing "the phallic opening
power of the male." Eric Neumann, *The Great Mother* (New York, 1955), p. 170.
At a point in the novel when Margaret and Henry are most deeply estranged, she
tosses him the doorkeys of Howards End and says contemptuously: "Here are your
keys." (HE, 352.) He does not pick them up.

The hesitations in that statement are some measure of Margaret's fastidiousness, her reluctance to "connect." Yet she is too intelligent not to see the dangers posed by effeminacy on the one hand and brutality on the other. Without connection, we have only the *idea* of what Arnold (and the Schlegels after him) called "culture"—a state of spiritual perfection—without the means for making it prevail. And this book can be read as the most explicit test of Arnold's notion of culture in our literature.

We first meet the Schlegel sisters living with their brother Tibby, a kind of comically diminished Cecil, at Wickham Place. Their parents dead, unattended by guardians, their situation is like that of Virginia and Vanessa Stephen living at Gordon Square with their brother Thoby ("Tibby"?) in the early days of Bloomsbury. The Schlegels too are considered "advanced," and Aunt Juley (Mrs. Munt), suspicious of this "politico-economical-aesthetic" establishment, predicts that the girls will soon "enter on the process known as throwing themselves away" (p. 14). They are thoroughly Bloomsbury: they entertain musicians, artists, and even an actress; they believe in literature, art, and personal relations; they are moralists and anti-Utilitarians; they have a snobbish faith in the rightness of their own sensibilities. And the process of "throwing themselves away" is that essential experiment with their own freedom, the bringing of the best that they (among others) have thought and said to the exploration, and perhaps the redemption, of the world.

Like Virginia and Vanessa Stephen, the Schlegels have been strongly shaped by the example and teachings of a father.* His influence still fills the house. Among his effects is a sword, once wielded in the wars of the Fatherland, but long since put away as a reminder of what men may perish by. An expatriate German, he rejected his homeland when it became a Great Power and "abstained from the fruits of victory" when he saw that victory (in the Franco-Prussian War) meant only material aggrandizement. An Imperial Germany was not his country: "If one classed him at all it would be as the countryman of Hegel and Kant, as the idealist, inclined to be dreamy,

* The Schlegel sisters were derived, Forster says, from the three sisters of Lowes Dickinson. "The Art of Fiction," p. 37.

whose Imperialism was the Imperialism of the air." Nowhere does Forster make more distinct his affiliation with the traditions of German (and Coleridgean) idealism, with its implicit separation of the utilitarian and the esthetic functions. Father Schlegel condemned his countrymen as "stupid" because they used the mind without caring about it, prizing only what they could use—money first, intellect second, imagination not at all. Pan-Germanism is as unimaginative and vulgar as English Imperialism:

"It is the vice of a vulgar mind to be thrilled by bigness,* to think that a thousand square miles are a thousand times more wonderful than one square mile. . . . That is not imagination. No, it kills it. . . . Oh yes, you have learned men, who . . . collect facts, and facts, and empires of facts. But which of them will rekindle the light within?" (pp. 30–31.)

The "light within" is the same as Arnold's "sweetness and light," and the state in which the father became a citizen was more a state of mind, a condition of grace, than it was a body politic.† "England" is used throughout the novel in this mystic sense;‡ it implies politics and economics and classes, but it transcends them—as Art transcends the individual work of art. Forster asks, as Mrs. Munt sets off on the road from the railway station to Howards End: "Into what country will it lead, England or Suburbia?" (p. 15.) Margaret, too, becomes resident in that ideal England:

---

* Compare Virginia Woolf: "Let us not take it for granted that life exists more fully in what is commonly thought big than in what is commonly thought small." "Modern Fiction," *The Common Reader, First Series* (London, 1957), p. 190.

† Arnold's nickname for the middle class, "the Philistines," was borrowed from the German. In his essay on Heine, Arnold defines a Philistine as "a strong, dogged, unenlightened opponent of the chosen people, of the children of the light" and points out that German representatives of the liberal spirit viewed themselves as "children of the light" and their adversaries as "humdrum people, slaves to routine, enemies to light; stupid and oppressive, but at the same time very strong." "Heinrich Heine," *Essays in Criticism* in *Matthew Arnold, Poetry and Prose*, ed. John Bryson (Cambridge, Mass., 1954), p. 399.

‡ "Mystic" is used here as Forster himself frequently uses it, to signify a "mystery" in the religious sense. He also frequently makes the term synonymous with "mystifying" or "mysterious," as in the following examples. "The *Times* has consecrated a long and a very mystical leading article to the Royal Tournament." "Notes on the Way," *Time and Tide*, XV (1934), 694. Again: "I find myself being invited to define wisdom, and becoming mystical about it." "De Senectute," *The London Magazine*, IV (1957), 17.

She forgot the luggage and the motor-cars, and the hurrying men who know so much and connect so little. She recaptured the sense of space, which is the basis of all earthly beauty, and, starting from Howards End, she attempted to realize England. She failed—visions do not come when we try, though they may come through trying. But an unexpected love of the island awoke in her, connecting on this side with the joys of the flesh, on that with the inconceivable. (p. 216.)

But is this exactly the connection we seek? Must we not make some accommodation to the motor-cars and the hurrying men rather than run away from them? To connect only a remembered feeling with an inconceivable idea suggests that solipsistic imprisonment in mind which Kant himself never escaped.* Is Forster showing us a real connection or a trick with words? Questions like this must be asked again and again, for connections between inner and outer are quite different from connections entirely within the mind; the first kind can solve the dramatic problem of this novel, the other can only evade it.

The Germans in *Howards End,* both patriate and expatriate, remind us that nations as well as classes must be connected, and Forster provides us, in the Schlegels' German "connections," a gallery of profiles as portentous as those in Katherine Anne Porter's *Ship of Fools.*[7] Forster's continental Germans are often comic, but their comedy threatens at every moment to lose its benignity. "Connection" to them is a matter of family or blood, of tribal rather than spiritual allegiances; and though they are relations they know nothing of "personal relations," the ground on which Forster feels nations as well as people must meet. The shadow of war which hangs over this book is but a lengthening of these private disabilities—the inability of these Red-bloods to know culture except as an empty ceremony or to imagine an internationalism of the spirit.

To the threat of war, as to all brutal and irrational impulses, the Schlegels oppose a kind of Dickinsonian politics: "In their own fashion they cared deeply about politics, though not as politicians would have us care; they desired that public life should mirror whatever is good in the life within." (p. 29.) It is an important statement. Schlegelian liberalism, when it is unchallenged by opposition, becomes more of an esthetic than a political attitude, lapsing into a quiescent

---

* A German cousin in the book puts this danger well: "One is certain of nothing but the truth of one's emotions." (p. 180.)

faith that somehow private good will radiate into the body politic. But the Schlegels know this and worry about it—it is one of their distinctions.

The question of the book, as Trilling points out, is "Who shall inherit England?" and the plot is about "the rights of property."[8] But this England and this property are essentially spiritual properties and a spiritual state, and the question of inheritance has as much to do with eternal kingdoms as with earthly real estate.* Can the spirit make bequests? Has the soul offspring? These are the questions Forster wants to probate in this novel, yet being a novelist, he is stuck with actual houses and lands, which actual people buy with money and credit. And these hard facts return him, as they do Margaret and Helen, to the hard world. "What would it profit Mr. Bast if he gained the whole world and lost his own soul?" Margaret is asked. "Nothing," she answers, "but he would not gain his soul until he had gained a little of the world."[9] Margaret is Shavian in seeing the intimate connection between moral health and £600 a year, and makes no bones about it. "Money forever!" she shouts to the shocked Mrs. Munt.† But she knows she is shocking; this is a radical idea, and her argument is no more based on a desire for social justice than was Clapham's love of the slave. Fair shares in food, clothes, or housing are not what matters, but the light within. Money is important only because there can be no "soul" without it, none of the health or leisure or culture that give England and Howards End their mean-

---

* That spiritual state is, in fact, identical with what Arnold means by the idea of *the State*; and the problem of realizing that state is the essential plot of this book. The following statement by Arnold provides a useful reference point: "What if we tried to rise above the idea of class to the idea of the whole community, *the State,* and to find our centre of light and authority there? Every one of us has the idea of country, as a sentiment; hardly any one of us has the idea of *the State,* as a working power. And why? Because we habitually live in our ordinary selves, which do not carry us beyond the ideas and wishes of the class to which we happen to belong. . . . By our every day selves . . . we are separate, personal, at war; we are only safe from one another's tyranny when no one has any power. . . . But by our *best self* we are united, impersonal, at harmony. We are in no peril from giving authority to this, because it is the truest friend we all of us can have." "Doing as One Likes," *Culture and Anarchy, The Portable Matthew Arnold,* pp. 523–24.

† Henry Wilcox declares to Margaret, at a crucial point in their relations: "I am not one of your Bernard Shaws who consider nothing sacred." (p. 320.)

ing. If this is so, should we not honor the strong ones who earn it—
or even marry them? Margaret acts and speaks the answer: "If Wilcoxes hadn't worked and died in England for thousands of years, you
and I couldn't sit here without having our throats cut. There would
be no trains, no ships to carry us literary people about in, no fields
even. Just savagery. . . . More and more do I refuse to draw my income and sneer at those who guarantee it." (p. 185.) It is bravely said,
but to be fairminded about Red-bloods is one thing—living with them
is another matter. We must turn to the Schlegels' experiments in connection.

3

The two sisters are quite different. Trilling suggests that the names
Margaret and Helen may derive from the heroines of the two parts
of *Faust,* "one the heroine of the practical life, the other of the ideal
life."[10] Forster has denied any borrowing, but the association, though
it fits the theme of the book better than it does the characters of the
girls, is suggestive. One of the book's narrative rhythms is their drawing apart and their final coming together.

Helen is ardent, impulsive, idealistic, and easily disillusioned. She
is the first one to meet the Wilcoxes. Spending a weekend at Howards
End, she is kissed by Paul, wires her sister that she has fallen in love,
and falls out again. Paul, a typical male Wilcox, is appalled at having
let passion touch his life, terrified lest anything so real as a personal
relationship disrupt his plans for a career in the colonies. Helen's
withdrawal is immediate and instinctive:

"Somehow, when that kind of man looks frightened it is too awful. It is
all right for us to be frightened, or for men of another sort—father, for instance; but for men like that! When I saw all the others so placid, and Paul
mad with terror in case I said the wrong thing, I felt for a moment that the
whole Wilcox family was a fraud, just a wall of newspapers and motor-cars
and golf-clubs, and that if it fell I should find nothing behind it but panic
and emptiness." (p. 27.)

"Panic and emptiness"! This is the first time we hear that important refrain, and it becomes her special phrase. It is her term of contempt for the Wilcox way of life, especially when these Red-bloods

fail to confirm her fantasies about what men should be and do; it is also the other side of her own manic enthusiasms. "The world is empty," writes Jung, "to him alone who does not understand how to direct his libido towards objects, and to render them alive and beautiful."[11] That is Paul and the other Wilcoxes, but it is also Helen herself; and as we observe her development we get ever clearer demonstrations, as with Hardy's Sue Bridehead, of her frigidity. Her connections with the world are almost all hysterical ones, frantic clutches after some otherness that would relieve her nun-like isolation, and they do not make others happy. The motif of "panic and emptiness" appears again when Helen and her sister, together with Tibby, Aunt Juley, and some German cousins, listen to Beethoven's Fifth Symphony at a concert. Margaret can "only see the music"; Tibby, "profoundly versed in counterpoint," derives his pleasure from "the transitional passage on the drum"; Aunt Juley wants to tap; Fräulein Mosebach remembers that Beethoven was "echt Deutsch"; Herr Leisecke can think of nothing but Fräulein Mosebach. But Helen translates the music into *literature,* the story of her recent experience with Paul, and sees "heroes and shipwrecks in the music's flood":

> "No; look out for the part where you think you have done with goblins and they come back," breathed Helen, as the music started with a goblin walking quietly over the universe, from end to end. . . . They were not aggressive creatures; it was that that made them so terrible to Helen. They merely observed in passing that there was no such thing as splendour or heroism in the world. . . . Panic and emptiness! Panic and emptiness! . . .
> And the goblins—they had not really been there at all? They were only the phantoms of cowardice and unbelief? One healthy human impulse would dispel them? Men like the Wilcoxes, or President Roosevelt,* would say yes. Beethoven knew better. The goblins really had been there. They might return—and they did. . . . Panic and emptiness! Panic and emptiness! (pp. 34–35.)

The music is to her a portent, summing up "all that had happened or could happen in her career . . . a tangible statement, which could never be superseded" (p. 36). This despair colors all her experiments

---

* Compare Dickinson: "We have divided men into Red-bloods and Mollycoddles. 'A Red-blood man' is a phrase which explains itself. . . . We have adopted it from a famous speech of Mr. Roosevelt." *Appearances* (London, 1914), p. 193.

in connection. In the final pages of the novel the prophecy is amply fulfilled, as Helen remarks: "I'm ended. I used to be so dreamy about a man's love as a girl, and think that for good or evil love must be the great thing. But it hasn't been; it has been itself a dream." (p. 356.) But these are the words of a woman who has never known love except as a brief and desperate self-immolation. She was "ended" before she began, for the "panic and emptiness" she saw in the Wilcoxes was only a projection of fears she felt in herself. When she learns that Margaret intends to marry Henry she reacts as Ansell reacts to Rickie's engagement, or Mr. Beebe to Lucy's, with a shudder of revulsion, as if before a horror. " 'Don't, don't do such a thing! I tell you not to—don't! I know—don't!'

" 'What do you know?'

" 'Panic and emptiness,' sobbed Helen. 'Don't!' " (p. 182.)

"Panic and emptiness" subsides only when Helen no longer tries to connect: "I can only do what's easy. I can only entice and be enticed. I can't, and won't, attempt difficult relations." (p. 205.) This solution, compared with Agnes's simpleminded connubial greed, seems hardly honorable, yet clearly Helen is, for Forster, within the circle of the saved and Agnes is among the damned. Why? It would seem that, as in *The Longest Journey,* Forster has divided his ego-representatives in two, Helen being a development on Rickie and Margaret on Stephen. Helen withdraws into absolutes and wants the quick route to heaven; though sex touches her life and she bears a child, she—like Rickie—withdraws from it. "You and I have built up something real," she says to Margaret, "because it is purely spiritual. There's no veil of mystery over us. Unreality and mystery begin as soon as one touches the body." (p. 205.) This may be the wrong answer, just as Rickie's life is a wrong kind of life, a failure; but we have no sense that the author withholds his sympathy from either. Helen's withdrawal gives Margaret, the heroic connector, her chance to work, just as Rickie's sacrifice gives Stephen his chance. It is significant that Margaret disapproves of Helen's methods:

All vistas close in the unseen—no one doubts it—but Helen closed them rather too quickly for her taste. At every turn of speech one was confronted with reality and the absolute. Perhaps Margaret grew too old for metaphysics, perhaps Henry was weaning her from them, but she felt that there was something a little unbalanced in the mind that so readily shreds the visible. The business man who assumes that this life is everything, and the mystic who asserts that it is nothing, fail, on this side and that, to hit the truth. "Yes, I see, dear: it's about halfway between," Aunt Juley had hazarded in earlier years. No; truth, being alive, was not halfway between anything.* It was only to be found by continuous excursions into either realm, and though proportion is the final secret, to espouse it at the outset is to insure sterility. (pp. 205–6.)

If Helen is guilty of the radicalism of extremes, Margaret, Forster's chief ethical representative, is presented as an example of "proportion." Her truth, we learn, is neither that of the yogi nor that of the commissar; it is rather a synthesis, an organic whole which is greater than the sum of its parts. To achieve this Moorean (or Arnoldian) state is the whole point of connecting, and Helen is finally reconciled to Margaret's marriage because she sees the action as a heroic attempt to "keep proportion" in spite of the goblins and their terrible universal message.

But the connections Helen makes are worth study, partly because it is her energy that gives the book much of its momentum. She is the first, we remember, to meet the Wilcoxes at Howards End, and these new connections briefly fascinate her.

The Wilcox children—Charles, Evie, and Paul—are all less pleasant versions of their father. Devotees of the outer life of "telegrams and anger" (rather than "sweetness and light"), they are known and know themselves in terms of stinking cars, cricket averages, and the financial pages of the *Times*. But Helen is at first swept off her feet; she even enjoys being bullied by Henry Wilcox into believing that all her fancy ideas about equality, votes for women, socialism, art and literature, are nonsense. "When Mr. Wilcox said that one sound man of business did more good to the world than a dozen of your social reformers, she had swallowed the curious assertion without a gasp, and had leant back luxuriously among the cushions of his motor-car." (p. 25.) These enchantments quickly became hateful, but one Wilcox

---

* The remark recalls one by Sir Charles Simeon: "Truth is not in the middle, and not in one extreme, but in both extremes. . . . Sometimes I am a high Calvinist and sometimes a low Arminian." J. C. Pollock, *A Cambridge Movement* (London, 1953), p. 6.

stands apart from the tribe and is exempted from Helen's general condemnation. Ruth, the mother, the unassertive presiding spirit of Howards End, is almost a myth-like figure, and seems to float rather than walk through the book. She inhabits the house of realism like some ghostly deity. It is Helen who first meets and admires her:

She seemed to belong not to the young people and their motor, but to the house, and to the tree that overshadowed it. One knew that she worshipped the past, and that the instinctive wisdom the past can alone bestow had descended upon her—that wisdom to which we give the clumsy name of aristocracy. High born she might not be. But assuredly she cared about her ancestors, and let them help her. (p. 23.)

But Helen's most vital relationship is with Leonard Bast, one of the most interesting and least convincing characters in the book.* Leonard, who bears some resemblance to Butler's Ernest Pontifex, is a poor insurance clerk who lives "at the extreme edge of gentility" with Jacky, a lower-class woman whom Forster treats with unqualified—and even cruel—contempt. Leonard has staked his salvation on his ability to acquire "culture." To this end he goes to Queen's Hall concerts, looks at pictures, and reads Ruskin,† Meredith, and George Borrow—believing that one day he will "push his head out of the grey waters and see the universe." Having no conception of "a heritage that may expand gradually," Leonard hopes "to come to Culture suddenly, much as the Revivalist hopes to come

* Forster admits that he had no "personal knowledge" of the "home-life of Leonard and Jacky," but adds: "I believe I brought it off." "The Art of Fiction," p. 33.

Leonard Woolf in *Growing* (1961), the second volume of his autobiography, gives a fascinating portrait of a British civil servant in Ceylon who "always reminded" him of Leonard Bast. He came from "that depressing, dun-coloured, lace curtain region where the lower middle-class merges into the working class or vice versa." He wrote poetry of "a sickly, sticky simplicity which, had I not read it . . . I should not have believed attainable by an adult in the 20th century," and his appearance was that of "a small, insignificant looking man, with hollow cheeks, a rather grubby yellow face, an apologetic moustache, and frightened or worried eyes behind strong spectacles." (pp. 63–64.)

† Ruskin comes in for some light critical chaffing by Forster. For example, in *A Room With a View* he writes: "There was no one even to tell her which, of all the sepulchral slabs that paved the nave and transepts, was the one that was really beautiful, the one that had been most praised by Mr. Ruskin." (p. 30.) See also RV, 125, and HE, 51–53, 56–57.

to Jesus" (p. 53), a vulgar error for which his author does not let him off lightly. No easy atonement is available to those not born in the ranks of the elect.

Leonard is a fictional test of Arnold's belief that Culture, if it is to be realized at all, has its best chance among the Philistines. "The era of aristocracies is over," wrote Arnold; "nations must now stand or fall by the intelligence of their middle class and their people." For all its grievous faults, the middle class is the broad base of the nation, its source of power, and England's hope lies in the possibility that this class can be transformed, "liberalised by an ampler culture, admitted to a wider sphere of thought, living by larger ideas, with its provincialism dissipated, its intolerance cured, its pettinesses purged away."[12] Here if anywhere, thought Arnold, can be recruited the "saving remnant," that community of the best who can rise above the interests of class and sect to the true equality: they can become the representatives of humanity and "the heavenly Gods."[13] Can Leonard qualify? Can the "pursuit of perfection" and "sweetness and light" operate as strongly in him as mere class interest? That is his test, and Forster is brutally clear about limiting the scope of this novel to that class which has, on Arnold's terms, some fair hope of achieving culture. That Forster is consciously testing Arnold's belief is evident from this rather shocking statement: "We are not concerned with the very poor. They are unthinkable, and only to be approached by the statistician or the poet. This story deals with gentlefolk, or with those who are obliged to pretend that they are gentlefolk." (pp. 47–48.)

Only those who have some chance of inheriting "England" are of interest, and once Forster has let Leonard into his novel, he seems pressed to decide whether he should let him stay, just as the Schlegels debate whether they should invite Leonard to Wickham Place. Is he good enough? Can he be made good enough? The name Bast is itself a satiric tag,* and Forster several times burlesques his character, as in the following internal monologue: "Oh, to acquire culture! Oh, to pronounce foreign names correctly! Oh, to be well informed!" (p. 41.)

---

* Besides the obvious connections with bastard, the name also could evoke St. Sebastian, who, full of the arrows of outrageous fortune, still manages to live on and

This is cheap playing to the Bloomsbury galleries. Nevertheless, it
is Leonard's connection with Helen and with Schlegel sensibilities
that gives this book its social conscience. Just as he stands on the
edge of the social "abyss," so he affords the Schlegels a glimpse into
it—increasing both their "panic and emptiness" and their guilt over
class and money. Money is a vital sub-theme in the book, and Margaret speaks for both sisters:

"You and I and the Wilcoxes stand upon money as upon islands. . . .

"Helen and I, we ought to remember, when we are tempted to criticize
others, that we are standing on these islands, and that most of the others are
down below the surface of the sea. The poor cannot always reach those whom
they want to love, and they can hardly ever escape from those whom they
love no longer. We rich can. Imagine the tragedy last June if Helen and
Paul Wilcox had been poor people, and couldn't invoke railways and motor-cars to part them.

". . . I'm tired of these rich people who pretend to be poor, and think it
shows a nice mind to ignore the piles of money that keep their feet above
the waves. I stand each year upon six hundred pounds, and Helen upon the
same, and Tibby will stand upon eight, and as fast as our pounds crumble
away into the sea they are renewed—from the sea, yes, from the sea. And
all our thoughts are the thoughts of six-hundred-pounders, and all our
speeches."[14]

This refusal to associate money with the devil, to repress the very
thought of it as something loathsome, as filthy lucre, is a measure
of her emancipation from Victorian mores. Only Margaret, however,
is ready to touch it forthrightly; Helen is so fearful of its contamina-
tion that (in a wildly altruistic gesture) she tries to give away £5,000
outright to Leonard—an act as full of hostility and disgust as of generosity.*

From Clapham onward the relationships between money on the
one hand and Nonconformist morality on the other were uneasy and
problematical; and Forster belongs to that class which felt these pres-

---

not despair. The connection of Leonard with "odours from the abyss" also brings
to mind that the Roman saint, after his martyrdom by stoning, was thrown into
a sewer.

* It is interesting that Ruth Wilcox carefully distinguishes between gifts of objects and gifts of money—objects being given to equals (as Howards End to Margaret) and money to servants. Since the Schlegels tend to share Mrs. Wilcox's values, Leonard is quite right in viewing this offer of money as humiliating. See HE,
85.

sures most acutely. *Howards End* reflects a critical stage that the problem reached around the turn of the century. Between 1880 and 1910 England gradually changed from the leading industrial power in Europe into the leading financial power, and along with this change went an ethical shift from what might be called Victorian work values to Edwardian money values. In that period, writes Noel Annan, "the restraints of religion and thrift and accepted class distinctions started to crumble and English society to rock under the flood of money. The class war, not merely between labour and owners, but between all social strata of the middle and upper classes began in earnest. . . . A new bitterness entered politics, a new rancour in foreign relations and a materialism of wealthy snobbery and aggressive philistinism arose far exceeding anything hitherto seen in England."[15]

When Britain awoke to discover that she was the world's leading money market, the knowledge had literary as well as ethical results. Money acquired by manipulation rather than by manual labor inaugurated a morality so much larger and more exciting than a pinchbeck calculus of right and wrong that writers found themselves in possession of a new and vital theme. *Erewhon Revisited, The Spoils of Poynton, The Awkward Age, The Way We Live Now, Belchamber, Major Barbara, New Grub Street,* and *Nostromo* are but a few of the works dealing with the corruption of society by money.[16] And *Howards End* perhaps heads this list of novels exploring ways the intellectual rich can live with their bank accounts and keep their consciences. The Schlegel sisters, trying to maintain spiritual canons of taste in an age increasingly dominated by pecuniary ones, are studies in the moral anxiety of living in a specialized world that has done away with the idea of dirty money as it has done away with the idea of original sin. They are the vanguard of those ethical possibilities seen by Keynes: "When the accumulation of wealth is no longer of high social importance, there will be great changes in the code of morals. . . . The love of money as a possession—as distinguished from the love of money as a means to the enjoyments and realities of life—will be recognised for what it is, a somewhat disgusting morbidity, one of those semi-criminal, semi-pathological propensities which one hands over with a shudder to the specialists in mental disease."[17]

Yet what of those, like Leonard, who neither love money nor have it? When Helen takes his umbrella by mistake at the Queen's Hall concert, he thinks she is trying to steal it: he has been "had" in the past, and "this fool of a young man thought that she and Helen and Tibby had been playing the confidence trick on him" (p. 37). His suspicions are not made believable, but the point is impressive: the poor cannot afford to trust people. Margaret "minds" his suffering, and teaches Helen to mind it too, but even as she considers inviting him to tea she is affronted by those "odours from the abyss" which cast his social and spiritual presentability in doubt. But "on the whole" (that Moorean measure) he is worth the risk:*

She wished that he was not so anxious to hand a lady downstairs, or to carry a lady's programme for her—his class was near enough her own for its manners to vex her. But she found him interesting on the whole—everyone interested the Schlegels on the whole at that time—and while her lips talked culture, her heart was planning to invite him to tea. (p. 39.)

The tea does not come off, but two years later their paths cross again when Jacky calls at Wickham Place to accuse the girls of stealing her husband. The plot is simply ridiculous at this point, but the Bast-Schlegel connection leads to some interesting confrontations. When Helen learns that Leonard, far from being off philandering, has gone for an all-night tramp across the Surrey countryside—"when darkness covered its amenities, and its cosy villas had re-entered ancient night"—she is unspeakably thrilled and admits him, momentarily, to equality. "You've pushed back the boundaries," Helen cries, exaltedly, "I think it splendid of you." To know that he could, even temporarily, drop his cultural anxieties and return to being "the naïve and sweet-tempered boy for whom Nature had intended him" was recommendation enough. Although he cannot (in their presence) yet talk about the Surrey countryside without dragging in Jefferies, Borrow, Thoreau, and R.L.S., he has nevertheless taken a step toward realizing "England." "Within his cramped little mind dwelt something that was greater than Jefferies' books—the spirit that led Jefferies to write them." (pp. 127–28.)

Thus do the Schlegels play the god, apparently without ever sus-

---

* It appears again in the mouth of Leonard: "Now, take me on the whole, I'm a quiet fellow." (p. 151.)

pecting that they are doing so. Margaret's analysis of Leonard, though shrewd, reveals a fantastic degree of aggressive snobbery:

One guessed him as the third generation, grandson to the shepherd or ploughboy whom civilization had sucked into the town; as one of the thousands who have lost the life of the body and failed to reach the life of the spirit. . . . Culture had worked in her own case, but during the last few weeks she had doubted whether it humanized the majority, so wide and so widening is the gulf that stretches between the natural and the philosophic man, so many the good chaps who are wrecked in trying to cross it. She knew this type very well—the vague aspirations, the mental dishonesty, the familiarity with the outsides of books. (pp. 121-22.)

Tibby stands with such pedants and esthetes as the Reverend Casaubon, Ralph Touchett, Marius the Epicurean, Sainty Belchamber, Stephen Undershaft, Des Esseintes, and Cecil Vyse*—a decadent and half-comic end-of-line aristocrat with intellectual pretensions. He is unable to love people and can love things only with a languid energy. Oxford suits him, as Forster deftly says, because "it wants its inmates to love it rather than to love one another. . . . His Oxford remained Oxford empty, and he took into life with him, not the memory of a radiance, but the memory of a colour scheme." (p. 111.) He is corrupted, if not by money, then by the leisure and softness money can bring. Nevertheless, Forster is his active partisan; he has twice the sympathy for Tibby that he has for the comparatively more attractive Henry Wilcox. *Howards End* displays in an aggravated form the problem of all humanistic fiction: that ordinary human beings must

---

* Cecil Vyse is actually referred to in this book, when Margaret and Tibby are discussing Tibby's possible choice of profession. Tibby, like Shaw's Stephen Undershaft, has just said that he prefers no profession whatever:

" 'I was thinking of Mr. Vyse. He never strikes me as particularly happy.'

" 'Yes-es,' said Tibby, and then held his mouth open in a curious quiver, as if he, too, had thought of Mr. Vyse, had seen round, through, over, and beyond Mr. Vyse, had weighed Mr. Vyse, grouped him, and finally dismissed him as having no possible bearing on the subject under discussion. That bleat of Tibby's infuriated Helen." (HE, 115–16.) As usual, Forster slips the names of some real people and places into his book. Mr. Dealtry, who appears on p. 49, bears a name important in Forster's family history; Munt was the name of Forster's first governess in the house in Hertfordshire ("The Art of Fiction," p. 37); and the Pomeranian references are probably accurate, p. 138.

serve both as absolute judges and as erring mortals in the same fable. Yet it is really an astonishing cultural prejudice that allows Forster to write, very much in earnest, that "Perhaps the keenest happiness he [Leonard] had ever known was during a railway journey to Cambridge, where a decent-mannered undergraduate had spoken to him" (p. 129). Can we really take seriously a happiness that depends on such desperate inequalities in the human condition? This book wants us to take it seriously, but the sight of the Schlegels capriciously dispensing largesse is enough to discourage any enthusiasm for *noblesse oblige*.

As Leonard is drawn more and more into Helen's orbit, he is more and more victimized by her idealism and absolutist zeal—and by Henry's advice. He quits his job on a false tip from Henry that his employer's firm is about to fail, and becomes "unemployable." Helen, infuriated at the injustice and at Henry's refusal to accept responsibility, flies with the "starving" Basts to Oniton, where the Wilcoxes have gone to celebrate Evie's wedding. She can get no justice. Margaret, when she learns that Jacky had been Henry's lover ten years before, is more nauseated than ever by the "odours from the abyss" and refuses to intercede. But Helen, turned salvationist, is obsessed with finding deliverance for the Basts ("the Basts were in her brain"), and, taking one of Margaret's own earlier theories literally, she tries to give them "the second most important thing in the world" —hard cash (pp. 134–35). Though he refuses the gift, Leonard has, ironically, come to believe the theory; he is on the verge of denying any role for "poetry" or the "diviner harmonies" in human life unless they are subsidized by money. Helen argues passionately against him, for his refusal of her bribe together with this new cynicism means the end of her power over him. She resorts to the desperate plea that a thing more real than money or injustice is *death*. Live in terms of this absolute, she begs; not in terms of these other "little things":

"Injustice and greed would be the real thing if we lived for ever. As it is, we must hold to other things because Death is coming. I love Death—not morbidly, but because He explains. He shows me the emptiness of Money. . . .

"The Wilcoxes are deeper in the mist than any. Sane, sound Englishmen!

building up empires, levelling all the world into what they call common sense. But mention Death to them and they're offended, because Death's really Imperial. . . .

" 'Death destroys a man: the idea of Death saves him.' Behind the coffins and the skeletons that stay the vulgar mind lies something so immense that all that is great in us responds to it." (pp. 252–53.)

But whatever she says, this is morbidity—as clear an expression of the death-wish as our literature offers. Hers is not simply a plea for the value of tragedy, for that awareness of death which increases incentives for life; it is rather a negative use of death as the great leveler, the evener of scores. Her notion of how to achieve deliverance for Leonard is "to cut the rope that fastened [him] to the earth" (p. 253), to set him loose on a journey upward, just as earlier she had exulted over his journey to "ancient night" in Surrey.* Leonard resists her deadly arguments, but his actual death at the end of the novel dramatically fulfills her program for him.

But if, in terms of the plot, this is an unfair and unjustified speech of Helen's, in terms of Forster's insight it is profound. Like Lawrence, Forster often writes bits of wisdom that are no less wise for not fitting into the narrative. Death destroys, but the idea of death saves—in seeing this, Forster is making his own break with the idealism of thinkers like Dickinson, and even Whitehead. Organisms like those in Dickinson's *Magic Flute* are without death and, hence, without individuality. To repress the idea of death is to kill the humanity of the individual. As Norman O. Brown says, "The precious ontological uniqueness which the human individual claims is conferred on him not by possession of an immortal soul but by possession of a mortal body."[18]

Helen sees the sickness inherent in this repression of death and sees also how deeply imbedded it is in the culture that Leonard is so sedulously aping. Her ideas are right; what is intolerable is her action, the unfairness of her setting herself up as absolute judge and executioner. And the sexual act preceding that finale and leading directly to it again shows Helen in the role of destroyer. Though the act produces

---

* Compare Mr. Beebe's image of Lucy as a kite in *A Room with a View* (p. 114). Just as Helen only ostensibly desires Leonard's freedom, so also does Mr. Beebe only ostensibly want Lucy's.

an heir for Howards End, for "England," it is nevertheless a "death" act, a kind of hysterical self-immolation verging on the suicidal:

> She and the victim seemed alone in a world of unreality, and she loved him absolutely, perhaps for half an hour. (p. 335.)

He *is* a victim, and the fleshly union is unreal. Though the scene negotiates with the ancient truth that he who would save his life must lose it, that truth suffers a terrible distortion. Her half-hour's sexual gift was an expression of "panic and emptiness" rather than love; and though she conceives a child, the father of that child is utterly repudiated, cut off from any continuing love, while Helen cloisters herself, not unhappily, against the possibility of any such sharing in the future. Why is he the victim, and not she? The answer is obvious: she has *title* to her inheritance, while he must *earn* his. And since his earning power has been destroyed, the best he can hope for is to provide a future heir and then pass quietly out of the picture, content that the Schlegels remember him with a few kind, or at least respectful, words.

4

We have seen that this morality play begins, as morality plays must, with certain prejudices in favor of the angels. But what about Margaret's "connection"? Less prudish and absolute than Helen, in her exogamic marriage to Henry Wilcox she makes a definite effort to join the prose and the passion. She knew Henry's faults and took the connubial risk with her eyes open. She says to Helen:

> "There is the widest gulf between my love-making and yours. Yours was romance; mine will be prose. I'm not running it down—a very good kind of prose, but well considered, well thought out. . . . I know all Mr. Wilcox's faults. He's afraid of emotion. He cares too much about success, too little about the past. His sympathy lacks poetry, and so isn't sympathy really. I'd even say"—she looked at the shining lagoons—"that, spiritually, he's not as honest as I am. Doesn't that satisfy you?" (p. 184.)

It is an astonishing statement to come from one who will soon be a bride. Is her honesty about Henry matched by an equal honesty in examining her own motives? The evidence is interesting.

First we must admit that the case against Henry is a strong one.*
He treats people as things; he turns Howards End (i.e., England) into
a warehouse; he is a prude and defensively conventional. He is mad
with rage over Helen's affair with Leonard, yet he cannot see that his
own adultery with Jacky is morally the same. When the Jacky affair
comes to light, Margaret, to save him from panic, has to help him
"rebuild his fortress and hide his soul from the world" (p. 261). He
can never admit to being wrong, whereas the Schlegels did not mind
being wrong: "To them nothing was fatal but evil." Margaret's frank-
ness even allows her to hope that someday, "in the millennium," her
husband's "type" will be expendable. But for the present, the Wilcox
virtues of "neatness, obedience, and decision" (though they kill imagination) remain necessary for the race's survival, and deserve homage
"from those who think themselves superior, and who possibly are"
(p. 171).

These thoughts about her husband-to-be bring out the missionary
in her. She thinks of her love as a means of setting "his soul in order"
(p. 232), of making him a "better man," of helping him "to the building of the rainbow bridge that should connect the prose in us with
the passion."[19] "How wide the gulf between Henry as he was and
Henry as Helen thought he ought to be! And she herself [Margaret]
—hovering as usual between the two, now accepting men as they are,
now yearning with her sister for Truth. Love and Truth—their warfare seems eternal." (p. 243.)

How easily Margaret turns from talking about Henry to talking
about "men"—as though Henry were not an individual but a symbol!
And this, in large part, is what her problem in connection comes to.
Seeing that her influence over him depends on what she calls "the
methods of the harem," she increasingly feels association with him to
be a humiliation, an aspect of the eternal contention between male
and female. When, for example, Henry owns up to his affair with
Jacky, Margaret knows that he is "not so much confessing his soul

---

* Yet one of the arcane ironies of this novel is that Henry is given almost exactly
the same features as Philip Herriton—the same high forehead, the same retreating
chin and ambiguous lips. To the degree that Philip is Forster himself, this is indeed
one of the neater "secrets" that Forster loves to keep from the reader. Compare
HE, 95, and WA, 78. See Chapter Seven, p. 177.

as pointing out the gulf between the male soul and the female" (p. 259). Again and again we hear echoes of the melioristic notion advanced by Carpenter and Dickinson of the emergence of a "third sex," a new synthesis that will transcend sex, as the notion of the classless society would transcend class: "Are the sexes really races, each with its own code of morality, and their mutual love a mere device of Nature to keep things going? Strip human intercourse of the proprieties, and is it reduced to this?"

> Her judgment told her no. She knew that out of Nature's device we have built a magic that will win us immortality. Far more mysterious than the call of sex to sex is the tenderness that we throw into that call. . . . We are evolving, in ways that Science cannot measure, to ends that Theology dares not contemplate. (p. 254.)

Is it possible for Margaret to love anyone who does not also hear this millennial call—to this "truth" which is greater than love? Implicit in her whole relationship with Henry is the nagging question of whether she should make do with "men" in the relativistic present, or anticipate the classless and sexless society, now, in her own sensual being.

Her decision—or better, her drift—is strongly influenced by the first Mrs. Wilcox. From the first, Margaret is touched and chastened by this uncontentious spirit. At a time when Margaret is "zig-zagging with her friends over Thought and Art" in the New English Art Club, Ruth Wilcox declares: "We never discuss anything at Howards End." "Clever talk alarmed her, and withered her delicate imaginings; it was the social counterpart of a motor-car, all jerks, and she was a wisp of hay, a flower." (pp. 81, 78.) This wisp of hay nevertheless can sting like a nettle, as Margaret discovers when she is snubbed for refusing Ruth's first invitation to visit Howards End—for failing to recognize the importance of Howards End and the favor that was being shown her. (Ruth is the only character with greater spiritual authority than Margaret, and she is merciless on lapses of intuition.) She acts as an influence rather than a mover, thinking it "wiser to leave action and discussion to men," but when called upon to "separate those human beings who will hurt each other the most," she moves with uncompromising dispatch. But there is no hurry in her character: "She took her time, or perhaps let time take her." (p. 83.)

Without any obvious messianic equipment, she moves on the earth as an incarnation of spiritual absolutes, an embodiment of "England's" best self. Even Henry Wilcox recognized her "unvarying virtue," the "wonderful innocence that was hers by the gift of God" (p. 94), and the tenderness of his grief when she dies is perhaps his highest recommendation. But their union raises some vexing questions: What could possibly have led her to marry him—the same motives that moved Margaret? Then why does her spiritual power not have a greater effect on her brood of Wilcox barbarians? Does this mean that Margaret, in her missionary attempts with Henry, is defeated before she starts—that prose and passion cannot mix? If Ruth had so little influence on Henry, what can Margaret do? These questions demonstrate, in part, the near impossibility of bringing the worlds of myth and of realism together in the same book. But the difficulty, one feels, is not just technical; the more one reads this novel, the more one is disturbed by its ethical evasiveness.

Howards End is Ruth's temple. To the Schlegels, as to Rickie, houses are "alive," whereas the Wilcoxes treat houses as things to buy, sell, lease, and improve. "We know this is our house," says Helen about Howards End, "because it feels ours" (p. 318). Though the Wilcoxes hold the "title-deeds" and the "door keys," these evidences of ownership do not impress the Schlegels. The clash between realism and romance is marked. When Margaret marries, in a sense she marries both Henry and Ruth—the one in the flesh, the other in the spirit. The first union gives her legal title to the house, but the second gives her spiritual title, and there is no doubt which one Forster respects more. Mrs. Wilcox alone had "possessed" Howards End, for she had loved it, had sensed its inner and continuing life. The ancient wych-elm, where pigs' teeth had been buried by the country people in the belief that the bark would then cure the toothache, is to her no mere curiosity, but a precious and true inheritance, the soul of the past impinging on the present. So when Mrs. Wilcox on her deathbed pencils a hasty note (which she fails to sign) leaving Howards End to Margaret, it is a spiritual rather than a material bequest (though the Schlegels ultimately get the material house as well). The Wilcoxes, of course, see in Ruth's act only illegality and "treachery":

To them Howards End was a house: they could not know that to her it had
been a spirit, for which she sought a spiritual heir. And—pushing one step
farther in these mists—may not they have decided even better than they supposed? Is it credible that the possessions of the spirit can be bequeathed at
all? Has the soul offspring? (p. 104.)

The joining of a house to a spirit, of treasure upon earth to treasure
in heaven, is part of Margaret's problem in connection; and Forster,
like the Claphamites, deals with spiritual questions in the language
of the court and the marketplace. But in exploring these "mists,"
Forster brushes against the more broadly symbolic issue of homelessness itself. The loss of the "mythical home, the mythical source,"
writes Nietzsche, is a cause of the "stupendous historical exigency of
the unsatisfied modern culture,"[20] and Forster is first among contemporary writers to exploit the symbolic reality of a house that is a
home, one of those simple universals evoking the critical need of modern man to "find his way back to a world in which he is no longer
a stranger."[21]

As the novel proceeds, Margaret becomes more and more identified
with Mrs. Wilcox, eventually assuming not only her married name
but much of her nature. Ruth represents the achievement of "proportion," an ideal which has always ranked highest with Margaret.
Margaret tells Helen,

"To be humble and kind, to go straight ahead, to love people rather than
pity them, to remember the submerged—well, one can't do all these things
at once, worse luck, because they're so contradictory. It's then that proportion comes in—to live by proportion. Don't *begin* with proportion. Only
prigs do that. Let proportion come in as a last resource, when the better
things have failed." (p. 77.)

In fact many of the "better things" do seem to have failed for Ruth
Wilcox: she no longer enjoys art, literature, conversation, sex, family
life, or even personal relations. Proportion amounts to Arnoldian
"disinterestedness," a kind of middle ground between partisanship
and indifference, a rising above competition, and Margaret drifts
toward it. Like Ruth, she becomes less and less "enthusiastic about
justice," saying to Helen at Oniton: "There is to be none of this
absurd screaming about justice. I have no use for justice." (p. 241.)
Nor, at last, does she care any more about "duty," art or literature,

political or social problems. "She had outgrown stimulants," writes
Forster, "and was passing from words to things" (pp. 276–77), moving
toward that strange spiritual autism which also is to overcome Mrs.
Moore in *A Passage to India*.

As part of this process, she turns against the city and toward the
country, as Ruth had done. Earlier, Margaret had been surprised to
hear Ruth say "there was nothing to get up for in London" (p. 73),
but as her eyes open to the architecture and the language of "hurry"
she too comes to despise cosmopolitanism. "This craze for motion,"
she says, "has only set in during the last hundred years. It may be
followed by a civilization that won't be a movement, because it will
rest on the earth" (p. 359). Earlier in the novel, Forster had written:
"Month by month the roads smelt more strongly of petrol, and were
more difficult to cross, and human beings heard each other speak with
greater difficulty, breathed less of the air, and saw less of the sky. Nature withdrew: the leaves were falling by midsummer; the sun shone
through dirt with an admired obscurity." (pp. 113–14.) The psychic
withdrawal of Ruth and Margaret is but an aping of Nature's defeat,
and a recognition that the city is a form of death. As Lewis Mumford
writes: "The metropolis is rank with forms of *negative vitality*. Nature and human nature, violated in this environment, come back in
destructive forms. . . . In this mangled state the impulse to live departs from apparently healthy personalities. The impulse to die sup-
plants it."[22] It is through Ruth, not through marriage, that Margaret
finds relief from "flux." It is through Ruth, not through Henry, that
she finds a home amidst the "civilization of luggage." Yet the "proportion" both the women achieve or seek is hardly anything more
than a form of the *negative vitality* Mumford speaks of, an opting
out of active life. Though Margaret's moves from Wickham Place to
Oniton to Howards End are all away from metropolitan deathliness,
away from the secular city to the holy country, she is nonetheless
tainted by this negativism, and led further into it by Ruth. Margaret
is no Christian "in the accepted sense" and does not "believe that God
had ever worked among us as a young artisan." But Ruth Wilcox is
evidence to her that God works in other ways, the living affirmation
that "it is private life that holds out the mirror to infinity" (p. 86).
The child of an unbelieving though churchgoing age, Margaret finds

in Ruth everything she can retain as religion. "Though it is impossible to tell," writes J. Hillis Miller, "whether man has excluded God by building his great cities, or whether the cities have been built because God has disappeared, in any case the two go together."[23] And Forster—with Margaret concurring—would agree with him that "life in the city is the way in which many men have experienced most directly what it means to live without God in the world":[24]

Certainly London fascinates. One visualizes it as a tract of quivering grey, intelligent without purpose, and excitable without love; as a spirit that has altered before it can be chronicled; as a heart that certainly beats, but with no pulsation of humanity. . . . Nature, with all her cruelty, comes nearer to us than do these crowds of men. . . . London is religion's opportunity—not the decorous religion of theologians, but anthropomorphic, crude. Yes, the continuous flow would be tolerable if a man of our own sort—not anyone pompous or tearful—were caring for us up in the sky. (p. 114.)

Margaret's following of St. Ruth is a direct consequence of her repudiation of London. But we feel it as a negative discipleship, an escape to a kind of pleasant despair; for the city remains and needs some good force to "connect" with it.

5

What, finally, can we say of Margaret's connection with Henry? Does she love him and give the marriage a fair trial, or does she only go through the motions? Her early feelings for him describe an ascending order of impatience: he had cheated on Ruth, he sells Oniton without consulting his wife, he is underhanded about the irregular will (this is discovered later), and he even refuses to let the pregnant Helen spend a night in Howards End. While he forgets his own immorality, he is conventionally outraged at Helen's, causing Margaret to deliver a speech that marks her final emotional deliverance from him. Though the word "love" is used after this, one feels it is only the return to a verbal habit.

"Not any more of this!" she cried. "You shall see the connection if it kills you, Henry! You have had a mistress—I forgave you. My sister has a lover—you drive her from the house. Do you see the connection? Stupid, hypocritical, cruel—oh, contemptible!—a man who insults his wife when she's alive and cants with her memory when she's dead. A man who ruins a woman for his pleasure, and casts her off to ruin other men. And gives bad financial advice, and then says he is not responsible. These men are you. You can't recognize them because you cannot connect. I've had enough of your un-weeded kindness. I've spoilt you long enough. . . . No one has ever told what you are—muddled, criminally muddled. Men like you use repentance as a blind, so don't repent. Only say to yourself, 'What Helen has done, I've done.' " (p. 325.)

Later, remembering her words, "her speech to him seemed perfect." "She neither forgave him for his behaviour nor wished to forgive him." "It had to be uttered," she claims, "to adjust the lopsidedness of the world"; and—significantly—"It was spoken not only to her hus-band, but to thousands of men like him—a protest against the inner darkness in high places that comes with a commercial age. . . . He had refused to connect, on the clearest issue that can be laid before a man, and their love must take the consequences." (p. 350.)

But has she adjusted the world's lopsidedness, or has she made it more lopsided? To address herself not just to Henry but to "men," to those imaginary "thousands," is evidence enough that she has, un-consciously perhaps, rehearsed this speech before. It is evidence, too, that her relation to him is not simply "personal," but abstract; he is in fact a figure in her personal allegory even as he is in her author's. In one of her ponderings Margaret reflects: "It is pleasant to analyse feelings while they are still only feelings, and unembodied in the social fabric" (p. 183). Yes, and it is equally pleasant to discuss love this way, before it is invested in a man. The purity of detachment strongly appeals to her, and it is impossible not to feel the profound relief, and even pleasure, in her casting-out speech to Henry. But to divide fact from feeling and love from flesh in this way is the essence of sentimentality; and Margaret's "love" is not exempt from the cruelty that so often accompanies the sentimental attitude. Before Henry, we are told, she had often loved, "but only so far as the facts of sex demanded: mere yearnings for the masculine, to be dismissed for what they were worth, with a smile" (p. 175). But why with a smile? Could her yearnings for the feminine, her loyalties to Helen and to Ruth, be dismissed so lightly? Something is indeed lopsided here. Henry's commitment to Margaret has of course its shortcomings —he could be "a little ashamed of loving a wife" (p. 197), and he is as ascetically furtive about sex as he is about money—but Margaret is essentially virginal from the start. Her real design is to save Henry, not to marry him; and their actual relations are a power struggle, as the following passage makes clear:

A younger woman might have resented his masterly ways, but Margaret... was, in her own way, as masterly. If he was a fortress she was a mountain peak, whom all might tread, but whom the snows made nightly virginal. Disdaining the heroic outfit, excitable in her methods, garrulous, episodical, shrill, she misled her lover much as she had misled her aunt. He mistook her fertility for weakness. (p. 194.)

Nor does an "invitation to disloyalty" toward Henry disturb her. When Miss Avery, the querulous and half-literate country woman who had served immemorially at Howards End, comments (referring to the family history) that "things went on until there were no men," Margaret is amused. She laughs again when this old crone declares: "But Wilcoxes are better than nothing, as I see you've found." (p. 289.) Although old servants are privileged in speech, Margaret's encouraging this rudeness effects a tacit alliance against her husband. Perhaps Margaret is laughing at "men" more than at Henry, but even so she is sexually hostile—or withdrawn—and clearly the marriage is hampered by her reluctance to meet Henry—or in fact any man—halfway. Her "fertility" is intellectual, and the connections she cares about most (as she makes clear in her speech to Henry) are connections of ethical ideas. She cannot love children and is "thankful to have none"; before the novel ends, "places" and "things" have become more important to her than people:*

"I can play with [children's] beauty and charm, but that is all—nothing real, not one scrap of what there ought to be. And others—others go farther still, and move outside humanity altogether. A place, as well as a person, may catch the glow. Don't you see that all this leads to comfort in the end?" (p. 357.)

But whose comfort? The book ends with the two girls and their misbegotten heir in complete and undisputed possession of Howards End, in its real as well as its spiritual estate—and with all the human creatures they connected with either maimed, imprisoned, or

---

* Margaret says: "I believe we shall come to care about people less and less, Helen. ...I quite expect to end my life caring most for a place." (p. 138.)

dead. Once again things had gone on until there were no more
men. Henry is still physically present, and we are told that Margaret
still loves him, but he is broken, a man no longer. Margaret had said
that she would make him see the connection if it "killed" him, and
she very nearly has had her wish. After Charles goes to prison convicted of manslaughter for his part in Leonard's death, Henry's "fortress" gives way, and he simply turns himself over to Margaret "to do
what she could with him." Margaret dismisses him dryly: "He has
worked very hard all his life, and noticed nothing. Those are the
people who collapse when they do notice a thing." (p. 355.) If there
is love in that remark, it is not recognizable in any ordinary sense.
Margaret's may be one of the unfairest marriages in modern fiction.

Leonard dies of "natural causes" after Charles, avenging Helen's
seduction, strikes him down with the flat of the old Schlegel sword.
Charles, an even more unbelievable character than Jacky, is a caricature of Wilcox chivalry, the comedy-hall avenger full of wooden
words and gestures.* But Helen has in effect killed Leonard long
before. She has "loved the absolute," and, appropriately, Leonard has
"been ruined absolutely" (p. 334). He becomes to her "not a man,
but a cause" (p. 329); and after that, even less. "I ought to remember
Leonard as my lover," she says. "I tempted him, and killed him, and
it is surely the least I can do. I would like to throw out my heart to
Leonard on such an afternoon as this. But I cannot. It is no good pretending. I am forgetting him." Even this small display of conscience
annoys Margaret: "I can't have you worrying about Leonard. Don't
drag in the personal when it will not come. Forget him." And then
follows an exhibition of the sisters' high-mindedness and high-
handedness:

> "Yes, yes, but what has Leonard got out of life?"
> "Perhaps an adventure."
> "Is that enough?"
> "Not for us. But for him."
> Helen took up a bunch of grass. . . .
> "Is it sweetening yet?" asked Margaret. (pp. 356–57.)

---

* To Tibby: "Who d'ye suspect, then? Speak out, man. One always suspects someone." (p. 328.) On Leonard, just arrived at Howards End: "Oh, is he there? I am
not surprised. I now thrash him within an inch of his life." (p. 343.)

Thus do the gods dispense their rewards, and thus are men ex-punged from their lives and from Howards End. In a highly sym-bolic scene after Helen's final return to Howards End, Margaret stands at the gate like a seraph, guarding it against Henry and Crane, the chauffeur, who have come to enforce Helen's removal: "A new feeling came over her; she was fighting for women against men. She did not care about rights, but if men came into Howards End, it should be over her body." (p. 306.) The house symbolizing England has become a feminine sanctuary, nor has it been preserved against effeminacy. The women are content with this state of things: "This is ours. Our furniture, our sort of people coming to the door." (p. 318.) And they smugly amuse themselves over the masculine spolia-tions of the past. The only convincing love scene in the book is that between Margaret and Helen, alone at last, exchanging endearments in the temple from which men have been excluded. It is almost in-cestuous, a love that has cast off all connections except those within the family—and with God's representative, Ruth Wilcox:

"I feel that you and I and Henry are only fragments of that woman's mind. She knows everything. She is everything. She is the house, and the tree that leans over it. People have their own deaths as well as their own lives, and even if there is nothing beyond death, we shall differ in our nothing-ness." (p. 331.)

We shall differ in our nothingness! Meaningless as the statement is, it brings to mind words that have recurred throughout the book—emptiness, abyss, darkness, panic, death. These words have been as conspicuous as the vocabulary of connection—proportion, wholeness, the light within. And they remind us, though we do not feel their author intended them to, that the struggles of the book are not solely between Red-bloods and Mollycoddles, but between forces of ideal-ism and nihilism within the company of the saved.

The Schlegel experiments in connection mean a little expansion outward of their femininity, a little relaxing of their frigidity and fear, and then a closing again into a tight circle of safety and inviola-bility. They make of Howards End a place of sterile quarantine for the best self of England, but there is no indication that these de-fenders will ever again do battle with the enemy. The symbolic hope, of course, is Helen's son. He is continuance. But we have no reason to suppose that Helen and Margaret will be better child-rearers than Ruth Wilcox. The burden of the book's conclusion is that Forster does not really want connection at all, but only the rewards of connection; he does not want sex, but only the heir. He wants, in short, ends without means. As Margaret says: "Alas! that Henry should fade away as reality emerged, and only her love for him should remain clear, stamped with his image like the cameos we rescue out of dreams." (p. 351.) This is the love of love, not the love of people, and while it may be sound Moorean ethics, it is a disastrous program for practical humanism. "She, who had never expected to conquer anyone, had charged straight through these Wilcoxes and broken up their lives." (pp. 360–61.) The girls are "finished" almost before they begin, yet Forster calls their retreat a "victory":

And all the time their salvation was lying round them—the past sanctifying the present; the present, with wild heart-throb, declaring that there would after all be a future, with laughter and the voices of children. Helen, still smiling, came up to her sister. She said, "It is always Meg." They looked into each other's eyes. The inner life had paid. (p. 315.)

The sisters' victory, to be sure, is not complete—it will take two thousand years of development to attain it fully—but they have won the battle.*

We end with sensitivity quarantined from impulse, and an attendant promise of decadence and brutality. It is too bad, for this is a fascinating and ambitious book, and few readers will easily believe that this is what Forster really wants his fable to say. The malignancy inherent in a spiritual-esthetic withdrawal is a subject Forster knows well, and has warned about in his essays.[25] But in fictionalizing the problem, he has presented a moral failure as a triumph—and, in the name of much that is beautiful and fine, has become the partisan of much that is sick and corrupt. The forces of value do not "connect," but pursue each other in a lonely and circular futility. And the circle is especially vicious because Forster seems to see only its "proportion" and not its "emptiness."

* Compare the vision of connecting the races in Faulkner's "Delta Autumn": *"Maybe in a thousand or two thousand years in America ... But not now! Not now!"* Go Down Moses (Harmondsworth, 1961), p. 272.

6

But as a technical experiment this is an important novel, and perhaps even a great one. Its thematic problems arise in part because
Forster tried to say and do too much. "I think *Howards End* is all
right," he wrote on his eightieth birthday. "But I sometimes get a
little bored with it. There seems too much, too many social nuances,
there."[26] This crowding, however, is part of the book's fascination:
into it Forster poured the splendid energies of a fine intelligence and
a writing talent at a high point of maturity. The texture of the prose
alone, even-voiced and urbane, makes it worth the reading—it is the
style of a man with an almost perfect ear for rhythmic decorums. But
its greatest interest comes from the fact that it is Forster's first major
experiment with the technique of "rhythm."

Forster and Bloomsbury as a whole held that Art, purely conceived, should transform the raw materials of temporal life into something transcending them. All the dualisms of *Howards End*—the seen
and the unseen, the outer and the inner, the public and the private,
motion and rest, city and country, men and women, Red-bloods and
Mollycoddles—represent possible poles of this transformation. Forster
does not aspire, as Virginia Woolf does, to create a fictional structure
which "is miraculously habitable without the help of walls, stair-
cases, or partitions," but he is as eager as she to take the novel beyond "story," beyond the stenography and photography of realism.
Though he begins with "people" and himself in particular, he aims
at anonymity, at a state, as Virginia Woolf says, that passes "beyond
the range of personality into a world which is not altogether the
world of fiction."[27] To describe this achievement Forster employs
the terms "fantasy" and "prophecy." Fantasy is here less relevant
than prophecy, which is a "tone of voice," a kind of music. "How will
song combine with the furniture of common sense?" Forster asks in
Aspects. Not very well, he answers, yet that is exactly what this book
tries to do—and is a main reason for its thematic failures.

But the novel is not prophetic on every page: the furniture of
common sense is by no means altogether slighted. Indeed, in the
scene where the Schlegel library tumbles down upon Leonard and
disarrays the tables and chairs, the furniture of common sense is very
literally present. Nor is Forster being prophetic when he describes

Henry as "one of those men who know the principal hotel by instinct" (p. 187), or Evie as "one of those who name animals after the
less successful characters of Old Testament history" (p. 149), or when
he says of Mrs. Warrington, "Like many other critics of Empire, her
mouth had been stopped with food" (p. 223). Humor is antipathetic
to prophecy, and much of the novel is humorous. Yet the book's main
flow is from lightness to seriousness; and even Tibby, in a casual way,
is carried in it: "Mellowing rapidly, he was a pleasanter companion
than before. Oxford had done much for him. He had lost his peevish-
ness, and could hide his indifference to people and his interest in
food." (p. 295.)

To read this novel as Forster would have us read it, we must conceive of it as a kind of musical score in which leitmotifs associated
with certain characters and situations are of special importance. And
it is the alternation of these leitmotifs that provides what, essentially,
Forster means by "rhythm." The book's rhythms are carried mainly by
key phrases, and words within these phrases, which are stated and
repeated in ever-widening circles of meaning. These circles are not
neatly concentric; like rings in water they vary according to the kind
of disturbance they meet with. The energetic Wilcoxes throw many
stones, and the spreading rings are broken up; the Schlegels, when
they have the sacred lake to themselves, throw one stone and are content to watch Nature complete the harmonious patterns in peace.
"Heaven works of itself," says Margaret—a condition of spiritual
laissez-faire which, finally, she and her sister try to emulate in their
own lives.

The displacement of Margaret's affections from people to places and
things is a movement from the rhythms of "telegrams and anger" to
those of Nature—a movement of expansion. For the city-dweller,
personal expansion is confined to the limits of the city, but for those
who live in the unspoiled country, where the horizons of the imagination widen to "space" itself, and the un-urgent rhythms of the land
(its little hesitations and rolling gradients) lead to infinity, there
sounds a universal music. The city is the outer life, a cacophony, a
huge interruption in the symphony of the spirit; it is the inner life
that spreads into thematic dominance and expands into the finale:

The mask fell off the city, and she saw it for what it really is—a caricature of infinity.... Helen seemed one with grimy trees and the traffic and the slowly-flowing slabs of mud.... Margaret's own faith held firm. She knew the human soul will be merged, if it be merged at all, with the stars and the sea. (p. 296.)

To list all the rhythmic statements and recapitulations is impossible, but we must follow a few, for they are in effect the score of this book.

"Panic and emptiness," Helen's term for the Wilcoxes and their way of life, first occurs to her as she listens to the Fifth Symphony; the words are always associated in her consciousness with Paul or Henry, or with the goblins, which are Red-bloods in fantastic disguise. But when Helen cuts herself off from the Wilcoxes, the phrase is never again heard in its wholeness. To be sure, the goblins return (as Beethoven predicted they would) at the very end of the book, on the occasion of Leonard's death,* but they then bring only a diminished memory of what to Helen had once been an overwhelming terror of "panic and emptiness." The phrase is last heard undiminished in what we might call the third movement of the book, during Helen's last conversation with Leonard. It refers, as usual, to the Wilcoxes and their breed: "and if you could pierce through him, you'd find panic and emptiness in the middle" (p. 248). Before the phrase finally dissolves, we hear it several times in fragments, the barest echoes of its early volume. Helen speaks of the "emptiness" of money (p. 252), and Margaret seeks to save Henry from "panic."

But in the coda it does not appear at all. Here Helen's phrase has become "Death destroys a man, but the idea of death saves him" (p. 342), a phrase that grows directly out of "panic and emptiness" and replaces it. The transference is ingenious. On the very page where "emptiness" is sounded for the last time (p. 252), this new phrase takes over, marking the point where Helen repudiates Henry once for all and embarks on her new career of saving Leonard. "Death destroys ... but the idea of death saves" works in two ways: as a final damning criticism of the Wilcoxes (they cannot face death), and as

---

* "Again and again must the drums tap, and the goblins stalk over the universe before joy can be purged of the superficial." (p. 342.)

an argument to win Leonard from his attachment to the kingdoms of this world. In a broader sense, it also marks the transition between Helen's concern with social problems and her attachment to universals; this movement, which dominates the whole book, is the movement toward "prophecy." Thus one motif fades into another. "Did Leonard grow out of Paul?" Helen asks at the end. The answer is obvious: it is another way of asking whether "the idea of death" grew out of "panic and emptiness."

Both Helen and Margaret move in and out of the Wilcox sphere of influence, but just as their personalities and motives are different so are their rhythms, or motifs, different. Both try to get in tune with the alien rhythms of "telegrams and anger," but Helen collides, creating some of the novel's most violent cacophony. Margaret, however —so we are told—connects throughout: "She connected though the connection might be bitter." (p. 220.) Her word is "proportion," and the phrases that express her inner and outer movements are mainly variations on the two metaphors of connection and proportion. As Mrs. Wilcox fades and dies, Margaret moves into her theme:

> Some leave our life with tears, others with an insane frigidity; Mrs. Wilcox had taken the middle course, which only rarer natures can pursue. She had kept proportion.... It is thus ... that we ought to die—neither as victim nor as fanatic, but as the seafarer who can greet with an equal eye the deep that he is entering, and the shore that he must leave. (p. 108.)

Proportion lies between frigidity and tears, and Margaret is credited with steering that nice course, avoiding the shipwreck threatened in Beethoven's symphony. The metaphor of the seafarer, repeated with variations again and again (once with reference to Tennyson's Ulysses), is always used to describe one who embarks without illusions on a difficult course, and who acquires knowledge in doing so.* This is Forster's benediction on Margaret's marriage: "They have weathered the storm, and may reasonably expect peace. To have no illusions and yet to love—what stronger surety can a woman find?" (p. 272.)

But just as Margaret fades into Mrs. Wilcox (she and Helen are "fragments of that woman's mind"), so a number of other characters are described and criticized in Margaret's "voice." This is to be ex-

---

* After Margaret forgives Henry, she finds everything "in proportion now and she, too, would pity the man who was blundering up and down their lives" (p. 257).

pected, for Margaret's voice comes closest to Forster's own, and he makes no attempt at all to hide his partisanship for her and her ideal of "proportion." The most important metaphor carrying that ideal is expressed in Matthew Arnold's famous line about Sophocles: "Who saw life steadily and saw it whole."[28] It is heard intact four times in the novel, at intervals of roughly one hundred pages, and it is heard at other times in fragments, scattering now into metaphors of clear-seeing and steady-seeing, and now into metaphors of wholeness. The phrase appears first with Leonard: "Oh, it was no good, this contin-ual aspiration. . . . To see life steadily and to see it whole was not for the likes of him." (p. 58.) Arnoldian culture is beyond him. Even Margaret at times is swept with little gusts of despair and her voice falters: "It is impossible to see modern life steadily and see it whole, and she had chosen to see it whole. Mr. Wilcox saw steadily." (pp. 170–71.) But when Margaret looks not at "modern life" but at the eternal life of the country, proportion seems a reality once more:

Here had lived an elder race, to which we look back with disquietude. The country which we visit at week-ends was really a home to it, and the graver sides of life, the deaths, the partings, the yearnings for love, have their deep-est expression in the heart of the fields. All was not sadness. The sun was shining without. The thrush sang his two syllables on the budding guelder-rose. Some children were playing uproariously in heaps of golden straw. . . . In these English farms, if anywhere, one might see life steadily and see it whole, group in one vision its transitoriness and its eternal youth, connect— connect without bitterness until all men are brothers. (pp. 283–84.)

But this is a momentary connecting, and Margaret knows that the modern symphony cannot close on that note: "Under cosmopolitan-ism, if it comes, we shall receive no help from the earth." (p. 275.)

Although Margaret is somewhat less adept at seeing clearly than at seeing whole, the Wilcoxes fail on both counts: "The breezy Wilcox manner, though genuine, lacked the clearness of vision that is imper-ative for truth." (p. 192.) Addicted as they are to the "visible," they cannot see even that—to say nothing of the "invisible"—in propor-tion. And Margaret, in her great denunciatory speech, takes as her theme Henry's failure to "*see* the connection," damning his failure to "*notice* things."* We are told that "she loved him with too clear

* Italics in original.

a vision to fear his cloudiness" (p. 233), but if she did not fear it she certainly hated it. The Wilcox way of seeing is to "concentrate," and that word—with all its implications of squinting, shrinking, peeking, focusing on details in the Benthamite fashion rather than on wholes,*—is part of the rhythmic rising and falling of the Arnoldian phrase over the course of the novel:

> He simply did not notice things, and there was no more to be said. He never noticed that Helen and Frieda were hostile, or that Tibby was not interested in currant plantations.... "My motto is Concentrate. I've no intention of frittering away my strength on that sort of thing!" "It isn't frittering away the strength," she protested. "It's enlarging the space in which you may be strong." He answered: "You're a clever little woman, but my motto's Concentrate." (pp. 197–98.)

"As is Man to the Universe, so was the mind of Mr. Wilcox to the minds of some men—a concentrated light upon a tiny spot, a little Ten Minutes moving self-contained through its appointed years." (p. 263.) Mrs. Munt, too, is associated with the word: "To history, to tragedy, to the past, to the future, Mrs. Munt remained equally indifferent; hers but to *concentrate* on the end of her journey, and to rescue poor Helen." (p. 15.)† Margaret's awareness of "space" and of the illimitable reaches of human possibility is, therefore, a rebuke to all those in the book who view life microscopically or through the focus of the "half-closed eye." The last echo of Arnold's phrase is heard as Leonard, defeated in his search for "Culture," rides countryward to Howards End. In passing Tewin Woods he notes—between the house and the graves of two old country eccentrics—"the villas of business men, who saw life more steadily, though with the steadiness of the half-closed eye" (p. 341). To Henry, "steadiness included all praise" (p. 95), whereas Margaret, Helen, and even Leonard were clear-seers, in the ranks of Arnold's "children of light."‡

Thus the words "clearness," "steadiness," "wholeness," and their variants, together with different ways of "seeing," join at times into

---

* "Henry treated marriage like a funeral, item by item, never raising his eyes to the whole." (p. 323.) See Chapter One, p. 5.

† Italics added.

‡ "But Leonard was near the abyss, and at such moments men see clearly." (p. 240.)

the full Arnoldian sentence and at other times break into fragments, as the vision of the characters involved approaches or falls short of proportion. The metaphor is one of seeing, but the joinings and partings of these words comprise a music as well, and impinge on the domain of sound. The Wilcox inability to "see" is also an inability to "hear," and when father and son are shown metaphorically stuffing their ears, we realize that their deafness is but a different form of their blindness:

Charles and his father sometimes disagreed. But they always parted with an increased regard for one another, and each desired no doughtier comrade when it was necessary to voyage for a little past the emotions. So the sailors of Ulysses voyaged past the Sirens, having first stopped one another's ears with wool. (p. 107.)

We could follow other rhythms, but the key ones are the dominant phrases of Margaret and Helen. From these centers the main themes expand, like rings in water, or like sound waves in air. They converge and set up disturbances, something new emerges, and finally all dissension closes on the "sacred centre": "He passed again and again amid whirring blades and sweet odours of grass, encompassing with narrowing circles the sacred centre of the field." (p. 354.) This is the same center as that of Cadbury Rings, or of Rickie's dell, or of the country inside the hedge: we are home again with mother (and her only child) and the bad father is once again punished for having died young. The "jangle of causes and effects" (p. 348) becomes stilled (and here is one of those points where we leave "story" for "prophecy"); we enter the peace of the country and of eternity. Throughout the novel Forster shows us more beauties of landscape than of people. Helen is called "beautiful" but we never see her face or body. The girls resemble spiritual transparencies, and they finally disappear into Howards End almost as Miss Beaumont disappears into a tree.

The book is full of other symbols: the motor-cars, the telegrams, the land, the houses, the characters themselves. Words and phrases other than those already discussed appear and disappear significantly throughout the novel; among them are "love," "reality," "personal relations," "tragedy," "light," "darkness," "grey," "immortality," and Biblical echoes like "inherit the earth." There is the "wisp of hay" that is Ruth, and there is Tibby's "hay fever." There are the "odours from the abyss"* that appear on the three occasions when Margaret encounters Jacky or Leonard. There is the "dust" raised by the Wilcox motor-cars, the Wilcox "grittiness," and the London smog's "red rust," all of which are in the same symbolic family. And there are the rabbits, a minor but not altogether negligible rhythmic "secret": the Howards End inhabited by Wilcoxes when the novel opens is called a "rabbit warren," Helen thinks the hay Ruth is continually smelling is "for rabbits or something," the Wilcoxes "breed like rabbits," the clerks in the Wilcox offices are "little rabbits" inhabiting "little rabbit-hutches faced with glass or wire," and at the end a farm boy hearing the girls mention their brother Tibby supposes him to be a rabbit.[29] To follow out all the book's thematic repetitions, major and minor, would not much reward us, and might in fact class us with the pedantic Tibby, to whom the whole Fifth Symphony was reduced to "the transitional passage on the drum." But what Forster wants us to feel is an effect "comparable to the effect of the Fifth Symphony as a whole, where, when the orchestra stops, we hear something that has never actually been played" (AN, 154), and this feeling, if attainable at all, can be attained only by the reader who follows the book's rhythms to the end—and beyond.

The rub is that music is not made of human beings and the novel is. "Music, though it does not employ human beings, though it is governed by intricate laws, . . . does offer in its final expression a type of beauty which fiction might achieve in its own way." (AN, 155.) When people *use* music, as when Mrs. Munt taps to the "dididy dum" of the Fifth, then the fiction operates in a human, if not always edifying, world; but when people are used by music, sublimed, so to speak, into sounds, then something happens to their humanity, and we can hardly expect any narrative or dramatic solutions of their problems. That is what happens to the Schlegels. Their final entry into Howards End is a passage out of this world into one of spiritual absolutes, into the music heard after the orchestra stops, into the future perfection (that all or nothing) which "has never actually been played." And this, essentially, is why they never do really "con-

---

* Margaret, just after her marriage, is removed from the Bast sphere of influence: "There was an unforeseen surprise, a cessation of the winds and odours of life." (p. 185.)

nect." We watch Leonard grow out of Paul, and see Paul "fade" as Helen abstracts her experience into "tragedy"; we watch Margaret merge with Ruth Wilcox and then try to connect with Henry, only to emerge from these alliances a new creature—detached, autonomous, preserving "proportion" like an egg for the future to hatch. The design of these movements is often intriguing and beautiful; but when people and their experiences are valued more as musical relations than as personal relations, when life is sacrificed to art, we can witness some cruel reductions of the human spirit. Tibby shows these perils in an extreme form: he can respond to Helen's tears only when they have an esthetic effect upon him: "He had known her hysterical—it was one of her aspects with which he had no concern— and yet these tears touched him as something unusual. They were nearer the things that did concern him, such as music." (p. 266.) In short, he likes her the way Browning's Duke likes his Duchess, dead and hanging on a wall. Is Helen any kinder than this to Leonard, or Margaret to Henry? Because they cannot bring these men into harmony with their private symphony, they destroy them in the loud noises of the fourth movement and quietly settle down to make their own kind of music.

There is ugliness in such beauty. It is a serene close for the elect, but a horror for those who fail to learn—or be born knowing—the tune. In the end the demands of "prophecy" and "rhythm" do not mesh successfully with the demands of a workable humanism. Forster unfairly criticizes Henry James on the count that "most of human life has to disappear before he can do us a novel" (AN, 147), but Forster is guilty of the fault himself. The Schlegels attain the "universal" only through the death or moral destruction of everyone who opposes them, everyone who cannot or will not sing to their tune. To assure their own salvation, they face with equanimity and even with pleasure the elimination of the men who could do no better than toot the horns and bugles of the ordinary world.

5 The Vallone Fontana Caroso, near Ravello, the scene that
inspired Forster's first short story.

The valley ended in a vast hollow, shaped like a cup, into
which radiated ravines from the precipitous hills around. . . .
The general appearance was that of a many-fingered green
hand, palm upwards, which was clutching convulsively to keep
us in its grasp.   ("The Story of a Panic")

16 "Pope Gregory appearing to Santa Fina," by Ghirlandaio (1445–94).
Fresco in the Collegiate Church, San Gimignano. Santa Fina is the
original of Santa Deodata in the novel.

*So holy was she that all her life she lay upon her back in
the house of her mother, refusing to eat, refusing to play,
refusing to work. The devil, envious of such sanctity,
tempted her in various ways. . . . He tripped up the mother and
flung her downstairs. . . . But so holy was the saint that she
never picked her mother up, but lay upon her back through all,
and thus assured her throne in Paradise.*
     (*Where Angels Fear to Tread*)

The Piazza, San Gimignano.

*The Piazza with its three great attractions—the Palazzo
Pubblico, the Collegiate Church, and the Caffè Garibaldi:
the intellect, the soul, and the body—had never looked more
charming.* (Where Angels Fear to Tread)

18 The towers of San Gimignano.

To her imagination Monteriano had become a magic city of
vice, beneath whose towers no person could grow up happy
or pure.   (Where Angels Fear to Tread)

19 View from Forster's undergraduate rooms at King's.

20 Forster in his rooms at King's, about 1901.

But Rickie . . . just then . . . loved his rooms better than any
person.   (*The Longest Journey*)

21 The original of the "dell" in *The Longest Journey*.

*The dell became for him a kind of church—a church where
indeed you could do anything you liked, but where anything
you did would be transfigured.*   (*The Longest Journey*)

22 Figsbury Ring, Wiltshire, the original of the "Cadbury Rings."
*Turn where he would, it encircled him . . . this double entrenchment
of the Rings.* (*The Longest Journey*)

23 Acton House, near Felton in Northumberland, the original
of Cadover, "the perilous house," in *The Longest Journey*.

Piazza della Signoria, Florence.

he great square was in shadow; the sunshine had come too
e to strike it. Neptune was already unsubstantial in
twilight, half god, half ghost....   (A Room with a View)

25 "Rooksrest," Stevenage, Hertfordshire—the original of "Howards End."
Forster, mother, and pony in foreground. About 1885.

26 View of "Oniton" from
    Clun Castle, Shropshire.

27 Clun Castle.

It . . . had suffered in the border
warfare between the Anglo-Saxon
and the Kelt, between things
as they are and as they
ought to be. (Howards End)

28 Some originals of the "Marabar" Caves—entrances to the Gopī and Vahiyākā Caves in the Barābar Hills, **Bihar**, India.

Having seen one such cave, having seen two, having seen three, four, fourteen, twenty-four, the visitor returns to Chandrapore uncertain whether he has had an interesting experience or a dull one or any experience at all.   (A Passage to India)

29 Two views of the Lomas Rishi Cave, Barābar Hills.

Fists and fingers thrust above the advancing soil—here
at last is their skin, finer than any covering acquired by the
animals, smoother than windless water, more voluptuous than love.
  (A Passage to India)

30. The Kauwādol, Barābar Hills.

The boulder . . . even moves when a crow perches upon it: hence
its name and the name of its stupendous pedestal: the Kawa Dol.
   (*A Passage to India*)

31 Adināatha Temple, Khajurāho.

*The World Mountain, on whose exterior is displayed life
in all its forms. . . all crowned at the mountain's summit
by the sun.* ("*The World Mountain*")

32 Detail of the south wall, Adinātha Temple.

> . . . life human and superhuman and subhuman and animal, life
> tragic and cheerful, cruel and kind, seemly and obscene. . . .
> ("The World Mountain")

Part III

The Great Round

Chapter eleven

A Passage to Alexandria

I believe that to go forward as a spiritual man it is necessary first to go back.
            —Theodore Roethke

Forster's sojourns in the Middle East and in India mark stages in his maturing as a man and a writer. As he moved further and further from home geographically, he came closer and closer to home spiritually. As he got to know Indians and Egyptians in the way he had earlier known Italians and Greeks, he experienced an increasing detachment from the hold of Sawston and its values. His writings suggest that by the time he reached Alexandria, rebellion was an accomplished fact; the need for fantasy was done, and the need for history was acute. Certainly his stay in the Middle East was a period of crucial development in a new line—a viewing of the past in conjunction with a war-wracked present, and a facing of his own creative doldrums.

Between November 1915 and January 1919, Forster was with the International Red Cross in Egypt, stationed at Montazah, a suburb of Alexandria. Though he was hardly in the thick of it, he was well into the periphery of the war that "spoilt everything," and he "realized" human history far more seriously than he had ever done before. "Middle-aged people ought to go away and get other experiences," said Forster about his own wartime separation from Cambridge.[1] It was quietly said, but these Middle Eastern experiences, though they did not alter Forster's fundamental attitudes, enriched and widened them. This period must be considered if we are to account for the movement from the relative failure of *Howards End* to the masterful achievement of *A Passage to India*.

The chief work of this period is *Alexandria, A History and a Guide,* written during the war but not published until 1922. It is a charming book, a historical Baedeker directing the reader through Alexandrian time and Egyptian space in something of the way that D. H. Lawrence directs one through ancient and modern Italy in *Etruscan Places.* Why did Forster turn to history? One answer is that he had always turned to it—for amusement, for inspiration, for "mental balance." It would have been surprising if the war that was finishing off his class and its culture did not prompt him to reappraise that inheritance; and for Forster as for others of that generation, the past seemed a stay against a tragic present. The "spongy tract" of fiction, we remember, is bounded by "the opposing ranges of Poetry and of History"; Forster, in art and out of it, is always aware of his place in time. "I belong to the fag-end of Victorian liberalism," he writes.[2] The Middle East, by its very distance from home, offered an excellent standpoint from which to view the bitter struggle which that liberalism now faced.

Alexandria, far from being typical of Forster's work from 1914 to 1924, was one of the few genuinely good things he was able to do in that period. His entire output was nonfictional, and most of it was abortive or downright bad. Between 1910 and 1914, in particular, the forces of anti-literature had been lively, and we cannot appreciate his later achievement unless we know of this time in the shallows.

Forster in 1914 had contracted to do a study of his "hero," Samuel Butler. The project had occurred to him as early as 1903, when *The Way of All Flesh* appeared, and was briefly revived in 1910 when he wrote a short essay on Butler.[3] The war killed the project at a time when Forster's desk was littered with other false starts or misconceived ventures. In 1911 he wrote a play, *The Heart of Bosnia,* which almost got staged in 1914, when the war interrupted.[4] In the spring of 1914 he began a novel tentatively called *Arctic Summer,* but discarded it after a few chapters.[5] The stories appearing in this period are his worst; but perhaps most illustrative of the blight on his work during this pre-war twilight are some pieces appearing in the Cambridge undergraduate magazine *Basileon.*

One piece satirizes a Victorian *Manual of Domestic Economy,* by J. H. Walsh. The satire is heavy and dull: "The audience it assumes regarded comfort as everything, personal relations as nothing, passion and beauty as nothing."[6] The other piece, entitled "An Allegory" by the student editors, is a painfully cute conversation between some high-minded watercraft on the Cam, including a Canoe, a Punt, a Motor Launch, the Punt's Sister, a Punt Pole, and a Double Sculler, as well as such non-aquatic speakers as Mown Grass Floating Away, Falling Blossoms of the Chestnut, and a Traction Engine. The pathetic fallacy has wedded the machine age:

> Traction Engine: Humph! What do we have here? Every one happy? This'll never do.
> Punt: It's a traction engine. It's reality, it's the hard facts of life. Oh what a lucky chance that it happened to be passing.
> Traction Engine: I shall pass often enough in the future.
> Punt: A Futurist! Better and better.
> Traction Engine: I see much amiss here. I see trees that must be lopped and turf that must be scarred out of recognition. I see buildings that ought never to have been built, or, if built, ought never to be put to the purposes for which they were originally intended. I shall destroy them.
> Punt: How perfectly splendid of you.
> Traction Engine: I am not splendid. Don't idealise me. I come to remind you of the filth of the lower reaches and the monotony of the sea, of the winds, not heroic, that blow ships further and further from joy.... I am the squalor of experience. I shall come.[7]

Another piece from this time, in *The Author,* begins with another dialogue between a Reader and a Writer; the Reader wants to know how books are written and the Writer (obviously Forster himself) cannot, or will not, tell him. ("It is a reality outside his ordinary self. He has created it but contains it no longer.")[8] In 1913, Forster apparently published only two pieces: a review of S. M. Mitra's *Anglo-Indian Studies* and an account of railway travel in India.[9] But the most important evidence of a creative block during this period is the trouble he had with *Passage* itself.

Forster began the novel in 1912–13 during his first visit to India and had "a great deal of difficulty" with it, even at one point thinking he would never finish. The war intervened, and his efforts were not renewed until 1921, during his service as private secretary to the Maharajah of Dewas State Senior. He records some of his struggles with the book in *The Hill of Devi* (1953):

I began this novel before my 1921 visit, and took out the opening chapters with me, with the intention of continuing them. But as soon as they were confronted with the country they purported to describe, they seemed to wilt and go dead and I could do nothing with them. I used to look at them of an evening in my room at Dewas, and felt only distaste and despair.* The gap between India remembered and India experienced was too wide. When I got back to England the gap narrowed, and I was able to resume. But I still thought the book bad, and probably should not have completed it without the encouragement of Leonard Woolf.[10]

The confession reveals the self-doubt that assailed him throughout this period. Forster needed distance from himself and from his subject in order to work, and the years between 1910 and 1924, by closing some gaps between memory and experience, helped prepare him for his great work.

In these years, for one thing, Forster harvested many new observations of places and people, living and dead. *Passage* is the book it is partly because its author is an expert on his subject, one who has observed, not casually or sentimentally, but with an objective and professional eye.

In 1914 and 1915, Forster wrote a great many articles on India and reviews of books about India. In 1916 he seems to have published nothing. Between 1917 and 1919 (in which year he produced 42 articles and reviews), his writing consisted mainly of articles for *The Egyptian Mail*, including a series called "Alexandria Vignettes." These pieces have no great merit, but they show the novelist reemerging, filling his notebook and renewing his energies. One deals with "Gippo English," the garbled English found on Egyptian shop signs;† another with a Sunday concert at San Stephano (also discussed

---

* This seems to contradict a point he made in the *Paris Review* interview: "I have always found writing pleasant, and don't understand what people mean by 'throes of creation.' " "The Art of Fiction," p. 41.

† Forster's wit has always depended on his keen eye for the outrageous. Here are a few of the signs he observed: "Here is Alexandre's garden where Australian heroes eat and shoot." On a barber shop: "Antiseptic Red Cross civility and cleanliness." On a restaurant:
                    "Whose for a feed at the old Angieterre.
                    A feed you know will carry you fare."
"Gippo English," signed "Pharos," in *The Egyptian Mail*, Alexandria, December 16, 1917.

in *Alexandria*), during which the audience talked and was happy, like the provincial opera audience in *Angels*. Here is part of his account of the concert:

It is better to be inattentive with Latins and Levantines than to attend with Teutons, and San Stephano . . . is not a censorious place. . . . Did ever sparrows chatter like the San Stephanese? A sparrow in a German concert-hall betrays no emotion except fear, but the sparrow here lives and loves and nests and fights close above a sixty-man-power orchestra. The ancient Romans would not have minded this. . . . They were curiously tender to sparrows. . . . And Anthony and Cleopatra, who once commanded music (this is certain) not far from San Stephano . . . must often have raised their eyes to such feathered dalliance. . . . Anthony and Cleopatra are gone, gone is their luxury which scandalised so many generations of historians and contrasts so unfavourably with the home life of modern monarchs. . . . The very city they admired is indistinguishable. Nothing of the Alexandria they knew survives except sea, sand, and little birds; remembering which, be tolerant if you can of that exasperating twitter, which has drowned whatever is still audible in the Beethoven symphony.[11]

This juxtaposing of the present and the past, the South and the North, the Pagan and the Christian, is an important anticipation of *Alexandria,* and of *Passage* as well.

Forster's slender volume called *Pharos and Pharillon* (1923) is a more direct anticipation. Although the articles gathered there appeared after *Alexandria,* they were all written before it. If one reads *Alexandria* first, these essays can be taken as an amusing comment upon the later works; they fill out details and supplement hints that are there undeveloped. Pharos is the famous lighthouse, one of the Seven Wonders of the ancient world, which stood in the harbor of Alexandria until about A.D. 700, when it fell into the sea. Pharillon is the square base of the building that the Arabs used as a beacon and watchtower until, in the fourteenth century, an earthquake caused it to slide "unobserved" into the Mediterranean (PP, 8). Pharos symbolizes the events of antiquity, Pharillon modern events and Forster's personal impressions of the modern city. The chapters in the first half touch on the building of the lighthouse, the deification of Alexander, the accession of Ptolemy V, the Jewish deputation led by Philo to the mad Caligula, and the furious quarrels of the Church Fathers. Not the least interesting thing in the book is the imaginative account of the reflections of one Timothy Whitebonnet, a monk who grew up at Canopus, "where the air is so thick with demons that only the most robust of Christians can breathe":

Foul influences had haunted it from the first. Helen, a thousand years ago, had come here with Paris on their flight towards Troy, and though the local authorities had expelled her for vagabondage, the ship that carried her might still be seen, upon summer nights, ploughing the waves into fire. In her train had followed Herodotus, asking idle questions of idle men; Alexander, called the Great from his enormous horns; and Serapis, a devil worse than any. . . . In their honour the Alexandrians used to come out along the canal in barges and punts, crowned with flowers, robed in gold, and singing spells of such potency that the words remained, though the singers were dead, and would slide into Timothy Whitebonnet's ear, when the air seemed stillest, and pretend to him that they came from God. Often, just as a sentence was completed, he would realize its origin, and have to expectorate it in the form of a toad—a dangerous exercise, but it taught him discernment, and fitted him to play his part in the world. (PP, 44.)

The modern chapters describe the visit to Alexandria of a Mrs. Eliza Fay,* a lively and spiteful eighteenth-century traveler; various places of interest in the city; and the poetry of C. P. Cavafy, the city's laureate. Cavafy, writes Forster, "though not afraid of the world, always stands at a slight angle to it" (PP, 79), a stance Forster knows well. Paradoxically, Alexandria is both on and off the main track and has had more great "tourists"—Alexander, Julius Caesar, Antony, and Napoleon—than great residents. The modern city is "scarcely a city of the soul." "Founded upon cotton with a concurrence of onions and eggs, ill built, ill planned, ill drained—many hard things can be said against it, and most are said by its inhabitants." (PP, 75.) The modern city is Pharillon, a fallen tower, but it inevitably implies the past.

Much of the material in *Alexandria* appears first in *Pharos* in a more relaxed and discursive form. *Pharos* shows Forster the historical biographer at the top of his form, working again in the manner of Lytton Strachey, as he had done earlier in such pieces as "Cardan" (1905) and "Gemisthus Pletho" (1905).† The *Pharos* essays are no

---

* See her *Original Letters from India, 1779–1815*, with introductory and terminal notes by E. M. Forster (London, 1925).

† Later Strachey-like pieces are "Captain Edward Gibbon" (1931), "Voltaire's Laboratory" (1931), "Ferney" (1940), and "Voltaire and Frederick the Great" (1941). See also "Fog over Ferney," *The Listener*, LXV (1958), 1029–30.

mere belletristic exercises, but attempts to capture the past in order to make ironic comments on the present. Forster is particularly adept at giving dryly malicious accounts of the Church Fathers, in the manner of Gibbon. The undogmatic Clement, for example, is handled rather gently by Forster, who clearly feels a certain warmth toward a man whose method was to mock rather than to denounce the pagan gods. In the hope that his world might pass "without catastrophe from Pagan to Christian," Clement stood in marked contrast to the Christians and the Christianity that followed:

Christianity, though she contained little that was fresh doctrinally, yet descended with a double-edged sword that hacked the ancient world to pieces. For she had declared war against two great forces—Sex and the State—and during her complicated contest with them the old order was bound to disappear.... Sex disquieted him, but he did not revolt against it like his successor Origen.... He lived in a period of transition, and in Alexandria. And in that curious city, which had never been young and hoped never to grow old, conciliation must have seemed more possible than elsewhere, and the graciousness of Greece not quite incompatible with the Grace of God. (PP, 34.)

Though *Pharos*, like *Alexandria*, renders an account of actual happenings, they are turned by the artist's hand into a humanistic argument.

Lionel Trilling, with some justice, has criticized *Pharos* for its "archness": "Under Forster's implacable gentleness, the past becomes what it should never be, quaint, harmless, and ridiculous." Yet the past is always in part what men need it to be, and Forster's playfulness with history reflects a legitimate yearning for benignity in life. But beneath the gay surface lies a private seriousness. When Forster describes the changing hellenism of Alexander the Great, for example, it is "an intimation of deep changes taking place in the 'hellenism' of ... Forster himself."[12]

One mover of these changes was the Alexandrian poet C. P. Cavafy, whom Forster, in the essay concluding *Pharos*, first introduced to the English-speaking world. The joining in Cavafy of a homosexual's sensibility with an acute historical sense was deeply appealing to Forster, and the Greek poet must be counted as a major influence on Forster's life. Cavafy found, writes Forster, "in the expanses and recesses of the past, in the clash of great names and the tinkle of small ones, in the certified victories and slurred defeats, in the jewels and the wounds and the vast movements beginning out of nothing and sometimes ending nowhere: he found in them something that transcended his local life and freshened and strengthened his art."[13] Forster, too, found this kind of inspiration in history. Moreover, Cavafy "can give the sense of human flesh and blood continuing through centuries that are supposed to be unsatisfactory."

Forster is especially impressed by "One of their Gods," Cavafy's poem telling of a god who visits, not some sacred place, but Seleukeia's brothel district: "The idea that the Divine should descend to misbehave, so shocking to the Christian, comes naturally enough to a paganizing Greek, and the poem (which I first knew in a Valassopoulo translation) sums up for me much that is characteristic."[14] Forster seems not only to have acquired broadmindedness toward the sensuality of the Orient, but to have accepted and delighted in it.

This was also the period that gave Forster, as Trilling has said, "a firm position on the Imperial question." If there is any doubt about Forster's capacity for serious social and political criticism, his chief work of this period should dispel it. His most ambitious piece is "Egypt," the Introduction to a long pamphlet entitled "The Government of Egypt, Recommendations by a Committee of the International Section of the Labour Research Department" (1920). Forster's Introduction is a brief history of Egypt's domination and exploitation by foreigners, and a criticism of British stewardship. He points out that even though as early as 1883 Gladstone's government had indicated a desire to end the British occupation as soon as possible, the British were still there in 1920, on the pretext of giving "advice" to the Egyptians. The pamphlet recommends that since the dislocations caused by the war can now be expected to subside, Britain should withdraw and recognize Egypt as an independent state. The proposal is made by the Committee, not by Forster, but he obviously agrees with it. His main criticism is that the colonial bureaucracy is hypocritical and inept*—especially in its failure to treat the Egyp-

---

* Forster wrote a review of Sir William Willcocks's *The Nile Projects* in "A Flood in the Office," *The Athenaeum*, No. 4658 (August 8, 1919), 717–18, in which Willcocks accused his superior, Sir Murdoch MacDonald, an engineer, of purposely overestimating the amount of Nile water available and of making technical errors

tians as individuals. Lord Cromer, for example, although he introduced useful reforms, "had a profound distrust of Orientals," and
"his sympathy with Nationalism was purely academic." But until the
war the "mild and cheerful Egyptians" (the "blacks," as colonial usage
designated them) were not hostile to the occupying power despite
serious provocation by the British troops. But by 1918–19 they were
definitely anti-British, Forster claims, owing to the imposition of a
ridiculously severe censorship, the conscription of Egyptians for the
Labour Corps, the high-handed commandeering of supplies from the
countryside, and other similar abuses. An uprising occurred in March
of 1919; belatedly, in December, a mission headed by Lord Milner
came to investigate the situation and ultimately to grant a constitution under the Protectorate. At the time of Forster's writing the mission's report was not in, but Forster had misgivings about it: "The
composition of the Mission naturally inspired distrust. Milner himself was known as a militant Imperialist, who sincerely believed that
the world would be happier if it were ruled by the British upper-
middle classes." Typical of Milner's attitude was this statement: "If
any man desires to help Egypt forward on the road of independence,
the worst and most short-sighted thing he can possibly do is to resist
the introduction of English control into any department of the Government." (GE, 7.) It is this kind of attitude among officials and military men that Forster mainly attacks.

An offender of a different stripe was Sir Wallis Budge, the eminent
and indefatigable collector of objects for the British Museum. In violation of every local Egyptian law, Budge removed "The Book of the
Dead" from Egypt to Britain. Though Budge was a sensitive man
who made many friends in the East, Forster sees a touch of the vulgar
adventurer in his merely competitive gathering of "national posses-

---

in the administration of his office. Forster seems to side with Willcocks: "Anyone
who had worked in an office knows how strong is the tendency to hush everything
up and how the subordinate is always sacrificed to save the superior." MacDonald
sued Willcocks for libel in Egypt, an action of which Forster at the time knew
nothing. But owing to the Egyptian action, the republication of Forster's review
in AH made it "automatically radioactive," as Forster put it. (Conversation, January
10, 1958.) The offending piece was omitted from all later editions of AH and the
matter was dropped.

sions." "Delightful" as the volumes of his book *By Nile and Tigris* are, they lack one quality, writes Forster: "they fail to enlist our sympathies with the author—the touch of the filibuster in him prevents it. . . . It is fun when he pushes the Turk into the Tigris, but it would have been funnier had he fallen in himself. We part from him with admiration, but without tenderness, and with an increased determination to rob the British Museum."[15]

A far more damaging offender, in Forster's opinion, was C. Leonard Woolley,* the archeologist whose *Dead Towns and Living Men* Forster reviewed in 1920. Woolley knew how to get "the most out of Orientals":

He pointed his pistol at the governor of a sub-province who tried to hold up his work, at a judge who had not decided in his favour, at other soldiers and civilians; he wrote bloodthirsty letters; he thwarted and rescued many Germans; he hobnobbed with savage Kurds in their tents. He is against routine and respectability; he is resourceful, brave, and young; he has half the qualities that are desirable east of Suez. But he has only half; to get the most out of Orientals is not by any means to get the East. For that final achievement poetry is needful, poetry with a touch of divine slackness in it. Kinglake in a past generation, Wilfrid Blunt and Marmaduke Pickthall in the present, have this rare and precious poetry; they, too, might hold up officials or visit Kurds, but they would do it differently, and would not leave the reader intimidated by their efficiency at the end.[16]

It is worthwhile to examine the nature of the three good men held up as examples here. A. W. Kinglake, one of the original Apostles, took a journey through the Middle East in 1835. His *Eöthen* (1844) reveals that he journeyed in order to understand, not to dominate, and was broad-minded enough to find beauty in paganism as well as in Christianity.[17] He was an early type of such later travelers as C. M. Doughty,[18] T. E. Lawrence, and, indeed, Forster himself. Marmaduke Pickthall was a novelist ("one of those rare writers who only feel at home when they are abroad")[19] who not only visited the East but became a cultural transvestite, adopting Eastern clothes and an Eastern identity. Forster lists two of Pickthall's many (inferior) novels, *Said the Fisherman* and *Children of the Nile*, among the sources he used in writing *Alexandria*; and he quotes from another book of Pick-

* Author of the popular *Digging Up the Past* (1930).

thall's, *Oriental Encounters,* with some admiration. Pickthall, says
Forster, "does not sentimentalize about the East, because he is part
of it"; he had developed a love for Arabs that his countrymen found
"hardly decent."[20] Forster quotes from the preface to *Oriental Encounters,* where Pickthall "hints at the youthful experiences that have
served his art so well." Pickthall was amazed at the "immense relief"
he felt in sharing the life of some Syrians with whom he fell in:

> In all my previous years I had not seen happy people. These were happy.
> ... Class distinctions, as we understand them, were not. Everybody talked to
> everybody. With inequality they had a true fraternity. ... I had a vision of
> the tortured peoples of the earth impelled by their own miseries to desolate
> the happy peoples. ... But in that easy-going Eastern life there is a power of
> resistance ... which may yet defeat the hosts of joyless misery.[21]

This is also, writes Forster, "the creed of Wilfrid Blunt, though
he has been too much of the grand seigneur to live down to it."[22]
Both a statesman and a poet, Blunt was educated for officialdom but
spent all his life "tilting against" it. Forster, in reviewing his *Diaries,*
recognizes him as a spiritual brother. In the first of his *Diaries,* those
he kept in 1888–1900, Blunt is revealed as the kind of enfant terrible
in politics that Samuel Butler was in art and literature.[23] He considered becoming a Muslim, but after his experiences with the Se-
nussi, he decided that "the less religion in the world perhaps, after
all, the better." Sometimes traveling with letters to the great, sometimes incognito, he sought out both the eminent and the obscure.
Forster's own "refusal to be great," which Trilling finds irritating,
was anticipated by Blunt.[24] He was, Forster writes, "in the best sense
of the word, an amateur—a lover of intellect, generosity, liberty and
tradition, all lovable things, but alas! no more capable of dwelling
in unity than are butterflies with fish."[25] Lacking the professional
heart ("He could not stand the insincerities that are customary between officials"),[26] he never rose to a high position, but Forster believes his amateurism ennobled him: it enabled his "friendliness and
kingliness," two qualities the East values highly, to flourish. In Blunt,
the "chivalrous free-lance who loves justice and beauty," Forster recognizes an old-fashioned kind of nobility, a quality reflected in
Cyril Fielding of *Passage.* Blunt lives in the "unwritten chronicles"
of the East, writes Forster:

... as one of the few really noble Englishmen, as one who not only championed the weak, but championed them in the right way and upheld their dignity without compromising his own, who was religious without fanaticism and cultivated without disillusionment, who had the sense of the appropriate, who was impressed by coincidence and not averse to omens, who appreciated conversation and horses, and who yearly observed, among the amenities of his Sussex home, the anniversary of the bombardment of Alexandria.[27]

Other notable travelers with eyes for the "real East" rather than the "faked East"[28] are James Morier, Charles Doughty, and Lucie Duff-Gordon.[29] And a few years later Forster met T. E. Lawrence, who became a close, if evasive, friend. Many people had trouble understanding Lawrence's passion for privacy, which was perhaps a little stronger than his passion for the limelight. Forster is no exception: he ingenuously explains Lawrence's re-enlistment after the War as a desire "to get into touch with people."[30] There is something a little pathetic in this attempt to assimilate Lawrence's motives to his own, but it is not surprising that Forster was drawn to this man of action. Lawrence demonstrated the possibility that action and sensitivity can be connected. He seemed to present an example of a whole man, and a man who "will always bewilder those excellent people who identify telling the truth and being true."[31] Lawrence epitomizes for Forster that rare success, a man who can be a hero, even in a machine age.

These considerations of men and issues are part of Forster's postwar engagement with history. Between 1920 and 1922, he reviewed many books on history, politics, anthropology, biography, and travel;[32] the section of *Abinger Harvest* called "The Past" covers a span of time from ancient Rome ("Macolnia Shops") to modern Clapham ("Battersea Rise"). "The past" for Forster is at least that wide, and in dealing with it he always attempts to effect some assimilation of history in its private and its public aspects. In an article entitled "The Consolations of History," he begins with a whimsical confession: "It is pleasant to be transferred from an office where one is afraid of a sergeant-major into an office where one can intimidate generals, and perhaps this is why History is so attractive to the most timid amongst us. We can recover self-confidence by snubbing the dead."[33] Still, his motive is not just to snub the dead, but to resurrect them, turn them into "literature." In our time, as Carl L. Becker has noted, "history is nothing but history, the notation of what has occurred, just as it happened,"[34] but to Forster history is more than this; it is an attempt to quicken the past through imagination, to join "information" to "poetry." In speaking of Theocritus, he writes: "Only through literature can the past be recovered and here Theocritus, wielding the double spell of realism and of poetry, has evoked an entire city from the dead and filled its streets with men."[35]

Forster's novels, and none more than *Passage,* are attempts to weave that "double spell." Far more than the other novels, *Passage* essays connections in time and in space, connections between ultimate beginnings and the here-and-now, and connections between peoples, classes, and races. Time in Forster's fiction is always, in some sense, "the enemy," but as his art grows, time tends to be assimilated rather than escaped. In *Passage* Forster seriously and brilliantly comes to terms with it—he creates that double spell by focusing the implications of past and future on a sharply realized present. The following paragraph, written in 1920, gives a glimpse into this new working of Forster's historical imagination:

The past once was alive and it is now dead, and if a writer succeeds in expressing these facts simultaneously, as Hardy does in "The Dynasts," and D'Annunzio in "La Città Morta," he has achieved a great literary effect. The expression must be simultaneous, there must be a complete fusion of all tenses, or the *spell* fails. Napoleon and Agamemnon are men and will not be men, were men and are not men at the same time.... The gates between the living and the dead fly open ... yet though the passage has become easy it has lost nothing of its Miltonic horror. The tenses have not fused in any philosophic sense; it is an aesthetic faith that has interwoven them, three in one and one in three, and made them a garment for poetry.[36]

To overcome that Miltonic horror may be one reason that *Alexandria* is so filled with humor. But if Forster intimidates generals and saints, he is not basically frivolous; though the book is in some sense a preparatory exercise, it nonetheless achieves "literature" in its own right.

The book is, exactly as the title says, both a history and a guide. The "History" is written in short sections, each of which is followed by references to the second part, the "Guide"; Forster intends these references to help the reader link the present and the past. The first half of the book covers the period from the city's founding in 331 B.C. to the British bombardment of 1882. The second half guides one down present-day streets to the places where the events of Alexandrian history occurred.*

Alexandria begins—like the "Caves" part of *Passage*—with an account of the alluvial and geological events that created the site, and made the two great harbors and the long southern frontage on Lake Mariout. Alexander the Great, recognizing the "perfect climate, fresh water, limestone quarries, and easy access to the Nile," ordered his city built here. Having done so he never returned, for the priest in the Siwan Oasis, which he visited soon afterward, declared him a god, "and henceforward his Greek sympathies declined. He became an Oriental. . . . He wanted to harmonize the world now, not to Hellenise it." (p. 9.) After his death, the city was ruled by the descendants of Ptolemy, one of Alexander's ablest generals. Forster distinguishes three Ptolemies: Ptolemy Soter, Ptolemy Philadelphus, and Ptolemy Eugertes. Under them the city grew and throve, although Philadelphus, who married his sister (as the Ptolemies were wont to do), was a weak link: "He could endow and patronise. But unlike Alexander, unlike his father, he could not create." (p. 17.) During the reign of the Ptolemies, the famous lighthouse, the Mouseion (Library), the Palace at Silsileh, and the Temple of Serapis were built. The Temple is important to Forster because the god Serapis, a composite creation, demonstrates something he prizes in the city at its best, namely its pagan latitudinarianism, its capacity to contain opposites and to live among religious contradictions without being upset. The main element of the god was Osiris, to which was added the bull god Apis of Memphis; together they formed the compound "Serapis." Although Egyptian in origin, the god was Greek in attributes and appearance, possessing qualities connected with Zeus, Aesculapius, Dionysus, and Pluto:

---

* Forster has never been one to despise the journeyman task of travel-writing, even of guidebook-writing. "I have always respected guidebooks," writes Forster, "particularly the earlier Baedekers and Murrays" (AHG, xv). After reading *Alexandria* we can have no doubt that Mr. Emerson is his spokesman in this exchange:

" 'But Miss Lavish has even taken away Baedeker.'

" 'Baedeker?' said Mr. Emerson, I'm glad it's *that* that you minded. It's worth minding, the loss of a Baedeker. *That's* worth minding.' " (RV, 32.)

The idea that one religion is false and another true is essentially Christian, and had not occurred to the Egyptians and Greeks who were living together at Alexandria. . . . Osiris-Apis-Dionysus-Zeus-Aesculapius-Pluto may seem to us an artificial compound, but it stood the test of time, it satisfied men's desires, and was to be the last stronghold of Paganism against Christianity. (pp. 20, 21.)

This is Forster's kind of Broad Church. We are repeatedly reminded that this is no impartial book but an Intelligent Tourist's Guide to Humanism, a marshaling of the past to discomfit Sawston and delight Bloomsbury. Hence the Rome that took over from the Ptolemies is viewed with some hostility:

The solid but unattractive figure of Rome . . . came forward with studied politeness as the protector of liberty and morals in the East. Legal and self-righteous, she struck a chill into the whole Hellenistic world. She was horrified at its corruption—a corruption of which she never failed to take advantage, and the shattered empire of Alexander fell piece by piece into her hands. (p. 24.)

Before entering its modern phase with the coming of Napoleon, the city had known three great periods: the Greco-Egyptian (Ptolemaic), from 331 B.C. until about 30 B.C.; the Christian (including the Rule of Rome and the Rule of the Monks), from 30 B.C. until about A.D. 641; and the Arab, from 641 until 1798. After summarizing the events of these periods, Forster devotes a section to discussing their cultures. Were they open or closed societies? That is to say, did they have one truth or did they tolerate difference? By their answers to this question he judges them.

The Ptolemaic civilization gets fair marks. In literature it boasted Callimachus, Apollonius of Rhodes, and Theocritus, and in scholarship the pedant Zenodotus; in science it achieved greatness with Euclid, Eratosthenes, and Claudius Ptolemy. But the close connection between the Palace and the great Library was ultimately stifling. "When, for instance, Queen Berenice the wife of Euergetes lost her hair from the temple where she had dedicated it, it was the duty of the court astronomer to detect it as a constellation and of the court poet to write an elegy thereon." (p. 31.) Its literature, snobbish and subsidized, tended toward over-ripeness: "To be graceful or pathetic or learned or amusing or indecent, and in any case loyal—this sufficed it." (p. 32.) One of the ominous signs of the dynasty's final decline appears in Claudius Ptolemy's corrections of Eratosthenes's map of the world. The original map appeared in 250 B.C., and Ptolemy's corrected version three hundred and fifty years later. But in Ptolemy we can trace "the decline of the scientific spirit" (p. 45). Though he added many facts and corrected many errors, he deliberately made one monumental mistake: he prolonged Africa into an imaginary continent and linked it up with China:

> It was a mere flight of his fancy: he even scattered this continent with towns and rivers. No one corrected the mistake and for hundreds of years it was believed that the Indian Ocean was land bound. The age of enquiry was over, and the age of authority had begun, and it is worth noting that the decline of science at Alexandria exactly coincides with the rise of Christianity. (p. 45.)

With this pointed Gibbonian non sequitur, Forster passes to Cleopatra. Before Christianity utterly spoiled things, the civilization had a great last fling. Cleopatra represented the victory of literature over history: she *became* poetry. (Forster appends the versions of her death written by Plutarch, Shakespeare, and Dryden.) But with her passing and the coming of Octavian, who succeeded Antony, the city is royal no longer: an aseptic age of prudence, parsimony, and efficiency begins. Octavian is one of the generals Forster enjoys intimidating: "He is one of the most odious of the world's successful men and to his cold mind the career of Cleopatra could appear as nothing but a vulgar debauch. Vice, in his opinion, should be furtive." (p. 29.)

With the coming of the Christian era these tendencies and worse ones are accentuated. It is in considering the complexities of this period that Forster develops his main ironies. He deals with three main groups: the Jews, the Greek Neo-Platonists, and the Christians, grouped under a variety of orthodox and heretical persuasions.

Just as the artist is a mediator between the work and the viewer, so the Alexandria of each of these groups was a mediator between East and West, past and present—a role it most obviously played during the Christian period. The Alexandrian Jews, Greek in spirit as well as in speech, found an intermediate between Jehovah and Man in "Sophia," or Wisdom. Later, through Philo, they sought this intermediate in the concept of the Logos or Word. "This Logos of Philo is, like 'Wisdom,' a messenger who bridges the gulf. He is the outward expression of God's existence." (p. 67.) The Neo-Platonic language used here by the Alexandrian Jews, writes Forster, "recalls and probably suggested" the opening of St. John's Gospel: "In the beginning was the Word, and the Word was with God."

The Greek Neo-Platonists whom Forster discusses are Longinus, Origen, and the greatest of them all, Plotinus. Plotinus's thought is a congenial subject to Forster: "The Christian promise is that a man shall see God, the Neo-Platonic—like the Indian—that he shall be God."[37] Of all these thinkers, Plotinus seems to Forster the most successful in bridging the gap between Man and God, East and West; and Forster playfully directs at him his gentlest and most admiring irony:

Plotinus was probably born at Assiout; probably; no one could find out for certain because he was reticent about it, saying that the descent of his soul into his body had been a great misfortune, which he did not desire to discuss. He completed his main training at Alexandria, and then took part in a military expedition against Persia, in order to get in touch with Persian thought (Zoroastrianism), and with Indian thought (Hinduism, Buddhism). He must have made a queer soldier and he was certainly an unsuccessful one, for the expedition suffered defeat, and Plotinus was very nearly relieved of the disgrace of having a body. (p. 69.)

When Christianity proper comes on the scene, Forster is less genial. The sectarianism, the furious contentions of the schismatics, the hardening of faith into dogma make unedifying history; and as religion becomes official, Forster's sympathies diminish. Yet his prevailing tone is mockery rather than fulmination, and he makes some fine entries in his comic hagiography. St. Macarius, for example (see Plate 35)—a minor saint if there ever was one—appears thus in Forster's Baedeker:

St. Macarius ... was an Alexandrian who was seen by another saint in a vision killing the apostate Emperor Julian (d. 363). He is also celebrated for a bunch of grapes that he refused to eat, and for a mosquito that he killed. Overcome with remorse at its death, he retired naked to the marshes near, and at the end of six months was so distended by stings that the brethren could only recognise him by his voice. He selected this site for his monastery on account of the badness of the communications and water supply. (AH, 224–25.)

And Forster takes sides in the quarrel between Athanasius and Arius instead of damning both houses, as one might have expected him to do. Athanasius, who "was accused by his enemies of looking like a snake, and of seducing, in the theological sense, 700 virgins" (p. 52), believed that God and Christ were of the *same* substance and therefore equal; whereas Arius believed that Christ, being the Son of God, was younger than God and, though not inferior, was of *like* substance, not of the *same* substance. At the Council of Nicaea, Athanasius's view was "stamped as orthodox," but Forster takes his stand with the loser:

It is easy to see why Arianism became popular. By making Christ younger and lower than God it brought him nearer to us—indeed it tended to level him into a mere good man and to forestall Unitarianism. It appealed to the untheologically minded, to emperors and even more to empresses. But Athanasius, who viewed the innovation with an expert eye, saw that while it popularised Christ it isolated God, and he fought it with vigour and venom. . . . But the strife still continues in the hearts of men, who always tend to magnify the human in the divine, and it is probable that many an individual Christian today is an Arian without knowing it. (pp. 80–81.)

Following the Arab conquest by Amr in 641, Alexandria underwent a long period of decay. Lacking any historical sense, the Arabs did not know the value of their prize, and "though they had no intention of destroying her, they destroyed her, as a child might a watch. She never functioned again for over 1,000 years." (p. 62.) In the modern period, following Napoleon, Alexandria has been held mainly by those who "cannot see," who cannot contemplate the divine Logos, and instead "look at the onions in the ground" (p. 68). The coming of the Arabs put God far away. We face the God of Islam, writes Forster, "as a God of power, who may temper his justice with mercy, but who does not stoop to the weakness of Love, and we are well content that, being powerful, he shall be far away." (p. 83.)

Thus human history to Forster—and perhaps especially the history of this city—is fundamentally the drama of whether God or the gods are near or far away, and how they meet when they meet at all. Alexandria, the crossroads city, mediated between the earthly and the divine as the artist does. But there must be a symbolic city in the present; the artist must, like Blake, attempt to build his New Jerusalem.

Such an attempt, in the wake of the cruelest war on record, is no light task, and Forster recognizes in himself the recurring temptation to escape from it into fantasy:

In the heart of each man there is contrived, by desperate devices, a magical island.... We place it in the past or the future for safety, for we dare not locate it in the present.... We call it a memory or a vision to lend it solidity, but it is neither really; it is the outcome of our sadness, and of our disgust with the world that we have made.[38]

A Passage to India is an attempt to create that holy city, to bring a memory of the past and a vision of the future onto one vast and all-encompassing present stage. The epic starts, as is proper, *in medias res.*

Chapter twelve

A Passage to India:
The Great Round

I hear my echo, that verbal shadow.
　　　　　　　—Theodore Roethke

There is a great God on the threshold of my lower self,
whom I fear while he is my glory.
　　　　　　　—D. H. Lawrence

Circles, containers, hollows, and swellings are, with Forster, basic symbols. His fiction is thick with dells, grottoes, hollow trees, rings, pools, rooms, houses, and in this last and greatest novel, with caves. "The Machine Stops" has its subterranean womb, "The Other Side of the Hedge" has its sacred enclosure, and "The Celestial Omnibus" concludes in a heaven bounded by the "widening curves" of the expanding sounds of rainbows. (cs, 49.) Expansion and contraction—functions of circular figures—are the prevailing motions of his art, and the prevailing images are those which arrest this motion and focus on it. Even the idea of flat and round characters may be seen as an expression of this same symbolism, as may the circularity of certain characters' experience—the self-return of a Philip or a Rickie after their timid investment in the active life.

Throughout his work, these feminine images operate in double roles—as prisons and as paradises, as dread enclosing coils and as cradles of an ideal, harmonious peace; they are obviously basic to Forster's fictive imagination. His work shows an increasing awareness of the elemental paradox that the tumescence of creation has always a dark underside of nothingness, that life lives on death. This vital awareness, part of Forster's matured private myth, is deeply embedded in the esthetic structure of *A Passage to India.*

The circle has an ancient symbolic lineage. In nearly all cultures it has stood for the cyclic unity of life, the inseparability of beginning and end, the eternal round of the seasons. The wheel of life and the serpent swallowing its tail are two of man's earliest imaginings; and an ancient phrase popular with Renaissance poets was "God is a Circle, whose Circumference is nowhere and whose Centre everywhere."[1] The notion of the Circle of Perfection, the conception of a perfect correspondence between macrocosm, geocosm, and microcosm (universe, world, and man), was widely held as late as the Elizabethan period, but with the advent of science and more skeptical attitudes that metaphor was shattered. "For three hundred years," writes Marjorie Nicolson, "men have vainly tried to put together the pieces of a broken circle."[2] One need not search far in modern literature to find evidences of the effort. Browning, anachronistically optimistic, writes: "On the earth the broken arcs; in the heaven a perfect round." Yeats cast the figure in more representatively modern terms: "Things fall apart; the centre cannot hold."[3]

A Passage to India is an attempt to put together the pieces of that broken circle; it is Forster's greatest effort to relate the broken arcs of his own experience to some final scheme of ultimate value. The book's fundamental structure consists of circle after circle echoing out from the caves at the center to the outermost fringes of the cosmos. Although the book teems with variety, it is contained by this unity.

But this narrative design, however beautiful and suggestive, again raises problems like those that came up in connection with Rickie's dell and the Schlegel's house. In those earlier books, "connection" was achieved through some degree of exclusion: the dell, despite Rickie's impulses of Shelleyan generosity, remained a private hideaway, a sanctuary for snobs; the house became a place of feminine quarantine, effete and sterile. Both represent a withdrawal of the libido from outward connections into a guilty and symbolically incestuous isolation. Will a similar withdrawal into a private retreat, or escape into a private heaven, take place here? Rickie, we remember, would have felt free of guilt had *everyone* been included in his dell; and in *Passage* such wholesale inclusion occurs, for the book's outer circles contain everything, all the plenitude of creation. Is the setting then paradise, the perfect environment? No: although the Great Round contains everything and everyone, men—caught in their own narrow circles—do not often see this great unifying context or hear the echoes that connect inner and outer, unconscious and conscious, microcosm and macrocosm. Their isolation is tragic, but it is an isolation depicted against an immense backdrop of implicit wholeness. Is the isolation complete and final? Is any communication possible between the near and the far? Is this backdrop representative of real or only of ideal value? These questions may seem to have more to do with the book as Forsterian gospel than as a work of art, but the gospel and the art cannot be separated. Unless we can believe in the book's symbolism, unless its myth has validity, the whole work goes soft at the center. It is that center we must examine first.

2

The nucleus of the Great Round is the cluster of empty places called the Marabar Caves.* This is the vital center. The caves include everything and are included in everything—just as they include nothing and are included in nothing. This is not a senseless paradox, as it might appear to be, but neither is it easy to understand, and we must approach the caves slowly and sympathetically.

The caves are a mystery to most people in the book, and were apparently at first a mystery to Forster himself. When he began the book he knew that "something important" happened in the caves "and that it would have a central place in the novel," but he did not know what that place would be. They were simply "a solid mass

---

* The Marabar Caves actually exist as the Barābar Caves, about 19 miles by road north of Gaya (6 to 8 miles east of Bela railway station) in Bihar Province. There are seven caves, the Sudāmā, the Lomas Rishi, the Karan Chaupār, the Viśva Jhoprī, the Gopī, the Vahiyākā, and the Vedathikā. Some of the cave entrances bear inscriptions, and one, the Lomas Rishi, is fairly elaborately carved; some of the caves have two chambers, some one, and most are highly polished. Some of the chambers are rectangular, others are circular or semi-circular; the largest chamber (Gopī cave) measures 44 ft., 7 inches long, 19 ft., 1 inch wide, and 6 ft. high. The Kawa Dol exists as the Kauwādol, about two miles south of the Marabar range of hills, and is the site of an ancient Silabhadra monastery. Though Forster has exaggerated the number of the caves and allowed "no carving, not even a bees'-nest or a bat" to distinguish one from another, his description is most remarkable for its fidelity to fact. See Sir John Houlton, *Bihar, The Heart of India* (Bombay, 1949), pp. 27–40; and Maulvī Muhammad Hamīd Kuraishī, *List of Ancient Monuments Protected Under Act VII of 1904 in the Province of Bihar and Orissa*, Archaeological Survey of India, New Imperial Series, Vol. LI (Calcutta, 1931), pp. 33–43. (See Plates 28, 29, and 30.)

ahead, a mountain round or over or through which . . . the story must somehow go." They represented, said Forster, an area in which "concentration" could take place. "They were something to focus everything up; they were to engender an event like an egg."[4]

But these "bubbles" within the Marabar Hills are far more than one writer's private metaphor. The mountain and its hollow core, the body and its cavity, or even more generally, the circle within the circle, are archetypal picturings of life's origin, of the primal inside and outside from which creation springs. The Marabar Caves, antedating human religion and history, are "not holy" to the Hindu, yet what happened in that engendering egg is instinctively understood by Professor Godbole, the Hindu, while it only terrifies, puzzles, or bores the others. The Hindus possessed India long before the latecoming Moslems and Christians,* and throughout the book it is they who are closest to elemental knowledge, to the meaning of ancient myth. It is a Hindu view of life that gives the book its final thematic and esthetic focus. "Cave-worship," writes Norman Douglas, "is older than any god or devil. It is the cult of feminine principle—a relic of that aboriginal obsession of mankind to shelter in some Cloven Rock of Ages, in the sacred womb of Mother Earth who gives us food and receives us after death."[5] The particular caves of the Marabar do not happen to be worshiped, but they have this universal symbolic meaning, a meaning that the Hindu preserves and venerates in the architecture of his temple. When Forster discovered the Hindu temple (years after *Passage* appeared), he did so with a delighted shock of recognition—as if the full meaning of his own book were only now opening to his expanding vision.

Forster first learned about the temple from reading Herbert Read and Stella Kramrisch,† and from viewing a photographic exhibition of Indian temples at the Warburg Institute in 1940, during the "dead of the war-night." He was taught to see the temple as the "World Mountain," a mountain "on whose exterior is displayed life in all its forms, life human and superhuman and subhuman and animal,

* Although India contains many sects and races, these three leading groups are allowed to represent the whole. Buddhism, for example, has virtually died out in India, the land of its birth.
† "I owe so much to Dr. Kramrisch that I find it difficult to review her book dispassionately." "The World Mountain," *The Listener*, XXXLII (1954), 977.

life tragic and cheerful, cruel and kind, seemly and obscene, all crowned at the Mountain's summit by the sun." In the interior of the mountain, he continues, there is "a tiny cavity, a central cell, where, in the heart of the world complexity, the individual could be alone with his god."[6] (See Plates 31 and 32.) In another article, written in 1940, he reveals that this discovery had personal meaning for him:

> I know some Hindu temples fairly well ... but I have never understood what they were about. ... Now I learn that the Hindu temple symbolises the world-mountain. ... The Hindu temple is not for community-worship. It is for the individual. Buddhism and Christianity have congregations, and monks and sermons, so they need large places to meet in. Hinduism doesn't, and however large and elaborate the Hindu temple is outside, the inner core of it is small, secret and dark. Today one hears of nothing but the community-spirit. ... I weary of it, and it was with relief and joy that I saw those great temples where the individual is at the last resort alone with his god, buried in the depths of the world-mountain. I came away feeling not only that Hindu art is a remarkable achievement—that I had always realized —but that it was an achievement that I might interpret in view of my own experiences and needs.[7]

The World Mountain may in a sense be taken as Forster's essential symbol, the symbol—imperfectly anticipated in dells and rooms and houses—for which he had been groping throughout his creative career. The architecture of *Passage* is the architecture of this temple. At the center is that "small, secret and dark" inner core—the ur-temple, the ultimate darkness—around which is clustered all the complexity of the daylight world of appearance. On the inside is the anonymous, humorless region of the "subconscious," of those primal forces antecedent to character and the source of the experience Forster calls "prophecy." On the outside is the world of ego, of consciousness and history, life in its tragedy, comedy, absurdity, abundance, and mess. Connecting the two is a simple, doorless corridor, inviting men to travel freely in either direction as they will. Although the World Mountain retains the old dichotomies between body and soul, seen and unseen, the connection between them is made superlatively easy. No chemistry of "transformation," no marrying of opposites is needed; all one need do is walk from the human to the divine and back, without fuss or ritual preparation. To be sure, Hinduism is far from being perfectly balanced between outer and inner: "However much

it wanders over the surface of the world-mountain it returns at last
to the mountain's heart."[8] Yet this metaphor mingles the outer and
the inner, the human and divine, in just the proportions Forster
wants. Dr. Kramrisch may have been the one who explained this symbolism to Forster, but Forster had been pursuing its truth for a long
time.

The true aim of the Indian artist, writes E. B. Havell, whose *Ideals
of Indian Art* (1911) "opened an epoch" for Forster,[9] "is not to extract
beauty from nature, but to reveal the Life within life, the Noumenon
within phenomenon, the Reality within unreality, the Soul within
matter.... There is nothing common or unclean in what God has
made, but we can only make life beautiful for ourselves by the power
of the spirit that is within us."[10] This emphasis is, of course, equally
familiar in Western romanticism, and Forster by no means had to
read Havell to get these ideas. Still, this book influenced him, and it
is unquestionable that after 1910 or 1911—and in *Passage*—Forster
makes less of these dualities than of the unity encircling them, less
of the old puritan antagonisms than of the single context in which
they exist. Forster would perhaps be reluctant to say that "there is
nothing common or unclean in what God has made," but after
Howards End he is able to accept the life on the outside of the World
Mountain with far less fastidiousness and moral worry than before.
To say that "God so loved the world that he took monkey's flesh upon
him" (p. 334) suggests a new mood of spiritual gusto, and the mud-
bespattered hilarity of the book's last section suggests that the repressed heir of Sawston has finally declared his independence. Redemption is of the earth, earthy, and of the water, watery; it is full
of filth and disorder, yet Forster mixes in it with joy. It almost seems
that prophecy and a sense of humor may not, after all, be utterly incompatible. However we read these signs, there is no question that
after his first visit to India in 1912, Forster's Protestant inheritance
seemed less than ever adequate, and Hinduism increasingly attractive. He writes in 1914:

Religion, in Protestant England, is mainly concerned with conduct. It is an
ethical code—a code with a divine sanction it is true, but applicable to daily
life. We are to love our brother, whom we can see. We are to hurt no one,
by word or deed. We are to be pitiful, pure-minded, honest in our business,
reliable, tolerant, brave. These precepts ... lie at the heart of the Protestant

faith, and no accuracy in theology is held to excuse any neglect of them. . . .

The code is so spiritual and lofty, and contains such frequent references to the Unseen, that few of its adherents realise it only expresses half of the religious idea. The other half is expressed in the creed of the Hindus. The Hindu is concerned not with conduct, but with vision. To realise what God is seems more important than to do what God wants. He has a constant sense of the unseen—of the powers around if he is a peasant, of the power behind if he is a philosopher, and he feels that this tangible world, with its chatter of right and wrong, subserves the intangible. . . . Hinduism can pull itself to supply the human demand for Morality just as Protestantism at a pinch can meet the human desire for the infinite and the incomprehensible. But the effort is in neither case congenial. Left to itself each lapses—the one into mysticism, the other into ethics.[11]

This division between Hebraism and Hinduism is a refinement of the one between Hebraism and Hellenism that had preoccupied him in earlier books. But *Passage* is less a dialectic of dualisms than it is a revelation that unity already exists—if men would but recognize it.*

The caves, however, are not spiritually identical with the inner cell of the World Mountain; they are only its archetypal form. The architecture of the temple is a late and sophisticated shaping of a dim racial memory—of something primal, elemental, antecedent to consciousness. The caves hint at something existing before gods, before differentiation, before value. Though the temple remembers this form, and shapes itself around it as a shell around an egg, it is at a far remove from the caves' "unspeakable" nothingness.

What are the caves? Forster's description is surely one of the triumphs of the English language:

There is something unspeakable in these outposts. They are like nothing else in the world, and a glimpse of them makes the breath catch. They rise abruptly, insanely, without the proportion that is kept by the wildest hills

---

* This joining is similar to what the Hindu calls Māyā, the identity of opposites, the fundamental unity of everything in God. "Māyā," as Heinrich Zimmer describes it, "is a simultaneous-and-successive manifestation of energies that are at variance with each other, processes contradicting and annihilating each other: creation *and* destruction, . . . the dream-idyll of the inward vision of the god *and* the desolate nought, the terror of the void, the dread infinite. Māyā is the whole cycle of the year, generating everything *and* taking it away." Heinrich Zimmer, *Myths and Symbols in Indian Art and Civilization*, ed. by Joseph Campbell (New York, 1962), p. 46.

elsewhere, they bear no relation to anything dreamt or seen. To call them "uncanny" suggests ghosts, and they are older than all spirit. Hinduism has scratched and plastered a few rocks, but the shrines are unfrequented, as if pilgrims, who generally seek the extraordinary, had here found too much of it. Some saddhus did once settle in a cave, but they were smoked out, and even Buddha, who must have passed this way down to the Bo Tree of Gya, shunned a renunciation more complete than his own, and has left no legend of struggle or victory in the Marabar.

The caves are readily described. A tunnel eight feet long, five feet high, three feet wide, leads to a circular chamber about twenty feet in diameter. This arrangement occurs again and again throughout the group of hills, and this is all, this is a Marabar Cave. Having seen one such cave, having seen two, having seen three, four, fourteen, twenty-four, the visitor returns to Chandrapore uncertain whether he has had an interesting experience or a dull one or any experience at all. He finds it difficult to discuss the caves, or to keep them apart in his mind, for the pattern never varies, and no carving, not even a bees'-nest or a bat distinguishes one from another. Nothing, nothing attaches to them, and their reputation—for they have one—does not depend upon human speech. It is as if the surrounding plain or the passing birds have taken upon themselves to exclaim "extraordinary," and the word has taken root in the air, and been inhaled by mankind.

They are dark caves. Even when they open towards the sun, very little light penetrates down the entrance tunnel into the circular chamber. There is little to see, and no eye to see it, until the visitor arrives for his five minutes, and strikes a match. Immediately another flame rises in the depths of the rock and moves towards the surface like an imprisoned spirit: the walls of the circular chamber have been most marvellously polished. The two flames approach and strive to unite, but cannot, because one of them breathes air, the other stone. A mirror inlaid with lovely colours divides the lovers, delicate stars of pink and grey interpose, exquisite nebulae, shadings fainter than the tail of a comet or the midday moon, all the evanescent life of the granite, only here visible. Fists and fingers thrust above the advancing soil—here at last is their skin, finer than any covering acquired by the animals, smoother than windless water, more voluptuous than love. The radiance increases, the flames touch one another, kiss, expire. The cave is dark again, like all the caves.

Only the wall of the circular chamber has been polished thus. The sides of the tunnel are left rough, they impinge as an afterthought upon the internal perfection. An entrance was necessary, so mankind made one. But elsewhere, deeper in the granite, are there certain chambers that have no entrances? Chambers never unsealed since the arrival of the gods. Local report declares that these exceed in number those that can be visited, as the dead exceed the living—four hundred of them, four thousand or million.

Nothing is inside them, they were sealed up before the creation of pesti-
lence or treasure; if mankind grew curious and excavated, nothing, nothing
would be added to the sum of good or evil. One of them is rumoured within
the boulder that swings on the summit of the highest of the hills; a bubble-
shaped cave that has neither ceiling nor floor, and mirrors its own darkness
in every direction infinitely. If the boulder falls and smashes, the cave will
smash too—empty as an Easter egg. The boulder because of its hollowness
sways in the wind, and even moves when a crow perches upon it: hence its
name and the name of its stupendous pedestal: the Kawa Dol. (See Plate
30.)

And within the caves, when disturbed by human voices, is sounded
a "terrifying echo" which is "entirely devoid of distinction."

Whatever is said, the same monotonous noise replies, and quivers up and
down the walls until it is absorbed into the roof. "Boum" is the sound as
far as the human alphabet can express it, or "bou-oum," or "ou-boum,"—
utterly dull. Hope, politeness, the blowing of a nose, the squeak of a boot,
all produce "boum." Even the striking of a match starts a little worm coil-
ing, which is too small to complete a circle, but is eternally watchful. And if
several people talk at once, an over-lapping howling noise begins, echoes
generate echoes, and the cave is stuffed with a snake composed of small
snakes, which writhe independently.[12]

The entire novel is implied in these descriptions, and they should
be meditated upon; for there is here hardly a word or idea that is
not put to use, that is not heard or felt again, in protean guises,
throughout the book. The lights and darks, the shapes and sounds,
the snakes and hollows of these descriptions are carried on waves of
rhythm across the "hundred Indias" to the uttermost limits of the
macrocosm. Like the gods of India, who fuse and melt one into the
other with infinite ease and complexity, the cave-born echoes move
out over the land, interfuse and separate, and render the Word—or
something before the Word—in a thousand confusing declinations.
More than leitmotifs, these words and phrases are (so to speak) there
all the time, but, such is human imperfection, we hear them only
at intervals.

For example, the caves are "unspeakable," horrible and wordless.
Forster plays upon the ambiguities of the word "unspeakable" in a
multitude of ways. "The breath catches," it is "difficult to discuss"
the caves, their reputation "does not depend upon human speech,"
and words put into their vacant mouths are reduced to that idiotic

ur-syllable "bou-oum" or "ou-boum." Similarly, "no," "not," and "nothing" echo hollowly out of the entrances like reverberations of infinite absence. The caves are "like nothing else in the world," "they bear no relation to anything dreamt or seen," "no carving, not even a bees'-nest or a bat distinguishes one from another," "nothing, noth- ing attaches to them," and if they were excavated, "nothing, nothing would be added to the sum of good or evil." The *nothing* in these phrases is like that in Wallace Stevens's vision of the Snowman: the "nothing that is not there and the nothing that is."[13] It is a substan- tive, not just an emptiness, a presence as well as an absence. That echoing "nothing" is carried across India to the ears of Hindu, Mos- lem, and Anglo-Indian alike, bringing a message of terror or of peace —depending on the individual's capacity to receive or to assimilate it. The caves are the primal womb from which we all came and the primal tomb to which we all return; they are the darkness before exis- tence itself. Some can contemplate that nothingness, others cannot.

Other phrases—echoes—appear and disappear. The word "ghosts" in the above passage is heard many times in the novel. The "bees'- nest" recalls the "wasp" that figures in an extrasensory perception in the consciousness of two of the characters. The "reputation" of the caves gets echoed in two forms—in the "rumors" that circle through this land where "nothing's private," and in the worry over worldly reputation that obsesses some of the more superficial characters.

But most important are the hollowness and roundness of the caves, and all the mythological evocations of these forms. The novel is one great echo chamber, one great round, but in so constructing it Forster is not simply creating a private fictional universe; he is re-creating the world of the Indian religious consciousness. He does so as a sympa- thizer rather than as a scholar, but his perceptiveness is astonishing— as his Indian appreciators acknowledge.[14] Heinrich Zimmer has said that "the myths and symbols of India resist intellectualization and reduction to fixed significations"—a fact that makes Forster's sure imaginative grasp of them particularly impressive.[15] The adept in Indian art and religion (they are the same) would recognize the snakes and flames, the "bou-oum" and the caves themselves as ancient sym- bols far transcending any one artist's private myth. "Caves," writes Stella Kramrisch, "were at all times sacred in India," and the innermost sanctuary of the temple is called the *garbhagriha,* or "womb-house."[16] Within the perimeter of the temple's central altar, a cairn "rises like a gigantic, solid bubble, which has the significance of the World Egg *(anda)*"[17]—analogous perhaps to the "egg" of the Kawa Dol in the novel. And the concept of the womb of the universe, the "great round," is, as Jung and Eric Neumann and others have shown, one of the universal archetypes.[18] Out of this dark and primal cavity issue all the transformations we call life, and everything so born is ultimately called back to its "womb of origination and death." But before any transformation takes place, before any life can break that egg and enter the outer world, a movement occurs within—the elemental stirrings of androgynous fertilization. This movement is commonly depicted as a wheel rolling upon itself, or as the "circular snake of the uroboros," which "at once bears, begets, and devours."[19] According to E. B. Havell in *The Ideals of Indian Art,* the pioneering study that first opened Forster's eyes to India, these symbols, with their thousand variants, are never entirely out of sight in Indian myth and art:

> The first . . . manifestation of the Unknowable, before creation itself, was . . . the Egg, or Womb of the Universe, and was afterwards symbolised in India by a female form, Kâlî, as the Mother of all the Gods. I believe that the first symbols in art ever used by the teachers of Vedic philosophy were those smooth, egg-shaped stones, untouched by human craftsmen, which are placed beneath sacred trees and still worshipped throughout the length and breadth of India. . . .
>
> The stones symbolise the First Germ, the Egg of the Universe. The tree . . . is the Universe itself: a well-known symbol of the One in many used by worshippers of Vishnu, the Preserver, in the present day. The snake which, carved in stone, is often worshipped at the same place, is a recognised symbol of reincarnation. . . . Thus the stone, the tree, and the serpent represent the birth and evolution of the cosmos, and the passage of the soul to its goal in Nirvana; and in this beautiful symbolism lies the root of Indian art.[20]

Forster came to read these evidences with a far deeper awareness of their ambiguities than Havell displays. This symbolism is, for one thing, by no means all "beautiful." Kali is not simply a kindly "mother." On the positive side she is indeed the nourisher and giver of life, but on the negative side she is the devourer, seducer, and poisoner—the "blood-drinking goddess of death."[21] Likewise Vishnu is both "Preserver" and "Destroyer," the Lord of Māyā; he goes through a cycle of changes comparable to all the phases of human experience, good and bad, happy and unhappy.* The snake, too, is both beautiful and deadly: the shedding of its skin represents reincarnation or rebirth, and its circular coils represent the evolution of life; but this circularity also describes an unbearable endlessness from which the Indian mystic seeks release (*Moksha, Nirvāna*). Earth, the great mother—whose womb is symbolized by the cave—is something to escape from as well as return to, for it imprisons as well as releases. The escape is commonly represented by a tree (or other vegetation symbol) "in which the plant bursts out of the dark womb of the earth and sees 'the light of the world.' "²² That escape is both a phylogenetic event and a psychological movement from unconsciousness to consciousness—and Forster, like the Indian artist, is deeply aware that the dark before and the light after are of equal value in a whole view of life.

Forster is particularly sensitive to the duality of consciousness and

---

* The cycle of Vishnu's spontaneous self-transformations is vividly described by Zimmer: "The cycle has completed itself. One day of Brahmā has elapsed. Vishnu, the Supreme Being, from whom the world first emanated ..., now feels growing within himself the urge to draw the outward cosmos back into his divine substance. Thus the creator and maintainer of the universe comes to the point of manifesting his destructive aspect: he will devour the sterile chaos and dissolve all animate beings, from Brahmā on high ... down to the ultimate leaf of grass. The hills and rivers, the mountains and the oceans, gods and titans, goblins and spirits, animals, celestial beings, and men, all are to be resumed by the Supreme.

"In this Indian conception of the process of destruction, the regular course of the Indian year—fierce heat and drought alternating with torrential rains—is magnified to such a degree that instead of sustaining, it demolishes existence. The warmth that normally ripens and the moisture that nourishes, when alternating in beneficent co-operation, now annihilate. Vishnu begins his terrible last work by pouring his infinite energy into the sun.... The whole world dries up and withers. ... And when the life-sap has entirely vanished from both the egg-shaped cosmic body and all the bodies of its creatures, Vishnu becomes the wind, the cosmic life-breath, and pulls out of all creatures the enlivening air.... All goes up in a gigantic conflagration, then sinks into smoldering ash. Finally, in the form of a great cloud, Vishnu sheds a torrential rain, sweet and pure as milk, to quench the conflagration of the world. The scorched and suffering body of the earth knows at last its ultimate relief, final extinction, Nirvāna.... the fecund water-womb receives again into itself the ashes of all creation. The ultimate elements melt into the undifferentiated fluid out of which they once arose. The moon, the stars, dissolve. The mounting tide becomes a limitless sheet of water. This is the interval of a night of Brahmā." Zimmer, *Myths and Symbols,* pp. 36–37. Much of the structure of *Passage* arises from this dramatic Indian conception of seasonal change.

unconsciousness. The snakes in the stones of the Marabar Caves are reflections of the match flame—light brought in from a newer and relatively rational world outside—but they make visible other flames, other snakes, which we are to imagine as inhabiting the stone from the beginning, before man forced an entrance. That is why "the two flames approach and strive to unite, but cannot, because one of them breathes air, the other stone." Consciousness and unconsciousness pursue each other in the novel, but they do not meet—and therein lies the world tragedy. The echoes too—the aural equivalents of the "snakes composed of small snakes, which writhe independently"—are made possible by that same outside air that feeds the flames, the air which carries waves of sound and through which light passes. The tree is not present in Forster's symbolism of the caves, but it is implied by the way the word "extraordinary" (uttered by passing birds) takes "root in the air" and is "inhaled by mankind." The air, the tree, the light, the human inhalation—all are aspects of consciousness, of life beyond and leading away from this dark and earthy ur-womb. Likewise the sounds "ou-boum" and "bou-oum" impinge on the ears of men in history as reverberations from that prehuman nothingness from which they, and all creation, emerged.*

Thus in the novel the visitors to the caves are making a return from consciousness to unconsciousness, going back to a prehistoric and pre-rational condition from which they have been released, but which is still a lurking—though repressed—presence in them all. Not to recognize this is not to understand the novel, for the main characters are defined by their reactions to the caves: some refuse to visit, others find them dull, still others experience there the hysteria of "panic and

---

* Glen O. Allen among others has pointed out that pronouncing and medi-tating upon the syllable "Om" is an important part of the discipline of those seek-ing Brahman: A, U, M representing (in one combination) the threefold manifes-tation of the godhead—Brahma, Vishnu, Siva. Glen O. Allen, "Structure, Symbol and Theme in E. M. Forster's *A Passage to India*," *PMLA*, LXX (1955), 942–43. The holy syllable is also part of Shri Krishna's song in the *Bhagavad-Gita*. See *The Song of God: Bhagavad-Gita*, trans. by Swami Prabhavananda and Christopher Isherwood (New York, 1954), p. 71:

> I am the essence of the waters,
> The shining of the sun and the moon:
> OM in all the Vedas,
> The word that is God.

emptiness"—that horror peculiar to Forster's novels which is here traced, so to speak, to its source. "The profound shock of the leap from animal to human status is echoing still in the depths of our subconscious minds," writes the biologist Loren Eiseley.[23] Forster's book is a reading of that shock and a study of some of its possible consequences.

3

Though the caves are at the center of this book, and the vaulting arches of the macrocosmos circumscribe it, these rounds are crossed and intersected and triangulated by all the multitudinousness of created life—all the confusion on the slopes of the World Mountain. "God's symbol was the circle, man's the straight line" is too simple a geometry for this book; yet it suggests the lesser orderings, the human attempts to bring method and arrangement to the chaos of existence.[24] Most conspicuous among these are triads and trinities.

The book is divided into three sections: Mosque, Caves, Temple.* These sections, according to Forster, correspond to the three sections of the Indian year: the cool spring, the hot summer, and the wet monsoon season of autumn. They also stand for Moslem, Anglo-Indian, and Hindu, and for the qualities of character and temperament associated with these ethnic groups. Since Moslem-Mosque and Hindu-Temple clearly go together, it would seem logical to link Anglo-Indian and Caves—as Glen O. Allen has tried to do, describing "the religion of caves" as a "devotion to reason, form, and the sense of purpose as the *sine qua non* of right behavior and attitude."[25] But actually the caves represent everything that the British, with their devotion to the daylight virtues of God, King, and Country, generally find incomprehensible or repugnant. If Forster had needed merely a parallel name, he could have called this middle section "The Club," which was Sawston-in-India's true church. But Mr. Allen is both perceptive and just in seeing that the three sections emphasize certain qualities of mind and soul—to the Moslem belongs the emotional nature, to the Anglo-Indian the intellect, and to the Hindu the capacity for love. These are not, of course, absolute, but the emphasis

* Gertrude White has compared these three sections to a Hegelian triad. See "*A Passage to India:* Analysis and Revaluation," *PMLA,* LXVIII (1953), 643-44.

is generally valid.* For example, Ronny and Adela—two "reasonable" Anglo-Indians—come closest to love in the first part of the novel, during the winter solstice when the sun (reason) is at its nadir and the moon (instinct) is full and high. The illumination of the moon and stars tempts these two, who normally live by the daylight of reason, to hazard some timid descents into the unconscious, into the dark of their buried passions. In Indian myth the moon and her offspring, the sun, are at eternal enmity, and the coming together of Ronny and Adela is threatened by these permanent hostilities of the universe:

> Her hand touched his, owing to a jolt, and one of the thrills so frequent in the animal kingdom passed between them, and announced that all their difficulties were only a lovers' quarrel. Each was too proud to increase the pressure, but neither withdrew it, and a spurious unity descended on them, as local and temporary as the gleam that inhabits a firefly. It would vanish in a moment, perhaps to reappear, but the darkness is alone durable. And the night that encircled them, absolute as it seemed, was itself only a spurious unity, being modified by the gleams of day that leaked up around the edges of the earth, and by the stars. (p. 92.)

It is a "spurious unity" because they have been victimized by consciousness, by an inhibiting Western education that has made feeling, passion, and love either sentimental or illicit.† And since their moral pride causes them to deny darkness, they cannot make a whole, for darkness is half of the diurnal round.

A further trinity is that of sky, water, and earth. The "overarching sky" harbors the sun and moon, whose antagonisms are reflected in the novel in the antagonisms between the sexes. In one version of the ancient myth, the light-bearing Queen of Night was the firstborn of

---

* Another analogue might be found in the three parts that Sankhya philosophy assigned to the mother archetype, which are usually translated as goodness, passion, darkness (*sattva, rajas, tamas*). These are, writes Jung, the three essential aspects of the mother: "her cherishing and nourishing goodness, her orgiastic emotionality, and her Stygian depths." (*Archetypes and the Collective Unconscious,* p. 82.) Though it might be hard to equate Anglo-India with "goodness," the attribution would work if goodness were thought of as a preoccupation with morality.

† In a broadcast talk to India during World War II, Forster said: "Besides our war against totalitarianism, we have an inner war, a struggle for truer values, a struggle of the individual towards the dark, secret place where he may find reality." "The Individual and his God," *The Listener,* XXIII (1940), 802.

the Primal Egg, the virgin daughter of the virgin Earth Mother, and far older than the sun. The sun, born of the same womb, turned to rape its mother and her other offspring; the moon even now loses half her kingdom to the sun's day and is monthly devoured, piece by piece, by this enemy. She is, as Forster says, "the exhausted crescent that precedes the sun" (p. 265), yet she survives with unending persistence. The sun creates and destroys, burns and nourishes; it also represents consciousness, and, in the form of the beacon at the peak of the World Mountain, it invites men to blessed release from the cycles of existence. But the moon is the lower fire, the fire of earth and woman, "which the male need only 'drill' out of her"[26]—even as men drilled passageways into the virginal geodes of the Marabar Caves. All this mythology is latent in the novel. When, for instance, near the close of the first section, the sun enters its season, the possibilities for human love retreat before its burning:

The sun was returning to his kingdom with power but without beauty—that was the sinister feature. If only there had been beauty! His cruelty would have been tolerable then. Through excess of light, he failed to triumph, he also; in his yellowy-white overflow not only matter, but brightness itself lay drowned. (p. 120.)

The sky also harbors the air, without which hearing and breathing would be impossible. The novel is full of breathing, as if it were itself an exercise in yoga—as in a sense it is. Aziz, the Moslem, "had breathed for an instant the mortal air that surrounds Orientals and all men, and he drew back from it with a gasp, for he was young" (p. 60). Earth, fire, trees—all breathe, all suck in part of their sustenance from the air, just as men receive the air and its "echoes" in their imperfect attempts to become one with the breathing universe.

Water, the source and sustainer of all life, rises to the heavens, falls upon the earth, and enters the bodies of men, of animals, and of plants, all of which are ultimately one interpenetrating environment. Water also symbolizes blood and milk, the basic sustaining and nourishing fluids of life. The Marabar Caves are dry, but in their very rocks are reflections of the primal moistness, the amniotic fluid of the Great Mother. Their sides are "smoother than windless water," and the tourists on entering first skirt a "puddle of water" and are then "sucked in like water down a drain" (p. 153). Just outside is "the Tank

of the Dagger." Water in its season conquers the ravishing sun, even
as the sun in its strength sucks up water. Water can drown as well as
nourish, but without it there can be no love. At the close of the novel,
water dominates the Hindu festival, where "the air was thick with religion and rain" (p. 310). Water brings a promise of Universal Love,
earth and sky temporarily cooperating ("The festival flowed on, wild
and sincere, and all men loved each other," p. 316), but this is only a
promise: the present still revolves in the cycle of seasons, where dry-
ness and famine will in their turn come again.*

The earth is *materia,* Mother, the material body in all its aspects.
Entered by sun and water, men and animals, and yielding its comfort
and sustenance, it is the mediator between darkness and light, between unconsciousness and consciousness. It is both the womb and
the grave. The sucking of the waters into the earth is like kissing
("After a silence—myriads of kisses around them as the earth drew the
water in," p. 332), but they are kisses of death as well as of life. The
earth wears vegetation like hair; cactuses stab the "purple throat" of
the sky. Forster's personification of Mother Earth is very thorough-
going; he refers, for example, to the "fists and fingers" of the Marabar
Hills and to their "skin"—"finer than any covering acquired by the
animals, smoother than windless water, more voluptuous than love"
(p. 131). The earth collects "bellyfuls of rain," and when the Ganges
is described as "flowing from the foot of Vishnu and through Siva's
hair" (p. 129), we are in the bloodstream of the natural as well as of
the supernatural.

Life animal, vegetable, mineral is another triad mixing with that
of sky, water, and earth. Indian animals have no "sense of an interior"
—houses to them are only "a normal growth of the eternal jungle,
which alternately produces houses trees, houses trees" (p. 37). In the

---

* The Mau Tank and the Hindu festival are drawn from Forster's personal experience. They are mentioned in *The Hill of Devi* but with particular relevance
in some fragments from an Indian notebook which Forster published in *Encounter*
in 1962. The description of the sky over the Mau Tank is similar in both book
and article. The article also mentions visits to caves and a murder case—
events which were clearly used in the novel. See "Indian Entries," *Encounter*,
XVIII (January 1962), 20–27. *The Hill of Devi* (1953), is a collection of letters and
comment covering Forster's two visits to Dewas State Senior in 1912–13 and 1921.
Forster visited India again in 1945. See also *E. M. Forster: A Tribute*, p. xi.

novel's opening chapter water and earth come together: "The very wood seems made of mud, the inhabitants of mud moving" (p. 9). Vegetation connects earth and water, earth and air: "the toddy palms and neem trees and mangoes and pepul" rise from gardens "where ancient tanks nourish them." "Seeking light and air, and endowed with more strength than man and his works, they soar above the lower deposit to greet one another with branches and beckoning leaves, and to build a city for the birds." (p. 10.) But above all is the "overarching sky":

> The sky settles everything—not only climates and seasons but when the earth shall be beautiful. By herself she can do little—only feeble outbursts of flowers. But when the sky chooses, glory can rain into the Chandrapore bazaars or a benediction pass from horizon to horizon. The sky can do this because it is so strong and so enormous. Strength comes from the sun, infused in it daily, size from the prostrate earth. (p. 11.)

The "arches" of the book extend through microcosm, geocosm, macrocosm, infinite in both directions: "Outside the arch there seemed always an arch, beyond the remotest echo a silence." (p. 56.)

The human beings in the novel are part of this enormous context and share in its predicament. Just as earth, sky, and water cooperate briefly for peace and plenty, only to become again antagonists in the hard-baked summer, so the people know only brief seasons of love and understanding. The book is a comment, from a great ironic height, on the stupidity of these divisions, for presumably humans—unlike the other orders of creation—can do something about them. But it is equally stupid for men to consider themselves above nature or to think they can, with impunity, ignore its determining power:

> Men yearn for poetry . . . and India fails to accommodate them. The annual helter-skelter of April, when irritability and lust spread like a canker, is one of her comments on the orderly hopes of humanity. Fish manage better; fish, as the tanks dry, wriggle into the mud and wait for the rains to uncake them. But men try to be harmonious all the year round, and the results are occasionally disastrous. The triumphant machine of civilization may suddenly hitch and be immobilized into a car of stone. (pp. 219–20.)

"Political views," Forster has remarked, are of "secondary or tertiary" importance in *Passage*—an obvious fact that nonetheless needs to be repeated.[27] Lionel Trilling misses much of the book's significance because he reads it mainly as a political and social comment, and to many of its Western readers the book is simply not interesting in any other terms.* Yet one of the aims of the book is to make people and their politics look small, to see them as petty actors on a gigantic stage. "It matters so little to the majority of living beings what the minority, that calls itself human, desires or decides," writes Forster. "Most of the inhabitants of India do not mind how India is governed. Nor are the lower animals of England concerned about England, but in the tropics the indifference is more prominent, the inarticulate world is closer at hand and readier to resume control as soon as men are tired." (p. 119.) It is an unusual political novel that admits the lower animals on a parity with other minorities and majorities; and to his reading of history Forster brings the geologist's rather than the historian's sense of time. One of the finest passages of the book is that describing the great antiquity of the Marabar Hills and the slow formations that made them. Forster makes use of scientific information, but does so, like Hardy, as a myth-maker:

The Ganges . . . is not an ancient stream. Geology, looking further than religion, knows of a time when neither the stream nor the Himalayas that nourished it existed, and an ocean flowed over the holy places of Hindustan. The mountains rose, their debris silted up the ocean, the gods took their seats on them and contrived the river, and the India we call immemorial came into being. But India is really far older. In the days of the prehistoric ocean the southern part of the peninsula already existed, and the high places of Dravidia have been land since land began, and have seen on the one side the sinking of a continent that joined them to Africa, and on the other the upheaval of the Himalayas from a sea. They are older than anything in the world. No water has ever covered them, and the sun who has watched them for countless aeons may still discern in their outlines forms that were his before our globe was torn from his bosom. If flesh of the sun's flesh is to be touched anywhere, it is here, among the incredible antiquity of these hills.

Yet even they are altering. As Himalayan India rose, this India, the primal, has been depressed, and is slowly re-entering the curve of the earth. It may be that in aeons to come an ocean will flow here too, and cover the

---

* Trilling says of *Passage*, rather surprisingly: "Always the pattern remains public, simple and entirely easy to grasp." Lionel Trilling, *E. M. Forster* (Norfolk, 1943), p. 144. This is true only if one concentrates on the public aspect of the book, on its characters and the drama of its events. It is not true if one reads the book in terms of its metaphysics and symbols, i.e., if one sees events and characters as they relate to the World Mountain.

sun-born rocks with slime. Meanwhile the plain of the Ganges encroaches on them with something of the sea's action. They are sinking beneath the newer lands. Their main mass is untouched, but at the edge their outposts have been cut off and stand knee-deep, throat-deep, in the advancing soil. There is something unspeakable in these outposts. They are like nothing else in the world, and a glimpse of them makes the breath catch. (pp. 129–30.)

The humans, who live by clock time rather than geologic time, are only presumptuous newcomers to this action, their politics only clouds of dust on the eternal plain.

4

To spend so many pages discussing the setting of a novel before turning to the narrative is an unusual critical procedure, but with *Passage* hardly any other will serve. For this setting, this great echo chamber, provides the book's chorus and prophetic voice; it at once creates and amplifies the meaning of the novel's action. Moreover, the book must be contemplated as well as read, for its design is that of a mandala—one of those encircled squares which have served men immemorially as archetypes of wholeness affording a vision of unity around a disordered multiplicity.[28] We come late to the people and plot because they come late in time, and the book insists that we see them, along with everything else, in perspective.

The most important triad of the book, on the human level, is that of Hindu, Moslem, and Anglo-Indian. The chief representatives of these groups are, respectively: Godbole, the mild and mystical absent-minded professor of Government College; Aziz, the volatile and hypersensitive physician employed by the British Civil Surgeon; and a collection of Anglo-Indians ranging from officials like Colonel Turton, Major Callendar, and Ronny Heaslop, to those capable of conceiving a greater destiny than "ruling India." Among these last are Cyril Fielding, Principal of Government College, a liberal humanist who values personal above public relations, and hence is suspect in the British colony. Also vaguely outside the ruling circles are two ladies from England: Adela Quested, the "queer and cautious girl" who comes out to see if she wants to marry Ronny; and Mrs. Moore, Ronny's mother, who comes out to arrange the match. Adela, repressed as she is, foolishly tries to see the "real India" (though she "hates mysteries"). She finds, like many another character of Forster's, that a Baedeker tour can involve an encounter with Pan, or with something worse. Mrs. Moore—the avatar of Mrs. Wilcox—succeeds where Adela fails, but as she encounters the darkness of the "hundred Indias" she suffers a catatonic withdrawal as extreme as Adela's panic, and more final.

All of these groups are divided within themselves as well as against each other. The Hindus, relatively withdrawn from social and political contentions, are yet the defenders of caste, and we are often reminded of the wheels within wheels of their ancient discriminations: "There were circles even beyond these—people who wore nothing but a loincloth, people who wore not even that, and spent their lives in knocking two sticks together before a scarlet doll" (p. 40). During the festival the "cleavage was between Brahman and non-Brahman; Moslems and English were quite out of the running, and sometimes not mentioned for days." Forster explains: "The fissures in the Indian soil are infinite: Hinduism, so solid from a distance, is riven into sects and clans, which radiate and join, and change their names according to the aspect from which they are approached" (p. 304). One of the most moving portraits in the novel is that of the Sudra, the untouchable, who pulls the punkah in the courtroom where Aziz is brought to trial:*

Almost naked, and splendidly formed, he sat on a raised platform near the back . . . and he seemed to control the proceedings. He had the strength and beauty that sometimes comes to flower in Indians of low birth. When that strange race nears the dust and is condemned as untouchable, then nature remembers the physical perfection that she accomplished elsewhere, and throws out a god. . . . This man would have been notable anywhere; among the thin-hammed, flat-chested mediocrities of Chandrapore he stood out as divine, yet he was of the city, its garbage had nourished him, he would end on its rubbish heaps. Pulling the rope towards him, relaxing it rhythmically, sending swirls of air over others, receiving none himself, he seemed apart from human destinies, a male fate. . . . The punkah wallah . . . scarcely knew

---

* In "Indian Entries" Forster writes: "March 25 [1913]. To court with Saeed, but he only signed documents. In the sub-judge's room more went on; civil surgeon giving evidence in murder case. Punkah boy, seated at end of table, had the impassivity of Atropos." (p. 25.) An American recently returned from India told me that this scene and that of the "bridge party" were two episodes that dated *Passage* for him. Electric fans are now omnipresent, and bridge parties went out with imperialism.

that he existed and did not understand why the Court was fuller than usual, indeed he did not know that it was fuller than usual, didn't even know he worked a fan, though he thought he pulled a rope. (p. 226.)

The swirls of air carried on the rhythms of that passage become part of the common respiration of all the races in that courtroom, but they do not remind them that they are one. Even Godbole, the Brahman, is separated from his god. In Fielding's house he sings a song to Shri Krishna, in which he mimes a milkmaid imploring the god to come: "Come, come, come, come, come, come. He neglects to come."[29]

The Moslems suffer more definite, if more superficial, forms of estrangement. Hindus bore or disgust them, and the Hindu religion, compared with the hard lucidities of Islam, seems a dark confusion of cow-dung and double-talk. The British are scarcely any better; they are amusing or infuriating, depending on one's tolerance, and they never let one forget that they are rulers and that natives are natives. Whichever way the Moslems turn, they feel alienated or humiliated. Their proud isolationism is complicated by a sentimental hope that all men can be brothers and the hundred Indias made one; and they are divided within themselves. Aziz, perhaps the finest portrait in Forster's work, is very much their representative.* At once superstitious and scientific, passionate and rational, political and

---

* Aziz is modeled after Syed Ross Masood, to whom the novel is dedicated. (See Plate 36.) "Saeed" figures prominently in "Indian Entries," where both his appearance and actions are described as they are in the novel. Saeed is handsome, a "dashing young dog," and is sentimental about the ancient poetry and past of Islam. Forster describes the way he and Saeed rode together, went to mosques together, and argued—especially about the qualities of the English in India. Saeed damns the English much as Aziz does at the end of *Passage*. Saeed, like Aziz, doesn't care for sightseeing, "especially when the sight is Hindu" (p. 27), and he has Aziz's sensual nature: "I think ideal friendship with a woman is better than other things, though it is love in a way, for one wants to kiss." Moreover, the discussion about money and debt between Aziz and Fielding, in which Urdu proverbs about money are swapped for those of Poor Richard (p. 167), is doubtless remembered. In "Indian Entries" there is a good deal about proverbs, and on March 30, 1913, Forster writes: "Conversation with S. about debt depressed me." (p. 27.) See "Syed Ross Masood" in TC, pp. 299–301. The identification is made in *E. M. Forster: A Tribute*, p. xii: "Aziz is modeled on Masood, my greatest Indian friend. To him I dedicated *A Passage to India*. Godbole is also modeled on a friend. But I think of them—of Aziz and Godbole—as people and not as religious types." The friend on whom Forster modeled Godbole could be the Maharajah of Chhatarpur, who once remarked to Lowes Dickinson, "Oh when will Krishna come and be my friend?" (GLD, 139.) The question is echoed in Godbole's invocation to that god.

apolitical, practical and visionary, Aziz is continually at war with himself. He is a scientist with his hands, not with his mind: "He loved poetry—science was merely an acquisition, which he laid aside when unobserved like his European dress." (p. 278.) But he could realize in poetry no theme beyond the ancient glories of Cordova or Samarcand, nor any mood greater than his natural "pathos or venom." Whenever Aziz and his co-religionists gather, the discussion usually meanders from politics ("whether or no it is possible to be friends with an Englishman") to the unsanitary Hindus ("All illness proceeds from Hindus") to their own intrigues and self-doubts ("India is in such a plight, because we put off things"). It nearly always ends, after present irritations are purged, in a poetic escape to the heroic past of Islam. Words create the reality, and the Moslems momentarily lose in fantasy their sense of inferiority and loneliness:

Aziz liked to hear his religion praised. It soothed the surface of his mind, and allowed beautiful images to form beneath. . . . He recited a poem by Ghalib. It had no connection with anything that had gone before, but it came from his heart and spoke to theirs. They were overwhelmed by its pathos; pathos, they agreed, is the highest quality in art; a poem should touch the hearer with a sense of his own weakness, and should institute some comparison between mankind and flowers. (p. 110.)

Aziz, and to some extent the rest of the Moslems, can be seen as mediating in a way between East and West. Aziz tries to be friends with an Englishman (Fielding); he worships Mrs. Moore, who was kind to him; and—in organizing the ill-fated expedition to the Marabar Caves—he is anxious to show that an Indian can be as efficient as a Westerner. But he cannot quite build the bridge. Just as when a Moslem servant (according to Forster) can easily pass from the wish that dinner were ready to an announcement that it is indeed ready, so Aziz can never sort out the processes of his mind into Western categories. But the greatest barrier to understanding is British insensitivity. Trust an Englishman and there always follows the inevitable snub or gaucherie (as when Adela in her "honest, decent, inquisitive way" asks Aziz whether he has one wife or more than one, p. 160). Friendship for Aziz is not a matter of honesty, decency, or justice, but a matter of feeling. The same goes for politics: "We can't build up India except on what we feel." (p. 122.)

The question of personal relations and friendship, therefore, is central to the book and subsumes the whole question of politics. But the impediments to friendship are subtle and insidious. It is impossible for Aziz to play "with all his cards on the table" (p. 127), as Fielding can, for what the West would call duplicity is, from his point of view, a kind of tact. He upholds the proprieties but cannot invest them with a "moral halo," believing as he does that "there is no harm in deceiving society as long as she does not find you out" (p. 107). This same duplicitous tact invades his personal relations and helps bring on the final estrangement from Fielding:

Aziz did not believe his own suspicions—better if he had, for then he would have denounced and cleared the situation up. Suspicion and belief could in his mind exist side by side.... Suspicion in the Oriental is a sort of malignant tumour.... He trusts and mistrusts at the same time in a way the Westerner cannot comprehend. It is his demon, as the Westerner's is hypocrisy. (pp. 290–91.)

Aziz has "no sense of evidence" (p. 282), nor is he warmed by British integrity and fair play. What the Indians want from the British, instead of their cold justice, is, in his view, kindness. Yet when Aziz himself tries to be kind and generous, his ego gets in the way of what a Westerner might recognize as unselfishness: "Like most Orientals, Aziz overrated hospitality, mistaking it for intimacy, and not seeing that it is tainted with the sense of possession." (p. 149.) Nor can he receive gifts without certain ritual gestures which, to most Westerners, convey insincerity. When Adela, at great personal cost, testifies to Aziz's innocence before her outraged countrymen, the Orientals cannot accept her offering:

If she had shown emotion in court, broke down, beat her breast, and invoked the name of God, she would have summoned forth his imagination and generosity.... But while relieving the Oriental mind, she had chilled it, with the result that he could scarcely believe she was sincere.... Truth is not truth in that exacting land unless there go with it kindness and more kindness and kindness again, unless the Word that was with God also is God. And the girl's sacrifice—so creditable according to Western notions—was rightly rejected, because, though it came from her heart, it did not include her heart.[30]

Moving from the heart to the head, we move from Moslems to Anglo-Indians, and to the kind of inner divisions we have met in Forster's earlier books. Both the British and the Moslems scorn the mysteries of India, its art and religion, for they are alike conquerors, and hence contemptuous of what they have hurt. Mrs. Moore is an exception, and so, to a degree, are Fielding and even Adela, but the officials never break their Sawstonian postures of defense. Ronny, accused by his mother of playing the god and enjoying it, declaims the Anglo-Indian creed in reply: "We're out here to do justice and keep the peace. . . . India isn't a drawing-room. . . . We're not pleasant in India, and we don't intend to be pleasant. We've something more important to do." (p. 53.) Mrs. Moore cannot take this smug public-school attitude as "the last word on India." That word, she increasingly feels, is with God and is God—though the longer she is in India the less Christian that God seems. Assuredly Ronny's self-satisfied voice from "the mouth moving so complacently and competently beneath the little red nose" has no divine overtones: "One touch of regret—not the canny substitute but the true regret from the heart—would have made him a different man, and the British Empire a different institution."[31]

On the political level, that is the theme of the book. Forster is not, of course, claiming that personal relations are a sufficient substitute for governments, though he is opposed to authority on principle.[32] Rather, he is pleading that we should put first things first and remember, as he says in *The Longest Journey,* that "it is in what we value, not in what we have, that the test of us resides" (LJ, 188). Mrs. Moore's comment that "the desire to behave pleasantly satisfies God" only embarrasses her son: "Ronny approved of religion as long as it endorsed the National Anthem, but he objected when it attempted to influence his life." (p. 55.) Such attitudes ("God who saves the King will surely support the police," p. 220) in a land saturated with religion virtually assure the British defeat. Although Forster is not worried about the political defeat, he is worried about the moral defects that make it inevitable—defects arising, as he explains elsewhere, from the "undeveloped heart." English public-school men

go forth into a world that is not entirely composed of public-school men or even of Anglo-Saxons . . . into a world of whose richness and subtlety they have no conception. They go forth into it with well-developed bodies, fairly developed minds, and undeveloped hearts. And it is this undeveloped heart that is largely responsible for the difficulties of Englishmen abroad. An undeveloped heart—not a cold one. The difference is important. . . .

For it is not that the Englishman can't feel—it is that he is afraid to feel. He has been taught at his public school that feeling is bad form. He must not express great joy or sorrow, or even open his mouth too wide when he talks—his pipe might fall out if he did. He must bottle up his emotions.* (AH, 13.)

Ronny's pathetic attempts to fall in love with Adela are of a piece with the occasional and pathetic attempts of the Anglo-Indians to build a "bridge" between the races and creeds. "I've finally decided that we are not going to be married, my dear boy" (p. 87), is Adela's way of announcing, during a low in their up-and-down relationship, her own condition of isolation. They laugh about it later ("We've been awfully British," p. 89), but, though they are happy about managing to be "decent" and avoiding a quarrel, they both dimly recognize that they are cut off from a great deal that is important in life. "I won't be bottled up," says Adela (thinking of her future with Ronny), but her excursion beyond the *cordon sanitaire* of her educated inhibitions into the dark bottles of the Marabar Caves sends her screaming back to the safety of British lines. Hers too is the tragedy of the undeveloped heart.

The other Anglo-Indians, particularly the women, are given less sympathy. From Colonel Turton (the Collector) to Major Callendar (the Civil Surgeon) to McBryde (the Police Inspector), the British public-school heart is revealed in a descending order of impairment. Turton believes honestly in law and order and is no racist ("I don't hate them, I don't know why," p. 222), but the others under pressure reveal the bare hate beneath the civilized masks. At Aziz's trial Callendar shows himself the unabashed blood patriot: the natives are "swine" or "buck niggers," the trial will "make them squeal and it's time they did squeal" (p. 224), and he titters "brutally" as he describes the condition of the loyalist Nureddin, who has been viciously beaten

* This essay, published in 1926 (though dated 1920 by Forster in AH), was written with Aziz partly in mind. In it he tells of a holiday on the Continent with an Indian friend with whom he argues about the question of emotions and the propriety of showing them. " 'What?' he cried. 'Do you measure out your emotions as if they were potatoes?' I did not like the simile of the potatoes, but after a moment's reflection I said, 'Yes, I do; and what's more, I think I ought to.' " That simile reappears in *Passage*: "Is emotion a sack of potatoes, so much the pound, to be measured out?" See AH, 14, and PI, 264.

by the police. McBryde, at the same trial, speaks like a Goebbels or a member of a White Citizens Council:

Oriental Pathology, his favourite theme, lay around him, and he could not resist it. Taking off his spectacles, as was his habit before enunciating a general truth, he looked into them sadly, and remarked that the darker races are physically attracted by the fairer, but not *vice versa*—not a matter for bitterness this, not a matter for abuse, but just a fact which any scientific observer will confirm. (p. 227.)

An anonymous heckler in the courtroom wants to know, "Even when the lady is so uglier than the gentleman?" and a native, picked at random by the police, is thrown out.

Anglo-Indian women are even more obnoxious than their men.* "It's our women," declares Turton, "who make everything more difficult out here" (p. 222). The female counterpart of McBryde is the young mother, "a brainless but most beautiful girl," who flees to the Club during the pre-trial disturbances and dares not return to her bungalow "in case the 'niggers attacked.' "[33] It takes two years—so Aziz and his friends believe—for the average Englishman in India to lose his humanity; it takes an Englishwoman only six months. All Englishwomen, they agree, "are haughty and venal" (p. 15). "Don't forget," Mrs. McBryde reminds Mrs. Moore. "You're superior to everyone in India except one or two of the Ranis, and they're on an equality." (p. 44.) No one bothers to learn the language except Mrs. Turton, who has "learnt the lingo, but only to speak to her servants, so she knew none of the politer forms and of the verbs only the imperative mood" (p. 45).

Such were the hostesses of the "Bridge Party," which Col. Turton had conceded to Adela by way of satisfying her desire to see the "real India." It is a horrible failure. The Indians gather on one side of the lawn and the Anglo-Indians on the other; at a signal from the Collector (he touches his wife with a switch), the rulers move across to pay their compliments to the submerged races. Only Fielding, Adela, and Mrs. Moore talk to the Indians as individuals. "The Englishmen had

---

* G. L. Dickinson writes H. O. Meredith from India (January 20, 1913): "It's the women more than the men that are at fault. There they are, without their children, with no duties, no charities, with empty minds and hearts, trying to fill them by playing tennis and despising the natives." (GLD, 141.)

intended to play up better, but had been prevented from doing so by their women folk, whom they had to attend, provide with tea, advise about dogs, etc." (p. 49.) The writer Santha Rama Rau remembers her mother saying, "Social insults will break up the British Empire just as fast as political injustice could."[34] Scenes such as these remind us that this is in some fundamental ways an Edwardian novel. Before the war (when this part of the novel was written) Indians were still interested in aping British manners and joining British society; by 1924 such desires were all but dead. Today, of course, the idea of anything resembling a Bridge Party would be preposterous; but if the notion that kindness could save the British Empire in India now seems sentimental or visionary, it was not entirely so when this book was conceived. The book truly records one of those lost chances in the history of international relations.

Like the Moslems, the Anglo-Indians are exiles, talking the language, wearing the clothes, and eating the food of exiles. Their loneliness is emphasized by the items on the Club menu:

Julienne soup full of bullety bottled peas, pseudo-cottage bread, fish full of branching bones, pretending to be plaice, more bottled peas with the cutlets, trifle, sardines on toast: the menu of Anglo-India. A dish might be added or subtracted as one rose or fell in the official scale, the peas might rattle less or more, the sardines and the vermouth be imported by a different firm, but the tradition remained. (pp. 50–51.)

For an Anglo-Indian to eat pan (betel nut)—as Forster is proud to have done—was unthinkable; its stain was the mark of the pariah.[35] Food, like everything else, emphasizes India's divisions. The problem over provisions for the Marabar expedition is enormous: Godbole can eat no meat and Aziz no ham, and the British need whisky-soda and port. Aziz, in organizing this expeditionary bridge party of his own, challenges "the spirit of the Indian earth, which tries to keep men in compartments" (p. 133). Forster comments:

How can the mind take hold of such a country? Generations of invaders have tried, but they remain in exile. The important towns they build are only retreats, their quarrels the malaise of men who cannot find their way home. India knows of their trouble.... She calls "Come" through her hundred mouths.... But come to what? She has never defined. She is not a promise, only an appeal. (pp. 142–43.)

Among the Anglo-Indians, Fielding, Adela, and Mrs. Moore seriously try to respond to that appeal. Fielding, too, gives a "bridge party" in his home to which he invites Adela, Mrs. Moore, Godbole, Aziz, and some others. His formula for seeing the "real India" is "meet Indians," and he extends the hand of friendship without formality or reserve. A Hellenist and a humanist, he confronts India without trying to change either her or himself. "After forty years' experience, he had learnt to manage his life and make the best of it on advanced European lines, had developed his personality, explored his limitations, controlled his passions—and he had done it all without becoming either pedantic or worldly." (p. 199.) Free of either racial prejudice or sexual anxiety, he "traveled light," like a "holy man minus the holiness" (p. 126). He tries to bring the light of reason, as it emerges in his beloved Hellenic Mediterranean—to whatever darkness he encounters:

Neither a missionary nor a student, he was happiest in the give-and-take of a private conversation. The world, he believed, is a globe of men who are trying to reach one another and can best do so by the help of good will plus culture and intelligence—a creed ill suited to Chandrapore, but he had come out too late to lose it. He had no racial feeling—not because he was superior to his brother civilians, but because he had matured in a different atmosphere, where the herd-instinct does not flourish. (pp. 65–66.)

He is, in short, a Bloomsbury intellectual,* liberal, decent, and sensitive. He brings to mind Samuel Butler and Leonard Woolf (who spent years in the Ceylon Civil Service); he possibly shares some of the qualities of Matthew Arnold's brother William, who was director of education in the Punjab in 1853.[36] But most of all he is a version of Forster himself, a middle-aged and much matured descendant of Philip, Rickie, and Cecil. Fielding is too parochial, too confined in his Westernism, ever to have written *A Passage to India,* but he could well represent, especially in his friendship with Aziz, the pre-Indian Forster to whom Masood showed an India greater than "a vague jumble of rajahs, sahibs, babus, and elephants."[37] Just as Fielding goes home from India and returns, so does Forster; and there is reason to believe that this older Forster occasionally felt as alienated from Hinduism as Fielding habitually did. After going from Dewas to

---

* He even talks briefly about Post-Impressionism with Aziz (p. 70).

Hyderabad in 1921, Forster wrote: "I have passed abruptly from Hinduism to Islam and the change is a relief. I have come . . . into a world whose troubles and problems are intelligible to me." (HD, 154.) The openness demanded by Hinduism, the lowering of psychic defenses, are more than Forster can permanently live with, and we can see in Fielding some of those curtailments of imagination that may be an oblique foreboding of Forster's own impending retirement from novel-writing.

The friendship between Fielding and Aziz is the novel's chief demonstration that a bridge between the races might be built. But at last, when Fielding becomes (in Aziz's eyes) fully identified with the Anglo-Indians through the acts of protecting Adela after the trial, marrying an English girl (Stella, the daughter of Mrs. Moore), and returning to India as a civil servant, they are irreparably estranged. Yet they do not understand the reasons for the estrangement: on his last ride with "his dear Cyril," Aziz is a fretful mixture of love and hate, amity and hostility. They wrangle about politics, but politics is only part of it, and perhaps Aziz feels a sexual as well as a racial betrayal. "We wanted to know you ten years back," Aziz exclaims. "Now it's too late.* . . . Clear out, clear out I say." (p. 334.) Fielding fights back by ridiculing

---

* This reflects an actual turn of political and social events in the early twenties, as Forster points out in "Reflections in India. I.—Too Late?": "The penalty is inevitable. The mischief has been done, and though friendships between individuals will continue and courtesies between high officials increase, there is little hope now of spontaneous intercourse between the two races. The Indian has taken up a new attitude. Ten or fifteen years ago he would have welcomed attention, not only because the Englishman in India had power, but because the etiquette and customs of the West, his inevitable destiny, were new to him and he needed a sympathetic introducer. He has never been introduced to the West in a social sense, as to a possible friend. We have thrown grammars and neckties at him, and smiled when he put them on wrongly—that is all." *The Nation and the Athenaeum*, XXX (1922), 614. Compare the incident of Aziz and the necktie in *Passage*, Chapter VII.

Note the letter in *The Hill of Devi* (November 12, 1921): "I have been with pro-Govt. and pro-English Indians all this time, so cannot realise the feeling of the other party: and am only sure of this—that we are paying for the insolence of Englishmen *and* Englishwomen out here in the past. I don't mean that good manners can avert a political upheaval. But they can minimise it, and come nearer to averting it in the East than elsewhere. English manners out here have improved wonderfully in the last eight years. . . . But it's too late. Indians don't long for social intercourse with Englishmen any longer. They have made a life of their own." (p. 155.)

the idea that the antique dignity of India will be at all enhanced by the trumpery of nationalism:

India a nation! What an apotheosis! Last comer to the drab nineteenth-century sisterhood! Waddling in at this hour of the world to take her seat! She, whose only peer was the Holy Roman Empire, she shall rank with Guatemala and Belgium perhaps! Fielding mocked again. And Aziz in an awful rage danced this way and that, not knowing what to do, and cried: "Down with the English anyhow. That's certain. . . . We may hate one another, but we hate you most. . . . We shall drive every blasted Englishman into the sea, and then"—he rode against him furiously—"and then," he concluded, half kissing him, "you and I shall be friends."

"Why can't we be friends now?" said the other, holding him affectionately. "It's what I want. It's what you want."

But the horses didn't want it—they swerved apart; the earth didn't want it, sending up rocks through which riders must pass single file; the temples, the tank, the jail, the palace, the birds, the carrion, the Guest House, that came into view as they issued from the gap and saw Mau beneath: they didn't want it, they said in their hundred voices, "No, not yet," and the sky said, "No, not there."[38]

It is a most important scene, but we misread it if we take it to express a final despair over the human condition. "Not now, not yet!" were the very words Forster used in commenting on H. G. Wells's millennial optimism,[39] but he meant thereby a postponement rather than an abandonment of hope. The failure of love between Aziz and Fielding is only a minor episode on the surface of the World Mountain and derives only partly from the unalterable nature of things. Although the land itself seems to rise up to enforce their divorce, and the horses seem to defy their desires, this is only a symbolic way of saying that the achievement of love involves a coming to terms with the inanimate and the irrational—with forces partly beyond men's control. The horse is a libido symbol, according to Jung: "It represents the libido . . . repressed through the incest prohibition."[40] These unconscious forces, universally symbolized in myth, are clearly operating here. The attempt to enter Mother India has failed; it is forbidden and will remain forbidden until men can hear and understand her echoes and know themselves as brothers within the great circle. Until men know and accept what they hold in common, they will suffer from their differences.

Both Fielding and Aziz grope for that commonality, but lack the insight to find it. They suffer not from the undeveloped heart or mind, but from the undeveloped soul—indicated in their inability to comprehend Hinduism or the caves. Fielding is curious about Hinduism as he is curious about everything, but when he declares, "What I want to discover is its spiritual side, if it has one" (p. 332), it is clear that he will never be admitted, or want to be admitted, to the dark mysteries of the World Mountain. His is a world of light and reason:

> Great is information, and she shall prevail. It was the last moment of the light, and as he gazed at the Marabar Hills they seemed to move graciously towards him like a queen, and their charm became the sky's. . . . Lovely, exquisite moment—but passing the Englishman with averted face and on swift wings. He experienced *nothing* himself; it was as if someone had told him there was such a moment, and he was obliged to believe. And he felt dubious and discontented suddenly, and wondered whether he was really and truly successful as a human being. (p. 199; my italics.)

This vague discontent (so delicately suggested), this half-heard message from the Marabar (which he doesn't visit), this puzzling experience of "nothing," are all Fielding can know of the unconscious life. And the separation of consciousness from unconsciousness that both Aziz and Fielding suffer is at the root of their separation from each other.

Fielding is in the same predicament as Adela. Both are prisoners of their intellectuality, of their words; yet beyond their words is a wordlessness that vaguely haunts them. Just as she and Aziz found "little to say" to each other, so she and Fielding, groping for verbal communion, dimly sense that behind their brave words is a *nothing* not accessible to words—which, being unknown, can terrify. After Adela's trouble in the caves, the two of them seek some scientific word—"telepathy" or "hallucination"—to explain it and the echoes she had heard. But reason alone is not an adequate guide in such darkness:

> A friendliness, as of dwarfs shaking hands, was in the air. Both man and woman were at the height of their powers—sensible, honest, even subtle. They spoke the same language, and held the same opinions. . . . Yet they were dissatisfied. When they agreed, "I want to go on living a bit," or "I don't believe in God," the words were followed by a curious backwash as though the universe had displaced itself to fill up a tiny void, or as though they had seen their own gestures from an immense height—dwarfs talking, shaking hands and assuring each other that they stood on the same footing of insight. (pp. 274–75.)

Mrs. Moore, however, meets the shadow face to face.* As she comes
to know the "real India," her character undergoes a strange metamorphosis, in which all her loyalties to religion, race, and family are
shaken to the roots. The change begins on the night she encounters
Aziz in the mosque, when he is so touched by learning that she came
in reverence and respect that he makes her an honorary Oriental.
Later, on the Marabar expedition, she jokes with Aziz: "We shall all
be Moslems together." But she does not become a Moslem. She slowly
moves toward a view of life that is Hindu, if anything—in which the
differences between races and sects become unimportant. The second
stage of her metamorphosis begins with hearing Godbole sing a song:

It so happened that Mrs. Moore and Miss Quested had felt nothing acutely
for a fortnight. Ever since Professor Godbole had sung his queer little song,
they had lived more or less inside cocoons, and the difference between them
was that the elder lady accepted her own apathy, while the younger resented
hers. (p. 139.)

Those feelings occur on the train ride to the Marabar Caves, and the
"cocoons" in which they feel "nothing acutely" are premonitory of
those toward which they are progressing. Adela will not be "bottled
up," and these psychic fears along with Mrs. Moore's acceptance of
boredom and apathy prepare us for their different reactions to the
catastrophe. Mrs. Moore grows discontented with "poor little talk-
ative Christianity" not because she is attracted to new creeds, but because she has, like Lazarus, apprehended something antecedent to
creeds, and even to words. As a result of hearing the echo in the caves,
she is overcome with a sense of accidie that gradually reduces the
entire Christian doctrine from "Let there be Light" to "It is finished"
to "boum":

Coming at a moment when she chanced to be fatigued, it had managed to
murmur, "Pathos, piety, courage—they exist, but are identical, and so is
filth. Everything exists, nothing has value." If one had spoken vileness in
that place, or quoted lofty poetry, the comment would have been the same—
"ou-boum." If one had spoken with the tongues of angels and pleaded for all
the unhappiness and misunderstanding in the world, past, present, and to
come . . . it would amount to the same, the serpent would descend and return to the ceiling. (pp. 156–57.)

---

* G. L. Dickinson, while in India, wrote a letter to a "Mrs. Moor," in which he
talked of Hindus and particularly noted a "wasp"—a creature of some importance
in the novel. (GLD, 140.)

She has caught a glimpse of Godbole's "ancient night," and her reaction can be explained to her sensible countrymen only as nerves or fatigue or old age. She withdraws more and more from social and family responsibilities. She becomes indifferent to bringing Ronny and Adela together, saying that "though people are important, the relations between them are not" (p. 141). And although she is convinced of Aziz's innocence, she will not testify on his behalf at the trial, nor will she visit Adela in her illness. She is not decent or likable or fair, and the old lady is certainly not "endearing," as Santha Rama Rau has seen her to be.[41] Totally unprepared by culture or religion for the vision India shows her, Mrs. Moore plans an ultimate retreat into "a cave of [her] own," and has arrived at "that state where the horror of the universe and its smallness are both visible at the same time—the twilight of the double vision in which so many elderly people are involved" (p. 216).* This is a Western kind of despair. She has seen what Godbole often sees, but it kills her desire to live instead of bringing her peace. Adela also experiences a "double relation" to the event in the cave ("Now she was of it and not of it at the same time," pp. 236–37), but she fights this doubleness as a sickness and wills a world that is a clean, well-lighted place. Like most of her countrymen, she is, in the words of D. H. Lawrence, "mad with the egoistic fear of [her] own nothingness."[42] But not Mrs. Moore.†

---

* Compare D. H. Lawrence's "twilight of both darknesses, the hush of the two-fold silence" in *The Rainbow* (Harmondsworth, 1949 [1915]), p. 202.

† In discussing her character with Forster, the author read aloud the following passage from *Women in Love* as suggesting the kind of state Mrs. Moore had reached. Forster was interested, asked to read the passage himself, and commented to this effect: "Yes, it's very like, isn't it? Though of course Lawrence was dealing with a relationship between the sexes, which doesn't apply to Mrs. Moore." (Conversation with Forster, March 12, 1965.) The passage is as follows:

"There is," he said, in a voice of pure abstraction, "a final me which is stark and impersonal and beyond responsibility. So there is a final you. And it is there I would want to meet you—not in the emotional, loving plane—but there beyond, where there is no speech and no terms of agreement. There we are two stark, unknown beings, two utterly strange creatures. . . . And there could be no obligation, because there is no standard for action there, because no understanding has been reaped from that plane. It is quite inhuman,—so there can be no calling to book, in any form whatsoever—because one is outside the pale of all that is accepted, and nothing known applies. One can only follow the impulse, taking that which lies in front, and responsible for nothing, asking for nothing, giving nothing, only each taking according to the primal desire." (New York, 1922), pp. 165–66.

She becomes a legend among the Indians. Though they know next to nothing about her, rumor puts her on their side; her name, mentioned during the trial, becomes magic. It is passed beyond the court to the crowd outside and taken up as a victory cry. After the acquittal, "Esmiss Esmoor" is chanted throughout Chandrapore as an invocation to the goddess who, in some mysterious way, has entered into Adela's testimony and saved them. No one knows how the chant started, nor can it be stopped. Following the trial there is a temporary Hindu-Moslem entente, and this incantation, penetrating the partitions of the Indian world, comes as a reminder that ultimately there is no privacy and that we are all naked within the same echoing cave. The echoes of the book, of which "Esmiss Esmoor" is one, are emanations from the unconscious. They get through everywhere—as nightmare and nervousness to those who stop their ears, as dreams of harmony and peace to those who do not resist. For the fearful ones, the Indian world is full of spies, secrets, and rumors. For example, Ronny one night finds, "as always, an Indian close outside the window ... picking up sounds" (p. 210). Even Fielding is not immune to such problems. "Fatigued by the merciless and enormous day," he on one occasion "lost his usual sane view of human intercourse, and felt that we exist not in ourselves, but in terms of each other's minds" (p. 259). But Mrs. Moore glimpses something more unprivate than even the nightmares of her countrymen could admit—a reality which, had she been prepared for it, might have been redeeming. It is entirely appropriate that she leave the action, depart from India, and die on the way back to England.*

5

Having passed from Hindu to Moslem to Anglo-Indian, we are, when we take up Mrs. Moore, back to the Hindu again. The circle is closing; the snake is finding its tail. The third section, "Temple," has struck some critics as tacked on, an afterthought, but this is a serious

---

* K. W. Gransden points out that Mrs. Moore seems also to occur as Mrs. March in the fragment "Entrance to an Unwritten Novel," which depicts a scene on a voyage home from India to Southampton: "Tired with the voyage and the noise of the children, worried by what she had left in India and what she might find in England, Mrs. March fell into a sort of trance." (*E. M. Forster*, p. 81.) In an archetypal sense, this is the mother, the sacred mother, finally dispatched. She is sad and unfulfilled, but that is not the message of this novel or of this fragment.

misjudgment. Insofar as it needs an excuse, Forster has excused it by saying: "It was architecturally necessary. I needed a lump, or a Hindu temple if you like—a mountain standing up. It is well placed; and it gathers up some strings. But there ought to be more after it. The lump sticks out a little too much."[43] It must be added that the section is not only architecturally but also thematically necessary, a fact brought to light in this comment by Noel Annan:

When I saw the play which was made out of *A Passage to India* and which ends with Aziz's acquittal, I was overwhelmed by the feeling that in the novel Forster was saying that there is no unified moral explanation of life; that neither Fielding's humanism nor Mrs. Moore's intuitionist morality could be sustained after the impact with India; that India shows up the narrowness and deceptive tidiness of Western morality. I said this to F. when we were discussing the play, and he said: "Ah, but of course in the novel there is the last section"—and I suppose it is in that section that deals with Hinduism and religion that Forster feels that the reconciliation can be made.[44]

Indeed the last section does play this role. The plot of the book, the part amenable to dramatization, could not seriously enter this final part because Hindu thought is essentially plotless: it attains its points of illumination through meditation rather than action, and when it acts it tends to be playful rather than purposeful. The birth of Shri Krishna is a kind of Hindu equivalent to the birth of Jesus, but the celebration commemorating it is such a riot of noise and color and horseplay that those who are accustomed to the relatively sedate Western Christmas might be shocked by its seeming irreverence and vulgarity. But the point of it all is a spiritual ravishment of the unknown beyond the reach of drama and almost beyond the reach of human imagination. Thus is the god born:

Infinite love took upon itself the form of SHRI KRISHNA, and saved the world. All sorrow was annihilated, not only for Indians, but for foreigners, birds, caves, railways, and the stars; all became joy, all laughter; there had never been disease nor doubt, misunderstanding, cruelty, fear. Some jumped in the air, others flung themselves prone and embraced the bare feet of the universal lover; the women behind the purdah slapped and shrieked; the little girl slipped out and danced by herself, her black pigtails flying. Not an orgy of the body; the tradition of that shrine forbade it. But the human spirit had tried by a desperate contortion to ravish the unknown, flinging down science and history in the struggle, yes, beauty herself. Did it succeed?

Books written afterwards say "Yes." But how, if there is such an event, can it be remembered afterwards? How can it be expressed in anything but itself? Not only from the unbeliever are mysteries hid, but the adept himself cannot retain them. He may think, if he chooses, that he has been with God, but as soon as he thinks it, it becomes history, and falls under the rules of time. (pp. 299–300.)

To dramatize this kind of event is almost impossible; nor is it easily made part of "a narrative of events in their time sequence." Yet it is this "mountain" that brings home the book's meaning. The festival, as we would expect, is all nonsense to Aziz and Fielding. "Oh, shut up," says Aziz to his friend on their last ride. "Leave Krishna alone, and talk about something sensible." So they talk politics. Mrs. Moore is not there in the flesh but only as a "memory or a telepathic appeal," but it is Godbole's duty, "as it was his desire, to place himself in the position of the God and to love her, and to place himself in her position and to say to the God, 'Come, come, come, come.' " (p. 303.) This is not stageable, nor is the Hindu notion of evil serviceable in police courts and murder trials. Thus Godbole:

"I am informed that an evil action was performed in the Marabar Hills, and that a highly esteemed English lady is now seriously ill in consequence. My answer to that is this: that action was performed by Dr. Aziz." He stopped and sucked in his thin cheeks. "It was performed by the guide." He stopped again. "It was performed by you." Now he had an air of daring and of coyness. "It was performed by me." He looked shyly down the sleeve of his own coat. "And by my students. It was even performed by the lady herself. When evil occurs, it expresses the whole of the universe. Similarly when good occurs." (pp. 185–86.)

He is, of course, right; we are all implicated in evil—and he happens to be right about ascribing some part of this particular evil to "the lady herself." But this kind of talk infuriates Fielding, even as Mrs. Moore's contemplation of human affairs from a great distance infuriates her countrymen. Yet it is the Godbole vision we must understand if we are to understand the book.

What is it, then, that Godbole and Mrs. Moore see? Or, to put the question more leadingly, what exactly did happen to Adela in the caves? *Nothing* happened to her, in two senses of that word. In a literal, legal sense no event occurred—Aziz was not even in the same cave. But *nothing* also occurred in a psychic sense: she had a glimpse into the everlasting no, the pit of *nada,* the ultimate negation lying at the bottom of the unconscious. She had seen what can be explained mythologically as the archetypal emptiness preceding existence itself. This is not to say that Mrs. Moore and Godbole had had the same experience as Adela, but only that they had looked into a similar cave. In clinical terms, Adela no doubt suffered a form of sexual hysteria. She had been tense all that day and, just before entering the cave, had suddenly noticed that Aziz was a very handsome man. She had just as suddenly realized that she and Ronny did not love each other. Moreover, she was in a near-panic about sex generally—virginal, frigid, afraid of being entered, afraid of that return downward and backward which is as illicitly tempting for women as for men.[45]

What does she encounter? Louise Dauner perceptively suggests that she met what Jung describes as the Animus, the male archetype that woman carries within her.[46] But this would not account for the terror of the experience (Miss Dauner herself quotes Neumann in calling it "an invisible stimulating, fructifying, and inspiring male spirit"), or for its profundity. The experience is, rather, what Jung describes as the Shadow, that deepest and darkest bottom of the unconscious which strikes unspeakable horror into those unequipped to encounter it.* The experience of the Shadow commonly involves an approach through a narrow passage, like the entrance to a cave, followed by a glimpse of a boundless expanse, which could be symbolized by the depths that seem to lie within the polished sides of the cave:

The meeting with oneself is, at first, the meeting with one's own shadow. The shadow is a tight passage, a narrow door, whose painful constriction no one is spared who goes down to the deep well. But one must learn to know oneself in order to know who one is. For what comes after the door is, surprisingly enough, a boundless expanse full of unprecedented uncertainty, with apparently no inside and no outside, no above and no below, no here and no there, no mine and no thine, no good and no bad. It is the world of water, where all life floats in suspension; where the realm of the sympathetic system, the soul of everything living, begins; where I am indivisibly this *and* that; where I experience the other in myself and the other-than-myself experiences me.[47]

---

* Forster declared: "I couldn't read Freud or Jung myself; it had to be filtered to me." "The Art of Fiction," p. 40.

This is the "twilight of the double vision"; it is the same experience that evokes in Godbole a sense of limitless compassion rather than of horror. But the Westerner not habituated to wandering in these depths experiences the Shadow as a kind of rape of the personality. In the realm of consciousness, writes Jung, we are our own masters, but "if we step through the door of the shadow we discover with terror that we are the object of unseen factors." This knowledge can, Jung continues, "give rise to primitive panic." After the event Adela "vibrated between hard common sense and hysteria" (p. 201) and could give no sure account of what happened; but it is clear that the "sort of shadow" she experienced was similar to the one Jung describes:

She would begin a speech as if nothing particular had happened. "I went into this detestable cave," she would say dryly, "and I remember scratching the wall with my finger-nail, to start the usual echo, and then as I was saying there was this shadow, or sort of shadow, down the entrance tunnel, bottling me up." (pp. 201–2.)

The panic of being bottled and the panic of being loosed in a boundless expanse is the same panic (claustrophobia and agoraphobia being counterparts). To meet oneself as something *other,* "something objective, self-subsistent, and living its own life," is for the intellectualized Westerner like Adela an almost unbearably abnormal experience. It is, says Jung, a modern sickness that man has built such resistances against assimilation of the unconscious; it is a form of his "irresponsibility," and the "man without a shadow"—"who imagines he actually *is* only what he cares to know about himself"—has become in the West the commonest human type.[48] Both Fielding and Adela are such types, yet they sense their "irresponsibility" and feel guilty about it. Adela experiences the event in the cave as a humiliation, sensing "in some vague way that she was leaving the world worse than she found it. She felt that it was her crime, until the intellect, reawakening, pointed out to her that she was inaccurate here, and set her again upon her sterile round." (p. 202.) Fielding, vicariously partaking of Adela's crisis, also feels an "emptiness like guilt." Adela believes that Mrs. Moore can tell her what the experience in the cave means, but Mrs. Moore, who knows it is beyond verbal explanations, keeps away: "And consequently the echo flourished, raging up and down like a nerve in the faculty of her hearing, and the noise in the cave, so unimportant intellectually, was prolonged over the surface of her life." (p. 202.)

That is to say that the echo (the shadow as sound) is an event in the sympathetic nervous system (rather than in the cerebrospinal), in those nerves that have no direct connection with consciousness, but that are nevertheless essential for maintaining balance in life. Jung's explanations of this essential point are most suggestive:

"Spirit" always seems to come from above, while from below comes everything that is sordid and worthless. For people who think in this way spirit means highest freedom, a soaring over the depths, deliverance from the prison of the chthonic world, and hence a refuge for all those timorous souls who do not want to become anything different.... The unconscious is the psyche that reaches down from the daylight of mentally and morally lucid consciousness into the nervous system that for years has been known as the "sympathetic." This does not govern perception and muscular activity like the cerebrospinal system, and thus control the environment; but, though functioning without sense-organs, it maintains the balance of life and, through the mysterious paths of sympathetic excitation, not only gives us knowledge of the innermost life of other beings but also has an inner effect upon them. In this sense it is an extremely collective system, the operative basis of all *participation mystique,* whereas the cerebrospinal function reaches its high point in separating off the specific qualities of the ego, and only apprehends surfaces and externals—always through the medium of space. It experiences everything as an outside, whereas the sympathetic system experiences everything as an inside.[49]

It is, in short, the inner cell of the World Mountain, as the world of mind and will is the surface, and the world of abstracting ideality the peak—or point of release. It is the sympathetic system that apprehends the general and the anonymous, what Jung calls the collective unconscious. The sympathy that all the inhabitants of Chandrapore feel in Mrs. Moore—her knowledge of "the innermost life of other beings" and the inner effect it has on them—is not sympathy in the moral or Christian sense; it is simply an opening of oneself to the unconscious part of life that civilized people habitually repress. The cry "Esmiss Esmoor" is the very voice of a *participation mystique,* the mob speaking as if in sleep or nightmare. "Esmiss Esmoor" is only "ou-boum" at a higher level of sophistication and development, and although the chant may invoke a goddess, it is a goddess without fixed attributes or character—an anonymous goddess that can stir a mob to hysterical fury as easily as to love.

When Mrs. Moore taps these anonymous depths in herself, she feels diminished and small ("the horror of the universe and its smallness [were] both visible at the same time"), for as a Christian she has been brought up to believe that value lies in "spirit," in something on or beyond the heights, something "large" that transcends earthly carnalities. The Schlegels at the close of *Howards End* are still looking toward those heights, averting their gaze from the abyss of "panic and emptiness." But Mrs. Moore looks and does not turn away:

> What had spoken to her in that scoured-out cavity of the granite? What dwelt in the first of the caves? Something very old and very small. Before time, it was before space also. Something snub-nosed, incapable of generosity—the undying worm itself. Since hearing its voice, she had not entertained one large thought, she was actually envious of Adela. All this fuss over a frightened girl! Nothing had happened, 'and if it had,' she found herself thinking with the cynicism of a wicked priestess, 'if it had, there are worse evils than love.' The unspeakable attempt presented itself to her as love: in a cave, in a church—Boum, it amounts to the same. (p. 217.)

What does this tell us? Forster is not recommending Hinduism or cave-worship as a way of life any more than he is recommending Mohammedanism or Christianity.* "Proportion" is still his recom-

---

* Several critics, wanting a hero for the story and seeing in Aziz the most likely candidate, have lamented that Aziz is not "large" enough for the cosmic stage on which his adventures are played. V. A. Shahane, influenced by the criticism of Gertrude White and N. Chaudhhuri, writes: "The fact remains that Forster should have given us a weightier Aziz." But actually he is meant to be no larger than the other main characters. They are all little people against that huge backdrop, and had Forster made Aziz as large as that setting he would have turned his book into some kind of romance or fantasy. Gertrude White, in particular, finds a disparity between comic matter and cosmic meaning in the book. The disparity is indeed there, but to see it as a fault is not to see it, as Forster intended, as a fact of life. How is one to mend it without falsifying things as they are? Is the human comedy not as distant from the soul of the world mountain as from its point of release? To make any facile synthesis would be to write a *Magic Flute*, not a *Passage to India*. It would be to realize these hopes of synthesis without any honest or realistic consideration of the resistance nature offers to the joining of the one and the many. See V. A. Shahane, *E. M. Forster: A Reassessment*, p. 115; Gertrude M. White, "*A Passage to India*: Analysis and Revaluation," *PMLA*, LXVIII (1953), 654–55; and Nirad C. Chaudhhuri, "Passage to and from India," *Encounter*, II (1954), 19–24.

mendation, but his perspective on what that includes has widened enormously. In these three faiths and races he symbolically samples what needs synthesis—the mind, the heart, and the soul. He honors the Hindu way in particular because it is the least resistant to the unconscious and the instinctual, the least dogmatic and theological, the least appalled by the vision of the shadow. Shadows and their echoes are not good, any more than death is good; but to be unable to acknowledge and be in touch with such facts of life, whether out of fear or fastidiousness or obtuseness, is to fragment life, to render it sterile, joyless, and fundamentally unreal. Hinduism, therefore—though nearly as lopsided as the others—is valuable in that it restores those things that the West (and some of the East) has most repressed and forgotten. The book exhorts our spiritually impoverished, symbol-less age to connect the conscious and the unconscious spheres of our being. It also emphasizes that unless such a connection is made we shall go on making our old mistakes—political, social, domestic—without knowing why, and go on wandering across the face of the World Mountain without realizing that it has a center. The separation between conscious and unconscious is what used to be called the separation between man and God; humanism, if it is to mean anything, must deal with this fundamental fact. Adela, so withdrawn, fastidious, desexed, urban, and intellectual, is a heartbreaking caricature of the modern condition. Although free from the sadism and racism that come out in the Turtons and the McBrydes, she is nevertheless a product of the same alienation that made them.

The theme which this book hammers home is that, for all our differences, we are in fact *one*. There is no getting out of this, our common boat. Not only are we related, each to each, as persons, but we partake also of the earth, sky, and water; of mud, temples, and bacteria; of oranges, crystals, and birds—and of the unseen as well. Physically of one environment, we are also psychically one, and it is reason's denial of our commonality, the repression of that *participation mystique,* which has caused man to rule his Indias and himself with such futility and blindness—and has in our era occasionally shown us the shadow incarnate as a Hitler or a Stalin. Without preaching, the novel asks us to be responsible, to integrate our selves, to link reason and instinct, to base our civilized arrangements on what the human race has in common instead of on what rives it into races, classes, religions, sexes, and divided personalities.*

A Passage to India, unlike Forster's earlier books, is almost totally lacking in didactic or editorial comment. It is presented objectively, in a dramatic present, and its theme is implicit rather than explicit— as the theme of a myth must be. Nevertheless, it is, in an old-fashioned sense, the most prophetic of Forster's books, carrying not only his most powerful warning about the human predicament, but also one of the most provocative analyses of that predicament to be found in modern literature. It is the warning that Jung in another medium (and in a growing company) has reiterated persistently within our century. Jung, probably more than anyone else, has taught us how to read the kind of myth that *Passage* is:

Separation from his instinctual nature inevitably plunges civilized man into the conflict between conscious and unconscious, spirit and nature, knowl- edge and faith, a split that becomes pathological the moment his conscious- ness is no longer able to neglect or suppress his instinctual side. The accu- mulation of individuals who have got into this critical state starts off a mass movement.... In accordance with the prevailing tendency of consciousness to seek the source of all ills in the outside world, the cry goes up for politi- cal and social changes which, it is supposed, would automatically solve the much deeper problem of split personality. Hence it is that whenever this demand is fulfilled, political and social conditions arise which bring the same ills back again in altered form. What then happens is a simple reversal: the underside comes to the top and the shadow takes the place of the light.... All this is unavoidable, because the root of the evil is untouched....

Our rational philosophy does not bother itself with whether the other per- son in us, pejoratively described as the "shadow," is in sympathy with our conscious plans and intentions. Evidently it does not know that we carry in ourselves a real shadow . . . which no man can overlook without the gravest risk to himself....

...We still go on thinking and acting as before, as if we were *simplex* and not *duplex.* Accordingly, we imagine ourselves to be innocuous, reason- able and humane. We do not think of distrusting our motives or of asking ourselves how the inner man feels about the things we do in the outside world. But actually it is frivolous, superficial, and unreasonable of us, as

---

* Shahane, for example, calls "Temple" "a symbol of harmony," whereas the Marabar echo is "a symbol of evil" (*E. M. Forster: A Reassessment,* p. 108). On the contrary, the caves are before ethics, nothing, the absence of right and wrong. Ethics is a matter belonging to the slopes of the mountain, not its inner cell.

well as psychically unhygienic, to overlook the reaction and standpoint of the unconscious. . . . It should be worthy of all the attention we can give it, especially today, when everyone admits that the weal or woe of the future will be decided neither by the attacks of wild animals nor by natural catastrophes nor by the danger of world-wide epidemics but simply and solely by the psychic changes in man. It needs only an almost imperceptible disturbance of equilibrium in a few of our rulers' heads to plunge the world into blood, fire, and radioactivity.[50]

6

Esthetically the novel is a masterpiece. At every point the grand design meshes with the narrative to make us aware that the physical and the metaphysical are but separate aspects of a single, interpenetrating reality. And never has "rhythm"—that informing principle of all Indian sculpture, painting, and architecture—been given a greater opportunity in fiction or achieved a greater success. Forster has realized his work, as does the Indian artist, from the inside out, expanding it from a spiritual center. As the yogi realizes the inner life through a discipline of controlled breathing, or as the Indian dancer feels the god flowing outward in the form of movements and gestures, so does this book demonstrate through the flow of its "echoes" a world of gross matter informed with spiritual intimations.

Rhythm is evident in manifold guises. It is incarnate in the doublings and triplings that saturate the book: Aziz's "two memories" (p. 132), Adela's "double relation" to her experience in the cave, Mrs. Moore's "double vision," and the "half-way moment" at the Hindu festival are some of the dualities that set up vibrations and call for reconciliation, even as the trinities* in their more complex and

* The book is full of what might be seen as travesties of the Hindu invocation to the three-in-one, A U M. When Aziz suggests to Godbole that the caves "are immensely holy, no doubt," Godbole answers "Oh no, oh no," and then, after a pause, "Oh no" again. The Anglo-Indians repeat the same incantation with their machinery: the train carrying the party to the caves speaks to the "timeless twilight": "Pomper, pomper, pomper." Even Mrs. Turton, when her passions are high, slips into the immemorial rhythms of ancient India: "You're weak, weak, weak," she says to her husband before reminding him that Indians should be made "to crawl from here to the caves on their hands and knees whenever an Englishwoman's in sight." The three arcades of the Mosque are repeated in the "three high arches of wood" in Fielding's house; and Aziz's "Madam! Madam! Madam!" to Mrs. Moore "echoes" those arches. (pp. 79, 142, 225, 21, 67, 22.)

exalted way occasionally give promise of reconciliation achieved. These doublings and triplings create "echoes," which manifest themselves as sound, touch, sight; as earth, air, water; or as a thousand other sublunary things. They are almost totally synesthetic, appearing and disappearing with more subtlety and ubiquity than Proust's "little phrase." Echoes take the form of wasps and bees, ghosts and holy ghosts, appearing sometimes in material form and sometimes as ideas (or mere puns) in the minds of the characters.

But rhythm appears most often as sound. The book is full of noise and music; out of India's hundred mouths comes a babel or a harmony, depending on one's ear. The sounds of India remind Aziz, in his mosque, of exile, and drive him back to his own faith for relief. He hears some Hindus drumming and knows they are Hindus because he finds the rhythm uncongenial. Christian church bells do not move him much more:

> He could hear church bells as he drowsed, both from the civil station and from the missionaries out beyond the slaughter house—different bells and rung with different intent, for one set was calling firmly to Anglo-India, and the other feebly to mankind. He did not object to the first set; the other he ignored, knowing their inefficiency. (p. 105.)

The echoes of these bells do not include the echoes of the caves; they do not begin at the beginning, but initiate their own beginnings— hence they carry only a superficial social meaning. The true Anglo-Indian hymn was the British national anthem, inviting God into partisan politics and causing a stiffening to attention, as if the listeners expected the King to drop in. Mrs. Moore heard its invitations with decreasing sympathy, for its "note had died into a new one" (p. 32). But the song echoing most persistently through the book is Godbole's appeal to the god to come. His song is without words, unlike those of Anglo-India or Islam, and although Fielding and Aziz agree that "Hindus are unable to sing" (p. 288), they are stirred by Godbole's song, with its hints of the silent commonality beneath and behind the world's noise: *

---

*Godbole's later song, which opens the "Temple" chapter, is not quite wordless, but is the reiteration of only two lines: "Tukaram, Tukaram,/Thou art my father and mother and everybody." Tukaram, writes V. A. Shahane, is the greatest mystic saint of Maharashtra. "Tukaram is the exponent of the Bhakti cult, man's union with God through love, which is the central issue in Hindu mysticism." (*E. M. Forster, A Reassessment*, p. 108.)

His thin voice rose, and gave out one sound after another. At times there seemed rhythm, at times there was the illusion of a Western melody. But the ear, baffled repeatedly, soon lost any clue, and wandered in a maze of noises, none harsh or unpleasant, none intelligible. It was the song of an unknown bird. (p. 83.)

The playing of "Nights of Gladness" by a European band during the festival did not interrupt the Hindu worshipers, for they "lived beyond competition" (p. 297). And Godbole's singing like an "unknown bird" reminds us that animal voices, too, join India's hundred others —as if claiming equal recognition in the family of creation. The squeals of a squirrel ("in tune with the infinite, no doubt, but not attractive except to other squirrels"), the creaks of brown birds, the "ponk ponk" of the coppersmith, are a few of these related echoes.

These songs and sounds are all, in their several ways, appeals from one living part of the universe to another to "come"—to come bringing food or love or relief from loneliness. Godbole's song doubles back in a dozen pathetic or comic variants. Aziz had installed wires for electricity in his bungalow, but "Electricity had paid no attention, and a colony of eye-flies had *come* instead" (p. 106). When City Magistrate Heaslop approaches, Aziz exclaims: "He comes, he comes, he comes. I cringe. I tremble." (p. 255.) The punctuality of this Anglo-Indian god comments ironically on the god who never comes. And "come" enters the idiom of the British, though no racial memory tells them how misdirected their appeal is. "Come along, Aziz, old man," says Fielding at the arrest, and when Aziz complies instead of flying, the Inspector sighs: "Ah, thank God, he comes" (p. 169). This word, like many others, has unnumbered variations, clustering and breaking apart like so many bees—or eye-flies.

Thus the great appeal is mimicked and travestied. The echoes of the book are transmuted into echoes within echoes, men understanding each other's noises no better than each other's languages. And beyond the echoes is silence (as beyond the light is darkness), the condition of the ultimate beginning and the ultimate end.

These evidences could be multiplied without end. Rhythm is more than a technique: it is the incarnation of the book's meaning. The interrelationships between earth-sea-sky, animal-vegetable-mineral, soul-heart-mind—together with the metaphors carrying them—have no point of final rest. They are the expanding waves of a continuum

flowing out from the earth's shadow-center to the silences of the outermost circumference, and back again. We never see this whole—not
even a Godbole sees it—but it is implied. The multitudinous echoes
accumulate into a body of circumstantial evidence that the Great
Round exists, that unity and harmony are the ultimate promises of
life. The circle is not closed before our eyes, but we are left believing
that it was closed once and may be again.

The beauty and brilliance of this esthetic design are such that they
are likely to turn the critic into a helpless appreciator. The book is an
endless mine of those secrets Forster likes to keep from the reader, and
its achievements in dialogue and humor far surpass Forster's earlier
work. "He persuades you," writes Santha Rama Rau, "by characterization and without a word of exposition, that his Indians are speaking to each other in their own language, and yet catches the special
lilt and idiom of Indian-English when they are talking to the colonial
British."[51] It is not easy to forget the Nawab Bahadur's "Half one
league onwards" (p. 91) as he directs his motor-car into motion, or
the characterization of old Mr. Graysford and young Mr. Sorley, the
parish missionaries down by the slaughterhouse (the sort of Christians
Gandhi loved). Laughter cannot be withheld, for these absurdities are
part of the human comedy on the World Mountain.

"In our Father's house are many mansions," [Mr. Graysford and Mr. Sorley]
taught, and there alone will the incompatible multitudes of mankind be
welcomed and soothed. Not one shall be turned away by the servants on
that verandah, be he black or white, not one shall be kept standing who
approaches with a loving heart. And why should the divine hospitality cease
here? Consider, with all reverence, the monkeys. May there not be a man-
sion for the monkeys also? Old Mr. Graysford said No, but young Mr. Sorley, who was advanced, said Yes; he saw no reason why monkeys should not
have their collateral share of bliss.... And the jackals? Jackals were indeed
less to Mr. Sorley's mind, but he admitted that the mercy of God, being infinite, may well embrace all mammals. And the wasps? He became uneasy
during the descent to wasps, and was apt to change the conversation. And
oranges, cactuses, crystals, and mud? and the bacteria inside Mr. Sorley? No,
no, this is going too far. We must exclude someone from our gathering, or
we shall be left with nothing. (pp. 40–41.)

Is there still some earnestness attached to the irony here? The question haunts the critic. And it invokes the final question: just how successful is this novel?

"The many gods of India would have no existence on earth," writes Stella Kramrisch, "were it not for their portraits in stone and bronze, and their temples."[52] It is a large claim for art, and yet Forster has from the beginning desired art to play such a role, to incarnate divinity itself. That is one reason it is valid to speak of his books as "myths," or chapters of a new "gospel."

But we may legitimately ask of a gospel that it be as true as it is beautiful, and here *Passage* raises some doubts. Though it is perhaps the greatest English novel of this century as an esthetic accomplishment, does it in fact succeed any better than the earlier novels in coming to grips with the issue of crude power? In bypassing politics, in failing to deal with any but personal kinds of resistance, the book has struck some readers as wayward, even irresponsible. Indeed, its theme could be read as a simple-minded declaration that nation-states are like people and that political divisions can be cured by what cures personal quarrels—by kindness and sensitivity and good-will—without any particular attention to political strategy or means. Forster goes much farther in scorning practical considerations than, say, Gandhi would have gone; and even Mrs. Moore's anti-social apathy is presented as at least an honorable way out.

There is some small truth in this view of the book. Always evident in Forster's work is the desire to get beyond the will, to pass away from the socio-political contentions on the sides of the World Mountain down to the dark, dull places of primal nothingness or up to the transcendent domain of spirit. His novels can accordingly be read in one sense as exalting nihilism or escape. Those will-less ones, like Mrs. Wilcox and Mrs. Moore, exist as beings lapsed almost to a state of nature. They could say, after the Jesus of Lawrence's *The Man Who Died*: "How good it is to have fulfilled my mission, and to be beyond it. Now I can be alone, and leave all things to themselves, and the fig-tree may be barren if it will, and the rich may be rich. My way is my own alone."[53]

But this state, so infuriating to the critics who see it only as a kind of social dereliction, is in fact a state that precedes and preconditions all fundamental creative human growth even as the fallowness of the earth precedes the growth of plants. That human growth, as Forster conceives it, must have its roots deep in the earth (caves) and aspire toward the sun (peak), but it must be achieved in part, like the

growth of seeds, by virtue of being left alone. The meddlesome ma-
nipulations of modern man have destroyed more than they have built,
and in the bargain are destroying love. Forster sees the imbalance of
modern life and wants to correct it. His books are one long testimony
to this desire—from the will-driven fantasies, with their appeal for
justice, justice, to the almost earthlike patience of *Passage,* with its
seeming (but only seeming) abandonment of hope. The effort to connect in *Howards End* failed partly because of the very anxiety that
went into it, but the myth of *Passage* is matured with the knowledge
of Lawrence's Jesus: "Having died, he was patient, knowing there
was time, an eternity of time."[54] Forster has not redefined the moral
or spiritual issue; he has redefined the ground on which it is to be met.

In short, the book is a masterpiece of *understanding.* It shows us
the context in terms of which all questions must be asked and all
action taken. By bringing our social separateness and our real inter-
relatedness within the compass of one vision, it unforgettably makes
the point that before we save the world we must save ourselves, before we can know anything we must know ourselves. The book's politics are millennial rather than practical: it will take hands other than
Forster's to remove the untouchables and the slaughterhouses from
the human scene. Forster is as reluctant here as always to deal in practical plans of action. But he has given us a myth that throws the political problems into focus, reminding the reader that the follies and
crimes of history stem as much from man's failures of insight as from
his wrongdoing, that our predicament stems as much from wrong
questions as from wrong answers.

The essential point is that understanding itself is a kind of action.
And here we come full circle. The bringing of the conscious and the
unconscious into contact, the removal of the barriers of prejudice
from the mind, the awareness that we are all bound by an invincible
commonality—these are psychic acts that may have enormous consequences. This book is the preparation for such an act, is itself such
an act. It is an object for contemplation, a mandala; not just a great
work of fiction, but one of the greatest modern efforts to write a myth
for our time.

Chapter thirteen

Criticism: The Near and the Far

> To try and approach truth on one side after another, not
> to strive or cry, not to persist in pressing forward, on any
> one side, with violence and self-will—it is only thus, it
> seems to me, that mortals may hope to gain any vision of
> the mysterious Goddess.
>
> —*Matthew Arnold*
>
> The strong are so stupid.
>
> —*E. M. Forster*

It is easy to think of Forster's work as ending with *Passage,* but that
novel marked a turning point rather than a finish. Though he doubtless would have gone on producing novels had he been able to do so,
his forty years' production of nonfiction after 1924 represents, to some
degree, a deliberate change of vocation.* "I wanted to write but did
not want to write novels"[1] is a statement to take seriously, for the
writer of prose has from the beginning contended with the poet, the

---

* A completed but unpublished novel dealing with the subject of homosexuality
was produced after *Passage,* and at least one unpublished story. Forster apparently
felt both to be unpublishable; those who have read the novel generally consider it
a failure. These two pieces of unpublished fiction are discussed in a letter that T. E.
Lawrence wrote to Forster on September 8, 1927: "I'm sorry your short story isn't
publishable. As you said, the other one wouldn't do for general circulation. Not
that there was a wrong thing in it: but the wrong people would run about en-
larging their mouths over you. It is a pity such creatures must exist. The *Royal
Geographical Journal,* and *Journal of the Central Asian Society,* two learned societies, both found *Revolt in the Desert* indecent. It seems almost incredible.

"I wanted to read your long novel, & was afraid to. It was like your last keep,
I felt: and if I read it I had you: and supposing I hadn't liked it? I'm so funnily
made up, sensually. At present you are in all respects right, in my eyes: that's because you reserve so very much, as I do. If you knew all about me (perhaps you do:
your subtlety is very great: shall I put it 'if I knew that you knew . . .'?) you'd think
very little of me. And I wouldn't like to feel that I was on the way to being able
to know about you. However perhaps the unpublished novel isn't all that. You
may have kept ever so much out of it. Everywhere else you write far within your
strength." *The Letters of T. E. Lawrence,* ed. David Garnett (New York, 1939),
p. 537.

moralist with the artist. Not that Forster felt his turning away from fiction to be altogether a defeat; nonfictional prose, he writes, since it is "a medium for daily life as well as for literature, is particularly sensitive to what is going on."[2] To be sensitive to what is going on becomes, after 1924, virtually Forster's vocation. One could, of course, consider this final phase entirely in terms of failure, and see Forster as suffering a loss of will and imagination before the "gigantic horror" of the modern situation.[3] Indeed, it is hard to read his later work without some sense of anticlimax. By itself it doubtless would make no compelling claim on our attention (ranking perhaps with the critical writings of a Desmond MacCarthy or an E. B. White). But as a postscript to a great creative achievement it has a special value and interest.

Elizabeth Bowen has claimed that Forster's work shows little development, that he was "adult when he began to write," and that "it took no term of years to show what would be inevitable."[4] As regards his fiction, this certainly needs serious qualification—between the stories and *Passage* there is an evolution of the artist from almost a child's to a man's estate—but as regards his work after 1924 the claim is valid. Although that work varies in quality, it can all be read as a single, continuing effort to enunciate a humanistic gospel, to advance the claims of the "aristocracy of the sensitive, the considerate, and the plucky."[5]

But in a narrower sense, it is not possible to find a single thematic line in this writing, which includes two biographies, an unpublished novel (maybe two), two pageants, and a libretto, as well as innumerable reviews, sketches, and critical articles.* Since 1924 Forster has published more than four hundred pieces. Though the subjects and themes are extremely various, everything is touched by a unique sensibility and style—the style of a democratic common man, colloquial and unpretentious, combined with the wit and delicate ironies of his own ideal aristocrat. This manner is inseparable from his humanism; his view of life is in part created by the gestures that express it. Forster exists as a moral influence as well as an artist. And it is largely the

---

* My study of Forster has been greatly facilitated by Oliver Stallybrass's excellent bibliographical work on Forster, which he generously allowed me to consult, and which has now been completed by Miss B. J. Kirkpatrick.

writing of this last period that has established him as an influence—especially with the generation that came to maturity during and after the Second World War. For every reader of that generation who knows Forster's novels there may be ten who know "What I Believe."

2

"Art is not enough, any more than love is enough," Forster writes in 1934; "but art, love and thought can all do something, and art, the most nervous of the three, mustn't be brushed aside like a butterfly."[6] During the Depression years and the war years following, Forster rang many changes on these generalizations, concluding in 1941 that "Love is a great force in private life . . . but love in public affairs does not work."[7] At a P.E.N. Conference in 1944 he brought laughs by stating: "I don't believe in love in Government offices."* These years at times show his idealism in strategic, and sometimes in near-panic, retreat before the unassimilable events of modern history. "Perhaps no one in our time," writes Lionel Trilling, "has expressed so simply as Forster the weariness with the intellectual tradition of Europe which has been in some corner of the European psyche since early in the 19th century."[8] His statement (recalling Mrs. Moore) that the best chance for future society "lies through apathy, uninventiveness, and inertia" makes him appear weary not only with intellectualism but almost with consciousness itself.[9] But Forster's disillusionment is by no means always this deep; his anxiety undergoes many changes in pitch and intensity. In 1939 he writes, "So, though I am not an optimist, I cannot agree with Sophocles that it were better never to have been born."[10] Actually he is never even close to such root-and-branch pessimism. The next year, with a war on and Hitler in mind, he writes: "Creation lies at the heart of civilisation like fire in the heart of the earth. . . . In this difficult day . . . it is a comfort to remember that violence has so far never worked."[11] After the war he writes: "Can we combine experience and innocence? I think we can."[12] And in 1957,

* "E. M. Forster's Intolerant Tolerance," *The Manchester Guardian*, August 28, 1944, p. 4. The P.E.N. Club is an international organization of poets, playwrights, essayists, and novelists aiming "to promote and maintain friendship and intellectual cooperation in all countries." Forster was president of the club in 1944, and made the main address at its annual meeting.

when he is seventy-eight years old, he warns against identifying old age with growing old, with that senescence which is a kind of despair.[13] Ennui and disgust with the modern world are among his strongest feelings—he compares the period between the wars to that which caused St. Augustine to write *The City of God*.[14] Nevertheless, he has no notion that our age is peculiar in its badness, or that our maladies are incurable:

This disharmony has sounded all through human history, there is nothing new about it, we can hear it in Lucretius, St. Augustine, Donne, Matthew Arnold, but it is loudest at times like the present when the ramparts of the world threaten to give way with a rush and to let loose upon the individual too much of the unknown at once.[15]

Forster's taste is more predictable than his opinions; he is, like Aziz, more faithful to "truth of mood" than to "verbal truth" or consistency. But critics who make him out to be basically another Mrs. Moore—a kind of spiritual catatonic who, having once glimpsed the caves, can thereafter do nothing but passively put in his days—have missed a main point of both *Passage* and the essays. Angus Wilson, for example (who says his sympathies with Forster's work "desert" him in the third part of *Passage*), asked Forster in an interview whether the collapse of Mrs. Moore was connected with Forster's ceasing to write novels. He received an answer that at first disappointed him: "It's a moment of negation. I suppose it's the same thing as the vision we have discussed with its back turned."[16] The vision, in short, though it has different aspects, is *one thing*, an organic whole; Forster sees the negation, but he also connects it with its context. What is not yet well understood in the criticism of Forster is that this negative vision, horrible as it is by itself, is absolutely necessary for a balanced and even sane view of life.

Nevertheless, there is no denying that Forster, compared with such *hommes engagés* as Julian Bell and André Malraux, has been a peaceful sojourner in his own vineyard. Like Matthew Arnold (albeit less actively) he has advocated disinterestedness in an age of gigantic conflict, and has found tolerable only "the slighter gestures of dissent." When asked whether he was apolitical for the same reasons as André Gide (because "there is no politics without fraud") he said, "No, not because of fraud (English politics have less fraud than French) but

because of their essential futility. It's preposterous to read of Gait-
skell's answer to Macmillan on economy on the same page as Sput-
nik!"[17] But in those areas where politics impinge on personal relations, threaten individual freedom, or impair civil liberties, he has
been an energetic partisan.

3

Throughout the decade of the thirties, Forster, along with many of
his cultured contemporaries, felt smoked out of the ivory tower and
driven into the public arena. Since they had no taste for politics,
they did not quite know what to do there; but the inescapable facts
of Depression, Fascism, Communism, the coming war—and all the
social repressions accompanying mobilization for crisis—seriously disturbed their complacency and consciences. In the twenties most English writers had been relatively isolated from the nation's social and
political life, assuming often a virtuous superiority to any show of
public-spiritedness or patriotism. Of this period George Orwell wrote:
"England is perhaps the only great country whose intellectuals are
ashamed of their own nationality."[18] But the thirties brought a haunt-
ing sense of the enemy at the gates, and any easy complacency
about the permanence of civilization began to seem frivolous and
forced. What worried Forster, however, was the enemy within the
gates, the invaders of private freedom who multiply in a besieged
society:

We can't build as we like or drink when we like or dress as we like. We can't
even undress as we like, but when we bathe must wear an increasing amount
of costume in the combined interest of British modesty and British trade. We
can't say what we like—there is this legend of free speech, but you try it on:
free speech and saying what you want to say are very different things. We
can't read or write what we like. Oh, by the way, some publishers of repute
intend to bring out an edition of Joyce's *Ulysses* in this country: I hope they
will get away with it, for it is an important work—but we shall see. And,
finally, we cannot go where we like. Escape is impossible. We can only get
out of England on a ticket of leave, issued if our conduct has been satisfactory.... This ticket of leave is called a passport.[19]

Above all, Forster believes that books must be kept free. In 1944, the
Tercentenary of the *Areopagitica,* he wrote an appreciation of Milton's classic statement, and found it a timely brief against the modern

censor: "The big mind having to apply for permission to the fidgety small mind."[20] Forster had made public his own libertarian position regularly since the late twenties. In reviewing St. John-Stevas's *Obscenity and the Law* (1956), he recalls a long list of literary suppressions since 1909 and his personal involvement in some of them. He remembers *The Spectator*'s denunciation of H. G. Wells's *Ann Veronica* in 1909 as a "poisonous book" populated by "a community of scuttling stoats and ferrets." Thomas Hardy (who was a friend of Forster's) headed the list of authors protesting, to which the editorial reply was: "We are not impressed with the list." Forster goes on:

Nor can I forget the *Well of Loneliness* case, when with forty other witnesses I repaired to the Old Bailey in a state of some trepidation. Most of us had never been in a court of law before and hated it, but felt obliged to testify that Miss Radclyffe Hall's book was well written, seriously intentioned, and devoid of obscenity.... The evidence of fellow-writers was disallowed, and with a mixture of mortification and relief we departed. All copies of the book were destroyed, and it is now on general sale.[21]

That was 1928. In October 1960, Forster again appeared at the Old Bailey, this time as a defense witness in the *Lady Chatterley's Lover* trial. In the interim Forster repeatedly denounced the public guardians of literary morality: William Joynson-Hicks (Jix), who backed the *Well of Loneliness* prosecution, and Sir David Maxwell Fyfe, the Home Secretary leading the "purity drive" of 1954—which had as its crowning incident the banning of *The Decameron* by the City of Swindon, thus elevating it to the ranks of the "Swindon Classics." In a joint letter written in 1928, Forster and Virginia Woolf protested the legal principle behind these prosecutions—the Campbell Act of 1857, which made it possible for a magistrate, on hearing a complaint that a book is obscene, to order the book to be seized and the sellers or publishers to appear and show cause why the book should not be destroyed. The letter asked for a ruling which would prevent mere policemen from passing judgment on more than the question of "pornography." Pornographic books, writes Forster, "ought to be suppressed, and they are easily detected and classified, for the reason that their aim is not literature but physical provocativeness."[22] The argument is naïve and high-minded, but its principles are shared not only by Virginia Woolf but by D. H. Lawrence. In *Pornography and*

Obscenity (1930), for example, Lawrence denounces pornography because (as Forster explains it) pornography "inclines the mind to run round and round in a circle instead of going forward and gaining strength." Lawrence, he says, condemns all forms of "self-enclosure" —not merely "the physical act of masturbation, but any emotional counterpart of it, any turning-inward upon itself of the spirit, any furtiveness and secrecy, any tendency to live in little private circles of excitement, rather than in the passionate outer life of personal exchange." Forster accepts some of these arguments timidly. He seems unsure, for example, of Lawrence's belief that "to define filth is to sterilize it," though he believes the book is remarkable as a polemic.

On blasphemy Forster took a bolder line. People should not be corrupted, he wrote, "but there is no reason why they should not be shocked. I am often shocked myself (for example by certain smug and loathsome advertisements of beer that defile our streets), but I bear up; everything in civilisation cannot suit everybody."[23] By 1939 Forster's taste and judgment on matters of free speech had become so well recognized that he was appointed by the Lord Chancellor to the committee to examine the Law of Defamatory Libel—perhaps the closest he ever came to *official* eminence.

A cause célèbre in the mid-thirties was the prosecution of James Hanley's novel *Boy,* which dealt with homosexuality. The book was defended by such writers as A. P. Herbert, A. A. Milne, J. B. Priestley, and H. G. Wells. T. E. Lawrence wrote to the publisher:

I saw E.M.F. while the case was pending and talked to him about it. He is one of the few writers who might dare lead an attempt at help. Most of them are afraid of the word sodomy. I wonder why?

I thought it would be more effective if I tackled E.M.F. before rather than after judgement. A subtle mind, that one.[24]

Hanley's book is boring, but Forster seems genuinely to have liked it and to have been interested in Hanley's other work. Throughout this period Forster sometimes confuses a defense of civil liberties with a defense of fine art, particularly if a book under attack deals with homosexuality. Forster speaks out strongly. "The subject has been recognised by science and is recognisable in history," he writes. "It exists as a fact among the many other facts of life."[25] Hence he believes it should neither be debarred from books nor be put in a class apart from other crimes of sex: "If homosexuality between men ceased to be *per se* criminal—it is not criminal between women—and if homosexual crimes were equated with heterosexual crimes and punished with equal but not with additional severity, much confusion and misery would be averted; there would be less public importuning and less blackmail."[26] In the debate over the Wolfenden Report, Forster takes —unsurprisingly—the liberal position. He is not hopeful of radical reform, but he is glad of the liberalization that has occurred since the trial of Oscar Wilde:

The law has not altered, nor is it likely to alter, since it is to the advantage of all governments to retain severe sexual laws—it gives them an additional hold over their subjects. But public opinion certainly has altered. Knowledge of psychology and physiology penetrates even into circles which have never heard their names. For example, the average man in 1895 went mad with genuine loathing or rage, he felt it his duty to spit in Wilde's face on Clapham Junction station, and to denounce all who befriended him. But the average man today would be merely indignant, disgusted, or bored.[27]

The issue of homosexuality is, of course, far more important to Forster than these judicious words would suggest. If Forster has generally been on the side of the underdog, it is at least partly because he has always sympathized with this alienated minority. And if the cause of art and sensitivity has seemed to him beleaguered, it is partly because society has forced some of its ablest practitioners to live half-secret lives. His liberalism is inseparable from these facts.

Racial and class prejudices are of a piece with sexual prejudice, and Forster tirelessly denounces them. In a 1938 radio talk he preached one of his most forthright sermons on brotherly love: "Don't snub your neighbour, don't make him look a fool, don't show him up, don't take him down, don't have things out with him, don't stand no nonsense from him; and, if you must do such things, don't be proud of it afterwards."[28] He also spoke decisively and with admirable coarseness about the color bar against Indians in hotels and restaurants: "The man who makes a row about Indians in a restaurant or hotel is usually some blustering lecher who is wanting to show off in front of his pickup. Why does the management not tell him to go to hell?"[29] The tensions of the time show in the phrasing; Nazi persecutions of the Jews were in everybody's mind, and Forster was not remiss in taking a stand: "The grand Nordic argument, 'He's a bloody capitalist so he must be a Jew, and as he's a Jew he must be a Red,' has already taken root in our filling-stations and farms."[30]

Forster is fundamentally distrustful of authority, and the bureaucratic mind draws his heaviest fire. One of his finest satires is "Our Deputation," in which he and four others take a complaint to some nameless Government Ministry, and encounter the fake civility of officialdom: "I reflected upon the technique which is employed by those in high authority when they desire to administer a snub.... They begin a sentence deeply, gruffly, gently; it moves along like a large friendly animal; then it twitters, turns acid and thin and passes right overhead with a sort of whistling sound."[31]

The military, that most brutal foe of personal relations, embodies a form of authority he particularly detests, partly because it insists that the business of war has something heroic about it. In the thirties he protests the Aldershot Tattoo (an annual military show) and the two minutes' silence honoring the dead of the past war. He objects to the "obscenities" concealed behind the show's propaganda: "In the past, sabres and cavalry charges and jolly Tommies and majors with medals and patriotic hymns had a certain heroic value.... They are now just advertisements through which a tradesman pushes his wares. The wares are poison gas and vesicant dew; the tradesman is the Devil."[32] His objection to the reverential silence was more audacious and drew a violent reaction: he saw in it "the thin edge of the wedge—the first instance in England of that drilled mass-emotion which plays such a large part in the street-life of Italy and Germany."[33] Though Forster backed the war against Hitler, he never backed war, and his evasive pacifism stirred and can still stir vexed responses from fellow liberals. Was not Hitler the greater Devil? Can such evil be turned away except by arms? Forster does not really answer such questions, except to say that the people whom he respects most "behave as if they were immortal and as if society was eternal."[34] That is to say, they behave like gods and live in terms of absolutes, not of expedients. Here, for Forster, is the difficulty of humanism, in art and out of it. He recognizes the fact of force, but he places himself at as great a distance as possible from its details, observing it from the long-range perspective of history:

I realise that all society rests upon force. But all the great creative actions, all the decent human relations, occur during the intervals when force has not managed to come to the front. These intervals are what matter. I want them to be as frequent and as lengthy as possible, and I call them "civilisation."[35]

Had Forster, like John Dewey, distinguished more explicitly between force and violence, he might have seen more clearly that force is always present in every creative action. Still, it was good that there were some few like Forster in those prewar times who took the long view and kept their countrymen in mind of the fact that the coming war was for "civilisation" and not just for victory.

One of Forster's most controversial protests was a recommendation that owners of investments sell their shares in any companies sweating labor or contributing to war preparations. He himself got rid of some South African mining stock and some shares in Imperial Chemicals, Ltd. ("70 ordinary and 50 deferred"), and he advised others to do the same. Though a moral gesture of this sort offers little enough help to the shareless and jobless, his position is nevertheless admirable compared with the unquestioning self-interest of most of his class. Still, his attitude has less to do with sharing the wealth than with salving the conscience. He wrote rather plaintively of his dilemma:

Ever since I have read *Widowers' Houses* I have felt hopeless about investments. It seemed impossible for a small private investor like myself to know where his money had actually gone or whether it was doing harm or good. When I ask those who are better informed than myself, they usually laugh at me and tell me not to worry, and I have got to feel that the world of finance is so complicated that—ethically speaking—it doesn't matter what I buy.

In a sense this is true. It is impossible for any one to have clean hands. I will wash my hands in innocency and so will I go to thine altar? Impossible. There's nowhere to wash. We are all messed up together in a civilization which is going badly askew and which may, as the Communists think, be skewing because of the institution of private property. No individual, however humble, can be guiltless. Yet resignation is a mistake, there are degrees of guilt, and now and then I have tried—very incompetently—to overhaul my investments and to direct them into more plausible channels.[36]

But Forster does not rebel, or go into exile, or sell all he has and give it to the poor.* Conscience does not demand so much. Besides, what

* In reviewing a translation of Tolstoy's *What, Then, Must We Do?*, Forster made explicit his position on money and poverty:
"When the Dean of Durham (officially representing the carpenter Jesus) enjoins

would be the point? Spending and consumption are the new virtues, not charity and saving. One man's wealth does not go far, but one man's influence might. Though there is something—if not holier-than-thou, at least richer-than-thou—in Forster's shuffling of shares, it was braver to speak out than to hide one's guilt.

If at this time (1934) Forster had had to choose between Communism and Fascism, he would have chosen Communism, but the choice repels him. His real desire, though he has no hope of realizing it, is capitalism cleaned up.[37] In his review of F. A. Hayek's *The Road to Serfdom* and Harold Laski's *Faith, Reason, and Civilisation* he expresses the wish that both books would explode and leave, "as their residue, the truth." According to Forster, Hayek's book claims that "the system of private property is the most important guarantee of freedom, not only for those who own property, but scarcely less for those who do not." Laski, admitting the shortcomings of the Russian Revolution and its crimes, nevertheless sees Communism as "the new faith," and sees an important parallel between its rise and the rise of Christianity. Forster, though sympathizing with Hayek's argument, ends by begging the question: "I myself am a sentimentalist who believes in the importance of love. . . . I don't know whether it can be thus [as a binding social force] utilised. I only believe that it is important in itself and that the desire to love and the desire to be loved are the twin anchor ropes which keep the human race human."[38] These are typical worries besetting Forster in this decade; and they are doubtless part of what kept him from returning to fiction. The honesty in such a passage as the following is as impressive as the confusion:

---

poverty upon me, I answer readily enough, 'Yea, Dean, yea,' because I know that when his sermon is over the Dean will go back to an excellent lunch, and leave me free to do the same. It is a put-up job between us, a farce that has gone on century after century, ever since Christianity became respectable. But Tolstoy is not like that. He does not go off to his lunch. He, too, had his insincerities of action, but they were not of the suave organised sort promoted and practised by clergymen. The bulk of him is sincere; he demands a sincere response, and that is why he is so painful to read. He exacts (in my case) a definite refusal. I believe that he is right, that poverty has been caused by wealth, and that it is impossible to help the poor without becoming poor oneself. But I will not do it, I will not part with the whole of my surplus. Will you? If so, discontinue (among other things) your subscription to the *New Leader*. . . . It is better that we should make this reply than remain vague, self-satisfied, and unseeing." "Poverty's Challenge. The Terrible Tolstoy," *The New Leader*, XII (1925), 11.

Talking with Communists makes me realise the weakness of my own position and the badness of the twentieth century society in which I live. I contribute to the badness without wanting to. My investments increase the general misery, and so may my charities. And I realise, too, that many Communists are finer people than myself—they are braver and less selfish, and some of them have gone into danger although they were cowards, which seems to me finest of all.... [But] their argument for revolution—the argument that we must do evil now so that good may come in the long run—it seems to me to have nothing in it. Not because I am too nice to do evil, but because I don't believe the Communists know what leads to what. They say they know because they are becoming conscious of "the causality of society." I say they don't know, and my counsel for 1938–39 conduct is rather: Do good, and possibly good may come from it. Be soft, even if you stand to get squashed.[39]

"Be soft, even if you stand to get squashed"! That statement is almost a summary of Forster's social and political position. When war came Forster supported it actively with pen and voice, yet he avoided chauvinism. He worried more about the survival of cultural values after the war than about winning battles. His P.E.N. speech in the autumn of 1941—addressed to a hall full of anti-Hitler writers and refugees, all highly committed—began, "I believe in art for art's sake."[40] At the height of the political storm, he was one of the very few still listening to the inner voice. Has any other war writer ever begun a piece with the words: "This pamphlet is propaganda"? Though he did not shirk the fact that all would have been lost if the totalitarians had won, he felt just as strongly that "all is equally lost if we have nothing left to lose."[41] He sorted the German good from the German evil, pointing to the culture the Nazis destroyed as a warning to Britain not to do the same. Germany's trouble was that she "allowed her culture to become governmental" whereas England's is "national" and has developed "slowly, easily, lazily." English prudishness, freakishness, hypocrisy, love of freedom, mild idealism, and good-humored reasonableness "have all combined," writes Forster, "to make something which is certainly not perfect, but which may claim to be unusual."[42] Forster is, after all, an intensely patriotic man; there is more than irony in Rickie's impulsive statement: "Thank God I'm English." If Forster's own ideal amateurism (which permits him to "know nothing about economics or politics") seems overprivileged and irresponsible in a world on the brink of disaster, one must see that, while he shares in the defects of the England he describes, he also exemplifies the ripeness of its easygoing virtues.*

After the war Forster continued to take part in the battles for freedom and culture. In 1948 he resigned his active role in the National Council for Civil Liberties when he thought their action opposing a Government purge of Communists was motivated by political rather than nonparty considerations.[43] He continued to be active in the P.E.N. Club, and in 1946 he opposed the vote of the Stockholm P.E.N. Convention to establish a blacklist of authors who had collaborated with the enemy during the war.[44] In 1941 he refused to broadcast over the B.B.C.† because of its refusal to employ artists who had supported the (Communist) People's Convention. Though Forster dis-

---

* Many critics, of course, are not willing to let Forster or his class off this easily. The Marxist critic D. S. Savage, when he attacks Forster's characters, is also attacking the postures and privileges of Forster's little society:

"The life of Forster's characters, as members of the English upper-middle classes, is based upon falsehood because it is based on unearned income, derived from nameless and unmentioned sources, and all their independence, freedom, culture, 'personal relationships' are only made possible by this fact. Their lives are lived in a watertight system abstracted from the larger life of society as a whole. They are out of touch with humanity, carefully, though for the most part unconsciously, preserving themselves, by means of their mental circumscriptions and social codes, from all encroachment of the painful and upsetting actualities which make their privileged existence possible. Unlike the rich of other times, their privileges carry with them no burden of responsibility, and thus possess no concrete social sanction. The penalty they pay for their social advantages is a heavy one—a fundamental unreality which vitiates the personal dramas which take place in the closed social circuit to which they are condemned. For an inner spiritual change which affects one's attitude to one or two other selected persons only, and does not extend itself to include every other human being irrespective of social distinction, is invalidated from the start." *The Withered Branch* (London, 1950), p. 56.

That there is validity in this criticism is undeniable. What Mr. Savage fails to see is that many civilized virtues are made possible by these class privileges, and that Forster has worked through his fiction and criticism to make inner spiritual changes a public as well as a private event. Mr. Savage seems to have misread the symbolism of *Passage* and hence to have missed that book's assimilation of private and public contexts.

† In this he was joined by Ralph Vaughan Williams, R. H. Tawney, Leonard and Virginia Woolf, H. G. Wells, Dame Sibyl Thorndike, H. W. Nevinson, and Bernard Shaw. In 1931 he had attacked the B.B.C. for yielding to pressure for the withdrawal of a German documentary on General Nobile's polar expedition (*Krassin Saves Italia*). "The Freedom of the B.B.C.," *The New Statesman and Nation* (n.s.), I (1931), 209-10. But Forster could praise as well. In 1957 he congratulated the

agreed with the aims of the Convention, he nevertheless felt that it was not "Quixotic to demand, when in no immediate danger ourselves, that no one shall be persecuted for his opinions."[45] Recently he has supported the ban-the-bomb demonstrations and the protest marches to Aldermaston: "I don't feel hopeful of our chances of escape," he writes, "while continuing to hope."[46]

In a war pamphlet, reflecting upon the Hitlerian *Walpurgisnacht*, Forster wrote: "The tragic view of the universe can be noble and elevating, but it is a dangerous guide to daily conduct, and it may harden into a stupid barbarism, which smashes at problems instead of disentangling them."[47] The last time he made serious use of "tragedy" as an idea was in *Howards End*. But the war that followed brought tragedy without catharsis, and world events since have done little to make the mode more popular. Heroism in the modern world has generally gone bad, producing more men like Stalin, Mussolini, or Hitler than like T. E. Lawrence or Gandhi. As a result Forster has seen a future in "softness" rather than in "hardness"—in those like Gandhi "who have sought something in life that is neither chaos nor mechanism, who have not confused happiness with possessiveness, or victory with success, and who have believed in love."[48] In short, Forster's program has been to keep alive in the present world as much old-time liberalism as can survive in our alien and hostile climate. The following statement from "The Challenge of Our Time" is virtually definitive of his position:

I belong to the fag-end of Victorian liberalism, and can look back to an age whose challenges were moderate in their tone, and the cloud on whose horizon was no bigger than a man's hand. In many ways it was an admirable age. It practised benevolence and philanthropy, was humane and intellectually curious, upheld free speech, had little colour-prejudice, believed that individuals are and should be different, and entertained a sincere faith in the progress of society. The world was to become better and better, chiefly through the spread of parliamentary institutions. The education I received in those far-off and fantastic days made me soft and I am very glad it did, for I have seen plenty of hardness since, and I know it does not even pay.[49]

B.B.C. for allowing the agnostic Professor Stephen Toulmin to voice his opinions, and criticized *Listener* readers who apparently endorsed prior B.B.C. policies discouraging the free expression of disbelief. "Mr. E. M. Forster and the B.B.C. Refusal to Broadcast. Protest Against the Political Veto," *The Manchester Guardian*, March 18, 1941, p. 8.

Least of all has hardness paid for those who have found themselves in bread lines and trenches and concentration camps, and Forster's lucky exemption from these symbolic situations of our time has, for some, impaired his authority as a moral spokesman. But Forster is not universal man, nor does he pretend to be. He is a private citizen, appreciative of his good luck, who has honestly striven to add his little light to the modern darkness.

4

Forster's literary and critical career since 1924 is that same striving under a different aspect, appearing mainly in the form of personal essays and book criticism. Much of this is minor work, but some of it reveals a critical commitment of major importance.

The essays include such pieces as "Mr. and Mrs. Abbey's Difficulties" (1922), "Notes on the English Character" (1926), "My Own Centenary" (1927), "Trooper Silas Tomkyn Comberbacke" (1931), "A Letter to Madan Blanchard" (1931), "Mrs. Grundy at the Parkers' " (1932), "Mrs. Miniver" (1939), "Voltaire and Frederick the Great" (1941), "George Crabbe and Peter Grimes" (1948), and "John Skelton" (1950); there are also some playful fantasies on his own work, like "A View Without a Room" (1958). In these pieces Forster is the urbane first-person commentator, employing a gentle irony with deadly aim.

"My Own Centenary" ("From *The Times* of A.D. 2027") is an ironic memorial piece similar to Swift's "Verses on the Death of Dr. Swift," in which Forster gets in some stabs at the inanities of official praise:

"He whose hundredth anniversary we celebrate on Thursday next is famous, and why?" No answer was needed, none came. The lofty Gothic nave, the great western windows, the silent congregation—they gave answer sufficient, and passing on to the final word of his text, 'men,' the Dean expatiated upon what is perhaps the most mysterious characteristic of genius, its tendency to appear among members of the human race.... There can be no doubt that his contemporaries did not recognize the greatness of Forster. Immersed in their own little affairs, they either ignored him, or forgot him, or confused him, or, strangest of all, discussed him as if he were their equal. We may smile at their blindness, but for him it can have been no laughing matter, he must have had much to bear, and indeed he could scarcely have endured to put forth masterpiece after masterpiece had he not felt assured of the verdict of posterity. (AH, 75.)

In a different line are the essays on Mrs. Miniver and the poets
Crabbe and Skelton. In the early war years Mrs. Miniver (both in Jan
Struther's novel and in the film starring Greer Garson) emerged as
the wartime heroine of things-as-usual, the imperturbable guardian
of the myth that England still had an aristocracy in the saddle. The
country that not long since had swallowed Chamberlain was swallowing her just as easily, and Forster, revolted, moved to expose her. She
came from Forster's own class—"the class which strangled the aristocracy in the nineteenth century, and has been haunted ever since by
the ghost of its victim"—and she was almost the ideal representative
of what Forster loathed in that class, especially in its women. He
takes pains to point out that, for all her poorishness, her shabby car,
her four servants, her "vaguely heraldic" name, her son at Eton, and
her distant connections with the McQuern of Quern, she is (though
a lady) no aristocrat; she is "top-drawer but one." When she walks
past, the villagers have to spit and "splutter a little smut" in order to
preserve their self-respect and get rid of a feeling of incompetence.

What answer can the villagers make to a lady who is so amusing, clever, ob-
servant, broad-minded, shrewd, demure, Bohemian, happily-married, triply-
childrened, public-spirited and at all times such a lady? No answer, no answer
at all. They listen to her saying the right things, and are dumb. They watch
her doing the right things in the right way, and are paralysed. . . . She is too
wonderful with the villagers, she has them completely taped. (TC, 305.)

Here again is Forster's own true subject, that upper-middle class which
he could never leave and never tolerate. These villagers splutter smut
on Forster's behalf as well, carrying on the protest against female-
dominated Sawston begun by those uncouth males, Gino, Stephen,
and the Emersons. Mrs. Miniver is Agnes Pembroke thirty-five years
later, the unrepentant daughter of a Benthamite class of tradesmen
and professional men and little Government officials that came to
power following the Industrial Revolution and Reform Bills and
Death Duties and "has never been able to build itself an appropriate
home." That homelessness is Forster's own condition—one reason he
hates Mrs. Miniver. But a deeper reason is that he, along with the villagers, regards her as a fake aristocrat. She lacks that "grace or grandeur," that "fierce eccentricity," that "sense of ancient lineage or
broad acres lost through dissipation," that "something which makes

patronage acceptable, even if it hurries the patron to the guillotine."
He also blames her class for such a phenomenon as the English Fas-
cist Oswald Mosley, asserting that Mosley appeals to "the boredom
which devastates people who are not quite sure that they are gentlemen." In short, the true aristocrat is not restless, the fake one is; and
the notion of a true aristocracy obsesses Forster: "Quality is everywhere imperilled in contemporary life. Those who value it, as I do,
are in a vulnerable position. We form as it were an aristocracy in the
midst of a democracy, yet we belong and desire to belong to the democracy."[50]

The old order had its faults and crimes, Forster admits, yet he is
incurably fond of it. Mrs. Miniver would "tidy" civilization up, but
Forster—never forgetful of the "human" qualities in disorder—loves
the old aristocrats for their prodigality and oddballism and contempt
for petty form. He is, for example, amused by faults in the Countess
von Arnim (for whom he worked in Pomerania) that he would have
hated in a Harriet or an Agnes. And in describing a certain Lithu-
anian nobleman, Forster goes out of his way to praise "the shabbi-
ness, the threadbare feudalism, the occasional aristocratic arrogance"
—acceptable qualities because they are connected with "warm-heart-
edness, hospitality, and a sense of the soil." Even a playboy aristocrat
like the Duke of Portland, whose *Reminiscences* Forster describes as
"more of a bag than a book," is easily forgiven his "touches of arrogance and patronage."[51] When the Duke fatuously comments, "I hope
the new world, though I do not always agree with its ways, holds as
many possibilities of happiness, good fellowship, and enjoyment of
life as that which I knew," Forster rewards the inanity by saying: "In
a sentence such as this the landed aristocrat seems the only democrat,
and our hearts go out to him."* The common reader can only say:
No, they don't.

Forster's most readable achievements in the personal essay are his
pieces on literary figures. In "John Skelton" Forster fuses literature
and history in an amalgam reminiscent of Virginia Woolf's sketches
in *The Common Reader*—or of his own writings on Alexandria.
Skelton, the poet who wrote verses defying Cardinal Wolsey, is also

---

* The fact that Lady Ottoline Morrell, Bloomsbury's pet aristocrat, was the Duke's
daughter may have influenced Forster's judgment.

shown training hawks in his church at Diss. An amusing conjunction, but Trilling could again accuse Forster of making history what it should never be—"quaint."

In "George Crabbe and Peter Grimes," one of his best pieces, Forster studies the connections between an artist's work and his environment, which in Crabbe's case were particularly strong. The story of Peter Grimes is inseparable from the "dull, harsh, stony, wiry, soft, slimy" North Sea coast at Aldeburgh, where the sea is inexorably gaining upon the land. Although Crabbe hated the place and its people, he could no more stay away from them than his character Peter Grimes could. In the story, Grimes, the hateful son of a hateful father, expresses his wrath by murdering his apprentices from the workhouse. This hostility against the father is one of the story's two "motives" that fascinate Forster. He writes of Grimes:

His father has brought him to disaster—that is his explanation, and the father-motive which preluded the tragedy has re-emerged. To push the motive too hard is to rupture the fabric of the poem and to turn it into a pathological tract, but stressed gently it helps our understanding. The interpretations of Freud miss the values of art as infallibly as do those of Marx. They cannot explain values to us, they cannot show us why a work of art is good or how it became good. But they have their subsidiary use: they can indicate the condition of the artist's mind while he was creating, and it is clear that while he was writing "Peter Grimes" Crabbe was obsessed by the notion of two generations of males being unkind to one another and vicariously punishing unkindness. It is the grandsire-grandson alliance against the tortured adult.

The other motive—also to be stressed cautiously—is the attraction-repulsion one. . . . The poet and his creation share the same inner tension, the same desire for what repels them. Such parallels can often be found between the experiences of a writer, and the experiences of a character in his books. (TC, 188–89.)

This is, of course, also true of *The Longest Journey,* where both the father motive and the attraction-repulsion motive are conspicuously present.

An opera made from "Peter Grimes" by Montagu Slater and Benjamin Britten was produced in 1948 at Aldeburgh. Perhaps stimulated by its success, Forster tried his own hand in the genre. In 1951 he and Eric Crozier wrote the libretto and Benjamin Britten the music for a four-act opera based on Melville's *Billy Budd,* which Forster calls that "song not without words."* A formula like that in "Peter Grimes" again appears: a "father motive" shows in the condemnation of Billy by the father-figure Vere; an "attraction-repulsion motive" in the ambiguities of loving what one kills and killing what one loves, as when Billy, sentenced by the drumhead court to hang, bursts out, "Starry Vere, God bless you!" In Forster's treatment Melville's Claggart, the natural enemy of Billy's beauty and innocence, loses most of his ambiguity and becomes instead a self-revealing, self-announcing villain of almost melodramatic simplicity. But the hint of homosexual attraction which Melville drops (when Claggart wore a look of "soft yearning," as if he "could even have loved Billy but for fate and ban") is, if anything, accentuated in the opera. Its style often reminds us of Dickinson's *The Magic Flute*;† it suffers, as a critic said, from "an exaggerated softness of feeling." The reason may be that Forster tended to read Melville's myth as a demonstration that hardness does not pay rather than as a revised version of the Fall.

5

It is not easy to find a unifying thread running through Forster's literary criticism. As opposed to the kind of prose we have been considering, it is an eclectic body of work, often brilliant but sometimes astonishingly irresponsible. It brings to mind Ian Jack's paradox that the English, "who have produced the greatest poetical literature in the world, have a deep instinctive preference for the third-rate."⁵²

---

* Forster's only other attempts at drama after the war seem to be "The Abinger Pageant," performed on July 14 and 18, 1934, at Abinger, Surrey, with Tom Harrison as producer and Vaughan Williams doing the music; and "England's Pleasant Land" (1940), a "pageant play" produced at Milton Court, Westcott, Surrey, on July 8, 1938, again with the assistance of Harrison and Vaughan Williams. Both pageants had as their purpose a protest against the destruction of the land and the old landmarks and ways of life by "progress." They were extraordinarily well received by the critics. (See Plate 40.)

† But also of certain scenes in *The Longest Journey*. There are times, stutter and all, when Stephen is Billy himself:

" 'Last Sunday week,' interrupted Stephen, his voice suddenly rising, 'I came to call on you. Not as this or that's son. Not to fall on your neck. Nor to live here. Nor—damn your dirty little mind! I meant to say I didn't come for money. Sorry. Sorry. I simply came as I was, and I haven't altered since.' ...

" '*I* haven't altered since last Sunday week. I'm—' He stuttered again. He could not quite explain what it was." (LJ, 281–82.)

Nevertheless, taken as a whole, Forster's critical writing (most of which appeared in the form of reviews) represents an important manifesto of taste. Although no theorizer, Forster is an expert reader. Literature to him is a "man-to-man business," which is presided over by the heart. "The final test of a novel," he writes, "will be our affection for it, as it is the test of our friends, and of anything else which we cannot define" (AN, 26). Consequently, the test of Forster's criticism is the condition of Forster's heart, which, though a sensitive organ, has the shortcoming of hearts generally: a tendency to indulge prejudices, to play favorites, to ignore evidence, to be soft on the young, and to prefer the familiar. Still, it is a good and often a stout heart. When it cooperates with Forster's fine literary intelligence, we have criticism of the first order.

His heart is not moved, as we would expect, by pedants, especially by pedants without style. It is not easy to forget his double-barreled review of Ford Madox Ford's erratic *The English Novel: From the Earliest Days to the Death of Joseph Conrad* and Ernest A. Baker's enormous *The History of the English Novel: Intellectual Realism, from Richardson to Sterne,* both of which appeared in 1930. Forster much preferred the lively Ford, in spite of all his misrepresentations, to the deadly scholar—and Baker was stirred to an indignant protest. Forster says of Ford:

> It is annoying, when one is an earnest seeker after truth and perhaps an examination candidate as well, to be told that ever since 1860 the *Pilgrim's Progress* and *Madame Bovary* have been among the four most popular books all the world over. It's untrue. They haven't been. And one's irritation is not diminished by being unable to say which have been. Anyhow, not those two. It's annoying, again, to be told that history has altered owing to the disuse of Plutarch, that Conrad, James and Crane are the three chief influences in contemporary fiction, that English fiction and fiction all the world over are identical, that Bach and Holbein are the world's two greatest artists, Anthony Trollope also running; that *Babbitt* was suggested by *Pamela,* that Our Lord and Tibullus used to be mentioned more frequently in conversation, and that Mr. Ford himself has never known anyone who has known Miss Virginia Woolf. Why, he dedicates this very work to a friend in common! Surely we can catch him slipping at last. But no, we cannot; because there is no such person as Miss Virginia Woolf. She is Mrs. Woolf.[53]

Ford had written a wildly critical review of *Aspects* in 1927, but Forster generously praises Ford for his brilliant editorship of *The*

English Review and his kindness to young writers, himself included.*
Though Ford tickled him, Forster "read with rage" comments like
the following: "although *Tom Jones* contains an immense amount
of rather nauseous special-pleading, the author does pack most of it
away into solid wads of hypocrisy at the headings of Parts or Chapters." But for the work of Professor Baker Forster finds no excuse
whatever:

The book is dull, badly written, and conventional in its judgments despite
its dalliance with modernity.... His work may contain original research
(I am not qualified to say), but it has none of the other merits of scholarship;
it cannot marshall facts plainly or discuss them philosophically, or give a
straightforward account either of a novelist's life or of the contents of a novel.
... Were the book less pretentious, one would not be severe, but ... it is the
fourth of a series which is apparently trundling down the centuries to the
present day.... We return with renewed appreciation to Mr. Ford.[54]

Whenever Forster encountered the trinity of dullness, bad writing,
and banality, he damned; and he was given a particularly good opportunity with Sir Sidney Lee's *King Edward VII: A Biography.*
When Sir Sidney mentions royalty, Forster writes, he "cannot be too
serious or swell himself out too large." Here is one of his "tumid,
gravid, authoritative, apoplectic, apocalyptic" sentences: "Despite
the restraints on boyish liberty and the educational discipline in
which the paternal wisdom chiefly made itself visible to the son, the
boyish faith in his dead father's exalted and disinterested motive
lived on." Comments Forster:

Such a sentence pops when trodden upon, like seaweed, yet it would be
wrong to say it contains nothing. A diplomatic residuum survives—something gummy, something as subtle in its way as literature, though it exudes
from the opposite end of the pen.[55]†

---

* Three of Forster's short stories were published in *The English Review*, but only
one ("Other Kingdom") during Ford's editorship (December 1908 to February
1910). It is interesting to note that there is a character named "Ford" in the
cast of that story.

† Among his other damning criticisms of bad books or plays are his reviews of May
Sinclair's *Mary Olivier: A Life* (1919) and Robert Hichens's *The Voice from the
Minaret* (1919). Of the first he writes: "The style ... is both jerky and monotonous,
and the book, as a whole, is a document rather than a work of art: it embalms many
precious facts about life, but not life itself." "A Moving Document," *The Daily
Herald,* July 30, 1919, p. 8. Of the second: "When a play is poorly constructed,

Great scholars, however, get no such treatment. R. W. Chapman's editing of Jane Austen is admirable and Forster praises it sincerely. Still, Forster does not forget that "confusing literature with education" is an occupational disease of professional academicians: although Jane Austen's novels are "so good that everything connected with the novelist and everything she wrote ought certainly to be published and annotated," should that generalization include even the letters—those boring, insignificant letters? Reluctantly, Forster answers no. The editing of the letters makes Mr. Chapman's impeccable scholarship look just a little silly; and Forster does not keep a straight face before erudition that investigates why Miss Austen wanted a coach line from Hungerford to Chawton, or that provides *eight* indexes. "Naturally," writes Forster, "when one invests in a concern one comes to value it, and Mr. Chapman is not exempt from this sensible rule. He has contended with the subject manfully, like St. Paul at Ephesus; and would he have done so if it was not worth while?"[56] The question is worthy of a Jane-Austenite.

For dealers in fantasy or whimsy—like Ronald Firbank, David Garnett, Edith Sitwell, and Forrest Reid, to say nothing of their forebear Laurence Sterne—Forster has an almost fatal tropism. Of Firbank he writes: "It is frivolous stuff, and how rare, how precious, is frivolity! How few writers can prostitute all their powers!"[57] David Garnett too is honored, but not so highly. Garnett, Forster writes,

is deliberately naïve, and has found in fantasy a serviceable ally rather than a fairy queen. In other words, he is not a pure fantasist. Unlike Firbank, he wants to do something, he wants to write a story, and we are here in the presence of a much more sophisticated mind.[58]

Fantasy and the exercise of will are not compatible, as Forster knows, and Garnett's fantasies, like his own, are hybrids. It is surprising, however, that the young Yeats displeased him, especially since Yeats is listed along with Blake, Morris, Huysmans, and Eliot as a writer who took him "into a country where the will is not everything."[59]

---

undistinguished in diction, conventional in character-drawing, devoid of beauty, and morally a fake, one might conclude that it is a bad play. The conclusion may be wrong. For there is another quality that can exist independent of all the above, and win the dramatist a triumph of a sort: grip." "Grip," *The Athenaeum*, No. 4662 (September 5, 1919), 852.

Apparently Yeats's fondness for astrology, Rosicrucianism, magic, incantation, séances, fairies, and the Great Wheel was more than Forster could take. His judgment is severe: Yeats, he says, "had no discrimination, and more enthusiasm than knowledge, and though he could say sharp things about his opponents, he had no critical sense."[60] Forster concedes that Yeats was a great poet, but everything following that concession is derogatory. He even finds the "slouching monster" of "The Second Coming" (surely one of Yeats's greatest poems) to be evidence that Yeats's voice is not authentic.[61] Never a completely reliable judge of poetry, Forster may have had some of these opinions at second hand from his Indian friend V. K. Narayana Menon, author of *The Development of William Butler Yeats* (1942).[62] Though Forster began in fantasy, he grew to disapprove of monsters and fairies, except when they came with the best of credentials. "I have an uneasy feeling," he writes in 1926, "that grown-up people ought to grow up and that when stout men and women clap at a performance of *Peter Pan* to proclaim their belief in fairies, there is something imbecile in Old England."[63]

However, another Irish myth-maker gets Forster's warmest approval. He is Forrest Reid, a friend of thirty-five years' standing (at the time of his death, in 1947) and the author of many novels, two of which were dedicated to Forster.* Reid is the artist of a city, Belfast, and its surrounding country, as Cavafy is of Alexandria. In Reid's pages, the commercial town of Belfast becomes, Forster says, "haunted by a ghost, by some exile from the realms of the ideal who has slipped into her commonsense, much as the sea and the dispossessed fields, avenging nature, have re-emerged as dampness and as weeds in her streets."[64] The best of Reid's writing is richly shaded by a gray sensuousness and a mystical sense of nature, but it is also, like his beloved River Lagan, sluggish—and conspicuously lacking in dramatic power, thematic invention, and psychological depth. What, then, did Forster find to like? The answer would seem to be simply that Forster liked Reid and therefore liked his books. The two men share common ground in their feeling for youth and innocence and in

---

* *Following Darkness* (1912) and *Peter Waring* (1937). The second is a revised and largely rewritten version of the first, but Reid regarded it as a "new book." See Russell Burlingham, *Forrest Reid: A Portrait and a Study* (London, 1953), p. 167.

their reverence for personal relations and the country. But Forster admired most what he called Reid's "moral fragrance":

He was elusive and sensitive, yet at the same time he was tough and he knew his own mind. He preached no dogma, and yet all his work is characterised by what he himself has beautifully called a sort of moral fragrance. Its final impact is ethical. Behind nature and the indwelling power in her, behind the Lagan and the Ulster countryside, behind Celtic or Hellenic fancies, behind his sympathy for youth and young people, for animals, for birds, there lurks that moral fragrance. Not moral precepts but moral fragrance. There is a profound difference.[65]

Behind this admiration is, as Russell Burlingham points out, the "secret understanding" of the sensitive, the considerate, and the plucky, "sending out little signals to each other like candles in the surrounding darkness."[66] Reid tried to send such a little signal to Henry James, with unhappy results. He dedicated his homosexual romance, *The Garden God,* to James without asking James's permission. James's reply was a permanent and chilling silence: the subject was one, writes Burlingham, "which Henry James viewed with both a shrinking distaste and, it now seems, a peculiar fascination."[67]

Loyalty to friends is the first premise of Forster's criticism—though happily friendship and literary excellence are sometimes found together. He never forgot Edward Garnett's generosity in noticing *Where Angels Fear to Tread,* and in return he did his best to say something good about Garnett's undistinguished *The Trial of Jeanne D'Arc and Other Plays.** Like Garnett, Forster tried hard to discover and encourage the genius of other writers. In 1932, for example, he puffed Rosamond Lehmann, L. A. G. Strong, John Collier, William Plomer, John Hampson, and Christopher Isherwood; he has recently backed such newer writers as Donald Windham, Michael O'Donnell, Robert Ivy, Peter Townsend, and John Coleman.[68] Nor has he been remiss in trying to advance the fortunes of Bloomsbury, among both

---

* Forster writes: "Long, long ago, when my first novel was published, Mr. Garnett and the late C. F. G. Masterman were the only critics who took any notice of it. I like to think it was his flair. I know it was his generosity. He picked up a book by an unknown writer which, in his opinion, was promising, he forced an enthusiastic review into a magazine, and so gave me a chance of reaching a public." "The Man Behind the Scenes," *The News Chronicle,* November 30, 1931, p. 4. Garnett's review appeared in *The Spectator,* XCV (1905), 1089-90.

the old guard and what might be called the newer (among them William Golding, John Lehmann, William Sansom, and Angus Wilson). Forster's support here is well grounded and not uncritical. Still, his freemasonry is obvious—indeed, he proclaims it. Distressed, for example, at some of the attacks on Strachey after Strachey's death, he proposed a kind of league to deal with those who snipe at Bloomsbury, the only condition of membership being that the words "highbrow" and "lowbrow" shall never be used. These words, Forster writes,

are responsible for more unkind feelings and more silly thinking than any other pair of words I know. They attempt to introduce into literature the cleavage which is so lamentable in the world of affairs: the cleavage between the brain worker and the manual labourer. I have used them myself in the past, greatly to my regret; now as penitents will, I want to found a league.[69]

Yet toward Virginia Woolf—close friend, esthete, artist, lover of Cambridge—Forster is deeply critical. Here, if anywhere, one might expect mutual admiration to flourish, for her esthetic program bears many similarities to Forster's own. She, more than any other writer, put Fry's esthetic into fiction, attempting an escape from the representational world into one of pure "relations," reducing time to the impressionistic moment and space (at times) to the dimensions of a mark on the wall.[70] But she carried these tendencies further than Forster did, and, though he admires her achievement, he feels little warmth for it. Her artistic development took her increasingly from a visible world of human action and actors into the unseen circles of the mind's dialogue, into a world of thoughts and feelings which are viewed with a hard, crystalline objectivity. Forster's, however, took him another way—away from such epistemological solitudes into a warm earthiness. He conquered time and space, so to speak, by embracing rather than escaping them. The thought coursing through Rhoda's mind in *The Waves*—"The world is entire, and I am outside of it, crying, 'Oh save me, from being blown for ever outside the loop of time!' "[71]—is exactly the nightmare *Passage* saves us from, for that book describes our inevitable participation in existence, not our exclusion from it. Forster does not share Virginia Woolf's basically nihilistic passion for the pure, sensing perhaps its close connection with the knowledge of Mrs. Dalloway: "the full

knowledge—inside knowledge—of what suicide is."[72] Forster recognizes Virginia Woolf's genius and originality, but senses something
wrong, fearing, among other things, that her impressionistic techniques will work like acid to dissolve the human beings in her fiction.
Although she affirms a belief that "human beings are the permanent
material of fiction," and although she developed the technique for
getting into her characters' minds, her people are not fully alive.[73]
If they live, they do not live "continuously," as do the characters of
Tolstoy:[74]

> She dreams, designs, jokes, invents, observes details, but she does not tell a
> story or weave a plot, and—can she create character? That is her problem's
> centre. . . . Plot and story could be set aside in favour of some other unity, but
> if one is writing about human beings, one does want them to seem alive. . . .
>   What wraiths, apart from their context, are the wind-sextet from *The
> Waves,* or Jacob away from *Jacob's Room*! They speak no more to us or to
> one another as soon as the page is turned. And this is her great difficulty.
> Holding on with one hand to poetry, she stretches and stretches to grasp
> things which are best gained by letting go of poetry.[75]

Forster has also offended in this particular, killing off characters to
suit the plot, but after *Howards End* human sacrifices and sudden
deaths disappear. Instead, the "round" human being, such as Aziz,
becomes of first importance. But Virginia Woolf's streams of consciousness, so lucid and cold, describe at last an inwardness that isolates the individual, cuts him off both from the outer world and, too
often, from the reader's sympathy. "The mind which asserts its own
autonomy," writes G. H. Bantock, "accepts the deadliest of tyrannies
—itself."[76] That is the essential point Forster wants to make. Virginia
Woolf's art ends in solipsism and is at odds with human love. Forster quotes a passage from *The Waves* that virtually defines their
alienation:

> But sympathy we cannot have. Wisest Fate says no. If her children, weighted
> as they already are with sorrow, were to take on them that burden too, adding
> in imagination other pains to their own, buildings would cease to rise; roads
> would peter out into grassy tracts; there would be an end of music and of
> painting; one great sigh alone would rise to Heaven, and the only attitudes
> for men and women would be those of horror and despair.

Hers is "an admirable hardness . . . so far as hardness can be admirable,"[77] but hardness, we know, does not even pay.

33 Forster at Montazah, Alexandria, about 1917.

34 Montazah Palace, Alexandria.

*During the recent war (1914–1919) Montazah became a Red
Cross Hospital; thousands of convalescent soldiers . . . will
never forget the beauty and the comfort that they found there.*
    (*Alexandria: A History and a Guide*)

painting of Saint Macarius, Camposanto, Pisa.

*Macarius . . . was an Alexandrian who was seen by another
. . nt in a vision killing the apostate Emperor Julian. . . . He is
. . so celebrated for a bunch of grapes that he refused to eat, and
. r a mosquito that he killed.* (Alexandria: A History and a Guide)

36 Forster and Syed Ross Masood, the original of Aziz in
    A Passage to India. At Tesserete, Switzerland, 1910.

37 *Left to right:* W. J. H. Sprott
Gerald Heard, Forster, and
Lytton Strachey, in the
early twenties.

38 Forster addressing the
*Congrès International
des Ecrivains,* Paris,
June 21, 1935.
To his left is Charles
Mauron; just visible behind
Mauron is André Malraux.

39 Forster and T. S. Eliot at the home of Leonard and Virginia
   Woolf, Lewes, Sussex, around 1930.

Forster at the production of
England's Pleasant Land,
at Milton Court, Westcott,
Surrey, July 9, 1938.
Left to right: Lady Allen
of Hurtwood, Forster,
Ralph Vaughan Williams,
and the bandmaster.

41 Forster with novelist
Forrest Reid, Belfast,
about 1937.

42 Forster with Charles Mauron at Saint-Rémy-de-Provence, September 1962.

While Forster credits Virginia Woolf with being the first to bring "the actual process of thinking" into the novel, the credit probably should go to Henry James.[78] This is one of many instances where Forster seems almost deliberately to misjudge and undervalue James. Yet *Aspects* clearly reveals that Forster had read the Master carefully. In *The Ambassadors* James "pursued the narrow path of aesthetic duty, and success to the full extent of his possibilities has crowned him. ... But at what sacrifice!" (AN, 146.) What is sacrificed is the characters, who are, says Forster, stretched on a Procrustean bed so that they will fit the novel's pattern. But if this is at all true of *The Ambassadors* it is even truer of Forster's own *Angels,* which is so strikingly similar to *The Ambassadors* in structure and plot as to suggest the possibility of direct influence. (Forster's book appeared in 1905, James's in 1903.) *Angels,* like James's book, contains two ambassadorial missions to a foreign land for the purpose of rescuing a young person from what the family at home sees as a corrupting amorous entanglement. Philip, the ambassador, becomes enchanted by the foreigner and his land, even as Strether is drawn to Paris by Mme. de Vionnet. Lilia is a kind of Chad (on whose behalf the ambassadorial missions are set in motion), Gino a kind of Mme. de Vionnet (the sexual bait). Harriet, in character and function, is nearly another Mamie—who is, as Forster points out, a favorite type of James's, appearing as Mrs. Gereth in *The Spoils of Poynton* and as Henrietta Stackpole in *The Portrait of a Lady.* Strether's final statement of defeat (quoted by Forster) could have come from Philip's mouth: "I have lost everything—it is my only logic." What does this show? Only that the young Forster may have been more indebted to James than he knew or wanted to acknowledge. And it reminds us that the timid young man who visited James in 1908 (and was not recognized) was already the author of three novels.* James, long since convicted of snobbery by Forster's Cambridge coterie, could scarcely have endeared himself by this lapse. Nor could it have become easier

---

* When Forster's relatives heard he was going to visit James they were "thrilled by the prospect," and Forster's aunt recalled having met James about 1888 and having told him that she had an aunt at Clapham, to which James replied: "I do wish I had an aunt at Clapham." When the aunt told the story to Forster's mother, the mother replied: "Laura! What an affected remark!" When Forster met James and told him he was living at Weybridge, James replied that he could see himself living at Weybridge. "Henry James and the Young Men," p. 103.

for Forster to admit any debts he may have had in that direction. In a diary entry at the time of the visit, Forster wrote: "First great man I've ever seen—not alarming but that isn't my road." Forster's refusal to be great is well known; but he may have understudied greatness more than he wished to confess.

Forster ends his discussion of James in *Aspects* with an account of the contretemps between James and H. G. Wells after the appearance of *Boon,* in which Wells criticizes James savagely: "The only human motives left in [James's] novels," says Wells, "are a certain avidity and an entirely superficial curiosity." It is most surprising that Forster, so sensitive to parts of James's achievement, should agree with this unfair judgment. But it brings home the fact that, for all their likenesses, the two men are fundamentally very different. James could never have put the caves at the center of a novel; the primitive and the chthonic are alien to him. Nor could Forster recognize James's moral sense: in his novels, Forster says, there is "nothing so crude as good or evil."[79]

George Meredith was a great name in Forster's youth, a "spiritual power," and Forster's generation was "inside his idiom" as a modern is inside Eliot's (AN, 85). Meredith offered a great deal to youths who were trying to free themselves from Victorianism: he was intellectual, witty, sexually emancipated, and wrote in a style and language that the philistines could not possibly understand. Moreover, Meredith's grandiose notions about "process," "blood," "work," "heroism," and "earth" could provide the arcane terms an apostate generation needed. Meredith's notions of "earth" may have been vaguely at work in the "Wiltshire" section of *Journey,* but Meredith is no Hardy or Lawrence, and Forster came to see him as "a chilly fake":

He could no more write the opening chapter of *The Return of the Native* than Box Hill could visit Salisbury Plain. What is really tragic and enduring in the scenery of England was hidden from him, and so is what is really tragic in life. When he gets serious and noble-minded there is a strident overtone, a bullying that becomes distressing. (AN, 86.)

Agnes reminded Rickie of "a heroine of Meredith's—but a heroine at the end of the book" (p. 82), that is to say, one that is played out. Like Carlyle, Meredith wielded an influence very difficult to understand today: the "unconscious insincerity" of his art seems painfully apparent.[80] What turned Bloomsbury away from him, according to Virginia Woolf, were the great Russian writers—Turgenev, Dostoevsky, and Tolstoy.[81]

Strangely enough, Forster discusses Tolstoy and Proust together, ranking *War and Peace* as the greatest novel and *A la recherche du temps perdu* as the second-greatest. It is a revealing conjunction, for these very different writers represent two antithetical tugs in Forster's own nature. First, Proust seems to represent "art" and Tolstoy "morality": Proust's great work "is not as warm-hearted or as heroic or as great as *War and Peace*. But it is superior as an artistic achievement."[82] Art, in Forster's view, can express only part of life; and in treating these two writers Forster is clearly bothered by the fact that Proust's great work of introspection—his epic testimonial of the inner chambers of decadence and disease, of love ritualized and intelligence hardened—does not satisfy the moral sense. (Compare Matthew Arnold's objections to Zola's "lubricity.") Second, Tolstoy is the novelist of space, while Proust is the novelist of time. The French writer, immured in his cork-lined room, ill and dying, found a kind of immortality through an imaginative defiance of time.* But Tolstoy's treatment of time seemed better: he uses time as "something regular, against which a chronicle could be stretched," whereas with Proust it is intermittent.[83] In that word "chronicle" we get a glimpse of the essential Forster. He likes his history plain (in novels and out of them), however much he may scorn "events in their time sequence." Only once in his fiction (in *The Longest Journey*) does Forster employ a flashback; he is as old-fashioned about fictional chronology as he is idiosyncratic about avoiding too much fictional illusion (the opening of *Howards End* reads, "One may as well begin with Helen's letters to her sister"). Among other reasons, Forster likes *War and Peace* because "it is an easy novel: there are no secrets in it, no artificiality, and all you have to do is to read—or listen until the story is finished."[84] However different this is from his own practice, it is fair to say that

---

* Forster claimed he learned most from Jane Austen and Proust—from Jane Austen "the possibilities of domestic humor," and from Proust "ways of looking at character ... the modern subconscious way. He gave me as much of the modern way as I could take." "The Art of Fiction: E. M. Forster," *The Paris Review*, I, 39–40.

this is his ideal—the novel he wishes he could have written, had the conditions of his life permitted such openness and simplicity. Time, as Forster tells us, is "the enemy," and the technique of "rhythm" is a fictional device for overcoming it. But though Proust is the master technician in that art, it is the far less sophisticated Tolstoy who brings rhythm to the perfection Forster cherishes for it: in Tolstoy the "rhythmic rise, fall, rise of the generations" and the great sweeps of space suggest infinity.[85] Tolstoy's space "leaves behind it an effect like music":

After one has read *War and Peace* for a bit, great chords begin to sound, and we cannot say exactly what struck them. . . . They do not come from the episodes nor yet from the characters. They come from the immense area of Russia, over which episodes and characters have been scattered, from the sum-total of bridges and frozen rivers, forests, roads, gardens, fields, which accumulate grandeur and sonority after we have passed them.[86]

Compared to Proust's chamber music, this is a symphony, and Forster hears at last something that has not actually been played.

Another important point is that Tolstoy is of the land, whereas Proust is of the city. Forster is cool toward James, Eliot, and Joyce, and warm toward Hardy and Lawrence for many reasons, but one big reason is his preference for natural simplicities over urban sophistication and complication. Tolstoy's faith is that "simple people are best." Proust, the clever neurasthenic metropolite, shares no such illusion—and hence comes off second-best.

Forster honors André Gide, another fictional experimenter, less for his art than for his humanism. "He has taught thousands of people to mistrust façades, to call the bluff, to be brave without bounce and inconsistent without frivolity. . . . *Il se sauva.*[87] He saved himself instead of being saved"—and showed the honor in this unheroic course. In one of his most earnest essays, Forster contrasts Gide, the "natural democrat," and Stefan George, the "natural aristocrat" (whose art and esthetic cult gave aid and comfort to the Nazis). Forster defines the humanist as one who possesses "curiosity, a free mind, belief in good taste, and belief in the human race," and Gide, with these qualities, made himself an example of how a humanist could be a force without resorting to force.[88] The other way was George's, the way of authority, of cultism, and Forster hated it. Both Gide and

George were homosexuals, a fact of special interest, for George's life demonstrated how personal relations could decay into tribalism. In *Aspects* Forster gives a great deal of space to Gide and uses *Les Faux Monnayeurs* to illustrate that type of modern novel in which plot is discontinuous and almost directionless—presumably like life itself. At the center of Gide's book is a discussion of the art of the novel by a character who, like Gide, also keeps a diary and is also writing a book called *Les Faux Monnayeurs*. That discussion, writes Forster, "contains the old thesis of truth in life versus truth in art":

What is new in it is the attempt to combine the two truths, the proposal that writers should mix themselves up in their material and be rolled over and over by it; they should not try to subdue any longer, they should hope to be subdued, to be carried away. As for a plot—to pot with the plot! Break it up, boil it down. Let there be those "formidable erosions of contour" of which Nietzsche speaks. All that is prearranged is false. (AN, 96–97.)

Forster is fascinated by the experiment but not finally convinced by it. Gide is a bit too cool, too un-English, too much the experimentalist at the cost of passion: he is, says Forster, "not well advised, if he wants to write subconscious novels, to reason so lucidly and patiently about the subconscious." (AN, 97.)

Another novelist who was "rolled over and over" by his material was James Joyce, and the material he rolled in was, in Forster's view, filth. When *Ulysses* came out in 1926, Forster was torn between admiration and disgust. Is it the "Book of the Age," he asks. The answer is no, and again art conflicts with reality. Although Forster modified his opinion about Joyce in later years, Joyce still seemed to him a dealer in dirt:

Joyce is horrified and fascinated by the human body; it seems to him ritually unclean and in direct contact with all the evil in the universe, and though to some of us this seems awful tosh, it certainly helps him to get some remarkable literary effects. . . . Joyce tries to spatter the universe with dirt, and to make all our habits and ideals (art, religion, and society in particular) seem ludicrous and repulsive.[89]

As a technical achievement, Forster thought it "the most remarkable work of our times" and declared that any reader who is also a writer must feel "that he has been shown a new possibility in art." Nevertheless, the book suffers, in Forster's view, from an "inverted Vic-

torianism." Arnold's sweetness and light may be a misleading formula, he feels ("the universe will never be revealed by a schoolmaster
in a surplice"), but "crossness and dirt" is no satisfactory substitute.
The book shocked not only Forster but Virginia Woolf and, surprisingly, D. H. Lawrence as well;* there was still plenty of un-
inverted Victorianism around. But, good or bad, a book has the right
to be read; and Forster whimsically defended it against the censors:

> Sir William Joynson-Hicks does not care for *Ulysses*—he thinks it may lead us
> to go to Night Clubs—and consequently it is not an easy book to obtain. Nor
> is it easy to read, being five times as long as most novels, nor easy to under-
> stand owing to its obscurity, nor easy to hold owing to its weight. It is in
> every sense a formidable work. Even the police are said not to comprehend
> it fully....[90]

Forster is distinctly ambivalent about T. S. Eliot. He admires and
does not admire. Eliot the social critic and Christian—the author of
Notes Towards the Definition of Culture and *The Cocktail Party*—
he finds unpleasant. *That* Eliot, he writes, has over the years "gone
both beyond me and behind."[91] But the poet, at least at times, is
another matter. Compared with Yeats, Forster felt that "here is someone authentic, someone who rings true through and through."[92]
Feeling is not criticism, but there is support for such intuitive methods in Eliot's own claim that a test of genuine poetry lies in its power
to "communicate before it is understood."[93] Still, Forster's criticism
is based more on moral and personal grounds than on any close understanding of the poetry. "We can have the poem," writes F. R. Leavis,
"only by an inner kind of possession"—our approach to literature, he
insists, "is personal or it is nothing."[94] Forster's possession of, say, *The
Waste Land* is certainly highly personal, but it is also highly idiosyncratic in a way Leavis would not approve. Forster liked the early
poems (including *The Waste Land*) for what he calls their "witty

---

* Virginia Woolf called the book "illiterate, underbred . . . the book of a self taught
working man . . . egotistic, insistent, raw, striking, and ultimately nauseating." *A
Writer's Diary* (New York, 1953), p. 46. D. H. Lawrence declared, "My God, what
a clumsy *olla putrida* James Joyce is! Nothing but old fags and cabbage-stumps
of quotations from the Bible and the rest, stewed in the juice of deliberate, jour-
nalistic dirty-mindedness." Quoted in F. R. Leavis, "Joyce and 'The Revolution of
the Word,'" in *The Importance of Scrutiny*, ed. Eric Bentley (New York, 1948),
p. 320.

resentment followed by the pinch of glory"—whatever that means.[95] And he first read them in a mood of war-weariness in 1917, during a convalescence in which he also read Huysmans, and was moved to exclaim: "Oh, the relief of a world which lived for its sensations and ignored the will—the world of des Esseintes! Was it decadent? Yes, and thank God." Forster did not all his life equate decadence and civilization, yet here was born the "fragmentary sympathy" for Eliot that has persisted over the years:

The poems were not epicurean; still they were innocent of public-spiritedness: they sang of private disgust and diffidence.... Here was a protest, and a feeble one, and the more congenial for being feeble. For what, in that world of gigantic horror, was tolerable except the slighter gestures of dissent? (AH, 106–7.)

Forster resents the obscurities of *The Waste Land* and Eliot's failure to sound any note of invitation to the reader ("Mr. Eliot does not want us in," AH, 113). But lurking behind these judgments is Forster's sense of the fact that Eliot is not only a snob but an American snob: "One has a feeling at moments that the Muses are connected not so much with Apollo as with the oldest county families. One feels, moreover, that there is never all this talk about tradition until it has ceased to exist, and that Mr. Eliot, like Henry James, is romanticizing the land of his adoption." (AH, 111.) Although Eliot was never a denizen of Bloomsbury, he was close enough to be subject to the family backbiting, and even Forster can be snide. When Forster's Indian friend K. Natwar-Singh confessed difficulty in reading Dylan Thomas's "Under Milk Wood," Forster gave him this interesting advice: "Read him backwards. I often do that with T. S. Eliot."[96]

But D. H. Lawrence, a man with no Bloomsbury credentials whatever, gets Forster's highest and most discerning praise. And interestingly enough, Eliot was among those who stirred Forster to utter that praise. In 1915 Lawrence made his one excursion into Bloomsbury. It was a symbolic encounter, Bloomsbury's major effort to make friends with a writer from the lower classes, and Lawrence's major flirtation with "culture." The meeting was not a success. Lawrence smashed some of the best Bloomsbury china and cursed some of the most revered Bloomsbury gods. He hated Francis Birrell almost at sight, openly despised Duncan Grant's paintings, and was made by

Keynes "mad with misery and hostility and rage."* He found a friend
in David Garnett (thanks largely to Garnett's warmth and even
temper); but the relationship begun with Bertrand Russell broke up
—after a stormy year of letters and meetings—in mutual recrimina-
tion. "I came to feel him," wrote Russell, "a positive force for evil and
. . . he came to have the same feeling about me."[97] But on the whole
—as Lawrence wrote to Lady Ottoline Morrell in April 1915—he could
abide none of the crew:

> To hear these young people talk really fills me with black fury: they talk end-
> lessly, but endlessly—and never, never a good thing said. They are cased each
> in a hard little shell of his own and out of this they talk words. There is never,
> for one second, any outgoing of feeling and no reverence, not a crumb or
> grain of reverence. I cannot stand it. I will not have people like this—I had
> rather be alone. They made me dream of a beetle that bites a scorpion. But
> I killed it—a very large beetle. I scotched it and it ran off—but I came on it
> again, and killed it. It is this horror of little swarming selves I can't stand.[98]

F. R. Leavis, in making Lawrence the culture-hero of the century,
has not left his hero unrewarded for thus helping him to pay off his
old scores against Bloomsbury.† But Forster gave both Leavis and
Lawrence something to admire. Though Lawrence preached at him
and they quarreled, Forster felt a warmth for Lawrence that was
returned.‡ On the occasion of Lawrence's death Forster made a state-

---

* See *D. H. Lawrence: A Composite Biography*, ed. Edward Nehls (Madison, Wis-
consin, 1957), pp. 301-2.

† See F. R. Leavis, "Keynes, Lawrence, and Cambridge," in *The Common Pursuit*
(London, 1952), pp. 255–60.

‡ Forster visited Lawrence for three days early in 1915. *D. H. Lawrence's Letters to
Bertrand Russell*, ed. Harry T. Moore (New York, 1948), p. 29. This is Lawrence's
letter to Russell, dated February 12, 1915, describing the visit: "We have had E. M.
Forster here for three days. There is more in him than ever comes out. But he is not
dead yet. I hope to see him pregnant with his own soul. We were on the edge of a
fierce quarrel all the time. He went to bed muttering that he was not sure we—my
wife & I—weren't just playing round his knees: he seized a candle & went to bed,
neither would he say good night. Which I think is rather nice. He sucks his dummy
—you know, those child's comforters—long after his age. But there is something
very real in him, if he will not cause it to die. He is *much* more than his dummy-
sucking, clever little habits allow him to be."

This encounter occurred about nine months before Forster sailed for his war
service in Egypt. The possibility that Lawrence may have helped snap Forster out
of his creative doldrums is intriguing. Forster said to Angus Wilson: "Lawrence
could be very trying. He spent one whole afternoon condemning my work. At last

ment that shocked and dismayed Bloomsbury, but one that Leavis
thinks will be "classical." Perhaps nothing that Forster ever said
more definitely shows his independence of mind:

Now he is dead, and the low-brows whom he scandalized have united with
the high-brows whom he bored to ignore his greatness. This cannot be
helped; no one who alienates both Mrs. Grundy and Aspatia can hope for a
good obituary Press. All that we can do . . . is to say straight out that he was
the greatest imaginative novelist of our generation.[99]*

The highbrows came out screaming. Clive Bell demanded to know
what Forster meant by "straight out" and "high-brows," and T. S.
Eliot wanted enlightenment on "greatest," "imaginative," and "novelist."[100] Forster thus replied to Eliot in the pages of *The Nation and
the Athenaeum*:

Mr. T. S. Eliot duly entangles me in his web. He asks what exactly I mean by
"greatest," "imaginative," and "novelist," and I cannot say. Worse still, I
cannot even say what "exactly" means—only that there are occasions when
I would rather feel like a fly than a spider, and that the death of D. H. Lawrence is one of these.[101]

Though Forster and Lawrence differ extremely in superficial ways,
the kinship between them is profound. They are both prophetic
vitalists, hating the machine civilization that has cut men off from
their roots, and revering what Aldous Huxley (like Forster one of the
few Bloomsburians on Lawrence's side) has called "the dark presence
of the otherness that lies beyond man's conscious mind."† Perhaps
only Conrad, Hardy, and—at a stretch—Meredith could share with
Forster and Lawrence what we might call the vision of the cave, the
encounter with the chthonic underworld of human experience. Certainly Forster's esteem for Lawrence defines certain qualities that set

---

I asked him if there was anything good in it. 'Yes,' he said, 'Leonard Bast. That was
courageous.' " Angus Wilson, "A Conversation with E. M. Forster," *Encounter*, IX
(November 1957), 54.

* Thirty years later, as a witness at the *Lady Chatterley's Lover* trial, Forster as-
serted that he would still hold to that judgment. See *The Trial of Lady Chatterley*, ed. C. H. Rolph (Harmondsworth, 1961), p. 112.

† *The Letters of D. H. Lawrence*, ed. Aldous Huxley, p. xi. Forster, however, must
have been saddened to learn that Lawrence had totally misread *Howards End*.
Lawrence wrote Forster from Taos on September 20, 1922: "You *did* make a nearly
deadly mistake glorifying those *business* people in Howards End. Business is no
good." *The Letters of D. H. Lawrence*, p. 552. (Italics in original.)

Forster dramatically apart from others in or near his circle; and F. R. Leavis has helped brilliantly to clarify that distinction by observing that "if you took Joyce for a major creative writer, then, like Mr. Eliot, you had no use for Lawrence, and if you judged Lawrence a great writer, then you could hardly take a sustained interest in Joyce."[102] The workability of that touchstone suggests something of the deep cleft between the urban writers of the period and those of the country, between those who deal with the social and the intellectual and those primarily interested in the mythic and the unconscious. Although Forster the Jane-Austenite loves the social surfaces, he has also gone, with Lawrence, into mines that lie far below. How similar, for example (to take one out of a dozen instances), is the character and psychic problem of Hermione Roddice in *Women in Love* (1920)—who is a portrait of Lady Ottoline Morrell—to that of Adela Quested. Both women are catastrophes of modern civilization —repressed, class-bound, over-intellectualized. When Hermione declares "And in so many things, I have *made* myself well. I was a very queer and nervous girl. And by learning to use my will, simply by using my will, I *made* myself right" she gives voice to precisely the malady that sends Adela screaming from the caves. To Birkin in Lawrence's novel, "Such a will is an obscenity," but Hermione is sure it is not:

Her voice was always dispassionate and tense, and perfectly confident. Yet she shuddered with a sense of nausea, a sort of seasickness that always threatened to overwhelm her mind. But her mind remained unbroken, her will was still perfect. It almost sent Birkin mad. But he would never, never dare to break her will, and let loose the maelstrom of her subconsciousness, and see her in her ultimate madness.[103]

This is not just to see a correspondence in talent or technique, such as there is between James and Forster; it is to see a sharing of the same vision of life. For that ultimate madness of Hermione is exactly what Forster did expose us to.

The kinship between the two writers has many other aspects. They are both pagans haunted by Christianity, trying to rediscover in the forms of creative imagination a new vision of the whole.[104] Both remember the old dualisms but want to transcend them: "I think there is the dual way of looking at things," writes Lawrence. "The other way is to try to conceive the whole, to build up a whole by means of symbolism, because symbolism avoids the I and puts aside the egotist."[105] That is very close to what Forster attempts in *The Longest Journey, Howards End,* and *Passage to India.* In the "great periods," writes Lawrence in the same letter, "when man was great, he has faced the *East*: Christian, Mohammedan, Hindu, all," and the very religions Lawrence lists are those Forster employs symbolically in *Passage*.[106] Lawrence writes further that

the old symbols were each a word in a great attempt at formulating the whole history of the soul of Man. They *are unintelligible* except in their whole context. . . . The Crucifixion of Christ is a great mucking about with part of the symbolism of a great religious Vision.[107]

For both Lawrence and Forster, the universe echoes with intimations of spiritual realities. Although Forster, less driven and angry than Lawrence, sometimes invokes the chthonic powers for comedy as well as for prophecy, both writers visit Pan on the residents of suburbia for the same reason—to awaken civilized society from its sleep of death. In their search for value they follow similar routes, from north to south, from the conscious to the unconscious, from the present into the past. Both revere the land. In *St. Mawr,* Lawrence sees the country around Taos, New Mexico, as a divine perfection: "The landscape lived, and lived as the world of the gods, unsullied and unconcerned."[108] For Lou, of *St. Mawr,* no less than for Margaret Schlegel, what is sought is a connection between the ideal of space, vastness, infinite expansion, and the immediate world around her feet: "The New England woman had fought to make the nearness as perfect as the distance: for the distance was absolute beauty."[109] This is a ranch with a view, another version of the view from Summer Street or from Howards End.

The Oedipus problem is central with both writers, showing most explicitly in *Sons and Lovers* and *The Longest Journey.* Both works are baldly autobiographical, and in both the authors are obviously struggling to gain possession of their own souls. Paul Morel resists the maternal smothering even as Rickie does (although Rickie's mother never directly enters the action). Since *The Longest Journey* appeared in 1907, Graham Hough's claim that *Sons and Lovers* (1913) is "the first Freudian novel in English" would seem to need some qualification.[110]

Even on the matter of sex both writers, superficially so different, are in essential agreement. Lawrence's final emphasis, most dramatically shown in *St. Mawr,* is less on sexual union than on asexual transcendence, on achieving a "world before and after the God of Love."[111] In the following speech by Lou, we can hear Margaret Schlegel: "I don't hate men *because* they're men, as nuns do. I dislike them because they're not men enough."[112] The male Wilcoxes, we remember, could not even go bathing without their "appliances." They are to Margaret not men, but tools of their tools—the half-men of the machine age, of whom Clifford in *Lady Chatterley,* the crippled capitalist in his motorized wheelchair, is another example.[113] Yet there are, of course, differences between Margaret and Lou. Margaret is far more nunlike, more fastidious, less committed to Lou's kind of wild eternal bridegroom. Lawrence recognizes a similar withdrawal in Forster and strikes out against it. Lawrence asks, "For what do I come to a woman?" and answers:

> To know myself. But what when I know myself? What do I then embrace her for, hold the unknown against me for? To repeat the experience of self discovery. But I have discovered myself—I am not infinite. Still I can repeat the experience. . . . That is, I can get a sensation. The repeating of a known reaction upon myself is sensationalism. That is what nearly *all* English people do now. . . . And this is like self-abuse or masterbation [*sic*]. The ordinary Englishman of the educated class goes to a woman now to masterbate himself. . . .
>
> When this condition arrives, there is always Sodomy. The man goes to the man to repeat this reaction upon himself. It is a nearer form of masterbation. But still it has some *object*—there are still two bodies instead of one. A man of strong soul has too much honour for the other body—man or woman—to use it as a means of masterbation. So he remains neutral, inactive. That is Forster.[114]

Though we may question Lawrence's diagnosis, we have seen that honorable neutrality reflected in Philip and Rickie, and in some of the women who took over their roles. We have seen it, that is, until *Passage,* where the agony of this kind of neutrality seems to have been replaced by something more positive and happy. One wonders whether Lawrence would have written of Forster in 1924 as he did in 1915. Nevertheless, Forster never idealizes sex. Like Lawrence, he believes that the ideal is something beyond the act. Among the gods, Forster writes, only Demeter has "true immortality." "The others continue, perchance, their existence, but are forgotten, because the time came when they could not be loved. But to her, all over the world, rise prayers of idolatry from suffering men as well as suffering women, for she has transcended sex."[115]

And finally, Lawrence and Forster are alike in loathing what the new world has done to the old. In a fine passage of *Lady Chatterley's Lover,* Lawrence expresses his hatred of the ugliness caused by industrialism. Lady Chatterley is driving through a working-class suburb:

The car ploughed uphill through the long squalid straggle of Tevershall, the blackened brick buildings, the black slate roofs glistening their sharp edges, the mud black with coal-dust, the pavements wet and black. It was as if dismalness had soaked through and through everything. The utter negation of natural beauty, the utter negation of the gladness of life, the utter absence of the instinct for shapely beauty which every bird and beast has, the utter death of the human intuitive faculty was appalling. The stacks of soap in the grocers' shops, the rhubarb and lemons in the green-grocers'! the awful hats in the milliners'! All went by ugly, ugly, ugly, followed by the plaster-and-gilt horror of the cinema with its wet picture announcements. . . . Standard Five girls were having a singing lesson, just finishing the la-me-do-la exercises and beginning a "sweet children's song." Anything more unlike song, spontaneous song, would be impossible to imagine: a strange bawling yell that followed the outlines of a tune. . . . What could possibly become of such a people, a people in whom the living intuitive faculty was dead as nails, and only queer mechanical yells and uncanny will power remained? . . .

Tevershall! That was Tevershall! Merrie England! Shakespeare's England! No, but the England of today, as Connie had realized since she had come to live in it. It was producing a new race of mankind, over-conscious in the money and social and political side, on the spontaneous, intuitive side dead, —but dead! Half-corpses, all of them: but with a terrible insistent consciousness in the other half. . . . Ah, God, what has man done to man? What have the leaders of men been doing to their fellow-men? They have reduced them to less than humanness; and now there can be no fellowship any more! It is just a nightmare.[116]

This is a nearer view of the "red rust" that Forster saw encroaching from the distance on Howards End. He too sees it not just as an eclipse of beauty and gladness, but as an eclipse of all that makes "personal

relations" possible. Birkin, of *Women in Love,* desires people "to like
the purely individual thing in themselves, which makes them act in
singleness," and Forster desires it too.[117] But, along with their prophetic hopes, both Forster and Lawrence have a nightmare vision of
a world in which only the mass man and his mass emotions can survive. They fear the kind of situation described by Cyril Connolly:

> Now the industrialization of the world, the totalitarian State, and the egotism
> of materialism have killed friendship; the first through speeding up the
> tempo of human communications to the point where everyone is replaceable,
> the second by making such demands on the individual that comradeship can
> only be practised between workers and colleagues for the period of their
> co-operation, and the last by emphasizing all that is fundamentally selfish
> and nasty in people, so that we are unkind about our friends and resentful
> of their intimacy because of something which is rotting in ourselves.[118]

Both Lawrence and Forster wanted to stop that rot, and both believed in a spiritual aristocracy. Lawrence reacted far more violently
than Forster to what seemed to him the vices of democracy; as Mark
Schorer has pointed out, three of Lawrence's novels—*Aaron's Rod,
Kangaroo,* and *The Plumed Serpent*—deliberately experiment with
undemocratic ideas. But Lawrence concludes, very much as Forster
does, that Great Men are not to be trusted: "The leader-cum-follower
relationship is a bore. And the new relationship will be some sort of
tenderness, sensitive, between men and men, and between men and
women."[119] (The original title of *Lady Chatterley's Lover* was *Tenderness.*) In a key speech of Mellors to Connie, we get most of what
Forster said in his essay on the "undeveloped heart" and most of what
he implied in his phrase the "aristocracy of the sensitive, the considerate, and the plucky." Lawrence's frank way of talking about sex is
no part of Forster's vocabulary, but the feeling Lawrence wants to
evoke is exactly his: "We're only half-conscious, and half alive. We've
got to come alive and aware. Especially the English have got to get
into touch with one another, a bit delicate and a bit tender. It's our
crying need."[120]

The differences between Forster and Lawrence are too obvious to
need emphasis. The similarities are what we are likely to overlook:
it is too easy to think of Forster only as the liberal humanist and forget
his prophetic vision, the force that gave heat and light to his human-

ism. Forster has written about Lawrence on several occasions; but the following is perhaps his best summation.[121] Lawrence, he says,

resembles a natural process more nearly than do most writers, he writes from his instincts as well as preaching instinct, so that one might as well scold a flower for growing on a manure heap, or a manure heap for producing a flower.

His dislike of civilisation was not a pose, as it is with many writers. He hated it fundamentally, because it has made human beings conscious, and society mechanical. Like Blake and the other mystics, he condemns the intellect with its barren chains of reasoning and its dead weights of information; he even hates self-sacrifice and love. What does he approve of? Well, the very word "approve" would make him hiss with rage, it is so smooth and smug, but he is certainly seeking the forgotten wisdom, as he has called it; he would like instinct to re-arise and connect men by ways now disused. . . . He does believe in individuality—his mysticism is not of the Buddhistic annihilistic sort—and, illogical as it sounds, he even believes in tenderness. I think here that the memory of his mother counts. Theirs was an attachment which cut across all theories. . . . Tenderness is waiting behind the pseudo-scientific jargon of his solar plexuses and the savagery of his blood-tests. It is his concession to the civilisation he would destroy and the flaw in the primitive myths he would recreate. It is the Morning Star, the Lord of Both Ways, the star between day and the dark.[122]

Forster claims no kinship, makes no cry of "Mon semblable, mon frère!," does not announce himself a Laurentian. But in the little collection of objective (and true) observations above, he has described not all, but the best part, of himself. Lawrence is a Stephen to Forster's Rickie, his half-brother, and the prophet of that same "forgotten wisdom" which Forster invokes with his Pans and Italians, caves and echoes. Their social criticism, too, stems from the same discontent. And nothing more clearly demonstrates Forster's independence from Bloomsbury, or any party line, than his frank and honest championing of a misunderstood and undervalued author.

6

To close with Lawrence is to remember what is most fundamental in Forster—that spiritual center from which all of his opinions and attitudes arise, and which was brought to maturity, to selfhood, over the course of four novels and many years. Until the caves, or something like them, were accommodated within his vision, he could not answer the questions raised in his early books or stem the anxieties that had prompted their writing. But with *Passage* he completed his own full circle and was home—and went home. From start to finish, his problem has been the accommodation of his nearer to his farther vision. Only once, and in a work of art, does he accomplish it. Outside of art, in the social and political realm, his achievement is more modest and troubled with both far- and near-sightedness. But even in this realm Forster has been in his own way dependable, and his position was never better summarized than in his Presidential Address to the 1944 P.E.N. Conference.

The Conference was meeting, Forster said on that occasion, for two reasons: "to get the mind clear about the future" and to consider how "the artist, the theorist, the dreamer" might, if not cut any ice in society, at least melt a little. He proposes, therefore, to divide potential speakers at the Conference into two classes, which he labels the "musts" and the "oughts." The "musts" appeal to history, characteristically making such statements as: "Economic changes must inevitably precede spiritual change. Let us therefore—so far as we are free agents—concentrate on material problems: better housing, food, clothing, etc.—for ourselves and our fellows: and perhaps when these problems are solved we shall have become better men. Anyhow . . . to put spiritual change first is to contradict the process of history." The "oughts" bear another set of recommendations. They make no appeal to history; they would agree with H. A. L. Fisher, "who could discern no rhythm, pattern or plot in the past, and who could predict for the future nothing except the play of the contingent and the unseen." Their concern is for the here-and-now: *What ought I to do now?* They attack the question "by appealing to something within—to conscience, to a sense of social duty, or to supernatural promptings." In which class, asks Forster, does he himself belong? "I am an impure 'ought,' " he replies:

I am certainly an "ought" and not a "must," for I can discern no inevitable process at work in society, whereas I can see something at work in myself— call it taste, call it conscience. It tells me—this inner voice or inner mumble —that the immediate need for humanity is spiritual, and that better men are more likely to produce better houses than *vice versa*. I want the better houses. The pure "ought" who says, "Let's be good and damn the consequences," is too bleak for me.[123]

The "musts" and the "oughts" are the extremes of Forster's own nearer and farther vision. He ends by standing between both camps in his own mild but firm independence. The "musts" live on the surface of the World Mountain; the "oughts" concentrate on its core and its peak. Forster has gone down to the core and up to the peak, and he has dwelt in patience and anger and wisdom and humor amid the social muddle on the mountain's sides. These have been deeply lived experiences, but above all they have been experiences which he has finally seen as parts of a whole, a multiplicity in a unity. That is why, though he is a prophet who has seen the shadow, he is at the same time—or in the next moment—a prophet who can laugh.

Notes

Chapter one

EPIGRAPHS: (1) "English Prose between 1918 and 1939," TC, pp. 281–82. (2) F. R. Leavis, *D. H. Lawrence: Novelist* (London, 1955), p. 162.

1. Alfred North Whitehead, *Science and the Modern World* (New York, 1946), p. 292.

2. Norman O. Brown, *Life Against Death, The Psychoanalytic Meaning of History* (New York, 1959), pp. 237–38.

3. C. G. Jung, *The Undiscovered Self* (New York, 1961), p. 86.

4. Eliot places the "dissociation" in the 17th century but claims we have "never recovered" from it. Though critics have seriously questioned Eliot's historicity, the phrase is nevertheless valuable as a cliché expressing a widespread feeling. See Frank Kermode, "Dissociation of Sensibility," *The Kenyon Review*, XIX (1957), 169–94. The quotation from Whitehead is from *Science and the Modern World*, p. 291.

5. John Stuart Mill, *Mill on Bentham and Coleridge*, ed. F. R. Leavis (London, 1959), p. 108.

6. *Ibid.*, p. 48.

7. Walter Stone, quoted by John Hall Wheelock in "Introductory Essay" to *Poets of Today*, VI (New York, 1959), p. 28.

8. Basil Willey, *Nineteenth Century Studies* (London, 1949), p. 4.

9. *Ibid.*

10. Samuel Taylor Coleridge, *Biographia Literaria* (London, 1949), p. 151.

11. John Keats, "Lamia," II, lines 230, 235–36.

12. Thomas Carlyle, "Characteristics," *Critical and Miscellaneous Essays*, III (New York, 1899), 16.

13. C. G. Jung, *The Archetypes and the Collective Unconscious*, in *The Collected Works*, Vol. IX, Part 1, Bollingen Series XX (New York, 1959), p. 23.

14. William Hazlitt, "On Poetry in General," *Selected Essays of William Hazlitt, 1788–1830*, ed. Geoffrey Keynes (London, 1948), p. 386.

15. "Art for Art's Sake," TC, p. 99.

16. "The Challenge of Our Time," TC, p. 71.

17. "Art for Art's Sake," TC, p. 103.

18. "E. M. Forster on his Life and Books," an interview by David Jones, *The Listener,* LXI (1959), 11.

19. "Death of a Poet: Birth of a Critic," *The Listener,* VI (1931), 333. See also G. H. Bantock, "The Social and Intellectual Background," *The Modern Age, The Pelican Guide to English Literature* (Baltimore, 1961), Vol. VII, p. 14.

20. *The Letters of Matthew Arnold to Arthur Hugh Clough,* ed. H. F. Lowry (London and New York, 1932), p. 128. Letter dated Feb. 12, 1853.

21. Letter from Arnold to Mrs. Forster dated August 6, 1858, in *Matthew Arnold, Poetry and Prose,* ed. John Bryson (Cambridge, Mass., 1954), p. 750.

22. "Sweetness and Light," in *Matthew Arnold, Prose and Poetry,* ed. Archibald L. Bouton (New York, 1927), pp. 259–63.

23. *Ibid.,* pp. 258–59.

24. "William Arnold," TC, p. 202.

25. Jonathan Spence, a letter from Forster in "E. M. Forster at Eighty," *The New Republic,* CXLI (1959), 21, 35.

26. *Ibid.*

27. "The Challenge of Our Time," TC, pp. 69–70.

28. "Aspect of a Novel," *The Bookseller,* September 10, 1960, p. 1230.

29. Conversation, March 10, 1965.

30. Prologue, "The Abinger Pageant," AH, p. 385.

31. "Our Second Greatest Novel?" TC, p. 231.

32. "The Last of Abinger," TC, p. 369.

33. "Notes on the Way," *Time and Tide,* XV (1934), 767. Compare Ursula in D. H. Lawrence's *Women in Love*: "The Universe is non-human, thank God." (New York, 1922), p. 301.

34. "The Enchaféd Flood," p. 276.

35. "The Last of Abinger," TC, p. 368.

36. " 'Snow' Wedgewood," TC, p. 208.

37. "What I Believe," TC, p. 83.

38. "English Prose between 1918 and 1939," TC, p. 282.

39. "The Art of Fiction, I: E. M. Forster," *The Paris Review,* I (1953), 30.

40. "What I Believe," TC, pp. 84–85.

41. *Ibid.,* pp. 83–84.

42. "Does Culture Matter?" TC, pp. 114–15.

43. "Our Second Greatest Novel?" TC, p. 232.

Chapter two

EPIGRAPHS: (1) From "Songs of Loveliness," *Daily News and Leader,* Jan. 27, 1920, p. 5 (a review by Forster of *More Translations from the Chinese* by Arthur Walz and *Japanese Poetry: The 'Uta'* by Arthur Waley). (2) "Stranger in the Village," in *Notes of a Native Son* (New York, 1964), p. 138.

1. William Cowper, "In Memory of the Late John Thornton, Esq.," *The Poetical Works of William Cowper,* ed. H. S. Milford (London, 1934), pp. 399–400.

2. "Recollectionism," *New Statesman and Nation* (n.s.) XIII (1937), 405.

3. *Ibid.*

4. David Spring, "The Clapham Sect: Some Political and Social Aspects," *Victorian Studies,* V (1961), 36.

5. E. M. Howse, *Saints in Politics* (Toronto, 1952), p. 10.

6. Standish Meacham, *Henry Thornton of Clapham, 1760–1815* (Cambridge, Mass., 1964), p. 1.

7. Noel Annan, *Leslie Stephen* (London, 1951), p. 3. See also "The Intellectual Aristocracy," in *Studies in Social History. A Tribute to G. M. Trevelyan,* ed. J. H. Plumb (London, 1955), pp. 241–87.

8. Howse, p. 25. Quoted from Sir James Stephen, *Essays in Ecclesiastical Biography.*

9. Howse, p. 119.

10. Annan, p. 5.

11. Howse, p. 126. His accounts for other years are as follows:

1790 Charity: £2,260	Other expenses: £1,543
1791 Charity: £3,960	Other expenses: £1,817
1792 Charity: £7,508	Other expenses: £1,616
1793 Charity: £6,680	Other expenses: £1,988

12. "Henry Thornton," TC, p. 197.

13. The Claphamites, however, never thought of themselves as a "sect." The term was probably first applied by Sir James Stephen in an article entitled "The Clapham Sect," *The Edinburgh Review,* LXXX (1844), 251–307. But possibly the name was invented by Sydney Smith. See R. de M. Rudolf, "The Clapham Sect," in *Clapham and the Clapham Sect* (Clapham, 1927), p. 89.

14. Howse, p. 185. Quoted from the London *Times,* July 29, 1933.

15. "Henry Thornton," TC, p. 198.

16. "E. M. Forster," in *The Importance of Scrutiny,* ed. Eric Bentley (New York, 1948), p. 296.

17. "Henry Thornton," TC, p. 199.

18. "Notes on the Way," *Time and Tide,* XVI (1935), 1571.

19. "The Ivory Tower," *The Atlantic Monthly,* CLXIII (1939), 53.

20. R. I. W. and S. W. Wilberforce, *The Life of William Wilberforce* (London, 1838), I, 106.

21. "Aspect of a Novel," *The Bookseller,* Sept. 10, 1960, p. 1229.

22. "The Raison d'Etre of Criticism in the Arts," TC, p. 130.

23. "Henry Thornton," TC, p. 201.

24. "Battersea Rise," AH, p. 282.

25. "Henry Thornton," TC, p. 199.

26. See Spring, p. 39, and Annan, p. 120. Jane Austen, too, is given to such metaphors, and Forster is a Jane Austenite. See Mark Schorer, "The Humiliation of Emma Woodhouse," *The Literary Review* II (1959), 547–63.

27. Alfred Kazin, *On Native Grounds* (New York, 1956), p. 74.

28. Howse, p. 129.

29. *Life of Wilberforce,* V, 36.

30. "Post-Munich," TC, p. 36.

31. *Ibid.,* pp. 35–36.

32. "The Challenge of Our Time," TC, p. 68.

33. From a speech of Wilberforce in Parliament, June 22, 1813; quoted in Eric Stokes, *The English Utilitarians and India* (Oxford, 1959), p. 31.

34. Charles Grant, *Observations on the State of Society Among the Asiatic Subjects of Great Britain, particularly with respect to Morals and on the Means of Improving It* (1792), p. 220; quoted in Stokes, p. 34.

35. "The Gods of India," *The New Weekly,* I (1914), 338

36. "Henry Thornton," TC, p. 220.

Chapter three

EPIGRAPHS: (1) "Cambridge," TC, p. 357. (2) "What I Believe," TC, p. 80.

1. Secrecy is a strict rule in the Society. No one boasts of membership, the rooms for meetings are secret, and only posthumously can Apostles be honored or otherwise publicly recognized as Apostles.

2. Letter to author from Noel Annan, June 5, 1963.

3. Frances M. Brookfield, *The Cambridge "Apostles"* (London, 1906), pp. 5–6.

4. A reliable list of the original membership is given by Noel Annan in his *Leslie Stephen.* Annan gets his information from an unpublished paper entitled "Old Bloomsbury" by Vanessa Bell. "The original members were Vanessa Bell, Virginia Woolf, Thoby and Adrian Stephen (the four children of Sir Leslie); Clive Bell and Leonard Woolf; J. M. Keynes, Duncan Grant and Roger Fry; Desmond and Molly MacCarthy; Lytton, Oliver, Marjorie, and James Strachey; Sydney Saxon Turner, musician and civil servant; H. T. J. Norton, mathematician and don; and on occasions E. M. Forster and Gerald Shove, who was a Fabian and a Cambridge economist, and married F. W. Maitland's daughter, whose great-aunt was Julia Stephen." *Leslie Stephen, His Thought and Character in Relation to His Time* (London, 1951), p. 123n.

Though Bloomsbury originated, according to Clive Bell, in a group that met in his rooms in 1899 and called itself "The Midnight Society," he was never invited into the Apostles. In his memoirs he records the defection of

Midnighters to the Society around 1903: "From London, with commendable regularity and a faint air of mystery, would come on Saturdays Bertrand Russell, E. M. Forster and Desmond MacCarthy: these also were friends, and I suspect they were the death of the Midnight." *Old Friends* (London, 1956), p. 28. His exclusion accounts, no doubt, for what he felt as "a faint air of mystery" in the others—and illustrates how cruelly Cambridge's little class-systems could operate.

It is R. F. Harrod who describes the ladies as "Apostles to the fingertips." *The Life of John Maynard Keynes* (New York, 1951), p. 177. The notion of women Apostles is, however, almost absurd. Though it could perhaps be debated today, it was in 1900 an impossibility not even conceived of. This masculine exclusiveness could enrage Virginia Woolf. In a letter to Lytton Strachey, May 21, 1912, she remarks: "How difficult it is to write to you! It's all Cambridge—that detestable place; and the ap–s–les are so unreal, and their loves are so unreal, and yet I suppose it's all going on still—swarming in the sun—and perhaps not as bad as I imagine. But when I think of it, I vomit—that's all—a green vomit, which gets into the ink and blisters the paper." *Virginia Woolf & Lytton Strachey, Letters*, Leonard Woolf and James Strachey, eds. (London, 1956), p. 38.

5. Keynes: "We did not see much of Forster at that time [Michaelmas 1902]; who was already the elusive colt of a dark horse." "My Early Beliefs," *Two Memoirs* (London, 1949), p. 81. "We did not see very much of him. . . . He was strange, elusive, evasive. You could be talking to him easily and intimately one moment, and suddenly he would withdraw into himself; though he still was physically there, you had faded out of his mental vision, and so with a pang you found that he had faded out of yours." Leonard Woolf, *Sowing, An Autobiography of the Years 1880–1904* (London, 1960), p. 171. Strachey, writes Woolf "nicknamed him the Taupe, partly because of his faint physical resemblance to a mole, but principally because he seemed intellectually and emotionally to travel unseen underground." *Sowing*, p. 172. See also *Frank Swinnerton, An Autobiography* (London, 1937), p. 345.

6. In an interview on November 6, 1957, Forster told me that he was not trained in philosophy, was not sure he had read *Principia Ethica,* and got most of his Moore indirectly—through his friend H. O. Meredith (to whom RV is dedicated). The quotation from Strachey is in GLD, p. 110; the one from Keynes is in "My Early Beliefs," p. 82.

7. Conversation with Clive Bell, May 1, 1958.

8. *Portraits from Memory* (London, 1956), pp. 9–10.

9. *Sowing,* p. 88.

10. See also "Breaking Up," *The Spectator,* CLI (1933), 110.

11. *Ibid.*

12. "Literature or Life? Henry W. Nevinson; the Boy Who Never Stuck," *The New Leader,* October 2, 1925, p. 14.

13. *The Georgian Literary Scene* (London, 1935), p. 408.

14. Brookfield, *The Cambridge "Apostles,"* p. 6.

15. *Autobiography of Charles Merivale,* ed. Judith Anne Merivale (Oxford, 1898), pp. 98–99.

16. Letter from Keynes to B. W. Swithinbank, March 27, 1906. Quoted in R. F. Harrod, *The Life of John Maynard Keynes,* p. 117.

17. Annan, *Leslie Stephen,* pp. 123–24.

18. L. E. Elliott-Binns, *Religion in the Victorian Era* (London, 1953), p. 400.

19. T. Wemyss Reid, *Life, Letters, and Friendships of Richard Monckton Milnes* (London, 1890), I, 51.

20. J. C. Pollock, *A Cambridge Movement* (London, 1953), p. 7.

21. Quoted in *ibid.,* p. 17.

22. Hallam Tennyson, *Alfred Lord Tennyson, A Memoir* (New York, 1898), I, 43.

23. Noel Annan, "The Strands of Unbelief," in *Ideas and Beliefs of the Victorians* (London, 1950), p. 154. For a good account of the reading of the early Apostles, see also John Connop Thirlwall, Jr., *Connop Thirlwall, Historian and Theologian* (London, 1936), pp. 55–58.

24. Annan, *Ideas and Beliefs,* p. 151.

25. Harold Nicolson, *Tennyson: Aspects of his Life, Character, and Poetry* (London, 1959), p. 76.

26. "My Early Beliefs," p. 96.

27. D. C. Somervell, *English Thought in the Nineteenth Century* (London, 1947), p. 19.

28. *Ibid.,* 19.

29. Standish Meacham, *Henry Thornton of Clapham, 1760–1815* (Cambridge, Mass., 1964), p. 13.

30. *Ibid.,* p. 141. Quoted from William Paley, *Reasons for Contentment: Addressed to the Labouring Part of the British Public* (1793).

31. Basil Willey, *Nineteenth Century Studies* (London, 1949), p. 139.

32. Quoted in Basil Willey, *The Eighteenth Century Background* (London, 1946), p. 85.

33. *Aids to Reflection* (New York, 1872), pp. 317–18.

34. "Table Talk," *The Complete Works of Samuel Taylor Coleridge,* W. G. T. Shedd, ed. (New York, 1884), VI, 412.

35. "My Early Beliefs," p. 97.

36. Meacham discusses Henry Thornton's linking of God and money. *Henry Thornton,* p. 137.

37. "My Early Beliefs," p. 83.

38. "Table Talk," pp. 364–65.

39. "Essay on Faith," *Works,* V, 559.

40. *E. M. Forster: The Perils of Humanism* (Princeton, 1962), pp. 19–36.

41. "Equality," in *Matthew Arnold, Poetry and Prose,* John Bryson, ed. (Cambridge, Mass., 1954), p. 590.

42. Quoted in Gertrude Himmelfarb, *Lord Acton, A Study in Conscience and Politics* (Chicago, 1962), p. 205.

43. *Ibid.,* pp. 205, 204.

44. *Ibid.*

45. *Ibid.,* p. 202.

46. *Ibid.,* p. 203.

47. E. H. Carr, "The Widening Horizon," *The New Republic,* CXLV (1961), 12.

48. *Ibid.*

49. Hallam Tennyson, *Memoir,* I, 69.

50. Clive Bell, *Old Friends,* p. 45.

51. Compare the poem "It is Different for Me," which Forster includes in AH, p. 31.

52. Quoted in Frederick Grubb, "In but not of: A Study of Julian Bell," *Critical Quarterly,* II (1960), 123. See also David Garnett, *The Familiar Faces* (London, 1962), pp. 159–67. Mauron is author of *The Nature of Beauty in Art and Literature* (1927), *Aesthetics and Psychology* (1935), and other books. He has translated Mallarmé with Roger Fry (1936), and he began a translation with Fry of *A Passage to India.* Mauron, writes Forster, was the friend who "has helped me with pictures most." "Not Looking at Pictures," TC, p. 142. Forster dedicated *Aspects of the Novel* to him. See Plates 38 and 42.

53. "In but not of," p. 123.

54. *Essays, Poems and Letters,* ed. Quentin Bell, Foreword by Lord Keynes (London, 1938), p. 391.

55. "War and Peace: A Letter to E. M. Forster," in *ibid.,* p. 388.

56. *Ibid.,* p. 341.

57. William A. Jamison, *Arnold and the Romantics* in *Anglistica,* X (Copenhagen, 1958), 27.

58. Lionel Trilling, Introduction to *The Portable Matthew Arnold* (New York, 1949), p. 4.

59. "My Early Beliefs," p. 96.

60. *Ibid.,* pp. 98–99.

61. See "Anonymity," TC, pp. 87–97.

62. "Dante," *The Working Men's College Journal,* X (1908), 261.

63. *Slavery and Freedom* (New York, 1944), p. 9.

64. "The Ivory Tower," *The Atlantic Monthly,* CLXIII (1939), 56, 58. Letter to the author from Forster, February 9, 1963.

65. McTaggart, "The Further Determination of the Absolute," *Philosophical Studies* (London, 1934), p. 216.

66. McTaggart, *The Nature of Existence* (Cambridge, 1927), II, 479.

67. GLD, p. 73. The remark was made by Desmond MacCarthy, no expert. There have been other ambitious metaphysicians since, for example Samuel Alexander in the twenties. C. D. Broad, McTaggart's best critic, writes that

"He knew little of science and cared nothing for history," so that "except for certain valuable materials provided by his emotional life, there was little but straw to be cut by the exquisitely fashioned dialectical machinery of his mind." C. D. Broad, *Examination of McTaggart's Philosophy* (Cambridge, 1938) II, 790.

68. G. Lowes Dickinson, *J. McT. E. McTaggart* (Cambridge, 1931), pp. 94–95. According to Dickinson's Introduction (p. vii), the materials for this book were mainly collected by Wedd with the assistance of Mrs. McTaggart, but owing to Wedd's illness were arranged into a book by Dickinson. It is therefore sometimes difficult to know who is the author of a specific statement.

69. *Ibid.*, p. 87.

70. See Harold Nicolson, *Swinburne* (London, 1926), p. 137.

71. Dickinson, *McTaggart*, p. 87.

72. *Studies in the Hegelian Dialectic* (1896), *Studies in Hegelian Cosmology* (1901), and *A Commentary on Hegel's Logic* (1910).

73. Russell writes of the relief of escaping from McTaggart's Hegelianism: "Moore first, and I closely following him, climbed out of this mental prison and found ourselves again at liberty to breathe the free air of a universe restored to reality." "The Influence and Thought of G. E. Moore," *The Listener*, LXI (1959), 755.

74. See Keynes, *Two Memoirs*, p. 82; GLD, p. 110, and Woolf, *Sowing*, pp. 131–49. In this last there is a particularly brilliant and amusing description of McTaggart.

75. See Moore, "The Refutation of Idealism," *Mind*, XII (n.s.) (1903), 433–53; see also reply by C. A. Strong, "Has Mr. Moore Refuted Idealism?" *Mind*, XIV (n.s.) (1905), 174–89.

76. See *The Philosophy of G. E. Moore*, ed. Paul Arthur Schilpp (Chicago, 1942); John Passmore, *A Hundred Years of Philosophy* (London, 1957); and J. K. Johnstone, *The Bloomsbury Group* (London, 1954).

77. Conversation with Forster, November 6, 1957.

78. "Aspect of a Novel," *The Bookseller* September 10, 1960, p. 1228.

79. *Principia Ethica* (Cambridge, 1956), p. 21.

80. *Ibid.*, pp. 188–89.

81. *Ibid.*, pp. 203–4. "Do you remember," writes Keynes, "the passage in which he discusses whether, granting that it is mental qualities which one should chiefly love, it is important that the beloved person should also be good-looking?" "My Early Beliefs," p. 92. Moore's difficulty arose from his attempt to link truth and beauty not only in art, but in the human relationship of love.

82. "My Early Beliefs," p. 94.

83. Woolf, *Sowing*, p. 156.

84. *Ibid.*

85. "Henry James and the Young Men," *The Listener*, LXII (1959), 103.

86. Conversation with Forster, October 23, 1957. On this occasion Forster said, "No, I wasn't conscious of following him. I knew Roger very well of course. He used to laugh at me for always wanting to look at the *picture*. I used to joke with him and ask why, if the representation didn't matter, he arranged his lines to look like recognizable people and landscapes. He would answer, 'I like them better that way.' " The quotation is not verbatim.

87. *Roger Fry, A Biography*, pp. 51–52. The emancipation Fry effected was in part the work of G. E. Moore, who broke the spell of McTaggartian Hegelianism on the Apostles. Russell writes: "This philosophy was supposed to offer a substitute for religion, but at a great expense. One must not permit oneself to believe in the expanses of the sea, or in the sun and moon, or in the great nebula in Orion. All these things were illusion—so we were told—from which Mind suffered when it forgot Hegel." "The Influence and Thought of G. E. Moore," *The Listener*, LXI (1959), 755. The visual arts could hardly prosper until one was ready to accept the reality of lines and colors.

88. "Some Questions in Esthetics," *Transformations, Critical and Speculative Essays on Art* (New York, 1956), p. 11.

89. *Ibid.*, p. 10.

90. "Indian Art," *Last Lectures* (Boston, 1962), pp. 150–51.

91. Once when Wedd attempted to get Shaw to speak at the College, Dr. B. F. Westcott of King's raised some doubts about Shaw's "ethical basis." Shaw, hearing about the matter, wrote Wedd a postcard saying "Tell the old boy that my E. B. is just the same as his." (Westcott was Regius Professor from 1870 until 1890, when he became Bishop of Durham.) *King's College Cambridge* (the annual report of the College Council . . . on the . . . condition of the College), Cambridge, 1940, p. 2. See also GLD, p. 96.

92. *King's College Cambridge*, p. 2.

93. A good article on Conway is Warren S. Smith, "Moncure Daniel Conway at South Place Chapel," *The Christian Century*, LXXX (1963), 77–80. Shaw heard Conway talk at the Shelley Society and "thought highly of him." Conway's essay *Christianity* (1876) closely parallels Shaw's Preface to *Androcles and the Lion*.

94. *Memoirs*, "Religion," pp. 30–33. Wedd's *Memoirs* consist of seven typescripts in the King's College Library, and represent the bulk of his writings. They are labeled as follows: "A Local Grammar School" (8 pp.); "Religion" (69 pp.); "G.L.D." (12 pp.); "Typed draft of account of University Life, pp. 3–23" (20 pp.); "King's in 1883" (53 pp. unnumbered); "The Square" (71 pp., concerning Trinity Square, Tower Hill, London, a place near Wedd's childhood home); and "The University" (137 pp. unnumbered). Also among Wedd's remains in the King's College Library is the ms. of an untitled novel, handwritten in an almost indecipherable script (about 170 pp).

95. "Religion," p. 38.

96. *Ibid.*, pp. 67–69.

97. "Typed draft of account of University Life," pp. 20–21.

98. *Ibid.*, pp. 12–13.

99. Introduction to *The Aeneid of Virgil,* trans. E. Fairfax Taylor (London, 1906), I, x–xi.

100. There are three letters from Forster to Wedd and one to Mrs. Wedd in the King's College Library. The letters to Wedd are worth citing in their entirety for the sense they give of the importance to Forster of Wedd's friendship:

> 10 Earl's Road
> Tunbridge Wells
> Tuesday [1901]

Dear Wedd

I went to see the O.B., and found him amiable but not encouraging. My one hope, he seems to think, is to fortify my degree with a certificate from a training college. He suggested my coming to his at Cambridge, but did not seem particularly enthusiastic about me. However I may as well apply for the papers on the subject. Thank you for the trouble you have taken about me.

I saw your lectureship in Monday's paper. I suppose you will lecture in Greek history.

I leave home next Saturday, and start on my round of visits. I shall try to learn some French in the vac: it is probably the most useful thing I can do.

I remain

> Yrs very sincerely
> E. M. Forster

> West Hackhurst
> Abinger, Dorking.
> Sept. 3rd, [1901]

Dear Mr Wedd,

I have finished all the Latin you suggested—except the last two books of the Nat. Deorum, which I have not been able to get hold of. I am just beginning the Greek, which I hope to get finished by October, as there is not much of it. Ought I to be doing anything about my history yet? I think I am getting to work quicker, which is some comfort. I was away till the beginning of August: three weeks of the time in Northumberland, where I suppose you are now. I liked Acton very much: we spent most of our time netting for salmon—or bull trout: I never could tell the difference—in the Coquet, and got a good many, to the great wrath of the Anglers' Federation, who own the opposite bank and may only use a rod, and have never yet been seen to get a fish. I have not seen anybody from King's, except Haward, with whom I spent a morning in London. Meredith has written once or twice to me: he seems to detest Germany very heartily. I am stopping here in Surrey for about a week.

Yours very sincerely

E. M. Forster

[Note: The Acton referred to is the original of "the perilous house" in LJ (See Plate 23). Meredith is Owen Meredith, Forster's good friend, who now resides in Belfast.]

2. Lung 'Arno delle Scazie

Pensione Simi, Firenze

Dec. 1. 01

Dear Wedd

You asked me to write to you when we last met, but I feel that I have little of interest to tell you. I have been living the life of the comfortable tourist for two months, which for letter writing at all events is a mistake. Having given up our house at T. Wells, we are able to do things in a comparatively luxurious and unexciting way. But the orthodox Baedeker-bestarred Italy—which is all I have yet seen—delights me so much that I can well afford to leave the Italian Italy for another time. I saw a little of it yesterday, when we went to Prato—do you know it?—which seems a little off the track. A small band of the inhabitants accompanied us to show the sights, and when we tried to buy postcards they thronged in till the shop was crammed, and advised us what to buy. I enjoyed the place very much, though the light was so bad that we c *dnt* see the Lippi frescoes, though we climbed up among the high altar candles for the purpose. The dean and chapter [?] of Prato suffered from stiff necks, and have tacked up a red cloth canopy all round the choir, cutting off the bottom and most beautiful of the frescoes.

I was let off the sermon this morning on condition we substituted for it Fra Angelico's frescoes in San Marco. But, as I remember you saying, he is almost too good, and when I got outside the church I refused, and went to see the Fry-belicked Spring in the Academy. [Forster's note, added in 1954: Roger Fry used to lick dirt off the Primavera when the custodian wasn't looking.] The flowers are now astonishingly bright. I was rather put off Fra Angelico by starting the day with Castagno's frescoes at St. Apollonia. Do you remember the portrait of Pippo Spani—a long legged ruffian who is bending his sword across his knees?

As to my past travels, I have been to Basle, Lucerne, Como, Cadenabbia, and Milan. In Florence we have been about 6 weeks, and leave on Thursday for Perrugia—possibly stopping two nights at Arezzo on the way. We stop a week or a fortnight at Perrugia, & then go to Rome. The above address or care Poste Restante Rome will be the best.

But the chief object of this letter is to tell you that a benevolent old lady has given me £50 to go to Greece with next Easter. I mean to go the Gardner trip, if it exists, and I am very much hoping that you will be coming too. I know you have been twice running, but I still hope I shall be lucky.

This letter is written between an Englishman and a Frenchman who are learning Italian together, and a Russian who is trying to explain the Spanish constitution in French. The other inmates are all females, and not very amusing. George Hodgkin and J. E. More are however both in Florence, which is very nice for me. I shall find Spencer in Rome—possibly Lubbock too, though I haven't heard from him for some time. It's a pity Meredith can't get away for Xmas. I have just had a letter from Dent, who is my chief Cambridge correspondent.

As to writing, I have done none since the summer, when however I did a certain amount. What with sight seeing, and reading up, and trying to learn Italian, I find my time crammed. I don't know when I shall be back; my mother finds it so pleasant to have no house that I expect the last housemaid will have died before our return.

I remain

Yours affect^{ly}

E. M. Forster

[The persons referred to are Percy Lubbock, Owen Meredith, and Edward J. Dent, a well-known musicologist.]

101. "E. M. Forster on his Life and Books," *The Listener,* LXI (1959), 11.
102. *King's College Cambridge,* p. 2.
103. Letter from Forster to the author, February 9, 1963.

Chapter four

EPIGRAPH: "Tolerance," TC, p. 58.
1. GLD, p. 238. "The truest words about him were said by his former bedmaker at Cambridge, Mrs. Newman: 'He was the best man who ever lived.' That is what I feel about him myself, and it is what those who knew Socrates say of Socrates at the close of the 'Phaedo.' " But Esmé Wingfield-Stratford recalls a bedmaker who said of Dickinson: "Never again do you catch me doing anything for that horriferous man." *Before the Lamps Went Out* (London, 1945), p. 176.
2. See *Before the Lamps Went Out,* p. 178. Sir Charles Tennyson attributes the sobriquet "Dirty Dick" to "his untidiness and natural opacity of complexion." *Stars and Markets* (London, 1957), p. 89.
3. *Before the Lamps Went Out,* p. 178.
4. *Julian Bell, Essays, Poems, and Letters,* p. 335.
5. *Before the Lamps Went Out,* p. 177.
6. "Songs of Loveliness," *The Daily News and Leader,* January 27, 1920, p. 5.
7. A complete bibliography by R. E. Balfour is appended to Forster's biog-

raphy. Some of Dickinson's more important works are: *The Greek View of Life* (1896), *The Meaning of Good* (1901), *Letters from John Chinaman* (1901), *A Modern Symposium* (1905), articles in *The Independent Review* (1903–6), *Appearances* (1914), *The Magic Flute* (1920), *The International Anarchy* (1926), and *After Two Thousand Years* (1930).

8. *Letters from John Chinaman* (London, 1946), p. 88.

9. Noel Annan argues that Dickinson was typical of a certain kind of don at the turn of the century, before the College had research students in the modern sense. Although as scholars they were amateurs, "as teachers of wisdom rather than of a subject" they were "unsurpassed." Letter to author from Noel Annan, King's College, June 5, 1963.

10. *Appearances, Being Notes of Travel* (London, 1914), p. 195.

11. "Typed draft of account of University life," pp. 3–4. It is interesting to note that the sets split over Tennyson. Tennyson "in his drawing-room moods" was, says Wedd, the best set's favorite poet. "The University," *Memoirs*, p. 120. But Dickinson and Forster cannot stand him. Dickinson: "Tennyson *will not do*; he's only half alive and that half is diseased." GLD, p.81. Forster (comparing him with George Meredith): "I feel indeed that he was like Tennyson in one respect: through not taking himself quietly enough he strained his inside." AN, p. 86. Leonard Woolf writes: "For us in 1902 Tennyson was out-of-date and we therefore underestimated his poetry." *Sowing*, p. 169. See also GLD, pp. 55–56.

12. See the description of Clive Bell in David Garnett, *The Flowers of the Forest* (London, 1955), pp. 23–24.

13. This society was founded "as the result of some popular lectures on philosophy which had been delivered by McTaggart." (GLD, p. 102.)

14. Letter to author from Noel Annan, June 5, 1963.

15. *The Greek View of Life*, with a Preface by E. M. Forster (London, 1957), p. vi.

16. "Prometheus Unbound," *The Times Literary Supplement*, January 17, 1958, p. 25.

17. "My Early Beliefs," in *Two Memoirs* (London, 1949), pp. 97–98. The earlier quotation is from *Before the Lamps Went Out*, p. 178.

18. *The Greek View of Life*, p. 155.

19. "A Great Humanist," *The Listener*, LVI (1956), 547.

20. See especially "Religion: A Criticism and a Forecast" (1905), "Religion and Immortality" (1911), and articles in *The Independent Review* and *The Hibbert Journal*. The first two essays were gathered in a 1946 edition of *Letters from John Chinaman* with an Introduction by E. M. Forster (London).

21. "Ecclesiasticism," *Letters from John Chinaman*, p. 115.

22. "Revelation," *Letters*, p. 135.

23. "Religion," *Letters*, p. 141.

24. See Ian Watt, *The Rise of the Novel* (Berkeley, 1959), p. 90.

25. "Faith," *Letters,* p. 157.

26. "Religion," *Letters,* p. 147.

27. *Ibid.,* p. 148.

28. "Faith and Knowledge," *Letters,* p. 159.

29. "Religion," *Letters,* p. 137.

30. "Is Immortality Desirable?" *Letters,* p. 200.

31. "Optimism and Immortality," *Letters,* p. 179.

32. "Faith and Knowledge," *Letters,* p. 167.

33. *Ibid.,* pp. 161–62.

34. *Ibid.,* p. 162.

35. *Ibid.,* p. 164.

36. "Euthanasia: Being Lines from the Note-Book of an Alpinist," *The Independent Review,* VII (1905), 476–77. Reprinted in *Letters,* p. 209. Cf. LJ, p. 128.

37. *Ibid.,* pp. 477–78 (or pp. 210–11).

38. "The Religious Symbol," *Daedalus,* LXXXVII (1958), 12.

39. GLD, p. 37. See also p. 63: "It becomes evident that there is no good like friendship; which indeed may be termed love; which love, it seems to me, is the one thing to be cherished if there is to be any purport in life."

40. Letter to author from Noel Annan, June 5, 1963. The preceding quotation is from *The Meaning of Good* (London, 1937), p. 185.

41. *After Two Thousand Years, A Dialogue Between Plato and a Modern Young Man* (London, 1930), pp. 186–87, 196.

42. "What I Believe," TC, p. 82.

43. See Edward Carpenter, *Towards Democracy* (London, 1912), p. 12. Quotation from G. Lowes Dickinson, "Edward Carpenter as a Friend," in *Edward Carpenter: in Appreciation,* ed. Gilbert Beith (London, 1931), p. 39.

44. "Edward Carpenter as a Friend," p. 41.

45. *Ibid.*

46. *The Intermediate Sex, A Study of Some Transitional Types of Men and Women* (London, 1909), pp. 16–18.

47. *The Greek View of Life,* p. viii.

48. *Ibid.,* pp. 189–90.

49. "Quo Vadis?" *The Independent Review,* VIII (1906), 149.

50. One of his best-known books is *The International Anarchy* (1926), which deals not only with the causes of the war but shows that anarchy, not this or that nation, causes wars. See GLD, p. 194.

51. GLD, p. 88. See "What I Believe," TC, p. 82.

52. *Appearances,* pp. 26–27.

53. *Ibid.,* p. 5.

54. *Letters,* pp. 27–28.

55. *War: Its Nature, Cause, and Cure* (London, 1923), pp. 34–35.

56. Letter to author from Noel Annan, June 5, 1963.

57. "Machiavellianism," *The Albany Review,* III (1908), 557–58.

58. "A Great Humanist," *The Listener,* LVI (1956), 546.

59. My italics. See Note, p. 85.

60. *The Magic Flute,* p. 98.

61. *Ibid.,* p. 127.

62. *The Greek View of Life,* p. 190.

Chapter five

EPIGRAPH: Stéphane Mallarmé, as quoted in W. B. Yeats, *The Autobiography of W. B. Yeats* (New York, 1958), p. 210.

1. The three essays (Besant's and James's are both entitled "The Art of Fiction"; Stevenson's is "A Humble Remonstrance") are all reprinted in *Realism and Romanticism in Fiction, An Approach to the Novel,* eds. Eugene Current-Garcia and Walton R. Patrick (Chicago, 1962), pp. 68–118.

2. See Ford Madox Ford, *Thus to Revisit* (New York, 1921), pp. 42–43.

3. C. J. Weber, *Hardy of Wessex* (New York, 1940), p. 17.

4. "The Book of the Age? James Joyce's 'Ulysses,' " *The New Leader,* March 12, 1926, p. 13.

5. AN, p. 27. Ford Madox Ford could not forgive Forster for this kind of remark. See "Cambridge on the Caboodle," *The Saturday Review of Literature,* IV (1927), 449–50.

6. See p. 117.

7. Introduction to D. H. Lawrence's *Psychoanalysis and the Unconscious* and *Fantasia of the Unconscious* (New York, 1960), pp. xix–xx.

8. "Anonymity," TC, p. 97. Forster attributes the idea to Shelley.

9. "The Raison d'Être of Criticism in the Arts," TC, p. 123.

10. *Ibid.,* p. 126.

11. *Ibid.,* pp. 125–26.

12. *Ibid.,* p. 126.

13. "Art for Art's Sake," TC, p. 99. The notion that the work of art is like a natural organism, a whole and relatively self-contained entity, has a long tradition in romantic criticism, beginning at least with Goethe. See M. H. Abrams, *The Mirror and the Lamp* (New York, 1958), p. 327.

14. *Ibid.,* p. 103.

15. *Ibid.,* pp. 100–101.

16. "Not Listening to Music," TC, p. 138. Originally appeared as "How I Listen to Music," *The Listener,* XXI (1939), 173.

17. Bradley, *Oxford Lectures on Poetry* (London, 1950), p. 5.

18. "The Raison d'Être of Criticism in the Arts," p. 126.

19. "Not Listening to Music," TC, p. 136.

20. *Ibid.,* pp. 136–37.

21. *Ibid.,* p. 137.

22. *Ibid.,* p. 138.

23. "The Raison d'Être of Criticism in the Arts," p. 128.

24. *Ibid.*

25. *Ibid.*

26. "Anonymity," p. 93.

27. *Ibid.*

28. *Ibid.,* p. 91.

29. *Ibid.*

30. *Ibid.*

31. *Ibid.*

32. "The Raison d'Être of Criticism in the Arts," p. 129.

33. *Ibid.*

34. "Not Listening to Music," p. 138.

35. See "What I Believe," TC, p. 78; "To ignore evidence is one of the characteristics of faith."

36. AN, p. 81. Though Forster does not care much about questions of point of view, he would not have the author take "the reader into his confidence about his characters," since "intimacy is gained . . . at the expense of illusion and nobility." He would, however, allow the author to take the reader into his confidence "about the universe." See Booth, *The Rhetoric of Fiction* (Chicago, 1961), p. 17n.

37. See the discussion of Kant's philosophy by Charles Frederick Harrold, "Introductory Survey," *English Prose of the Victorian Period* (New York, 1938), p. xlii.

38. AN, p. 147. Geoffrey Tillotson has replied to Forster's attack on James. *Criticism and the Nineteenth Century* (London, 1951), pp. 244–69.

39. "Henry James and the Young Men," *The Listener,* LCII (1959), 103.

40. See the illuminating discussion of "Rhythm" in James McConkey, *The Novels of E. M. Forster* (Ithaca, 1957), pp. 94–160.

Chapter six

EPIGRAPHS: (1) Roger Fry, writing on Corot in *Transformations* (New York, 1956), p. 50. (2) "The Unpoetic Compromise: On the Relation Between Private Vision and the Social Order in Nineteenth-Century Fiction," *Society and Self in the Novel* (New York, 1956), p. 41.

1. "The Art of Fiction," *The Paris Review,* I (1953), 37.

2. "A Book That Influenced Me," TC, p. 227.

3. Conversation with Forster, October 23, 1957.

4. "A Book That Influenced Me," p. 196.

5. From *Delusion and Dream,* as quoted in *Modern Continental Literary Criticism,* ed. O. B. Hardison, Jr. (New York, 1962), p. 243.

6. "Mr. and Mrs. Abbey's Difficulties," AH, p. 266.

7. Woolf, *Sowing*, p. 152.

8. "The Prince's Tale," *The Spectator*, CCIV (1960), 702.

9. "Butterflies and Beetles," *Life and Letters*, III (1929), 3.

10. *Ibid.*, pp. 5–6.

11. *Ibid.*, p. 3.

12. Conversation with Forster, January 10, 1958.

13. "The Art of Fiction," p. 36.

14. Introduction, CS, p. 5.

15. *Ibid.*, p. 6. This may be the experience remembered in LJ, pp. 161–62.

16. *Ibid.*

17. *Ibid.*

18. *Ibid.*

19. *Ibid.*

20. *Ibid.*, p. 5.

21. *Ibid.*

22. W. R. Irwin, "The Survival of Pan," *PMLA*, LXXVI (1961), 167.

23. *Ibid.*, p. 162.

24. *Ibid.*, p. 162.

25. *Ibid.*, p. 160.

26. Lionel Trilling, *Matthew Arnold* (New York, 1949), p. 119.

27. "The Novels of E. M. Forster," *The Death of the Moth and Other Essays* (London, 1947), p. 108.

28. *Ibid.*

29. William Hale White ("Mark Rutherford"), *The Autobiography of Mark Rutherford, Dissenting Minister* (London, 1936), p. 65.

30. Joseph Frank, "Spatial Form in Modern Literature," in *Critiques and Essays in Criticism, 1920–1948*, ed. R. W. Stallman (New York, 1949), p. 325.

31. *The Works of John Ruskin*, ed. E. T. Cook and Alexander Wedderburn (London, 1909), XXXVI, xxxiv.

32. Constance Sitwell, *Flowers and Elephants* (London, 1927), p. 23.

33. *Ibid.*, p. 33.

34. "Albergo Empedocle," *Temple Bar*, CXXVIII (1903), 677.

35. *Ibid.*, p. 684.

36. *Ibid.*

37. *Ibid.*, p. 667.

38. CS, p. 97. Compare RV: "Italy is heroic, but Greece is godlike or devilish—I am not sure which, and in either case absolutely out of our suburban focus." (p. 218.) See Forster's letter to Wedd from Florence, December 1, 1901, in which Forster indicated his intention of going to Greece. Doubtless the story was written during or shortly after the trip. See Note 100, pp. 401–2.

39. See James Joll, *The Anarchists* (Boston, 1964), p. 17.

40. "The Novels of E. M. Forster," p. 109.

41. See LJ, p. 25 and Plate 21: "If the dell was to bear any inscription, he would have liked it to be 'This way to Heaven' painted on a sign-post by the high-road."

42. CS, p. 41. I am indebted to H. J. Oliver for noticing that Bons is "snob" spelled backward. *The Art of E. M. Forster* (Melbourne, 1960), p. 21.

43. CS, p. 41. Those who "shriek" or "yell" with laughter are always, in Forster's fiction, among the damned. See HE, p. 235.

44. Forster first heard *The Ring* in November 1904 at Dresden. This story was written in 1908. See "Revolution at Bayreuth," *The Listener,* LII (1954), 755.

45. See "Art for Art's Sake," TC, p. 103. See also p. 8 above.

46. Quoted in Wayne C. Booth, *The Rhetoric of Fiction* (Chicago, 1961), p. 394.

47. *The Letters of D. H. Lawrence,* ed. Aldous Huxley (New York, 1932), p. 97.

48. "The Novels of E. M. Forster," p. 105.

49. See "Notes on the English Character," AH, pp. 11–24.

50. See above, p. 63.

51. See below, pp. 280–82.

52. See "A Novel that 'Went Wrong,'" *The Manchester Guardian,* June 13, 1951, p. 3; and "The Art of Fiction," *The Paris Review,* I (1953), 30–31.

53. "The Art of Fiction," p. 30.

54. "The Challenge of Our Time," TC, p. 67.

55. "T. S. Eliot," AH, p. 106.

56. "The Novels of E. M. Forster," p. 106.

57. Søren Kierkegaard, *The Sickness Unto Death,* trans. Walter Lowrie (New York, 1954), p. 164.

Chapter seven

EPIGRAPH: "The Love Song of J. Alfred Prufrock."

1. AN, p. 117. See pp. 115–18 above.

2. Compare the marriage of Forster's mother, a Whichelo, into the Thornton family. MT, pp. 249–62, and pp. 31–32 above.

3. Compare Philip and Caroline with Rickie and Agnes of LJ, Colonel Leyland and Miss Raby of "The Eternal Moment," and Harry and Emily of "The Curate's Friend."

4. See Herbert Marcuse, *Eros and Civilization. A Philosophical Inquiry into Freud* (Boston, 1955), pp. 11–20.

5. WA, p. 165. See also p. 161.

6. "The Art of Fiction: I, E. M. Forster," *The Paris Review,* I (1953), 38; reprinted in *Writers at Work,* ed. and intro. by Malcolm Cowley (New York, 1958), pp. 23–35.

7. *Ibid.,* p. 37.

8. *Ibid.,* p. 38.

9. Quoted in Charles Burton Marshall, "Why the Russians are There," *The New Republic,* October 1, 1962, pp. 9–10.

10. "Howard Overing Sturgis," AH, pp. 148–49.

11. "Peter Quince at the Clavier."

12. WA, p. 200. Compare the behavior of the horses at the end of *Passage.*

13. AN, p. 136. Compare Nietzsche: "Who among you can laugh and be elevated at the same time?" *Thus Spoke Zarathustra,* Third Part, in *The Portable Nietzsche,* trans. by Walter Kaufmann (New York, 1954), p. 260.

Chapter eight

EPIGRAPHS: (1) "Esthétique du Mal." (2) *The Sickness Unto Death* (New York, 1954), p. 163.

1. "Virginia Woolf," TC, p. 259.

2. Richard Gilman, "Why Mailer wants to be President," *The New Republic,* February 8, 1964, p. 20. The statement is attributed to Diana Trilling.

3. "Aspect of a Novel," *The Bookseller* (September 10, 1960), p. 1230.

4. See especially *The Spectator,* XCIX (1907), 24–25; and *The Athenaeum,* No. 4151 (May 18, 1907), 600–601.

5. "The Art of Fiction," *The Paris Review,* I (1953), 38.

6. See MT, pp. 174–98, and p. 210 n below. Uncle Willie may also be referred to in "The Raison d'Être of Criticism in the Arts," TC, p. 122.

7. "The Art of Fiction," p. 37.

8. LJ, p. 182. In the letter he wrote to Wedd in 1901, Forster mentions a "round of visits" he must make to relatives during the vacation. This he does in the book too. See also LJ, pp. 38ff. There is also an eccentric Jackson in MT, pp. 189–90.

9. "Aspect of a Novel," p. 1230.

10. *Anatomy of Criticism* (Princeton, 1957), pp. 302–14.

11. Wayne C. Booth, *The Rhetoric of Fiction* (Chicago, 1961), p. 136.

12. Quoted in Cyril Connolly, *The Unquiet Grave* (London, 1946), p. 69.

13. *Anatomy of Criticism,* p. 304.

14. See Booth, pp. 53–60.

15. Robert Lee Wolff, "The Three Romes," *The Making of Myth,* ed. Richard M. Ohmann (New York, 1962), p. 137. Aeschylus's use of the trilogy form to suit his particular cast of thought may also be relevant here.

16. *Ibid.,* pp. 137–38.

17. Compare AN, p. 82.

18. "The Tragic Fallacy," *The Modern Temper* (New York, 1929), p. 94.

19. I am indebted to Joseph Wood Krutch for many of the ideas in this paragraph. See "The Tragic Fallacy," *passim.*

20. *Anatomy of Criticism,* p. 308.

21. "Aspect of a Novel," p. 1228.

22. See Forster on Jane Austen: "Yet with all the help in the world how shall we drag these shy, proud books into the centre of our minds?" AH, p. 175.

23. Henry James, *Notes on Novelists* (New York, 1914), p. 387. James's italics.

24. Conversation with Forster, November 6, 1957. See above, p. 63.

25. LJ, pp. 72–73. When this book was published Forster was 28 to Rickie's 20.

26. Ansell tells Rickie, after meeting Agnes, "I saw no one." As Gerald dies, he repeatedly tells Agnes—in an unwitting parody of Ansell—"I can't see you." Ansell again, when urged to visit Rickie by Widdrington, remarks: "It is no good me going. I should not find Mrs. Elliot: she has no real existence." LJ, pp. 23–24, 62, 202.

27. Friedrich Nietzsche, *The Birth of Tragedy* and *The Genealogy of Morals*, trans. Francis Golffing (New York, 1956), pp. 218, 221.

28. C. J. Jung, "The Sacrifice," *Psychology of the Unconscious*, trans. Beatrice M. Hinckle (New York, 1963), p. 429.

29. *Ibid.,* p. 428. Italics in original.

30. "Aspect of a Novel," p. 1228.

31. René Wellek, "Literary Criticism and Philosophy," in *The Importance of Scrutiny*, ed. Eric Bentley (New York, 1948), p. 29.

32. The lines are quoted as they appear in LJ, p. 146, but there are slight variations in wording and punctuation from Shelley's published versions. D. H. Lawrence often expresses identical ideas. Consider this passage from the chapter "Man to Man" in *Women in Love*: "The way they shut their doors, these married people, and shut themselves in to their own exclusive alliance with each other, even in love, disgusted him. It was a whole community of mistrustful couples insulated in private houses or private rooms, always in couples, and no further life, no further immediate, no disinterested relationship admitted: a kaleidoscope of couples, disjointed, separatist, meaningless entities of married couples." (New York, 1922), p. 226.

33. LJ, p. 72. See note 25 above.

34. LJ, p. 24. See note 26 above.

35. Agnes Pembroke is the same blind carrier of the Life Force as Ann Whitefield, and interestingly enough Ann's betrothed is also named Ricky ("Ricky Ticky Tavy").

36. LJ, p. 87. Compare Mrs. Failing: "Isn't it odd ... that the Greeks should be enthusiastic about laurels—that Apollo should pursue anyone who could possibly turn into such a frightful plant?" LJ, p. 106.

37. Walter Pater, "The School of Giorgione," *The Renaissance* (New York [n.d.]), p. 111.

38. LJ, p. 172. See also p. 71.

39. *The Victorian Frame of Mind, 1830–1870* (New Haven, 1957), p. 242.

The active life comes in for considerable discussion in the book. After Rickie goes to work in the school, Forster reflects: "It is so easy to be refined and high-minded when we have nothing to do. But the active, useful man cannot be equally particular. Rickie's programme involved a change in values as well as a change of occupation." LJ, p. 174. And Ansell, who has been accused of inaction by Widdrington, exclaims: "Action! Nothing's easier than action; as fools testify. But I want to act rightly." LJ, p. 204.

40. "Aspect of a Novel," p. 1228. The Rings also appear briefly in HE, p. 176.

41. See HE, p. 304: "How dare these men label her sister! . . . 'Were they normal?' What a question to ask! And it is always those who know nothing about human nature, who are bored by psychology and shocked by physiology, who ask it."

42. LJ, p. 207. Note the heroic vocabulary.

43. "The Art of Fiction," p. 32.

44. "The Sacrifice," pp. 453–55.

45. "The Tragic Fallacy," p. 95.

46. Introduction to D. H. Lawrence, *Psychoanalysis and the Unconscious* and *Fantasia of the Unconscious* (New York, 1960), p. x.

Chapter nine

EPIGRAPH: Friedrich Nietzsche, *Thus Spake Zarathustra,* trans. Thomas Common (New York, n.d.), p. 165.

1. *Letters of D. H. Lawrence to Bertrand Russell,* ed. Harry Moore (New York, 1948), p. 29. Letter dated February 12, 1915.

2. *Letters of D. H. Lawrence to Bertrand Russell,* p. 31.

3. "A View Without a Room: Old Friends Fifty Years Later," *The New York Times Book Review,* July 27, 1958, p. 4.

4. *Ibid.*

5. *Ibid.* See also Forster's statement in "The Art of Fiction": "I got that far, and then there must have been a hitch." *The Paris Review,* I (1953), 36.

6. William Dean Howells, *The Rise of Silas Lapham* (Boston, 1884), p. 73.

7. RV, p. 205. The same phrase appears on p. 15.

8. "E. M. Forster and Samuel Butler," *PMLA,* LXI (1946), 804–19.

9. *Ibid.,* p. 812. RV, p. 246.

10. "E. M. Forster and Samuel Butler," 812n.

11. RV, p. 244. It is doubtless significant that Mr. Beebe had "never heard of" *The Way of All Flesh.* See RV, p. 153.

12. RV, p. 42. See also p. 113.

13. Friedrich Nietzsche, *The Birth of Tragedy from the Spirit of Music,* I, as quoted in *Modern Continental Literary Criticism,* ed. O. B. Hardison, Jr. (New York, 1962), p. 231.

14. RV, p. 135. This is another repetition of the theme of "Other Kingdom."

15. LJ, p. 264.

16. TC, pp. 370–71.

17. RV, pp. 249–50. Compare "The Machine Stops."

18. "A View Without a Room," p. 15.

Chapter ten

EPIGRAPHS: (1) *The Works of John Ruskin,* ed. E. T. Cook and Alexander Wedderburn (London, 1903–1912), VII, 464. (2) "Democracy," *The Portable Matthew Arnold,* ed. Lionel Trilling (New York, 1949), pp. 462–63.

1. Mark 5:36.

2. See Arthur Koestler, *The Yogi and the Commissar* (New York, 1946). "The Commissar's emotional energies are fixed on the relation between [the] individual and society, the Yogi's on the relation between the individual and the universe." p. 5.

3. Alfred North Whitehead, *Science and the Modern World* (New York, 1946), p. 287.

4. *E. M. Forster* (Norfolk, 1943), pp. 114–15.

5. I am indebted to Mr. Randall Reid for this question and phrasing.

6. Letter from Forster, April 20, 1964.

7. The German elements in this novel undoubtedly owe something to Forster's own experience as tutor in the household of the Countess "Elizabeth" von Arnim at Nassenheide in Pomerania in 1904. In 1908, Elizabeth, with husband and family, moved to England, and in 1910 her husband died, an event which did not distress her unduly: "Perhaps husbands have never altogether agreed with me." Leslie de Charms, *Elizabeth of the German Garden* (London, 1958), p. 150. Subsequent suitors included H. G. Wells and Francis Lord Russell, whom she later married. She always called her first husband "The Man of Wrath." A question put by Forster to the three little girls who were his charges at Nassenheide was: "If there was a war between England and Germany, which would you want to win?" Their answer was: "If there was a war between England and Germany, I shouldn't care which won: I should run away as fast as I could." *Elizabeth,* p. 104. See also Countess M. A. (B.) Russell, *Elizabeth and Her German Garden* (London, 1898), and HE, pp. 109–10.

8. *E. M. Forster,* p. 118.

9. HE, p. 135. Compare LJ, p. 256. The idea is also prominent in Butler and Shaw.

10. *E. M. Forster,* p. 134.

11. C. J. Jung, "The Unconscious Origin of the Hero," *Psychology of the Unconscious* (New York, 1963), p. 193.

12. "A French Eton; or Middle Class Education and the State," *Matthew Arnold, Poetry and Prose*, ed. Bryson, p. 342. Preceding quotation from Lionel Trilling, *Matthew Arnold* (New York, 1949), p. 229.

13. "Equality," *The Portable Matthew Arnold*, ed. Trilling, p. 581.

14. HE, p. 64. Note the surprising statement: "Where there is no money and no inclination to violence tragedy cannot be generated." HE, p. 130.

15. "The Intellectual Aristocracy," *Studies in Social History. A Tribute to G. M. Trevelyan*, ed. J. H. Plumb (London, 1955), pp. 252–53.

16. *Ibid.*

17. John Maynard Keynes, *Essays in Persuasion* (New York, 1963), p. 369.

18. Norman O. Brown, *Life Against Death, The Psychoanalytical Meaning of History* (New York, 1959), p. 104.

19. *Ibid.*, 196. A rainbow bridge, with explicit Wagnerian references, also appears in "The Celestial Omnibus." See Chapter Six, p. 148. The leitmotif technique of this book is also Wagnerian. Note Margaret's statement about Wagner, p. 41.

20. *The Birth of Tragedy from the Spirit of Music*, in *Modern Continental Literary Criticism*, ed. O. B. Hardison, Jr. (New York, 1962), p. 238.

21. C. J. Jung, *The Archetypes and the Collective Unconscious*, trans. R. F. C. Hull (New York, 1959), p. 110.

22. Lewis Mumford, *The Culture of Cities* (New York, 1938), pp. 271, 291–92. Italics in original.

23. "The Theme of the Disappearance of God in Victorian Poetry," *Victorian Studies*, VI (1963), 209.

24. *Ibid.*

25. See "Virginia Woolf," TC, p. 253. Strangely enough, most recent critics fail entirely to see the hostile qualities in Margaret's character and marriage. Frederick C. Crews says, for example, "she resolves the antagonism between body and soul by accepting her role of wife in the fullest sense." *E. M. Forster: The Perils of Humanism* (Princeton, 1962), p. 121. Frederick P. W. McDowell even regards the girls as "victims," along with Leonard, "of the Wilcox moral arrogance," whereas it is clearly the girls who have won and Henry and Leonard who have lost. " 'The Mild Intellectual Light' : Idea and Theme in *Howards End*," *PMLA*, LXXIV (1959), 454. Only James McConkey seems to recognize the "victory as well as defeat" in her experience. *The Novels of E. M. Forster* (Cornell, 1957), p. 119.

26. "E. M. Forster on his Life and Books," *The Listener*, LXI (1959), p. 11.

27. *Granite and Rainbow* (London, 1958), p. 135. Consider Virginia Woolf's remark in *The Voyage Out*: "I want to write a novel about Silence [about] the things people don't say." (London, 1949), p. 262.

28. Forster mentions Arnold in several articles: Arnold's poem "To A Friend" is discussed in an interesting essay, "A Note on the Way," AH, pp.

87–91, reprinted from *Time and Tide*, XV (1934), 723–24. See also "A Note on the Way" appearing November 2, 1935, in the same magazine. Briefer references to Arnold occur in the following pieces: "William Arnold," TC, pp. 202–6; "Aspect of a Novel," *The Bookseller*, September 10, 1960, p. 1228; The Book of the Age?" *The New Leader*, March 12, 1926, p. 13; "De Senectute," *The London Magazine*, IV (1957), 15; "Victorian Writers," *The Athenaeum*, No. 4735 (1921), 93–94.

29. These references to rabbits are found on pp. 6, 4, 289, 196, 207, 316. I am indebted to Mr. Jerry A. Dibble for pointing out the sequence to me.

Chapter eleven

EPIGRAPHS: (1) Forster, "Gemisthus Pletho," AH, p. 208. (2) "Open Letter," *Mid-Century American Poets*, ed. John Ciardi (New York, 1950), p. 69.

1. "E. M. Forster on his Life and Books," *The Listener*, LXI (1959), 11.

2. "The Challenge of our Time," TC, p. 67.

3. "The Legacy of Samuel Butler," *The Listener*, XLVII (1952), 955.

4. Lionel Trilling, *E. M. Forster* (Norfolk, 1943), p. 136. The play is not lost, as Trilling suggests, but is in Forster's possession.

5. Forster read this unfinished novel at the Aldeburgh Festival in June 1951. See "A Novel that 'Went Wrong,' " *The Manchester Guardian*, June 13, 1951, p. 3; and "The Art of Fiction," *The Paris Review*, I (1953), 29–41.

6. "Mr. Walsh's Secret History of the Victorian Movement," *Basileon Z*. No. 13 (June 1911), 7.

7. "An Allegory," *Basileon H* (June 1912), 6–7.

8. "Inspiration," *The Author*, XXII (1912), 281.

9. The Mitra review was listed in the Bibliography compiled by Oliver Stallybrass, but the periodical in which it appeared had not been located. The other piece is: "Iron Horses in India," *The Golden Hynde*, No. 1 (December 1913), 35–39.

10. *The Hill of Devi* (London, 1953), p. 155.

11. "Sunday Music," *The Egyptian Mail*, Alexandria, September 2, 1917, p. 10.

12. G. D. Klingopoulos, "E. M. Forster's Sense of History: and Cavafy," *Essays in Criticism*, VIII (1958), 159.

13. "The Complete Poems of C. P. Cavafy," TC, p. 248.

14. *Ibid.*, p. 249.

15. "For the Museum's Sake," AH, p. 329. Originally "The Objects," *The Athenaeum*, No. 4697 (1920), 599–600.

16. "Archaeology" (Review of *Dead Towns and Living Men* by C. Leonard Woolley and *Discovery in Greek Lands* by F. H. Marshall), *The London Mercury*, II (1920), 763–64.

17. S. L. B. Bensusan, Introduction to *Eöthen* (Philadelphia [n.d.]), p. 15.

18. See Forster, "Cousin X—," *The Daily News and Leader,* February 3, 1920, p. 5. (Review of *Mansoul* by C. M. Doughty.)

19. "Salute to the Orient!" AH, p. 291. Compare the remark of James Justinian Morier, another Eastern traveller, in the Dictionary of National Biography: "He was never at home but when he was abroad."

20. "Salute to the Orient!" pp. 291–92.

21. *Ibid.,* p. 292. Comparisons with André Gide's experience are relevant here. See *Si le grain ne meurt.*

22. *Ibid.*

23. "Wilfrid Blunt," AH, pp. 310–11.

24. See Raymond Mortimer, "A Refusal to be Great?" *The Sunday Times,* June 24, 1962, p. 25. (Review of *The Achievement of E. M. Forster* by J. B. Beer, and *E. M. Forster* by K. W. Gransden.)

25. "Wilfrid Blunt," p. 311.

26. *Ibid.,* p. 310.

27. *Ibid.,* pp. 315–16.

28. "Salute to the Orient!" p. 290.

29. *Ibid.,* p. 288. James Justinian Morier (1780?–1849) is the author of *Journey through Persia, Armenia, and Asia Minor to Constantinople in the Years 1808 and 1809* (1812); *A Second Journey through Persia* (1818); *The Adventures of Hajji Baba of Ispahan* (1824); and numerous other books with Oriental themes.

Charles Montague Doughty (1843–1926) is the author of *Travels in Arabia Deserta* (1888); *The Dawn in Britain* (1906–7); *Adam Cast Forth* (1908); *The Cliffs* (1909); *The Clouds* (1912); *The Titans* (1916); and *Mansoul* (1920).

Lucie Duff-Gordon (1821–1869), is the author of *Letters from Egypt 1863–65* (1865) and *Last Letters from Egypt* (1875), among many other books.

30. " 'The Mint' by T. E. Lawrence," *The Listener,* LIII (1955), 279.

31. *Ibid.* Forster says of *The Seven Pillars of Wisdom*: "It is the book of a man who cannot fit in with twentieth-century civilization, and loves the half-savage Arabs because they challenge it." "English Prose between 1918 and 1939," TC, p. 287.

32. Among the more interesting of the reviews and articles not here discussed are the following:

"Literature and History," *The Athenaeum,* No. 4679 (Jan. 2, 1920), 26–27. Review of *Etudes et fantasies historique,* 2e série, by E. Rodocanachi.

"Frenchmen and France," *The Daily News and Leader,* Jan. 3, 1920, p. 7. Review of *French Ways and Their Meanings,* by Edith Wharton.

"Civilisation," *The Daily Herald,* Jan. 21, 1920, p. 8. Review of Georges Duhamel's book of that title.

"Where There is Nothing," *The Athenaeum,* No. 4687 (February 27, 1920), 270–71. Review of Georges Clemenceau's novel, *The Strongest*—along with some trenchant comments on the author.

"The Mosque," *The Athenaeum*, No. 4960 (March 19, 1920), 367–68. Review of *Moslem Architecture*, by G. T. Rivoira, trans. G. McN. Rushworth.

"Jehovah, Buddha and the Greeks," *The Athenaeum*, No. 4701 (June 4, 1920), 730–31. Review of *Hellenism*, by Norman Bentwich, and *Hellenism in Ancient India*, by Gauranga Nath Bannerjee.

"The Boy Who Never Grew Up," *The Daily Herald*, June 9, 1920, p. 7. Review of *Letters of Travel*, by Rudyard Kipling.

"A Great History," *The Athenaeum*, Nos. 4705, 4706 (July 2–9, 1920), 8–9, 42–43. Review of *The Outline of History*, Vol. I, by H. G. Wells. "Mr. Wells' 'Outline,'" *The Athenaeum*, No. 4725 (Nov. 19, 1920), 690–91. Review of *The Outline of History*, Vol. II.

"Big Stick and Green Leaf," *The Athenaeum*, No. 4707 (July 16, 1920), 76. Review of *Recreation*, by Viscount Grey of Fallodon.

"Luso-India," *The Athenaeum*, No. 4713 (August 27, 1920), 268. Review of *The Book of Duarte Barbosa*, Vol. I, and *History of the Portuguese in Bengal*, by J. J. A. Campos.

"A Cautionary Tale," *The Nation*, XXVIII (1920), 47–48. Review of *Europe and the Faith*, by Hilaire Belloc.

"Missionaries," *The Athenaeum*, No. 4721 (Oct. 22, 1920), 545–547. Review of *In Unknown China*, by S. Pollard; *The Rebuke of Islam*, by W. H. T. Gairdner; and *Character Building in Kashmir*, by the Rev. C. E. Tyndale-Biscoe.

"The Untidy Gentleman," *The Nation*, XXVIII (1920), 344, 346. Review of *The New Jerusalem*, by G. K. Chesterton.

"Reflections in India, I: Too Late?" *The Nation and the Athenaeum*, XXX (1922), 614–15.

"Reflections in India, II: The Prince's Progress," *The Nation and the Athenaeum*, XXX (1922), 644–46.

"The Emperor Babur," *The Nation and the Athenaeum*, XXXI (1922), 21–22. Review of *Memoirs of Babur*, trans. Leyden and Erskine, annot. and rev. by Sir Lucas King.

"The Mind of the Indian Native State," *The Nation and the Athenaeum*, XXXI (1922), 146–47, 216–17.

"India and the Turk," *The Nation and the Athenaeum*, XXXI (1922), 844–45.

"Our Graves in Gallipoli," *The New Leader*, Oct. 20, 1922, p. 8.

33. AH, p. 191.

34. Carl L. Becker, *The Heavenly City of the Eighteenth-Century Philosophers* (New Haven, 1932), p. 18.

35. AHG, pp. 37–38.

36. "Literature and History," *The Athenaeum*, No. 4679 (January 2, 1920), 26. Review of *Etudes et Fantasies Historiques* by E. Rodocanachi in original.

37. AHG, p. 72. Dickinson was also a student of Plotinus. GLD, pp. 51–60.

38. "Happiness!" AH, p. 49.

Chapter twelve

EPIGRAPHS: (1) Theodore Roethke, "Comment. The Poet and His Critics," A Symposium edited by Anthony Ostroff, *New World Writing*, 19 (New York, 1961), p. 215. (2) *Kangaroo* (Harmondsworth, Middlesex, 1950), p. 151.

1. Marjorie Nicolson, *The Breaking of the Circle* (New York, 1962), p. 47.

2. *Ibid.,* p. 123.

3. "Abt Vogler" and "The Second Coming."

4. "The Art of Fiction," *The Paris Review,* I (1953), 30–31.

5. Norman Douglas, *Old Calabria* (Harmondsworth, 1962), p. 37.

6. "The World Mountain," *The Listener,* XXXLII (1954), 978.

7. "The Individual and His God," *The Listener,* XXIII (1940) 801–2.

8. "The World Mountain," p. 978.

9. *Ibid.* "The information might be imperfect, the deductions unsound, but Havell was first in the interpretative field."

10. E. B. Havell, *The Ideals of Indian Art* (London, 1920), p. 24.

11. "The Gods of India," *The New Weekly,* May 30, 1914, p. 338.

12. PI, pp. 130–32; 154. According to Mr. Glen O. Allen, the word "Kawa Dol" in Hindustani means "the crow's swing."

13. "The Snowman," *Harmonium* (New York, 1950), pp. 16–17.

14. See *E. M. Forster: A Tribute, With Selections from His Writings on India,* edited and with an Introduction by K. Natwar-Singh (New York, 1964).

15. Zimmer, *Myths and Symbols in Indian Art and Civilization,* ed. Joseph Campbell (New York, 1962), p. 41.

16. Stella Kramrisch, *The Art of India. Traditions of Indian Sculpture, Painting and Architecture* (New York, 1954), p. 20.

17. *Ibid.,* p. 16.

18. See *The Archetypes and the Collective Unconscious, Collected Works,* Vol. IX, Part I (New York, 1959), p. 294; and Erich Neumann, *The Great Mother* (New York, 1955).

19. Neumann, *Great Mother,* p. 30.

20. Havell, pp. 58–59.

21. Neumann, *Great Mother,* p. 72.

22. *Ibid.,* p. 65.

23. *The Immense Journey* (New York, 1961), p. 92.

24. Nicolson, *The Breaking of the Circle,* p. 48.

25. Allen, "Structure, Symbol and Theme," p. 937. See note, p. 310.

26. Neumann, *Great Mother,* p. 310.

27. Conversation between Forster and Sir John Wolfenden on KPFA-FM, San Francisco, March 2, 1960, rebroadcast from the B.B.C.

28. See C. J. Jung, *The Archetypes and the Collective Unconscious,* p. 388; note especially the illustrations.

29. PI, p. 84. In an article called "A Soul in Trouble," Dickinson writes about a conversation with an Indian who says: "Here all the needs of my soul rise up and cry: Why does not my Krishna come? Will he never come?" *Basileon I. (Being the Ninth Book of King's)*, No. 16 (June 1914), 2.

30. PI, pp. 254–55. These are thoughts of Hamidullah, another Moslem.

31. PI, p. 54. Mr. O. G. W. Stallybrass (in "The Wobblings of E. M. Forster," *The Guardian*, June 20, 1960, p. 5) quotes some of the original versions of the manuscript of *Passage,* most of which show Forster trimming his style toward a fine simplicity. The original of this went as follows: "One touch of regret—not conversational regret, but the stab that goes down to the soul—would have made him a different man, and she would have worshipped him.

32. After India got her independence, though he still had innumerable friends there, Forster became very critical of Nehru and Indian policy.

33. PI, p. 189. See also p. 191: "They had started speaking of 'women and children'—that phrase that exempts the male from sanity when it has been repeated a few times."

34. *E. M. Forster: A Tribute,* p. 61.

35. See "Luso-India," *The Athenaeum,* No. 4713 (Aug. 27, 1920), 268; and "Pan," *The Criterion,* I (1923), 402–8 (reprinted as "Adrift in India, 5: Pan," in AH, pp. 352–59).

36. See "An Arnold in India," *The Listener,* XXXII (1944), 410–11 (reprinted in TC, pp. 202–6).

37. "Syed Ross Masood," TC, p. 299. See also *E. M. Forster: A Tribute,* pp. 88–91.

38. PI, pp. 335–36. This is drawn from a remembered experience. In "Indian Entries," Forster writes: "Kept quietish all day, but rode in evening, and most successfully. Horse played no tricks and we trotted and cantered over open country to Mahratta village. Saeed burst out against the English. 'It may be 50 or 500 years but we shall turn you out.' He hates us far more than his brother does. Horse curvetting all the time in the sunset. Very jolly. Patches of green among the barren—we rode from one to another to admire. Horse played no tricks: S. made his play—an amiable show-off. Energy and sense at the bottom. He is a reckless talker, but realises one has few friends." Entry for March 27, 1913. *Encounter,* XVII (1962), 13.

39. "Mr. Wells' 'Outline,'" *The Athenaeum,* No. 4725 (November 19, 1920), 690. Nearly all critics, however, see Forster in this last novel as expressing a pessimistic, skeptical, or negativistic view of human existence. David Shusterman says: "Though more despairing, the world of his last novel is essentially the same as that he has written about in his earlier novels." "The Curious Case of Professor Godbole: *A Passage to India* Re-

examined," *PMLA*, LXXVI (1961), 427. Frederick P. W. McDowell writes that *Howards End* "is largely free from the negative effects upon Forster's art of his later skepticism." "The Mild Intellectual Light," PMLA, LXXIV (1959), 453. Frederick C. Crews writes: "What finally confronts us is an irreparable breach between man's powers and his needs" (p. 163), and, speaking of his humanism, that Forster as a novelist "finds himself drawn more and more to its negative side." *E. M. Forster: The Perils of Humanism* (Princeton, 1962), p. 6. James McConkey, who gives a most perceptive reading of *Passage,* concludes that "the way of Godbole is the only possible way" (p. 159), which, to the Westerner, is bound to seem a pessimistic way. *The Novels of E. M. Forster* (Ithaca, N.Y., 1957). Alan Wilde and K. W. Gransden alone among recent critics seem to have fully appreciated the complexities of Forster's vision in *Passage.* Alan Wilde writes, "the abyss remains, no matter what man does, but man can do something nonetheless." *Art and Order: A Study of E. M. Forster* (New York, 1964), p. 157. K. W. Gransden, in one of the best books on Forster, "The terrifying insights of the caves, the joyous ones of the temple, seem to be put forward as not only morally better but as more sensible than the constantly failing simplifications . . . of the will to power." *E. M. Forster* (Edinburgh, 1962), p. 105.

40. C. J. Jung, *The Psychology of the Unconscious,* trans. Beatrice M. Hinckle (New York, 1963), p. 316.

41. *E. M. Forster: A Tribute,* p. 59.

42. *The Man Who Died* (New York, 1959), p. 184.

43. "The Art of Fiction," pp. 32–33. The critic who has most clearly seen the importance of this last section is V. A. Shahane in *E. M. Forster, A Reassessment* (Delhi, 1962), p. 108. The Hindu festival, he writes, "is not functionless. It brings to bear upon Aziz, Fielding, Adela, Ronny, Stella, Ralph, a feeling of reconciliation, however momentary this might be."

44. Letter from Noel Annan to the author, June 5, 1963. The play was done by Santha Rama Rau.

45. See C. J. Jung, "The Sacrifice," *The Psychology of the Unconscious,* p. 274.

46. Louise Dauner, "What Happened in the Cave? Reflections on *A Passage to India,*" *Modern Fiction Studies,* VII (1961), 268.

47. Jung, *The Archetypes and the Collective Unconscious,* pp. 21–22.

48. Jung, *The Structure and Dynamics of the Psyche* (New York, 1960), p. 346.

49. Jung, *The Archetypes and the Collective Unconscious,* pp. 19–20.

50. Jung, *The Undiscovered Self* (New York, 1958), pp. 93–97.

51. *E. M. Forster: A Tribute,* p. 57.

52. Kramrisch, *The Art of India,* p. 26.

53. D. H. Lawrence, *The Man Who Died,* p. 180.

54. *Ibid.,* p. 178.

Chapter thirteen

EPIGRAPHS: (1) Preface to *Essays in Criticism,* First Series (London, 1875), pp. vii–viii. (2) "What I Believe," TC, p. 80.

1. "E. M. Forster on his Life and Books," *The Listener,* LXI (1959), 11.
2. "English Prose between 1918 and 1939," TC, p. 291.
3. "T. S. Eliot," AH, p. 107.
4. Miss Bowen writes further: "With some artists the attempt at self-discovery is, itself, the art. But Mr. Forster, though his first novels were published when he was in the twenties, seems to have been adult when he began to write. Then he took up without hesitation, in fact with evident certainty, the position with regard to life that he has occupied since. . . . At all events, he went with that first book direct to his personal maturity—and in an artist that is more than a private matter. The thirty-three years since *Where Angels Fear to Tread* have given him further data, but have not changed his conclusions. . . . His 'development' has been a matter of equipping himself more fully, and with wider and wider reference, to express what he has from the first felt." *Collected Impressions* (London, 1950), p. 123.
5. "What I Believe," TC, p. 82.
6. "A Note on the Way," *Time and Tide,* XV (1934), 723. Reprinted in AH, p. 89.
7. "Tolerance," TC, p. 56.
8. *E. M. Forster* (Norfolk, 1943), pp. 173–74.
9. "Art for Art's Sake," TC, p. 100.
10. "What I Believe," TC, p. 81.
11. What Would Germany Do To Us?" TC, p. 54.
12. "The Raison d'Être of Criticism in the Arts," TC, p. 127.
13. "De Senectute," *The London Magazine,* IV (November 1957), 15–16.
14. "English Prose between 1918 and 1939," TC, p. 286.
15. "Notes on the Way," *Time and Tide,* XVI (1935), 1571.
16. Wilson also made the following observation: "Apart from inner moral grace, there is in your work the idea of momentary vision—onwards from stories in 'Celestial Omnibus.'" Forster denied that Mrs. Munt had this vision, but said that Stephen "had something of the sort." "A Conversation with E. M. Forster," *Encounter,* IX (November 1957), 54.
17. T. S. Eliot," AH, p. 107. *The Journals of André Gide,* III (New York, 1949), 338. Conversation, November 6, 1957.
18. George Orwell, "England Your England," *A Collection of Essays* (New York, 1954), p. 279.
19. " 'Seven Days' Hard,' " *The Listener,* XI (1934), 452.
20. "A Tercentenary of Freedom," *The Listener,* XXXII (1944), 633–34; reprinted in TC, p. 63.
21. "The Swindon Classics," *The Observer,* March 11, 1956, p. 17.
22. "The 'Censorship' of Books," *The Nineteenth Century,* CV (1929), 444.

23. *Ibid.* Preceding quotation from "Mr. D. H. Lawrence and Lord Brentford," *The Nation and the Athenaeum,* XLVI (1930), 509.

24. Letter to C. J. Greenwood, May 4, 1935, *The Letters of T. E. Lawrence* (New York, 1939), p. 864.

25. "The Censorship of Books," p. 445.

26. "Society and the Homosexual: A Magistrate's Figures," *The New Statesman and Nation* (n.s.), XLVI (1953), 509.

27. "The Feast of Tongues," *The Spectator,* CLXI (1938), 194. Review of Frank Harris's *Oscar Wilde.*

28. "Here's Wishing!" *The Listener,* XXI (1939), 18.

29. "Indians in England," *The New Statesman and Nation* (n.s.), XVI (1938), 312.

30. "Comment and Dream: Jew-Consciousness," *The New Statesman and Nation* (n.s.), XVII (1939), 7–8. Reprinted in TC, p. 25.

31. "Comment and Dream: On a Deputation," *The New Statesman and Nation,* XVII (1939), 43–44. Reprinted as "Our Deputation," TC, p. 28.

32. "The Next War," *The New Statesman and Nation,* III (1932), 90.

33. "Mr. E. M. Forster Replies," *Time and Tide,* XV (1934), 829. (A reply to letters arising from his series of "Notes on the Way," June 2–23, 1934.)

34. "What I Believe," TC, p. 81.

35. *Ibid.,* p. 80.

36. "Notes on the Way," *Time and Tide,* XV (1934), 696.

37. See "Notes on the Way," *Time and Tide,* XV (1934), 766, and the good statement in his review of Christopher Caudwell's *Studies in a Dying Culture:* "The Long Run," *The New Statesman and Nation* (n.s.), XVI (1938), 971.

38. "A Clash of Authority," *The Listener,* XXXI (1944), 685–86. See also notes 5–7 above.

39. "The Long Run," *The New Statesman and Nation* (n.s.), XVI (1938), 971–72.

40. See "The New Disorder," *Horizon,* IV (1941), 379. A somewhat different version of this speech is included in *Writers in Freedom,* ed. Herman Ould (London, 1942), pp. 74–77. Much of it is rewritten and incorporated in "Art for Art's Sake," *Harper's Magazine,* CIC (1949), 31–34, and reprinted in TC, pp. 98–104.

41. *Nordic Twilight* (London, 1940), p. 3, and "Post-Munich," TC, pp. 34–35.

42. "Culture and Freedom," TC, p. 43.

43. "The N.C.C.L.," *The New Statesman and Nation* (n.s.), XXXV (1948), 396.

44. "Black List for Authors?" *The Listener,* XXXVI (1946), 174.

45. "Mr. E. M. Forster and the B.B.C. Refusal to Broadcast. Protest Against the Political Veto," *The Manchester Guardian,* March 18, 1941, p. 8.

46. In Philip Toynbee, *The Fearful Choice* (Detroit, 1959), p. 82.

47. *Nordic Twilight* (London, 1940), p. 11.

48. "Mahatma Gandhi," *E. M. Forster: A Tribute, With Selections from his Writings on India*, ed. K. Natwar-Singh (New York, 1964), p. 81.

49. "The Challenge of Our Time," *The Listener*, XXXV (1946), 451; reprinted in TC, pp. 67–71.

50. "Fifth Anniversary of the Third Programme," *The Listener*, XLVI (1951), 540.

51. "A Duke Remembers," TC, p. 303. Aldous Huxley has expressed Forster's attitude perfectly: "Eccentricity.... It's the justification of all aristocracies. It justifies leisured classes and inherited wealth and privilege and endowments and all the other injustices of that sort. If you're to do anything reasonable in this world, you must have a class of people who are secure, safe from public opinion, safe from poverty, leisured, not compelled to waste their time in the imbecile routines that go by the name of Honest Work. You must have a class of which the members can think and, within the obvious limits, do what they please. You must have a class in which people who have eccentricities can indulge them and in which eccentricity in general will be tolerated and understood. That's the important thing about an aristocracy." *Chrome Yellow* (New York, 1955), p. 50. Forster has written a good deal on eccentrics and eccentricity. See especially "The Cambridge Theophrastus: The Early Father," *Basileona*, No. 2 (November 21, 1900), 23–24; "Literary Eccentrics," *The Independent Review*, XI (1906), 105–6; "The English Eccentrics," *The Spectator*, CL (1933), 716; "Eccentric Englishwomen, 7: Luckie Buchan," *The Spectator*, CLVIII (1937), 986–87.

52. Steven Marcus, "The Limits of Literary History," *The New York Review of Books*, II (April 2, 1964), 10. Review of Ian Jack, *English Literature, 1815–1832* (Volume X in the Oxford History of English Literature).

53. "The Hat-Case," *The Spectator*, CXLIV (1930), 1055.

54. *Ibid.*

55. "Edward VIII," *The Calendar of Modern Letters*, I (1925), 156. See Virginia Woolf, "The New Biography," in *Granite and Rainbow* (New York, 1958), pp. 149–55.

56. "Jane Austen," AH, p. 182. First quotation on p. 368 is from: "An Approach to Blake," *The Spectator*, CLXVIII (1932), 474.

57. "Butterflies and Beetles," *Life and Letters*, III (July 1929), 5–6.

58. *Ibid.*, pp. 6–7.

59. "A Note on the Way," AH, p. 90.

60. "An Indian on W. B. Yeats," *The Listener*, XXVIII (1942), 824. Based on reading *The Development of William Butler Yeats*, by V. K. Narayana Menon.

61. *Ibid.*

62. See "An Indian on W. B. Yeats" and *E. M. Forster: A Tribute*, pp. 3–14.

63. "Escaping the House of Common-Sense," *The New Leader,* April 16, 1926, p. 11. See also "Ghosts Ancient and Modern," *The Spectator,* CXLVII (1931), 672: "Satanism . . . must be presented forcibly, or it becomes owlish. Not all who say 'abracadabra' shall enter the kingdom of darkness, not all unfrocked priests and pagan emblems can lead us into paths of unrighteousness."

64. "The Work of Forrest Reid," *The Nation,* XXVII (1920), 47. (Review of *Pirates of the Spring.*)

65. Forrest Reid Memorial: *Addresses Delivered at the Unveiling of the Plaque at 13 Ormiston Crescent . . . , Belfast, 10th October 1952* (Foxton, England, 1952), pp. 5–6.

66. Russell Burlingham, *Forrest Reid: A Portrait and a Study* (London, 1953), p. 167.

67. *Ibid.,* p. 70.

68. "Not New Books," *The Listener,* VIII (1932), 951. See the introduction by Forster to Donald Windham, *The Warm Country* (New York, 1960), and Forster's Introduction to the *Cambridge Anthology,* ed. Peter Townsend (London, 1952).

69. "Not New Books," p. 951.

70. See "The Mark on the Wall," *Monday or Tuesday* (New York, 1921), pp. 99–116. The story is a series of free-associations surrounding the observation of a mark on a wall (which turns out to be a snail). Some of those free-associations are extremely interesting: "Why, if one wants to compare life to anything, one must liken it to being blown through the Tube at fifty miles an hour—landing at the other end without a single hairpin in one's hair! Shot out at the feet of God entirely naked!" (p. 102).

71. *The Waves* (London, 1955), p. 15.

72. "The Novels of Virginia Woolf," *The New Criterion* (April 1926), 277–86, and [same title], *The Yale Review,* XV (1926), 505–14. Reprinted as "The Early Novels of Virginia Woolf," AH, p. 130.

73. "The Early Novels of Virginia Woolf," AH, p. 132.

74. *Ibid.*

75. "Virginia Woolf," TC, p. 258.

76. "The 'Private Heaven' of the Twenties," *The Listener,* XLV (1951), 419.

77. "Virginia Woolf," TC, p. 264.

78. "The Early Novels of Virginia Woolf," AH, p. 132.

79. "Henry James and the Young Men," *The Listener,* LXII (1959), 103.

80. Quoted in Edith Wharton, *A Backward Glance* (New York, 1934), p. 232.

81. *Granite and Rainbow,* p. 48. We meet Meredith now, Virginia Woolf writes, "as some hero so ardently admired once that his eccentricities are now scarcely tolerable; they seem to preserve too well the faults of our own youth."

82. "Our Second Greatest Novel?" TC, p. 229.

83. "Proust," AH, p. 117.

84. "Tolstoy's *War and Peace,* Introduction to the Series of Broadcasts," [Wembley]: B.B.C., January 1943, p. 7. This is very similar to "Tolstoy's *War and Peace," The Listener,* XVII (1937), 87.

85. "Proust," AH, p. 116.

86. AN, pp. 39–40.

87. "André Gide," *The Listener,* XLV (1951), 343. Reprinted as "Gide's Death," TC, p. 237.

88. "Humanist and Authoritarian," *The Listener,* XXX (1943), 242. Reprinted as "Gide and George," TC, p. 233.

89. "The Book of the Age? James Joyce's 'Ulysses,'" *The New Leader,* March 12, 1926, p. 13.

90. *Ibid.*

91. "T. S. Eliot," AH, p. 107.

92. "An Indian on W. B. Yeats," *The Listener,* XXVIII (1942), 824.

93. "Dante," *Selected Essays: 1917–1932* (New York, 1932), p. 200.

94. "Literary Studies," *Scrutiny,* IX (March 1941). Reprinted in F. R. Leavis, *Education and the University* (New York, 1948), pp. 66–86.

95. "T. S. Eliot and his Difficulties," *Life and Letters,* II (1929), 417–25; reprinted as "T. S. Eliot," AH, p. 107.

96. *E. M. Forster: A Tribute,* p. 68.

97. "D. H. Lawrence," *Portraits from Memory* (London, 1956), pp. 104–5.

98. David Garnett, *The Flowers of the Forest* (London, 1955), p. 53.

99. "D. H. Lawrence," *The Nation and the Athenaeum,* XLVI (1930), 888. Letter dated March 29, 1930. Forster's "Aspatia" is usually "Aspasia."

100. "D. H. Lawrence," *The Nation and the Athenaeum,* XLVII (1930), 109.

101. *Ibid.* (April 12, 1930), 45.

102. Leavis, *D. H. Lawrence, Novelist* (London, 1955), p. 10.

103. *Women in Love* (New York, 1922), p. 158.

104. See Graham Hough, *The Dark Sun* (New York, 1956), p. 190.

105. Harry T. Moore, *The Intelligent Heart: The Story of D. H. Lawrence* (New York, 1962), p. 227.

106. *Ibid.*

107. *Ibid.*

108. *St. Mawr* and *The Man Who Died* (New York, 1960), p. 148.

109. *Ibid.*

110. *The Dark Sun,* p. 40.

111. *St. Mawr* and *The Man Who Died,* p. 151.

112. *Ibid.,* p. 158.

113. *Lady Chatterley's Lover,* p. 223.

114. *Lawrence's Letters to Russell,* pp. 33–34.

115. "Cnidus," AH, p. 201.

116. *Lady Chatterley's Lover,* pp. 180–82.

117. *Women in Love,* p. 36.

118. [Palinurus], *The Unquiet Grave* (London, 1946), p. 29.

119. Quoted by Mark Schorer in Introduction, *Lady Chatterley's Lover,* p. xv.

120. *Lady Chatterley's Lover,* p. 334.

121. Note the pieces cited above in Notes 99–101. In addition, the following articles should be consulted: "Mr. D. H. Lawrence and Lord Brentford," *The Nation and the Athenaeum,* XLVI (1930), 508–9; "D. H. Lawrence," *The Listener,* III (1930), 753–54; "The Cult of D. H. Lawrence," *The Spectator,* CXLVI (1931), 627. See also AN, pp. 68, 132–33.

122. "D. H. Lawrence," *The Listener,* III (1930), 754.

123. The quotations in this paragraph are from Forster's Presidential Address published in *Freedom of Expression,* ed. Hermon Ould (London, 1945), pp. 11, 112.

Acknowledgments and Credits

I am grateful to the publishers of Forster's works, in England and the United States, for permitting me to quote from works of which they own the copyright: to Edward Arnold (Publishers) Ltd. and Alfred A. Knopf, Inc. (Random House, Inc.) for their permission to quote from *Where Angels Fear to Tread* (1905), *The Longest Journey* (1907), *A Room with a View* (1908), and *Howards End* (1910); to Edward Arnold Ltd. and Harcourt, Brace & World, Inc. for their permission to quote from *A Passage to India* (1924), *Aspects of the Novel* (1927), *Goldsworthy Lowes Dickinson* (1934), *Abinger Harvest* (1936), *Two Cheers for Democracy* (1951), *The Hill of Devi* (1953), and *Marianne Thornton* (1956); to Alfred A. Knopf, Inc. (Random House, Inc.) for permission to quote from *The Celestial Omnibus* in *The Collected Tales of E. M. Forster* (1947); to Harcourt, Brace & World, Inc. for permission to quote from *The Eternal Moment and Other Stories* in *The Collected Tales of E. M. Forster*; and to Sidgwick & Jackson Ltd. for their permission to quote from *The Collected Short Stories of E. M. Forster* (1948); to the Hogarth Press and to Alfred A. Knopf, Inc. (Random House, Inc.) for their permission to quote from *Pharos and Pharillon* (1923); and to Doubleday & Co., Inc. for their permission to quote from *Alexandria: A History and a Guide* (1922).

I wish further to thank the following for permitting me to quote from works to which they hold the rights: the British Broadcasting Corporation for permission to quote from Forster's many *Listener* articles; the Bollingen Foundation for permission to quote from Erich Neumann's *The Great Mother* (1955), and C. G. Jung's *The Archetypes and the Collective Unconscious* (1959) and *The Structure and Dynamics of the Psyche* (1960); to Faber and Faber Ltd. and to Harcourt, Brace & World, Inc. for their permission to quote a few lines from T. S. Eliot's "The Love Song of J. Alfred Prufrock" in *Collected Poems 1909–62*; to John Farquharson Ltd. for permission to quote from *The Withered Branch* (1950) by D. S. Savage; to John Murray for permission to quote from E. B. Havell's *Ideals of Indian Art* (1920); to George Allen & Unwin Ltd. for permission to quote from the following works by G. Lowes Dickinson: *The Meaning of Good* (1901), *Letters from John Chinaman* (1901), *Appearances* (1914), *The Magic Flute* (1920), *War: Its Nature, Cause and Cure* (1923), and *After Two Thousand Years* (1930); to the Gotham Book Mart for permission to quote from *D. H. Lawrence's Letters to Bertrand Russell*, edited by Harry Moore (1948); to the Grove

Press, Inc. for permission to quote from D. H. Lawrence's *Lady Chatterley's Lover* (1959); to Harper & Row and the Bollingen Library for permission to quote from Heinrich Zimmer's *Myths and Symbols in Indian Art and Civilization* (1946); to Alfred A. Knopf, Inc. for permission to quote from three poems of Wallace Stevens: "Peter Quince at the Clavier," "Esthétique du Mal," and "The Snowman"; to Little, Brown and Co. and the Atlantic Monthly Press for permission to quote from C. G. Jung's *The Undiscovered Self,* trans. by R. F. C. Hull (1957); to Methuen & Co. and to Crowell-Collier for permission to quote from G. Lowes Dickinson's *The Greek View of Life* (1896); to the *New Statesman* and *The Observer* for permission to quote from Forster's articles in those magazines; to *The Paris Review* for permission to quote from an important interview with Forster by P. N. Furbank and F. J. H. Haskell that appeared in its first issue (Spring 1953) and has been reprinted in the Viking volume *Writers at Work*, edited and introduced by Malcolm Cowley (1958); to Rupert Hart-Davis for permission to quote from John Maynard Keynes's *Two Memoirs* (1949); to *The Spectator* for permission to quote from Forster's articles in that magazine; and to Leonard Woolf for permission to quote from the three volumes of his autobiography—*Sowing* (1960), *Growing* (1961), and *Beginning Again* (1964)— all published by his own house, The Hogarth Press.

Pictures are courtesy of E. M. Forster, except as follows:
    Plate 2, Jonathan Cape Ltd.; Plate 8, Eva Reichmann, London, and the Provost and Fellows of King's College, Cambridge (photo by Edward Leigh); Plates 11 and 12, the Master and Fellows of Trinity College, Cambridge; Plate 13, the Provost, Fellows, and Librarian of King's College, Cambridge; Plate 15, Istituto Italiano di Cultura, New York (photo by Maniglia Luigi, Fotografo, Ravello); Plate 16, Fratelli Alinari, Florence; Plate 17, Electa Editrice, Milan; Plate 18, Italian State Tourist Office, New York; Plates 19 and 21, by John Slater, and courtesy of Arthur and Jonathan Sale, Cambridge; Plate 22, Ministry of Defence, United Kingdom, and J. K. St. Joseph (British Crown Copyright Reserved), from the Cambridge University Collection of Aerial Photography; Plate 24, Verlag Ernst Wasmuth, Tübingen; Plates 26 and 27, S. E. Rogers, Clun, Shropshire; Plate 28, Archaeological Survey of India, New Delhi; Plate 29, Archaeological Survey of India, Linda Hess, and S. D. Kapoor; Plate 30, Linda Hess and S. N. Das; Plates 31 and 32, Madame Eliky Zannas; Plate 33, United Arab Republic Tourist and Information Center, New York; Plate 35, Aldo Martello, Milan, and the Index of Christian Art, Princeton (photo by E. Carli); Plate 42, Charles Mauron.
    Plates 1, 3, and 25 have been previously published in MT. Plate 2 is a rare photograph that originally appeared in *Battersea Rise* (1934) by Dorothy Pym. Plate 10 was made up as a postcard and sent by Carpenter to Forster in Alexandria, 1916.

In addition I should like to thank those many others who helped me find, take, or reproduce pictures. Though only a fraction of those pictures ended up in the book, I am grateful for the kindness and generosity which I encountered, and sorry that my gratitude must be limited to a list of names: Joseph A. Belloli, Trudy Born, Florence H. Chu, Edmund V. Corbett, William L. Crosten, Edwin J. Doyle, Guelfo A. Frulla, Claireve Grandjouan, Albert Guerard, Christine Gwynn, Rupert Hart-Davis, Matthew S. Kahn, Verdel A. Kolve, Edward Leigh, Joan McCord, George Rawlings, William F. Rogers, Lawrence Ryan, Isabel Sewell, R. P. Singh, Ramshewr Singh, Barbara Solomon, Wallace Stegner, Lorie and Tanya Tarshis, Vincenzo P. Traversa, Wayne S. Vucinich, and Patrick Wilkinson.

I thank also the following organizations: the Cambridge University Library; the Clapham Permanent Building Society, London; the Indian Consulate, San Francisco; the Italian State Tourist Office, San Francisco; the Istituto Geografico de Agostini, Novara, Italy; the New York Public Library; Orient Longmans, Ltd., Calcutta; the Royal Geographic Society, London; Opera della Primaziale, Pisa; the London *Sun*; Thomson Newspapers, Ltd., London; and the United Arab Consulate, San Francisco.

W. S.

Index

Abinger Hammer, 14

Abinger Harvest. See under individual essays

"Abinger Pageant, The," 365n

Acton, Lord, 52–53

Aeneid, The, 69

After Two Thousand Years, 86–87

"Albergo Empedocle," 127n, 129, 144–45

Alexander the Great, 285, 292

Alexandria: A History and a Guide, 280, 291–97; sources, 283f, 288

"Alexandria Vignettes," 282

"Allegory, An," 281

Allen, Glen O., 310n, 311

Anglo-Indians, 91; in *A Passage to India,* 317, 319–27, 342

Annan, Noel, 25, 250, 333; and Bloomsbury, 41n, 46–47, 52, 394; on Dickinson, 79, 84n, 403

"Anniversary Postscript," 217, 233n, 234

"Anonymity," 103, 108–9

"Apostles, the," 44–45, 54–55, 58, 78; membership of, 40, 60, 394f; and Forster, 41ff; and Clapham, 46–51; and Julian Bell, 56f; and Fry, 66; mentioned, 52f

Appearances, 91

Arctic Summer, 158, 236n, 280

Aristotle, 114

Arnold, Matthew, 9; culture, 10–11, 239, 248; and Forster, 14, 20f, 350, 415f; on Bloomsbury, 42, 52; and *Howards End,* 239f, 248, 259, 271–73; on *the*

State, 54, 242n; mentioned, 26, 82, 172, 375, 378

Art, as Forster's doctrine, 7–8, 18–20, 101–10, 375; definition of, 66; in *The Longest Journey,* 184–85; and *Howards End,* 267; and love, 349

"Art for Art's Sake," 103

"Art of Fiction, The" (in *The Paris Review*), 18, 122, 129, 158, 176, 186, 210, 214n, 282n, 301, 333

Aspects of the Novel, 101, 103, 110, 121; on poetry, 7; and Fry, 66; characters, 111–14, 117; plot, 113–15; fantasy and prophecy, 115–16, 117f, 174, 175n; humor, 116–17; pattern and rhythm, 118–20, 267; Ford's review of, 366; on James, 373f; on Gide, 377

Augustine, St., 350

Austen, Jane, 162, 221, 224; *Persuasion,* 112–13; and Forster, 116, 368, 375n, 394, 410

Author, The, 281

Baker, Ernest A., 366f

Bantock, G. H., 372

Barābar Caves, 300n

Basileona, 55, 280

Bast, Leonard. *See Howards End*

Battersea Rise, 15ff, 26f, 29

"Battersea Rise," 290

Beach, J. W., 101

Becker, Carl L., 290–91

Beethoven, Ludwig van, Fifth Symphony, 120, 270, 274

Bell, Clive, 54, 65n, 381, 394–95; mentioned, 41, 78
Bell, Julian, 55–57, 60, 73; mentioned, 51, 350
Bell, Vanessa. *See* Virginia and Vanessa Stephen
Benson, E. F., 66
Bentham, Jeremy, 4–5, 20. *See also* Utilitarianism
Benthamite-Coleridgean dualism, 3–14 *passim*, 20; and Apostles, 47–51
Berdyaev, Nikolai, 59–60
Bergson, Henri, 163
Besant, Walter, 101
Billy Budd, 364–65
Blakesley, J. W., 54
Bloomsbury Group, 52–55, 179, 184; and Clapham, 23, 28, 36f, 46–47, 50f, 57; and Forster, 23, 28, 39, 58ff, 91, 98, 370–71; membership of, 41, 394–95; and Julian Bell, 55–56; and McTaggart, 61; and Moore, 63–65; and Fry, 66; and Dickinson, 76, 85, 87, 90f, 98; its esthetics, 101f, 107, 118; and *Howards End*, 235, 239, 267; and Meredith, 375; and D. H. Lawrence, 379, 381, 387; mentioned, 42, 45, 78, 125, 130
Blunt, Wilfred, 289
Booth, Wayne, 112, 187, 406
Bowen, Elizabeth, 348, 420
Bradley, A. C., 58, 104–6
Britten, Benjamin, 364
Brontë, Emily, 117
Brookfield, Frances, 40
Brothers Karamazov, The, 90n, 174–75
Brown, Norman O., 3f, 254
Browning, Oscar, 69, 77
Browning, Robert, 9, 82, 142f, 299; "Saul," 61; and Oscar Browning, 69n; "Cristina," 141; James on, 192
Bryan, William Jennings, 93
Buddhism: in India, 301n, 302
Budge, Sir Wallis, 287–88
Burlingham, Russell, 370
Butler, Bishop Joseph, 50
Butler, Samuel, 172, 221–22, 229n, 250, 289; *The Way of All Flesh*, 41, 48, 150, 280; *Erewhon*, 123–24, 153
Byron, George Gordon, 127

Cadbury Rings, 206–7, 273
"Cambridge Conversazione Society," 40

Cambridge University, 40, 42–45, 52, 66f; in *The Longest Journey*, 29, 42–43, 63, 187n, 189, 194–95, 205; and Moore, 63; and Dickinson, 77f, 84f, 93–94; mentioned, 28, 60, 69
Campbell Act of 1857, 352
"Cardan," 284
Carlyle, Thomas, 6, 8
Carpenter, Edward, 87–88, 196n, 257
Carr, E. H., 53f
Cavafy, C. P., 284–86, 369
Cave symbolism: in *Passage*, 298–311 *passim*, 338, 387, 419
Celestial Omnibus, The, 128–29; title story, 129f, 148–52, 298, 420; "The Curate's Friend," 129, 156–57; "Other Kingdom," 63, 129, 157–58, 199; "The Other Side of the Hedge," 129, 147–48, 298; "The Road from Colonus," 129, 145–47; "The Story of a Panic," 122n, 129–38, 224
"Challenge of Our Time, The," 37, 360
Chapman, R. W., 368
Characters: Forster on, 111–15, 117, 375n
Christianity, 3, 11, 19f, 121; and "Apostles," 48–49; in *Alexandria*, 295–96; in *Passage*, 302, 330
Circle symbolism: in *The Longest Journey*, 195n, 206–7, 211; in *Passage*, 298–301, 344; the Great Round, 299f, 307f, 344
Clapham Sect, 27–29, 34–36, 39, 393; and Forster's family, 21–27, 31–32; attitude toward India, 37–38, 66; and Apostles, 40, 43, 46–47, 49–51; mentioned, 33, 57, 60
Clough, A. H., 9
Coleridge, Samuel Taylor, 4, 6, 8, 20; and Forster, 59, 118; and Dickinson, 76; on poetry, 106n; *The Rime of the Ancient Mariner*, 109. *See also* Benthamite-Coleridgean dualism
Collected Short Stories, 129n, 130. *See also Celestial Omnibus, The; Eternal Moment, The*
Collected Tales of E. M. Forster, The. *See Collected Short Stories*
Comedy. *See* Humor
Communism: and Forster, 357–59
Comte, Auguste, 189–90
Connelly, Cyril, 386
Conrad, Joseph, 118, 381

Continuance, family, 27; in *The Long-est Journey*, 208, 211–12, 214; in *A Room with a View*, 232, 234; in *Howards End*, 265
Conway, Moncure Daniel, 68
"Co-Ordination," 129, 158–59
Crabbe, George. *See* "George Crabbe and Peter Grimes"
Crews, Frederick C., 52, 114n, 413, 419
Cromer, Lord, 287
Crozier, Eric, 364
"Curate's Friend, The," 129, 156–57

Dante, 59, 147, 150–51
Dauner, Louise, 335
Decameron, The, 352
Dell symbolism, 298, 408; in "The Story of a Panic," 131; in "The Machine Stops," 154; in *The Longest Journey*, 195–200, 207, 273, 299; in *A Room with a View*, 230
Dent, E. J., 176f
Descartes, René, 141
Despair (accidie), 179, 330
Dickens, Charles, 35, 44, 102; *Hard Times*, 4
Dickinson, G. Lowes, 40, 71–98, 156, 402; his books, 41, 72, 74n, 79–80, 86–96 *passim*, 115, 161, 365; and Apostles, 41–42, 58–70 *passim*, 101, 104, 120, 231, 398; and *The Independent Review*, 53, 83; on Oscar Browning, 69n; Mollycoddles and Red-bloods, 77–78, 84, 90f, 93, 236–37, 244n; as humanist, 80–85; as homosexual, 85–89; his politics, 89–94; and Shelley, 149; his sisters, 239n; a "third sex," 257; and India, 324n, 330n, 418; on Tennyson, 403
Dostoevsky, Feodor Mikhailovich, 90n, 116ff, 174–75
Douglas, Norman, 301

"Ear-rings through the Keyhole," 129
Earth imagery and symbolism, 309, 312–15
Egg symbolism, 308
"Egypt," 286–87
Egyptian Mail, The, 282
Eiseley, Loren, 311
Eliot, George, 102, 175n, 232
Eliot, T. S., 9, 188, 368, 381; "dissociation of sensibility," 4, 391; and Pru-

frock, 116n, 159n, 162, 182; *The Waste Land*, 228, 378–79
Elliot, Ebenezer, 35n
Elliot, Rickie, 33, 210, 214–15, 411; his homelessness, 16, 29–30; his father, 30; and Cambridge, 63, 67, 193–203; his religion, 64; dream, 83n; and fantasy, 124; his stories, 127, 137, 203, 224n; as Forster, 162, 176, 177n, 185f; as hero, 187, 189–93, 211–13; his dell, 195–200, 207, 273, 299; his marriage, 201–9; and *A Room with a View*, 224n, 225; and *Howards End*, 236, 245; mentioned, 42–43, 118, 216, 234n, 358
Eminent Victorians, 41n, 47
Encounter, 314n
England: of *Howards End*, 240, 242, 248, 250, 255, 265; Forster on, 351, 358
"England's Pleasant Land," 365n
English Review, The, 366–67
Eternal moment, concept of: in Forster's stories, 141–44; in *The Longest Journey*, 201f
Eternal Moment, The, 128, 129n; "Co-Ordination," 129, 158–59; "The Eternal Moment," 68n, 129–31, 137–44; "The Machine Stops," 129, 152–56, 298; "The Point of It," 57, 73n, 129f, 158f, 161; "The Story of the Siren," 122n, 127n, 129, 158–60

Family: Forster on, 15–16, 27; continuance of, 208, 211–12, 214, 232, 234, 265
Fantasy, 297, 368; in the novel, 115, 118; in Forster's stories, 123–28, 151, 157, 160–61; in *The Longest Journey*, 189; in *Howards End*, 267
Fascism, 357, 363
Faust (Goethe), 243
Feminine symbolism and imagery, 131, 238, 298
Figsbury Rings, 206
Firbank, Ronald, 368
Fisher, H. A. L., 388
Ford, Ford Madox, 366–67, 405
Forster, E. M., 7–8, 18–20; his family, 15–16, 21–36 *passim*, 49n, 164n, 186, 204, 210n, 233; his school, 43–44; features of, 177, 256n; his travels, 279–80; and politics, 35–59; mentioned, 11, 56n, 57. *See also* Elliot, Rickie
France, Anatole, 118

Frank, Joseph, 142
Freud, Sigmund, 124, 131n, 135, 172, 335n, 384
Fry, Roger, 399, 401; his esthetics, 19, 66–67, 101–6 *passim*, 120; *Transformations*, 53, 66; Virginia Woolf on, 65n, 371; and Dickinson, 77, 94; mentioned, 40, 60, 63, 70
Frye, Northrop, 187f, 191
Fyfe, Sir David Maxwell, 352

Gandhi, 345, 360
Ganges River, 314, 316–17
"George Crabbe and Peter Grimes," 361f, 364
Garnett, David, 115, 368, 370, 380
Garnett, Edward, 370
"Gemistus Pletho," 223n, 284
George, Stefan, 376–77
Germany, 355, 358; and *Howards End*, 239–41, 412
Gide, André, 187, 219, 350, 376–77
Gods of India, The, 38
Goethe, Johann Wolfgang von, 58, 77, 172, 187
Golding, William, 371
Goldsworthy Lowes Dickinson, 41–42, 60. *See also* Dickinson, G. Lowes
Gransden, K. W., 332n, 419
Grant, Charles, 35, 38
Grant, Duncan, 379, 394
Great Round, the. *See under* Circle symbolism
Greece: in "The Road from Colonus," 145–46, 407; in "A Room with a View," 230
Greek ideals, 80; and Wedd, 69; and Dickinson, 86–89, 97; Neo-Platonists, 294–95
Greek View of Life, The, 79–80, 88–89, 96

Hall, Radclyffe, 352
Hallam, Arthur, 40, 51, 54
Hamlet, 190–91
Hand imagery, 131, 133
Hanley, James, 353
"Happiness," 177n
Hardy, Thomas, 101, 118, 352; mentioned, 9, 30n, 244, 381
Havell, E. B., 303, 308
Hayek, Friedrich A., 37n, 357
Hazlitt, William, 6f

Heart of Bosnia, The, 280
Hebraism, 304
Hegel, G. W. F., 48, 58, 62, 190, 311n, 398f
Hero, 188–89, 237; fainting, 148, 206, 210; unheroic, 180, 186, 207, 212; prophetic, 190–91, 213–14; tragic, 190, 213
Herriton, Philip. *See under Where Angels Fear to Tread*
Hichens, Robert, 367n–68n
Hill of Devi, The, 281–82, 314n, 327n
Himmelfarb, Gertrude, 52
Hinduism, 37–38, 91, 303–5; its temple, 301–2, 308; in *Passage*, 311, 314, 317–20, 327, 332–33, 339, 419. *See also* World Mountain
Hitler, Adolf, 190, 349, 355, 360
Holt, Lee Elbert, 222, 229n
Homosexuality, 347n, 353–54; and McTaggart, 61; and Dickinson, 85–88, 96; in "The Story of a Panic," 135–36; in *Angels*, 182; in *The Longest Journey*, 193; and Forrest Reid, 370
Hough, Graham, 383–84
Houghton, Walter, 204
House symbolism, 16, 29; in *Howards End*, 237–38, 259, 265, 299
Howards End, 150, 235–75, 375; Henry Wilcox, 5, 157, 177n, 246, 255–58, 261–63; Mrs. Wilcox, 146, 233n, 247, 257–61; passing of countryside, 11–12, 260–61, 385; monetary and spiritual concerns, 33, 34n, 35–36, 249–50, 253, 259; Margaret Schlegel, 107n, 235, 240–43, 255–65, 270–71, 338, 384, 413; inheritance in, 143, 242, 248, 255, 258, 265; symbolism in, 237–38, 259, 273–74, 299, 383; and D. H. Lawrence, 381n, 383; mentioned, 18, 64, 303, 346, 360, 419
Howse, E. M., 25, 393
Humor, 116–17, 375n; in *Angels*, 163–76 *passim*, 217; in *A Room with a View*, 217–18, 220, 222, 232–33; in *Howards End*, 268; in *Alexandria*, 291
Huxley, Aldous, 152, 381, 422
Huxley, T. H., 48
Huysmans, Joris Karl, 252, 379

Independent Review, The, 53–54, 68, 83, 130
India, 18, 37–38, 316–17, 418; its art and religion, 66–67, 303, 307–13 *passim*,

341; and Dickinson, 91; sounds of, 342–43
"Indian Entries," 318n, 319n, 418
Inglis, Sir Robert, 25
"Inspiration," 185n–86n
International Anarchy, The, 72, 74n, 94–95
Irwin, W. R., 134
"Ivory Tower, The," 28, 103

Jack, Ian, 365
James, Henry: and Forster, 66, 102, 119, 275, 373–74, 379; on Browning, 192; and Forrest Reid, 370; mentioned, 101, 179n, 223, 250, 252, 382
Joachim of Fiore, 189f
"John Skelton," 361–64
Joyce, James, 118, 187, 382; *Ulysses*, 102, 351, 377–78
Joynson-Hicks, William, 352, 378
Jung, C. G., 6, 188, 244, 312n; "split consciousness," 4; collective unconscious, 108; "incestuous libido," 197–98, 212; "great round," 308; horse symbolism, 328; the Shadow, 335–37, 340–41

Kant, Immanuel, 48, 58, 107–8, 241
Keats, John, 6, 124
Kemble, John, 40
Kermode, Frank, 391
Key symbolism, 238n
Keynes, John Maynard, 36, 179, 394, 398; and Apostles, 40f, 46, 49–54 *passim*, 58, 65; and Dickinson, 78, 80; on wealth, 250; and D. H. Lawrence, 380
Kierkegaard, S. A., 160–61
Kinglake, A. W., 288
Kingsley, Charles, 75
Koestler, Arthur, 235
Kramrisch, Stella, 301, 303, 307–8, 345
Krutch, Joseph Wood, 190, 214
Kuno. *See* "The Machine Stops"
Künstlerroman, 187, 193

Lady Chatterley's Lover, 352, 381n, 385f
Laissez-faire, 37
Lampedusa, Giuseppe di, 126
Laski, Harold, 357
"Last of Abinger, The," 230
Lawrence, D. H., 114, 118, 121n, 172, 227n, 378–87; *Women in Love*, 106n, 199n, 331n, 382, 386, 410; and "The

Machine Stops," 155; *The Lost Girl*, 165n; on Forster, 216–17; *Etruscan Places*, 280; *Kangaroo*, 298; *The Man Who Died*, 345f; *Pornography and Obscenity*, 352–53; *Lady Chatterley's Lover*, 352, 381n, 385f; *St. Mawr*, 383f; *Sons and Lovers*, 383–84; mentioned, 15, 114, 116f, 254
Lawrence, T. E., 288, 290, 347n, 353, 415
League of Nations, 93
Leavis, F. R., 3, 27, 45, 157n, 378, 380ff
Lee, Sir Sidney, 367
Lessing, Doris, 187
"Letter to Madan Blanchard," 361
Letters from John Chinaman, 92, 161
Longest Journey, The, 11, 33–34, 185–92, 203–10, 364; Stephen Wonham, 23, 186, 205–14, 229, 245, 365n; Stewart Ansell, 29, 33, 186, 193–99 *passim*, 203, 208–14 *passim*, 410f; and Swinburne, 62; Cambridge, 63, 193–203; title, 85n; and Dickinson, 97; sudden deaths in, 109; and Henry James, 119n; Mrs. Failing, 186, 203–6; Agnes Pembroke, 189, 194, 199–208, 245, 410; Wiltshire, 189, 210–15, 374; and *A Room with a View*, 216n, 227, 231n, 234; and *Howards End*, 237; and *Passage*, 322; use of flashback, 275; Oedipus problem, 383; mentioned, 22, 44, 123, 170n, 384. *See also* Elliot, Rickie; Sawston
Lubbock, Percy, 101, 114
Luce, G. H., 91
Lynd, Helen Merrell, 54n–55n

MacCarthy, Desmond and Molly, 40, 65n, 348, 394, 395, 397
"Machine Stops, The," 129, 152–56, 298
Magic Flute, The, 90n, 94–96, 365; mentioned, 72, 86n, 161
Mailer, Norman, 184
"Macolnia Shops," 290
Malraux, André, 350
Marabar Caves, 300–313 *passim*, 320, 323, 330
Marabar Hills, 314, 316, 329
Marianne Thornton, 23, 26, 30n, 32, 72
"Mark on the Wall, The," 423
Martin, E. O., 38
Marxism, 3, 50, 51n, 190
Masood, Syed Ross, 319n
Masterman, C. F. G., 370n

Maurice, F. D., 40, 75
Mauron, Charles, 56, 102, 397
Mau Tank, 314n
Māyā, 304n
McConkey, James, 206n, 406, 413, 419
McDowell, Frederick P. W., 146n, 413, 418–19
McTaggart, J. M. E., 40, 58–65 *passim*, 104, 397–99; his Absolute, 61, 70, 120, 198; mentioned, 82, 111
Meacham, Standish, 49n
Melville, Herman, 117f, 364–65
"Menace to Freedom, The," 62n
Menon, V. K. Narayana, 369
Meredith, George, 82, 92, 105, 374–75, 381, 423
Meredith, H. O. 395
Merivale, Dean, 45
Mill, James, 36n
Mill, John Stuart, 3–5, 20
Miller, J. Hillis, 261
Milner, Lord, 287
Milnes, Monckton, 40, 47
Milton, John, 225, 291, 351–52
Mitra, S. M., 281
Modern Symposium, A, 87, 89
Mollycoddles. *See* Red-bloods and Mollycoddles
Money: Forster on, 23, 32–37, 210, 396, 416; in *Howards End*, 249–50, 253
Moore, G. E., 40, 58–66 *passim*, 395, 398f; *Principia Ethica*, 41, 50n, 53, 63, 101, 158, 395; his "good," 64, 109, 120, 198; and *The Longest Journey*, 193; and *A Room with a View*, 230; mentioned, 51, 58, 103f, 119
More, Hannah, 28
Morrell, Lady Ottoline, 363, 380, 382
Moslems: in *Passage*, 317–21
Mosley, Oswald, 363
Mountain symbolism, 301. *See also* World Mountain
"Mr. Andrews," 127–29, 158
"Mr. and Mrs. Abbey's Difficulties," 361
"Mrs. Grundy at the Parkers'," 361
"Mrs. Miniver," 361–63
Muir, Edwin, 101
Mumford, Lewis, 260
Music and musical effects, 106–7, 120–21, 376; in *The Longest Journey*, 201; in *Howards End*, 244, 270, 274
"My Own Centenary," 361
Mythology: Pan, 131–38, 224, 318, 383; in "The Road from Colonus," 146;

in "Other Kingdom," 157–58; Apollonian and Dionysian, 172, 209, 225; Pasiphae, 181; Demeter, 211, 385; in *A Room with a View*, 224; in *Alexandria*, 292–93

Naturalistic Fallacy, 64
Nature: Forster on, 12, 14–15; symbolism, 131n
Natwar-Singh, K., 379
Neumann, Eric, 308, 335
Nicolson, Marjorie, 299
Nietzsche, F. W., 207n, 209n, 211n, 225, 259; "bad conscience," 197; mentioned, 191, 213
Nordic Twilight, 421, 422
"Not Listening to Music," 106
"Note on the Way, A," 413–14
"Notes on the English Character," 361
Novel. *See Aspects of the Novel*

Old School, The, 203n
Oliver, H. J., 408
Orwell, George, 152, 351
"Other Kingdom," 63, 129, 157–58, 199, 273
"Other Side of the Hedge, The," 129, 147–48, 298
"Our Deputation," 355

P.E.N. Club, 349, 358f, 388
Paley, William, 49f
Pan, 131–38, 224, 318, 383
Pan Pipes, 137
Passage to India, A, 297, 317–41, 345–46; as turning point, 8, 11, 347f, 350, 388, 418; and Dickinson, 92, 97; Adela Quested, 138n, 317–41 *passim*; Cyril Fielding, 229, 289, 317–36 *passim*, 342f; Mrs. Moore, 146, 233n, 260, 322, 324, 326, 330–38, 341f, 345, 349f; beginning of, 281–82; time and rhythm, 291, 341–44; circle symbolism, 298–300; setting of, 300–17; Godbole, 301, 317, 319, 325f, 330–36 *passim*, 341n, 342–47, 419; Aziz, 313, 317–30 *passim*, 334–35, 338n, 341ff, 372; mentioned, 279, 292, 371, 383f
Pater, Walter, 141–42, 201, 252
"Peter Grimes." *See* "George Crabbe and Peter Grimes"
Pharos and Pharillon, 283–85
Pickthall, Marmaduke, 288–89
Plato, 54, 58, 77, 80, 86–89, 141

Plomer, William, 30n, 370
Plotinus, 295
Poetry, 18, 104–10 *passim*, 184; and prose, 5–11; Shelley on, 104n, 105, 115n, 120n; Browning on, 143
"Point of It, The," 57, 73n, 129f, 158f, 161
Point of view, 105, 113f, 406
Pornography: Forster on, 352–53
Porter, Katherine Anne, 241
Portland, Duke of: *Reminiscences*, 363
Prometheus Unbound, 151n
Prophecy: in the novel, 115–19; in Forster's stories, 126; in *Angels*, 167, 174–76; in *The Longest Journey*, 213–14; in *Howards End*, 267, 275
Protestantism, 81–82, 303–4
Proust, Marcel, 120, 375–76; mentioned, 26, 141

Raby, Miss. *See* "Eternal Moment, The"
Rahv, Philip, 90n
"Raison d'Etre of Criticism in the Arts, The," 103
Rau, Santha Rama, 325, 331, 344, 419
Raven, Canon C. E., 234
Read, Herbert, 301
"Recollectionism," 21–23
Red-bloods and Mollycoddles, 77–78, 84, 90f, 93; and *Howards End*, 236–37, 244n, 265, 267, 269
"Reflections in India. I.—Too Late?," 327n
Reid, Forrest, 127, 369–70
Reviews, by Forster, 38, 281, 357, 366f, 367n–68n
Rhythm, 113, 118–21, 376, 406; in *Howards End*, 267–75; in *Passage*, 341–46
Rieff, Philip, 102–3, 215
Ring symbolism. *See* Circle symbolism
Rise of Silas Lapham, The, 220
"Road from Colonus, The," 129, 145–47
"Rock, The," 129
Roethke, Theodore, 298
Room with a View, A, 111n, 216–34; Cecil Vyse, 175f, 217–19, 226–33 *passim*, 252n; George Emerson, 217–32 *passim*; Lucy Honeychurch, 217–34, 254; continuance in, 232, 234; humor in, 232–33; mentioned, 10n, 132n, 137n
Ruskin, John, 9, 75f, 143, 196n, 235
Russell, Bertrand, 53, 380, 398f; mentioned, 40, 43, 62

St. John-Stevas, Norman, 352
St. Joseph, J. K. S., 206n
Sartre, Jean-Paul, 112n
Savage, D. S., 359n
Sawston, 43–44, 279, 303, 362; and *Angels*, 165–73 *passim*; in *The Longest Journey*, 187n, 189, 203–10; and *A Room with a View*, 219f
Schiller, Ferdinand, 10, 77, 87
Schlegel, Margaret. *See under Howards End*
Schopenhauer, Arthur, 198, 209n
Schorer, Mark, 386
"Scuffles in a Wardrobe," 129
Serapis, 292
Shahane, V. A., 338n, 340n, 419
Shaw, Bernard, 82, 196n, 199, 250, 252, 359n, 399
Shelley, Percy Bysshe, 77, 82, 85n, 192, 410; Wedd on, 68; "A Defense of Poetry," 104n, 105, 115n, 120n; in "The Celestial Omnibus," 148–49; *Epipsychidion*, 198
Sheppard, J. T., 65n
Shusterman, David, 418
Sidgwick, Henry, 40, 45–46
Simeon, Sir Charles, 47–48, 246n
Sinclair, May, 367n
Sitwell, Constance, 143–44
Skinner, B. F., 147
Sky symbolism, 312–13, 315
Slater, Montagu, 364
Smith, Logan Pearsall, 93
Smith, Sydney, 24n
Spinoza, B., 136
Stallybrass, Oliver, 348n, 414, 418
Stein, Gertrude, 111
Stephen, Sir James, 47n
Stephen, Leslie, 87
Stephen, Thoby, 40, 65n, 239
Stephen, Virginia and Vanessa, 41, 46, 239, 394
Sterling, John, 48, 51
Stevens, Wallace, 181, 184, 307
Stevenson, Robert Louis, 101
Stone, Walter, 391
"Story of a Panic, The," 122n, 129–38, 224
"Story of the Siren," 122n, 127n, 129, 158–60
Strachey, Lytton, 40–41, 46f, 65n, 98, 284, 371, 394–95
Sturgis, H. O., 180, 250, 252
Sun symbolism, 312–13

"Sunday Music," 171n
Swift, Jonathan, 361
Swinburne, Algernon Charles, 61–62
Swinnerton, Frank, 44

Tennyson, Alfred, Lord, 40, 45–51 *passim*, 403; "Ulysses," 89n, 136, 270; and Joyce's *Ulysses*, 102; *Tithonus*, 157; mentioned, 8f, 28
Theocritus, 291
Thirlwall, Connop, 40
Thomas, Dylan, 379
Thornton, Henry, 21–36 *passim*, 49n, 210n
Thornton, Marianne, 22, 31f, 164n, 204; her biography, 23, 26, 30n, 32, 72
Tillich, Paul, 84
Time: in novels, 111; and *Passage*, 291; and rhythm, 376
Tolstoy, Leo, 356n–57n, 372, 375–76
Tomlinson, George, 40
Tonbridge, 43–44
Tree symbolism, 310
Trench, Richard, 49
Trevelyan, G. M., 26, 93
Trevelyan, R. C., 91
Trilling, Lionel, 57, 289, 349, 364; and "The Story of a Panic," 136; and *Howards End*, 237, 242f; and *Pharos*, 285f; and *Passage*, 315–16
Trinity: Forster's use of, 59, 190, 312, 317, 409
"Trooper Silas Tomkyn Comberbacke," 361
Two Cheers for Democracy. See under individual essays

Utilitarianism, 4, 36f, 49f

Vaughan Williams, Ralph, 365n
"View Without a Room, A," 361
"Voltaire and Frederick the Great," 361
Von Arnim, Countess "Elizabeth," 196n, 363, 412

Walsh, J. H., 280
Water symbolism, 312–15
Waves, The, 371f
Weber, Max, 81
Wedd, Nathaniel, 67–70, 187, 399–403; and Dickinson, 75, 78, 84; mentioned, 40, 60, 63, 128, 156

Wellek, René, 85n
Wells, H. G., 328, 352, 353, 359n, 379, 412; *The Time Machine*, 152
Westcott, B. F., 399
Wharton, Edith, 17n, 34
"What I Believe," 40, 54, 62n, 221n, 349
Where Angels Fear to Tread, 164–76; comedy in, 162–64, 169, 171, 176, 182–83; Caroline, 172–73, 179, 181–82, 232; Philip, 176–83, 216, 256n; and *The Ambassadors*, 373; mentioned, 189n, 217, 283, 370
Whewell, William, 40, 50
White, Gertrude, 311n, 338n
White, William Hale ("Mark Rutherford"), 142, 187
Whitehead, Alfred North, 3f, 40, 53, 236
Wilberforce, William, 24ff, 28, 36f, 46
Wilcox, Henry, or Mrs. Wilcox. *See under Howards End*
Wilde, Alan, 419
Wilde, Oscar, 145, 161, 354
Willcocks, Sir William, 286n–87n
Willey, Basil, 6
Wilson, Angus, 205n, 350, 370, 380n, 420
Wingfield-Stratford, Esmé, 72–73, 80, 402
Wolfe, Thomas, 188
Wolfenden, Sir John, 354, 417
Wolff, Robert Lee, 189
Wooley, C. Leonard, 288
Woolf, Leonard, 125, 247n, 282, 394; and Apostles, 40f, 43, 46n, 53, 65n
Woolf, Virginia, 184, 239, 363, 371–73, 394–95, 423; and Fry, 65n, 66, 371; and "The Eternal Moment," 140–42; and "The Other Side of the Hedge," 147; and *Howards End*, 240n, 267; and the Campbell Act, 352; on Meredith, 375, 423; and *Ulysses*, 378; mentioned, 41, 46, 155, 160, 359n, 366
Wordsworth, William, 9, 15, 141
Working Men's Council Literary Society, 59
World Mountain, The: and Forster, 301–2, 345, 389; and *Passage*, 302–4, 311, 328f, 337, 339, 344; and the sun, 313

Yeats, W. B., 368–69, 378

Zimmer, Heinrich, 304n, 307, 309n

Redwood Library and Athenaeum
NEWPORT, R. I.

Selections from the Rules

New fiction is issued for 7 days, new non-fiction for 14 days, and other books for 28 days with the privilege of renewal.

Books overdue are subject to a fine of 2 cents a day.

All injuries to books and all losses shall be made good to the satisfaction of the Librarian.

5 volumes may be taken at a time and only 5 on 1 share or subscription.